Access Contested

Information Revolution and Global Politics
William J. Drake and Ernest J. Wilson III, editors

Access Contested

Security, Identity, and Resistance in Asian Cyberspace

edited by Ronald Deibert, John Palfrey, Rafal Rohozinski, and Jonathan Zittrain

International Development Research Centre
Ottawa · Cairo · Dakar · Montevideo · Nairobi · New Delhi · Singapore

The MIT Press
Cambridge, Massachusetts
London, England

MIT Press books may be purchased at special quantity discounts for business or sales promotional use. For information, please email special_sales@mitpress.mit.edu or write to Special Sales Department, The MIT Press, 55 Hayward Street, Cambridge, MA 02142.

The online edition of this work is available from IDRC and at http://www.access-contested.net.

International Development Research Centre
PO Box 8500, Ottawa, ON K1G 3H9, Canada
info@idrc.ca / www.idrc.ca <http://www.idrc.ca>
ISBN 978-1-55250-507-6 (IDRC e-book)

This book was set in Stone Sans and Stone Serif by Toppan Best-set Premedia Limited. Printed and bound in the United States of America.

Library of Congress Cataloging-in-Publication Data

Access contested : security, identity, and resistance in Asian cyberspace / edited by Ronald Deibert . . . [et al.].
    p.   cm. — (Information revolution and global politics)
Includes bibliographical references and index.
ISBN 978-0-262-01678-0 (hardcover : alk. paper) — ISBN 978-0-262-51680-8 (pbk. : alk. paper)
1. Cyberspace—Government policy—Asia. 2. Computer security—Asia. 3. Computers—Access control—Asia. 4. Internet—Government policy—Asia. 5. Internet—Censorship—Asia. I. Deibert, Ronald.
HM851.A253   2011
303.48′33095—dc23

                                                                                    2011031273

10   9   8   7   6   5   4   3   2

Contents

Acknowledgments

The OpenNet Initiative would not exist without the vital contributions of dozens of very talented and often courageous researchers from around the world.

Jacqueline Larson provided invaluable editorial input for the entire book. The authorship and editing of the country profiles were led by Marianne Lau (Citizen Lab), Adam Senft (Citizen Lab), and Jillian York (Berkman Center). Other written contributions were made by Roxana Farahmand (Pakistan), Lindsey Massar, Guangye He (China), Rebekah Heacock, Yu Ri Jeong (South Korea), Arnav Manchanda (China), Pirongrong Ramasoota (Thailand), James Tay (China), and Vee Vian Thien (Malaysia).

Masashi Crete-Nishihata (Citizen Lab), Robert Faris (Berkman Center), James Tay (Citizen Lab), and Jillian York (Berkman Center) help to manage the ONI research enterprise on an ongoing basis. Their professional stewardship keeps the ONI on track. The ONI software development team is led by Clayton Epp (Citizen Lab), Elias Adum (Citizen Lab), and Eran Henig (Citizen Lab). Jonathan Doda (Citizen Lab) acted as the lead technical engineer and analyst for the ONI in 2008 and 2009. Shishir Nagaraja (Cambridge University) did the same in 2007. Jane Gowan (Citizen Lab) designed the cover art for *Access Contested* and provided additional design input to the ONI project.

ONI regional deputies Helmi Noman (Middle East and North Africa) and Stephanie Wang (Asia, 2007–2009) coordinated field research across their respective regions. The ONI would like to acknowledge the invaluable contributions of the Secdev Group in implementing the OpenNet Asia project, together with the resulting contributions that went into this volume from the regional coordinators, Francois Fortier and Al Alegre, the project manager Deirdre Collings, and research assistants Arnav Manchanda and Antoine Nouvet as well as the entire OpenNet Asia project team. The ONI is grateful to all members of OpenNet Eurasia, in particular the regional coordinator Tattugul Mambetalieva. The ONI is also grateful to the University of Amsterdam Digital Methods Team, especially Professor Richard Rogers, Erik Borra, Esther Weltevrede, and Anat Ben-David, for participating in the ONI's April 2009 analysis workshop at the Citizen Lab, Munk School of Global Affairs, University of Toronto.

The ONI is grateful to MIT Press: William Drake, Ernest Wilson III, and Marguerite Avery.

The Citizen Lab would like to thank Catherine Antoine and the RFA team, Ramtin Amin, Kristen Batch, Carolina Botero, Larid Brown, Jessica Daggers, Jakub Dalek, Neil Desai, Luis Carlos Díaz, Victor Elvino, Sahar Golshan, Robert Guerra, Seth Hardy, Gus Hosein, Andrés Izquierdo, Vanessa Johan, Dylan Jones, Andrej Karpathy, Elana Koren, Lucinda Li, Daniel Lister, Jamie Liu, Rishi Maharaj, Isaac Mao, Margaret McKone, Miriam McTiernan, David Naylor, Kay Nguyen, Palantir Technologies, Ginger Paque, Wilhelmina Peter, Anna Postelnyak, Psiphon Inc., Xiao Qiang, Juliana Rincón, Ewald Scharfenberg, Anand Sharma, Sunil Shrestha, Janice Stein, Jamie Uhrig, Jeremy Vernon, Nart Villeneuve, Chris Walker, Greg Walton, Sean Willet, Peter Wills, and Greg Wiseman.

The Berkman Center for Internet and Society would like to thank Renata Avila, Ellery Biddle, Catherine Bracy, Rafik Dammak, Zsuzsa Detrekoi, Alexey Dolinskiy, Alex Fayette, Eric Fish, Effi Fuks, Urs Gasser, Cickek Gurkan, Sarah Hamdi, Sanjana Hattotuwa, Eric Johnson, Ismael Kathtan, Mohamed Keita, Colin Maclay, Katitza Rodriguez Pereda, Anas Qtiesh, Daniel Rosenberg, Amin Sabeti, Zinta Saulkalns, Gbenga Sesan, Chris Soghoian, Shiham Thabreez, Firuzeh Shookoh Valle, Seth Young, and Ethan Zuckerman.

The Secdev Group would like to thank the Eurasia I-Policy Network, and Psiphon Inc., Emin Akhundov, Asommadin Atoev, Ali Bangi, Alexsei Bebinov, Alexandra Belyaeva, Vadim Dryganov, Moses Hakobyan, Alexsei Marciouc, Lindsey Massar, Maksat Sabyrov, Nick Shchetko, Zviad Sulaberidze, Nart Villeneuve, and Yury Zisser.

The ONI is very grateful for support from the following institutions: The John D. and Catherine T. MacArthur Foundation, The International Development Research Centre (Canada), The Canada Centre for Global Security Studies, and the Donner Canada Foundation.

Production of this volume was made possible through the generous support of the International Development Research Centre. The ONI would like to especially thank Laurent Elder (IDRC), Phet Sayo (IDRC), and Kathleen Flynn-Dapah (IDRC) for their support and encouragement of OpenNet Asia and this volume.

The ONI would like to specially acknowledge numerous researchers and contributors to our research and other activities who have chosen to remain anonymous. We dedicate this volume to their courage.

Author Biographies

Erwin A. Alampay   is an associate professor at the National College of Public Administration and Governance, University of the Philippines.

Masashi Crete-Nishihata   is the research manager of the Citizen Lab at the Munk School of Global Affairs, University of Toronto, and a member of the OpenNet Initiative and Information Warfare Monitor.

Ronald Deibert   is the director of the Canada Centre for Global Security Studies and the Citizen Lab at the Munk School of Global Affairs, University of Toronto. He is a founder and principal investigator of the OpenNet Initiative and Information Warfare Monitor projects, and a coeditor of the ONI's two previous volumes: *Access Denied* and *Access Controlled*.

Regina M. Hechanova   is an associate professor and the executive director of the Ateneo Center for Organization Research and Development, Department of Psychology, Ateneo de Manila University.

Heike Jensen   is a postdoctoral researcher affiliated with the Department of Gender Studies of Humboldt University of Berlin, Germany. Her research has concentrated on gender and Internet governance, and she has been engaged in feminist advocacy in the civil society constituencies of Internet Corporation for Assigned Names and Numbers (ICANN), World Summit on the Information Society (WSIS), and the Internet Governance Forum (IGF).

Jac sm Kee   is the women's rights advocacy coordinator of the Association of Progressive Communications. She leads a five-country research project on sexuality and the Internet (EROTICS) and the Take Back the Tech! global campaign.

Rebecca MacKinnon   is a Bernard L. Schwartz Senior Fellow at the New America Foundation. She is cofounder of Global Voices Online, an international citizen media network, and a founding member of the Global Network Initiative, a multistakeholder initiative for the protection of free expression and privacy in the ICT sector.

Milton L. Mueller   is a professor at Syracuse University's School of Information Studies. He is a founder of the Internet Governance Project and has been active in the Internet Corporation for Assigned Names and Numbers (ICANN), the World Summit on the Information Society (WSIS) civil society, and the Internet Governance Forum. He is the author of *Networks and States: The Global Politics of Internet Governance*.

Joselito C. Olpoc   is an instructor at the John Gokongwei School of Management, Ateneo de Manila University.

John Palfrey   is the Henry N. Ess III Professor of Law at Harvard Law School and a faculty codirector of the Berkman Center for Internet and Society at Harvard University. He is a founder and principal investigator of the OpenNet Initiative and a coeditor of the ONI's two previous volumes: *Access Denied* and *Access Controlled*.

Pirongrong Ramasoota   is the deputy dean of graduate studies at the Faculty of Communication Arts, Chulalongkorn University in Thailand. She is cofounder and director of the Thai Media Policy Center (Thai-MPC), a research/advocacy unit that investigates and advocates on issues related to media policy and regulation in Thailand and overseas.

Sonia Randhawa   produces a radio show, *Accent of Women*, broadcast through the Community Radio Network in Australia. She is an editor of GenderIT.org and director for the Centre for Independent Journalism, Malaysia.

Hal Roberts   is a fellow at the Berkman Center for Internet and Society at Harvard University, where he researches a variety of topics around new media and Internet control.

Rafal Rohozinski   is the CEO of the SecDev Group and Psiphon Inc., and a senior scholar at the Canada Centre for Global Security Studies, Munk School of Global Affairs, University of Toronto. He is a founder and principal investigator of the OpenNet Initiative and Information Warfare Monitor projects, and a coeditor of the ONI's two previous volumes: *Access Denied* and *Access Controlled*.

Vee Vian Thien   is a researcher at the Berkman Center for Internet and Society at Harvard University. Her LLM long paper for Harvard Law School in 2010 focused on the Malaysian blogosphere, and she researches Internet regulation in the Southeast Asian region.

Gayathry Venkiteswaran   is executive director of the Southeast Asian Press Alliance, a network representing media freedom groups from four countries in the region. Previously she was director of the Centre for Independent Journalism, Malaysia. She has worked as a journalist and has also taught journalism and media history in private colleges.

Nart Villeneuve is a researcher who focuses on malware, botnets, and the cybercriminal underground. His technical research led to the discovery of two cyber-espionage networks, GhostNet—which compromised diplomatic missions around the world—and ShadowNet—which extracted secret information from the Indian government.

Jonathan Zittrain is a professor of Law at Harvard Law School, where he cofounded its Berkman Center for Internet and Society, and a professor of Computer Science at Harvard's School of Engineering and Applied Sciences. He is a founder and principal investigator of the OpenNet Initiative and a coeditor of the ONI's two previous volumes: *Access Denied* and *Access Controlled*.

Ethan Zuckerman is a senior researcher at the Berkman Center for Internet and Society at Harvard University where his research focuses on the digital public sphere. He is cofounder of international citizen media aggregator Global Voices.

Foreword

As we enter the second decade of the 21st century, cyberspace has emerged as a leading sphere of contestation between largely democratic forces seeking to use the Internet and related "liberation technologies" to expand and enhance freedom, knowledge, and connectivity and autocratic states eager to stifle that potential. This volume is the most compelling and informed account and analysis of the new contestation in cyberspace that is now available.

The Arab Spring highlighted the importance of new social media networks, which were vital tools used by activists in mounting the historic revolutions in Tunisia and Egypt. But as we know, the Jasmine Revolution also caused dictatorships to tighten their controls. It is important to bear in mind that the ultimate outcome of the Arab Spring and similar uprisings will not be determined by technological factors alone, because authoritarian regimes also appreciate the political potential of cyberspace to advance their own objectives. Indeed, there is more than ample evidence of the sharpening contestation in cyberspace, from the Egyptian government's crude wholesale closure of the Internet during the Tahrir Square protests (following a precedent set by Burma's ruling junta during the 2007 Saffron Revolution) to the Syrian and Iranian regimes' more sophisticated use of Facebook and other social media to identify, monitor, and repress activist networks.

Similarly, as this volume details, with the Internet's center of demographic gravity shifting to Asia, China is adopting proactive approaches to contesting cyberspace by supplementing long-established filtering, censorship, and surveillance techniques with more aggressive measures, including cyber attacks on dissident Web sites. Pakistan's use of blasphemy laws to ban Facebook, as well as Bangladesh's blocking of access to YouTube because of politically embarrassing video footage, demonstrate that regimes are using regulation as a pretext for restriction, replicating the backlash against terrestrial civil society in cyberspace. Governments are striving to suffocate the liberating potential of cyberspace through the monitoring of Internet café users, "just-in-time" targeted Internet blocking, and the establishment of "national cyber zones" to ensure state control.

As the editors of this volume make clear, cyberspace is "now considered a domain equal in importance to land, air, sea, and space as the medium through which commerce, education, hobbies, politics, and war all take place." It is "an object of geopolitical competition" between democratic and autocratic forces, in which Asia is proving to be one of the most contested and strategically significant terrains, principally because of the role of China—host to the world's largest cohort of Internet users and its most sophisticated censorship and monitoring regime. Beijing's ruling Communist authorities censor or deny Internet access because of its proven benefit in enhancing freedom of information, expression, and association. The regime is also an increasingly proactive player—employing its "50 Cent Army" to monitor and counter its critics—in what Rebecca MacKinnon calls "networked authoritarianism."

The country-based and issue-specific case studies in *Access Contested* provide an indispensable guide to the politics of Asia's contested cyberspace. The volume also provides a valuable historical overview of the four phases of cyber regulation:

1. The "open commons" phase—up to 2000—during which it was expected that the Internet would inform, empower, and liberate citizens "in a noisy but robust web of support for global civil society."
2. The "access denied" phase—from 2000 to 2005—in which states like China and Saudi Arabia erected filters to block access to information,
3. The "access controlled" phase—from 2005 to 2010—in which states developed more variable, sophisticated, and aggressive interventions, including registration, licensing, and identity regulations to facilitate online monitoring and promote self-censorship.
4. The current "access contested" phase—in which cyberspace is becoming normalized as a terrain on which states, companies, citizens, and groups conflict, compete, and even collaborate, as evidenced by the militarization and attempted "nationalization" of cyberspace.

This current phase has also witnessed the emergence of coalitions like the Global Network Initiative, which convenes activists, academics, and companies like Google, Yahoo!, and Microsoft to help ensure that Internet regulations safeguard access, privacy, and basic rights.

The current dynamics and forces at play in contesting cyberspace provide grounds both for concern and optimism.

Worryingly, the threat to cyberspace's liberating potential is not only coming from authoritarian states but also from democracies. France is leading calls for the G8 to impose tighter regulations, while Turkey's new Internet regulations establish a surveillance system under which citizens are only allowed Internet access via one of four state-regulated filters and citizens can be monitored via a compulsory online profile.

On the other hand, as the editors of this volume note, the contestation of cyber-space has a silver lining: "What was once an arcane discussion restricted to engineers, intelligence agencies, and a small segment of policymakers is being broadened into public policy and popular circles." With the constitution and rules governing cyber-space still to be determined, it is imperative that democratic states and global civil society mobilize to counter the authoritarian tendencies among its would-be "found-ing fathers." *Access Contested* will be an invaluable source of instruction and inspiration in this seminal struggle.

Carl Gershman
President of the National Endowment for Democracy

Part I   Access Contested: Theory and Analysis

1 Access Contested

Toward the Fourth Phase of Cyberspace Controls

Ronald Deibert, John Palfrey, Rafal Rohozinski, and Jonathan Zittrain

November 2009, Sharm el-Sheikh, Egypt. At a large conference facility in the middle of a desert landscape, the Internet Governance Forum (IGF) is in full swing. Thousands of attendees from all over the world, lanyards draped over their chests, bags stuffed with papers and books, mingle with each other while moving in and out of conference rooms. Down one hallway of the massive complex, a large banner is placed outside a conference room where a book launch is about to begin. The OpenNet Initiative (ONI) is holding a small reception to mark the release of its latest volume, *Access Controlled: The Shaping of Power, Rights, and Rule in Cyberspace*. As part of the planned proceedings, members of OpenNet Asia plan to show clips of a short documentary they have produced on information controls across Asia.

Before the event gets under way, an official from the United Nations—the forum's host—asks to speak to the ONI's Ron Deibert. The official is upset about the distribution of small pamphlets that invite attendees to the book reception, in particular about the reference to Tibet on the back (which he encircles in pen to make his point). He asks that no more such pamphlets be distributed. Deibert reluctantly agrees, since the event is about to begin.

But one incident leads quickly to another. An ONI research associate is now carrying the large banner back from the hallway, this time escorted by the same official, another official, and a security guard. The banner is placed on the floor while discussions take place. Deibert asks what the problem is now, to which the official replies that the reference to the "Great Firewall of China" is unacceptable to one of the state members and that the poster must be removed. An animated discussion follows, with people gathering. The growing crowd of onlookers pulls out mobile phones, snaps photos, starts rolling videos, and sends tweets out to the Internet about the furor. The security guards remove the banner from the book reception, and the event continues.

Following the reception, people assemble videos of the controversy and post them to YouTube. Press inquiries begin, and soon there are stories and posts about the event, including an image of the banner in question on BBC, CBC, and other news outlets around the world. What was a sleepy book reception has turned into a political melee.

Onlookers' accounts differ from those made by the IGF executive coordinator, Markus Kummer, and these differences stir up confusion. Kummer claims the reason the banner was removed had nothing to do with the reference to China, but rather that no banners or posters are allowed in the IGF, a claim that is clearly contradicted by dozens of other commercial banners spread throughout the massive complex.

The now-infamous IGF ONI book reception illustrates in one instance the current state of cyberspace contestation. Rather than overt censorship, a member state pressures UN officials at the IGF to remove a poster that alludes to practices (in this case, technical censorship) they would prefer not be mentioned. Meanwhile China is engaging in a forthright campaign to neutralize the IGF, pushing instead for Internet governance to be moved to a more state-exclusive forum. Perhaps not surprisingly, the IGF president seems loath to annoy the member state, perhaps for fear of stirring up yet more animosity toward the IGF. But the quiet show of authority does not go unchallenged—documented by dozens of social-media-enabled activists and attendees, accounts of the event ripple outward to become a media storm.

A little over a year later, events in Egypt take a dramatic turn as the country is embroiled in protests. The contests in the street are to an unknown degree organized over the Web and documented there, with the Egyptian authorities ordering all Internet service providers (ISPs) to shutter services.[1] While the country is effectively severed from the Internet, supporters of the Egyptian demonstrators worldwide share strategies on repairing the broken connections. Everything from ham radios and satellite phones to primitive dial-up connections is employed. Eventually, the Egyptian authorities relent on the blackout, but the contests in cyberspace continue. Egyptian authorities order the country's main cell phone carriers to send out mass SMS texts urging pro-Mubarak supporters to take to the streets and fight the assembled protestors.[2]

Digital technologies play an increasingly important role in terms of how we express ourselves and communicate with one another. Those who hold public office, along with those who speak to power, recognize the growing importance of the Internet and related technologies, which together forge the domain of cyberspace. It is now considered a domain equal in importance to land, air, sea, and space and is the medium through which commerce, education, hobbies, politics, and war all take place.

Not surprisingly, cyberspace has become an increasingly contested space—an object of geopolitical competition. This contestation is illustrated on a daily basis, from the formation of military cyber commands to the filtering of social media tools by repressive regimes to the creation of new tools and methods designed to circumvent them. The tussles over cyberspace are the result of a gradual entanglement of competing strategic interests mutually dependent on and targeting a common communications and information space. It bears constant reminding that the environment we are talking about is only several decades old, and in a short period of time it has gone through a massive growth that continues unabated.

Over the last eight years, through a pioneering interuniversity and public/private collaboration, we have been witness to these transformations and the growing struggles to shape and control cyberspace. Our collaboration started out animated by a simple and astonishingly unanswered puzzle: if someone connects to the Web in a country like China or Saudi Arabia, will that person experience the same Internet as a person connecting from Canada or the United States? We built a fairly elaborate methodology designed to answer this question, even as it evolved over time. Although we have documented with a good degree of precision the growing number of countries that attempt to filter access to information and services online, we have also observed an entirely different struggle to shape practices and norms around cyberspace. While it is still essential to have something like what we call a "gold standard" for testing Internet filtering on a comparative basis, the range of controls being exercised by a growing number of actors, as well as the resistance to those controls, present challenges to our research.

As with its predecessor, *Access Controlled*, which focused on member states of the Organization for Security and Cooperation in Europe, we take a regional view in *Access Contested*, focusing primarily on the cyberspace contests playing out in Asia. Although cyberspace can be viewed as an undifferentiated whole, it is important not to lose sight of important regional variations. Nowhere is the battle for the future of rights and freedoms in cyberspace more dramatically carried out than in the Asian region. At the epicenter of this contest is China—home to the world's largest Internet population and, in our view, the world's most advanced Internet censorship and surveillance regime. China struggles to balance national/cultural security and regime stability against the exploding aspirations of ethnic and social groups who strive for identity and recognition, and commercial ventures seeking connectivity to worldwide markets. The resistance to its controls ranges from grassroots human rights groups to corporate giants like Google. Recent revelations of cyber espionage, patriotic hacking, and theft of intellectual property have thrust China into a tense rivalry with regional and global powers, such as India and the United States.

The drama of security, identity, and resistance evident in China is played out across Asia, but in a form unique to each country's national context. India is an emerging information and communications technology (ICT) superpower but like China struggles to balance economic development, identity, and resistance through surveillance and censorship of its own. Burma is among the world's most repressive regimes and has shown a willingness to take drastic measures to control online dissent, including shutting down the Internet altogether during protests in 2007 known as the Saffron Revolution. In Thailand, street protests have spilled online, leading authorities to take unusually harsh measures to limit access to social networking and other mobilization services.

Throughout Asia, a diverse mixture of controls and local resistances has created a unique regional story around the contests to shape cyberspace. Most importantly, by focusing on cyberspace contests in Asia we are taking a glimpse into the future. There is a major demographic shift in cyberspace under way, as the center of gravity of the Internet's population slowly shifts from the North and West to the South and East. These nations are entering into cyberspace with a much different set of customs, values, and state-society relations than those, like the United States and Europe, out of which the Internet was developed and first took shape. Just as West Coast Californian culture motivated the first generation of Internet practices and principles, so too should we expect the next phase of these practices and principles to reflect a different regional flavor.

Four Phases of Cyberspace Regulation

Since 2006 when we began our global comparative approach to Internet filtering research, we have mapped content-access control on the Internet in 70 states, probed 289 ISPs within those states, and tested Web access to 129,884 URLs. Based on the data we have collected and the work of other researchers asking similar questions, we argue that there are four phases of Internet access and content regulation. The phases are the "open commons" period, from the network's formation through about 2000; "access denied," through about 2005; "access controlled," through 2010; and "access contested," the phase we are now entering, which is the subject of this volume.

Phase 1: The Open Commons (the 1960s to 2000)

The first phase, roughly from the Internet's initial formation in the 1960s through about 2000, is the period of the "open commons." This phrase is intended to convey descriptive, predictive, and normative meanings. During this initial period of the network's development, the dominant theory about its regulation—to the extent that anyone was thinking seriously about regulation at all—was that the Internet itself was a separate space, often called "cyberspace." The concept of cyberspace melded the creativity of the science fiction writer with the aspirations of the democratic theorist dreaming of a fresh start. Up until the late 1990s, most states tended either to ignore online activities or to regulate them very lightly. When states did pay attention to activities online, they tended to think about and treat them very differently from activities in real space. While the idea of an open commons seemed to work as a description, it proved inaccurate as a prediction. Of course, on a normative level, there is still salience and widespread attachment to the concept of an open commons.

Though the era of the open commons as a description of cyberspace is long past, there are important elements of the theory behind it that persist today. For example, there is truth to the argument that the Internet allows us to hear more speech from more people than ever before. The Internet can allow greater freedoms than citizens previously enjoyed, especially in closed regimes where the state controls the mainstream media. Governments can use the same technologies to increase openness and transparency in their operations. Moreover, cross-cultural understanding can flourish as never before, or so the theory goes, now that digital networks connect people from all around the world in new and important ways at very low cost. An individual in nearly any country on earth, assuming he or she has an Internet connection, can already access a vast store of information, much greater than what people a century ago could have imagined.

The great power of the Internet as a force for democratization is in collective action. Individuals can use these cheap technologies as organizing tools to pull others around them together and, through collective action, have a greater effect on a political process than they might have had otherwise. A vast amorphous set of communities known as the blogosphere cuts in and across political, ethnic, and other boundaries in a noisy but robust web of support for global civil society. However, any careful examination of the blogosphere and its subsets will demonstrate, too, that there are also problems associated with what people do in these spaces. This is true whether the context is the United States or Burma. Few would argue that there are sound reasons for any state to seek to restrict online speech and to practice increased surveillance, from child protection to routine law enforcement. While we celebrate the ways in which ICTs, whether digital or not, are useful to those who would bring democracy about around the world, it is equally important to realize that the same tools can be useful to those who would harm other people. Nearly all the problems that arise in offline space find their way into the online environment and in turn give rise to control strategies and contestation over them.

Though the rhetoric of the open Internet was (and remains, in some respects) compelling, it was inaccurate as a prediction. It was wrong in large measure because nothing in the technology is unrelated to human behavior. We have simply been wrapping our lives into this hybrid reality that is both virtual and analog—all of it "real"—at the same time. All the actions we take in using these technologies, whether on a virtual or a real platform, are effectively interconnected and could be regulated. As we have immersed more of our lives into cyberspace, the stakes have grown and the contests over those stakes and their related regulations have become more intense.

The technology of cyberspace is also not fixed in a way that lends itself to the sorts of predictions laid out by early enthusiasts. Indeed one of the hallmarks of cyberspace is its rapid cycles of innovations. It is a space characterized by powerful generativity— any of its millions of users can create software that ripples across the Internet with system-wide effects.[3] Whether these changes are benign or not, and regardless of their utility, these innovations ensure that cyberspace is in constant motion. At one level, the Internet's central characteristic is rapid change.

But the myth of openness that characterized this first phase remains an attractive model for citizens to collectively aspire to, even as it is carved up and colonized by powerful actors and competing interests. The core elements of an open commons have now become the touchstones for a set of constitutive principles to be shored up and defended, as opposed to assumed away as invincible. Perhaps ironically, what were once assumed to be the immutable laws of a powerful technological environment are now potentially fragile species in a threatened ecosystem.

Phase 2: Access Denied (2000 to 2005)

We call the second phase of Internet development, from roughly 2000 to 2005, the "access denied" period. During this second era, states and others came to think of activities and expression online as things that needed to be managed in various ways. The initial reaction to the mainstreaming of the Internet, by states such as China and Saudi Arabia, was to erect filters to block people from accessing certain information. In this second phase, governments shook off their laissez-faire approach to Internet regulation and began to intervene more assertively in cyberspace.

The world may appear borderless when seen from cyberspace, but sovereign state lines are in fact well established online, as is regional variation. It was the prospect of these lines emerging that formed the underlying rationale for the ONI as a joint research project among our respective institutions in 2002. We initially focused much of our research on states in the Middle East and North Africa, Asia, and Central Asia, where the world's most extensive filtering takes place. Our research has since come to cover states in every region of the world, including North America and Western Europe, where forms of speech regulation other than technical Internet filtering at the state level are the norm. A central component of our research is fieldwork conducted in situ. Two regional networks we helped form and continue to support—OpenNet Eurasia and OpenNet Asia—aim to monitor censorship and surveillance practices in their respective regions. OpenNet Eurasia was formed at the beginning of the ONI and consists of researchers, technologists, and lawyers from across the Commonwealth of Independent States (CIS). Building on our work in the CIS, we formed OpenNet Asia in 2007 through support from the International Development Research Centre. OpenNet Asia is composed of 14 academic and advocacy partners from 11 Asian countries. OpenNet Eurasia made key contributions to *Access Controlled*, and similarly we draw on contributions from members of OpenNet Asia in this volume to provide a grounded perspective on information controls in the region.

Filtering practices and policies vary widely among the countries we have studied. China continues to institute the most intricate and fast-acting filtering regime in the world, with blocking occurring at multiple levels of the network and covering content that spans a wide range of topic areas. Though its filtering program is widely discussed,

Singapore, by contrast, blocks access to only a handful of sites, each pornographic in nature. Most other states that we study implement filtering regimes that fall between the poles of China and Singapore, each with significant variation from one to the next. These filtering regimes are properly understood only in the political, legal, religious, and social context in which they arise.

The blocked content spans a wide range of social, religious, and political information. Our studies have combined a review of whether individual citizens could access sites in a "global basket" of bellwether sites to test in every jurisdiction across a variety of sensitive areas—akin to a stock index sorted by sector—as well as a list of Web sites likely to be sensitive in certain countries only. We found that in some instances governments justify their filtering by referring to one content category, such as pornography, while eliding the fact that other content categories were also being blocked. We also noted the tendency toward what we called "mission creep"—that is, once filtering systems were adopted for whatever reason, state authorities would be tempted to employ them to deal with other vexing public policy issues.[4] For example, while Pakistan began by blocking access to blasphemous content, it expanded its filtering regime to include Web sites of opposition groups and insurgencies.[5] We also discovered that governments tend to block local-language content more than that expressed in English, and locally relevant sources of information more than general global content.

The extent, locus, and character of Internet filtering vary from state to state and over time. Web filtering is inconsistent and prone to error. Numerous examples from our research noted the tendencies of overblocking and underblocking, whereby content is either missed or mistakenly included in block lists because of sloppy filtering techniques. What is hosted where is constantly changing (for example, IP addresses are often recycled for other uses while states' IP blocking lists are not updated), and Web content at any particular site is constantly changing, a fact that poses a problem for the censors. Mobile devices and social networks have further complicated the task of speech regulation online. No state we have yet studied, including China, seems able to carry out its Web filtering in a comprehensive manner (i.e., consistently blocking access to a range of sites meeting specified criteria). China appears to be the most nimble of the states that we have studied at responding to the shifting Web. This ability likely reflects a devotion of the most resources and political will to the enterprise of technical Internet filtering.

It would be a mistake to infer that Internet filtering is a phenomenon that takes place only in states with histories of hostility to free expression. Democratic states participate in extensive regulation of the Internet, just as authoritarian states do. We have documented Internet filtering in northern Europe, for instance, associated with child pornography. In the United States, the state regulates what children can see in libraries and schools, as one of many means of limiting access to information deemed to be harmful to them. One may feel differently about these child-protection measures than one does about the blocking of activists' speech on the fringe of nondemocratic societies, but the practices involve similar technical mechanisms, as well as pitfalls, in both types of settings. These practices have made Internet filtering a growing and pervasive global norm.

Citizens with technical knowledge can generally circumvent filters that a state has put in place. Some states acknowledge as much: the overseer of Saudi Arabia's filtering program, under the state-run Internet Services Unit, admits that technically savvy users can simply not be stopped from accessing blocked content. Expatriates in China, as well as those citizens who resist the state's control, frequently find up-to-date proxy servers or virtual private-network services through which to connect to the Internet and through which they can evade filters in the process. While no state will ultimately win the game of cat-and-mouse with those citizens who are resourceful and dedicated enough to employ circumvention measures, a preponderance of users will never do so—rendering filtering regimes at least partially effective despite the obvious workarounds.

Some of the earliest theorizing about control in the online environment, from the open-commons period, suggested that such state-run control of Internet activity would not work.[6] States like China have proven that an ambitious regulatory body can, by devoting substantial technical, financial, and human resources, exert a large measure of control over what their citizens do online. If they want, states can erect digital gates at their borders, even in cyberspace, and can render these gates effective through a wide variety of modes of control. These controls have proven right the claims of Lawrence Lessig, Jack L. Goldsmith, Tim Wu, and others who have emphasized the extent to which the online environment can be regulated and the ways in which traditional international relations theory will govern in cyberspace as in real space.[7]

Phase 3: Access Controlled (2005 to 2010)

The third phase, from 2005 roughly to the present day, is the "access-controlled" phase. Access controlled characterizes a period during which states have emphasized regulatory approaches that function not only like filters or blocks, but also as variable controls. The salient feature of this phase is the notion that there is a large series of mechanisms (including those that are nontechnological) at various points of control that can be used to limit and shape access to knowledge and information. These mechanisms can be layered on top of the basic filters and blocks established during the previous era or implemented separately altogether in their absence.[8] They reflect a more nuanced understanding of the range of tools available to authorities to shape and control, as opposed to block, access to information and freedom of speech. Notoriously, such tools include the use of more "offensive" (compared to passive or defensive) methods, including computer network attacks, espionage, and the projection of ideas favorable to a state's strategic interests.

The mechanisms of the access-controlled period are more subtle and nuanced than the first-generation filtering and blocking mechanisms that they complement. These controls can change over time to respond to changing political and cultural environments that arise online and offline. Filtering mechanisms can be made to work "just in time," in order to block content and services at politically sensitive moments, as the Chinese government did in reaction to ethnic riots in the autonomous region of Xinjiang in 2009 or as the Egyptian regime did in extreme form in response to the January 2011 protests.[9]

Many states also use registration, licensing, and identity requirements to control what people do online and to create a climate of self-censorship. In some jurisdictions, in order to publish information lawfully on the Internet, one needs to register oneself with the state as a publisher. The first-order controls associated with censorship are combined with legal controls and surveillance, the effect of which is to ensure that those publishing online know that they are being watched and that the state is capable of shutting them down or putting them in jail. These methods of regulation, working in combination, are highly effective, both as a means of law enforcement and through a chilling effect on online speech.[10]

During this access-controlled period, states have also increased the number of control points that are possible on this network and their use. While the image of the "Great Firewall of China" is evocative and, to some extent, accurate as a description, it is misleading insofar as it tells only a small part of the story of control online, in China and elsewhere. States control the online environment not just at the national border, as information flows in and out of the state, but in many environments within states. For instance, in order to go into an Internet café to log on to the Internet in Burma, one has to establish one's identity and log in at the front of the store so that the proprietor can link online activities to a certain machine and IP address and period of time.[11] These registration and logging requirements are combined with surveillance cameras that are trained on computer users in Internet cafés. Law-enforcement officials, in turn, can monitor or later re-create the digital tracks of the large population of Internet users who rely upon Internet cafés, especially in developing countries where fast connectivity to the home is prohibitively expensive or nonexistent.

Although new laws are being drafted to create a regulatory framework for cyberspace, in some cases old, obscure, or rarely enforced regulations are cited ex post facto to justify acts of Internet censorship, surveillance, or silencing. In Pakistan, for example, old laws concerning "blasphemy" have been used to ban access to Facebook, ostensibly because there are Facebook groups that focus on cartoons of the Prophet Mohammed.[12] Governments have also shown a willingness to invoke national-security laws to justify broad acts of censorship. In Bangladesh, for example, the government blocked access to all of YouTube because of video clips showing Prime Minister Sheikh Hasina defending her decision to negotiate with mutinous army guards. The

Bangladesh Telecommunications Commission chairman, Zia Ahmed, justified the decision by saying, "The government can take any decision to stop any activity that threatens national unity and integrity."[13]

Although many of these controls are initiated by states, other actors are implementing them either of their own accord or as a consequence of outsourcing. States themselves cannot implement the level of control that they seek over network activity directly, so their control strategies have expanded to include pressure on private-sector actors. Soon after China erected its Great Firewall, it became clear that this approach would not be sufficient as a means of exercising the extent and kinds of control that the state wanted to carry out over time. It has turned to private companies to do most of the blocking or the surveillance at the source, leading to a highly public, multiyear showdown between the state's regulators and the companies' executives.

While legal measures create the regulatory context for denial of access, for more immediate needs, authorities can make informal "requests" of private companies. Most often such requests come in the form of pressure on ISPs and online service providers to remove offensive posts or information that supposedly threatens "national security" or "cultural sensitivities." Google's 2010 decision to reconsider its service offerings in China reflects, in part, that company's frustration with having to deal with such informal removal requests from Chinese authorities on a regular basis. Some governments have gone so far as to pressure the companies running infrastructure to render services inoperative to prevent their exploitation by activists and opposition groups, as was the case in Egypt in January 2011. In some of the most egregious cases, such as the TOM-Skype case in China (discussed later in this section), outsourced censorship and monitoring controls have taken the form either of illegal acts or of actions contrary to publicly stated operating procedures and privacy protections.

For governments in both the developed and developing worlds, delegating censorship and surveillance to private companies keeps these controls on the front lines of the networks and among the actors who manage the key access points and hosting platforms. If this trend continues, we can expect more censorship and surveillance responsibilities to be carried out by private companies, cloud-computing services, Internet exchanges, and telecommunications companies—often drawing upon wide company discretion to implement a vague government mandate. Such a shift in the locus of controls raises serious issues of public accountability and transparency for citizens of all countries. In light of such regulations now creeping in the world over, it is instructive to note that many private companies collect user data as a matter of course and reserve the right in their end-user license agreement to share such information with any third party of their choosing. In the absence of government policies, Internet service providers, operators of social networking sites, and Web-hosting companies may make decisions based on business interests or on their own terms-of-service agreements. Not surprisingly, these decisions can be inconsistent, ad hoc, and sometimes discriminatory against marginal or radical groups.

Disabling or attacking critical information assets at key moments in time—during elections or public demonstrations, for example—may be one of the most effective tools for influencing political outcomes in cyberspace. Today, computer-network attacks, including the use of distributed denial-of-service attacks, can be easily marshaled and targeted against key sources of information, especially in the developing world, where networks and infrastructure tend to be fragile and prone to disruption. The tools used to mount botnet attacks thrive in the peer-to-peer architectures of insecure servers, personal computers, and social-networking platforms. Botnets can be activated against any target by anyone willing to pay a fee. There are cruder methods of just-in-time blocking as well, such as shutting off power in the buildings where servers are located or tampering with domain-name registration so that information is not routed to its proper destination. This kind of just-in-time blocking has been empirically documented by the ONI in Belarus, Kyrgyzstan, Tajikistan, Nepal, Burma, and most recently in Egypt.[14]

The attraction of just-in-time blocking to regulators is that information is disabled at key moments only, thus avoiding charges of Internet censorship and allowing for the perpetrators' plausible denial. In regions where Internet connectivity can be intermittent and unreliable, just-in-time blocking can be easily passed off as just another technical glitch with the Internet. When such attacks are contracted out to criminal organizations, it is nearly impossible to identify those responsible.

One unusual and important characteristic of cyberspace is that individuals can take creative actions—sometimes against perceived threats to their country's national interest—that have system-wide effects. Citizens may bristle at outside interference in their country's internal affairs or take offense at criticism directed at their governments, however illegitimate those governments may appear to outsiders. Those individuals who possess the necessary technical skills have at times taken it upon themselves to attack adversarial sources of information, often leaving provocative messages and warnings behind.

Such actions make it difficult to determine the provenance of the attacks. Are they the work of the government or of citizens acting independently? Or are they perhaps some combination of the two? Muddying the waters further, some government security services informally encourage or tacitly approve of the actions of patriotic groups. In China, for example, the *Wu Mao Dang*, or Fifty Cent Party (named for the amount of money its members are supposedly paid for each Internet post), patrols chat rooms and online forums, posting information favorable to the regime and chastising its critics.[15] In Russia, it is widely believed that the security services regularly coax hacker groups to fight for the motherland in cyberspace and may plant instructions on prominent nationalist Web sites and forums for hacking attacks.[16] In late 2009 in Iran, a shadowy group known as the Iranian Cyber Army compromised Twitter and some key opposition Web sites, defacing the home pages with their own messages.[17] Although no formal connection to the Iranian authorities has been established, the groups responsible for the attacks posted proregime messages on the hacked Web sites and services.

Accessing sensitive information about adversaries is one of the most important tools for shaping political outcomes, so it should come as no surprise that great effort has been devoted to targeted espionage. In 2008 the Information Warfare Monitor discovered that TOM-Skype (the Chinese version of Skype) was actively collecting the logs and records of any text and voice calls placed to users, including full-text chat logs that contained politically sensitive keywords.[18] The TOM-Skype example is only one of many such next-generation methods now becoming common in the cyber ecosystem. Infiltration of adversarial networks through targeted "social malware" (software designed to infiltrate an unsuspecting user's computer) and "drive-by" Web exploits (Web sites infected with viruses that target insecure browsers) is exploding along the dark underbelly of the Internet. Among the most prominent examples of this type of infiltration was a targeted espionage attack on Google's infrastructure, which the company made public in January 2010.[19]

The OpenNet Initiative's experiences in this third phase have proven to be challenging on a number of levels. Our methods were calibrated to check for basic Internet filtering as the primary mechanism of information shaping and denial. However, the hallmark of the access-controlled phase is the use of nontechnological methods of shaping cyberspace in combination with selective filtering. Many of these methods are based on social, as opposed to technical, means and do not lend themselves well to technical fingerprinting in ways that were more obvious in the access-denied phase, when our methods were born. In addition, some of the controls are applied selectively at key moments, when our testing regime may not be present, thus escaping our notice entirely. For the ONI to remain relevant, it must adapt to the exigencies of the new modes of cyberspace controls.

Phase 4: Access Contested (2010 and Beyond)

Today we are headed into a fourth phase that we call "access contested." Although the central characteristics of the previous phases remain relevant, the key notion of this phase, as outlined by Ronald Deibert and Rafal Rohozinski in chapter 2 of this volume, is that the contest over access has burst into the open, both among advocates for an open Internet and those, mostly governments but also corporations, who feel it is now legitimate for them to exercise power openly in this domain. There is, and will be more, pushback against some of these controls from civil society, supported in many instances by the resources of major governments, like the United States and the European Union. But that pushback is met by a more vigorous commitment by many governments (including, ironically, the United States itself) to develop and refine offensive actions in cyberspace against adversaries, however they are defined.

There is an ongoing contest over what this hybrid environment will look like over time and a growing realization of the battle's stakes among all groups. Most importantly, as Deibert and Rohozinski argue, the contests reach down to the very inner workings of the Internet architecture and call into question principles and protocols that were once assumed away as noncontroversial as governments like China and Russia assert their interests for a different vision of cyberspace.

In chapter 9, Milton Mueller provides an analysis of China's international strategies for cyberspace, a component of its Internet control regime that is often overlooked but growing in importance. Unwilling to accept a cyberspace determined by others, particularly as the number of Chinese Internet users expands, China is asserting a more ambitious foreign policy for cyberspace. These strategies are naturally bumping up against others' interests but also finding support from like-minded governments and international organizations.

The growing centrality of online activities to life in general is the primary driver of cyberspace contests. From the perspective of Internet users, online activity is increasingly a part of everyday life—not a separate sphere to which they travel occasionally, as if on vacation. The metaphor of cyberspace as a space, akin to "real space," breaks down in this respect. The technological mediation of these activities changes some things—for instance, the technology brings with it specific affordances for the activist in getting her word out and the spy in snooping on Internet traffic as it passes—but it does not change the underlying dynamics of states, companies, individuals, and groups.

In accordance with this deep immersion, we are seeing cyberspace contests playing themselves out among institutions at all levels of society, including within those not otherwise known for extensive technical filtering practices. For example, although the Philippines is not a country that has a national Internet-filtering regime, Erwin A. Alampay, Joselito C. Olpoc, and Regina M. Hechanova show in chapter 6 how information controls in the country are exercised in a variety of institutions, such as places of work and study, often with greater effect than if they were imposed by government regulation. Likewise, chapter 4 by Heike Jensen, Jac sm Kee, Gayathri Venkiteswaran, and Sonia Randhawa provides an insight into how long-standing social norms, in this case those related to gender and sexuality, can affect cyberspace practices in a country like Malaysia, where national-level Internet filtering is minimal. In chapter 3, Vee Vian Thien takes a different tack on Malaysia, showing how heavy-handed state controls in the traditional sector, combined with intimidation and arrests, have unintentionally bolstered resistance from the blogosphere.

Her analysis is mirrored to a certain degree in chapter 5 by Pirongrong Ramasoota on cyberspace controls in Thailand. As Ramasoota shows, cyberspace contests are particularly acute around major events and traumatic political episodes. Ramasoota documents how an emerging online public sphere in Thailand quickly became threatened following a military coup in the country with the introduction of more restrictive laws and regulations. However, civic groups have challenged these laws vigorously and through various methods in ways that demonstrate a continued vitality of the civil society sector.

In the access-contested phase, the regulation that states imposed in the earlier phases is giving rise to strong responses from civil society, from other states, and also from the private sector. Companies are implementing new strategies for coping with the spread of regulation and liability that they face as Internet intermediaries. And as we described, in response to mounting pressure from states including China and Vietnam, companies such as Google, Microsoft, and Yahoo! have joined together with human rights groups and academics to establish an organization, the Global Network Initiative, to help implement a code of conduct for handling such demands in a manner than upholds civil liberties.[20] And companies compete, directly and indirectly, in how extensively they carry out censorship online. Search engines, for instance, vary in terms of how and to what extent they filter keywords. Regulation online is increasingly a blend of the public and the private.[21] In her contribution to this volume (chapter 10), Rebecca MacKinnon compares pressures companies face in authoritarian China over surveillance and censorship to those in the democratic regimes of South Korea and India. Through this comparison she explores the challenges for corporate social responsibility and upholding universal principles of free expression and privacy in the region.

States, too, are now actively engaged in a contest with one another over cyberspace. Military officials increasingly think of the online environment as a strategic domain and a potential zone of warfare. The militarization of cyberspace indicates how states have built up offensive information-warfare capabilities in recent years.[22] Not surprisingly, there have been a growing number of incidents of computer-network attacks for political ends in recent years, including those against Burmese, Chinese, and Tibetan human rights organizations, as well as political-opposition groups in former Soviet Union countries. Two chapters look at these issues from different levels of analysis. In chapter 8, Nart Villeneuve and Masashi Crete-Nishihata trace the evidence around attacks on prominent Burmese-related independent media and reach some surprising conclusions that muddy the waters around attribution. For their part, Hal Roberts, Ethan Zuckerman, and John Palfrey take a more comprehensive view of the global situation regarding distributed-denial-of-service attacks against civil society groups and find the frequency and qualities of such attacks a growing concern (chapter 7).

Citizens around the world are beginning to awaken to some of these issues. Public reaction to Internet regulation also points to the contest that is beginning to play out in public arenas globally. For example, demonstrators in Pakistan in 2010 made plain their disagreement with the state's decision to increase the incidence of Internet blocking.[23] China's mandate that hardware providers install Green Dam filtering software on new computers before they shipped met with substantial resistance and was pulled back.[24] The Malaysian state has publicly struggled with political pressure to start filtering.[25] Plans to institute state-mandated filtering in Australia were shelved after extensive public pushback.[26] The last chapter has yet to be written in the back-and-forth between Google and China about whether unfiltered search results can be presented to Chinese Internet users. And in contrast to most other examples, there appears to be vocal public support in favor of pornography filtering in Indonesia.[27] These and many other contests like them will play out in the years to come.

The perspective of most states on Internet regulation has changed substantially from where it began in the open-commons era. The premise today is not whether the Internet can be regulated, but rather how it must be regulated and how that regulation should be carried out most effectively. States have also come to realize that the activities of other states online need to be constrained in various respects. State interests in what transpires online—the activities of other states, private companies, individuals, and groups—have become much clearer over the past decade, and the competitions have become more intense as a result. As Deibert and Rohozinski emphasize, there is an arms race in cyberspace today between states and their adversaries.

The early theorizing about Internet regulation centered on the extent to which states could, and would, regulate the activities of individuals in cyberspace. This kind of state-to-individual regulation is a given today. Contests now concentrate not only on other kinds of regulation in which states are involved but also on those exercised by a multitude of other actors with a stake in cyberspace policies and practices. It is important to remember that most of cyberspace is owned and operated by private parties, and its protocols are developed and refined through processes that straddle the public and the private. As the frontline operators of the network, these actors are being asked or otherwise compelled to regulate the spaces they own and operate in ways that constitute a de facto exercise of authority. Not surprisingly, many of these companies are moving into spaces of public policy deliberation where such policies are likely to become more prominent features. It is not too far-fetched to think of companies like Google, Facebook, and Research in Motion having foreign policies. The same could be said of networks of civil society groups across all parts of the political spectrum. Cyberspace contestation is made up of a complex patchwork of competing interests and actors of all types. A key feature of the access-contested period will be the interplay and clash between these often-competing interests and values.

These contests among private and public actors reach deep into the heart of the very foundational principles upon which the Internet was formed. Almost everything is now up for grabs and open for debate. Reflecting the essentially contested nature of the space, some have even gone so far as to argue that the Internet itself should be "reengineered" from the ground up, or that political authorities should have the capacity to turn it off entirely. As Deibert and Rohozinski claim in their chapter, one senses in these debates a watershed moment for the future of cyberspace. How it will all be resolved will have an enormous impact not just on global communications, but also on the future of democracy and human rights worldwide.

Notes

1. James Cowie, "Egypt Leaves the Net," Renesys, January 27, 2011, http://www.renesys.com/blog/2011/01/egypt-leaves-the-internet.shtml.

2. Darren Pauli, "Vodaphone Sent Mubrark SMS Propaganda," ZDNet, February 4, 2011, http://www.zdnet.com.au/vodafone-sent-mubarak-sms-propaganda-339308969.htm.

3. Lawrence Lessig, *Code and Other Laws of Cyberspace* (New York: Basic Books, 1999); Jonathan Zittrain, *The Future of the Internet—And How to Stop It* (New Haven, CT: Yale University Press, 2008).

4. Ronald Deibert and Nart Villeneuve, "Firewalls and Power: An Overview of Global State Censorship of the Internet," in *Human Rights in the Digital Age,* ed. Mathias Klang and Andrew Murray (Portland, OR: GlassHouse, 2005), 111–125.

5. See the Pakistan country profile in this volume.

6. David Post, "Governing Cyberspace," *Wayne Law Review*, 23 (1996): 155–171.

7. Lessig, *Code and Other Laws of Cyberspace*; Jack L. Goldsmith and Tim Wu, *Who Controls the Internet: Illusions of a Borderless World* (Oxford, UK: Oxford University Press, 2006); Jack L. Goldsmith, "Against Cyberanarchy," in *Who Rules the Net? Internet Governance and Jurisdiction,* ed. Adam Thierer and Clyde Wayne Crews, Jr. (Washington, DC: Cato Institute, 2003), 71–90.

8. Ronald Deibert and Rafal Rohozinski, "Beyond Denial: Introducing Next Generation Information Access Controls," in *Access Controlled: The Shaping of Power, Rights, and Rule in Cyberspace,* ed. Ronald Deibert, John Palfrey, Rafal Rohozinski, and Jonathan Zittrain (Cambridge, MA: MIT Press, 2010), 3–12.

9. "China Shuts Down Internet in Xinjiang," OpenNet Initiative Blog, July 6, 2009, http://opennet.net/blog/2009/07/china-shuts-down-internet-xinjiang-region-after-riots; "Egypt's Internet Blackout: Extreme Example of Just-in-Time Blocking," OpenNet Initiative Blog, January 28, 2011, http://opennet.net/blog/2011/01/egypt%E2%80%99s-internet-blackout-extreme-example-just-time-blocking.

10. Ronald Deibert and Rafal Rohozinski, "Control and Subversion in Russian Cyberspace," in *Access Controlled: The Shaping of Power, Rights, and Rule in Cyberspace,* ed. Ronald Deibert, John Palfrey, Rafal Rohozinski, and Jonathan Zittrain (Cambridge, MA: MIT Press, 2010), 24–28.

11. See the Burma country profile in this volume.

12. Reporters Without Borders, "List of Blocked Websites Gets Longer," May 20, 2010, http://en.rsf.org/pakistan-court-orders-facebook-blocked-19-05-2010,37524.html.

13. "YouTube Blocked in Bangladesh after Guard Mutiny," *Daily Telegraph*, March 9, 2009, http://www.telegraph.co.uk/news/worldnews/asia/bangladesh/4963823/YouTube-blocked-in-Bangladesh-after-guard-mutiny.html.

14. OpenNet Initiative, "Special Report Kyrgyzstan: Election Monitoring in Kyrgyzstan," April 15, 2005, http://opennet.net/special/kg/; OpenNet Initiative, "The Internet and Elections: The 2006 Presidential Election in Belarus (And Its Implications)," May 3, 2006, http://opennet.net/blog/2006/05/oni-releases-belarus-internet-watch-report; OpenNet Initiative, "Nepal," May 10, 2007, http://opennet.net/research/profiles/nepal; OpenNet Initiative,"Pulling the Plug: A Technical Review of the Internet Shutdown in Burma," 2007, http://opennet.net/research/bulletins/013; OpenNet Initiative, "Tajikistan," December 1, 2010, http://opennet.net/research/profiles/Tajikistan; OpenNet Initiative Blog, "Egypt's Internet Blackout: Extreme Example of Just-in-Time Blocking."

15. David Bandurski, "China's Guerrilla War for the Web," *Far Eastern Economic Review*, July 2008, http://feer.wsj.com/essays/2008/august/chinas-guerrilla-war-for-the-web.

16. Deibert and Rohozinski, "Control and Subversion in Russian Cyberspace."

17. "'Iranian Cyber Army' Hits Twitter," BBC News, December 18, 2009, http://news.bbc.co.uk/2/hi/8420233.stm.

18. Nart Villeneuve, "Breaching Trust: An Analysis of Surveillance and Security Practices on China's TOM-Skype Platform," Information Warfare Monitor, 2008, http://infowar-monitor.net/breaching-trust.

19. Google, "A New Approach to China," January 12, 2010, http://googleblog.blogspot.com/2010/01/new-approach-to-china.html.

20. Global Network Initiative, http://www.globalnetworkinitiative.org.

21. Jonathan Zittrain and John Palfrey, "Reluctant Gatekeepers: Corporate Ethics on a Filtered Internet," in *Access Denied: The Practice and Policy of Global Internet Filtering*, ed. Ronald Deibert, John Palfrey, Rafal Rohozinski, and Jonathan Zittrain (Cambridge, MA: MIT Press, 2008), 103–122; Colin Maclay, "Protecting Privacy and Expression Online: Can the Global Network Initiative Embrace the Character of the Net?" in *Access Controlled: The Shaping of Power, Rights, and Rule in Cyberspace*, ed. Ronald Deibert, John Palfrey, Rafal Rohozinski, and Jonathan Zittrain (Cambridge, MA: MIT Press, 2010), 87–108.

22. Ronald Deibert, "Black Code Redux: Censorship, Surveillance, and the Militarization of Cyberspace," in *Digital Media and Democracy: Tactics in Hard Times,* ed. Megan Boler (Cambridge, MA: MIT Press, 2008), 152–157.

23. See the Pakistan country profile in this volume.

24. See the China country profile in this volume.

25. See the Malaysia country profile in this volume.

26. OpenNet Initiative, "Australia and New Zealand," 2010, http://opennet.net/research/australia-and-new-zealand.

27. OpenNet Initiative Blog, "Indonesia and Its Porn Troubles," August 6, 2010, http://opennet.net/blog/2010/08/indonesia-and-its-porn-troubles.

2   Contesting Cyberspace and the Coming Crisis of Authority

Ronald Deibert and Rafal Rohozinski

[Essentially contested concepts are] concepts the proper use of which inevitably involves endless disputes about their proper uses on the part of their users.
—W. B. Gallie[1]

In its short life span, the Internet has evolved from a laboratory research tool to a global immersive environment—called cyberspace—that encompasses all of society, economics, and politics. It is the communications environment in which all other activities are now immersed. From the beginning, one of its central characteristics has been its unusual dynamism—a characteristic facilitated by a distributed architecture formed around a basic common protocol. Typically, innovations can come from anywhere in the network, at any of its constantly expanding edge locations, and from any member of its exponentially increasing user base. As the network grows, so do the innovations—leading to yet more dynamism and unpredictability.

Over several phases of the Internet's evolution, however, a different pressure has begun shaping the character of cyberspace—the actions of major institutions, such as states and corporations. Originally conceived of as being too slow, cumbersome, and antiquated to deal with the swiftly evolving trajectory of digital media, states have moved rapidly to regulate, shape, intervene, and exercise power in cyberspace across all its spheres. There is now a burgeoning market for cyber security methods and services that has emerged as a consequence of, and contributor to, the securitization of cyberspace. These interventions have been met with growing resistance as users and others become aware of the stakes involved and as the struggles mount to preserve cyberspace as an open commons. Cyberspace has thus become an object of intense contestation in ways that have been unparalleled in its evolution. The impact is only just beginning to be felt but will have enormous consequences for its character and, by extension, for global politics.

In this chapter, we examine the increasing struggle for superiority and the competition for power, influence, and control that defines the contestation of cyberspace. We lay out the major driving forces of cyberspace contests: the continued rapid expansion of cyberspace throughout all aspects of society, including the rapid rise of mobile access devices; a demographic shift from the North and West to the South and East as a new generation of digital natives outside the industrialized West logs on and brings with them a new set of values and interests and resistance to state and private-sector controls; the increasingly dynamic competition among states for influence in and through cyberspace, manifest in the creation of dedicated cyber armed forces and an arms race in cyberspace; and more aggressive measures taken by authoritarian and democratically challenged states to counter antiregime mobilization through offensive activities.

The contests we outline cannot be categorized in simple dualisms, but reflect a patchwork of competing interests and values. These contests are reaching down into the very inner workings of cyberspace, into areas previously assumed to be noncontroversial and immutable components of its core operating infrastructure. Everything is up for grabs as cyberspace opens itself up to intense debate, negotiation, and competitive struggle. Principles and rules that were once cherished and sacred have been questioned and challenged: from network neutrality, to basic peering and routing arrangements, to the legitimacy of denial-of-service and other offensive computer attacks. The contests in cyberspace that we outline, therefore, represent a serious crisis of political authority and legitimacy of existing norms, rules, and principles, as the emerging domain, along with the largely private-sector-controlled infrastructure on which it rests, clashes with the territorially based system of sovereign rule and widely varying perceptions of national interest and identity.

We conclude, however, on a relatively optimistic note. The crisis of authority in the domain opened up by contestation throws into question that entire edifice of cyberspace governance—from the infrastructure, to the code, to the regulatory realms. But in doing so, it also turns everything inside out, so to speak, laid bare for everyone to examine and begin again anew. Of course, such an opening presents serious risks for long-cherished principles and norms. But as they are questioned, an opportunity opens up for a comprehensive discussion of first principles: how the space should be defined and constituted, what behavior is appropriate for this space, and what should be the relationship, responsibilities, and rights of the actors who control it and the political jurisdictions through which it is embedded. Out of the rubble and chaos left in the wake of the perfect storm may arise an opportunity to rethink some conventional wisdom and assumptions that for too long have been taken for granted—not only about cyberspace, but also about the relationship between private and public authority, territory and political rule, and the character of global governance.

Drivers of Cyberspace Contestation

Driver 1: The Continuously Dynamic and Constantly Evolving Ecosystem of Cyberspace

It may seem obvious, but it is no less important a fact that cyberspace is deeply embedded in all aspects of life, growing continuously and dynamically. This growth and dynamism is one of the most important drivers of cyberspace contests. In a very short period of time cyberspace has moved from a research tool to which one connects to a space for online engagement separate from the "real world," to something that is all encompassing and all engrossing. We now depend on it for more of our daily activities, in the home, workplace, culture, politics, health, and other sectors. We store business and personal information on "clouds." We connect 24 hours a day through a continuously evolving range of devices. According to UN estimates, the number of SMS messages tripled from 2007 to 2010 to reach a staggering 6.1 trillion, with an average of close to 200,000 text messages sent every second.[2]

The Internet's infrastructure, relatively trivial at one time, has now become a critical component of society, economics, and politics, and ranked as one of the top security priorities for governments of the world. Downtime of a telecommunications network, even for a few minutes, can trigger huge financial losses for customers and clients. For example, even though Egypt has a relatively low Internet penetration rate of 24.3 percent,[3] the Organization for Economic Cooperation and Development estimated that the five-day shuttering of the Internet in early 2011 contributed to a loss of USD 90 million in direct revenues, and a substantially higher amount in secondary economic impacts for which it did not account.[4] It is noteworthy in this respect that the shuttering of the Internet did not initially include the Internet service provider (ISP) Noor, whose clients include the Egyptian stock exchange, five-star hotels, and corporate clients ranging from Coca-Cola to Pfizer.[5] Had the government shuttered that ISP at the same time as other providers, the losses would have been significantly larger.[6] In a more advanced industrialized setting, downtimes of minutes can cause major losses for the financial sector, including banks and stock exchanges.

Such an enormous shift from something separate to something so deeply immersive is going to raise the stakes for not only the rules of the game, but also the nature of the game itself, particularly around norms, rules, and principles that have previously been taken for granted or assumed away as noncontroversial. As more individuals, groups, and organizations become dependent on cyberspace, the clashes of interests, values, and ideologies become increasingly acute. There are more players with more at stake, and thus a more active interest in how regulatory and other shifts affect their strategic interests. Naturally, this creates conditions for disagreement and intense lobbying. What was once a tool for a relatively narrow segment of society (university researchers) has over time become the infrastructure for all of society itself. Not surprisingly, the rules of the game, once considered sacred by an inner sanctum of technologists, are now up for grabs for all of global society.

It has become widely acceptable to refer to cyberspace as a "commons." But it is, in fact, a rather curious commons because it is one that is parceled up, owned and operated by a multitude of private-sector actors. Not surprisingly, part of cyberspace contestation involves the spotlighting of the conditions by which these companies mediate our experiences with it, an issue that has become more complex as the range of devices connecting to each other through common protocols expands. Consider, for example, debates over intermediary liability: whether private actors that control Internet services should be held responsible for the content that passes through their networks.[7] In the past, such debates centered mostly on one type of actor: ISPs or telecommunications carriers. Today, questions of intermediary liability are relevant to a wide range of companies and services, from cloud computing platforms, to online hosting companies, mobile phone devices, and online forums and video-sharing sites. As these market-based actors create, constitute, and control the spaces of the Internet, their activities come under increasing scrutiny, regulatory and other pressures, and legal oversight from a growing number of political jurisdictions. In cases like China, for example, intermediary liability is a sine qua non of operating within that political jurisdiction. Internet service providers and other companies are legally and otherwise compelled to police content associated with their service offerings. Such intrusive pressures are not surprising among authoritarian regimes. But even outside authoritarian contexts, the pressures bearing down on intermediary liability are growing, for copyright-protection and other reasons.[8] In many democratic industrialized countries, legislation has been proposed that puts greater burdens of liability on intermediaries for the content they manage for a variety of reasons, from concerns over copyright violations to antiterror and hate speech. In Italy, for example, Google executives found themselves facing criminal charges for failing to remove a video from YouTube that was deemed offensive by Italian prosecutors.[9] In India, laws have been passed that hold ISPs accountable for maintaining "public order, decency, and morality."[10]

There has also been a major shift in the way we conduct our communications experience, with a rapid change from fixed to wireless-enabled mobile devices. The number of mobile cellular subscriptions in the Asian region grew from 22.5 per 100 inhabitants in 2005 to 67.8 per 100 inhabitants in 2010.[11] The shift to mobile not only has made connecting to cyberspace more convenient, but also has increased the number and type of Internet-connected devices and thus points of potential control, resistance, and contestation. Mobile technologies have been behind some of the most spectacular examples of social mobilization, as demonstrated by SMS-enabled mass protests in Iran, Egypt, and elsewhere. With greater mobility and constant one-to-one connectivity it may seem intuitive to think that we are untethered and thus increasingly empowered and free. But mobile connectivity also enhances the potential for fixing individual's communications with precision in time and space that would make the greatest tyrants of days past envious. For example, the latest (fourth-generation) mobile devices are standardly equipped to include metadata about the geolocational information of images and videos that are captured. Unwitting users who upload them to public Web sites and social networking platforms may not realize that the metadata can be harvested by anyone viewing the pictures and videos on those sites and services.

Not surprisingly, regimes aiming to control popular uprisings fueled by mobile technologies have turned to these and other methods to identify, isolate, and contain organizers and participants. These actions, in turn, have generated fear, intense scrutiny, widespread condemnation, and often very vocal criticism of the companies who operate the infrastructure and services and are forced or otherwise compelled in some manner to collude with the regimes.

For example, in Egypt in 2008, one of the country's largest cell phone carriers, Vodaphone, turned over information on users who employed the service to organize food protests. Later, in 2011, the company admitted that it had sent messages on behalf of state security services, encouraging Egyptians to take to the streets to counter the mass uprising in that country.[12] Both cases caused public outrage and calls for boycotts against the company from human rights and privacy advocates. Similarly, in a much-publicized set of squabbles, Research in Motion (RIM), the maker of the popular Blackberry device, has found itself facing demands from governments ranging from the United Arab Emirates to India and Indonesia for access to its encrypted data streams. In 2011, RIM agreed to implement content filtering on its Web browser in response to requests made by the Indonesian government to block pornography.[13] The controversy has brought about scrutiny into RIM's mobile architecture that otherwise would have likely never existed, pitted governments against each other, and generated criticism of RIM itself by human rights advocates suspicious that the company has made secret deals that violate due process and public accountability.[14] As cyberspace grows exponentially, embedding itself deeper into our everyday lives through a greater range of connected devices and services, the contests over the rules and protocols by which such a complex domain is organized naturally intensify as well.

Driver 2: A Demographic Shift in Cyberspace: Next-Generation Digital Natives

The massive growth, dynamism, and penetration of digital technologies are well known. What is less well known is that there is a major demographic shift occurring in cyberspace as the center of gravity of cyberspace users moves from the North and West to the South and the East. Although cyberspace was born in the United States and other Western industrialized countries, and thus embodies many of the values of users from those regions, Internet users in places like China, India, Latin America, and Southeast Asia will soon dwarf these early adopting constituencies. With these new digital natives will come a different culture of governance and a new set of strategic interests. Although it is not assured that these values, norms, and interests will clash wholesale with the prevailing modes of cyberspace practices, they are bound to do so in various ways that will invariably lead to contestation. Already the signs of such contestation are visible and seem destined to grow in scale and importance.

Images and metaphors of cyberspace are a useful way to portray its dominant characteristics. William Gibson, the science fiction author who coined the term "cyberspace," paints a picture of the domain as a virtual reality matrix in which users would physically plug their minds into and escape into a world of "endless city lights receding."[15] The image evokes clean spheres and precise mathematical coordinates—like the contours of 3D computer graphics. Gibson was influenced by his experiences of the game arcades that peppered downtown Granville Street in Vancouver, Canada, where he lived. For many cyberspace users today, this consumerist abstraction is still the dominant impression.

Elsewhere, we have characterized cyberspace as a kind of gangster version of New York—private and public actors intermixing with criminals and quasi authorities in a myriad of overlapping rules and regulations.[16] For the next phase of its evolution, the more appropriate image is perhaps the *favela*, or the shantytown—which better describes from where the next billion cyberspace users are likely to come. The majority of new Internet users in 2010 came from the developing world.[17] While many Western analysts like to think of cyberspace as the realm of high-tech chrome and virtual light, it is in the back streets of the developing world, with its intermittent power, crowded Internet cafés, and burgeoning wireless access points, that the future of the Internet is now being forged.

These next-generation digital natives are very different from the ones that until now have ruled and shaped cyberspace. These digital natives are also emerging under much different contexts than those that applied to the Silicon Valley generation. For this next generation, the Internet has not been a public (and often free) resource that they have encountered in libraries, schools, offices, and living rooms. It is, rather, a relatively precious resource that has to be bought, built, or stolen, and carefully weighed against other competing expenses and needs. Whereas for the Silicon Valley generation the dream of cyberspace had to do with access to information, freedom of speech, social connections, and entrepreneurial flair, for the new digital natives cyberspace may be something completely different, as well as a means for following dreams that are otherwise thwarted in their local contexts. For these new digital natives, cyberspace may offer the best means not only for routing around structural barriers to socioeconomic advancement; it offers a way to gain access to global markets—and gain economic riches far in excess of those available locally. Such access does not require venture capital or a leased office space and a large staff; it requires intelligence, boldness, and access to the Internet through a cheap consumer device.

Just as the social setting of universities and West Coast libertarian culture of the early Internet technologists influenced the constitutive values that informed cyberspace, so too will the much different social setting of the next generation of digital natives. At present, the Asian region comprises 42 percent of the world's Internet population (the most by region), but it ranks only sixth in terms of penetration rates at 21.4 percent, meaning that there is an enormous population yet to be connected, most of them young.[18] In China, for example, 60 percent of Internet users are under the age of 30.[19] According to the International Telecommunication Union (ITU), among the roughly 5.3 billion mobile subscriptions by the end of 2010, 3.8 billion are in the developing world.[20] It is important, although perhaps disturbing, to know that of the top 55 countries with the highest Internet penetration growth rates from 2008 to 2009,[21] 18 are considered by the United Nations to be the world's least developed countries, "representing the poorest and weakest of the international community."[22]

To understand the future of cyberspace, we need to understand the aspirations and needs of this next generation. From the crumbling tenements of the former Soviet Union, from the shantytowns of Nairobi, Manila, or Brazil, or from the crowded Internet cafés of Shanghai, a new wave of users is entering into the cyberspace domain. With them will come an entirely fresh suite of ideas, interests, and strategic priorities. Although not as wealthy in absolute terms, these actors are as smart and motivated as their Silicon Valley predecessors. And they are exploiting opportunities for economic advancement that follow different rules. At least a significant proportion of them realize that playing through the gray areas of sovereign state jurisdiction and the virtually endless methods of obfuscation can render law enforcement meaningless, allowing them to work in relative impunity in the profitable world of cybercrime (which we outline in the next section).

Not only are the demographic shifts that occur in cyberspace bringing new motivations and desires, but they are also bringing the weight of entire national collective identities and state interests hitherto largely absent or irrelevant to cyberspace governance issues. Although English has been the "operating system language" for the Internet since its inception, if present growth rates continue Chinese will be the dominant language on the Internet in five years.[23] Such a shift alone will have repercussions for how cyberspace is constituted as a public commons of information.[24] But more practically, it will begin (and already has begun) to put pressure on the governance of cyberspace routing. Already, the desire to encourage linguistic communities to express themselves online has triggered serious questions about how the systems that support them are managed and resources allocated, particularly around allocation and management of country top-level domains. What was once a purely technical and then commercial issue has thus been transformed into a broader political and social question of forging, expressing, and maintaining collective identities.

As this demographic shift occurs, the contests over cyberspace will take on a different hue as the center of gravity of the user base moves South and East, away from the petri dish of experimentation out of which it emerged. The actors that represent the majority of users today, stakeholders from the South, the developing world, and the non-English segments of the net, will do more to shape the future of cyberspace than any discussions at the Pentagon or in policy circles in North America and Europe. To understand how and in what ways cyberspace will be characterized in years to come we need to think beyond the beltway, beyond Silicon Valley, and into the streets of Shanghai, Nairobi, and Tehran. The contests occurring in those spaces deserve our attention today, if for no other reason than that they provide a glimpse of the types of global issues that will drive cyberspace governance in the future.

Driver 3: The Dark Driver of Cyberspace Contestation—Cybercrime

A driver of cyberspace contestation, related in various ways to the previous two drivers, is the massive growth of cybercrime. Although cybercrime has formed a hidden shadow and a kind of evil doppelgänger to every step of the Internet's long history from its very origins, its growth has suddenly become explosive in recent years by virtually any estimate. According to the security company Sophos, its global network of labs received around 60,000 new malicious software (malware) samples every day in the first half of 2010; every 1.4 seconds of every day, a new malware sample arrives.[25]

The reasons for this sudden surge in cybercrime can be connected back to the previous two drivers. Our expanding and constantly evolving communications ecosystem of extensive social sharing of data, mobile networking from multiple platforms and locations, and increasing reliance on "clouds" and social networking services operated by thousands of companies of all shapes, sizes, and geographic locations has emerged with such swiftness that organizations and individuals have yet to adapt proper security practices and policies. While convenient and fun, this environment is also a dangerous brew and an opportunity structure ripe for crime and espionage to flourish. A largely hidden and massively exploding ecosystem is parasitically thriving off of insecure data-sharing practices and vulnerable browsers, servers, and Web sites.

Ever since the Internet emerged from the world of academia and into the world-of-the-rest-of-us, its growth trajectory has been shadowed by a gray economy that has thrived on the opportunities for enrichment that an open, globally connected infrastructure has made possible. In the early years, cybercrime was clumsy, consisting mostly of extortion rackets that leveraged blunt computer network attacks against online casinos or pornography sites to extract funds from frustrated owners. Over time, it has become more sophisticated, more precise: like muggings morphing into rare art theft.[26] It has become one of the world economy's largest growth sectors—Russian, Chinese, and Israeli gangs are now joined by upstarts from Brazil, Thailand, and Nigeria—all of whom recognize that in the globally connected world, cyberspace offers stealthy and instant means for enrichment. Effecting a digital break-in of a Manhattan victim at the speed of light from the slums of Lagos or the terminal grayness of Moscow is elegant and rewarding—certainly more so than pulling a knife in the slums for a fistful of cash. It is a lot less risky too. Cybercrime has elicited so little prosecution from the world's law enforcement agencies it makes one wonder if a de facto decriminalization has occurred. Not surprisingly, it is seen as a safe yet challenging way out of structural economic inequality by the burgeoning number of educated young coders of the underdeveloped world.

What is most concerning, however, is that the market for the wares of the cybercriminal is expanding and broadening, moving from the dregs of identity theft and credit card fraud to the high-powered politics of interstate competition. As the Information Warfare Monitor has shown in the *GhostNet* and *Shadows in the Cloud* reports, and recent events in Iran, Burma, and Tunisia have demonstrated, the techniques of the cybercriminal are being redeployed for political purposes, including espionage and infiltration of adversaries.[27] With the recently revealed Stuxnet worm, developed to target the software used to control nuclear facilities in Iran, we have entered a new age where the techniques of cybercrime are being employed for advanced targeted warfare.[28]

The growth of cybercrime is much more than a persistent nuisance; it has become a highly ranked risk factor for governments, businesses, and individuals. The consequences for cyberspace contestation of this exploding threat vector are going to be numerous and wide-ranging, leading (among other things) to pressures for greater state regulation, intervention, and even exploitation—a fourth driver to which we now turn.

Driver 4: Assertions of State Power and National Identity in Cyberspace

The technological, demographic, and social shifts outlined previously are happening simultaneously with a sea change in the way that governments are asserting themselves in cyberspace. Whereas once the dominant metaphor of Internet regulation was "hands off," today the dominant descriptors involve intervention, control, and increasingly contestation. In our previous volume, *Access Controlled,* we outlined several generations of cyberspace control strategies employed by a growing number of states.[29] These strategies are now spreading virally, from regime to regime, as legitimate means to assert state power and control and disable adversaries. The types of assertions of state power vary, depending on the nature of the regime, but all states are approaching cyberspace in a much different way than they did a decade ago. They are driven by the need to control dissent and opposition, protect and promote national identity and territorial control, or simply respond to the growing pressures to regulate cyberspace for copyright control, child protection, or antiterrorism measures. Among the most impressive drivers is the perceived need to develop armed-forces capabilities in cyberspace, which in turn has triggered an arms race in cyberspace. Naturally, such assertions of state power are generating countermovements and resistance from individuals, civil society groups, and other states, which in turn create conditions for multiple contestations.

Although there are many cases that have become emblematic of this complex dynamic, perhaps the most potent is that of Iran in 2009. Thirty years before, the country had experienced firsthand how small media could cause a revolution, in that case through distributed cassette tapes spreading the message of resistance on behalf of the Ayatollah Khomeini regime. During the summer of 2009, mass mobilization occurred rapidly following disputed elections and charges of widespread fraud. Protests spilled into the streets of Tehran and other urban centers, fueled by new technologies and connected to networks of support over global social networking sites and among civil society groups worldwide. An important catalyzing moment was the shooting death of Neda Agha-Soltan, whose murder was captured by amateur video loaded onto YouTube and other video-sharing sites, and then went viral on a global scale. The video and the colors of the Green Revolution became a symbol of democratic solidarity. For many in the Western press, academia, and the cognoscenti, the groundswell of support was evidence of the unstoppable might of social networks. It was not uncommon to see headlines referencing a "Twitter Revolution." At one point, members of the Obama administration reportedly lobbied Twitter to keep the service reliable and running in order to support the protests in the streets of Tehran.[30]

But in and around the street demonstrations and social networking, the authorities worked systematically to disable, disrupt, and neutralize opposition through a variety of means. At the most basic level, the regime employed first-generation controls of Internet filtering to block access to social networking services and the sites and tools used by dissidents and others to circumvent the controls. In and of themselves, these first-generation methods would easily have been bypassed and nullified had that been the limit of the Iranian regime's tool kit. However, the Iranian authorities had several other means at their disposal, employing the full range of second- and third-generation control techniques. They instituted new laws and regulations that prevented the use of circumvention technologies and the distribution of information threatening to the regime or insulting of Islam, which created an additional level of self-censorship and a climate of fear. Notably, the Iranian authorities defined content that was defiling Islam or insulting to the regime as "cybercrime."

More importantly, though, authorities began to employ more offensive, active techniques of information shaping and denial. The European telecommunications company Nokia-Siemens had provided Iranians with high-grade surveillance and data-mining technologies that were employed with precision to identify communication networks and arrest individual protesters.[31] The Iranian authorities also harvested information from social networking sites, like Facebook and Twitter. It became quickly apparent that the very same technologies that were fueling dissidents and activists were being exploited with precision to identify, preempt, and disable them. A cloud of paranoia swept through Green Movement activists and their supporters as if a poisoned pill had been dropped into the well of social networking.

An even more ominous development was the emergence of a shadowy group known as the Iranian cyber army during the Green Revolution, which, in a very public fashion, began attacking opposition Web sites and hosting services connected to the revolution's supporters.[32] The evidence was not entirely clear at first, with the group making claims of support for the Iranian regime but leaving considerable speculation as to their actual attribution. Some more recent reports have surfaced providing circumstantial evidence linking the Iranian cyber army to the country's Revolutionary Guard. But whether evidence exists or not, the impact is clear enough: a menacing band of mercenaries took very vigorous offensive actions against adversaries.[33]

The Iranian case illustrates that cyberspace has become both a means and a battleground for intense, multivaried contestation. A revealing portrait of this complex space was recently undertaken in a joint analysis by Morningside Analytics and the Berkman Center for Internet and Society, which mapped the Iranian blogosphere.[34] The mapping shows the relative place and size of the conservatives and moderate/reformist components of Iranian cyberspace as represented by blogs, Web sites, and individuals. The main takeaway of this analysis is that cyberspace does not neatly or symmetrically line up in a sharp division between states and subjects. It is a complex domain of dynamic interaction, contestation, and conflict that involves links between segments of governments, the private sector, religious movements, and both civil and uncivil society. Big Brother may not be so big anymore: she can live next door. He can be your neighbor, the storekeeper down the street, your colleague from work, or the relatives who are living in Los Angeles or Toronto, as well as in Tehran.

It is important to emphasize that the newly invigorated cyberspace control strategies are not exclusive to authoritarian regimes like Iran. Some of the norms driving cyberspace controls are emanating from policies taken by liberal-democratic and advanced industrialized countries. Within these regimes, governments are developing wide-ranging and ambitious interventionist strategies in cyberspace, from the setting up of units within their armed forces dedicated to fighting and winning wars in cyberspace to introducing legislation on surveillance, data retention, and sharing. To give just one example, the *New York Times* recently reported that about 50,000 "national security letters" are sent out each year by U.S. law enforcement to companies in which sealed requests are made to disclose information about its users, such as one recently made to Twitter for information about supporters of Wikileaks.[35]

It would be misleading to equate these policies with the types of pressures that such companies face in jurisdictions like Iran or Belarus where there are no meaningful checks and balances or spaces for an adversarial press to report on them without considerable risk. But they do provide a justification for such actions, albeit in a different context and wrapped in a different rationale. As the Iranian case illustrates, what is deemed cybercrime in one context can be translated into something entirely different in another, all under the rubric of legitimizing regulation of cybercrime as a global norm. Recently, for example, South Korea bolstered its capacity to enforce cybercrime laws that make it illegal to host pro–North Korean messages on Web sites and forums. Between January and June 2010, the new South Korean cybercrime team of the National Policy Agency forced Web site operators to delete 42,787 pro–North Korean posts from their Web sites—an increase from 1,793 deletions under the previous liberal Roh Moo-hyun administration in 2008.[36]

Assertions of state power in cyberspace mesh with one of the other drivers mentioned earlier: the demographic shift in cyberspace to the South and East. In these regions, many states have a well-established tradition of government intervention and state control, particularly of the mass media and the economy. Already having such a tradition in place, they are also coming into cyberspace at a much different historical juncture than the "early adopters" of the technology in the North and West. For the latter, cyberspace was either something to be cordoned from government intervention altogether or a mystery best left untouched. For the former, they are coming at cyberspace from the perspective of a much different security context surrounding cyberspace and a much greater understanding of its contested terrain. They are doing so building upon the knowledge and practices of prior experiments and are adopting and sharing best practices of information control and denial.

One area where these best practices may be increasingly shared and policies coordinated is among regional security organizations. Until recently, the Shanghai Cooperation Organization (SCO),[37] the Arab League,[38] the Gulf Cooperation Council (GCC),[39] the Association of Southeast Asian Nations (ASEAN), the North Atlantic Treaty Organization (NATO), and others had not dealt with cyberspace issues in a concerted fashion, but that situation is changing. Recently, there have been indications that regional security organizations may be harmonizing laws, practices, and doctrines around cyberspace operations. After its 2010 Lisbon Summit, for example, the NATO alliance affirmed a greater commitment to joint cyberspace operations and doctrine. Although the activities of some of the other regional organizations, like the SCO, are much more opaque, there is evidence of coordination around "information security" practices, including evidence of joint exercises to counter mass social mobilization. Reflecting a regime stability view of cyber security, an August 2009 SCO summit approved a Russian proposal defining "information war" as an effort by a state to undermine another's "political, economic and social systems" including "mass psychologic [sic] brainwashing to destabilize society and state."[40] The GCC states have coordinated Internet policies perhaps the longest of the regional organizations. As far back as 1997, the GCC member states met to address the challenges for national security and "traditional practices and religious beliefs" of growing Internet connectivity. More recently, at the 2008 ITU Regional Cybersecurity Forum, held in Doha, representatives from the GCC were joined by Arab League states to discuss coordinated national security policies. The group issued a "Doha Declaration on Cybersecurity" at the conclusion, which emphasized the need for greater harmonization around cyberspace controls.[41]

Assertions of state power in cyberspace can exacerbate interstate rivalries and competition. After revelations of major breaches of the Indian national security establishment were made by the Information Warfare Monitor, for example, the Indian government stepped up its cyberwarfare and exploitation capabilities.[42] Legislation was even briefly proposed that would have legalized patriotic hacking in India in response to what was perceived to be a tolerance and exploitation of such activities in China.[43] The Indian government also took measures to restrict imports of high technology from China.[44] After the Operation Aurora attacks that compromised Google, the U.S. National Security Agency was called in to investigate the matter, and many inside and outside Congress pointed to the incident as a justification for an urgent expansion of offensive cyber capabilities.[45] Reflecting these sentiments, retired Air Force General Kevin P. Chilton argued that the United States should undertake a major and very public exercise of its offensive cyber capabilities for deterrent effects on other countries, presumably such as China.[46]

The militarization of cyberspace that we have described has touched off an arms race in the domain as governments and others rush to develop offensive capabilities. But it is also cultivating a normative milieu where offensive actions taken against adversaries and threats are given wider latitude and justification. Although within U.S. policy circles a tight lid is still kept on revelations of offensive cyber attacks, public discussions, like those of General Chilton, are becoming much more common. Likewise, although distributed denial of service (DDoS) attacks can be traced back decades, there has been a rash of more politically motivated ones, including those seemingly undertaken by or in support of governments against opposition groups and by citizens against states and corporations, such as the crowd-sourced Anonymous attacks directed against Tunisia and Egypt, and Visa, Mastercard, and Paypal.[47] In early 2011, in what will likely stand as one of the more brazen public hacks, Anonymous breached the servers of a security firm that was investigating its actions, called HBGary. The group defaced its Web site, took over the Twitter and LinkedIn accounts of some of its executives, and released more than 70,000 company e-mails into the public domain.[48]

Responses to this incident have yet to unfold, but seem certain to fuel more urgent calls to police cyberspace and control anonymity.

Driver 5: The Political Economy of Cyber Security

The assertion of state power in cyberspace is feeding into and in turn being driven by a massively exploding market for cyber security products and services. The size of this market is difficult to pinpoint with precision, in part because it is stretched across so many different economic sectors but also in part because a great deal of it is hidden within military and intelligence "black budgets" and withheld from public scrutiny. There are estimates that the global cyber security market is anywhere between USD 80 and 140 billion annually.[49] The market has triggered a major business restructuring and the emergence of a new cyber industrial complex, particularly in the United States where the market for products and services is the largest. Traditional military industrial giants like Northrup Grunman, Boeing, and Lockheed Martin have shifted to the cyber security markets, alongside a wide range of new niche players providing specialized services and tools.

It is important to underline that the political economy of cyber security not only responds to market demands, but is also a constitutive force that shapes and affects the realm of the possible, including strategic policy. New products and services, such as those providing deep packet inspection, surveillance and reconnaissance, data mining and analysis, filtering and throttling, and even computer network attack and exploitation present new opportunities for authorities and other actors that might never have been imagined. OpenNet Initiative research has tracked the sale of filtering technologies to authoritarian regimes for many years, but the market has expanded considerably.[50] Companies like Narus, for example, market products and technologies that allow precise identification and throttling of packets and protocols, including those used by censorship-circumvention projects and services. One of its products, Hone, parses through massive amounts of social networking data from disparate sources to connect individuals to separate accounts.[51] Its services came under scrutiny when it was revealed that its products were being employed to track dissidents and activists in Egypt and Saudi Arabia.[52] A growing number of firms now offer offensive computer network attack capabilities, which are being marketed as "solutions" for states and corporations.[53] Not surprisingly, the market can encourage the type of offensive actions against adversaries outlined earlier that push the boundaries of acceptable behavior online. For example, a Bollywood studio in India contracted a cyber security firm to engage in DDoS attacks against film download and torrent file trading sites.[54] As this type of market continues to expand, we should expect tools and services such as these to inform and drive state control practices.

Conclusion: Toward a Crisis of Authority

The drivers of cyberspace contestation outlined in the preceding sections reflect deep and powerful social forces that are not easily reversed. On the contrary, the momentum around each of these drivers of contestation is escalating and compounding daily. They are also mutually reinforcing. Although there are many implications of these contests, for cyberspace they reach down deep into and call into question some of its core constitutive norms, rules, and principles. Everything seems to be up for grabs. In such circumstances, it is fair to say that we have reached a point where cyberspace is an essentially contested space, to borrow a phrase form the philosopher W. B. Gallie. There is a crisis of authority in cyberspace, reflecting a fundamental disagreement about everything from acceptable behavior and rules of the road to the basis upon which the network itself is structured and governed globally.

In such circumstances, we should expect architectonic shifts—that is, alterations to the very nature of cyberspace itself that could change its character. Here it is important to emphasize that cyberspace is a human-made domain and therefore subject to a variety of technical rules and systems, all of which can be manipulated or subject to reversal and alteration. Such architectonic shifts could come by the introduction of shortsighted measures based out of fear and insecurity that have long-lasting and radical repercussions. One can see glimpses of such measures in disparate areas: in the growing number of cases of network disruption, from Nepal, China, Burma, Iran, and Egypt, as well as in "Internet kill switch" legislation proposals that would empower U.S. authorities to shut down the network in times of "crisis"; in discussions of mandatory Internet identity requirements and the abolition of online anonymity or discussions about reengineering the Internet; and most shockingly, in brazen offensive cyber attacks unleashed against supporters and detractors of Wikileaks, including theft and public release of proprietary e-mails. Principles and rules that were once considered fundamental and largely sacred have been subject to reexamination and questioning and outright dismissal—from network neutrality, to peering and domain name routing arrangements, to the legitimacy of DDoS and other types of offensive computer attacks.

It is against this backdrop that several developments on the horizon loom large and hold out the prospect for major design shifts in the architecture of cyberspace. According to many analysts, 2012 is the year in which the present IP addressing system, labeled IPv4, will run out of space and network operators and services will be required to adopt a new solution. The rapid expansion of Internet access in the Asian region is cited as one of the major factors contributing to the hasty exhaustion of the 4.3 billion spaces originally allocated in 1977.[55] At present, the main alternative to the existing system, IPv6, is one that offers much less anonymity and gives operators of networks considerably more power to identity individuals connected to specific devices.

The shift to mobile devices was outlined earlier, but the point bears repeating here. At present and into the future, the majority of individuals will be accessing cyberspace through a handheld device. Though constituting a part of cyberspace, and often connecting through the Internet, mobile systems employ a unique architecture of routing, which offers an opportunity for network operators to build insularity from other networks, as well as to isolate users into segments in granular ways that previous devices, like PCs, could not. As more cyberspace use takes place through mobile networks, a new architecture may supersede and ultimately displace the existing one. When considered together, IPv6 and mobile ecosystems present probably the most important watershed moment for cyberspace design.

Another looming set of issues concerns mounting pressures toward territorialized Internet access. The trend toward cyberspace territorialization, which started with national technical filtering, is now being reinforced by economic strategies. Countries recognize that economic barriers can be just as effective, and offer a much lower political cost, than traditional censorship. Many are throwing state support behind national cyberspace development projects, which are now defined as a critical economic sector. For example, Kazakhstan and Tajikistan make available access to the Internet that is restricted to the national domain at a lower cost than access to the global Internet. Russia has determined that the construction of a national search engine is in that country's strategic interest.[56] China Mobile Communications and Xinhua News Agency have signed an agreement to create a homegrown search engine.[57] Iran proposed the creation of a national e-mail system as a competitor to Gmail that, while not meeting much support, shows the same strategic inclination.[58] National-level services and technologies like these can be justified as being in the national economic interest while also being easier to subject to political controls and regulations. They also complement the emergence of linguistic domains, which allow governments like China and Russia to control the registration of domains in national languages. Together, these further the severing of nonterritorial networks around which cyberspace has been constituted.

While these mutually reinforcing drivers certainly hold out a daunting prospect for the future of the cyberspace commons, there is a silver lining. With a deeply contested space comes a crisis of authority, and the entire edifice of cyberspace governance is thrown into question and laid bare for reexamination. A lid is lifted on the Internet, allowing for a closer examination of what goes on beneath the surface, including that which has been obscured by state secrecy or intellectual property concerns. Arguably, as cyberspace contestation continues apace, a growing number of citizens worldwide now can include in their daily lexicon issues of deep packet inspection, content filtering, encryption, and circumvention. What was once an arcane discussion restricted to engineers, intelligence agencies, and a small segment of policymakers is being broadened into public-policy and popular circles. Although the prospects are strong that the present circumstances could see the introduction of radical and shortsighted measures, there is an equal opportunity for a discussion of "first principles" of cyberspace. With a crisis of authority, in other words, could come a constitutional moment for cyberspace.

Notes

1. W. B. Gallie, "Essentially Contested Concepts," *Proceedings of the Aristotelian Society,* 56 (1956): 167–198.

2. International Telecommunication Union (ITU), "ITU Estimates Two Billion People Online by End 2010: Access to Mobile Networks Available to Over 90% of World Population; 143 Countries Offer 3G Services," October 19, 2010, http://www.itu.int/net/pressoffice/press_releases/2010/39.aspx.

3. International Telecommunication Union (ITU), "Internet Indicators: Subscribers, Users and Broadband Subscribers," 2009 Figures, http://www.itu.int/ITU-D/icteye/Reporting/ShowReportFrame.aspx?ReportName=/WTI/InformationTechnologyPublic&ReportFormat=HTML4.0&RP_intYear=2009&RP_intLanguageID=1&RP_bitLiveData=False.

4. Organization for Economic Cooperation and Development (OECD), "The Economic Impact of Shutting Down Internet and Mobile Phone Services in Egypt," February 4, 2011, http://www.oecd.org/document/19/0,3746,en_2649_33703_47056659_1_1_1_1,00.html.

5. Noor, "Clients," http://www.noor.net/Clients.aspx.

6. Noor was eventually shut down on January 31, 2011. Earl Zmijewski, "Egypt's Net on Life Support," Renesys Blog, January 31, 2011, http://www.renesys.com/blog/2011/01/egypts-net-on-life-support.shtml.

7. Ethan Zuckerman, "Intermediary Censorship," in *Access Controlled: The Shaping of Power, Rights, and Rule in Cyberspace*, ed. Ronald Deibert, John Palfrey, Rafal Rohozinski, and Jonathan Zittrain (Cambridge, MA: MIT Press, 2010), 71–85.

8. Rebecca MacKinnon, "Will Google Stand Up to France and Italy, Too?" *The Guardian*, January 13, 2010, http://www.guardian.co.uk/commentisfree/libertycentral/2010/jan/13/google-china-western-internet-freedom.

9. Rachel Donadio, "Larger Threat Is Seen in Google Case," *New York Times,* February 24, 2010, http://www.nytimes.com/2010/02/25/technology/companies/25google.html.

10. Yamini Lohia, "Shackling the Net," *Times of India*, April 12, 2010, http://timesofindia.indiatimes.com/home/opinion/edit-page/Shackling-The-Net/articleshow/5784887.cms.

11. International Telecommunication Union (ITU), "Key Global Telecom Indicators for the World Telecommunication Service Sector," 2010 Figures, http://www.itu.int/ITU-D/ict/statistics/at_glance/KeyTelecom.html.

12. Vodafone, "Statements—Vodafone Egypt," February 3, 2011, http://www.vodafone.com/content/index/press/press_statements/statement_on_egypt.html.

13. Reporters Without Borders, "BlackBerry Filters out Porn Sites in Response to Government's Demand," January 20, 2011, http://en.rsf.org/indonesia-blackberry-filters-out-porn-sites-20-01-2011,39371.html.

14. Ronald Deibert, "Cyberspace Confidential," *Globe and Mail*, August 6, 2010, http://www.theglobeandmail.com/news/opinions/cyberspace-confidential/article1665125.

15. William Gibson, *Neuromancer* (New York: Ace Books, 1984).

16. Ronald Deibert and Rafal Rohozinski, "Liberation vs. Control: The Future of Cyberspace," *Journal of Democracy*, 24, no. 1 (October 2010): 43–57.

17. The ITU estimated that in 2010, 162 million of the 226 million new Internet users in 2010 would be from developing countries. International Telecommunication Union, "ITU Estimates Two Billion People Online by End 2010," October 19, 2010, http://www.itu.int/net/pressoffice/press_releases/2010/39.aspx.

18. Internet World Stats, "World Internet Usage and Population Statistics," June 30, 2010, http://www.internetworldstats.com/stats.htm.

19. Paul Budde Communication Pty Ltd. "China—Key Statistics, Telecom Market, Regulatory Overview and Forecasts," July 7, 2010.

20. International Telecommunication Union, "ITU Estimates Two Billion People Online by End 2010," October 19, 2010, http://www.itu.int/net/pressoffice/press_releases/2010/39.aspx.

21. Internet World Stats, "The Internet Big Picture: World Internet Users and Population Stats," 2010, http://www.internetworldstats.com/stats.htm, accessed February 18, 2011.

22. According to the UN, least developed countries "represent the poorest and weakest of the international community. Extreme poverty, the structural weaknesses of their economies and the lack of capacities related to growth, often compounded by structural handicaps, hamper efforts of these countries to improve the quality of life of their people. These countries are also characterized by their acute susceptibility to external economic shocks, natural and man-made disasters and communicable diseases." Office of High Representative for Least Developed Countries, Landlocked Developing Countries and Small Island Developing States, "Least Developed Countries: About LDCs," http://www.unohrlls.org/en/ldc/25.

23. Alex Wilhelm, "Chinese: The New Dominant Language of the Internet [Infographic]," The Next Web, December 21, 2010, http://thenextweb.com/asia/2010/12/21/chinese-the-new-dominant-language-of-the-internet-infographic.

24. For further discussion, see Milton Mueller, "China and Global Internet Governance: A Tiger by the Tail," chapter 9 in this volume.

25. Sophos, "Security Threat Report: Mid-year 2010," White Paper, 24, https://secure.sophos.com/sophos/docs/eng/papers/sophos-security-threat-report-midyear-2010-wpna.pdf.

26. Joseph Menn, *Fatal System Error* (New York: Public Affairs, 2010).

27. Information Warfare Monitor, *Tracking GhostNet: Investigating a Cyber Espionage Network*, March 29, 2009, http://www.tracking-ghost.net/; Information Warfare Monitor and Shadowserver Foundation, *Shadows in the Cloud: An Investigation into Cyber Espionage 2.0*, April 6, 2010, http://shadows-in-the-cloud.net/; "Websites of Three Burmese News Agencies in Exile under Attack," *Mizzima News,* September 17, 2008, http://www.mizzima.com/news/regional/1052-websites-of -three-burmese-news-agencies-in-exile-under-attack.html; Alexis Madrigal, "The Inside Story of How Facebook Responded to Tunisian Hacks," *The Atlantic,* January 24, 2011, http://www .theatlantic.com/technology/archive/2011/01/the-inside-story-of-how-facebook-responded-to -tunisian-hacks/70044; and Alexis Madrigal, "Most Sophisticated Malware Ever Targets Iran," *The Atlantic*, September 22, 2010, http://www.theatlantic.com/technology/archive/2010/09/ most-sophisticated-malware-ever-targets-iran-possibly-state-backed/63420.

28. James Farwell and Rafal Rohozinski, "Stuxnet and the Future of Cyber War," *Survival* 53.1 (2011), 23–40.

29. Ronald Deibert and Rafal Rohozinski, "Control and Subversion in Russian Cyberspace," in *Access Controlled: The Shaping of Power, Rights, and Rule in Cyberspace,* ed. Ronald Deibert, John Palfrey, Rafal Rohozinski, and Jonathan Zittrain (Cambridge, MA: MIT Press, 2010), 15–34.

30. Sue Pleming, "U.S. State Department Speaks to Twitter over Iran," Reuters, June 16, 2009, http:// www.reuters.com/article/2009/06/16/us-iran-election-twitter-usa-idUSWBT01137420090616.

31. Eddan Katz, "Holding Nokia Responsible for Surveilling Dissidents in Iran," Electronic Frontier Foundation, October 13, 2010, http://www.eff.org/deeplinks/2010/10/saharkhiz-v-nokia.

32. Hamid Tehrani, "Iran: Cyber Islamic Militarism on the March," Global Voices, February 19, 2010, http://globalvoicesonline.org/2010/02/19/iran-cyber-islamic-militarism-on-the-march.

33. Reports that were made in confidence to one of the authors of this chapter indicate that the Iranian cyber army had been able to penetrate deep into Green Revolution social movements through the use of sophisticated malware. If these reports are credible, and there is a good possibility that they are, the unquestioned assumption often made about the one-way impact of information and communications technologies (ICTs) on social and political liberation would need some serious qualification.

34. Bruce Etling and John Kelly, *Mapping Iran's Online Public: Politics and Culture in the Persian Blogosphere,* Berkman Center Research Publication No. 2008–01, 2008, http://cyber.law.harvard .edu/publications/2008/Mapping_Irans_Online_Public.

35. Noam Cohen, "Twitter Puts Spotlight on Secret F.B.I. Subpoenas," *New York Times,* January 1, 2011, http://www.nytimes.com/2011/01/10/business/media/10link.html?_r=1&partner=rss&emc=rss.

36. Lee Tae-hoon, "Censorship on Pro-NK Web Sites Tight," *Korea Times*, September 9, 2010, http://www.koreatimes.co.kr/www/news/nation/2010/09/113_72788.html.

37. The member states of the SCO are China, Kazakhstan, Kyrgyzstan, Russia, Tajikistan, and Uzbekistan. India, Iran, Mongolia, and Pakistan are observers.

38. The member states of the Arab League are Algeria, Bahrain, Comoros, Djibouti, Egypt, Iraq, Jordan, Kuwait, Lebanon, Libya, Mauritania, Morocco, Oman, Palestine, Qatar, Saudi Arabia, Somalia, Sudan, Syria, Tunisia, the United Arab Emirates, and Yemen.

39. The member states of the GCC are the United Arab Emirates, Bahrain, Saudi Arabia, Oman, Qatar, and Kuwait.

40. Tom Gjelten, "Seeing the Internet as an "Information Weapon," National Public Radio, September 23, 2010, http://www.npr.org/templates/story/story.php?storyId=130052701&sc=fb& cc=fp.

41. International Telecommunication Union, "Arab Region Presses for Heightened Cybersecurity: Doha Declaration on Cybersecurity Adopted at ITU Forum," February 21, 2008, http://www. itu.int/newsroom/press_releases/2008/NP01.html; ITU Regional Cybersecurity Forum 2008, "Draft Meeting Report: ITU Regional Workshop on Frameworks for Cybersecurity and Critical Information Infrastructure Protection (CIIP) and Cybersecurity Forensics Workshop Doha, Qatar, February 18–21, 2008," (RWD/2008/01-E), February 21, 2008, http://www.itu.int/ITU-D/cyb/ events/2008/doha/docs/doha-cybersecurity-forum-report-feb-08.pdf.

42. "Cyber War: Indian Army Gearing Up," Times of India, July 19, 2010, http://timesofindia .indiatimes.com/tech/news/internet/Cyber-war-Indian-Army-gearing-up/articleshow/6187297 .cms.

43. Joji Thomas Philip and Harsimran Singh, "Spy Game: India Readies Cyber Army to Hack into Hostile Nations' Computer Systems," Economic Times, August 6, 2010, http://economictimes. indiatimes.com/news/news-by-industry/et-cetera/Spy-Game-India-readies-cyber-army-to-hack -into-hostile-nations-computer-systems/articleshow/6258977.cms.

44. Heather Timmons, "India Tells Mobile Firms to Delay Deals for Chinese Telecom Equipment," New York Times, April 30, 2010, http://www.nytimes.com/2010/05/01/business/global/01delhi .html.

45. John Markoff, "Google Asks N.S.A. to Investigate Cyberattacks," New York Times, February 4, 2010, http://www.nytimes.com/2010/02/05/science/05google.html?_r=1.

46. Bill Gertz, "Show of Strength Urged for Cyberwar," Washington Times, January 27, 2011, http://www.washingtontimes.com/news/2011/jan/27/show-of-strength-urged-for-cyberwar/ ?page=1.

47. Jose Nazario, "Politically Motivated Denial of Service Attacks," in The Virtual Battlefield: Perspectives on Cyber Warfare, ed. Christian Czosseck and Kenneth Geers (Amsterdam: IOS Press, 2009), 163–181; Christopher R. Walker, "A Brief History of Operation Payback," Salon, December 9, 2010, http://mobile.salon.com/news/feature/2010/12/09/0.

48. Nate Anderson, "Anonymous vs. HBGary: The Aftermath," February 24, 2011, Ars Technica, http://arstechnica.com/tech-policy/news/2011/02/anonymous-vs-hbgary-the-aftermath.ars.

49. Deepa Seetharaman, "Arms Makers Turn Focus from Bombs to Bytes," Reuters, September 10, 2010, http://www.reuters.com/article/2010/09/10/us-aero-arms-summit-cybersecurity -idUSTRE6893EI20100910.

50. See, for example, Helmi Noman, "Middle East Censors Use Western Technologies to Block Viruses and Free Speech," OpenNet Initiative, July 27, 2009, http://opennet.net/blog/2009/07/middle-east-censors-use-western-technologies-block-viruses-and-free-speech.

51. Robert McMillan, "Narus Develops a Scary Sleuth for Social Media," IT World, March 3, 2010, http://www.itworld.com/internet/98652/narus-develops-a-scary-sleuth-social-media.

52. Ryan Singel, "Lawmaker Calls for Limits on Exporting Net-Spying Tools," *Wired*, February 11, 2011, http://www.wired.com/epicenter/2011/02/narus.

53. Dancho Danchev, "Should a Targeted Country Strike Back at the Cyber Attackers?" ZD Net, May 10, 2010, http://www.zdnet.com/blog/security/should-a-targeted-country-strike-back-at-the-cyber-attackers/6194.

54. John Leydon, "Bollywood 'Recruits DDoS Hired Guns to Fight Movie Pirates,'" *The Register*, September 10, 2010, http://www.theregister.co.uk/2010/09/10/bollywood_cyber_vigilantes_fight_movie_pirates.

55. Laurie J. Flynn, "Drumming Up More Addresses on the Internet," *New York Times*, February 14, 2011, http://www.nytimes.com/2011/02/15/technology/15internet.html?ref=technology.

56. "Russia Said to Be Developing National Search Engine—Vedomosti," Automated Trader, July 7, 2010, http://www.automatedtrader.net/real-time-dow-jones/3574/russia-said-to-be-developing-national-search-engine-_vedomosti.

57. Owen Fletcher, "The Chinese State Enters Online Search," *Wall Street Journal*, August 16, 2010, http://blogs.wsj.com/digits/2010/08/16/the-chinese-state-enters-online-search.

58. "Oh Lord: Why Iran's National Search Engine Will Likely Fail," Radio Free Europe/Radio Liberty, August 29, 2010, http://www.rferl.org/content/Oh_Lord_Why_Irans_National_Search_Engine_Will_Likely_Fail/2140725.html.

3   The Struggle for Digital Freedom of Speech

The Malaysian Sociopolitical Blogosphere's Experience

Vee Vian Thien

Beginning in July 2008, sodomy was featured in most Malaysian sociopolitical blogs and the headlines of Malaysian dailies for several months—a curious phenomenon given that a majority of Malaysians are either deeply religious or morally conservative, or a combination of both. Also, sodomy is a criminal offense in at least 78 countries including Malaysia.[1] The media interest was inspired by the unique identification of sodomy with the political career of a single man, Anwar Ibrahim. Anwar was charged with the offense once in 1998 when he held office as deputy prime minister of Malaysia, and again in 2008, as de facto leader of the opposition coalition, Pakatan Rakyat (PR). The timing of both trials could not be more significant. In 1998, the global spotlight was on Malaysia as host of the 1998 Commonwealth Games and for its upcoming 1999 general elections in the midst of the Asian financial crisis. On March 8, 2008, Anwar led PR to a new political dawn as a meaningful adversary to the ruling regime, Barisan Nasional (BN), in the 12th Malaysian general elections. For the first time in Malaysian history, PR stripped BN of its two-thirds majority in the federal parliament.[2]

The thriving, vibrant, and active Malaysian political blogosphere in its current form owes much to the Anwar sodomy saga. First, Anwar's trial attracted severe domestic and international criticism, which in combination with the Asian financial crisis created a hostile political atmosphere prior to the 1999 elections for his former mentor, the incumbent prime minister Dr. Mahathir Mohamad. Mahathir responded by pledging to boost Internet penetration in Malaysia through a series of programs.[3] Cumulatively, these programs effected changes necessary for the development of the Malaysian sociopolitical blogosphere. They laid the requisite physical infrastructure for access to broadband connection, that is, high-speed fiber-optic wires and ISPs, and trained a generation of "digital natives."[4]

Second, Anwar's swift coup-style removal from high political office stunned Malaysians into action. In 1998, they formed Reformasi, a grassroots movement protesting his dismal record that united disparate segments of civil society for the first time. This relatively diffuse, single-issue movement transformed into PR, a formidable opponent to BN in 2008. Notably, on both occasions, PR and Reformasi relied heavily on the Internet to evade long-standing governmental control and surveillance of the mainstream media. The year 1998 saw the beginning of political activism on the Internet with the proliferation of pro-Reformasi Web sites.[5] In 2008, PR ran a successful campaign on blogs and Web sites, managing to elect blogger-politicians.[6] Third, because the constrained and censored mainstream media were unable to satiate the Malaysian public's hunger for details of Anwar's high-profile first sodomy trial, this news vacuum enabled Malaysiakini, an award-winning online news portal, to launch itself successfully into the role of a reliable and objective source of uncensored information.

Since 2008 the Malaysian government has made numerous attempts at asserting control over the relatively unfettered Internet, citing maintenance of racial harmony in ethnically diverse Malaysia as its regulatory justification.[7] These attempts, whether an extension of existing laws or a tabling of regulatory proposals, have been met with ferocious online resistance, especially by the Malaysian blogosphere. To date, the Malaysian government has backed down from its three most drastic regulatory proposals: implementation of a nationwide filter on the Internet, registration of bloggers, and identifying "professional" as opposed to "nonprofessional" bloggers. Although the government has not formally acknowledged these acts as a concession to online pressure, the concession can be inferred from the circumstances. This social pressure is significant in its context—the Malaysian government is not known for retracting or repealing unpopular measures, especially those infringing on civil liberties.[8]

Malaysian sociopolitical blogs, a subcategory of blogs on matters concerning the governance of state and socioeconomic concerns, figure prominently in the general Malaysian public consciousness and were especially influential in the run-up to the 2008 elections, according to a study conducted by Zentrum Future Studies, a media studies research group.[9] Zentrum's survey polled eligible voters between the ages of 21 and 41 during the election campaign period running from February 20 to March 5, 2008. Zentrum reported that 54.1 percent of 21,000 eligible voters in its nationwide sample designated the online media, that is, blogs and news portals like Malaysiakini, as their preferred source of information, as opposed to mainstream newspapers.[10] Of the 11,360 sampled voters who preferred online media, 58.5 percent ranked blogs as their primary source.[11] Blogs had a much stronger following among younger voters than their older counterparts, as figure 3.1 illustrates. Given their visibility, these blogs and their administrators have been the main Internet regulatory target of the Malaysian government.

This chapter situates the regulatory drama currently unfolding in Malaysia within the OpenNet Initiative theoretical framework of next-generation controls, as conceptualized by Ronald Deibert and Rafal Rohozinski in the context of the Commonwealth of Independent States (CIS).[12] It then identifies structural and normative features of the Malaysian political blogosphere that have enabled it to successfully contest the

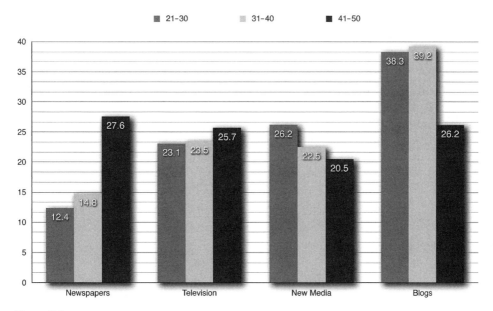

Figure 3.1
Age-based comparison of Malaysian voters' preferred media sources during the 2008 Malaysian general elections.
Source: Reproduced by permission from Zentrum Future Studies.

Malaysian government's imposition of *linear* regulatory measures, defined as traditional top-down imposition of state power. The chapter concludes by describing the recent emergence of third-generation controls in Malaysia and hypothesizing that it may be part of a wider shift toward subtler, covert, and, most importantly, *nonlinear,* participatory, and competitive forms of regulating the Internet in Malaysia. This shift in regulatory methodology also demonstrates the advent of a singular, unprecedented, bilateral dialogue between the Malaysian government and its regulatory subjects, namely, the sociopolitical blogosphere. I suggest that the direction of this conversation is still susceptible to influence by the Malaysian blogosphere.

Linear Regulatory Attempts: Hierarchical Top-Down Application of First- and Second-Generation Controls

Around 2007 the Malaysian government moved from publicly denouncing sociopolitical bloggers as untrustworthy to taking concrete steps against these vocal critics. In lieu of its well-known 1998 pledge of noncensorship of the Internet, the Malaysian government resorted mainly to second-generation controls.[13] It took a two-pronged approach in its attempt to extend traditional, unidirectional, top-down, and hence what I call "linear," imposition of state power over cyberspace. First, it expanded its application of existing defamation, sedition, and "offensive content" laws to bloggers. Second, it proposed regulatory measures specifically targeted at bloggers or the Internet.

In January 2007, a landmark defamation suit was instigated by NSTP Corporation, a publication company with close ties to BN, against two prominent political bloggers.[14] Subsequently, the government began detaining blogger-critics under various national security laws from 2007 to 2008. Floods of complaints were also filed with the Malaysian Communications and Multimedia Commission (MCMC), the main Internet regulatory body, against sociopolitical bloggers for the criminal offense of posting "offensive content" online.[15]

Malaysian Internet service providers (ISPs) are required by law to comply with written requests from MCMC to assist in preventing the commission of criminal offenses, including the improper use of the Internet to circulate "offensive content."[16] On August 27, 2008, MCMC issued an order to all Malaysian ISPs to deny access to the controversial but popular Malaysia Today run by Raja Petra Kamarudin.[17] Only TMNet, the main Malaysian ISP, complied with this order, applying a domain-name block on Malaysia Today. This type of block is known as DNS tampering. It was significant for its unprecedented utilization of MCMC's broad statutory powers against a Web site for *offensive* as opposed to *fraudulent* content. The timing of the block also coincided with a highly symbolic parliamentary by-election in Permatang Pauh on August 26, 2008, which saw the official return of Anwar Ibrahim to parliament after his incarceration in 1998.

Subsequently, the two main distributed denial of service (DDoS)[18] attacks on Malaysia Today occurred in September 2009 and September 2010, after Raja Petra released stories on governmental corruption running to billions of ringgit that were corroborated by leaked classified documents.[19] As with the 2008 DNS block, these attacks were strategically timed, occurring when Internet traffic to the site was exceptionally high. Raja Petra has suggested that the intermittent and focused nature of the attacks indicates that its instigators were professional for-hire hackers.[20] Two other sites, Anwar Ibrahim's blog and Free Malaysia Today, an independent news portal, also reported DDoS attacks on September 10, 2010.[21]

In 2007, the Malaysian government announced plans to introduce two additional regulatory measures specific to the political blogosphere. First, a Singapore-styled registration scheme was proposed, which would have rendered registration compulsory for bloggers designated as "political" by MCMC.[22] In Singapore this scheme has arguably chilled online political speech. In 2001 the founder of a popular and active Singaporean political discussion board, Sintercom, chose to shut the site down upon receiving notification that Sintercom had been designated "political" because registration would hold him personally liable for *all* content appearing on Sintercom. This includes anonymous libelous comments, thus exposing him to the risk of ruinous defamation suits.[23] Second, the government also proposed a labeling regime distinguishing government-backed "professional" from "nonprofessional" bloggers.[24] A third measure—far more drastic and wide-ranging than the first two—was announced on August 6, 2009. The Malaysian government declared plans to implement an Internet filter to curb access to pornography and "racially inflammatory" material. Reuters reported that a filter tender was issued to software companies on the same day.[25]

2007–2010: The Blogosphere's Backlash

Within hours of service of a defamation suit against Jeff Ooi and Ahiruddin Attan by NSTP, a blog dedicated solely to their cause was launched, a fund set up, and a solidarity logo "Bloggers United" mushroomed all over the Malaysian blogosphere.[26] After Nathaniel Tan became the first blogger to be detained under national security laws in Malaysia, a forum was held on July 20, 2007, to protest his arrest. The "Say 'NO!' to a Police State in the Malaysian Blogosphere" forum drew an audience of more than 150 individuals, and its panelists included many of the same individuals who rallied in support of Ooi and Attan, the first indicator of continuity in collective action by the blogosphere.[27]

When news of MCMC's order to ISPs to block Malaysia Today broke in 2008, in addition to resounding condemnation of the block, methods of circumventing the DNS block were posted immediately on other political blogs. The September 2010 DDoS attack on Malaysia Today was ultimately futile as copies of documents that the attack was apparently intended to block reappeared on another blog. Despite the 2009 and 2010 DDoS attacks, older Malaysia Today articles were shared on other sociopolitical blogs, mirroring the response to the DNS block in 2008.[28]

Responding to First- and Second-Generation Regulatory Proposals

The government's registration-of-bloggers scheme was reported on April 4, 2007. On April 5, 2007, a group of core sociopolitical bloggers met in person, formed an unregistered society of bloggers, the National Alliance of Bloggers (NAB), and elected its pro tem committee.[29] Members of NAB and other bloggers presented a unanimous front in condemning both registration and labeling proposals.[30] NAB organized a gathering on May 19, 2007, and hosted the forum "Blogs and Digital Democracy" five months later on October 3, 2007. Although ministerial statements indicate that the government was still contemplating new laws as of July 2007,[31] no draft legislation was ever reported, and by May 2009 the information minister affirmed that no new laws would be introduced against bloggers.[32] Anecdotal evidence and an observation of the chronology of events indicate that the fierce and quick-fire backlash by political bloggers, combined with widespread criticism, was at the very minimum a significant factor in the government's decision to retract its regulatory plans. Following 2009 proposals of a Malaysia-wide Internet filter, politicians and civil-society activists greeted this proposal with furious criticism on the blogosphere. Less than a week later, the Malaysian government retreated from this proposal, contradicting a Reuters report that it had already issued tenders to software companies.[33]

A Malaysian Form of "Flash Mobs": Continuity in the Blogosphere's Collective Action

In October 2010 police reports were lodged against three popular political blogs for postings alleging corruption involving the information minister, coincidentally a long-time critic of Malaysian bloggers.[34] These provided the impetus for another "real-world" mobilization of sociopolitical bloggers. A week after the police reports were filed, a group of bloggers, including former members of NAB, met in person and resolved to replace NAB with Bloggers for Malaysia (BfM), whose objectives are significantly less ambitious than NAB's, perhaps in response to the difficulties faced by NAB in obtaining consensus on universal standards of blogger conduct. Instead, BfM focuses on simply looking out for bloggers.[35] Both NAB and BfM share much in common with "flash mobs," powerful groups that form and dissolve rapidly. Much like NAB's relative dormancy after the initial uproar over legislative proposals in 2007, there has been little reported action by BfM since October 21, 2010. However, the distinguishing feature of these Malaysian "flash mobs" lies in the continuity of their identity and composition.

The Wider Roles of the Malaysian Sociopolitical Blogosphere

In addition to gaining electoral visibility in 2008 and contesting linear regulatory proposals between 2007 and 2010, the Malaysian political blogosphere plays several other roles often associated in developed democracies with the mainstream press.

Blogs as the Fifth Estate

Falling through an Internet loophole in licensing and registration regimes that constrain the Malaysian mainstream media, Malaysian bloggers have taken it upon themselves to act as watchdogs of the government.[36] They report on issues omitted by the mainstream media, set the public agenda in doing so, and provide refreshing, alternative viewpoints. For example, in early 2003, East Asia was afflicted by the fatal severe acute respiratory syndrome (SARS) epidemic. Fearing widespread panic, the Malaysian government required the mainstream media to downplay reporting on the issue, prompting a frustrated Jeff Ooi to comb the Internet for international sources, collating and posting his findings on his blog, Screenshots. Unexpectedly, Screenshots became a central hub for information on SARS, propelling Ooi's blog to international and domestic prominence.

Blogs as Catalysts for Mobilizing General Collective Action

One of the most highly visible accomplishments of the Malaysian blogosphere is its ability to rally huge protests and mobilize collective action. In a country where a gathering of three or more persons could constitute an assembly, thereby requiring a police permit, rallies, protests, and riots are rare.[37] From independence in 1957 until the emergence of the sociopolitical blogosphere circa 2005, there have been three major instances of riots. By contrast, civil society marched to protest on five separate occasions in 2007. All five were heavily publicized and coordinated by means of the Malaysian Internet and blogosphere, including the BERSIH rally calling for fair and clean elections, which attracted tens of thousands of protestors.

Blogs as Instructive Platforms of Expression

The mainstream Malaysian media steer clear of many pertinent political issues that are racially charged for fear of revocation of their printing licenses or of prosecution for sedition. By contrast, the blogosphere is strident and transparent about the "racial perspectives" taken, by both bloggers and readers who leave comments. However, "racially inflammatory" online content has not disrupted public order to date and is increasingly less commonplace, suggesting that the blogosphere may act as a "safety valve," a place to air grievances peaceably without resorting to violence and to discuss racial relations without descending to name calling.[38]

The Janus-Faced Malaysian Sociopolitical Blogosphere: A Medium of Communication and a Peer-Production System of Political Discourse

The question of how the Malaysian blogosphere has coordinated successful pushback against linear governmental regulatory attempts raises a related question of how it resolves the problem of information overload. Put simply, if anyone with access to the Internet can speak, how is anything meaningful being said or heard? The answer to both queries lies in unique features of the Malaysian political blogosphere.

Physical Clustering of Malaysian Sociopolitical Bloggers

In a 2006 study, Jun-E Tan and Zawawi Ibrahim report that Malaysian bloggers are geographically clustered.[39] An overwhelming 63.3 percent of them are located in Selangor and Kuala Lumpur, which is unsurprising given that this is the heartland of

Malaysia's IT-development projects and demographically has the highest percentage of top earners.[40] A 2008 study by Brian Ulicny reports that the active Malaysian sociopolitical blogosphere probably consists, at most, of 500 to 1,000 bloggers, "with a small, very active core of about 75 to 100 bloggers."[41] Based on the size of the political blogosphere and the geographical clustering of bloggers, the core community seems relatively easy to mobilize on short notice, especially if it is based on relationships that predate the blogosphere.

The Strength and Importance of Real-World Networks in Malaysia

There is a high degree of coincidence between the blogging community and civil-society activists in Malaysia, attributable in part to the initial lack of Internet censorship in the country. Political bloggers' demographics corroborate this overlap even further. A 2010 study by Brian Ulicny, Christopher J. Matheus, and Mieczyslaw M. Kokar observes that although 26.7 percent of their sample of random Malaysian bloggers are students, they make up a mere 5.9 percent of sociopolitical bloggers.[42] Also, the age range is correspondingly higher for this subset of Malaysian political bloggers, at an average age of 31.9 as opposed to the average of 20.5 for the sample of random Malaysian bloggers.[43]

A considerable number of top Malaysian sociopolitical bloggers are public figures in their capacity as civil-society activists, politicians, or prominent journalists. In a sample of 46 of the top sociopolitical blogs, drawn from a combination of the 2006 and 2010 studies, 34 bloggers reveal their identities. Of these, at least 20 fall within one of the three categories mentioned earlier. In addition, civil society strongly supports bloggers. The National Press Club hosted both 2007 and 2010 meetings establishing NAB and BfM, respectively. Also, the four Bloggers Universe Malaysia events to date have been jointly coordinated by NAB and the Center for Policy Initiatives, a nonprofit reformist think tank populated by bloggers.

Several propositions can be extrapolated from these observations and data. The higher median age of most sociopolitical bloggers provides a partial explanation for sustained participation within the blogosphere—Malaysian political bloggers are unlikely to be transitory college students. The significant number of these bloggers who were public figures prior to blogging accounts for the blogosphere's visibility, with its speakers drawing on their existing offline audiences. The remarkably rapid and impassioned responses by the blogosphere to regulatory proposals are unsurprising when juxtaposed against the Internet's intimate and multifaceted relationship with civil society. A comparison with Singapore illustrates the final point. By contrast to the thriving and active Malaysian sociopolitical blogosphere, its Singaporean counterpart is less visible and vocal despite Singapore's vastly superior Internet penetration rate. This contrast is especially stark when one compares Internet political activism during the countries' respective general elections, Singapore in 2006 and Malaysia in

2008. One academic reports the difference like this: "In the case of Singapore, the Internet merely exerted *some* pressure on the preexisting laws and state-imposed norms governing free speech; in contrast, in Malaysia, the Internet was a major contribution to what has been described as a 'political tsunami' during the recent general election."[44] Even allowing for Singapore's tighter online controls, election-specific regulations disallowing political videos and podcasts, and lack of explosive political scandals, academics attribute the general disparity to the preexisting strength of the offline Malaysian civil society.[45]

The observation that the success of the Malaysian sociopolitical blogosphere owes much to the existing civil society movement suggests another identifying feature of Malaysian sociopolitical bloggers: their motivations are nonpecuniary and social-psychological in nature.[46] Tan and Ibrahim report that most political bloggers cite influencing public opinion and performing a civic duty as their rewards for blogging.[47] This finding is highly relevant because it rationalizes the vehement rejection of the 2007 proposed labeling regime. To these pundits, political blogging is less attractive when government incentives are introduced because it reduces the social-psychological rewards they derive from blogging. They could be perceived as hypocritical and less credible for accepting government-backed labels while claiming to act as watchdogs of an administration accused of corruption.

On the basic premise that rewards have to outweigh costs for people to act, up until 2007 participation in the Malaysian sociopolitical blogosphere came at a low cost, because infrastructure remained inexpensive with Malaysia's aggressive IT policy. However, from 2007, the combined threats of defamation suits, detention, and MCMC persecution have raised the cost of blogging significantly, as was made evident by Raja Petra's drastic step of fleeing the country to avoid repeated incarceration. Nevertheless, the Malaysian political blogosphere remains vibrant, active, and responsive, with Raja Petra continuing to contribute from abroad in spite of the high personal costs of his participation.

Norms: The Invisible "Glue" That Binds the Malaysian Sociopolitical Blogosphere

The final missing piece of the puzzle of necessary and sufficient factors for the Malaysian blogosphere's sustained existence lies in the presence of norms. Tan and Ibrahim report that Malaysian political bloggers believe that it is *right* to double-check one's sources, that it is *better* to identify oneself openly, and that it is *wrong* to hurl racial abuse in comment boxes.[48]

The distinction between norms and social practices lies in the internal perspective of obligation, an expectation of nonlegal sanctions. One *expects* social sanctions for noncompliance with the regular practice of removing one's hat in church but not for failure to attend the cinema on a weekly basis.[49] Norms can be further subdivided into two categories.[50] Abstract norms rely on full internalization and unanimous endorsement by participants of a social practice.[51] By contrast, concrete norms need only a desire for esteem, a much shallower mode of internalization, which in turn enables easier amendment or abandonment of these concrete norms without overall destruction of the abstract norms from which they stem.[52] This conceptual distinction has powerful explanatory force for the Malaysian sociopolitical blogosphere. From a combination of general observations and the 2006 and 2010 studies mentioned earlier, I argue that there are four abstract norms supported by a total of twelve concrete norms in the Malaysian blogosphere. The four abstract norms are as follows.

Responsible Blogging   Tan and Ibrahim report that Malaysian bloggers are, in general, not exceedingly conscientious about the veracity of facts in their postings.[53] By contrast, 63.0 percent of *sociopolitical* bloggers interviewed in 2006 claim to double-check facts before posting.[54] This practice is supported by two concrete norms: the "see-for-yourself" norm of linking to original materials and the norm of disclosing one's real-life identity. This abstract norm's operation is illustrated by Anwar Ibrahim's 2007 allegations of political tampering with judicial nominations. These claims were accepted by bloggers once they had viewed a corroborating video clip uploaded by Anwar.[55]

Expectation of Bias   Readers are ultimately responsible for checking the truthfulness of blog posts and making their own judgments on credibility. Out of 476 readers polled by Tan and Ibrahim who trust blogs, merely 13.2 percent admit to "strongly trust[ing]" these blogs.[56] This distrust is grounded in the subjective practice of blogging, commencing with what *bloggers* care about most, in sharp distinction to objective, neutral, public-interest reporting by professional journalists. This feeds into two separate concrete norms. First, bloggers are expected to disclose their ideologies and motivations. Second and correspondingly, readers are expected to be the final judge of content quality once bloggers have made their relevant disclosure. Criticisms of MCMC proceedings against Nose4News, a popular satirical blog known for its outlandish mock reports, demonstrate this abstract norm in practice. The blogosphere defended the blogger by pointing to clear disclaimer notices on Nose4News as sufficient discharge of the blogger's responsibilities to his readers.

Inclusivity   This abstract norm has enabled relatively unknown individuals, such as Jeff Ooi, to join the ranks of A-list sociopolitical bloggers. Inclusivity is highly significant in two ways. First, it maintains conversations between bloggers and readers, albeit weighted in favor of the blogger. Bloggers are expected to enable the comment function on their blogs and to consider readers' contributions as potential sources of information. Second, as between bloggers, a concrete norm of mutual links, whether in-line citation or the maintenance of blogrolls, sustains the existence of a community of political bloggers through clustering. The conceptual distinction between abstract and concrete norms is most relevant here. Based on a sample I created of 46 of the most popular A-list political blogs, 19 do not maintain blogrolls. Nine of these belong to blogger-politicians, some of whom kept blogrolls prior to the 2008 elections. This omission may stem from a risk-adverse political calculation, but it does not substantially weaken the overarching abstract norm of inclusivity.

Another concrete norm stemming from inclusivity is the granular and heterogeneous nature of participation in the blogosphere.[57] "Granular" means that the degree of contribution to discourse in the political blogosphere can be as minimal or extensive as one is able to make it. Contributions are also "heterogeneous"—the *type* of contribution made depends on the blogger's expertise or interest. For example, Haris Ibrahim as a trained lawyer posts on legal issues, and Tony Pua, now an elected MP, blogged almost exclusively on education in the past.

Topicality   The value articulated by this abstract norm is that the determinative criteria for mutual- or cross-linking are the quality, relevance, and subject matter of the materials, not simply how well-connected they already are.[58] It is manifested in three concrete norms. First, political bloggers are expected to be motivated by nonpecuniary rewards. Second, listing in a blogroll is based on the host blogger's judgment on topicality, which is crucial in race-divided Malaysia. Most significantly, topicality is embodied in the third concrete norm requiring removal of racial slurs from blogs. These comments are not considered valuable contribution to political discourse, and racial tensions are universally acknowledged to be especially damaging in Malaysia (table 3.1).[59]

Table 3.1

SUMMARY OF ABSTRACT AND CONCRETE NORMS IN THE MALAYSIAN SOCIOPOLITICAL BLOGOSPHERE	
Abstract Norms	**Concrete Norms**
1. "Responsible blogging"	• Double-check one's facts before posting online.
	• "See for yourself" links to original source
	• Reveal one's identity where possible.
2. Expectation of bias	• Disclosure of blogger's ideologies, motivations, or intentions
	• Readers are the ultimate judge of content quality.
3. Inclusivity in participation	• Permit comments to be left by readers.
	• Grant consideration to readers' e-mails/comments as potential sources of materials.
	• Mutual links encouraged by maintaining blogrolls and mutual citation
	• Granularity and heterogeneity are expected in contributions.
4. Topicality	• Incentive for blogging not pecuniary, but passion
	• If a blogroll is maintained, sites are selected based on topicality or language, not race.
	• Bloggers are responsible for removing racist comments, posts, and trolls.

The Malaysian Sociopolitical Blogosphere: A Peer-Production System
of Political Discourse

The Malaysian blogosphere mobilizes collective action effectively and avoids plunging into a chaotic abyss of information overload by operating as a self-organizing, networked, peer-production system of political discourse. It operates much like Wikipedia insofar as it is decentralized and dependent on social cues over market prices, and its participants are motivated by social-psychological rewards. The blogosphere's topological features and norms organize the production of political conversations through a three-step process of intake, filtration, and synthesis.[60]

Intake   The first step of this system of production is the intake of material. Überblogs function as central points of entry for information. Bloggers' main sources of information are online news portals, other blogs, and readers' e-mails. In addition, the elected politicians among Malaysian A-list bloggers will often have firsthand information on parliamentary proceedings or regulatory proposals. Although Malay is the official language in Malaysia, many Malaysian A-list bloggers act as links out to foreign blogs. These bloggers are linguistic bridges, translating English posts to Malay and vice versa. This practice is evident in my sample of 46 of the most popular Malaysian sociopolitical bloggers. More than half, 56.5 percent, cross-link across languages, and 32.6 percent of these blogs are themselves bilingual. Also, politician bloggers have a vested interest in maintaining multilingual blogs to reach a broader electorate base.

Filtration   The relevance of content is assessed by the posting bloggers who make judgments congruent with the norms of topicality and responsible blogging. Accreditation by fellow bloggers is an important aspect of the filtration mechanism. Although readers ultimately determine the reliability of a post for themselves, the blogosphere assists this process through a form of peer review reliant on "signals." The norms of topicality and responsible blogging together maintain a pool of vocal and vigilant individuals who will make their disagreement, if any, with a speaker-blogger's views known. Corroborative posts and/or the lack of contradictory posts thus form the first signal. The next two signals are general indicators of approval—listing on a blogroll is a personal stamp of approval by the listing blogger, and hit counters form a crude indicator of any one blog site's popularity.

The blogosphere's filtration mechanism played a visible role during the campaign season of a 2010 federal by-election. The Hulu Selangor by-election saw "blogwars" explode between BN and PR supporters over circulation of "evidence" that PR's Muslim candidate consumed alcohol. When the grainy photograph first emerged on two pro-BN blogs, discerning and unaffiliated sociopolitical bloggers immediately began commenting on the awkwardness of the candidate's arms in that photograph. Eventually, these unaffiliated bloggers located the original undoctored photograph from a newspaper clipping, concluding the debate over its authenticity.

Synthesis   The final stage of peer production in the blogosphere lies in synthesizing the material into blog posts. The stability of this stage depends on bloggers abiding by the norms of verification and the expectation of bias. Additionally, the concrete norm of granularity and heterogeneity is triggered at this stage, when bloggers delve into as much depth as they want on a particular topic or take a particular spin on it. Note also the continuing responsibility of bloggers to monitor comments and remove racist slurs.

Cycling back to the two questions I asked at the outset of this discussion (How does the Malaysian sociopolitical blogosphere successfully coordinate pushback against linear, unidirectional regulatory attempts and fulfill the wider roles ascribed to it?), we must recall the relevant baseline. The Malaysian mainstream media suffer two major weaknesses; they are heavily censored and are divided by language. Unlike the mainstream media, the blogosphere emerged free from licensing regimes and thus has not been forced to adopt a similarly strong norm of self-censorship. Also, while multilingual columns in Malaysian daily papers are rare, a majority of the top Malaysian sociopolitical bloggers serve as linguistic bridges. The plotted link structure of the Malaysian political blogosphere by Ulicny, Matheus, and Kokar in figure 3.2 indicates this relationship. It also suggests that there is no extreme BN/PR polarization problem (yet) akin to the Republican/Democratic divide in the U.S. blogosphere.

Figure 3.2
Link structure of the Malaysian sociopolitical blogosphere as of 2010.
Source: Reproduced by permission from Brian Ulicny, Christopher J. Matheus, and Mieczyslaw M. Kokar, "Metrics for Monitoring a Social-Political Blogosphere," IEEE Computer Society 34 (2010).

Because the blogosphere is a decentralized peer-production system, individual detentions and defamation suits did not cripple the system as a whole, nor could the government assert comprehensive control by usurping centralized corporate ownership. In addition, more people are speaking to each other through the medium of the Malaysian blogosphere across racial and linguistic divides that exist offline. Existing real-world relationships, networks, and civil-society activism provide a strong starting point of publicity for the political blogosphere that has been enhanced and sustained by norms. With the relative geographical proximity of Malaysian sociopolitical bloggers, these factors cumulatively enable rapid, powerful responses both online and offline to linear regulatory attempts.

A Shift Away from Linear Regulation: Third-Generation Controls

It would be a misstatement to describe BN as still being the underdog in the digital race for votes.[61] After its 2008 debacle of losing the Internet war, the incumbent BN that still controls the Malaysian federal government has demonstrated a willingness to compete for cyberspace. Recent governmental actions indicate an inception of third-generation controls that are competitive, participatory, and nonlinear. Instead of traditional, unidirectional imposition of state power on the regulatory target, these measures focus on counterinformation strategies where the state is an active player competing for online reader attention. Such measures can broadly be divided between general and election-specific measures.

Most BN politicians launched their own Facebook pages, blogs, and Twitter accounts after 2008. Joining a global trend of e-transparency, the Malaysian government launched MyProcurement.com in April 2010. MyProcurement.com is an online portal displaying all nonclassified governmental tenders and successful bids. This is a peculiarly bold and risky move because these contracts form a recurrent theme in Malaysian corruption scandals. MyProcurement.com has received mixed reviews and has led to further uncovering of corruption by PR politicians. Another notable example of online engagement occurred in August 2010. Thousands of Malaysians responded to the prime minister's invitation on his blog 1Malaysia for suggestions and comments on the 2011 national budget that was due to be tabled before Parliament.

There has also been a significant increase in anonymous disruptive attacks on both PR and independent blogs. "Cybertroopers" is now a common Malaysian catchphrase. It was coined around 2007 and refers to pro-BN Internet activists who actively monitor the Malaysian political blogosphere for antigovernmental postings. Cybertroopers are often accused of being responsible for online attacks on PR politicians. For example, on August 31, 2010, a doctored photograph depicting a Chinese PR minister slaughtering a cow during the Ramadan month of fasting was circulated online. It was thought to be the work of a BN cybertrooper and was quickly identified as a doctored image.

The intention behind circulation of the photograph was clear: it was an attempt at rupturing relations between PR's component non-Muslim and Muslim parties.[62]

Post-2008 by-elections have seen PR, BN, and independent political bloggers all establish event-specific blogs.[63] These blogs exist for a limited period of time but are updated very regularly for that short campaigning period leading to the by-election. Blogs affiliated with PR and BN post comprehensive information on their offline schedules and event venues, while their independent counterparts tend to provide neutral commentary on the candidates. Recently, Malaysiakini reported unconfirmed rumors of a BN-cybertrooper fund, valued at MYR 10 million (almost USD 3.3 million), reserved for an upcoming Sarawak state election.[64] BN has unequivocally adopted an antipodal position to Internet campaigning and the "trustworthiness" of blogs in the years since its dismissive and ultimately costly stance in 2008.

Conclusion

The battle for control of Malaysian cyber-informational space is far from over, and its lines have shifted dramatically since the 2008 general elections. By contrast to the pre-2008 identification of online activism with civil society or PR, there is now a perceived three-way cleavage in the Malaysian sociopolitical blogosphere between BN supporters, PR supporters, and independent commentators. However, even so-called BN-affiliated bloggers have not escaped the government's heavy-handed reliance on existing laws criminalizing sedition or "offensive content." One explanation for NAB's reformation as BfM on thinner grounds of commonality lies in the inadequacy of political affinity as a shield from governmental persecution. Both PR-controlled state governments and BN's federal administration have filed numerous MCMC complaints against bloggers, regardless of political identity.

The recent surge of third-generation controls against the Malaysian sociopolitical blogosphere suggests two emerging patterns. First, there is a growing governmental preference for covert, subtle, and mostly nonlinear forms of *general* Internet regulatory controls in Malaysia. Although detention of Malaysian bloggers has ceased since 2008, there has been a less-publicized exponential increase in the number of MCMC proceedings against bloggers and independent news portals.[65] I consider MCMC action to be a subtler, albeit linear, form of control because its reasons for action are not necessarily traceable to the state—it is statutorily empowered to act on its own initiative or on receipt of complaints from individuals.[66] Further, this general movement is also reflected by the shift in the *type* of technical attacks launched against blogs and independent news portals. Following public outcry against the 2008 DNS block on Malaysia Today, all subsequent denial-of-access incidents affecting blogs and portals have been DDoS attacks. Because it is nearly impossible to trace the source of these attacks, blame cannot be attached to the state with any certainty.

The blogosphere is less able to respond effectively to these new measures than to overt, linear regulatory controls. For example, MCMC's broad interpretation of its statutory powers is harder to utilize as a rallying point to mobilize the masses, when compared to the state's 2007 overwhelmingly disproportionate reliance on national security laws to detain bloggers. Similarly, the blogosphere could neither marshal technical resources to effectively resolve DDoS attacks nor concentrate criticism on state actors to attract international sympathy, unlike its public campaign to evade the DNS block. Although the blogosphere uncovered original photographs in the incidents involving circulated doctored images, criticism was limited to and directed against pro-BN bloggers when no direct state-link was conclusively established.

Reasons for this shift are manifold. One view rests on a cynical assumption that the Malaysian government's actual goal is to extend existing state control over the mainstream media to the Internet. By this account, the shift is simply the result of a discovery that nonlinear controls have the twofold benefits of efficacy and a lower political price, as they are inherently more difficult to attribute to the state—which is especially appealing to the embattled BN administration. An opposite interpretation sees these controls as a positive sign of increased engagement between the state and its subjects. Regardless of which view is taken, the pivotal point here is that the government *has* changed tack. Its change is significant in the historical context because the Malaysian government is rarely swayed by public pressure. For example, the most widely circulated newspaper, *The Star*, was once a vocal critic of the Malaysian government. The state responded swiftly in 1987, revoking *The Star*'s publishing license in a concerted strike against growing political dissent. When reinstated several months later, *The Star* was and remains a pale version of its former self. Thus the Malaysian government's willingness to react and adapt to the blogosphere's resistance, regardless of its motivations for doing so, is unique.

My second suggestion is that there is now a dialogue between the state and the political blogosphere. A combination of factors has created fertile ground for the Malaysian blogosphere to take deep root in its current form in the Malaysian public consciousness. They range from the inadvertent, such as a decade-old pledge not to censor the Internet and BN's current political vulnerability, to the unexpected, such as the continuing Anwar sodomy saga and the fervency of online civil society activism. Arguably, the blogosphere has more successfully contested linear forms of governmental control than any other nonstate actor, forcing the Malaysian government to engage in an asynchronous dialogue. The script of this colloquy is as follows: the government initiated contact by attempting to impose hierarchical control over the blogosphere and was met with ferocious resistance. This prompted the state to retreat and rechannel its efforts instead through subtler means and competing with its own information campaign. Features of the sociopolitical blogosphere that enabled this initial exchange may now work to its disadvantage. For example, its decentralized structure, low barriers to entry, and norm of inclusivity mean that BN supporters cannot be excluded despite their flouting the norm of responsible blogging by initiating vicious, unfounded attacks on non-BN bloggers. The ball is now in the political blogosphere's court; if it wishes to develop positive aspects of this conversation, the blogosphere needs to innovate and evolve in order to seize the lead in the precious, but increasingly precarious, dialogic space it has managed to create.

Notes

1. International Lesbian, Gay, Trans and Intersex Association, "World: Illegality of Male to Male Relationships," http://ilga.org/ilga/en/article/about_ilga.

2. See the Malaysia country profile in this volume for further details.

3. These programs include the Multimedia Super Corridor, described in further detail in the Malaysia country profile in this volume.

4. John Palfrey and Urs Gasser, *Born Digital: Understanding the First Generation of Digital Natives* (New York: Basic Books, 2008), 1–15, define "digital natives" as people born after 1980 who "all have access to networked digital technologies. And they all have the skills to use those technologies" (1).

5. Agus Sudibyo, "Reformasi According to Malaysiakini," *Southeast Asian Press Alliance*, May 12, 2010, http://www.seapabkk.org/announcements/fellowship-2004-program/46-reformasi-according -to-malaysiakini.html.

6. See the Malaysia country profile in this volume for further details.

7. Ibid.

8. See, for example, the government's insistence on going ahead with deeply unpopular plans to build another megatower in Malaysia; "Anti–100 Storey Tower Group Calls for 'Cake Party,'" November 15, 2010, Malaysiakini, http://www.malaysiakini.com/news/148257. Note in particular its persistent refusal to repeal the draconian Internal Security Act, which permits detention without trial, despite long-running calls for its abolishment. Amnesty International, "Malaysian Parliament Should Abolish Internal Security Act," September 4, 2008, http://www.amnesty.org/en/news-and -updates/news/malaysian-parliament-should-abolish-internal-security-act-20080905.

9. Zentrum Future Studies Malaysia, "Pilihanraya umum Malaysia ke 12: Pengaruh kepercayaan terhadap media dan kesannya terhadap bentuk dan corak pengundian Malaysia—Tumpuan pada kumpulan responden 21–41 tahun" [12th Malaysian general elections: The extent of faith in the media and its effect on Malaysian voting shapes and patterns—Focus on the age group of 21–41 of respondents] (Edisi PDF untuk rujukan dan naskah lengkap kajian [PDF edition for reference and a complete study]), http://www.scribd.com/doc/8751281/Zentrum-Studies-Pru12. (The group was headed by Associate Professor Abu Hassan Bin Hasbullah of the University of Malaya.)

10. Calculated from data available in Zentrum, "Pilihanraya umum," 5 Jadual 4 [Table 4].

11. Ibid.

12. Ronald Deibert and Rafal Rohozinski, "Control and Subversion in Russian Cyberspace," in *Access Controlled: The Shaping of Power, Rights, and Rule in Cyberspace*, ed. Ronald Deibert, John Palfrey, Rafal Rohozinski, and Jonathan Zittrain (Cambridge, MA: MIT Press, 2010), 22–28.

13. For more details, see the Malaysia country profile in this volume.

14. Ibid.

15. Ibid.

16. Malaysian Communications and Multimedia Act 1998, sec. 263(2).

17. On August 27, 2008, MCMC issued an order to all Malaysian ISPs to deny access to Malaysia Today. As of 6:00 p.m. local time that day, only TMNet subscribers reported problems accessing the site—other ISPs' subscribers were still able to access the site. The DNS block lasted less than two weeks. The government decided to lift the ban on September 11, 2008, but detained Malaysia Today's administrator, Raja Petra Kamarudin, the following day. See generally, Debra Chong and Shannon Teoh, "Cyberspace Crackdown Limited to Malaysia-Today Website . . . for Now," *Malaysian Insider*, August 28, 2008, http://www.malaysianbar.org.my/legal/general_news/cyberspace_crackdown_limited_to_malaysia_today_website_for_now.html; Sim Leoi Leoi and Florence A. Samy, "MCMC Told to Unblock Malaysia Today (Update 2)," *The Star*, September 11, 2008, http://thestar.com.my/news/story.asp?file=/2008/9/11/nation/20080911145128&sec=nation. Note also that some commentators classify Malaysia Today as a news portal because it aggregates news from other sources. For my purposes, Malaysia Today is counted as a blog because Raja Petra self-identifies as a blogger. In addition, his *views*, not the site's aggregation of news, are arguably the main attraction of Malaysia Today.

18. For further details on DDoS attacks, see Hal Roberts, Ethan Zuckerman, and John Palfrey, "Interconnected Contests: Distributed Denial of Service Attacks and Other Digital Control Measures in Asia," chapter 7 in this volume.

19. On September 15, 2009, after Raja Petra posted a story on an MYR 12.5 billion (approximately USD 4 billion) corruption case involving the prime minister, which he corroborated by releasing PDFs of leaked classified cabinet documents, "suspicious activity" was reported attacking the site on the next day, September 16, 2009. The first round of hacking damaged the site on September 17, 2009, but the site's technical team managed to permit access to Malaysia Today by 6:00 p.m. local time. Subsequently, DDoS attacks ranging from 227 to 835 Mbps from proxy servers crippled the site's Singaporean node with the overwhelming traffic on the next day. See Raja Petra Kamarudin, "The Attacks on Malaysia Today," Malaysia Today, September 29, 2009, http://www.malaysia-today.net/archives/27311-the-attacks-on-malaysia-today-udpated-with-chinese-translation. A year later, Raja Petra again released a slew of documents from August 15 to August 27, 2010, this time on a controversial governmental buyback of Malaysian Airlines at the same price at which it was privatized, despite the MYR 8 billion (USD 2.6 billion) in losses accumulated

during its privatized state. DDoS attacks began on September 7, 2010, after his posting of another story on corruption involving the prime minister on September 5, 2010. Malaysia Today was inaccessible for 24 hours on September 7, 2010, and was intermittently inaccessible for seven days until September 14, 2010. See Malaysia Chronicle, "Fears for RPK's Safety as Attacks on Malaysia Today Continue," September 14, 2010, http://www.malaysia-chronicle.com/2010/09/attacks-on-malaysia-today-continue.html.

20. Raja Petra, "The Attacks," http://www.malaysia-today.net/archives/27311-the-attacks-on -malaysia-today-udpated-with-chinese-translation.

21. Neville Spykerman, "Cyber Attack: Anwar's Blog Latest to Be Hit," Malaysian Insider, September 10, 2010, http://www.themalaysianinsider.com/malaysia/article/fmt-malaysia-today-not -accessible-after-attacks.

22. "Bloggers May Have to Reveal Identities," Malaysiakini, April 5, 2007, http://www .malaysiakini.com/news/65558.

23. T. H. Tan, "Sintercom Founder Fades Out of Cyberspace," *Straits Times*, August 22, 2001. Note that Sintercom has since reemerged as Newsintercom, but its reincarnation is hosted abroad and run by anonymous administrators.

24. "Zam Recommends Labels for Bloggers," Malaysiakini, May 5, 2007, http://www .malaysiakini.com/news/66854.

25. Niluksi Koswanage and Royce Cheah, "Update 1—Malaysia Plans Internet Filter, Tougher Controls," Reuters, August 6, 2009, http://www.reuters.com/article/2009/08/06/malaysia-internet -idUSSP39843320090806.

26. Jeff Ooi, "Bloggers Legal Fund Being Finalised," Screenshots, January 24, 2007, http:// asiancorrespondent.com/6403/bloggers-legal-fund-being-finalised/.

27. Joyce Tagal, "A Resounding NO to Police State," Malaysiakini, July 20, 2007, http:// malaysiakini.com/news/70200.

28. Examples of these routing-round posts include "Three Ways to Access Blocked Malaysia Today," Liewcf.com, August 28, 2008, http://www.liewcf.com/3-ways-to-access-blocked-malaysia -today-3835/, and "How to Access Malaysia Today by Proxy and Beat the Block," Uppercaise, September 20, 2009, http://uppercaise.wordpress.com/2009/09/20/proxy-bookmarks-for-malaysia -today/.

29. Jeff Ooi, "Register the Bloggers? NAB and BUM," Screenshots, April 6, 2007, http:// asiancorrespondent.com/6201/register-the-bloggers-nab-bum/.

30. Jeff Ooi, "MarinaM on Blogging 101 for Lame Politikus," Screenshots, May 9, 2007, http:// asiancorrespondent.com/6107/marinam-on-blogging-101-for-lame-politikus/.

31. "Nazri Warns Bloggers Face Harsh Laws," Malaysiakini, July 25, 2007, http://malaysiakini .com/news/70375. (It was alleged that the government was "looking at formulating new laws to allow it to monitor and act against offending bloggers.")

32. "Rais Decries Dodgy Enforcement of Blogging Laws," Malaysiakini, May 13, 2009, http://malaysiakini.com/news/104230. (Rais Yatim, the Malaysian information minister, declared that existing laws were adequate to prosecute and regulate bloggers, but was critical of the enforcement of these laws.)

33. Niluksi Koswanage, "Malaysia to Cancel Internet Filter Study—Source," Reuters, August 12, 2009, http://in.reuters.com/article/2009/08/12/malaysia-internet-idINKLR52289420090812?pageNumber=1.

34. Cecilia Victor, "Rais Yatim Lodges Report over Allegations against Son," *Malay Mail*, October 12, 2010, http://www.mmail.com.my/content/52046-rais-yatim-lodges-report-over-allegations-against-son.

35. Tony Yew, "Bloggers for Malaysia," Bloggers for Malaysia, October 21, 2010, http://bloggersformalaysia.blogspot.com/.

36. Note that this "loophole" may soon be closed, as legislative amendments are being proposed to extend licensing requirements to online news portals and blogs. See the Malaysia country profile in this volume for further details.

37. Malaysian Police Act 1976, sec. 27.

38. Xiang Zhou, "The Political Blogosphere in China," *New Media and Society* 11 (2009): 1017 (referring to M. Jiang, "Authoritarian Deliberation: Public Deliberation in China," paper presented at sixth annual Chinese Internet Research Conference, Hong Kong, June 13–14, 2008).

39. Jun-E Tan and Zawawi Ibrahim, *Blogging and Democratization in Malaysia: A New Civil Society in the Making* (Petaling Jaya, Malaysia: SIRD, 2008).

40. Ibid., 44.

41. Brian Ulicny, "Modeling Malaysian Public Opinion by Mining the Malaysian Blogosphere" (First International Workshop on Social Computing, Behavioral Modeling and Prediction, Phoenix, AZ, April 2008), http://vistology.com/papers/VIS-SBP08%20.pdf.

42. Brian Ulicny, Christopher J. Matheus, and Mieczyslaw M. Kokar, "Metrics for Monitoring a Social-Political Blogosphere," *IEEE Computer Society* 34 (2010): 34–44, 36 (table 1).

43. Ibid.

44. Hang Wu Tang, "The Networked Electorate: The Internet and the Quiet Democratic Revolution in Malaysia and Singapore," *Journal of Information Law and Technology* 2 (2009): 3.

45. Cherian George, "The Internet's Political Impact and the Penetration/Participation Paradox in Malaysia and Singapore," *Media, Culture and Society* 27, no. 6 (2005): 903, DOI: 10.1177 (general observation); Tang, "The Networked Electorate," 10–11 (elections-specific). For an interesting flipside analysis of the online replication of offline relationships and networks, see Heike Jensen, Jac sm Kee, Gayathri Venkiteswaran, and Sonia Randhawa, "Sexing the Internet: Censorship, Surveillance, and the Body Politic(s) of Malaysia," chapter 4 in this volume.

46. For an in-depth analysis and discussion of social-psychological motivation and the diversity of motivations for action, see Yochai Benkler, "Coase's Penguin," *Yale Law Journal* 112 (2006): 371–446.

47. Tan and Ibrahim, *Blogging*, 52.

48. Ibid., 50–60.

49. H.L.A. Hart, *The Concept of Law* (Oxford, UK: Oxford University Press, 1994), 9–11.

50. Richard McAdams, "The Origin, Development, and Regulation of Norms," *Michigan Law Review* 96 (1997): 378–381.

51. Ibid.

52. Ibid.

53. Tan and Ibrahim, *Blogging*, 55.

54. Ibid.

55. Nathaniel Tan, "Audio Clip Further Incriminates Mahathir, Vincent Tan and VK Lingam," Jelas.info (blog), September 19, 2007, http://jelas.info/2007/09/19/.

56. Tan and Ibrahim, *Blogging*, 61 (figure 5.4).

57. I borrow and build on Yochai Benkler's definition of "granularity" and "heterogeneous," first used in the context of commons-based peer-production systems, that is, *Wikipedia* and *Slashdot*. See Benkler, "Coase's Penguin," 378–379.

58. Yochai Benkler, *The Wealth of Networks* (New Haven, CT: Yale University Press, 2006), 253.

59. See the Malaysia country profile in this volume for further details.

60. Benkler, *Wealth*, 254.

61. "Alternative Media: BN vs. PR—Who's Winning?" *Malaysian Digest*, March 15, 2010, http://www.malaysiandigest.com/features/2541-alternative-media-bn-vs-pr-who-is-winning.html. (The report finds BN having more Twitter and Facebook fans overall at 19,596 and 164,335 as opposed to PR's 17,176 and 109,472.)

62. PR's component parties include the mostly non-Muslim Democratic Action Party (DAP) and the Parti Islam Se-Malaysia (PAS), an Islamist political party.

63. See generally, Gabrielle Chong, "By-elections Cyber War Escalates," Malaysiakini, March 28, 2009, http://malaysiakini.com/news/101175.

64. Leven Woon Zheng Yang, "PBB Denies RM10 Mil Cybertrooper Fund," Malaysiakini, December 21, 2010, http://malaysiakini.com/news/151367.

65. See the Malaysia country profile in this volume for further details.

66. Malaysian Communications and Multimedia Act 1998, sec. 68, 69, and 70.

4   Sexing the Internet

Censorship, Surveillance, and the Body Politic(s) of Malaysia

Heike Jensen, Jac sm Kee, Gayathry Venkiteswaran, and Sonia Randhawa

The scholarly investigation of digital censorship and surveillance has moved from an initial focus on fact finding—what was filtered, who was under surveillance, and how this was accomplished technologically—to more contextualized investigations of the political, economic, and social dimensions of specific censorship and surveillance practices. A gender-sensitive approach is arguably more important now than ever for fully understanding the meanings and struggles over censorship and surveillance regimes. For instance, consider the central finding reported by Jonathan Zittrain and John Palfrey: "The Internet content blocked for social reasons—commonly pornography, information about gay and lesbian issues, and information about sex education—is more likely to be the same across countries than the political and religious information to which access is blocked."[1] Why should this be the case? And which logic has encouraged the common suppression of such disparate content?

The logic at issue is the logic underlying the nation-state and its task of perpetuating itself through the reproduction and renegotiation of its internal social hierarchies. We use Malaysia as a case study to point out some of these dimensions of national reproduction, tied as they are to the reproduction of citizens within national borders. At issue here is a nation's patriarchal policing of gender roles and their appropriate forms of (potentially procreative) sexuality, from an overall heteronormativity to finely tuned divisions based on class, race, region, and other salient markers.[2] This policing has been increasingly transferred to the digital realm, because this space has in unprecedented ways accommodated both the proliferation of alternative takes on the established gender and sexual order and the policing of citizens through censorship and surveillance.

Gender-sensitive research is thus urgently needed in this field of study, and our exploratory chapter is meant to chart some of the prime issues that need to be tackled.[3] To begin with, a change of perspective is required to see that the social issues in digital censorship and surveillance are not "soft" and relatively unimportant compared to "hard" issues such as political or religious persecution, but are in fact the central matters that go directly to the root of the social fabric. Attention to the reproduction of gender and sexuality within the framework of the nation-state is essential for understanding the morality debates that have increasingly come to dominate discussions about Internet governance and digital censorship and surveillance. Such a focus is essential because different kinds of political and economic tensions within a nation-state can be mediated by contesting morality issues and related gender and sexual issues in the digital realm.

Employing a gender lens fundamentally shifts the very definitions of censorship and surveillance to include a basic lack of freedom of expression and privacy. It shows how most women and many disenfranchised men have been kept from contributing to the public sphere by social and economic structures and agents other than state censors, and how many women have been placed under surveillance by their social peers rather than state agents. In drawing attention to these circumstances, a gender lens generates a more comprehensive understanding of the agents of censorship and surveillance, showing that the state is only one among several entities and institutions that systematically hinder specific groups of people from expressing themselves freely or from enjoying a self-determined degree of privacy.

Such an augmented understanding of censorship, surveillance, and its agents is crucial for understanding the precise stakes and scope of state-initiated censorship and surveillance systems. It additionally creates a useful familiarity with agents beyond the state precisely at a time when there is growing evidence that nonstate actors have become increasingly recruited by certain states to carry out undercover censorship and surveillance missions. This practice was identified by Ronald Deibert and Rafal Rohozinski as "next-generation information controls."[4]

Similarly, as it is becoming increasingly obvious that the absence of state-imposed digital censorship and surveillance in a nation does not mean that all its citizens enjoy freedom of expression and privacy, research needs to dig deeper into the multilayered mechanisms that regulate speech and privacy. Such conditions can be illustrated quite well by our case study of Malaysia. While we could not detect any state-level Internet filtering in Malaysia when we conducted the testing for the OpenNet Initiative (ONI) in 2008 and 2009,[5] and previous ONI testing had similarly not yielded any evidence of Internet filtering,[6] censorship and surveillance have nevertheless played important roles. Before looking through a gender lens on recent developments in this field in Malaysia and in particular focusing on the significance of sexuality and morality for its body politic, we will provide further methodological grounding to our framework and hypotheses.

Agents of Censorship and Surveillance

Following the logic of international human rights law such as the International Covenant on Civil and Political Rights (ICCPR), state authorities are the agents that may potentially curb their citizens' freedom of expression and privacy. In reality, however, distinct sociopolitical entities can be crucial agents in censorship and surveillance. Regarding regulation including censorship, Lawrence Lessig has developed a useful model that identifies the interrelated levels of norms, laws, markets, and architecture.[7] Laws constrain through the punishment they threaten; norms constrain through the stigma a community imposes; markets constrain through the price that they exact; and architectures, including hardware and programming code, constrain through the physical burdens or obstacles they impose.[8] Lessig makes the point that norms, markets, and architectures may generate their own regulatory effects, or they may be regulated by laws and thus pass on this state regulatory endeavor indirectly.

Jean K. Chalaby's work adds important dimensions of censorship to those identified by Lessig.[9] Most notably, she also recognizes media administration as well as outright state violence. Media administration includes obligations to obtain licenses, registrations, or authorizations and the requirement to deposit financial guarantees for entities wanting to establish media. Tactics of state violence encompass arbitrary arrests or physical attacks, and violent forms of censorship can also be exercised by nonstate agents, either at the behest of authorities or on their own. In fact, as recent research by the ONI in the Commonwealth of Independent States has shown, indirect and at times unlawful forms of Internet censorship instigated by states seem to play an increasing role. These next-generation information controls are often kept secret by states and may be outsourced to private or even illegally operating networks, including botnets that commit denial-of-service attacks. Next-generation controls even go beyond blocking content and services and include outsourced information campaigns designed to mislead, intimidate, fragment, confound, or hinder those perceived as enemies of the state.

Implicit in much of the literature addressing censorship is thus a definition that is not restricted to the suppression of content already produced. Censorship also means erecting enough hurdles to systematically keep specific content from reaching a social group, either at all or in a meaningful way, or to keep people from producing content in the first place. Experiences of censorship can in turn lead to self-censorship—the "slow internalization of the mechanisms of suppression."[10]

Surveillance, like censorship, can be instigated and carried out by different actors. States generally practice surveillance with the same rationales they cite for censorship, that is, to enhance national security and maintain order. They do so either directly, often within legal frameworks, or indirectly by requiring other actors to collaborate in surveillance, most notably media administrators, businesses, software writers, and other social entities. Big market players are also important agents of surveillance in their own right, and their motive is profit maximization, either by selling data trails left by customers or by using these data trails for marketing and advertising. Software writers may also be considered as autonomously involved in surveillance, at least to

Table 4.1

AGENTS, LEVELS, AND FORMS OF CENSORSHIP AND SURVEILLANCE				
	State Censorship	Nonstate Censorship	State Surveillance	Nonstate Surveillance
Laws	Direct	n/a	Direct	n/a
Violence	Direct	Direct	n/a	n/a
Administration	Indirect	Direct	Indirect	n/a
Business	Indirect	Direct	Indirect	Direct
Norms/society	Indirect	Direct	Indirect	Direct
Architecture, including code	Indirect	Direct	Indirect	Direct

the extent that they voluntarily offer or embed surveillance functions in their programming. Finally, private individuals engage in surveillance on their own, often in accordance with social norms. The dimensions of censorship and surveillance just discussed are systematized in table 4.1.

The Malaysian Nation

Turning to our exploratory case study of Malaysia, to apply a gender lens first of all requires us to "defamiliarize" ourselves with the nation-state as the unit of analysis that has become self-evidently applied in much of the research on digital censorship and surveillance.

The nation-state has traditionally been defined by a sovereign government ruling over the permanent population living within its demarcated territory, and it has thus been principally concerned with organizing people and boundaries.[11] In Malaysia, race relations have significantly textured the social, political, cultural, and economic makeup of the nation. Formal politics have been contested on the grounds of ethnic interests, and the singular ethnic conflict that occurred on May 13, 1969,[12] has resulted in two national policies[13] that continue to define a nation that is artificially split into two. Although the 27.6 million[14] population of Malaysia consists of a plurality and hybridity of ethnicities and backgrounds, formally Malaysians are hailed as either *bumiputera*[15] or *non-bumiputera*—each constituting roughly half the total population. The two groups form a hierarchy in which the *bumiputera*—Malays constitutionally defined as Muslims,[16] together with some 70 groups and subgroups of indigenous peoples—are afforded a privileged position in the constitution.[17]

The state is compelled to reify the differences between the two categories of citizenship to maintain and manage the continued legitimization of its hierarchy. Gender and sexuality are at the heart of this process. Ideologically, sexual norms and the enforcement of moral cultures serve to define the boundaries between different categories of citizen-subjects. Quite materially, these ideologies are meant to guide and police procreative (hetero-) sexuality and women's reproductive choices. The body thus becomes both a figurative and a real site for social order and control, where gender, sexuality, ethnicity, and religion are relationally constituted through and in each other.

The regulation of sexuality plays an important role in establishing the moral rights and supremacy of a particular ethnicity, which in turn helps to solidify the differences between the groups. At times of flux, the policing of these boundaries becomes accentuated. Paying attention to how sexual speech, discourse, and acts are regulated and placed under surveillance can provide important indicators on current national concerns and uncover the directions that censorship and surveillance will take.

Beyond the significance of gender and sexuality for internal stratification within the nation, these concepts are also central for the ideology of the nation as a whole. The national collective identity, or, in Benedict Anderson's influential terminology, the "imagined community," is usually based on the ideologies of the privileged groups in the nation.[18] Notably, the nation has often been imagined as female, evoking the hegemonic ideals of femininity favored by the ruling classes. Nationalism concurrently is described by Inderpal Grewal and Caren Kaplan as "a process in which new patriarchal elites gain the power to produce the generic 'we' of the nation. The homogenizing project of nationalism draws upon female bodies as the symbol of the nation to generate discourses of rape, motherhood, sexual purity, and heteronormativity."[19]

But what about real women? How are they situated in Malaysia? There is still a substantial gender disparity in terms of health, politics, and economic development. This can be seen in Malaysia's low Gender Empowerment Measure (GEM) ranking, coming in at 68 out of 109 countries, and its Gender Development Index (GDI) that ranks lower (76) than its Human Development Index (66).[20] These rankings point to systemic and structural barriers for women's equal opportunities and access to resources, which are also reflected in terms of decision-making positions. Women made up only 27.3 percent of senators in 2009, and only 10.4 percent of members of Parliament.[21] The figures do not improve much in the private sector, with only 6.1 percent of women participating at boardroom levels in the corporate sector.[22] As a result, women are significantly removed from most decision-making processes, including determining the boundaries of acceptable and unacceptable expression in the public sphere.

Media, the Internet, and Gendered Publics

A prime tool for the ideological creation of any nation has been the establishment of its public sphere, in relation to which freedom of expression and censorship have generally been theorized. The public sphere has always been created and maintained by media, from earlier mass media/news media to the more recent Internet. In Malaysia, the flow of information, speech, and expression has traditionally been tightly regulated in multiple ways with respect to the mass media. Regulation has included a monopoly over institutions of mass media,[23] stringent and punitive licensing administration,[24] numerous laws[25] and reiterative cautions on the possible recurrence of ethnic conflicts like the one of May 13, 1969.[26] Jointly, these measures have effectively circumscribed speech perceived as "sensitive" and threatening to disrupt social relations. Self-censorship has consequently been widely practiced, from members of the mass media to the everyday person.[27]

Although the development of the Internet in Malaysia was expressly promoted by the state in the late 1990s to catalyze the nation into fully developed status,[28] it has simultaneously destabilized governmental control over the flow of information and expression in the public domain. To attract foreign investment in the Multimedia Super Corridor (MSC) and to mitigate the government's reputation for exercising strict state control of the information and communications public domain, consultations were held with several key industry leaders including Microsoft and IBM. Business here acted as an anticensorship agent, and the MSC Bill of Guarantees that came out of these consultations included the promise that there would be no censorship of the Internet.[29] This was supported through Article 3(3) of the Malaysia Communications and Multimedia Act (MCMA)—the primary piece of legislation that regulates the Internet—which expressly states that "nothing in this Act shall be construed as permitting the censorship of the Internet."[30]

Given this formal guarantee, the Internet became a unique "public" space in Malaysia. Although stemming from economic interest, this relative freedom presented opportunities for civil society to engage in and proliferate the public discourse with previously prohibited speech and information. Several alternative news sites have sprung up since the late 1990s to early 2000s, among them Malaysiakini,[31] Malaysia Today,[32] and more recently, Malaysian Insider[33] and The NutGraph.[34] They are maintained by "technopreneurs," bloggers, and journalists aiming to fill the palpable gap of independent and unbiased information not directed by the ruling political party.[35] New sites also include community sites for people of diverse and marginalized sexualities.

It may also be noted that as Internet access began to proliferate in Malaysia, not only men but also a large number of women gained access. From 2000 to 2008, the percentage of the population with Internet access grew from 15 to nearly 70 percent.[36] Data collection on access to the Internet and infrastructural reach has often not been gender-disaggregated, but the latest survey conducted in 2008 on household use[37] of the Internet[38] stated only a slight difference between the percentage of male home users (51.9 percent) and female home users (48.1 percent).

Nevertheless, the general predominance of men as principal communicators in the public sphere has not been successfully challenged in the course of the rise of the Internet. In particular, the most influential bloggers tend to be men.[39] What consequently has also remained largely intact, despite the new communicators' claims to "unbiased" information, is the "male definition of news value."[40] It means that the public sphere of politics as well as other spheres of "hard news" such as the economy, finance, and science have remained defined as masculine or, to be more precise, defined as "neutral" from a male point of view.

The global pervasiveness and longevity of this gender imbalance in both offline and online news, as well as national variations of it, have been traced by the Global Media Monitoring Project (GMMP), conducted every five years since 1995 in all parts of the globe.[41] The gender disparity in terms of what constitutes "newsworthiness" is reflected in the 2010 Malaysia GMMP report, where women make up only 15 percent of all news subjects compared to men, who make up 85 percent.[42] The report also found that women were more likely to be featured as celebrities, homemakers, students, activists, teachers, and nonmanagement workers, whereas men were more likely to be represented as royalty, politicians, government officials, police officers, diplomats, and service professionals. This result clearly indicates that gender stereotypes predominate.

The censorship of women and their points of view has come about through their structural and ideological exclusion from the public sphere and its media, but it has also happened more directly through the use of sexist language and threats of sexual violence. Both strategies to silence women's speech continue to thrive on the Internet. Take for instance, Pamela Lim's experience on a popular Web site, http://www .loyarburuk.com, which provides a platform for discussing current topics in Malaysia. On October 10, 2010, she posted a video of two police officers who she claimed had behaved in an intimidating manner after stopping her car and asking her for a bribe to overlook an alleged traffic offense.[43] This video post received an unprecedented number of hits on the site and more than 700 comments. A majority of the comments that disagreed with her action were made up of personal attacks and employed racist and sexist language to condemn her act of citizen journalism. For example, one of the comments read, "Oh pammy, you remind me of my f*ck buddy a couple of years ago. A real 'miss-know-it-all.' She just couldn't shut up even if she tried. There was really only one way to keep her quiet and yes, she was a guzzler!"[44]

Here we find a pattern common to many media, in which women as a gender group tend to be predominantly confronted with attempts of censorship by nonstate actors. Meanwhile the state might even promote equal opportunities, but without striking at the commercial, social, and normative roots of gender-based discrimination, these initiatives generally do not go far. This is why authors like Sharzad Mojab see the "censorship of feminist knowledge" as a root problem, stating, "I believe that the subtlest censorship is denying feminist knowledge a visible role in the exercise of power. The state, Western and non-Western, rules through privileging androcentric knowledge as the basis for governance."[45]

The Malaysian state did try to encroach on the Internet to bring it more in line with the tight restrictions on "traditional" media. This effort has led to a situation in which the Internet is free from censorship only from the point of view of Internet law and, as ONI found, free from systematic Internet filtering.[46] Meanwhile, existing and non-Internet-specific laws such as the Sedition Act,[47] Official Secrets Act,[48] Internal Security Act,[49] and Defamation Act[50] have been used to restrict the kinds of content and speech that are allowed online. However, given the laws' reputation as tools of state repression and intimidation, their application was swiftly critiqued (and amplified over the Internet) by civil-society actors as constituting a breach of the initial promise of a censorship-free Internet.

This response presented a dilemma for the state, augmented by new and irrefutable evidence that the leading political group itself was actually at stake. The 2008 general elections in Malaysia saw the ruling coalition lose two-thirds of its majority in Parliament for the first time since the nation's independence. The Internet was credited with playing a significant role in the outcome of this election, providing a relatively freer and more independent avenue for information exchange and dissemination, and even fund-raising.[51] This signaled a time of transformation, in which the established social order was threatened by a new form of political engagement that appeared to reject familiar race-based politics.

It is at such points of status and boundary anxieties that the policing of sexuality becomes pronounced, so that a restoration of the symbolic cohesion and social order is attempted through reinstating the integrity of the material and sexed body, with its accompanying morality discourse. The apparent "free flow" of the Internet has become increasingly scrutinized and regulated vis-à-vis the subject of sexuality. Two major state strategies can be identified in this regard, to which we turn in the next section.

Sexualizing Censorship and Surveillance

The first strategy consisted of a consolidation of state power over the Internet through a reconfiguration of the government machinery responsible. In 2009 newly elected Prime Minister Mohd Najib Razak formed the Ministry of Information, Communications, and Culture (KPKK). The communications sector was removed from the Ministry of Energy, Water, and Communications, and merged with the highly powerful Ministry of Information and, interestingly, the Ministry of Unity, Culture, Arts, and Heritage. This change clearly signaled that information and communications technology (ICT) was no longer seen as primarily a matter of infrastructure as it had been in the late 1990s. Instead, its role in shaping the nation and its internal boundaries through information exchange, discourse proliferation, and expression was being recognized. Consequently, it has become anchored to the state machineries responsible for both the "hard" aspects of intelligence and state propaganda (information) and the "soft" aspects of arts and culture. This change also means that the minister who presently holds such a wide ambit of power is also responsible and much empowered under the MCMA.

The second strategy involved attempts to create a sense of moral legitimacy for Internet regulation by infusing it with a paternalistic framework of sexuality. Again, this strategy was attempted because other tactics of state censorship were met with harsh public criticism. In the early months of 2009 there were increased prosecutions under various pieces of legislation including the MCMA for the publication of materials online. Section 233 of the MCMA makes it an offense to transmit, create, or solicit any content that is "obscene, indecent, false, menacing or offensive in character with the intent to annoy, abuse, threaten or harass another person."[52] For the first time in its history, it was used to convict an Internet user for posting a comment on a Web site that was deemed insulting to the monarchy. A hefty fine of MYR 10,000 (USD 3,000) was imposed with the expressed rationale of acting as a deterrent and warning to members of the public from freely posting their thoughts online.[53] In view of the political transformations during that period, this fine significantly challenged the credibility of the act.

At the same time, a huge public debate was raised on the issue of online privacy in response to an incident where private photographs of a popular female public official from the opposition party were posted online as a tactic to shame or discredit her, an increasingly common practice in the "Web 2.0" context in many parts of the world.[54] The incident rendered visible the lack of laws against sexual harassment (both online and offline). However, instead of taking any steps to finally legislate on a sexual harassment bill or a data protection act—both having been in the pipeline for almost a decade—the same Section 233 of the MCMA was put forward as providing viable legal remedy for the protection of women against online sexual harassment, or blackmail by spouses who threaten to publish private and sexualized photographs online.[55]

This disregard for the actual recommendation by women's rights groups,[56] together with the wide interpretation of the law, indicate that the goal is not so much to realize and protect women's rights on the Internet as to strengthen the scope of the MCMA and to recover its moral legitimacy. It is also interesting to note that censorship was being proposed as a viable measure to counter the public invasion of a woman's privacy. After being mooted since 1998, the Personal Data Protection Bill 2010 was finally passed on April 5. However, the scope of the law is limited to the processing of personal data in commercial transactions, and the government is exempted from its purview. This provision effectively compromises its potential to act as an effective counterbalance to the impact of surveillance and self-censorship.

Religious material[57] and material related to sexuality[58] published online in Malaysia are also subjected to scrutiny.[59] Advocates and organizations that defend the rights of Muslim women, such as Sisters in Islam (SIS), face constant attacks because they not only directly challenge the power of the state overdefining "Islam," but they do so from a standpoint of gender equality and women's rights. In 2008, SIS's publication on progressive interpretations of Islam was banned,[60] and its Web site has been repeatedly compromised[61] since the opposition Islamic political party (PAS) called for an investigation and ban of the organization in 2009.[62]

However, due to the "informal" nature of such censorship efforts, which confirm a trend found by ONI's research,[63] they are rarely visible in reporting or documented in efforts to monitor the space for public expression and information exchange. Yet it is clearly evident that these censorship efforts respond to the perceived threats to the nation's constitution posed by groups such as SIS and their promotion of alternative discourses on gender, sexuality, and religion.

Finally, in August 2009, in synchronicity with the global thematic trends of Internet content regulation, the KPKK minister announced the government's intention to implement Internet filtering to reduce "Malaysian children's exposure to online pornography."[64] Despite renouncing the proposal after being met with alarm by content producers, in particular alternative online media providers and bloggers, the minister acknowledged that the Malaysian Communications and Multimedia Commission (MCMC) has been tasked to find appropriate solutions to the as-yet-unsubstantiated claim of the threat to children's safety from pornography.[65] This development presents a merging of both technical and discursive solutions in regulating the unruly online space.

Even though business acted as promoters of free speech in the consultations for the MSC Bill of Guarantees, industry self-regulation does not necessarily by extension equate with free speech. When the Communication and Multimedia Content Forum (CMCF) was formed by the MCMC together with industry players, academics, civil-society organizations, and selected prominent individuals, it developed a content code that includes provisions promoting rights-based and nondiscriminatory forms of content. However, application of the code is voluntary, and it appears that private companies prefer to implement their own individual policies and guidelines to meet potential concerns and liability. In fact, particularly with regard to sexual content, private companies have become central, autonomously acting agents of censorship, whose sustained background actions have both "normalized" this censorship as any company's "right" and have largely shielded it from public scrutiny and debate.

For example, the Web hosting company Exabytes changed its policy in May 2008 to prohibit "adult content" on their servers. This ban included Web sites "related to gay and lesbian"[66] content, conflating pornographic content with any type of content produced by, about, or for an already peripheral and discriminated-against section of society. However, after several complaints about this policy, the explicit mention of "gay and lesbian" was removed and replaced with the company's overriding right to decide what falls under the "adult" category. Internet service providers (ISPs) also appear to act as moral guardians by blocking access to sites with sexual content, such as pornography-sharing sites like YouPorn[67] and RedTube,[68] as well as Gutter-Uncensored,[69] a site that solicits and publishes private videos and images that are sexual in nature, including those of local celebrities and politicians. These blockings have remained almost unnoticed beyond the sites' users, who share advice on how to circumvent them.[70] The augmented censorship role of the private sector, along with the limited redress that ordinary users have, creates a power imbalance that is strangely reminiscent of the power imbalance between the traditional mass media and their audience. How the ISPs' censorship role in the area of sexuality relates to the various stakes of the state in this regard remains to be seen.

As a last example, cases surrounding the Malaysian national identity card MyKad offer interesting insights into how programming code has been used to discipline citizens and how the data constituting gender, race, and religion are assigned and controlled through laws, culture, and norms in order to police sexualities and desires. The MyKad contains personal data (name, date of birth, address, race, and religion), photo identification, and a biometric fingerprint. It is required for any formal transaction, and every Malaysian is obligated to carry it.[71] As a result, the MyKad potentially enables the government to comprehensively place individuals under surveillance. But, in addition, the card is the digital artifact that defines and produces, and in fact attempts to "freeze," the Malaysian citizen-subject in socially acceptable positions. This fact is evident in several cases of Malaysian citizens attempting to get the data in their MyKads changed, notably after conversions from Islam or after sex-reassignment surgery. In all cases, the individual struggles over self-definition and citizenship rights became a symbolic site for the struggle over what constitutes the nation and its internal social hierarchy and order, as it is coded through race, religion, and appropriate heterosexual contracts between citizens.[72]

Conclusion

In our Malaysian case study, we have illustrated how recent, publicly available information about the development of the Internet and its regulation at various levels and through various means acquires a fuller meaning when analyzed in a gender-sensitive framework and with attention to gender indicators for this country. The overall framework we have proposed for our interpretation posits that the maintenance of the body politic within a nation requires the disciplining of women and men along specific heterosexual and gender lines, interarticulated with other social hierarchies. The public sphere and its mass media, including the Internet, have constituted a vital area in which this disciplining is negotiated, particularly around notions of sexuality and morality.

Censorship by the state and by other entities constitutes an important form of intervention in this ideological battle, and the Malaysian case has provided evidence for the overall trend in several countries, as traced by ONI testing, that direct and sustained, state-ordered filtering of the Internet may not play a crucial role in this context and may in fact be much less important than other mechanisms of censoring and silencing people employed by state actors as well as nonstate actors. In addition, the deployment of a moralistic discourse of the state's duty to regulate sexuality has become the central framework employed by the state to distract from and thus negotiate tensions between the economic objectives of Internet development in the country and the Internet's disturbing capacity to shape and disrupt ideas of the Malaysian nation and its citizens.

The Malaysian case illustrates the clash between the potential power of the Internet to instigate far-reaching economic and social changes on the one hand and the established power of political and social elites on the other hand, which tries to perpetuate itself under new conditions. Under these conditions, the initial promise of a Malaysian Internet free from censorship was not upheld by the state, which has increasingly encroached upon this medium through a variety of direct and indirect means. These include the application of peripheral laws to rein in transgressive discourse, as well as administrative procedures and identity-based surveillance designed to foster a culture of self-censorship and conformity with gender and sexual rules. Further gender-sensitive research into censorship and surveillance, in Malaysia and elsewhere, would be welcome to unearth more of the inner workings of such negotiations, as well as the circumstances and factors that may complicate these processes and could theoretically also spur many unintended consequences in the gender and sexual order of a nation.

Notes

1. Jonathan Zittrain and John Palfrey, "Internet Filtering: The Politics and Mechanisms of Control," in *Access Denied: The Practice and Policy of Global Internet Filtering*, ed. Ronald Deibert, John Palfrey, Rafal Rohozinski, and Jonathan Zittrain (Cambridge, MA: MIT Press, 2008), 35.

2. Heteronormativity refers to the privileging of heterosexuality through institutions, structures of understanding, and practical orientations. See Lauren Berlant and Michael Warner, "Sex in Public," *Critical Inquiry* 24, no. 2 (1998): 548.

3. This chapter was written by the OpenNet-Asia Gender Research Framework development team, coordinated by the Association of Progressive Communications, Women's Networking Support Programme, in partnership with the Centre for Independent Journalism, Malaysia. The full framework is available at http://www.genderit.org.

4. Ronald Deibert and Rafal Rohozinski, "Control and Subversion in Russian Cyberspace," in *Access Controlled: The Shaping of Power, Rights, and Rule in Cyberspace*, ed. Ronald Deibert,

John Palfrey, Rafal Rohozinski, and Jonathan Zittrain (Cambridge, MA: MIT Press, 2010), 22–28.

5. However, there have been individual cases of sites being blocked, especially by TMNet—Malaysia's main ISP. A widely known "just-in-time" blocking example is of the popular sociopolitical blog http://www.MalaysiaToday.com, which was blocked during an important by-election in 2008 that saw the return of the opposition party's de facto leader (see Vee Vian Thien, "The Struggle for Digital Freedom of Speech: The Malaysian Sociopolitical Blogosphere's Experience," chapter 3 in this volume). More sustained and less noticed blocking has targeted popular sites featuring sexual content, discussed later.

6. See the Malaysia country profile in this volume for further details.

7. Lawrence Lessig, *Code Version 2.0* (New York: Basic Books, 2006). See chapter 11 and especially 123 and 234.

8. Ibid., 123–124. Lessig explains that protection as well as regulation has been exercised at these levels.

9. Jean K. Chalaby, "New Media, New Freedoms, New Threats," *International Communication Gazette* 62, no. 1 (2000): 19–29.

10. Brinda Bose, "The (Ubiquitous) F-Word: Musings on Feminism and Censorships in South Asia," *Contemporary Women's Writing* 1, no. 1/2 (2007): 17–18.

11. Anne McClintock, Aamir Mufti, and Ella Shohat, eds., *Dangerous Liaisons: Gender, Nation, and Postcolonial Perspectives* (Minneapolis: University of Minneapolis Press, 1997).

12. On May 13, 1969, existing racial tensions sparked a series of violent clashes between the Malay, Chinese, and Indian communities in Kuala Lumpur. This unrest led to the declaration of a state of emergency and the suspension of Parliament. See Martin Vengadesan, "May 13, 1969: Truth and reconciliation," *The Star*, May 11, 2008, http://thestar.com.my/lifestyle/story.asp?file=/2008/5/11/lifefocus/21181089; Wong Chin Huat, "Watershed elections of 1969," *The Sun*, July 26, 2007, http://may131969.wordpress.com/2008/09/27/watershed-elections-of-1969.

13. Economic Planning Unit, New Economic Policy, Prime Minister's Department, Malaysia, 1971.

14. Department of Statistics Malaysia, "Preliminary Count Report, Population and Housing Census, Malaysia, 2010," last accessed April 20, 2011, http://www.statistics.gov.my/portal/index .php?option=com_content&view=article&id=350%3Apreliminary-count-report-population -and-housing-census-malaysia-2010&catid=102%3Apreliminary-count-report-population-and -housing-census-malaysia-2010&lang=en.

15. The term *bumiputera* (literally "sons of the earth") was introduced through the New Economic Policy, and is in reference to Article 153(1) of the Federal Constitution.

16. Article 160 of the Federal Constitution defines "Malay" as "a person who professes the religion of Islam, habitually speaks the Malay language, conforms to Malay custom [sic]."

Federal Constitution (as of June 1, 2007) (Petaling Jaya, SDE: International Law Book Series, 2007), 198.

17. Article 153(1), Federal Constitution (as of June 1, 2007) (Petaling Jaya, SDE: International Law Book Series, 2007), 188.

18. Benedict Anderson, *Imagined Communities: Reflections on the Origin and Spread of Nationalism* (New York: Verso, 1983).

19. Inderpal Grewal and Caren Kaplan, "Postcolonial Studies and Transnational Feminist Practices," *Jouvert: A Journal of Postcolonial Studies* 5, no. 1 (2000), available at http://english.chass.ncsu.edu/jouvert/v5i1/grewal.htm (accessed October 4, 2009), paragraph 6.

20. "Human Development Report 2009—Country Fact Sheets—Malaysia," n.d., last accessed October 20, 2010, available at http://hdrstats.undp.org/en/countries/country_fact_sheets/cty_fs_MYS.html.

21. Zulkifli Abd Rahman, "30% Quota for Women in Decision-Making Posts," *The Star*, July 4, 2009, last accessed 20 October 2010, available at http://www.anugerahcsrmalaysia.org/2009/07/04/30-quota-for-women-in-decision-making-posts.

22. Sam Haggag, "Women at Work," *Malaysian Business*, April 1, 2010, last accessed October 20, 2010, at http://findarticles.com/p/articles/mi_qn6207/is_20100401/ai_n53096425.

23. For one of the most comprehensive surveys conducted to date, see Article 19 and SUARAM, *Freedom of Expression and the Media in Malaysia* (Kuala Lumpur: Article19 and SUARAM, 2005).

24. Print media are tightly controlled through the Printing Presses and Publications Act, and the majority of newspapers are owned directly or indirectly by political parties.

25. Laws that have an impact on freedom of expression include the Sedition Act, the Official Secrets Act (OSA), the Internal Security Act (ISA), the Defamation Act, and the Penal Code (Article 19 and SUARAM, *Freedom of Expression, and the Media in Malaysia*).

26. Vengadesan, "May 13, 1969: Truth and reconciliation"; Huat, "Watershed elections of 1969."

27. See note 24.

28. Roger W. Harris, "Malaysia's Multimedia Super Corridor—An IFIP WG 9.4 Position Paper," 1998, last accessed January 20, 2010, available at http://is2.lse.ac.uk/ifipwg94/pdfs/malaymsc.pdf.

29. Point 7 of the Bill of Guarantees states simply, "ensure no internet censorship," last accessed January 20, 2010, available at http://www.mscmalaysia.my/topic/MSC+Malaysia+Bill+of+Guarantees.

30. Laws of Malaysia, Act 588—Malaysia Communications and Multimedia Act, 1998 (incorporating all amendments up to January 2006).

31. Available at http://www.malaysiakini.com.

32. Available at http://www.malaysia-today.net.

33. Available at http://www.themalaysianinsider.com.

34. Available at http://www.thenutgraph.com.

35. For an analysis of the emergence of the Malaysian sociopolitical blogosphere, see Vee Vian Thien, "The Struggle for Digital Freedom of Speech," chapter 3 in this volume.

36. Statistics culled from ITU and MCMC, published by Internet World Statistics, "Malaysia Internet Usage and Telecommunications Reports," last accessed January 20, 2010, available at http://www.internetworldstats.com/asia/my.htm.

37. This constitutes a large part of all Internet use, with 39.4 percent of all subscriptions being for home use.

38. SKMM, "Household Use of the Internet Survey—Statistical Brief Number Seven," 2008, http://www.skmm.gov.my/link_file/facts_figures/stats/pdf/HUIS08_02.pdf.

39. Brian Ulicny, Christopher J. Matheus, and Mieczyslaw M. Kokar, "Metrics for Monitoring a Social-Political Blogosphere: A Malaysian Case Study," *Internet Computing* 14, no. 2 (2010): 36.

40. Gaye Tuchman, *Making News: A Study in the Construction of Reality* (New York: Free Press, 1978), 138.

41. See the self-description on the home page, last accessed October 15, 2009, available at http://www.whomakesthenews.org/gmmp-background.html.

42. National Report: Malaysia (Global Media Monitoring Project 2010), last accessed October 20, 2010, available at http://www.whomakesthenews.org/images/stories/restricted/national/Malaysia.pdf.

43. Pamela Lim, "Police Intimidation Caught on Video" (video), LoyarBurok, October 10, 2010, http://www.loyarburok.com/the-system/bolehland/video-police-intimidation-caught-on-video.

44. Ibid. See comments section.

45. Shahrzad Mojab, "Information, Censorship, and Gender Relations in Global Capitalism," *Information for Social Change* 14 (2001–2002), http://www.libr.org/isc/articles/14-Mojab.html.

46. See the Malaysia country profile in this volume for further details.

47. For example, see R.S.N. Murali, "Reckless Bloggers Can Be Prosecuted," *The Star*, August 18, 2009, http://thestar.com.my/news/story.asp?file=/2009/8/18/nation/4540459&sec=nation.

48. For example, see SEAPA, "Blogger Arrested under Official Secrets Act, Another under Investigation; Symptomatic of Clampdown on Online Expression, Says SEAPA," IFEX, July 16, 2007, http://www.ifex.org/malaysia/2007/07/16/blogger_arrested_under_official/.

49. For example, see Committee to Protect Journalists, "Malaysian Blogger Jailed for Two Years under Security Act," September 23, 2008, http://www.cpj.org/2008/09/malaysian-blogger-jailed-for-two-years-under-secur.php.

50. For example, see "Malaysian Blogger Charged with Criminal Defamation," Committee to Protect Journalists (CPJ), July 23, 2008, http://www.unhcr.org/refworld/country,,CPJ,,MYS,4562 d8cf2,48a5754433,0.html.

51. Tommy Thomas, "Election 2008: Crossing the Rubicon," Aliran, April 30, 2008, http://aliran .com/720.html?.

52. Laws of Malaysia, Act 588—Malaysia Communications and Multimedia Act, 1998 (incorporating all amendments up to January 2006).

53. Jacqueline Ann Surin, "Fined RM 10,000 for Insulting Sultan," The Nutgraph, March 13, 2009, http://thenutgraph.com/fined-rm10000-for-insulting-sultan.

54. Lee Yuk Peng, Wani Muthiah, Loh Foon Foong, and Sim Leoi Leoi, "Nude Pix Scandal Hits PKR Rep (Update 7)," *The Star*, February 16, 2009, http://thestar.com.my/news/story.asp?file=/2009/ 2/16/nation/20090216115814&sec=nation.

55. "Privacy: Does It Exist in Malaysia? Is It Time to Legislate?" Malaysian Bar, http://www .malaysianbar.org.my/human_rights/privacy_does_it_exist_in_malaysia_is_it_time_to_legislate _.html.

56. NGO Shadow Report Group, "NGO Shadow Report on the Initial and Second Periodic Report of the Malaysian Government: Reviewing the Government's Implementation of the Convention on the Elimination of All Forms of Discrimination against Women (CEDAW)," 2005, http://www .iwraw-ap.org/resources/pdf/Malaysia_SR.pdf.

57. Committee to Protect Journalists, "Malaysian Blogger Jailed for Two Years under Security Act," September 23, 2008, http://www.cpj.org/2008/09/malaysian-blogger-jailed-for-two-years -under-secur.php.

58. For example see "Malaysia Says NO to Internet Porn—But What's Wrong with Health Sites?" Softpedia, June 30, 2005, http://news.softpedia.com/news/Malaysia-Says-NO-to-Internet-Porn-4044 .shtml.

59. For example see "Stern Warning to Those Who Violate Laws on Net," *The Star*, August 20, 2009, http://thestar.com.my/news/story.asp?file=/2009/8/20/nation/4556160&sec=nation.

60. An SIS publication entitled *On Muslim Women and the Challenges of Islamic Extremism* was banned by the Home Ministry in 2008, under Section 7 of the PPPA, on the grounds that it was "prejudicial to public order," as reported by Lisa Goh, "Book Ban Is Irrational and against Constitution: SIS Lawyers," *The Star*, October 28, 2009, http://thestar.com.my/news/story.asp?file=/ 2009/10/28/nation/20091028201322&sec=nation. SIS challenged the order, and in the High Court quashed the Home Ministry's ban on January 25, 2009. *SIS Forum (Malaysia) v. Dato Seri Syed Hamid Albar bin Syed Jaafar Albar* [2009].

61. Interview of the authors with Mas Elati, communications officer of Sisters in Islam, October 18, 2009.

62. "42 'Deeply Disturbed' Groups Urge PAS to Recant Call to Ban SIS," *The Star*, June 14, 2009, http://thestar.com.my/news/story.asp?file=/2009/6/14/nation/4117613&sec=nation.

63. Deibert and Rohozinski, "Control and Subversion in Russian Cyberspace."

64. "Najib: Govt Will Not Censor the Internet (Update)," *The Star*, August 7, 2009, http://thestar .com.my/news/story.asp?file=/2009/8/7/nation/20090807143305&sec=nation.

65. Ibid.; Mazwan Nik Anis, "Govt to Study 'Negative Impact' of the Net," *The Star*, August 13, 2009.

66. A copy of an e-mail by Exabytes that details this policy is reproduced in a blog that followed the protest by various individuals about the change in policy (last accessed January 20, 2010), available at http://lainie.tabulas.com/2008/04/25/i-will-not-like-it-if-your-website-host-is -exabytes./.

67. Available at http://www.youporn.com.

68. Available at http://www.redtube.com.

69. Available at http://www.gutteruncensored.com.

70. See Gutteruncensored.com "How to Access Gutteruncensored.com from Malaysia?" Facebook page, last accessed January 9, 2011, available at http://www.facebook.com/topic.php?uid=71689 381800&topic=9595; "Accessing Youporn, Gutter Uncensored or Other Blocked Websites within Malaysia," Programming-Is-Fun.com, September 18, 2008, http://www.programming-is-fun.com/ 2008/09/accessing-yourpon-from-malaysia.html.

71. Annie Freeda Cruez, "Malaysians Told: Carry ICs or Risk Detention," *New Straits Times*, May 14, 1998.

72. See Jane Perez, "Once Muslim, Now Christian and Caught in the Courts," *New York Times*, August 24, 2006, http://www.nytimes.com/2006/08/24/world/asia/24malaysia.html; "Sex Change Won't Validate Same Gender Marriage: Tan," Daily Express Newspaper Online, November 15, 2005, http://www.dailyexpress.com.my/news.cfm?NewsID=38393. In the case of *Wong Chiou Yong v. Pendaftar Besar/Ketua Pengarah Jabatan Pendaftaran Negara* [2005] 1 CLJ 622, the High Court ruled that Wong, a female-to-male transsexual, could not alter the gender assigned to his identity card after his sex-change operation without an act of Parliament.

5   Internet Politics in Thailand after the 2006 Coup

Regulation by Code and a Contested Ideological Terrain

Pirongrong Ramasoota

In 2009, Thailand joined the rank of "a new enemy of the Internet," according to Reporters Without Borders.[1] This status is ironic, given the fact that the country's name means "land of the free" in Thai. This development marked a significant regress from a decade earlier when there was no cyber law and no regulator, only open Internet architecture and freedom as the central norm among first-generation Thai Internet users. Despite economic doldrums that followed a financial meltdown in 1997, freedom of expression and freedom of information in Thailand were markedly stable in the late 1990s.[2] The Thai Internet regulatory landscape gradually shifted, however, first with the establishment of the Ministry of Information and Communication Technology (MICT)[3] in 2002, which introduced the first Internet filtering policy, and later with the passing of the computer crime law in 2007, following the September 2006 military coup that overthrew the country's longest-ruling civilian administration in modern Thai history.

The period following the 2006 coup saw Thai politics bitterly divided between two opposing camps: red-shirted supporters[4] of the self-exiled former prime minister, Thaksin Shinawatra, who was ousted from power on charges of corruption and for disloyalty to the crown; and those who back the country's "network monarchy"[5]— a loose alliance of the palace, the military, the ruling Democrat Party, and the People's Alliance for Democracy (PAD), or the "yellow shirts."[6] This contest has also exhibited itself in the online sphere as powerful members of the network monarchy exercised control over Internet communication to maintain political stability while red-shirt dissidents and their supporters evaded and resisted the control through circumvention and online civic mobilization. Notably, the new computer crime law has been a potent force in constraining the behavior of Internet users as well as service providers through the new regulatory framework it imposes. In the postcoup years, the lèse-majesté offense—insulting the monarchy—has also been increasingly used to charge anyone writing or posting material deemed to be defamatory of Thailand's King Bhumibol Adulyadej or the royal family, and in blocking Internet content or shutting down Web sites.

In *Codes and Other Laws of Cyberspace,* Lawrence Lessig notes that four major regulatory elements are at play in Internet regulation—social norms, markets, technology (what he calls architecture), and law. Each of these elements, he argues, can directly limit individuals' actions in cyberspace through the different type of constraint each imposes, or they may work in combinations to constitute the "code" that regulates Internet users' behavior, that is, "regulation by code."[7] Norms constrain through the stigma that a community imposes; markets constrain through the price they exact; architecture constrains through the physical burdens it imposes; and law constrains through the punishment it threatens. Lessig emphasizes that architecture is the most sensible and influential modality of regulation. Nevertheless, he also notes that law can also change the regulation of architecture, especially when architecture (how the network is built and designed) is changed in order to realize a particular social end.

To extend Lessig's notion of regulation by code a bit further, a classical Marxist theory of ruling ideology is relevant if one considers the Internet beyond its role as conduit technology and thinks more deeply about its content and communication dimensions. In Internet-restrictive countries, "code" writers tend to shape the Internet as a means to promote a certain set of views and ideas—the ideology of the ruling class—and to exclude alternative or opposition ideas or views.

Drawing on this theoretical framework, this chapter examines the recent evolution of Internet filtering in Thailand, focusing in particular on the period following the September 19, 2006, coup and on the regulation of political content and communication. I address two main questions: (1) What are the major regulatory modalities in the Thai Internet filtering regime in the post-2006-coup era, and what are their major consequences for Internet stakeholders? (2) What are the reactions from civil society, and what mechanisms for addressing Internet filtering issues have emerged in Thailand?

The study relies on extensive analysis of laws and related policies, as well as in-depth interviews with stakeholders, policymakers, regulators, and members of civil society related to Internet regulation in Thailand. The discussion shows how the Internet in Thailand has turned into a contested terrain for competing values since the political change in 2006. What had been evolving as an emerging online public sphere became threatened and eroded in the postcoup years with the introduction of content-restrictive cybercrime law, an ID-enabled architecture, and the buttressing of a dominant social norm, which together constitute a schematic regulation by "code." However, civic groups and conscientious users who do not condone this controlling scheme have resisted it by projecting freedom and transparency as underlying values while challenging the legitimacy of Internet filtering and censorship through different means. While the contested nature of these Internet politics is not exactly equivalent to the color-coded politics that Thailand has been infamous for in recent years, there are definitely strong connections and shared implications.

Background

While Internet filtering has been actively practiced in Thailand since 2002, it did not become a political issue until after the military coup d'état of September 19, 2006.[8] The coup overthrew the highly popular Prime Minister Thaksin Shinawatra[9] and marked the beginning of a tumultuous chapter in Thai political history. In the aftermath of the coup, the self-exiled Thaksin and his red-shirt supporters have exploited the Internet as a primary channel for political communication.[10] Meanwhile, much political expression in Thailand has resorted to cyberspace, which has enjoyed relatively greater freedom of expression than have other forms of mass media. While broadcast media in Thailand have historically been controlled through state monopoly of the airwaves,[11] and print media generally had a lukewarm attitude toward the coup,[12] throughout the postcoup period (which international observers call color-coded politics for its red and yellow shirts), the Internet has emerged as a major public sphere.[13] Different online political forums, online newspapers, and political Web sites have become important platforms for expression, exchanges, and debates that represent a wide spectrum of political ideologies and orientations. As a result, authorities have increasingly zeroed in on Internet content as a target for censorship and surveillance in the post-2006-coup period.

Since September 2006, Thailand has seen four different governments led by four different prime ministers. The first postcoup PM was an appointee of the military junta, the Council for National Security (CNS), while the other three were MPs elected in 2007. The fourth prime minister—Abhisit Vejjajiva, leader of the Democrat Party, rose to power after the abrupt dissolution of the People's Power Party (PPP)[14] in late 2008, and the subsequent shift of alliance by a major faction in the preceding coalition government. The Democrat-led government, which was approved by the yellow shirts (the PAD) and the network monarchy, appeared to be brokered in by the military, and this alleged political illegitimacy was consistently used as a rationale by the United Front of Democracy against Dictatorship (UDD) in staging a series of protests against the Democrat-led government in 2009 and 2010.

In March to May 2010, when the red shirts took Bangkok in a protest calling for parliament's dissolution and a fresh election, the survival of the Abhisit government was again put to the test. Repeated negotiations failed to set an election date. The protests escalated into prolonged violent confrontations between the protesters and the military, and attempts to negotiate a ceasefire failed. More than 90 civilians and scores of soldiers were killed, with a total of more than 2,100 injured by the time the military successfully cracked down on the protesters on May 19. However, unrest rapidly spread throughout Thailand as red-shirt supporters clamored for justice. Many of these grievances were pouring out into cyberspace through social media where many dissidents were active.

Despite assuming office under unusual circumstances—over doubts regarding his government's sustainability and amid grievances against government mismanagement of the 2010 bloody crackdown—Abhisit completed his second year of administration with powerful backing still intact. In 2011 he was continuing to pursue his proclaimed goals of national reform and reconciliation.

To a number of observers and political experts, Thailand's wrenching political struggle over the past few years also boils down to another daunting question—the fate of the country after the end of the ailing 83-year-old King Bhumibol Adulyadej's reign. Other than the issues of support for Thaksin and the September 19, 2006, coup's legitimacy, Thai politics has also been polarized around loyalty to the monarchy. The right-wing conservatives and pro-status-quo forces in the military and current government, the main core of the network monarchy, are insecure and fearful of what will happen after the king passes from the scene.[15] During these dubious times, cases of lèse-majesté, involving prosecution of alleged insults to the immediate royal family, have dramatically increased. Critics see charges of lèse-majesté as an effective means to silence dissent, including on the Internet.

Insofar as online political communication is concerned, lèse-majesté has been the keyword in clamping down alternative viewpoints and in blocking Web sites related to Thaksin or the UDD (the red shirts). On more than one occasion, Abhisit and the Democrat-led government publicly announced that any lèse-majesté speech would not be tolerated offline or online. As part of their much-publicized policy to promote national reconciliation, the Abhisit-chaired cabinet approved a new agency in June 2010 to look after violations of the Computer-Related Offenses Act, in particular to protect and take care of the royal institution.[16]

This complex context is necessary for a nuanced understanding of the Internet-filtering regime in post-2006-coup Thailand. At least three regulatory elements can be delineated in this emerging filtering scheme: law, architecture, and social norms.

Law, Architecture, and Social Norms: Primary Regulators of the Thai Internet Filtering Regime

Law, architecture, and social norms are the dominant forms of regulation in Thailand's post-2006 Internet filtering regime. While Internet industry operators play a role, their regulatory influence emanates largely from the enforcement of law.

Law: Computer Crime Law and Lèse-Majesté

From September 2006 until the end of 2009, Thailand saw four different governments, two periods of massive political unrest, persistent insurgency, and an unprecedented level of political polarization. In this highly volatile context, four major legal measures have been used to control online communication:

1. The Council for Democratic Reform's Order No. 5/2549 (2006)[17] on the Ministry of Information and Communication Technology's control of information disseminated through information technology systems (known as the CDR's Order No. 5).
2. The Computer-Related Offenses Act B.E. 2550 (2007).
3. The Emergency Decree on Government Administration in a State of Emergency B.E. 2548 (2005) and the Internal Security Act B.E. 2551 (2007).
4. Lèse-majesté provisions.

Since the CDR's Order No. 5 was enforced concurrently with martial law in the period immediately after the coup, it will not be discussed here.

The Computer-Related Offenses Act B.E. 2550 (2007)

The Computer-Related Offenses Act B.E. 2550, better known as the Computer Crime Law, was the very first legislation to be passed by the CNS-appointed National Legislative Assembly (NLA), an interim legislature after the coup.[18] Although the initial drafting of the law began in 1996, it was not actually passed until 2007, following an international controversy in April 2007 when the junta-appointed minister of MICT banned video clips deemed insulting to the Thai king and threatened to sue YouTube for carrying them. This threat of a lawsuit came after failed requests to YouTube to take down the problematic clips.[19]

Since its enactment, the computer crime law has been controversial, particularly its negative implications for online freedom of expression. Unlike conventional cybercrime law, which does not regulate content,[20] the Thai Computer-Related Offenses Act classifies content offenses committed on a computer as another major offense category in addition to offenses committed against computer systems or computer data. Section 14 of the law defines offenses as the import into a computer system of

• forged or false computer data, in a manner that is likely to cause damage to a third party or the public.
• false data in a manner likely to damage national security or to cause public panic.
• data constituting an offense against national security under the penal code; and pornographic data in a manner that could be publicly accessible.[21]

According to recently published research on online censorship through law and policy in Thailand, two major types of offenses can be delineated from prosecution charges filed under the 2007 Computer-Related Offences Act:[22] (1) offenses against computer systems or data and (2) offenses against content published online. Statistics in the three years since the new law came into effect show that 45 cases fall into the first

Table 5.1

STATISTICS OF OFFENSES CHARGED UNDER THE COMPUTER-RELATED OFFENSES ACT B.E. 2550 (2007) FROM JULY 2007 TO JULY 2010		
Types of Offenses	Number of Cases	Percentage
Offenses related to computer system	45	24.32
Offenses related to content	128	69.19
Cannot be clearly categorized	12	6.49

Source: Suksri, Sawatree, et al., *Situational Report on Control and Censorship of Online Media through the Use of Laws and the Imposition of Thai State Policies* (Bangkok: Heinrich Böll Foundation Southeast Asia, 2010).

type (24.32%), 128 cases into the second type (69.19%), and 12 cases (6.49%) cannot be clearly categorized, as shown in table 5.1.

The data in table 5.1 show that the main emphasis in the enforcement of the new law is on content regulation rather than computer crimes that use computers as tools or aim at computer system as targets. National security is the main keyword for content offenses, most likely because it includes lèse-majesté (insulting the royal family), which is a taboo and a serious crime in Thai society.

The law also imposes severe sanctions for violators. For offenses against computer systems or computer data, the penalties include imprisonment of between six months and 20 years and/or a fine of between THB 10,000 (approximately USD 300) and 300,000 THB (approximately USD 9,036) while penalties for content offenses range from imprisonment for up to five years and/or a fine of up to THB 100,000 (approximately USD 3,012).[23]

Furthermore, the law grants broad powers to officials to investigate and gather evidence of a suspected offense committed by computer. Rather than suggesting the least intrusive action that will support their investigation, the law allows broad-based surveillance, censorship, and control of Internet-based activities. Competent officials, who are appointed by the minister of ICT, are authorized to do a range of things including summoning alleged parties to appear; requesting information and evidence; duplicating, decrypting, censoring, and accessing computer information; and confiscating or "freezing" computer systems.

In addition to granting these powers, the enforcement of the Computer-Related Offenses Act has important consequences for the regulation of Thai cyberspace, as follows:

1. *Legalizing blocking of Internet content*
Prior to the passing of the computer crime law, blocking of Internet content, which has been practiced since 2002 by the MICT, was always criticized for lack of legal

grounds. Critics have alluded to constitutional provisions that guarantee freedom of expression when attacking the blocking's illegality. For instance, the first clause in section 45 of the constitution reads, "A person shall enjoy the liberty to express his or her opinion, make speeches, write, print, publicize, and make expression by other means." The section goes on to prohibit the shutdown of media outlets like newspapers and broadcasting. While the Internet is never addressed in this constitutional provision, many cyber libertarians still see the Internet as a form of mass media that warrants the same protection. But with the passing and enforcement of the new computer crime law, blocking of Internet content is now legalized, falling as it does under the category of an offense. As section 20 of the law reads:

In case the offences according to this law involve the publicizing of computer information that may have negative implications to national security as indicated in Part II of this law or as prescribed in 1/1 of the penal code or which may violate public order or good morals of the people, the competent officials, with approval from the appointed Minister, may petition, with supporting evidence, to the court within the jurisdiction, to halt the spread of such computer information.

If the court issues an order to block the spread of information as in clause 1, competent officials may block the spread of that information themselves or request service providers to block the spread of that information.[24]

As a result, Internet filtering, which was a controversial issue in the past, is now considered legal. Since the act first came into effect, the MICT has applied section 20 to order thousands of Web sites alleged to contain lèse-majesté or pornographic materials to be blocked. Cracking down on lèse-majesté content has been identified as the MICT's policy priority.[25]

While the law specifies that a court warrant is mandatory, the actual enforcement has not been entirely strict. Based on interviews conducted as part of this study with selected Internet service providers, "requests for cooperation" from government agencies like the MICT and the Department of Special Investigation (DSI) do not always come furnished with court orders. The usual objectives of such requests are obtaining log files of Internet traffic, blocking problematic Web sites, and deleting problematic postings in online discussion forums. The requests often plainly make reference to provisions in the Computer-Related Offenses law, but without court orders. Although many service providers have qualms about blocking Internet content, they do not have any option but to comply.

2. *Indirect regulation via intermediary providers and self-censorship of online content providers*
The computer crime law enables the state to regulate intermediary providers who in turn regulate users. Section 15 of the law creates the burden of intermediary liability by imposing the same penalty on offenders as on intermediaries, regardless of prior

knowledge or intent. It claims that "any service providers [who] knowingly or unknowingly support or allow offenses indicated in Section 14 to be committed in the computer or system under his control *shall receive the same penalties as offenders under Section 14*"[26] (my emphasis).

According to the law, no distinction is made between network providers who act as mere conduits and content providers who actually host content in the way they are held liable for harmful or illegal content. Whether or not the providers have actual knowledge of the content in question or whether they quickly remove the content after becoming aware of it does not grant any immunity. However, the law does not extend liability to search engines and portals that provide links to illegal content.

Because of this intermediary liability enforcement, Internet intermediaries—network and content alike—have set up new measures to regulate content and in the process are passing regulatory constraints onto users. These measures are summarized in table 5.2.

Keeping a log file of Internet traffic is intended for investigation purposes, but the real target is the identity of users. In Thailand, where a civil registration system has been an inherent part of society for almost a century, it is relatively easy to pair IP addresses with citizen identification, since all service applications require the 13-digit citizen-identification number. While larger operators like Internet service providers (ISPs) can integrate this legal requirement into their existing operation, smaller providers—operators of Web sites, Web-hosting services, online discussion forums, and providers of institutional servers—have to set up some new form of identification and certification clearance system that makes users' network access conditional on providing credentials. In the case of Internet cafés, since they do not provide network service, customers are required to sign their names and citizen IDs in a logbook before using the service.

Meanwhile, medium to large organizational servers—academic institutions, companies, government agencies, and some Internet cafés—that provide Internet access

Table 5.2

SERVICE PROVIDERS' NEW REGULATORY MEASURES THAT CREATE INDIRECT REGULATION OF USERS AS A RESULT OF THE COMPUTER-RELATED OFFENSES ACT
New Content Regulation Measures Passed by Intermediaries Due to the 2007 Computer-Related Offenses Act
1. Keeping a log file of Internet traffic, including users' IP addresses, for 90 days
2. Identification and certification clearance requirement for users at institutional servers and for subscribers to online discussion forums
3. Installing filtering software at organizational servers to enable content filtering
4. Setting up a 24-hour monitoring system for online discussion forums
5. Incorporation of provisions of the law into codes of ethics/practice and terms of services

are increasingly installing filtering software on their systems, using a keyword or groups of keywords as criteria. Filtering criteria depend mainly on the policy of each organization, but the types of content offenses provided in the computer crime law are usually included.

Internet service providers also administer surveillance on interactive Web sites like online discussion forums and chat rooms that have registered IP addresses under their networks. For instance, CAT Telecom, a major ISP, administers this content-monitoring scheme through an in-house unit called Internet Data Center (IDC). An IDC staff member will periodically examine exchanges in online discussion forums, particularly political forums. If lèse-majesté content is found, IDC will inform the moderators of the particular online forum and give them 30 minutes to remove the content. If the content is not deleted within that time, CAT Telecom will block access to the IP address that hosts the online discussion forum.

As for operators of online discussion forums themselves, a 24-hour monitor of postings on the forum has been in place since the law came into force. While moderators of such forums make it part of their daily routine to remove illegal or harmful content, most feel reluctant and view the new law with much apprehension. The Web moderator of Prachatai (http://www.prachataiwebboard.com), Chiranuch Premchaiporn, who is now awaiting trial on intermediary liability charges filed under this law, described the main effect of the law being "a transfer of censorship from state agencies to webmaster, with the law as choker."[27] The late Somkiat Tangnamo,[28] webmaster of http://www.midnightuniv.org, admitted that he self-censored on lèse-majesté to an unprecedented level during the Abhisit government's rule. Evidently, self-censorship has become the prevalent practice for moderators of online forums, particularly politically oriented ones. See table 5.3 for a summary of such self-censorship/regulation practices during the post-coup period.

Although there has not yet been a study to examine online citizen reporters and their reaction to Internet filtering, related research shows that bloggers engaged in citizen journalism regulate content through codes of practice. In the case of OK Nation Blog, a popular journalistic blog, member bloggers develop their own sets of codes and practices, which closely observe provisions in the computer crime law and related laws like lèse-majesté.[29] In effect, legal provisions are incorporated into citizen reporters' codes and thereby become a framework for the self-regulation of bloggers.

The Emergency Decree on Government Administration in State of Emergency B.E. 2548 (2005) and the Internal Security Act B.E. 2551 (2007)

The Emergency Decree was passed in 2005 during the Thaksin administration, with the main objective of quelling the endemic insurgency in Southern Thailand. The

Table 5.3

SUMMARY OF SELF-CENSORSHIP PRACTICES IN ONLINE POLITICAL DISCUSSION FORUMS IN THE POST-2006-COUP PERIOD

Name of Online Discussion Forum	Self-Censorship/Self-Regulation Practices
www.midnightuniv.org	After lifting of the ban on the Web site in the days following the coup, the webmaster changed the site's comment-posting procedure by having all the posters send him an e-mail message rather than posting directly onto the forum so that he could filter all the postings firsthand. The practice, however, put off many regular visitors to the forum, which became a read-only forum without direct interaction among the forum users. Lèse-majesté has been the key criterion in monitoring postings, with particular sensitivity noted during the coup-installed government and the Abhisit Vejjajiva government.
www.prachathaiwebboard.com	Working staff have taken turns to maintain 24-hour monitoring of the forum to keep the postings under close watch, with lèse-majesté content a top priority. A distributed system of content monitoring was set up to enable Web moderators and users (with membership longer than one month) to mutually develop a watch list of problematic postings by flagging them. Web moderators look into the watch list and make final judgments about which postings ought to be deleted.
www.pantip.com* (Rajdamnoen room)	Webmaster installed a one-person-one-account regulation system in which each member has to register with a citizen ID number. Only registered members are eligible to post in the forum. This way, all members/posters know that they are traceable. Web site policy states that the Web moderator has the right to remove all postings regardless of direction (positive or negative) related to the royal family.

*www.pantip.com, or *pantip* for short, is a popular Web site that specializes in online forums. Its many forums and chat rooms encompass almost all topics of common interest, ranging from politics, science, sports, and fashion to entertainment. Its political online forum is named Rajdamnoen after a major thoroughfare in Bangkok where the Democracy monument is located and where many historic prode-mocracy street protests took place. Transliterated in Thai, *pantip* means a thousand tips. The name derived from Pantip Plaza, a very famous computer mall in Bangkok.

Internal Security Act (ISA) B.E. 2551 was passed in November 2007 by the military-installed legislature—the NLA. The ISA establishes an Internal Security Operations Command (ISOC), directed by the prime minister and the commander-in-chief of the army. The ISOC has the power to have relevant government officials implement any action or withhold the implementation of any action.

Both laws have imposed far-reaching restrictions on the right to free expression, peaceful assembly, and freedom of movement, and the right to a fair judicial process. During the political turmoil in April 2009, both laws were invoked on more than one occasion in certain districts of Bangkok during demonstrations by the United Front of Democracy against Dictatorship (UDD). The enforcement of these laws enabled the MICT and other government agencies to exercise broad-based censorship and surveillance of the media, including the Internet.

During the "Red Shirt Protests" from April to May 2010, a significant number of red-shirt sites were targeted and blocked, following a block list issued under the Emergency Decree that ordered 36 Web sites to be filtered. During this period ONI conducted tests on two major ISPs—state-run TOTNET and TRUE, a private telecommunications conglomerate. The testing found blocked sites under common content categories in both ISPs as follows: free expression and media freedom, gambling, political reform groups, and social networking. However, TOTNET was found to have filtered almost twice the number of sites (29 URLs) than TRUE and more content categories. For example, anonymizer and circumvention sites were blocked by TOTNET but not by TRUE. Significantly, neither TRUE nor TOTNET filtered the entire block list, with TOTNET blocking only 10 URLs from the list and TOTNET filtering this same set and an additional 13 for a total of 23 URLS.[30] Meanwhile, community radio stations and cable television stations were raided, and satellite television stations' signals were cut off.[31] While it is in effect, the Emergency Decree supersedes all other laws. It has been attacked by critics as an authoritarian piece of legislation that allows unprecedented state control.

Lèse-Majesté Provisions

Lèse-majesté—damaging or defaming the king and royal family—has been the single offense most frequently applied by the Thai authorities against Internet users and service providers under the computer crime law, largely because of the postcoup political crisis. Lèse-majesté provisions in Thai law include sections 8 and 9 of the 2007 constitution and section 112 of the penal code. Section 8 of the 2007 constitution notes that "the King shall be enthroned in a position of revered worship and shall not be violated. No person shall expose the King to any sort of accusation or action."[32]

Lèse-majesté is also classified under Offenses Relating to the Security of the Kingdom in Thailand's penal code. It has always been part of the code and rarely subject to change since its inception in 1957. Thai authorities treat lèse-majesté as a matter of national security, and cases of lèse-majesté usually entail severe punishment. This fact is evident in section 112 of the penal code, which reads, "Whoever defames, insults, or threatens the King, the Queen, the Heir-apparent or the Regent, shall be punished with imprisonment of three to fifteen years."[33] The royalist Democrat government, which has ruled since late 2008, recently proposed to Parliament a legal amendment that will raise prison sentences for lèse-majesté to a maximum of 25 years. The amendment will also add a maximum fine of one million baht (about USD 28,500). Currently, lèse-majesté carries no fine.

An analysis of legal prosecutions related to Internet content since the 2006 coup shows that lèse-majesté was the leading offense. When bringing charges of defaming the monarch on the Internet, the police will usually cite section 14 of the computer crime law together with section 112 of the penal code, since the offense is covered by provisions in both pieces of legislation. See table 5.4 for analysis of prominent cases of Internet content offenses during the post-2006-coup period.

Of all the content offenses charged, the only unresolved case is that of Chiranuch Premchaiporn, webmaster of Prachatai. The interesting point about Chiranuch's case is that she was first charged with only the computer crime law under an intermediary liability charge because the alleged lèse-majesté comment was posted by a forum user and not by herself. However, in September 2010 she was arrested on multiple charges including lèse-majesté for an interview published on the Web site in 2008 with a man who was arrested and charged with lèse-majesté for refusing to stand up during the royal anthem in a movie house.[34]

It should be noted that lèse-majesté cases have also increased offline. From 2008 to 2009, at least four cases were charged, alongside those in cyberspace:

• A local man, Chotisak Onsoong, went to a movie and refused to stand up while the royal anthem played before the movie. He was later arrested after the movie operator reported him to the police for an act deemed an insult to the king.[35]
• An Australian man, Harry Nicolaides, was arrested and sentenced to three years in prison for having published a book that defames the crown prince.[36] He later received a royal pardon and was immediately deported to Australia.
• Political science professor Giles Ungpakorn was summoned for questioning for an alleged lèse-majesté charge. He later fled to England, for fear of not getting a fair trial.[37]
• Political activist Daranee Chancheongsilapakul, also known as Da Torpedo, was convicted of lèse-majesté and sentenced to a combined jail term of 18 years. Daranee reportedly made a series of inflammatory speeches against the king and the 2006 coup at one of the red-shirt political rallies.[38]

Table 5.4

Date of Incident	Type of Offense Allegedly Committed	Summary of Incident	Legal Measures Taken
September 2007	Lèse-majesté (section 8 of the constitution, and section 112 of the penal code); input into a computer system of data that were an offense against national security or terrorism according to the criminal code [section 14(3) of the Computer-Related Offenses Act]	An alleged lèse-majesté comment against the monarchy on the now-defunct political forum Web site www.propaganda.forumotion.com by a man using the pseudonym of Praya Pichai. The man was brought into custody and jailed for two weeks but charges could not be filed for lack of evidence.	The Web site was shut down and Praya Pichai faced ten years of continued surveillance and a threatened prison term if he posts a political comment online again.
April 2008	Input into a computer system of pornographic computer data that are accessible to the public [section 14(4)] of the Computer-Related Offenses Act	Owner of 212 café online forum was arrested for hosting a link to a pornographic Web site. At the arrest time, the police could not specify the problematic URL of the link. Although the forum webmaster immediately shut down the Web site, a month later, the police raided his home office and appropriated his servers and computer devices.	The forum owner was summoned to appear at a police station and to submit the names and contact list of all the forum's clients (about 28,000 people). He eventually spent one night in jail and later posted bail for THB 100,000 (USD 3,250).
January 2009	Lèse-majesté (section 8 the constitution, section 112 of the penal code), input into a computer system of computer data that is an offense against national security or terrorism according to the penal code [section 14(3) of the Computer-Related Offenses Act]	A blogger was arrested and convicted for having uploaded royally defaming materials on the www.youtube.com Web site. He was held in custody for three months before a lèse-majesté verdict was announced in April, resulting in a ten-year imprisonment. In June 2010 his petition for a royal pardon was answered and he was released from prison.	The police (through the high-tech crime unit and DSI) kept the convicted blogger on surveillance for about six months before the arrest.

Continued

Table 5.4
(continued)

Date of Incident	Type of Offense Allegedly Committed	Summary of Incident	Legal Measures Taken
March 2009	Intermediary liability or consent/negligence of operators for offenses to be committed (section 15 of the Computer-Related Offenses Act)	Webmaster of the independent online newspaper www.prachatai.co.th was arrested because alleged lèse-majesté comments were posted on the Web site's online discussion forum at www.prachataiwebboard.com—though she said that she had removed them immediately after the first notice from the police. She is currently undergoing trial.	Prior to the arrest, Prachathai had reportedly received "requests" from the military to remove from its Web site articles and commentaries on the monarchy and the military.
November 2009	Import of false computer data that could threaten national security or cause public panic [section 14(2) of the Computer-Related Offenses Act]	Two brokers were arrested for having posted information on two political online forums—www.prachataiwebboard.com and www.sameskyboard.org. One of the postings was a translation of a Bloomberg news service article on a rumor about the king's deteriorating health. The postings allegedly helped the market to plunge 7 percent during trading on October 14 and 15, 2009. However, the webmaster of www.prachataiwebboard.com contradicted the police theory that the two brokers were helping spread the rumors for financial gain by confirming that both were long-standing members of the forum.	High-tech crime division and DSI have been keeping both political forums under constant surveillance throughout the postcoup period. When the suspects were arrested, their apprehension was in the context of a stock market manipulation. But a police official in charge did mention that their spreading of rumors took place on "two politically problematic and controversial Web boards."

Table 5.4

(continued)

Date of Incident	Type of Offense Allegedly Committed	Summary of Incident	Legal Measures Taken
September 2010	Lèse-majesté (section 112 of the penal code); inciting unrest by publication (section 116 of the penal code); input into a computer of system computer data that are an offense against national security or terrorism according to the penal code [section 14(3) of the Computer-Related Offenses Act]; and intermediary liability or consent/ negligence of operators for offenses to be committed (section 15 of the Computer-Related Offenses Act)	Webmaster of www.prachatai.co.th was stopped at an immigration checkpoint and arrested at Bangkok International Airport after returning from the Internet at Liberty 2010 conference in Budapest, Hungary. Her arrest warrant was based upon an interview published in www. prachatai.co.th about a man who was charged with lèse-majesté for failing to stand up for the royal anthem in a movie theater in 2008.	The arrestee was bailed out on THB 200,000 (USD 6,600) bail. She was expected to report to Khon Kaen provincial police station, where the arrest warrant was issued, once a month until the case is either dismissed or filed to the public prosecutor.

Architecture: From Automatic URL Filtering to an ID-Enabled Cyberspace

Automatic URL Filtering

After the September 2006 coup, the MICT was faced with mounting complaints over lèse-majesté cases, which were reportedly mushrooming on anticoup and pro-Thaksin Web sites. The existing IP-based filtering at ISP levels, based on block lists circulated by MICT, was deemed ineffective and was also criticized for overblocking. The interim minister of ICT thus revisited the idea of an automatic Internet filtering system, which was discussed in the later years of the Thaksin administration but did not materialize. As a result, a feasibility study was carried out, and a pilot project was commissioned to local researchers. The new automatic filtering system was installed at the level of international Internet gateway (IIG),[39] which is a higher level of networking than national Internet exchange (NIX) or ISPs.[40] All IIGs under CAT Telecom Plc were the first to be installed with the new automatic filtering system, since CAT Telecom is a state enterprise and reports directly to the MICT. The filtering technology was developed by a group of computer-engineering researchers at the Bangkok-based Kasetsart University. The URL filtering technique was originally developed to filter out unwanted content such as spam but could also be used to filter Web access by blocking at application layers or at URL levels.[41] The system began a trial run in 2008 and has been fully operational since early 2009.

Essentially, the URL filtering technique uses what Robert Faris and Nart Villeneuve call proxy-based filtering strategies.[42] Internet traffic passing by the filtering system is reassembled, and the specific HTTP address being accessed is checked against a list of blocked URLs or blocked keywords in the URL. When users attempt to access these URLs, they are subsequently blocked. But instead of showing an MICT block page indicating that the site has been blocked (as would be the case of IP blocking at ISP level), the new system has created a block page that looks like the browser's default error page, possibly to disguise the fact that the government is blocking these sites.

ID-Enabled Cyberspace

Largely because of enforcement of the computer crime law, online service providers (OSPs)—those that host social networking services, blogs, and Web sites—have increasingly set up a system that enables "traceability regulation."[43] To access content and services on these Web sites, users are required to provide some sort of identification or certification first. Using traceability regulation as a framework, we surveyed popular local online services like online discussion forums, blogs, social networking services, portals, and online newspapers. The results are shown in table 5.5.

Table 5.5

Type/Name of Web site	Identification/ Certification upon Login	Identification/Certification upon Registration			Remark
	User Name/ Password	E-mail	13-Digit Citizen ID	Name/ Address/ Phone	
Online discussion forums					
pantip.com	√	√	√	√	Member registration requires citizen ID and a personal photo
mthai.com	√	√			
forum.serithai.net	√	√			
Blog					
blogging.com	√	√	√	√	Membership bundled with that of pantip.com
exteen.com	√	√	√		
oknation.net	√	√	√	√	Member registration requires citizen ID and a personal photo
blogger.com	√				Login via Google account
gotoknow.org	√	√		√	Member registration requires real name
asiancorrespondent .com	√	√			English-language blog. Covers politics and situation in southern part of Thailand. Provides analyses of news from the *Bangkok Post* and *The Nation.*
Social networking service (SNS)					
facebook.com	√	√			

Continued

Table 5.5

(continued)	Identification/ Certification upon Login	Identification/Certification upon Registration			
Type/Name of Web site	User Name/ Password	E-mail	13-Digit Citizen ID	Name/ Address/ Phone	Remark
Twitter.com	√	√			
Hi5.com	√	√			
MySpace.com	√	√		√	Member registration requires name and birth date
Portal					
hunsa.com	√	√	√	√	Does not require citizen ID. User will be entered into "lucky draw" and able to join online auction if citizen ID is provided.
sanook.com	√	√			
kapok.com	√	√			
th.yahoo.com	√	√		√	Member registration requires name and birth date
Online newspaper					
thairath.co.th	√	√	√	√	Membership is required to search historical news
manager.co.th	√	√		√	Member registration requires name, birth date, and postal code
posttoday.com	√	√			Member registration requires name and birth date

Table 5.5

Type/Name of Web site	Identification/ Certification upon Login	Identification/Certification upon Registration			Remark
(continued)					
	User Name/ Password	E-mail	13-Digit Citizen ID	Name/ Address/ Phone	
komchadluek.net	√	√	√	√	Membership is required to receive e-newsletter and to post comments on the news
Others (video and photo sharing, satellite TV)					
voicetv.co.th	√	√		√	Member registration requires name and birth date
youtube.com	√	√			Can watch and upload video clips
flickr.com	√	√		√	Automatically registered with Yahoo account

The most minimal forms of identification and certification required in all surveyed OSPs are user name and password for logging into the system. For registration, all providers require an e-mail address as a precondition for access, while some require name, address, and phone number, and a few require the 13-digit citizen identification number. In any case, it is apparent that an architecture of identification has been established in the Thai cyberspace as a result of the new computer crime law.

Social Norms: A Benevolent and Inviolable Kingship

While lèse-majesté may sound peculiar to non-Thais, it has been a deep-seated concept in Thai culture for centuries. The monarchy has always been a central institution in Thai society. Despite the 1932 revolution that changed the governing regime from absolute monarchy to constitutional monarchy, the king was still allowed to exercise sanctioning prerogatives of legitimization. At that time, the first constitution was regarded as a royal gift, while the throne was generally viewed as holding a position of moral superiority over the new political leadership. This view still appears to prevail today.

In past and present constitutions, the monarch, as the head of state, has these privileges:

1. He is to be unreservedly respected: his person is inviolable, and he is not subject to the jurisdiction of the courts.
2. He is the Head of the State.
3. He is the soul of the nation and the font of national harmony.
4. He is above politics.
5. He is politically neutral, without aligning with any political group or party.
6. He can do no wrong (constitutionally).

Furthermore, the Thai conception of kingship is a combination of the Hindu divine right of *deva raja* and the Buddhist patriarchal kingship in which the king rules according to the law or dharma. Therefore, the legitimacy of the monarch is derived not only from divine right but also from his own conduct and commendable deeds. The present king, Bhumibol Adulyadej, who is now the world's longest-reigning monarch, has been credited for his lifelong dedication to rural development and the livelihoods of his poorest subjects. He is thus well loved and respected by the general Thai public. In 2006 on the 60th anniversary of his coronation, the entire country glowed yellow as loyal supporters of the king donned special yellow royal shirts in celebration everywhere throughout the year.

With exceptional privileges, conceptual dominance, and public reverence, the Thai monarchy has been used as a source of legitimacy in Thai politics. A former prime minister (1957–1963) and military dictator, Field Marshal Sarit Thanarat, made extensive use of the monarchy to legitimize his regime both domestically and internationally. This legitimization often happens at the expense of free speech. In the past, dissidents who were charged with lèse-majesté were usually social critics or those who openly resented military involvement in politics. Meanwhile, filers of lèse-majesté suits were typically from the military.

Traditionally, the monarchy has been identified as one of the core values to be protected under national security, which includes three things—the monarchy, religion (Buddhism), and the Thai nation. Any attempt to undermine these so-called three pillars of Thai society would be viewed as a threat to national security. As these core values are usually fused together, it is not uncommon for a show of disrespect, including criticism of the king, to be interpreted as "unpatriotic."

There has always been tension between free speech and royalism in Thailand, but never has the anxiety been so great as in the age of the Internet and a time of foreseeable royal succession. With the borderless and robust nature of the Internet, it is no longer feasible to keep the king virtually beyond criticism in the virtual world. But no matter how futile and ultraconservative lèse-majesté filtering may appear to some liberal people, there are those who support it and even participate in monitoring Web sites and reporting lèse-majesté to authorities. Statistics released by the MICT show that the greatest number of complaints received on Internet content had to do with lèse-majesté.[44]

Reaction from Civil Society and Mechanisms for Addressing Internet Filtering

In response to Internet filtering issues, members of civil society have reacted in a number of ways and used varying strategies to deal with new regulatory constraints. Members of civil society also contest what they conceive to be the government's abuse of power and violation of free speech online.

Online Security Caution

According to interviews with selected civil society activists, tightening up security in their online use seems to be the top strategy in coping with authorities' censorship and surveillance. This approach was manifested most frequently in their technological choice. For instance, a few Internet advocacy activists said they deliberately gave up the more popular Windows platform and opted instead for Linux as an operating system. Some also chose to disable the conversation-recording feature of Gtalk and turn on the secure access feature (SSL) in Gmail. The majority are very cautious about their passwords. Not only do they keep their passwords as their most confidential information, but they also change passwords frequently. Their choice of password is also crucial. One online activist said he avoided words in the dictionary and used multiple layers of password protection. In using social media like Facebook or Twitter, a few activists noted that they exercise more caution in accepting friends or in setting the circle to which their personal information will be accessible. Similarly, in using online discussion forums, these activists are careful in posting comments and in registering their personal information to the Web sites. Usually, they do not give anything beyond their e-mail address to avoid being identified.

Evasion and Circumvention

When it comes to Web censorship, a number of users wishing to access blocked Internet content can find easy ways around it by using proxy or VPN or using Google translate or Google cache. But with Web 2.0 applications and social media, things are a bit more complicated to get around. At this level, OSPs that rent out server space to a large number of Web site developers and operators of social media platforms are becoming increasingly important as intermediary censors for online content. Ethan

Zuckerman refers to OSPs' role in Internet filtering as "intermediary censorship."[45] They have become important choke points for Web users who publish content on Web servers they do not control. Such censorship is observed in at least three online political discussion forums that the research team studied in the postcoup period. These findings are summarized in table 5.6.

The summary in table 5.6 clearly shows that because a number of smaller Internet providers rely on them to publish content, OSPs can be powerful entities in controlling online speech. But the same summary also shows that this newer generation of Internet publishers is savvy enough to circumvent such intermediary filtering systems by exploiting alternative hosting services overseas. While this strategy may not solve their problem entirely—since the state can still block through URL-filtering at the IIG level—it still suggests that cyber citizens make efforts to redress the problem with whatever technological options are available.

Campaigning for Local and International Support

Based on interviews with civil society members, their most immediate concern about Internet filtering in Thailand is the new computer crime law. To them, the new law is more of an effort by the after-coup government to curb threats against national security and the monarchy, rather than to stop cybercriminality. In response to arrest cases under this very law, several rights-based groups have campaigned in support of the arrestees. The most obvious case is that of Chiranuch Premchaiporn, who has been arrested twice with charges under the same law. (See details about Chiranuch's arrest in table 5.4.) Because Chiranuch is a member of the prominent online freedom advocacy group—the Thai Netizen Network (TNN)[46]—her case has been continuously reported in Prachatai (until it was blocked by the emergency decree during the red-shirt crisis of March to May 2010) and in other alternative online media including mailing lists of TNN. Ever since Chiranuch's first arrest in March 2009, campaigns to support her and Internet freedom, using her case as a rallying point, have been growing steadily.

First, only the TNN and alliance organizations like Campaign for Popular Media Reform (CPMR)[47] and Freedom against Censorship Thailand (FACT)[48] joined forces. Gradually, other local human rights nongovernmental organizations (NGOs) joined the campaign to free Chiranuch (also known by her nickname Jiew) by submitting an open letter seeking the immediate dropping of charges against her and dissuading public prosecutors from pursuing trial. These include the Network of Human Rights Lawyers, the Project on Legal Environment, and the Association for Civil Rights and Liberties. Subsequently, the circle grew to more regional participation with the Southeast Asian Press Alliance (SEAPA), Southeast Asian Media Legal Defense (SEAMLD), which is a regional spin-off from the global Media Legal Defense Initiative (MLDI),

Table 5.6

SUMMARY OF ONLINE SERVICE PROVIDERS' ROLE AS INTERMEDIARY CENSORS OF ONLINE DISCUSSION FORUMS IN THAILAND

Name of Online Discussion Forum	Intermediary Censorship Experience	Reaction
www.midnightuniv .org*	The Web-hosting company from which the forum rented server space was blocked during the aftermath of the coup and discontinued service to the forum thereafter.	Forum moderator decided to change to a new Web-hosting company and introduced a new filtering system for forum postings.
www .prachataiwebboard .com†	During the period of intense political conflict in 2008–2009, the contracted Web-hosting company decided to terminate service to the Prachatai online forum, evidently out of fear of the political sensitivity of the forum's content.	Webmaster decided to separate hosting services used for the online newspaper and for the online political discussion forum. The latter moved to rent from an overseas Web-hosting service, to avoid blocking problem.
www.sameskyboard .org‡	The contracted Web-hosting service company was reportedly pressured by the MICT to abruptly halt service for www.sameskybooks .org/ and its other online services. The MICT's interference also wiped out the affiliated online forum—www.sameskyboard. org—and all the database kept by the online publisher for the previous five years.	The editor of the www.sameskybooks .org/ publicly condemned MICT for their alleged interference and opened a temporary Web site and a new online forum. Later, the service shifted to an overseas hosting company for all its online services.

*The site www.midnightuniv.org, known as Midnight University, is a leading alternative educational Web site that compiles academic resources on various sciences including social science and anthropology. The site also provides a forum for the public to exchange opinions on matters of interest. A group of progressive-minded academics, a number of whom are from Chiang Mai University, run this Web site and the political discussion forum attached to it. After the 2006 coup, www.midnightuniv.org attracted a lot of media attention because it represented very rare voices in society that condemned the coup and denounced the postcoup (2007) constitution.

†The site www.prachatai.co.th, or Prachatai for short, is an online newspaper that is very famous for its leftist and highly critical political standing. Prachatai is also openly anti-2006-coup. Founded in 2004 by a well-known social activist, it aims to be an independent medium free from state control, after the model of the famous Minda News (http://www.mindanews.com) in the Philippines. Prachatai's initial funding was allocated by the Thai Health Promotion Foundation. Later, when the foundation blacklisted it for probing into the foundation's spending, its supporter shifted to overseas sources such as the Rockefeller Foundation and Open Society Institute. Prachatai also runs a famous left-wing online discussion forum—www.prachataiwebboard.com, of which the political room is most popular.

‡The site www.sameskyboard.org, or samesky for local users, is a popular left-wing online political discussion forum attached to www.sameskybooks.com, an online site of local publishers of *Samesky* magazines. *Samesky* magazine is well-known for its progressive and critical viewpoints on politics and society.

and Asian Human Rights Commission (AHRC), among others. At the time of writing (October 2010), a global campaign to support Chiranuch was well under way, with leading media advocacy and human rights organizations such as the Electronic Frontier Foundation (EFF), Committee to Protect Journalists (CPJ), International Court of Justice (ICJ), Open Society Institute (OSI), Human Rights Watch (HRW), and Amnesty International involved. These organizations' main criticism is directed at Thailand's censorship policy and its impact on human rights and free speech, especially in cyberspace. Both the new computer crime law and lèse-majesté have been criticized as tools to suppress dissent and persecute political opponents.

After Chiranuch's second arrest in September 2010, a wider circle of Internet users promoted her cause through social media. Examples include a campaign using "free jiew" as a tag on the popular micro-blogging site Twitter (https://twitter.com/search?q =%23freejiew); blogs dedicated to the cause (http://freejiew.blogspot.com); and a platform set up by Digital Democracy to receive donations in support of her bail (http:// digitaldemocracy.chipin.com/free-jiew).

Public Advocacy and Policy Lobbying

Alongside campaigning for support at local and international levels for Chiranuch's case, civil society organizations have also been active in advocating for public awareness about Internet restrictions in Thailand. In fact, advocacy work through public education has been the core work of the TNN, of which Chiranuch is a founding member. For the past two years, TNN has been at the forefront in organizing meetings, seminars, and public forums on issues related to Internet freedom. For instance, in August 2010, TNN, together with Media 4 Democracy and SEAPA, organized a high-profile seminar on the Computer-Related Offenses Act, on its third anniversary. A former information minister, an online newspaper webmaster, a popular blogger, a media watch representative, and Chiranuch herself shared comments on the computer crime law's impact on democratization in Thailand. The common sentiment is that restrictive law and careless enforcement during political polarization will contribute negatively to democracy because self-censorship becomes the rule for safety, hence deterring debate and the climate of opinion that are so fundamental to democracy.

In addition to public education, civil society has also used policy lobbying as another avenue to redress Internet control issues. In early 2009, several rights groups, including TNN, CPMR, and FACT, submitted an open letter to current Thai Prime Minister Abhisit Vejjajiva demanding an amendment of the computer crime law to make it more transparent and less politically motivated. Although Abhisit stressed civil liberties in his inauguration speech in December 2008, he has ruled out a repeal of the computer crime law.

Ambivalence and Indifference

In contrast to the stance and strategies taken by NGOs and activists, key institutional bodies responsible for human rights in Thailand are not only slow in responding to complaints about impediments to freedom from enforcement of the new computer law, but they have also been ambivalent in the face of lèse-majesté and the protection of national security. According to the chairperson of the National Human Rights Commission (NHRC), a post-1997 reform independent organization, the MICT's Internet blocking is a new challenge for many organizations, including NHRC. There are still few complaints at NHRC about Internet filtering as a violation of the freedom of expression—compared to other more pressing issues such as exploitation of natural resources, abuse of power, and governmental malpractice. The complicated nature of the Internet has also contributed to Thai institutions' limited understanding of the seriousness of the situation.

The NHRC usually refers ICT-related complaints, including online blocking, to the National Telecommunications Commission (NTC), an independent telecommunications regulator and now interim regulator of broadcasting. While acknowledging that violations of freedom do exist on the Internet, the NHRC also admitted they lack the necessary technical and legal expertise to deal with the problem.

Apart from the NHRC, another avenue where people can address Internet filtering issues is through human-rights-related commissions attached to the House of Parliament and the Senate. However, an interview with one chairperson of such a commission—the House commission on human rights, freedom, and consumer protection—revealed a rather conservative stance. Absolute freedom, this person argued, can threaten national security, especially when it involves the monarchy. The reverence of the monarchy, he stressed, is unique to Thai society and shall not be compromised at any cost. In this light, the new computer crime law is a justified effort by the government to properly regulate Internet use by balancing freedom of expression with national security. The chairperson feels that the judicial system is always open for online civil rights groups to tap if the rights to communicate and freedom of expression online are violated by the law.

Conclusion

At a glance, the politics of Internet filtering in Thailand may only reflect the larger political struggle between pro- and anti-Thaksin forces or between pro- and antimonarchy forces. But a closer examination yields another type of politics beyond the dominant color-coded politics. This politics of the Thai Internet code involves a subtle relationship between different elements in the regulation of Thai cyberspace.

In the post-2006-coup experience, the Computer-Related Offenses Act of 2007, a product of the coup-installed legislature, appears to be a major driving force in shaping the cyber experience in Thailand. A number of new regulatory practices have resulted, including the following:

• Legalizing of blocking at network levels.
• Indirect regulation by intermediary providers, which gave rise to intermediary censorship by online service providers and self-censorship of online content providers.
• Creating an ID-enabled architecture that promotes traceability regulation.
• Incorporating censorship into the cyber community's code of practice.
• Self-censorship by users in the online public sphere.

Other laws such as the Emergency Decree, the Internal Security Act of 2007, and lèse-majesté laws also help intensify regulatory restraints with the elements of surveillance and punishment. Gradually, Internet operators—network, service, and content— and Internet users in Thai society have learned to integrate these legal provisions into their cyber behavior. While it is true that lèse-majesté law has been in existence since 1957, its actual enforcement or looming possibility of enforcement has never been as evident as in the present period. I for one still remember the early days of the Internet in the early 1990s in which Thai Net users exchanged opinions on the future of the monarchy on Bulletin Board Service (BBS) using anonymous e-mails. The Internet was free and unregulated because it was difficult to identify the user or poster of comments. This is no longer true in Thai cyberspace, since everyone is now visible and traceable through the new ID-enabled architecture.

Notably, the increased transparency of the Thai Internet is made possible by indirect regulation from the new law. As users are forced to give self-authenticating facts to service providers in order to gain access to the Net, they have contributed directly to the regulation of their own behavior in cyberspace. The new law has changed the regulation of architecture through design constraints that condition netizens' access to cyberspace.

Meanwhile, automatic URL filtering, which involves more subtle filtering design than IP blocking, has also led to a greater technical capability to deny access to information resources while reducing the possibility of blockers being discovered. Though not directly related to the new law, this new technological design has indeed made filtering more malleable and more effective.

The law and the architecture aside, social norms also have a powerful role to play in the Thai politics of Internet filtering. The respect and reverence for the monarchy, particularly for the current king who has reigned for more than 62 years, is a deep-rooted norm in Thai society. Whether lèse-majesté is legitimate or not may be a moot point. What is clear is that this enigmatic norm carries with it high sensitivity in cyberspace as well as in the "real" world. Alongside the increase in prosecution cases related to lèse-majesté speech online and offline, there has also been growing evidence of participatory forms of censorship—by service providers, content operators, and users—against lèse-majesté. While this participatory censorship is partly a consequence of the climate of fear arising from the new computer law and strict enforcement of lèse-majesté law, the law is not an isolated cause. After all, as Lessig rightly notes, norms constrain through the stigma that a community imposes, while law constrains through the punishment it threatens. In the Thai scenario, both elements apply.

Post-2006 Thailand is an interesting time and place to study Internet censorship and control. In this unique context, an ideological struggle is being played out between the old norm of preserving the sanctity of a revered institution that unites the nation and the new norm of free speech that could disrupt national order. If this ideological contest continues, we are likely to see more filtering, more cyber surveillance, more cyber policing, and more "rule of law" being used to suppress and undermine human rights and free speech online. In the meantime, civil society will employ more tools and options to circumvent politically motivated censorship through wider and higher circles of advocacy, to ultimately prove that freedom is not a crime.

Notes

1. Reporters Without Borders, "Is Thailand a New Enemy of the Internet?" January 12, 2009, http://en.rsf.org/thailand-is-thailand-a-new-enemy-of-the-12-01-2009,29945.

2. This was a result of the 1997 reform-oriented constitution that promoted transparency, accountability of government, and people's rights, liberties, and participation.

3. The Ministry of Information and Communication Technology (MICT) was set up as part of the bureaucratic reform introduced by Thaksin Shinawatra, then the new prime minister. From its inception, the MICT's main policy has been Internet regulation. This began with introducing filtering through the unit called "Cyber-inspector," aimed largely at pornographic content. Later in 2003, the MICT passed regulatory measures to regulate online gaming in response to moral panic in Thai society.

4. The "red shirts" is the informal name for the United Front of Democracy against Dictatorship (UDD), a major political organization in the post-coup period. Members of the UDD are known for wearing red clothes during antigovernment protests. Established in 2006 as Democratic Alliance against Dictatorship (DAAD), the main objective of the red shirts then was to fight against its arch rival—the People's Alliance for Democracy (PAD)—and to support the ousted former Prime Minister Thaksin Shinawatra. Supporters of the UDD are largely rural grassroots people who benefited from Thaksin's populist welfare policy, but also include the urban middle class who admire Thaksin's business-oriented administrative policy and action.

5. Duncan McCargo, "Political Outlook: Thailand," *Regional Outlook* (2010–2011), 54–58.

6. The People's Alliance for Democracy (PAD) originated from the mass movements preceding the September 2006 coup that ousted Thaksin from the premiership. The PAD, also known as the yellow shirts, spent much of 2008 protesting against two successive Thaksin-nominated governments—led by the late Samak Sundaravej and Somchai Wongsawat (Thaksin's brother-in-law)—that arose from the December 2007 election. The PAD's 190-day protest in 2008 was marked by the seizure of the Government House and the Suvarnabhumi International Airport in Bangkok, which had devastating and lasting effects on the Thai economy. In 2009, leaders of the PAD entered electoral politics by establishing the New Politics Party.

7. Lawrence Lessig, *Codes and Other Laws of Cyberspace* (New York: Perseus, 1999), 15–30.

8. This coup took place after a 15-year interval. The previous coup was staged in 1992 by the so-called National Peace-Keeping Council (NPKC), led by then Supreme Commander-in-Chief General Sunthorn Kongsompong. The NPKC overthrew General Chatichai Choonhavan, a civilian prime minister, who led a coalition government for less than two years.

9. Thaksin Shinawatra, founder of the Thai Rak Thai (TRT) Party, was a famous telecommunications tycoon, having made his fortune from satellite and mobile phone concessions through Shin Corporation. Thaksin was also a popular political leader who led the longest democratic and civilian rule—six years—in contemporary Thai history. Thaksin's popularity was largely attributed to populist policies that featured income redistribution, cheap health care, microcredit schemes, and many policy innovations in support of globalization and neoliberal economy. Thaksin is not well liked by a large number of urban or middle-class voters who are repulsed by his arrogance, authoritarian tendencies, and policy discrepancy while in power. He was also widely accused of disloyalty to the crown, an accusation that was largely used as a justification for the September 19, 2006, coup.

10. For instance, Thaksin reportedly launched and managed www.thaksinlive.com on his own before moving on to social media like Facebook and Twitter with http://twitter.com/Thaksinlive, in addition to making periodic video-linked appearances via satellite at the red-shirts' rallies. In late 2009, his family launched an Internet television site called Voice TV, which can be accessed on the Web at http://www.voicetv.co.th.

11. Up until 2001 when the first community radio station aired, all broadcast frequencies—524 for radio and six for national television stations—were controlled by state agencies. Major controllers of the airwaves include the Department of Public Relations (PRD), the Mass Communication Organization of Thailand (MCOT), and the Ministry of Defense, mainly through the army.

12. The Thai printed press, which has always been an important institution in shaping public opinion and setting public agenda, came under heavy criticism for condoning the coup. Notably, three leaders of professional media organizations/associations were appointed by the junta to be in the National Legislative Assembly (NLA), an interim legislature. Also, the printed media were able to push for the passage of a liberal print notification law to replace the draconian and authoritarian print law during the NLA term.

13. According to a nationwide survey of Internet users in 2009 by the National Electronics and Computer Technology Center (NECTEC), Thailand has 18.3 million Internet users, of which 1.8 million are broadband users.

14. The PPP shared the same fate as its predecessor—the TRT Party—when it faced dissolution by a ruling from the Constitutional Tribunal in November 2008 over charges of election fraud.

15. Thitinand Pongsudhirak, "The Search for a New Consensus," *Journal of International Security Affairs,* no. 17 (Fall 2009), http://www.securityaffairs.org/issues/2009/17/pongsudhirak.php.

16. Available at http://www.bangkokpost.com/tech/computer/39215/ministers-sign-computer -related-crime-mou.

17. Immediately after the coup, the coup makers made themselves known to the public as the Council for Democratic Reform under Constitutional Monarchy but usually used Council for Democratic Reform (CDR) as a shorter title. Later they changed the name to Council for National Security, or CNS.

18. The Computer-Related Offenses Act (also referred to as the cybercrime or computer crime act) was in the pipeline since 1992, involving several changes and draft versions.

19. "Thais to Sue Google over King Video" Al Jazeera, May 8, 2007, http://english.aljazeera.net/ news/asia-pacific/2007/05/2008525131444839889.html.

20. For example, the Council of Europe's Cybercrime Convention, which is the main international standard in this field and provides a guideline for the development of national legislation as well as a framework for international cooperation, does not address content regulation but instead calls for self-regulation or coregulation in relation to Internet content. Council of Europe, Convention on Cyber Crime CETS No. 185, http://conventions.coe.int/Treaty/Commun/ QueVoulezVous.asp?NT=185&CL=ENG.

21. Translation of the Computer-Related Offenses Act, Vol. 124, Section 27 KOR., Royal Gazette, 18 June 2007, p. 7. Available at http://www.itac.co.th/index.php?option=com_content&view =article&id=90.

22. Sawatree Suksri, et al., *Situational Report on Control and Censorship of Online Media through the Use of Laws and the Imposition of Thai State Policies* (Bangkok: Heinrich Böll Foundation Southeast Asia, December 8, 2010), http://www.boell-southeastasia.org/downloads/ilaw_report_EN.pdf.

23. Sinfah Tunsarawuth and Toby Mendel, *Analysis of the Computer Crime Act of Thailand,* http:// www.law-democracy.org/wp-content/uploads/2010/07/10.05.Thai_.Computer-Act-Analysis.pdf.

24. Translation of the Computer-Related Offenses Act, Vol. 124, Section 27 KOR., Royal Gazette, 18 June 2007, p. 7. Available at http://www.itac.co.th/index.php?option=com_content&view =article&id=90.

25. "Web Censoring Needs a Debate," *Bangkok Post,* January 6, 2009, http://www.bangkokpost .com/opinion/opinion/9202/.

26. Translation of the Computer-Related Offenses Act, Vol. 124, Section 27 KOR., Royal Gazette, 18 June 2007, p. 7. Available at http://www.itac.co.th/index.php?option=com_content&view =article&id=90.

27. Interview with Chiranuch Premchaiporn and the author.

28. Somkiat Tangnamo passed away in July 2010.

29. Nida Moryadee, "OK Nation Blog as Citizen Journalism," unpublished master's thesis, Chulalongkorn University, 2009, 2–12.

30. See the Thailand country profile in this volume for further details.

31. Reporters Without Borders, "Government Uses State of Emergency to Escalate Censorship," April 8, 2010, http://en.rsf.org/thailand-government-uses-state-of-emergency-08-04-2010,36968.

32. Translation of Constitution of the Kingdom of Thailand B.E.2550 (2007). Available at http://www.isaanlawyers.com/constitution%20thailand%202007%20-%202550.pdf.

33. Translation of Thai Penal Code B.E. 2499 (1956), Section 112. Available at http://thailaws.com/law/t_laws/tlaw50001.pdf.

34. Standing during the royal anthem in a movie theater is a customary practice in Thailand to show respect and allegiance to the king.

35. "Thailand: Moviegoer Faces Prison for Sitting during Anthem," *New York Times*, April 24, 2008, http://query.nytimes.com/gst/fullpage.html?res=9506E1DF1E31F937A15757C0A96E9C8B63&fta=y.

36. "Aussie Author Gets Three-Year Sentence for Lèse-Majesté," *Bangkok Post*, January 20, 2009, http://www.bangkokpost.com/news/local/10026/aussie-author-gets-three-year-jail-sentence-for-lese-majeste.

37. "Lèse-Majesté Suspect Flees," *Bangkok Post*, February 10, 2009, http://www.bangkokpost.com/news/local/136371/lese-majeste-suspect-flees.

38. "Eighteen Years in Jail for Da Torpedo," *Bangkok Post*, August 28, 2009.

39. Based on data of the National Electronic and Computer Technology Center (NECTEC), Thailand has six international Internet gateways (IIGs): CAT Telecom Plc, TOT Plc, TRUE Corporation, Thai Telephone and Telecommunications (TT&T), ADC, and CS Loxinfo. These six IIGs also serve as National Internet Exchange (NIX). Of these six IIGs, two—CAT Telecom Plc and TOT Plc—are former state enterprises and monopoly telecommunications companies that have been corporatized, while two others—TRUE and TT&T—are long-time telecommunications concessionaires. Only ADC and CS Loxinfo are new market entrants and fully private entities. NECTEC's data also show that only 20 ISPs are actually carrying regular Internet traffic despite the fact that more than 40 ISPs hold licenses to operate.

40. Of the 20 operating ISPs, half are semiconcessionaires, as 35 percent of their shares are by default held by CAT Telecom, the long-standing international carrier monopoly. Although CAT Telecom's shares are wholly controlled by the Ministry of Finance, the corporatized state enterprise is under the bureaucratic structure of another government agency—MICT. This bureaucratic structure also helps explain the line of control in monitoring and filtering Web sites in Thailand. A number of ISPs are not under this bureaucratic structure, however. These are new operators that emerged as a result of a telecommunications reform process that has been ongoing since

the 2004 establishment of the National Telecommunications Commission (NTC), the country's first independent regulator of telecommunications. NTC has been issuing licenses for telecommunications services and Internet services since 2005. So far, a total of 130 licenses have been issued for telecommunications service and 132 for Internet. This description, therefore, reflects a two-tiered structure of Internet regulation. On one side, there are the pre-reform semiconcessionaires who are highly liable to CAT Telecom, which answers directly to MICT. On another side, there are the postreform ISPs that operate under licenses issued by NTC. This structure leads to somewhat of a double standard in Internet regulation and filtering.

41. URL filtering is one of the Web-content-filtering techniques. Content filters act on either the content or the information contained in the network packet header or body. URL filtering focuses on the URL and is suitable for blocking a Web page or sections of Web sites. There are two common approaches for URL filtering—pass-through filtering and pass-by filtering. Unlike pass-through filtering in which network traffic (a stream of packets) must pass through the filtering engine (firewall, proxy, or application gateway) for content inspection and can cause extra delay, pass-by filtering network packets do not have to "go through" the filtering engine. The filtering engine normally connects to a mirror port of a switch/gateway and passively monitors packets that pass through the switch (hence the term *pass-by*). Pass-by filtering is more flexible and therefore chosen for the Thai URL filtering system.

42. Robert Faris and Nart Villeneuve, "Measuring Global Internet Filtering," in *Access Denied: The Practice and Policy of Global Internet Filtering*, ed. Ronald Deibert, John Palfrey, Rafal Rohozinski, and Jonathan Zittrain (Cambridge, MA: MIT Press, 2008), 87.

43. Lawrence Lessig describes "traceability regulation" as a requirement by the state for service providers to employ software that facilitates traceability by making access conditional on the users' providing some minimal level of identification. Lessig, *Codes and Other Laws of Cyberspace*.

44. Warapong Theprongthong, "Content Regulation of Political Online Discussion Forums, after the Enforcement of the Computer-Related Offenses Act 2007," unpublished master's thesis, Chulalongkorn University, 2010, 54.

45. Ethan Zuckerman, "Intermediary Censorship," in *Access Controlled: The Shaping of Power, Rights, and Rule in Cyberspace*, ed. Ronald Deibert, John Palfrey, Rafal Rohozinski, and Jonathan Zittrain (Cambridge, MA: MIT Press, 2010), 71–85.

46. Thai Netizen Network (TNN) is an interest group of Internet users who gathered to advocate on five basic principles—right to access information, freedom of expression, right to privacy, self-regulation, and creative commons—for online media. The group was founded in 2008 and comprises mainly people of the Net generation from various occupational backgrounds. See Thai Netizen Network, http://thainetizen.org.

47. Campaign for Popular Media Reform (CPMR), formerly the Committee to Monitor the Implementation of Article 40, was founded in 1997 by networks of academics, nongovernment organizations, mass-media practitioners, and civic media groups. These founders have played an active role in campaigning and participating in the course of Thai media reform since 1992.

CPMR's objective is to democratize communication in Thailand by promoting the transparency of media structure and the creation of a public sphere for communication. See Campaign for Popular Media Reform, "About Us," http://www.media4democracy.com/eng/about_us.html.

48. Freedom against Censorship Thailand (FACT) describes itself on its Web site as "a network of people who disagree with state censorship. We are a member organization in the Global Internet Liberty Campaign (GILC) and the Global Internet Freedom Consortium and cooperate with 200+ organisations around the world." See Freedom against Censorship Thailand, "About," http://facthai.wordpress.com/about.

6 Competing Values Regarding Internet Use in "Free" Philippine Social Institutions

Erwin A. Alampay, Joselito C. Olpoc, and Regina M. Hechanova

The Internet is used within institutions to expand access to knowledge, to improve communications, to manage information, or to increase productivity. But users also download movies, write blog posts, and chat with friends. In other words, people do not always use the Internet for the original purpose for which an institution provided it. Though it is value neutral, there are often competing values in the intentions of those who use Internet technology in an organization: between openness and control, privacy and security, participation and efficiency. These competing values are not necessarily emphasized equally, and may differ from unit to unit, even within the same type of institution. Emphasizing one value can hamper the pursuit of another, depending on the context and structures influencing an organization's choice.[1] Quinn and Rohrbaugh in their model on competing values, for instance, hypothesize that common tensions arise out of internal versus external issues, and between concern for control and a desire for flexibility.[2]

Since information systems can be designed for a range of purposes, it is relatively easy to observe how competing values lead to tensions in access and use. In the case of the Internet, how it is used and adopted within institutions also undergoes similar contestations, even in countries such as the Philippines, where access to it is relatively unfettered.[3]

This chapter explores three institutions in the Philippines: the government, educational institutions, and private corporations. Through a series of case studies, we analyze how these institutions struggle with implementing policies on Internet use, while highlighting competing values among stakeholders on how to take advantage of the benefits that the Internet provides. These cases highlight some of the issues, concerns, and competing views with respect to using Internet facilities in the workplace that emerged from two separate surveys conducted by OpenNet Asia in 2008–2009. The first survey collected the views of information and technology managers and human resources managers on why they provided Internet in the workplace and how they monitored and disciplined employees. The second survey investigated the same issues from the perspective of the employees. Comparing the views of both sides, patterns of dispute regarding the online space the organization provided were evident: one side tried to control use (e.g., monitoring; disciplining for misuse, etc.), while the other side explored the boundaries of the space (e.g., performing tasks not originally intended, deliberately circumventing policies that restrict use).

The first set of cases deals with how the current government uses new media. Governments see in new media the opportunity to encourage citizen participation and a venue for more transparent government. The second set of cases involves educational institutions. It analyzes universities internally providing Internet access to increase access to online knowledge, while at the same time trying to regulate what students access. The last set of cases analyzes corporations and how they tackle Internet abuse by employees, and their ways to control external stakeholders whose use of the Internet also has an impact on how these organizations are perceived.

These cases are analyzed using Quinn and Rohrbaugh's model, which describes four important values that differ in their preference for control (controlling versus flexibility) and locus (internal versus external), namely: internal process value, open system value, rational goal value, and human relations values. Internal process value emphasizes control and internal focus while stressing information management, communication, and stability. Rational goal, in contrast, focuses on the external and on control, using terms like *plans* and *productivity*. Human relations values the flexibility provided, while focusing on the internal and stressing better cohesion, morale, and human resources. Finally, open systems also look at the external and how to provide the organization with flexibility, while stressing growth, resource acquisition, and external support.[4]

Three Philippine institutions illustrate how competing values apply in contested Internet use: government, schools, and corporations. In these cases, clear positions, protocols, or policies have yet to take hold. In each venue, different sides debate the balance of how the Internet can or should be used by or within these institutions. These incidents, in turn, help define their respective institutions' future policies. Although not as dramatic as the contestations that occur at the international level, they nonetheless touch on similar themes: security, control, privacy, access to information, transparency, and freedom of speech.

Government Bureaucracy: Using the Internet for Participation, Transparency, and Efficiency

The new administration of President Benigno Aquino III won the May 2010 elections, which were partly fought through new media. Political candidates made use of social media including Facebook, YouTube, Twitter, and text messages on mobile phones. Since new media helped the administration get elected, the government eventually wanted to harness it for governance.

However, there are mixed sentiments regarding its utility in government service. A newly elected congressman, Federico Quimbo, through House Resolution 184, claims that "unabated and unregulated use of the Internet by government officials and employees during office hours adversely affects their productivity and the quality of service they provide." He estimates that all 900,000 state workers use government computers for at least two hours every day for unauthorized online social networking activities, and that the government stands to lose an estimated PHP 103,158,000 (approximately USD 2.3 million) every month from electricity expenses alone. He also claims that the Home Development Mutual Fund, where he previously served as president and chief executive officer, gained a significant increase in profit from PHP 2.7 billion (just over USD 61 million) in 2001 to PHP 9.8 billion (USD 221 million) in 2009 when it regulated the use of the Internet.[5] While this purported gain is difficult to prove as due solely to well-regulated Internet use, such sentiments on better organizational regulation are not unique to government institutions. In an OpenNet Asia survey of Philippines organizations in 2008, 77 percent of respondents said they had some restrictions in Internet access, of which more than half (51 percent) reported blocking social networking sites.

The Aquino administration, however, has a different perspective. It believes that Congress does not have to pass a law regulating the use of social networking sites like Facebook and Twitter in government offices. The heads of government departments and agencies are left to "state their policies on social media if the productivity of the employees is affected by their use of social networking sites."[6] In fact OpenNet Asia's organizational survey found that almost two-thirds of government agencies already had a form of Internet use policy in place. This includes policies on permissible sites to visit, use of Yahoo! Messenger, and access to social networking sites. About half of all government agencies restrict use of Yahoo! Messenger, while a third do not allow Skype, and 8 percent prohibited use of e-mail. Overall, use of social networking applications in the office or workplace was the third most common application blocked after pornography and gaming.[7]

Upon assuming office the new administration created a group specifically tasked with managing new media.[8] Their motivation in doing this was to be more transparent, obtain feedback, and get the sentiments of the public. However, because using new media for governance is relatively uncharted in the Philippines, the hard lessons of how to actually make them work as an instrument for state and civil society exchanges and discussion are just becoming evident.

The following is among the first cases of how the new administration used online social networks in a very prominent national issue. The case involves the events and investigation surrounding an ill-fated rescue of 25 tourists held hostage in a bus in Manila that led to the death of eight Hong Kong nationals.

Failed Rescue of Hong Kong Nationals

On August 23, 2010, a tourist bus with 25 people mainly from Hong Kong was hijacked by a disgruntled police officer recently dismissed from the service. The hostage drama unfolded before the eyes of the public and was made more spectacular by a zealous press. When negotiations fell apart, the hostage taker started firing shots, which forced the police to launch an assault. The hostage taker was killed in the final police assault, along with eight Hong Kong tourists.[9]

As the event was unfolding, it was broadcast live over national television and online. Hong Kong's chief executive, Donald Tsang, tried to contact President Aquino. However, even though the president had an official telephone, mobile phone, and e-mail and had a new media staff that presumably made him accessible on Twitter and Facebook, Tsang was unable to connect with him as the crisis was escalating. In the hours after the surviving hostages had been rescued, the president visited the site of the carnage, and his pictures and message were again beamed through various media, including the Internet.

This very open coverage is typical in the Philippines, where press freedom is highly valued and the media are considered an active influence in keeping government in check. This particular coverage, however, was also seen as contributing to the breakdown of negotiations, and also led to negative sentiments, not only from local citizens but also from Hong Kong residents, which was all documented in many social media, including the president's official Facebook page.[10]

To their credit, President Aquino's social media team initially did not filter the angry postings by Chinese residents to his Facebook account during the highly emotional and tragic events. Some of the messages posted said:

"Shame on you and your government. Tender your resignation now."

"*Maaari po sana na paki training ang mga kapulisan at ang SWAT team o kaya naman sibakin na po lahat. . . . nakakakahiya sa international community ang daming namatay* [Please either train the SWAT teams or fire them all. It is embarrassing to the international community that many people died.]."

"Your incompetence of leading your untrained stupid police force caused such a tragedy."

"We Hong Kong people are very angry for your comments. Please apologize to those who were affected."

"He's [President Aquino's] slowly killing our country coz [sic] of his stupidity."

"You see, our president is a retard who has done nothing but smirk in front of the TV cameras after all that has happened."

The administration's openness, in this case, allowed people to vent anger, as it was meant to do. At one point, Aquino's new media team had to change his profile picture from a smiling one (which some found offensive or insensitive given the situation) to a more solemn pose. Eventually, as some postings became more offensive and were deemed "below-the-belt" attacks on the president, some of the comments posted on his Facebook page were filtered.[11]

Subsequently, the government created an independent commission headed by the secretary of justice, called the Incident Investigation and Review Committee (IIRC), to look into the apparent systemic failure in the hostage incident. The president promised that all those found accountable by the commission would be charged and punished.

After two weeks of hearings, the IIRC submitted an 82-page report that found ten officials liable for administrative and criminal sanctions. Three close supporters of the president were among those included in the recommendations. According to Malou Mangahas of the Philippine Center for Investigative Journalism, the president wanted palace lawyers to first review the report and, if possible, strike out the names of three of his close allies. He was quoted as saying, "*Napatapang 'ata masyado ah. Bakit kasama pa sila* Puno, Lim, *at* Verzosa?" [It's too strongly worded. Why are we implicating Puno, Lim, and Verzosa?][12]

The administration then announced that a copy would be first supplied to the Chinese government as a form of courtesy, but promised to publish the complete report in time on the Office of the President's Web site (http://www.op.gov.ph), and quickly uploaded pages 1 to 60 of the report. However, it did not include the subsequent 22 pages that had the committee's conclusions on accountability or its recommendations and highlights of the report.

As these two cases illustrate, the government's intent to use the Internet for opening discussions and more transparency has not been completely fulfilled. For the former goal, there are fears that unfettered regulation could potentially lead to greater discord and disharmony rather than better understanding. For the latter, sociopolitical considerations still factor into what gets said.

Educational Institutions

Internet access is becoming a fundamental need in schools and universities, since it provides students with access to more knowledge and information.[13] As a result, access to the Internet in schools is becoming a norm, despite negative and unwanted experiences that result from its use.[14]

Access and Availability

Among educational institutions in the Philippines surveyed, 73 percent provided Internet access to everyone (faculty, students, and employees), while the rest had provisional access depending on the person's role in the institution.[15]

The degree to which the Internet is provided in Philippine schools varies, especially when considering the costs attached to it. For some, especially in private schools, the cost is already embedded in other fees. For others, the cost of using computers and the Internet is part of individual courses, with limited time use, any excess of which entails additional payments.

Access can also vary depending on the kind of user and the manner in which she or he obtains access. Some universities provide stand-alone computers with Internet access that do not require individual passwords to log on. In these cases, individual use of computer terminals cannot be effectively monitored. In other schools, students have to register their computer unit or log on using university-issued accounts, requirements that make it easier for dedicated information technology departments to monitor online use.

Restriction, Privileges, and Appropriate Use

Varying restrictions are implemented in educational institutions. For instance, generally, all of the universities in the OpenNet Asia organizational survey agree that access to pornography should be blocked.

However, for liberal arts programs, especially those with fine arts and literature courses, pornography can be a contentious issue. In some specific cases, technical tests conducted for OpenNet Asia in 2008 in the Philippines reveal that some sites that clearly have LGBT content were blocked. These include http://www.gayhealth.com, which promotes the belief that "lesbian, gay, bisexual and transgender men and women need and deserve their own source for health information," and http://www.samesexmarriage.ca, a Canadian site that advocates for equal rights for same-sex couples. Regardless of the reasons for the blocking of these sites, the danger in censoring sites is that decisions are dependent on the discretion of gatekeepers and, at times, are left to purely automated systems that cannot discriminate between sites.[16]

Some universities provide some leeway with these restrictions by giving users temporary access to blocked content provided that they give justification for why they want to access a Web site. In the OpenNet Asia survey study one university noted that it grants requests for temporary access provided that it is for research and instruction purposes. However, student respondents in a focus group found this process cumbersome, especially when action on the request takes time (if it comes at all) and when access can be alternatively obtained from public Internet cafés or from private Internet accounts. The same university has relaxed restrictions for its faculty, giving them access to alternative proxy servers. However, faculty members have to register in order to gain such access. Hence, people surrender certain liberties, which in this case may be privacy, in order to be included and gain privileges.[17] In fact, a computer science professor interviewed says that once a person logs on to the university network, that person's account can already be monitored, whether he or she uses the university-issued e-mail or commercial e-mail.

Another issue among universities regarding Internet usage pertains to accessing "high-bandwidth" consumer sites. OpenNet Asia testing conducted in a state university found YouTube and subsequently news content such as http://youtube.com/AlJazeeraEnglish and http://youtube.com/zamboangajournal blocked. The reason for this block, at the time of testing, was bandwidth concerns. In larger campuses with bigger student populations, the quality of Internet access varies. Some students complain that the quality of Internet access also varies within the same building. These quality issues were a network infrastructure problem, whereby quality diminishes with distance from the source. In other instances, there are individual units and colleges that provide wireless access independently, and in these cases they provide layers of restrictions in addition to those that the university already provides.

A recent study on the Filipino youth's digital media use found research and schoolwork to be the most common use for the Internet.[18] However, the same study found accessing entertainment and YouTube ranked second. As a result, one university proposed regulating high-bandwidth sites. Its recommendation was based on its internal Internet traffic report in 2008 that showed that six of the top 20 sites being accessed by its users pertained to online videos and downloading/file-sharing sites (table 6.1).[19] The proposed restriction, however, was not accepted by the student body. The students argued that since they are already paying fees for the service and since the cost of bandwidth was actually going down, funds should not be a problem if additional bandwidth is necessary.

These examples illustrate how Internet use in schools is developing rapidly, and how much is to be learned on how to make it effective and safe for students to use. Even though there is no prescriptive remedy to ensure Internet responsibility, schools find they cannot rely on a single solution.[20]

Corporations

Corporations recognize the impact on and contribution to their business of information technology like the Internet and "smart phones." A study on Philippine organizations revealed that 65 percent of employers provide Internet access to all their employees. Employers cited the importance of technology in enabling communication, enhancing productivity among employees, and obtaining information.[21]

There are also data to suggest that employee use can include unproductive, negligent, illegal, and counterproductive activities. In an OpenNet Asia survey that was distributed to 1,033 employees in 86 companies all over the Philippines, respondents were asked if they "know of any employee being disciplined due to violation of Internet use policy at work."[22] They were then asked to explain some details about the

Table 6.1

TOP SITES BROWSED IN A PHILIPPINE UNIVERSITY WHERE INTERNET ACCESS IS UNREGULATED			
Web Site	Bytes	Percent	Description/Remarks
1 http://veoh.com	28,660,474,919	13.29	Online videos
2 University home page (total)	17,656,553,028	8.19	Probably default home page of browsers
3 Google (total)	17,415,538,849	8.08	Various Google pages (aggregated)
4 http://onemanga.com	16,933,337,623	7.85	Japanese anime Web site
5 http://yimg.com	15,645,486,702	7.26	Yahoo! images server (provides the images in the main Yahoo! pages)
6 Facebook (total)	10,940,882,497	5.07	Social networking Web site
7 http://googlevideo.com	9,873,551,602	4.58	Online videos
8 http://vo.llnwd.net	7,558,115,507	3.51	Peer-to-peer networking
9 http://rapidshare.com	6,316,262,412	2.93	File-sharing/downloading site
10 http://megavideo.com	6,046,856,378	2.80	Online videos (like YouTube)
11 Yahoo! (total)	5,088,233,299	2.36	Various Yahoo! pages (aggregated)
12 http://multiply.com	4,340,471,199	2.01	Personal blogging/social networking Web site
13 http://liveupdate. symantecliveupdate.com	4,209,346,563	1.95	Symantec update services
14 http://animemagicbox.com	4,083,513,115	1.89	Japanese anime Web site
15 http://myspace.com	3,561,970,100	1.65	Personal blogging/social networking Web site
16 http://megaupload.com	3,389,124,492	1.57	File-sharing/downloading site
17 http://node1.otakuworks.net	3,321,871,362	1.54	Japanese anime Web site
18 http://tudou.com	3,297,361,598	1.53	Online videos (like YouTube, Chinese version)
19 http://friendster.com	3,251,756,770	1.51	The original social networking Web site
20 *.l.google.com	2,692,012,762	1.25	Top Google cache server (but counted in item 3)
Totals	174,282,720,777	80.84	

violation and any sanction imposed. Eleven percent, or 114, of the respondents reported knowing of a coworker who committed some technology abuse at work. Out of the 114 respondents, 73 gave details about the type of Internet-use-related abuse. The top two technology abuses or violations were "pornography related" and "downloading of video files, audio files, or unauthorized applications."[23]

Thus, like other employers across the globe, Filipino employers are at risk. They struggle to balance the productive uses of information and communication technologies for saving time and enhancing productivity, while also trying to curtail the abuses that can threaten their internal security and lead to legal liabilities.[24] At the same time, the experiences of employers highlight tensions in corporate values—equal treatment/benefits versus cost, privacy versus security, and freedom of expression versus risk of defamation.

Equal Treatment versus Cost

The use of policies to regulate information and communications technology (ICT) use is still not widespread among Philippine organizations. Less than half (48 percent) have an ICT-use policy in place. These policies typically cover the use of the Internet, e-mail, and instant-messaging applications. A minority have policies on mobile phone use (16 percent) and use of camera phones (11 percent).[25]

Beyond the existence of policy, a dilemma appears to be emerging in its implementation. On one hand, there is a need for any policy to apply to all members of an organization. On the other hand, actually implementing the policy uniformly may place an organization at a bigger risk. This dilemma appears to be especially salient in the case of pornography.

In the case of Company A (a bank) two incidents of accessing pornography were mentioned. The first was a case of an employee directly caught by the president of the company. The president happened to pass by his cubicle and saw the employee viewing a pornographic movie. The employee was terminated on the same day.

The second incident occurred during the height of a sex video release involving some popular show-business personalities. The IT security director of the bank was directed by the president to investigate the downloading of these videos in their system. Since they kept audit logs of Web sites that their employees visit and any Internet activities that they engage in, employees caught during the audit would be sanctioned according to the company's policies. With his investigation, the IT security director informed the president that should the prescribed sanctions be imposed on those who were caught, more than half of the company's management committee would not be present in the next board meeting. In the end, the president decided to release a memo informing everyone that a number of employees had been caught during the audit and a stern warning was issued (instead of termination).

Access to Information versus Security

The Internet has become a valuable resource for Philippine organizations and workers in obtaining information. A previous study revealed that one of the most popular reasons for using the Internet is research.[26] Yet the value of providing employees access to information is also tempered with concerns about security. Companies are facing bigger and bigger risks from viruses and malicious programs that are intentionally or unintentionally downloaded while employees are online. Companies also lose some level of productivity because the large size of some files can clog up the bandwidth, degrade the network, and consume valuable corporate storage space.

In qualitative responses from the employee survey, employees mentioned that those who were caught were downloading movie files (e.g., TV series or pornographic movies), music files, or pirated/unlicensed software. These files were then stored or installed on their work computer or, in the case of one incident, stored on the shared drive of the whole company. Employees who were caught downloading files were warned, suspended, or put on probation depending on the number of times they were caught downloading files that were considered unauthorized by the company.

To deal with the tension of access versus security, one approach of employers is to place restrictions on Internet use. For example, the OpenNet Asia survey reveals that 58 percent of employers block specific sites (although for 37 percent, blocked sites can be accessed if permission is requested). For a quarter of employers, accessible sites are dependent on the nature of their job (23 percent) or are limited to specific computers (21 percent).[27]

Freedom of Expression versus Risk of Defamation

Information and communication technology is used to facilitate communication, whether within the organization or between the organization and its publics. One emerging tension emerging from this communication is that freedom of expression can create a space for defamation, especially in the case of blogs.

Data show that a fifth of organizations surveyed by Lingao and Tordecilla already have ICT policies pertaining to personal blog postings.[28] These policies are also more common among financial and manufacturing firms. However, this is an emerging policy area among all types of organizations, as illustrated by the two following cases.

The first case is the first libel suit against a Philippine blog. It was filed in August 2005 against the institutional blog of the Philippine Center for Investigative Journalism (PCIJ) by Jonathan Tiongco. He filed six libel suits against the PCIJ, including one case for sedition. All of them were related to the posting of the "Hello Garci" audio recordings in PCIJ's institutional blog. These recordings were supposed conversations between then-president Gloria Macapagal-Arroyo and a commissioner for elections regarding vote manipulations in the presidential election. The Supreme Court threw out the petition to remove the recordings in October that year and said the constitutional right to free expression was paramount, even if it was just in a blog.[29]

The second case involved Pacific Plans, Inc. (PPI), an educational savings firm that offers educational plans to families. In 2005 the company was in near collapse and applied for rehabilitation with the Makati Regional Trial Court in 2005. The court issued a stay order on April 12, 2005, that allowed PPI to stop payment of tuition fee benefits to the traditional, open-ended plan holders and unilaterally substitute what its educational plan holders considered a patently disadvantageous scheme without any consultation with them. As an immediate reaction to this unexpected and unconscionable move of PPI, parents (plan holders) who converged at Kamagong Street in Makati on April 14, 2005, began to mobilize to be heard, and the Parents Enabling Parents (PEP) Coalition was born.

As a result, the Yuchengco group of companies and Pacific Plan holders are locked in a legal battle in connection with the savings firm's admission of financial difficulty, making it hard pressed to honor its commitment to fund the education of its 34,000 plan holders.

The Yuchengcos filed the libel case on October 18, 2005, before the city prosecutor of Makati City in connection with the alleged "highly defamatory" article posted by PEP members on its PEP Coalition blog alleging mismanagement and mishandling of their fund.[30] The case was later dismissed by a Makati court and by the court of appeals.

Blogging-related controversies are of course not just a concern among private corporations, but also a problem in public institutions as well as schools. In a public high school in the Philippines, for instance, a principal handed a ten-day suspension to four students as a penalty for posting a blog critical of her and other school officials. The principal argued that the blog postings were damaging to her role as principal and to the school and that they caused alarm to the school's alumni. She then imposed a penalty that she said was based on the school's rules and regulations.[31]

Student editors' guilds protested, calling the suspension a form of campus repression that undermined students' rights to freedom of speech and expression. The Commission on Human Rights chairman was also of the opinion that the students' rights may have been violated. The Department of Education eventually stepped in to rescind the order and transferred the principal.[32]

In these three cases, it is apparent that legal measures and harassment are being implemented to curtail freedom of expression. Even though the first two cases were dismissed from court, from an organizational perspective, legal costs of employee postings are very real concerns. Posting on an internal corporate blog, for instance, can be sensitive and potentially damaging because it has an institutional name attached to it. Likewise, external blogs of consumer groups can also become a public relations problem. All types of organizations are therefore becoming more wary of what occurs in the blogosphere.

Conclusion

The issues highlighted in the cases in this chapter illustrate the struggle to balance different objectives with competing values with regard to the Internet in the Philippines (figure 6.1).

The Internet can be used internally to strengthen internal systems and communications, just as it can be used externally to support communications with clients and obtain knowledge from outside the organization. Likewise, it can be used to control not only information, but also members of an organization, since it allows institutions to monitor their members. Similarly, with the increasing mobility of new devices and ever-expanding content online, the Internet also offers flexibility to members of organizations, assuming that institutions providing access to these services allow them to be used in this manner.

The problem, as the cases illustrate, occurs when institutions or their stakeholders want to use the Internet for purposes that conflict, contradict, or compete with another purpose. For instance, government prioritizes both national security and transparency and encourages external support through people's participation. However, these are inherently competing values, with the former being internally focused and requiring greater control, while the latter is focused externally and encourages more flexibility in its use. Similar contradictions were seen in how schools provide access to the vast knowledge in the Internet, and yet want to control how their students use that knowledge because of harmful content.

Resolving Competing Values

In democratic governments that espouse participation and transparency, regulating people's comments and controlling information that is made public by a government's own services remains a delicate balance. In educational institutions, rules of access and use of the Internet are also just being developed. Likewise, corporations try to balance using these technologies to ensure efficiency and better communications with issues such as privacy and worker/citizen rights.

The space is being contested in various ways. In cases where there are system-level information systems, there is discretion on how Internet-use policies are automated. In some cases, content is actually filtered, not as a policy, but rather as a result of using preinstalled corporate software. While this eliminates discretionary action among managers, discretion actually still exists in how the systems programs are implemented. These decisions are made by programmers, IT managers, and systems administrators.[33]

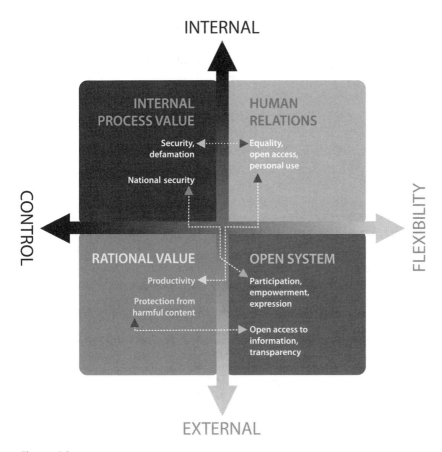

Figure 6.1

Competing values framework as applied to institutional Internet use.

Source: Figure adapted from Robert Quinn and John Rohrbaugh, "'A Spatial Model' of Effectiveness Criteria: Towards a Competing Values Approach to Organizational Analysis," *Management Science* 29 (1983): 363–377.

Even as formal rules and regulations are beginning to appear at the organizational level, legal avenues are also being used as a threat to control individual actions. Individual organizations are also becoming party to monitoring what happens online, especially for posts that may have an impact on their reputation, but also for internal posts that could have legal implications.

For individuals, the lesson here is that even as democratic societies offer space online, this access does not mean that an individual's online presence and actions are not monitored or unhindered. People who know that there is limited privacy in using the Internet within institutions are more careful of how they tread, what they view, and what they post. For the unwitting, what one does online may actually end up being a violation of their organization's rules and therefore subject to discipline, punishment, and dismissal. In some instances, behavior may be monitored by stakeholders outside the organization and can also be subject to prosecution.

As institutional policies begin to develop, organizations must consider the primary objective of providing access to the Internet. Do they want to promote participation and transparency in government? To encourage liberal ideas and access to knowledge in educational institutions? To ease communications, service improvement, and productivity in corporations? While organizations do have the right to develop their respective policies, they also have to make sure that the controls and regulations they impose do not end up curtailing their primary reason for providing Internet access in the first place.

To a certain extent, the tensions illustrated in the institutional-level cases mirror similar struggles to control the Internet at the national and global levels. For instance, institutions can be sensitive to, if not wary of, contrarian views to the point that they filter or censor online messages, file charges, or implement authorized-use policies to discourage such views. Likewise, network security is another concern mentioned among governments, schools, and corporations that want to monitor and limit access and use of Internet facilities. However, some of these practices are not based on well-thought-out or formally stated policies and are unknown to the employees themselves, so that these practices not only are selective in their implementation but also impinge on the privacy of employees. While policies in institutions cannot be prescriptive, the process of developing policies needs to involve management, administrators, users, and clients, just as with states and their citizens. Even then, however, contestations cannot be avoided, given the different priorities and competing values each side holds.

Notes

1. Victoria Buenger, Richard Daft, Edward Conlon, and Jeffrey Austin, "Competing Values in Organizations: Contextual Influences and Structural Consequences," *Organization Science* 7, no. 5 (September-October 1996): 557–576.

2. Robert Quinn and John Rohrbaugh, "'A Spatial Model' of Effectiveness Criteria: Towards a Competing Values Approach to Organizational Analysis," *Management Science* 29 (1983): 363–377.

3. Technical tests that the OpenNet Initiative conducted on Internet service providers in the Philippines from 2009 and 2010 found no evidence of Internet filtering.

4. Quinn and Rohrbaugh, "'A Spatial Model' of Effectiveness Criteria"; Buenger et al., "Competing Values in Organizations."

5. Amita Legaspi, "Lawmaker Seeks to Regulate Facebooking in Government Offices," GMANews .TV,http://www.gmanews.tv/story/198315/lawmaker-seeks-to-regulate-facebooking-in-govt-offices.

6. Jam Sisante, "Palace: No Need for Congress to Pass Law on Facebook Use," GMA News.TV, http://www.gmanews.tv/story/198401/palace-no-need-for-congress-to-pass-law-on-facebook-use.

7. Erwin Alampay and Ma. Regina Hechanova, "Monitoring Employee Use of the Internet in Philippine Organizations," *Electronic Journal of Information Systems in Developing Countries* 40 (2010): 10, http://www.ejisdc.org/ojs2/index.php/ejisdc/article/view/648.

8. At present, the Official Facebook page of the president is managed by a newly created new media team under the Presidential Communications Operations Office.

9. "Hong Kong Hostages Killed in Manila Bus Siege," BBC News, August 23, 2010, http://www .bbc.co.uk/news/world-asia-pacific-11055015.

10. One irony in the new administration's use of new media in this recent crisis was that even with cell phones, telephones, Facebook, and Twitter, at the height of the crisis Hong Kong's highest official could not get in touch with the president. In this case, the problem was not the technology, but rather unfamiliarity with protocols among the new administration and its counterpart in Hong Kong.

11. "Aquino Censors Facebook Page over Hostage Crisis Bashing," Inquirer, August 26, 2010, http://newsinfo.inquirer.net/breakingnews/infotech/view/20100826-288827/Aquino-censors -Facebook-page-over-hostage-crisis-bashing.

12. Malou Mangahas, "From Day 1, P-Noy Wanted to Save Lim, Puno, Verzosa," Philippine Center for Investigative Journalism, October 12, 2010, http://pcij.org/stories/from-day-1-p-noy -wanted-to-save-lim-puno-versoza/.

13. Marcell Machill, "Internet Responsibility at Schools: A Guideline for Teachers, Parents, and School Supervisory Bodies in Kids On-line," In *Promoting Responsible Use and a Safe Environment on the Net in Asia,* ed. Kavitha Shetty (Singapore: Asia Media Information and Communication Centre and SCI-NTU, 2002).

14. Shetty, *Promoting Responsible Use and a Safe Environment on the Net in Asia.*

15. Alampay and Hechanova, "Monitoring the Use of the Internet in Philippine Organizations."

16. In one of the universities in Malaysia for which the testing was performed, Ku Klux Klan Web sites were blocked, but similar Malay sites were not. This finding indicates that preselected

blocking was already part of the installed settings of commercial automated software some institutions use.

17. David Lyon, *The Electronic Eye: The Rise of Surveillance Society* (Minneapolis: University of Minnesota Press, 1994).

18. Liane Pena Alampay and Ma. Emy Concepcion Liwag, "Growing Up Digital (in the Philippines)," Paper presented in the Living the Information Society 2.0 Conference, October 1–2, 2009, Ateneo de Manila, Quezon City, Philippines.

19. A Universal-McCann survey found Filipinos to be the top Internet video viewers in the world. "Filipinos are World's Top Internet Video Viewers," GMA News, August 27, 2010, http://www8 .gmanews.tv/story/199588/filipinos-are-worlds-top-internet-video-viewers.

20. Machill, "Internet Responsibility at Schools."

21. Alampay and Hechanova, "Monitoring the Use of the Internet in Philippine Organizations."

22. Joselito Olpoc, Ma. Regina Hechanova, and Erwin Alampay, "Internet in the Workplace: Employees Perspective," paper presented to the seminar on Technology in the Workplace. Trendwatcher Series, November 6, 2009, at Rockwell, Makati City.

23. Ibid.

24. Nancy Flynn, *The e-Policy Handbook: Rules and Best Practices to Safely Manage Your Company's Email, Blogs, Social Networking and Other Electronic Communication Tools*, 2nd ed. (New York: AMACOM, 2009).

25. Alampay and Hechanova, "Monitoring the Use of the Internet in Philippine Organizations."

26. Ibid.

27. Ibid.

28. Ibid., 8.

29. Ed Lingao and Jaemark Tordecilla, "Blogs Targets of Libel Suits, Regulation," April 9, 2010, GMA News, http://www.gmanews.tv/story/188041/blogs-targets-of-libel-suits-regulation.

30. "CA Junks Yuchengco Libel vs. Parents Group," GMA News, April 10, 2009, http://www .gmanews.tv/story/173792/ca-junks-yuchengco-libel-vs-parents-group.

31. "Ex Adviser: Penalized Student Bloggers Not Notorious Kids," GMA News, January 16, 2009, http://www.gmanews.tv/story/144601/ex-adviser-penalized-student-bloggers-not-notorious -kids.

32. Aie See, "QCHS Principal to Be Transferred Amid Blog Controversy," February 3, 2009, GMA News, http://www.gmanews.tv/story/147191/qcshs-principal-to-be-transferred-amid-blog -controversy.

33. Mark Bovens and Stavros Zouridis, "From Street-Level to System-Level Bureaucracies: How Information and Communication Technology Is Transforming Administrative Discretion and Constitutional Control," *Public Administration Review* 62, no. 2 (March/April 2002): 174–184.

7   Interconnected Contests

Distributed Denial of Service Attacks and Other Digital Control Measures in Asia

Hal Roberts, Ethan Zuckerman, and John Palfrey

In early 2008 the Vietnamese government announced plans to mine bauxite, the mineral used to make aluminum, in the Central Highlands of Vietnam in cooperation with a Chinese company. These plans became the subject of increasing protest beginning in 2008 and continuing thereafter. Protesters have expressed environmental concerns about damage to mined areas and toxic by-products of bauxite mining. While some activists involved with the bauxite protests have been connected to banned prodemocracy movements, others have been protesting the Chinese-backed mine on grounds of environmental concern or national pride.[1]

In 2009 a group of activists distributed a petition and created a Web site named http://bauxitevietnam.info to protest the bauxite mining. According to reports from Vietnamese free-speech advocates, both the bauxitevietnam.info site and the larger bauxite protest movement have been under constant attack since 2009. The government has repeatedly detained and interrogated both the founders of bauxitevietnam.info and many of those who signed the petition. Forged e-mails, purportedly by the founders of the Web site, have been distributed online, falsely claiming that the leaders were quitting the protest. Activists report that the Vietnamese government broke into the site's servers to steal protester information and shut down the site.[2]

In January 2010 a flood of traffic from compromised computers overwhelmed bauxitevietnam.info, making it inaccessible not only in Vietnam but also throughout the entire Internet.[3] Political actors increasingly use this type of attack, known as a distributed denial of service (DDoS) attack, to control content on the Internet. Vietnam has routinely filtered Internet sites the government considers to be controversial, preventing users in Vietnam from accessing them without taking unusual steps. In contrast, a DDoS attack makes a Web site inaccessible to all online audiences by disabling a targeted Web server under a flood of traffic.

This particular DDoS attack used a botnet, an army of "zombie" computers that have been taken over, in the vast majority of cases, without their owners' knowledge. These zombie computers are generally used to commit some sort of fraud on the network. For example, some computers controlled by botnets are used to sign up for thousands of free e-mail addresses and send spam. In this case, the zombie computers sent an extraordinary number of requests to http://bauxitevietnam.info, crashing the site.

Shortly after the DDoS attacks on the site began, Google announced that it would no longer censor its search results in China[4] because of attacks on its Gmail service, which it found had originated from within China. While investigating the source of those Gmail attacks, Google found evidence that the botnet attacking bauxitevietnam .info—though not involved in the Gmail attacks—consisted largely of computers that had been infected by a malicious program hidden by an attacker within a program called VPSKeys.[5]

Technicians at Google and at the antivirus firm McAfee then unraveled the story of the bauxitevietnam.info DDoS attacks. VPSKeys is the most popular Vietnamese keyboard input program. Distributed by the Vietnamese Professionals Society (VPS), it allows Vietnamese users to enter Vietnamese characters easily using Western keyboards. Some months before the attacks on bauxitevietnam.info, likely in late 2009, the Web site hosting the VPSKeys software had been compromised. The attacker replaced the VPSKeys program with a Trojan version designed to infect the host computer with botnet software. The attackers also alerted thousands of VPSKeys users by e-mail that a new (secretly infected) version of the software was available. Many Vietnamese users updated their software in response. It is likely that the attackers were able to obtain the mailing list used to send this e-mail through a separate attack—possibly intrusions that seized membership databases of popular Vietnamese discussion forum sites in 2009.

Tens of thousands of users downloaded the Trojan software, which infected the host computers and added them to a botnet before the Trojan software was discovered. The makers of VPSKeys replaced the infected software with a clean version, but not before the Trojan software had created the network of compromised computers. This botnet was used to mount the DDoS attack on bauxitevietnam.info and may have been used against additional targets.

Why did the attackers go through the effort of compromising computers and creating their own botnet? There is a thriving underworld business devoted to the sale of lists of infected computers, which in essence allows attackers to rent these computers for the purpose of a one-time attack like the one on bauxitevietnam.info.[6] A plausible explanation is that a botnet of computers based in Vietnam would be difficult for a site administrator to defeat through geographic filtering. If bauxitevietnam.info were attacked by thousands of computers located in South Korea, an administrator might respond by blocking all requests to the Web site from that country. But blocking requests from Vietnam would defeat the purpose of raising awareness within Vietnam itself. It is also possible that the botnet was an added benefit in a scheme that primarily sought to monitor the activity of Vietnamese-speaking users around the world. The botnet was certainly capable of spying on the owners of the infected computers, possibly logging keystrokes and capturing passwords to online accounts, even possibly collecting the list of e-mail addresses used to encourage more people to download the Trojan software.

The administrators of bauxitevietnam.info defended the site from the DDoS attack by mirroring the site on multiple hosting providers. They created mirrors at http://bauxitevietnam.info, http://boxitvn.org, http://boxitvn.net, http://boxitvn.info, http://boxitvn.blogspot.com, and http://boxitvn.wordpress.com. The last two of these mirroring environments are especially important, because they are hosted by large blog-hosting services, Blogger (run by Google) and WordPress. These large-scale services offer highly DDoS-resistant services at no direct financial cost to the activists.

It is very rare that an observer can come to identify the owner of any botnet, as Nart Villeneuve and Masashi Crete-Nishihata also find in their fine-grained review of DDoS and defacement attacks in Burma in chapter 8 of this volume. It is the nature of a botnet to be distributed across a broad range of computers infected without the knowledge of their owners. Accordingly, no one (including Google and McAfee, two of a handful of actors most capable of diagnosing this sort of attack) has managed to determine who controlled the botnet during the course of the Bauxitevietnam attacks—or, for that matter, who controls it at the time of this writing. But there are indications that some DDoS attacks against Vietnamese sites have involved more than tacit approval of the Vietnamese government. Viet Tan, a Vietnamese prodemocracy dissident group, reports that their site is routinely subject to DDoS attacks and that many of the attacking computers are based in Vietnam.[7] Since http://viettan.org is generally blocked in Vietnam, these attacks require that authorities lift the blocks on attacked sites to permit attacks from zombie computers in Vietnam. It is difficult to verify this claim without access to Viet Tan's server logs documenting such an attack.

This example—by no means extraordinary, particularly in Asia—shows how DDoS attacks accompany a range of interventions that involve malware and related intrusions into the computers of ordinary Internet users. It demonstrates that governments and other political actors are using a broad array of intertwined methods to contest online (and offline) content that they find offensive. For example, the methods of attack in this case include the following:

- DDoS attacks
- Technical Internet filtering
- Surveillance
- Intrusion by means of malware
- Trojan software
- Online identity forgery
- Offline harassment

The difficulty of diagnosing (and defending against) these attacks is further complicated by the large set of actors, many of whose precise roles are unclear. For example, the attacks on http://bauxitevietnam.info may have involved the following:

• *Attackers*   A set of attackers, which may or may not have included the Vietnamese and Chinese governments, whose precise identity is unknown and who are responsible for a number of DDoS attacks, intrusions, and forgeries; the hundreds or thousands of compromised computers used to attack http://bauxitevietnam.info, most likely without knowledge of their owners.
• *Defenders*   The administrators of bauxitevietnam.info, and administrators of the hosting services and Internet service providers (ISPs) they use.
• *Affected third parties*   The Vietnamese Professionals Society (which inadvertently distributed malware), McAfee (which detected the attack), and Google (responsible for both investigating the DDoS attack and defending against the attacks via Blogger).

The use of malware particularly complicates this type of analysis. Researchers usually consider malware the province of commercial actors who compromise computers to participate in schemes designed for financial gain. This type of example demonstrates how malware is now playing a major role in how political actors seek to constrain Internet users both within and beyond their borders.[8] These interconnected controls make diagnosing DDoS attacks an enormous challenge in many cases simply because it is difficult to understand the full array of methods used with the attacks as well as who is executing those methods. In this case, it is likely that some of the computers that attacked bauxitevietnam.info were owned by individuals who supported the goals of the organization. This possibility, in turn, made the attack even harder to block because distinguishing between legitimate and attack traffic was impossible to do on an IP basis.

Finally, this example demonstrates what relatively sophisticated activists can do to defend themselves from DDoS attacks. A common strategy is to diversify hosting and, especially, to flee to large blog hosts, often based in the United States, for cover. While simple to understand and implement, the strategy is extremely effective, allowing the activists behind bauxitevietnam.info to maintain an online presence in the face of a sustained attack without paying for a fee-based DDoS-protection service, the most effective of which start at thousands of dollars per month.

DDoS and Other Next-Generation Control Measures

This chapter is a deep dive into the growing phenomenon of DDoS attacks. We seek to describe the state of DDoS attacks in the context of the interconnected contests to control online content. Our central goal is to situate the phenomenon of DDoS attacks within the theoretical framework developed in OpenNet Initiative (ONI) research. In particular, this in-depth review of the DDoS phenomenon builds on the observation that the types of control mechanisms that states and others may employ have evolved from the first-generation Internet control process of technical filtering to the second- and third-generation controls that we have observed emerging since the middle part of the 2000s.[9] As Ronald Deibert and Rafal Rohozinski say of these next-generation controls in the opening chapter of *Access Controlled*:

Although there are several tactics that can be employed within this rubric—deliberate tampering with domain name servers, virus and Trojan horse insertion, and even brute physical attacks —the most common is the use of DDoS attacks. These attacks flood a server with illegitimate requests for information from multiple sources —usually from so-called "zombie" computers that are infected and employed as part of a "botnet." The ONI has monitored an increasing number of just-in-time blocking incidences using DDoS attacks, going back to our first acquaintance during the Kyrgyzstan parliamentary elections of 2005.[10]

A group of ONI researchers have also tracked other early instances of DDoS attacks in the Belarus elections of 2005, the Russia-Estonia dispute in 2007, and the Russia-Georgia conflict of 2008.[11] In this chapter, we build upon these previous findings of our ONI partners in this broad-based review of DDoS attacks that were independent of particular sensitive political moments, as well as the detailed research on the 2008 Web defacement attacks in Burma in chapter 8.

Our research method in studying DDoS was multifaceted. We conducted an in-depth analysis of media reports on human-rights and independent media-connected DDoS attacks, surveyed independent media and human rights sites, conducted confidential interviews, and hosted a working meeting with participants from multiple related sectors in Cambridge, Massachusetts, in 2010. We shared our results with knowledgeable peers before disseminating them and discussed possible responses to the rising DDoS threat. Although our research was meant to cover DDoS broadly around the world, Asia proved to be one of two regions we focused on, along with the Commonwealth of Independent States (CIS). Our respondents in Asia came in particular from Burma, China, and Vietnam, and we focus on cases from those countries here.

We sent a survey on DDoS attacks to a sample of 317 independent media and human rights sites. We generated the sample by asking at least three local experts in each of the nine target countries for the most prominent independent media in their countries. We translated the survey into the primary Internet language of each surveyed country and also translated the recruitment e-mail to the primary language of each site. We received full responses from 45 sites, for a response rate of 14 percent.

These survey methods limited our findings in several ways. The sample involved was not large. Despite this limitation, we perceive that the 45 responses amount to a decent response rate for such a survey, given a series of special factors involved. These factors included the difficulty of reaching a key actor at each site, the inherent sensitivity of the survey subject, and the early stage of research in this field. We used neutral language that did not explicitly refer to DDoS attacks when querying the experts for the list of sites, but some of the experts were familiar with our work and therefore likely to bias their lists of independent media toward sites known to suffer DDoS attacks. It is likely that the 14 percent of responding sites overrepresents sites that have suffered a DDoS attack, since a survey on DDoS attacks may seem more interesting—and worth responding to—to DDoS attack victims. These two factors make the results of the survey less useful for answering questions about overall prevalence of DDoS attacks. We cannot, for these reasons, answer questions about what percent of all independent media sites in our surveyed countries have suffered DDoS attacks. But we believe that the responses are useful for investigating the nature of attacks reported by the surveyed sites and the defenses used by those sites.

We conducted interviews in person, over Skype, and by e-mail with administrators of 12 sites that experienced DDoS attacks. We contacted every survey respondent who reported having been subject to a DDoS attack and requested a more in-depth interview. Six of the interview participants were recruited through this method. We found the rest of the interview participants through media analysis or through referrals from researchers and other contacts in the field. We interviewed administrators of sites based in Australia, Burma, China, Iran, Russia, and Vietnam. The interviews involved a series of questions and answers tailored to each interviewee exploring the technical details of attacks and the experiences of the administrators dealing with them. In a few cases, we obtained and analyzed logs of attacks. We cannot publish the interviews themselves for security reasons, but we include a number of findings, in aggregate form, from the interviews.

Additionally, we studied as many published reports of DDoS attacks as we could find by tracking accounts posted to the Web over the course of six months. Our sample set includes 329 reports of attacks against more than 800 sites going back to 1998. We also had the unexpected opportunity to study a DDoS attack that happened to occur during the course of our research. Our research home, the Berkman Center for Internet and Society at Harvard University, hosts the site of a sister research project, the Citizen Media Law Project, which happened to be attacked by a sustained denial of service attack. We were able to study that attack in progress, as it happened, for which we are grateful to the unknown attackers.

Interconnected Methods of Contesting Information Online

A core finding from our survey and related methods is that DDoS attacks exist within a portfolio of different attacks suffered by these sites. We also found that the same site usually suffers from multiple types of attacks. During the past year, of the surveyed sites,

- 72 percent experienced national network filtering of their sites.
- 62 percent experienced DDoS attacks.
- 39 percent experienced an intrusion.
- 32 percent experienced a defacement.
- Of those experiencing a DDoS attack, 81 percent also experienced at least one of the following other content controls: Internet filtering, intrusion, or defacement.

These numbers provide strong evidence that DDoS attacks are not an isolated problem for independent media sites. Instead, DDoS attacks exist within a larger range of different kinds of attacks against the sites. In addition to the specific range of attacks reported, the surveyed sites reported a high level of unexplained downtime during the past year:

- 61 percent experienced unexplained downtime.
- Of those respondents who experienced unexplained downtime, 48 percent experienced seven or more days of unexplained downtime.

Unexplained downtime can be the result of factors other than attacks. Independent media sites often suffer from a lack of experienced system administrators, leading both to downtime and to the inability to diagnose the reasons for downtime. Still, the very high amount of unexplained downtime experienced by these sites suggests more, and possibly more complex, attacks than described by the answers to the preceding DDoS question.

Our finding that a significant number of sites have experienced 21 days or more of downtime suggests that there is a serious shortage of technical capacity available to respond to threats to independent media and human rights Web sites. Arbor Networks, a leading DDoS mitigation firm, surveys large ISPs annually about their experience with DDoS. Their survey of tier-one and -two ISPs suggests that most administrators of large ISPs respond to a typical DDoS attack within an hour.[12] The administrators we interviewed were unable to bring their sites back online in such a timely fashion.

Our in-depth interviews provided further support for the findings, in both our survey and media research, that DDoS attacks are often accompanied by intrusions, defacements, filtering, and offline attacks. One administrator of more than a dozen independent media sites reported DDoS attacks followed by offline extortion intended to force him to retract a story. (He refused.) That same administrator reported being subject not only to DDoS attacks but also to daily virus-laden e-mails targeting him personally and about topics of confidential interest to him; to weekly intrusion attacks based on guessed passwords; and weekly defacement and complete deletion of at least one of the sites under his control.

Another administrator had been subject to weeks-long, multigigabit DDoS attacks but reported that a greater problem was the harassment of participants in the publication's discussion forums: attackers broke into the discussion forum to steal and publish the identities of its users and also posted inflammatory content to the forum to trigger governmental prosecution. Yet another administrator reported that intruders had repeatedly accessed internal databases to learn about stories before they were published. And another reported that attackers broke into his site to insert malicious code with the intent of triggering antivirus warnings for the site and thereby scaring users from accessing it. He also reported intrusions to his site that inserted code that slowed the Internet connections of his users by causing them to download large packages of Trojan horse software. In all cases, the DDoS attacks may have been the most visible manifestation that a site was under attack. But the attacks that accompanied the DDoS attacks were often of far more concern and import to the affected administrators.

DDoS attacks vary greatly in their nature and magnitude. In our interviews, we heard about a range of attacks, extending from multi-Gbps floods of traffic that overwhelmed the network connectivity of the affected sites to attacks that used as few as a few dozen requests per minute to cripple sites by exploiting holes in Web servers and other applications. Five of the interview participants reported attacks in the range of 500 Mbps to 4 Gbps. One participant, who was the administrator of a large service provider working for an independent media site, reported an attack of greater than 10 Gbps. Some of these attacks may have been bigger, since at greater than 1 Gbps, many local ISPs become saturated and drop any additional traffic. One interview subject, whose site experienced several DDoS attacks in the previous four years, reported an escalation of the size of attacks over time. His site had been successfully disrupted in 2007 with a 1 Gbps DDoS attack, and he moved to more robust, DDoS-resistant hosting provider. His contract with the provider specified that he would be protected from attacks up to 2 Gbps. When an attack in 2010 involved 4 Gbps of traffic, his host took his site offline, offering him the option of either increasing his monthly payments or remaining offline until the attack ended.

Three interview participants reported application attacks at low—even very low—bandwidths that caused significant downtime. One was taken down by fewer than 40,000 requests per day, another by less than ten machines hitting his search page. Two participants reported long-term success using mitigation strategies—caching and Web application optimization—which would be effective against only relatively low bandwidth attacks. We believe these attacks exploited known holes in application software, such as the Slowloris attack against Apache Web servers.[13]

It is likely that most or all network attacks that we encountered in our research involved the use of botnets to generate incoming traffic. Other indicators suggest that some of the attacks involved the use of rented botnets. Two interview subjects reported that attacks began and ended at the top of an hour, suggesting that a botnet had been rented for a specific duration. The DDoS attack against the Berkman Center's Citizen Media Law Project offered further evidence of rented botnet attacks. The DDoS attack was an application attack using HTTP GET requests originating from a shifting set of exactly 500 IP addresses. The attack was highly effective, rendering the site inaccessible for 12 hours, despite steady work from the Berkman Center's highly experienced technical staff to keep the site online. That the attack came from a round number of attacking IPs and that the IP addresses in use shifted in real time in response to defenses suggests that the application attack came through a rented botnet.

We also saw a strong correlation between DDoS, filtering, defacement, and intrusion attacks in our media analysis. These techniques were often used in conjunction, and may have synergistic effects—making a site more DDoS resistant can make it more difficult to access using a Web proxy, for instance, which makes state-based filtering more effective. Independent media organizations participating in the working meeting repeated the same theme: sites suffer from multiple types of attacks, including DDoS, which in turn have complicated impacts on one another.

A key example of these impacts was the problems that a prominent Burmese independent Web site experienced from a combination of DDoS attacks and national filtering. The Web site has moved to a DDoS-resistant hosting provider to protect itself against high-bandwidth-traffic attacks. The site in question is routinely filtered by the Burmese government, so people within the country must use proxies to access the site. Burmese users gravitate toward a small set of proxies discovered through word of mouth. All the traffic from each of those proxies appears to come from the same IP address. One method the DDoS-resistant hosting provider uses to protect against attacks is to block IP addresses that are submitting too many requests. Since the proxies submit many more requests than other IP addresses, the hosting provider often bans them, to the end effect of blocking Burmese audiences from accessing the site. It is possible to address this problem by providing the hosting provider with a white-list of proxy servers, but that list is difficult to maintain because users in Burma keep seeking new proxies to stay one step ahead of government efforts to block them.

Non-DDoS attacks on a site are often more serious and less tractable than DDoS attacks. A common method for intrusions is to compromise the computer of someone who has administrator-level access to the target server. Access to the server is then used to delete sites; to discover the identities of dissidents, authors, and sources for further on- and offline harassment; to deface the target site; or to implant malware on the target site either to discredit the target site or to execute a DDoS attack on another site or both. Administrators of human-rights-related independent media consistently report being frequently subject to specifically targeted e-mail viruses, often connected to content tailored to be of interest to the administrator in question. These specifically targeted attacks are very difficult to defend against, requiring a high level of training and support for the victims. But many or most of the independent media organizations struggle to maintain even very simple client-side technology infrastructures.

For example, one participant—an administrator of a well-funded and prominent Asia-based nonprofit organization—reported that his organization shared two desktop computers among its staff of several dozen people. Many of these staff members had never touched a computer before working for the publication. Defending client computers that are so widely shared and used by such novice users, and that are specifically and aggressively targeted, is an enormously difficult problem to solve for even one organization, let alone for the field as a whole. We know of at least one organization focused on political rights in Asia that has a policy of reformatting the hard drive of laptop computers that have been removed from the office and used on other networks. Most organizations do not have nearly this level of concern or technical competence, even though most targeted organizations likely need to operate at this level of caution.

Two of the independent media site administrators we interviewed reported multiple types of attacks coming from multiple sources, as well as confusion about the source of the attacks. One participant was subject to a DDoS attack when he published a story about a prominent government actor, and then was approached separately both by the government actor with demands to take down the offending story and by the group of cybercriminals who were carrying out the attacks with demands for money. Another participant claimed that his site is sometimes attacked by the government when it is unhappy with a particular story and sometimes attacked by activists in opposition to the government when they are unhappy with a story (and sometimes the activists have taken credit for attacks that the participant thought were certainly coming from the government). Others we surveyed suggest that, in many cases, the effectiveness of DDoS attacks was a matter of gaining press coverage rather than success in taking and keeping a site down. In other words, even when DDoS is the only attack a site faces, the actors and their motivations may be complex and multilayered.

Site Administrators Worry about DDoS, among Other Attacks

Despite their prevalence, DDoS, intrusion, and defacement attacks are not the primary concern for most independent media sites. Asked to rank the impact of various issues, participants placed DDoS, intrusion, and defacement attacks squarely in the middle of the pack among other Internet content-control issues. The issues were ranked in the following order, with the most important issue listed first and with the average rank out of five noted (a higher number implies a lower priority):

- Blocking access to the publication's site by the government (2.47)
- Persecution of authors, publishers, or sources by the government (2.53)
- Intrusions, defacements, and denial of service attacks (2.89)
- Financial support for the publication (3.00)
- Technical issues other than defending against attacks (3.89)

While DDoS attacks are an increasingly prevalent form of Internet control, our respondents listed conventional government filtering as the most serious problem they face. Only 11 percent of respondents chose DDoS, intrusion, and defacement attacks as the most pressing issue, and only 32 percent chose these attacks as one of the two most pressing issues. These are particularly interesting findings given the bias of the study toward respondents facing such attacks. By comparison, 68 percent of respondents chose persecution of authors, publishers, or sources by the government as one of the two most pressing issues. Issues directly related to censorship and control (filtering, persecution, and DDoS and other attacks) all ranked higher than the two issues not directly related to censorship and control (finance and nonattack technical issues).

Effective Responses to DDoS Attacks Are Elusive

A common response to a DDoS attack is to turn to the hosting ISP during the time of the attack. The survey respondents had mixed luck getting their ISPs to defend them against attacks. Of those who experienced a DDoS attack in the past year,

- 55 percent had their site shut down by their ISPs in response to the attack.
- 36 percent report that their ISP successfully defended them against a DDoS attack.

The number shut down by their ISPs is surprisingly high, considering that an ISP will usually shut down an attacked site only when subject to a traffic-based attack (since other type of attacks generally do not directly affect the ISP's network or other customers). The fact that 55 percent of respondents suffering a DDoS attack had been shut down by their ISPs at least once indicates that at least 55 percent, and almost certainly more, of the sites had been subject to a traffic-based attack. This fact, along with the fact that only 36 percent of the respondents subject to DDoS attack had an ISP that defended them against attack, indicates that for many independent media, the local ISP is a weak point rather than a strong ally. We do not know whether the reason for this poor defense of sites by their ISPs is that independent media sites are customers of sites outside the core of ISPs able to respond to an attack in under an hour or whether the reason is that the independent media sites are customers of the core ISPs but are not able to pay for the DDoS protection that those ISPs generally sell as an add-on service.

In our survey, we also asked site administrators about the defenses they had tried when hit by a DDoS attack and how effective those defenses had been. Their responses can be read as a map of how independent media escalate defenses against DDoS attacks:

- 83 percent had fixed problems with their existing Web application software, with 80 percent reporting that this measure was "somewhat effective" or "effective."

• 75 percent had installed security software or hardware on their existing servers, with 92 percent reporting that this measure was "somewhat effective" or "effective."

• 62 percent had upgraded their Web server hardware, with 88 percent reporting that this measure was "somewhat effective" or "effective."

• 43 percent had downgraded the functionality on their existing sites, with 33 percent reporting that this measure was "somewhat effective" or "effective."

• 40 percent had subscribed to a denial-of-service-protection or other security service, with 100 percent reporting that this measure was "somewhat effective" or "effective."

• 38 percent had hosted content temporarily on a large hosting provider (Blogger, LiveJournal, etc.), with 67 percent finding that this measure was "somewhat effective" or "effective."

• 36 percent had changed their hosting providers, with 80 percent reporting that this measure was "somewhat effective" or "effective."

• 29 percent had changed their Web application software, with 75 percent reporting that the change was "somewhat effective" or "effective."

The vast majority of sites that experience DDoS attacks try to update the configurations of their local computers by fixing the existing Web application software, installing local security hardware or software, and installing upgraded local Web server hardware, or some combination of these three approaches. These basic strategies can all be taken by individual sites without help from core network providers, though in some cases core technical expertise may be needed to properly apply these upgrades. Each of these approaches rates as at least somewhat effective against DDoS attacks, insofar as these basic changes prove somewhat effective against further attacks.

A much smaller number of sites escalate their responses either by implementing more aggressive (and costly) defenses at the edge—downgrading functionality or changing Web application software—or by moving closer to the core of the network: subscribing to expensive protection services, hosting content on large providers, or changing hosting providers. The success of these defenses is more mixed than the simple edge-based fixes, perhaps because these are the defenses that are valid responses to network attacks, which are much more difficult to fend off than application attacks.

Our results indicate that the number of attacks against each site increased for a slight majority of participating sites:

• 16 percent reported many more attacks in 2010.

• 36 percent reported somewhat more attacks in 2010.

• 48 percent reported no change or fewer attacks in 2010.

ISPs—who are best positioned to defend sites against many types of DDoS—are often unable or unwilling to defend their customers. This finding leads us to speculate that many of the sites we surveyed are (or were, as many have been dropped by those providers) tier-three providers, who may lack a fiscal incentive to protect their customers. Tier-three Web-hosting providers sell their services for a small margin over costs—the hours worth of system administration time necessary to fend off a DDoS attack is more costly than the annual profit for the average account. These providers evidently do not see a reputation risk in failing to fend off a DDoS, and they find it more profitable to end relationships with "troublesome" customers than to provide protection to them.

The apparent efficacy of upgrading servers and fixing Web server software strongly suggests that attacks are not all based on clogging network connectivity (where these defenses would be ineffective) and point to application-level vulnerabilities. These sorts of fixes are only really helpful for either very small traffic attacks or application attacks, both of which can be reasonably dealt with by individual publishers at the edge of the network.

Best Practices for Human Rights and Independent Media Sites Are Emerging for DDoS Response

According to experts with whom we consulted, the responses that a site might take to a DDoS attack include the following:

• Blackholing the IP address of the attacked site (i.e., taking the attacked site offline).
• Deploying additional network and server infrastructure for the attacked site.
• Downgrading the content and/or functionality of the attacked site to reduce resource consumption.
• Filtering out attack traffic.
• Using a service with a distributed architecture to scale and absorb attacks on demand.

These responses range from the simplest to implement (taking the site offline, which is essentially giving up in the face of an attack) to complicated and difficult to implement.

Blackholing the IP address of the attacked site fulfills the aims of the attacker by making the site unavailable. But this response also makes the attack traffic disappear entirely from the Internet. In so doing, it protects the network hosting the site. This is the approach taken by many ISPs that are faced with a large traffic-based attack that is either too big or too expensive for them to defend against.

An attacked site may deploy additional servers and bandwidth to protect itself. Our survey results show that this is indeed the most popular method of protection. But for all but the biggest sites, deploying additional infrastructure for a single site is cost effective for small, application-based attacks only, because the peak traffic of a large, traffic-based DDoS attack will be orders of magnitude larger than the peak legitimate traffic of a site.

An alternative to increasing the server resources is to reduce the resource consumption of each page, allowing the server to handle more traffic with the existing server and network. There are some methods for reducing resource consumption that are effective and have little cost, such as caching dynamic content to reduce database queries. As attack size increases, though, an attacked site has to make changes that have costly side effects, like disabling site functions that require expensive database queries, reducing or eliminating images and streaming media, or creating an entirely separate failover site with simpler and less-interactive content.

Another way to reduce resource consumption is to distinguish attacking traffic from legitimate user traffic and filter out the attacking IP address. This approach is frequently used, and several of our meeting and interview participants reported success with this method, but only when the number of attacking machines is small and relatively static. It is simple for a competent system administrator to find and block a hundred static IP addresses that are flooding a site with requests for a single page, but that job becomes much, much more difficult when there are tens of thousands of IP addresses that are rotating every couple of hours and actively trying to make their traffic look legitimate. In these cases, it is sometimes possible to filter attacking traffic based on a signature for the particular traffic, but this approach can be very difficult against a moderately skilled attacker even for a highly skilled defender. It is possible to defend against a range of common attacks by using ModSecurity, an open-source attack-filtering system. But this sort of filtering helps against generic attacks only, and it uses up machine resources for the process of filtering and can therefore make the site more vulnerable to traffic-based attacks.

Finally, a site can protect itself by paying for a hosting or DDoS protection service to serve the content of the Web site. There are many services capable of handling all but the biggest attacks, and a few capable of handling the biggest observed attacks, simply because they have sufficient bandwidth and server resources to accept and process the attack traffic. The advantage of using such a service is that these services have economies of scale both in learning how to defend against particular attacks and in the necessary bandwidth and servers. When using such a service, the attacked site needs to pay for the peak attack traffic only while the attack is happening, rather than paying for the entirety of the resources needed to handle peak attack traffic.

These services, however, can command a very high markup on those resources. Even without the high markup, simply paying for the bandwidth to handle the peak attack traffic can be prohibitively expensive, especially for an independent media site. An attacked site may be able to hire a provider capable of handling millions of requests per second but not be able to afford the resulting bandwidth charges. The economies of scale work best for these sites if a large proportion of the site is not likely to be attacked at the same time, which is important to keep in mind given the model we found in interviews of a single local expert managing many sites from a given area (meaning that all or many of those are likely to be attacked at critical times for the country). As we noted previously, sometimes an attack will outstrip an administrator's ability to pay the associated bandwidth charges, and the site will be forced to go dark until the attack ceases.

Given the trade-offs of the various defense mechanisms, it is critical for sites that know they are likely to be attacked to weigh the various options before they are affected by DDoS. For instance, site administrators will need to know whether to pay the startup costs to hire a protection service, how much to pay a service to withstand a traffic-based attack, and at what point to accept that the cost of defending against a given attack is too high.

Hiding Their Tracks? Ample Suspicion, but No Hard Evidence, That States Are Involved in DDoS

Most sites participating in the interviews expressed a strong belief that the national government of the country their site reported on was ultimately responsible for the attacks. None, however, had clear evidence of state responsibility. One participant had reported a large, ongoing attack to the state's security service but got no help since "it is very difficult to look into this because it is very difficult to catch yourself." He asserted that the security service shut down its own attack only when other publications better connected to the government complained. One Vietnamese site pointed to a press report of a Vietnamese military official claiming responsibility for the attacks.[14] As mentioned previously, a Viet Tan administrator noted that his site was normally filtered from within Vietnam but that the filtering was taken down at precisely the time that a botnet from within Vietnam attacked the site. Most interview participants asserted the opinion that the national government was responsible for the attacks but did not claim any direct evidence for the responsibility. This inability to attribute direct responsibility for DDoS attacks is typical for the attacks. The distributed nature of the attacks makes it difficult to assign responsibility—it is certainly possible that either a government or progovernment individuals could attack a site critical of a specific regime, and our inability to trace the attack would not be an unusual circumstance. Our findings in these respects are consistent with the findings of Villeneuve and Crete-Nishihata in chapter 8.

As a related matter, we also found no obvious connection between the particular ideology of an attacker and the choice of DDoS as an attack method. We saw attacks from ostensibly right- and left-wing groups, attacks that targeted governments, and attacks that suggest government involvement. Neither is there an apparent geographic pattern to the DDoS attacks we saw in our media analysis. We found attacks reported in widely disparate corners of the world. Asian states were a common site for DDoS attacks, but certainly not the only region where they appear. While there is speculation that some attacks are traceable to governments—for instance, the example of http://bauxitevietnam.info—it is unclear that this is an assumption with any merit. DDoS is a technique used by individuals, groups, and, perhaps, states. The accessibility of easy-to-use tools and the apparent success of single-user attacks on small Web sites, as well as the technique's visibility in the media, suggest that aggrieved individuals may look to DDoS as an easy way of making a political point or settling a score. We note, too, that the widely reported DDoS attacks in the context of the release of U.S. State Department cables by Wikileaks in the fall of 2010 involved attacks both on Wikileaks itself and on major banks and others in apparent retaliation. In an ironic and perhaps inevitable twist, 4chan—an online community that claimed responsibility for many retaliatory attacks—was taken down by a DDoS on December 28, 2010. As with other Internet control mechanisms, DDoS is an approach used by a variety of actors to accomplish a variety of ends.

Conclusion: Situating DDoS in the Context of "Next-Generation Controls" and Other Online Contests

In response to the growing usage of next-generation Internet controls, citizens may be banding together to fend off DDoS and related attacks, at least on a modest scale. In three of our interviews, we heard of local technical experts acting as hubs of technical expertise for their countries (in Vietnam, China, and Iran, specifically). The most productive and satisfied of these local experts was far along in the process of moving sites in his country to a common infrastructure well supported by a hosting provider that was well connected to the core of the Internet (in all senses of "core": community, expertise, and resources). He was able to exert a great deal of control over the structure of the moved sites, including imposing onerous security and posting restrictions on the sites' administrators. The most concerned and least content of these local experts was struggling daily with many poorly written sites on broken, incompatible code bases, often reinstalling a site from scratch following an intrusion and manually fighting off the simpler of the constant DDoS attacks. He told us that he had the desire, but not the resources, to fix the underlying problems with the supported sites, as well as gratitude for the help he has received from other individuals, but he was frustrated by his inability to fend off high-bandwidth traffic attacks.

The threat of DDoS attacks is inextricable from other security considerations, including human resources concerns, technical resources, and community connections. Ultimately, what human rights and independent media organizations face, in Asia and elsewhere around the world, is a combination of a shortage of skilled site-administration skills, the bandwidth needed to fend off large network attacks, and the community connections needed to ask core network operators for help to fend off attacks. The difficulty of responding effectively to DDoS attacks is a symptom of a larger problem: most small, independent organizations simply do not have the talent, bandwidth, or connections to administer independent Web sites in the face of potential attack. The online environment not only offers new ways to reach a broad audience, inside a state and beyond, but also poses new challenges in keeping that online accessible in the face of the many types of attacks described in this book.

There is a final twist to the story. Citizens who wish to publish independent media sites but who do not have significant technical savvy are most likely to be able to resist DDoS and related attacks by signing up with a large, free hosting service. These services, such as Google's Blogger or WordPress, are often run by large, for-profit companies that are not based locally where the activists are situated. This approach was the strategy used by http://bauxitevietnam.info in the attacks described at the beginning of this chapter, which Google ultimately diagnosed and then defended the site by providing resistant hosting. The interconnected nature of these attacks, along with the possible responses, puts citizens in Asia and elsewhere in common cause with multinational companies based elsewhere, pitted together against an elusive opponent that may or may not include their own state. Rebecca MacKinnon takes up this topic in greater detail in chapter 10 of this volume.

Though increasingly unavoidable, this allegiance between human rights organizations and large corporations can be a tenuous and complicated one. In the fall of 2010, when Wikileaks was subject to a DDoS attack after releasing U.S. State Department cables, they turned to Amazon.com to serve their Web site.[15] A few days later, Amazon.com decided to stop hosting Wikileaks, which continued to be subject to DDoS attacks, just as the perceived allies of Wikileaks launched DDoS attacks against large banks and others perceived to have turned against Wikileaks.[16] While these independent media sites may have interests aligned with large corporate players to some extent, their allegiance may break down in the context of pressure from states or other powerful interests. It is important to note, however, that any ISP providing services to Wikileaks would likely have come under political pressure from the U.S. government. It is possible that other providers would have acquiesced under similar pressure.

The days of simple filtering of offensive Web sites, in the manner pioneered by Saudi Arabia and a few other states roughly a decade ago, are long past. The interplay of this range of public and private actors and next-generation mechanisms in cyberspace is becoming increasingly complicated and unpredictable. Independent media and human rights operations, especially in Asia, have a much harder job than ever before to keep their Web sites accessible in times of conflict.

Notes

1. BauxiteVietnam Blog, http://boxitvn.wordpress.com/; Bauxite Vietnam Web site, http://bauxitevietnam.info; John Ruwitch, "Web Attacks Hit Vietnam Bauxite Activists: Google," Reuters, April 2, 2010, http://www.reuters.com/article/idUSTRE62U0TM20100402.

2. Ben Stocking, "2 Popular Web Sites Blocked in Vietnam," *Sydney Morning Herald*, February 27, 2011, http://news.smh.com.au/breaking-news-technology/2-popular-web-sites-blocked-in-vietnam-20100211-nupw.html.

3. Viet Tan, "Denial of Service: Cyberattacks by the Vietnamese Government," April 27, 2010, http://www.viettan.org/spip.php?article9749.

4. In January 2006, Google launched google.cn, a search engine hosted in China and censored to comply with Chinese law. In January 2010, Google shut down google.cn and redirected traffic to their unfiltered Google.com.hk site.

5. Neel Mehta, "The Chilling Effects of Malware," Google Online Security Blog, March 30, 2010, http://googleonlinesecurity.blogspot.com/2010/03/chilling-effects-of-malware.html.

6. See the Shadowserver Foundation's resources on botnets and related activity at http://www.shadowserver.org/wiki/pmwiki.php/Information/Botnets for some of the most detailed analysis about the formation, growth, and application of botnets. One of the best of the white papers posted on the Shadowserver site, which addresses this question of rented botnets, is Krogoth, *Botnet Control, Construction, and Concealment: Looking into Current Technology and Analyzing Future Trends*, March, 2008 (special version for Shadowserver Web site), http://www.shadowserver.org/wiki/uploads/Information/thesis_botnet_krogoth_2008_final.pdf (see especially section 2.5, "Motivation and Usage"). See also *PC Magazine* Encyclopedia's entry on botnets: "Also called a 'zombie army,' a botnet is a large number of compromised computers that are used to create and send spam or viruses or flood a network with messages as a denial of service attack. The computer is compromised via a Trojan that often works by opening an Internet Relay Chat (IRC) channel that waits for commands from the person in control of the botnet. There is a thriving botnet business selling lists of compromised computers to hackers and spammers." Available at http://www.pcmag.com/encyclopedia_term/0,2542,t=botnet&i=38866,00.asp.

7. Viet Tan, "Denial of Service."

8. There have been an increasing number of reports of malware-related attacks on human rights organizations that may or may not have involved states. See, for instance, the path-breaking reports by our colleagues at the Information Warfare Monitor, available at http://www.infowar-monitor.net/research/.

9. For a description of first-generation Internet controls, see Robert Faris and Nart Villeneuve, "Measuring Global Internet Filtering," in *Access Denied: The Practice and Policy of Global Internet Filtering*, ed. Ronald Deibert, John Palfrey, Rafal Rohozinski, and Jonathan Zittrain (Cambridge, MA: MIT Press, 2008). For discussion of second- and third-generation controls, see Ronald Deibert and Rafal Rohozinksi, "Beyond Denial: Introducing Next-Generation Internet Controls," in *Access Controlled: The Shaping of Power Rights and Rule in Cyberspace*, ed. Ronald Deibert, John Palfrey, Rafal Rohozinski, and Jonathan Zittrain (Cambridge, MA: MIT Press, 2010).

10. Deibert and Rohozinksi, "Beyond Denial," 8.

11. Ibid.; OpenNet Initiative, "The Internet and Elections: The 2006 Belarus Presidential Election (and Its Implications)," OpenNet Initiative Internet Watch Report 001, April 2006, http://opennet.net/sites/opennet.net/files/2006%20Internet%20Watch%20Report%20Belarus.pdf.

12. Danny McPherson, Roland Dobbins, Michael Hollyman, et al., "Worldwide Infrastructure Security Report: Volume V, 2009 Report," Arbor Networks, January 19, 2010, http://staging .arbornetworks.com/dmdocuments/ISR2009_EN.pdf.

13. Christian Folini, "Apache Attacked by a 'Slow Loris,'" LWN.net, June 24, 2009, http://lwn .net/Articles/338407/.

14. Radio Free Asia, "Hackers in Vietnam: Do Not Confess Also That," May 19, 2010, http://www. rfa.org/vietnamese/programs/ReadingBlogs/%20VN-police-general-confesses-state-s-hacking-cb -s-web-and-blog-NHien-05192010161301.html.

15. Andrew R. Hickey, "Wikileaks Turns to Amazon Cloud to Dodge DDoS Onslaught," CRN, November 30, 2010, http://www.crn.com/news/cloud/228400232/wikileaks-turns-to-amazon -cloud-to-dodge-ddos-onslaught.htm.

16. Chloe Albanesius, "DDoS Attacks Continue to Plague Human Rights Sites," *PC Magazine*, December 22, 2010, http://www.pcmag.com/article2/0,2817,2374654,00.asp.

8 Control and Resistance

Attacks on Burmese Opposition Media

Nart Villeneuve and Masashi Crete-Nishihata

Burma is consistently identified by human rights organizations as one of the world's most repressive regimes. Human rights violations occur with regularity, especially in connection with the country's long-standing armed conflict. The ruling military junta, the State Peace and Development Council (SPDC), is best known for its political prisoners and its systematic denial of universal human rights such as freedom of expression.[1] The government's efforts to silence dissent pervade cyberspace and its system of Internet control is one of the most restrictive in Asia.

Despite the heavy hand that the regime wields over cyberspace, information communication technologies (ICTs) have provided Burmese opposition groups with the means to broadcast their message to the world and challenge the government. The ongoing battle between these two sides makes Burma a stark example of contested Asian cyberspace. The role of ICTs in this struggle can be framed by contrasting theories that view them either as "liberation technologies" that can empower grassroots political movements[2] or as tools that authoritarian governments can use to suppress these very same mobilizations.[3]

This contestation is dramatically illustrated by the series of protests that erupted across the country in 2007—in a movement popularly known as the "Saffron Revolution." During these protests, Burmese activists managed to bring the uprising to the world's attention by making images and videos of the demonstrations and subsequent government crackdown available on the Internet. Realizing the potential political impact of these images, the government severed Internet connectivity in the country for nearly two weeks.[4] This drastic action demonstrated that the regime had learned a significant lesson: although Burma's technical filtering system was successful in censoring access to information coming into the country from opposition media Web sites, it was unable to prevent information from flowing out of the country to these sites for global consumption.

As the one-year anniversary of the protests neared, the Web sites of the three main Burmese independent media organizations were attacked and effectively silenced. The Democratic Voice of Burma[5] and The Irrawaddy[6] were rendered inaccessible following a distributed denial of service (DDoS) attack. While these attacks were under way, Mizzima News[7] was also compromised and its Web site was defaced.[8] Periodic attacks on Burmese opposition media sites continued through 2009 and 2010.[9] In late September 2010, around the third anniversary of the Saffron Revolution, Burmese opposition media were once again silenced by a series of DDoS attacks and Web site defacements.[10]

The timing of these attacks and the content of the messages in the Web site defacements indicate a political connection, and although the identity and capabilities of the attackers—as well as any relationships they may have with the government—remain unknown, it is widely believed that the government played a role in the attacks. This belief prevails because the Burmese government has consistently demonstrated an interest in controlling and censoring the communications environment in the country.

This chapter explores the complexities of information control and resistance in Burma based on an investigation conducted by the Information Warfare Monitor (IWM)[11] on the attacks launched against the Mizzima News Web site in 2008. Through technical evidence obtained from our investigation and field research conducted in Burma, we were able to uncover and analyze the characteristics and capabilities of the suspected attackers. We found that these attacks are consistent with government and military interest in information control and censorship of the Internet as well as a pattern of ongoing attacks against Burmese political opposition. However, they cannot be conclusively attributed to the military or government of Burma. Our investigation found that the attack on the Mizzima News Web site appeared to have been a result of a combination of two factors: political motivation and the availability of a target of opportunity. The attackers are certainly unfavorable toward the Burmese opposition media, but cannot be simplistically characterized as "progovernment" either. Their primary motivation appears to be nationalism and a belief that the opposition media demean the public image of their country. The timing of the attacks provided a strategic utility that would normally have been beyond the attackers' means. While Burma maintains a robust Internet censorship system that prevents its citizens from accessing alternative news media, these attacks effectively prevented global access to opposition media sites during a sensitive period.

We proceed by describing the spectrum of information controls in Burma that includes pervasive Internet filtering, repressive legal frameworks, and recurring cyber attacks. We then provide a detailed technical and contextual analysis of the Mizzima News defacement attacks and highlight the difficulty of determining the actors involved and motivations behind such attacks as well as questions surrounding state attribution. Finally, we situate the case study in the wider context of information controls in Burma and argue that gaining an understanding of threats to freedom of expression in cyberspace requires a holistic analysis that accounts for the unpredictable and contested nature of the domain.

Information Controls in Burma

The SPDC maintains tight authoritarian rule over all forms of media and communications in the country. All local television, radio stations, and daily newspapers are owned and controlled by the state.[12] Within the country there are 100 private publications, which are also heavily restrained and censored by state authorities.[13] The Printers and Publishers Registration Act, implemented in 1965, prohibits printed publications from being critical of the government and requires all printers and publishers to register with the government and submit materials for review.[14] The Video and Television Law applies similar regulations to television and film media.[15] Together, these restrictions have stifled what was once a vibrant free press.[16]

Amid this repression of traditional media the Internet has become an important source of information on Burma. Beginning in the early 1990s, Burmese expatriates and journalists living in exile set up news groups, mailing lists, and Web sites to disseminate information on the human rights and political situation in the country.[17] Today, the most popular independent Burmese Web sites operate outside of the country, with Mizzima News based in India, The Irrawaddy in Thailand, and the Democratic Voice of Burma in Norway. These Web sites receive reports from citizens within the country and provide an alternative to state-controlled media that often includes content critical of the regime. While these media organizations have become important outlets for international audiences to receive information on Burma, they are heavily censored within the country.

The regime aggressively denies, shapes, and controls online information in Burma. Internet penetration is very limited with an estimated online population of less than 1 percent.[18] OpenNet Initiative (ONI) testing has consistently found that the only two Internet service providers (ISPs), Yatanarpon Teleport (or Myanmar Teleport, formerly known as Bagan Cybertech) and Myanmar Posts and Telecom, extensively filter Internet content by targeting circumvention technologies, foreign e-mail providers, communications tools such as Skype and Gtalk, material related to human rights and the Burmese democratic movement, and independent news Web sites.[19] The Web sites of Mizzima News, the Democratic Voice of Burma, and The Irrawaddy have been filtered by the country's ISPs for years. Filtering is achieved through technology linked to U.S. companies Fortinet and Bluecoat despite an embargo that places limits on exports to Burma.[20] These technical restrictions are paired with hard legal enforcement, and bloggers and journalists in the country face a constant threat of prosecution for publishing dissenting material. The Reporters Without Borders's Press Freedom Index of 2010 ranked Burma 174 out of 178 countries, and in 2009 the Committee to Protect Journalists deemed Burma the worst country in the world to be a blogger.[21] These repressive controls create a climate of self-censorship in which citizens avoid publishing and seeking out banned content.

The Saffron Revolution was the scene of the most dramatic example of Internet controls and resistance in Burma. A small number of peaceful protests organized by Burmese social and political activists began on August 17, 2007, in reaction to a 500 percent increase in the retail price of fuel.[22] These initial demonstrations were quickly suppressed by the government, but peaceful protests spread throughout the country under the leadership of Buddhist monks. By mid-September the number of participants had swelled to 100,000, including 10,000 Buddhist monks.[23] The government reacted with a severe crackdown from September 26 to 29. During this time, a number of serious human rights violations occurred, including killings, mass beatings, and arrests.[24] Burmese independent media outlets, including Mizzima News, The Irrawaddy, and the Democratic Voice of Burma, along with numerous bloggers and citizen journalists, played a crucial role in disseminating reports of the crackdown to the international community. Despite the heavy restrictions enforced by the regime, activists and citizen journalists managed to upload images and videos of the protests and crackdown to the Internet. The dissemination of these images to the world did not go unnoticed by the SPDC, and on September 29, 2007, it employed a blunter tactic of information denial than its standard filtering practices.

Through its comprehensive control over Burma's international Internet gateways, the SPDC implemented a complete shutdown of Internet connectivity in the country that lasted for approximately two weeks.[25] Only two other states have taken such drastic measures. In February 2005, Nepal closed all international Internet connections following a declaration of martial law by the king.[26] On January 26, 2011, the Egyptian government ordered national ISPs to shut down in reaction to major protests in the country.[27] Severing national Internet connectivity in reaction to sensitive political events is an extreme example of *just-in-time-blocking*—a phenomenon in which access to information is denied exactly at times when the information may have the greatest potential impact, such as elections, protests, or anniversaries of social unrest.[28] The crude but effective means of information denial implemented by the SPDC shows the extent the junta is willing to go to restrict bidirectional flows of information in Burma. It also serves as an example of Internet control beyond filtering that is focused on denying information to international users rather than just blocking domestic access.

Silencing voices critical of the regime during key events is an ongoing occurrence in Burma, and there exists a long history of cyber attacks against Burmese activists and independent media organizations, which include a range of attack vectors from malware to DDoS attacks. In 2000, for instance, Burmese political activists received numerous e-mail messages containing viruses that many believe were part of an organized campaign perpetrated by state agents.[29] More recently, Burmese independent news organizations have confronted waves of attacks on their Web sites during the anniversaries of key political events in the country (table 8.1). As coverage of the one-year anniversary of the 2007 crackdown was emerging, the servers of The Irrawaddy

Table 8.1

TIMELINE OF MAJOR POLITICAL EVENTS AND RECENT CYBER ATTACKS AGAINST BURMESE OPPOSITION WEB SITES	
Date	Event
August 8, 1988	Massive protests led by student activists in Burma known as the 8888 uprising
August–October 2007	Series of antigovernment protests led by Buddhist monks in Burma dubbed the "Saffron Revolution"
September 27, 2007	Military junta shutdown of access to the Internet within Burma
October 13, 2007	Internet access in Burma reconnected
September 2007	The Irrawaddy Web site infected with Trojan
July 2008	DDoS attack on Mizzima News Web site
July 2008	DDoS attack on Democratic Voice of Burma Web site
September 17, 2008	DDoS attack on Democratic Voice of Burma Web site
September 17, 2008	DDoS attack on New Era Journal Web site
September 17, 2008	DDoS attack on The Irrawaddy Web site
October 2008	Defacement attack on Mizzima News Web site
August 8, 2009	DDoS attack on Mizzima News Web site
September 2010	DDoS attack on Mizzima News Web site
September 2010	DDoS attack on Democratic Voice of Burma Web site
September 2010	DDoS attack on The Irrawaddy Web site

Sources: "Burmese Exiles' Leading Media Websites under Attack 20 July 2008," Burma New International, July 30, 2008, http://www.bnionline.net/media-alert/4590-burmese-exiles-leading-media-websites-under-attack-30-july-2008.html; "Press Release: DVB Web Site Hit by DDoS Attack," Democratic Voice of Burma, July 25, 2008, http://www.dvb.no/uncategorized/press-release-dvb-web-site-hit-by-ddos-attack/1256; "Websites of Three Burmese News Agencies in Exile under Attack," All Burma IT Students' Union, September 17, 2008, http://www.abitsu.org/?p=2502; Aung Zaw, "The Burmese Regime's Cyber Offensive," The Irrawaddy, September 18, 2008, http://www.irrawaddy.org/opinion_story.php?art_id=14280; Muchancho Enfermo, "Burma: Sri Lanka–Based Myanmar Media Website Attacked Again," Ashin Mettacara, March 17, 2009, http://www.ashinmettacara.org/2009/03/burma-sri-lanka-based-myanmar-media.html; http://www.ashinmettacara.org/2009/01/burma-myanmar-sri-lanka-based-burmese.html; "Fresh Attack on Mizzima Website," Mizzima News, August 8, 2009, http://www.mizzima.com/news/inside-burma/2599-fresh-attack-on-mizzima-website.html; Alex Ellgee, "Another Opposition Website Shut Down by Hackers," The Irrawaddy, June 19, 2010, http://www.irrawaddy.org/article.php?art_id=18759; Committee to Protect Journalists, "Burma's Exile Media Hit by Cyber-attacks," http://cpj.org/2010/09/burmas-exile-media-hit-by-cyber-attacks.php.

and the Democratic Voice of Burma were hit with DDoS attacks that overloaded the Web sites and rendered them inaccessible.[30] Similar attacks have occurred on subsequent anniversaries of the Saffron Revolution and the 1988 student protest known as the "8888 Uprising." The timing and coordination of these attacks suggest that the motivation behind them may be to censor the Web sites from commemorating the protests and possibly mobilizing new political actions.

It is unclear who was behind the attacks, although it is widely believed that the military or government played a role, since the regime maintains a strong interest in information control and actively seeks to silence opposition voices.[31] Opposition groups have come under persistent cyber attacks over the years and many believe such attacks are part of a wider campaign of state-sanctioned harassment.[32] However, positively determining attribution, motivations, and the extent of the attackers' abilities is a difficult task.

Mizzima News Defacement Attack

One example of the persistent attacks on Burmese independent media is the compromise and defacement of the Mizzima News Web site (http://www.mizzima.com) on October 1, 2008.[33] The original content of the site was replaced with a message from the attackers (figure 8.1):

Dear MIZZIMA Reader. . . . Listen please, Why Hack This Website? . . . Because We are Independence Hackers from Burma. We Born for Hack Those Fucking Media Website, Which are Ever Talk about Only Worse News For Our Country. We Very Sorry for Web Admin, You Need To More

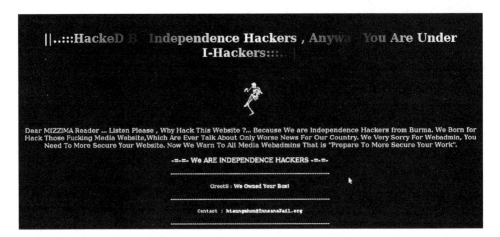

Figure 8.1
A screen capture of the defacement of Mizzima.com.

Secure Your Website. New We Warn to All Media Webadmins That is "Prepare to more Secure your Work."

This case demonstrates how attackers mask their identity, thus making it difficult to determine those responsible for the attacks. The attackers who defaced Mizzima News—which is blocked by ISPs in Burma—used censorship-circumvention software to perpetrate the attack hosted on servers that had IP addresses allocated to the United States, France, and Germany in order to make it appear as if the attacks originated in those countries.[34] Mizzima News reported on October 1, 2008, that the attacker's IP address originated in the United States. On October 10, 2008, Mizzima News reported: "While it is still difficult to technically trace who is behind the hacking attempts, Mizzima's technical staff said the main attempt is found to have originated from Russia with cooperation from other hackers in Germany, France and India."[35] The incident highlights the difficulty in tracing the geographic location of the attacks, let alone determining the identity and intent of the attackers. In the absence of sufficient evidence to attribute attacks, analysts often turn to the political context to fill in the gaps. In view of the persistent efforts by the government and military to crack down on political dissent, it is clear that they have an interest in silencing critics such as Mizzima News. However, a careful examination of the technical evidence, as well as an exploration of alternative explanations, is critical to understand the characteristics of the attackers.

Investigating the Attack

Following the October 1, 2008, defacement of the Mizzima News Web site, the IWM offered to assist Mizzima News with an investigation of the attack, and the organization provided us with access to their Web server logs and sample copies of c99shell (a backdoor program that provides attackers with remote access to a victim's machine) that were found on the compromised Mizzima News Web server.[36] We processed these log files and isolated the IP addresses that connected to and issued commands on the c99shell backdoor program. We removed the IP addresses of the legitimate administrators who had later connected to test c99shell. We were left with a set of IP addresses that we identified as belonging to a censorship-circumvention proxy service. While some variation existed in the IP addresses, there were consistent browser user-agents[37] that (1) connected from the circumvention proxy service IP addresses and (2) connected to and executed commands on the c99shell backdoor. We collected and analyzed all log entries in which the identified IP addresses connected to and issued commands on instances of the c99shell backdoor.

We identified five attackers. The two primary attackers appeared to be working in tandem with one another. Although we believe that the remaining three attackers are distinct individuals, there is the possibility that they are the two primary attackers using different browsers (and/or operating systems).

The log files indicate that in the days before and after the defacement, the attackers browsed the Mizzima News Web site from sites with Burma-related content such as http://komoethee.blogspot.com (September 10, 2008) and http://baganland.blogspot. com (September 30, 2008). They connected to Mizzima News from articles that referred to the ongoing DDoS attacks against The Irrawaddy and the Democratic Voice of Burma and were thus well aware of the scope of the attacks targeting opposition news media.[38] Just six hours before the defacement, the attackers visited Mizzima News from an article that detailed Burma's cyberwarfare capabilities and that claimed the attacks "may have been conducted by Myanmar military officers trained or undergoing training in Russia and China."[39] The attackers then accessed a variety of articles on the Mizzima News Web site. It is likely that at this stage they determined that the Mizzima News Web site was based on the Joomla! Customer Management System (CMS).[40]

Beginning on September 19, 2008, the attackers attempted to exploit a number of known vulnerabilities in the Joomla! CMS that the Mizzima News Web site was running on. After a series of unsuccessful attempts, Attacker 2 finally managed to exploit a password reset vulnerability in Joomla! and immediately logged in as the administrator. This "remote admin password change" exploit is very simple and can be conducted through any Web browser. The exploit was publicly available by August 12, 2008, about two months before it was used to compromise Mizzima News.[41]

After acquiring administrator privileges by exploiting the password reset vulnerability, Attacker 2 shared administrator access with Attacker 1. Both attackers attempted to download c99shell onto the compromised server, and within 20 minutes both attackers had set up the Trojan tool and began exploring the directories of the Mizzima News Web servers. Eventually, the attackers shared access with a third attacker and gained access to several My SQL databases. They deleted parts of the databases, and by 4:56 PM on September 30, 2008, they had defaced the Mizzima News Web site.

The attackers returned several times and installed more instances of c99shell as well as pBot, an Internet Relay Chat (IRC) bot with both Trojan and DDoS capabilities, while Mizzima's administrators attempted to delete the malicious files. The attackers also defaced the Mizzima News Web site repeatedly after Mizzima administrators tried to restore the original content. The attackers were finally locked out on October 4, 2008. They attempted—unsuccessfully—to return on October 5 and 6.

We approached the censorship-circumvention software provider that the attackers used with convincing evidence of the attacks and the use of their tool and asked if they could confirm that the attackers used the IPs we traced back to their services. The software provider confirmed that Attacker 1 and Attacker 2 logged in to the circumvention service from IP addresses assigned to Burma, which is interesting because the Mizzima News Web site is filtered by Burmese ISPs and inaccessible to Internet users in Burma. Therefore, the attackers had to bypass this ISP-level filtering in order to attack the Web site. They also probably believed that using the service would shield their identities.

To summarize, the evidence suggests there were two primary attackers working in collaboration with one another other to exploit and "Trojan" the Mizzima News Web server. These attackers appear to have shared links to the Trojans that they had installed with additional attackers. In total, there appear to have been five attackers working together to maintain control over the Mizzima News Web server. The attackers deleted portions of Mizzima's database and defaced the Web site repeatedly. Over the course of seven days, they continued to attack Mizzima's server while the Mizzima administrators worked to delete the different backdoors that the attackers frequently installed. By the fifth day they were shut out of the system, although they continued to check for access on the sixth and seventh days but were denied. We further confirmed that the attacks originated from Burma and used the proxy service to bypass national-level filtering of Mizzima News.

Investigating the Attackers

We investigated the identities of the attackers by analyzing the versions of the backdoor program c99shell and the IRC bot pBot they used, the specific attackers who downloaded these files, and the location they retrieved the programs from. What follows is an analysis of the data trail we followed by analyzing and linking the information contained in these files.

The c99shell backdoor program is a widely available Trojan backdoor written in the PHP programming language.[42] The versions of c99shell that the attackers tried to download to the Mizzima News Web server were slightly modified to include text in the interface reading, "Hacked by doscoder—oGc Security Team—#cyberw0rm @ oGc" (figure 8.2).

Based on this information, we could infer that the tool had been modified by "doscoder"—who is a member of the "oGc Security Team" and IRC channel "#cyberw0rm" on an IRC network called "oGc." However, these data points do not necessarily

Figure 8.2
Screen shot of the modified interface for the c99shell backdoor program.

attribute the attacks to these aliases, since it is possible the attackers could be using someone else's tools.

Where the attackers downloaded the Trojan programs they used in the attack revealed further evidence. The attackers downloaded c99shell and pBot from two separate locations. The version of c99shell at both locations was identical. The pBot was functionally identical, but the connection information in the pBot configuration file was different. Attacker 1 and Attacker 3 both made attempts to download the same instance of c99shell from a compromised server. However, only Attacker 2 was able to successfully download c99shell from the Web site 0verkill.co.cc and upload it to the Mizzima Web server.

Attacker 2 made attempts to download an instance of c99shell as well as another file, an instance of pBot, from 0verkill.co.cc. 0verkill.co.cc was registered to "Charlie Root" with the e-mail address ir00t3r@gmail.com. It was registered from an IP address in Burma.[43]

The pBot that Attacker 1 attempted to download from 0verkill.co.cc was configured to connect to an IRC server, overkill.myanmarchat.org (with the prefix "vesali") to IRC channel "#jail." The pBot that Attackers 2 and 3 attempted to download from a compromised server, videovideo.it, was configured to connect to an IRC server at 64.18.129.9 with the prefix "soul" (figure 8.3).

To collect further information we attempted to connect to 64.18.129.9, but were unable to obtain access. We were able to briefly connect to the overkill.myanmarchat. org IRC server until we were kicked out and banned. The "overkill" subdomain was subsequently removed and failed to resolve. When connecting to the overkill.myan-marchat.org IRC server, the network names "irc.doscoder.org" and "irc.vesali.net" were displayed. Only one user was seen on the server:

[xer0] (~xero@overkill.name): xero
[xer0] @#jail
[xer0] irc.doscoder.org:Over Kill Over The WorlD
[xer0] is a Network Administrator
[xer0] is available for help.

The IRC server information indicated that there was some still-unknown relationship between "doscoder" and "0verkill." It is important to recall that modifications were made to c99shell by doscoder—a member of the "oGc Security Team" and the "#cyber-w0rm" channel on the oGc IRC network. Now, "doscoder" emerged as the host name for the overkill.myanmarchat.org IRC server. A Web search turned up a relationship between the file name and location path of the c99shell at now defunct locations on doscoder.t35.com. In addition, much of the code in the defacement page posted on the Mizzima News Web servers was similar to the code in another unrelated defacement by doscoder. However, no further information was found concerning the doscoder alias.

```
<?

set_time_limit(0);
error_reporting(0);
echo "ok!";
ini_set("max_execution_time",0);
class pBot
{
var $config = array("server"=>"overkill.myanmarchat.org",
                    "port"=>"443",
                    "pass"=>" ",
                    "prefix"=>"[]vesali[]",
                    "maxrand"=>"5",
                    "chan"=>"#jail",
                    "chan2"=>" ",
                    "key"=>" ",
                    "modes"=>"+p",
                    "password"=>"overkill",
                    "trigger"=>".",
                    "hostauth"=>"overkill.name"
                    );
var $users = array();
function start()
```

Figure 8.3
The configuration of Attacker 2's pBot.

Although the overkill.myanmarchat.org IRC server disappeared soon after we connected to it, we discovered another IRC server hosted on "irc.myanmarchat.org." This server is one of the IRC servers for the Olive Green Complex (oGc), an IRC network founded in 2004 by Burmese students studying at the Moscow Aviation Institute (MAI) in Russia, which provides advanced training in computer engineering and informatics[44] and is currently subject to a U.S. embargo for its alleged role in supplying nuclear weapons technology to Iran.[45] According to Aung Lin Htut, a former deputy ambassador to Washington, the attacks against the Burmese opposition Web sites were conducted by "Russian technicians" based in "Burma's West Point cyber city"—a reference to Myanmar's Academy of Defense Services in Pyin Oo Lwin, Mandalay Division, Myanmar.[46] Aung Lin Htut further stated that Burmese military officers are trained at the MAI.[47]

The oGc is described by members as being an IRC group for those interested in information technology and computer engineering.

oGc is a non-profit organization and it intends for all people who interest in Information Technology. We all are students and all of members are interesting in learning IT. The main of oGc Network is to give outs free psyBNC account, email and others free services to people in learning more about unix and linux features. We [would] be glad if you would find any useful information on oGc and trust that we will not have disappointed you with the fruits of our efforts. Finally, the oGc was born and we [would] like to thank to all people who [participated] and helped us get oGc off the ground. We dedicated to use Myanmar IRC gateway. We started it at November 2004.[48]

The students also operate an IRC server at irc.olivegreen.org that has the same IP address as irc.myanmarchat.org. The oGc IRC network is accessible by several domain names. According to registration information, some of these domains were registered by students at the MAI. The server is frequented by students studying in Burma, Russia, China, and Singapore. There is also a server, irc.mmustudent.org, for students of the Myanmar Maritime University, which has a computer science department.[49] The earliest domain name registrations indicated that oGc originated in Russia. However, the most recent activity on the server was traced to Burma.

In our observations of the oGc IRC network we found the group's members and frequent chatters were friendly and generally interested in information technology. There was the occasional discussion about an exploit or Web defacement, but that was not the focal point of the conversation. The oGc IRC network appears to be a legitimate IRC network as opposed to a specifically "hacker"-related network.

As our investigation progressed we provided the circumvention software provider with the aliases of several suspects from the oGc IRC network and asked to confirm if they had them in their system. We found that three of these nicknames were among some 20 account names on the circumvention software service utilized from the same installation as one of the attackers. Based on these correlations, we had substantial evidence that members of the oGc may have been involved in the attack.

On the oGc IRC network we found an operator identified as the administrator of oGc who, through our analysis, was revealed to be using multiple aliases associated with the alias found in the configuration of the pBot Trojan used in the attacks against Mizzima, as well as related accounts on the circumvention software service. We initiated IRC chats[50] with the oGc administrator and other oGc members and asked why they thought Mizzima News was defaced. Their general response was that the opposition highlights only the negative aspects of Burma and generally produces "nonsense." The oGc administrator suggested that there were "rules of every country" and implied that Mizzima News had broken those rules, noting "u should know, what kind of articles are written there." In general, the oGc administrator and other members of the group did not appear to be "progovernment" and acknowledged that issues of government corruption were legitimate. However, they were very proud of their country and nationalistic, and they did not approve of the foreign media's portrayal of Burma. Although the oGc administrator denied being responsible for the deface-ment of Mizzima, he was often vague and implied that it may have been him. He was also aware of "doscoder" and "0verkill" but refused to discuss them.

Based on our correlative evidence, we directly accused the oGc administrator of defacing Mizzima in our IRC chat by linking his various aliases to the circumvention software used in the Mizzima attacks. The oGc administrator never directly accepted responsibility, but he used tongue-in-cheek responses that alluded to his involvement. For instance, although he said his involvement was "impossible," he added emoticon smiley faces to his replies. He also suggested that he was being framed and that a well-known hacker, Lynn Htun, was the person responsible for the attacks.

Lynn Htun, better known by his handle "Fluffi Bunni," defaced high-profile infor-mation-security-industry Web sites such as the SANS Institute with humorous, taunt-ing text and images between 2000 and 2003. Lynn Htun was arrested in London on April 29, 2003, while attending the InfoSecurity computer security conference, for his failure to appear in court on (unrelated) forgery charges. He formerly worked in the U.K. offices of Siemens Communications.[51]

In response to a post on Myanmar IT Pros (http://myanmaritpros.com)—a popular forum for Burmese information technology professionals—Lynn Htun posted the fol-lowing analysis of the oGc:

Their server is called irc.olivegreen.org . . . they set up irc servers and rent them out to botnet owners, in return, they are allowed to use the botnet to ddos once a month or so. They didn't hacked the drones for the botnet, they are simply providing the server(s) for harvesting the botnet. So in other words, there's no real skills there. . . . You should contact their service provider and tell them to shutdown the botnet hub that is running on the following VPS. . . . All the above IPs are bound to a FreeBSD box running on a VPS. You wont find the bots on their server when you join because they are all in a secret channel with umode flags set to hide them from normal users.[52]

Lynn Htun's accusation that the oGc occasionally uses a botnet constructed by others for DDoS attacks as a form of payment infuriated the oGc administrator, who denied the claims vigorously when we mentioned them during our IRC chats with him. During one chat a strange coincidence occurred when an IRC user with the nickname "lynn" appeared in the oGc IRC channel, purporting to be Lynn Htun. The two times that "lynn" connected to the server, the following information was displayed:

lynn (~xero@bagan-3634EE84.childminder.co.uk)
Lynn (humm@bagan-888BA9F1.uk2net.com) has joined #Bagan
[Lynn] (humm@bagan-888BA9F1.uk2net.com): xero

Recall that the information seen when a user enters the overkill.myanmarchat.org server was "~xero overkill.name irc.doscoder.org xer0 H*:1 xero." It may be a coincidence but the "xero" is present in both. It is difficult to assess whether lynn was in fact Lynn Htun. In the chat, "lynn" appeared to backpeddle from the post made on Myanmaritpros.com, raising questions about whether the user was actually Lynn Htun.

Lynn Htun's profile on Myanmaritpros.com indicates that he works for Myanmar Online. The IRC group for Myanmar Online has an apparent rivalry with oGc, and if anyone creates a channel with a name associated with oGc, such as "ogc," he or she is kicked from the channel and given the following message: "You have been kicked from the chat room by ChanServ with the reason 'lamer channel' and cannot send further messages without rejoining."

In some of his posts on Myanmaritpros.com, Lynn Htun expresses views that appear unfavorable toward the Burmese political opposition but do not necessarily reflect a "progovernment" position either. His perspective appears to be nuanced and stems from what he refers to as the "excessive politicization of our daily lives"[53] as well as the "collateral damage" that emerges as a result of tying economics to political reform through the use of sanctions:

Unfortunately our beloved politicians have [intertwined] the development of the country with political process. As such, as long as there are political deadlocks, our country's developments will be [hampered] and our IT industry will be stuck in a limbo forever more. I would like to show your posting to those who claim that sanctions are working and that they are essential for political transition. Insisting that economic and social development goes hand in hand with political progress is like saying prostrate cancer can be cure[d] with cough medicine. Yet, knowingly many insist that enforcing sanctions on Myanmar is a good thing because it serve[s] the greater cause and of course all the negative side effects are acceptable collateral damage.[54]

General discontent with opposition media is reflected in a thread on Myanmaritpros.com in which Lynn Htun and others expressed frustration over the coverage of a competition to develop a search engine sponsored by the Myanmar Computer Professional Association. After The Irrawaddy posted an article suggesting that the competition may have been "designed by the Burmese military junta in order to increase its Internet restriction technology and ability to control Web sites and blogs,"[55] Lynn Htun called them "democrazies" and suggested that The Irrawaddy was opposed to improving the state of information technologies in Burma: "I don't think that is on the agenda of the 'democrazies,' politicians and exiled media outlets. . . . Looks like they already cooked up some nasty accusations:-(."[56] This incident appears to illustrate a tension in the Burmese IT community that suggests how viewing the sociopolitical climate and its relation to technology in the country in black-and-white terms may overly simplify the situation.

Burmese Hacker Community

As part of our investigation, an IWM researcher traveled to Burma to gain insight into the local hacker community and assess their motivations. The hacker culture in Burma, as in many places around the world, appears to be oriented toward touting one's skills in order to improve business opportunities. One source within the information technology community indicated that the motives behind the attacks on Mizzima News may very well not have been political. Instead, they may have been motivated by a desire to demonstrate the hackers' skills online for personal gratification as well as to advance personal economic interests. He explained that by drawing attention to their expertise through such attacks, hackers may have hoped to attract demands for "protection" from network administrators. Essentially, they could have been creating a demand and, in turn, supplying the protection.

Hackers such as Fluffi Bunni have become respected members of Burma's information technology community and have commercialized their skills. While they do not support the political opposition, they are not necessarily hostile to it. Rather, they seem to believe that apolitical policies are better suited toward advancing both the economy and the ICT sector within Burma. As a result, they are critical of expatriate Burmese media that oppose the country's government and military.

In contrast, other sources within Burma indicated that political motivations were behind the attacks. They said that since very few people within Burma actually have an Internet connection, these attacks are likely the work of Russian-trained hackers. This view aligns with the charges made by Burmese opposition groups.

Ultimately, none of our sources could clarify whether those behind the attacks acted independently or alongside government interests. What we found in our field investigation is that there is a lively hacker community in Burma, but information regarding their relationship with the government and military is extremely scarce, and the information that is available is inconclusive.

The information obtained during the field investigation also provides context to the ongoing attacks against the Burmese opposition media. As we mentioned, the opposition Web sites are already blocked and inaccessible to Internet users in Burma. According to our sources in the country, the political opposition in Burma actually avoids using the Internet because they perceive communications over the Internet as being insecure, and using the Internet, as opposed to other forms of communication, makes them more vulnerable to government interception. In addition, computer literacy levels are very low, and few of those who use the Internet are familiar with security practices such as encryption. As a result, the opposition within Burma uses the Internet primarily for the dissemination of information through anonymous blogs and news reporting. The importance of sites like Mizzima News is not necessarily that they provide information to people within Burma, but rather that they provide information about Burma to a global audience. This observation helps to explain why opposition media sites are routinely attacked despite the fact that they are inaccessible to Internet users within Burma.

Assessing Threat and Attribution

To assess the capabilities of computer network attackers, John Arquilla has defined three useful categories that indicate the skill and resources required to carry out various levels of attacks:

Simple-Unstructured   The capability to conduct basic hacks against individual systems using tools created by someone else. The organization possesses little target analysis, command and control, or learning capability.

Advanced-Structured   The capability to conduct more sophisticated attacks against multiple systems or networks and possibly to modify or create basic hacking tools. The organization possesses an elementary target analysis, command and control, and learning capability.

Complex-Coordinated   The capability for coordinated attacks capable of causing mass-disruption against integrated, heterogeneous defenses (including cryptography). Ability to create sophisticated hacking tools. Highly capable target analysis, command and control, and organizational learning capability.[57]

Analyzing the attacks within this framework grounds political context in technical data in a way that provides a clearer picture of the identity and intent of the attackers.

Our analysis suggests that the attackers have significant knowledge of information technology, which enables them to launch attacks by leveraging basic, publicly available exploits and software tools. They may also have access to botnets capable of DDoS attacks, but they do not create or own the botnets themselves. In the attack against Mizzima News, the attackers employed basic means to mask their identities, but did not or were unable to escalate their user privileges to "root" administrator level on the server or successfully cover their digital tracks. They maintained a low level of operational security and left behind significant pieces of evidence. The evidence implicates members of the oGc in the attacks, and in particular the oGc's administrator. The relatively low sophistication of the attack and the capabilities of the attackers indicate that they are best placed within the "Simple-Unstructured" category of Arquilla's framework. However, the fortuitous timing of the attack provided the attackers with a "strategic utility" that would normally be beyond their means.

Despite the correlative evidence, there are several alternative explanations concerning attribution that we have to explore. The administrator of the oGc often suggested in our IRC chats that Lynn Htun was responsible for the attacks. Lynn Htun has a history of prolific defacements and is critical of opposition media sites. An IRC user reporting to be Lynn Htun had xer0 in his connection information, which matched a user in a channel on "overkill.myanmarchat.org" that was used by the attackers. However, it is unclear if the user we spoke with was really Lynn Htun. In addition, oGc and Lynn Htun's Myanmar Online appear to be rival IRC networks, a fact that may explain why the oGc administrator implicated Lynn Htun in the attacks.

Another explanation concerns the use of the oGc's IRC infrastructure as a platform for the attackers. It is possible that the attackers used the oGc infrastructure through some arrangement with oGc or that the oGc simply tolerated their presence. This scenario is consistent with Lynn Htun's charge that the oGc provides hosting for botnets in return for the ability to occasionally use them for DDoS targets. Another consistent explanation is that the oGc could have also supplied access to censorship-circumvention proxies to their general membership. The administrator's accounts of oGc on the circumvention software network could have been shared across members of the oGc.

Based on the evidence we collected, we assessed that the suspected attackers in this case are not particularly favorable to the Burmese opposition but cannot be simplistically characterized as "progovernment" either. Their hostility toward the Burmese opposition appears to stem from feelings of nationalism and a belief that the opposition promotes a negative image of their country. Most appear to be concerned with gaining employment and improving the state of information and communications technology in Burma. Although they have both the skills and motivation to attack opposition Web sites, they may have attacked such Web sites without formal connections to the government. While our investigation provides indications of the possible identities of the attackers, it presents more questions than answers around state involvement in the ongoing cyber attacks against Burmese opposition groups.

The characteristics of the attackers and the opportunistic nature of the attacks may reflect a "swarming effect" in which private individuals, inspired by patriotic sentiments, voluntarily participate in cyber attacks during political events without clear approval or direction from state entities. This phenomenon has been observed in a number of recent conflicts and political events, including the 2008 Russia-Georgia war, the 2009 Gaza conflict, and the 2009 Iranian elections.[58] Our investigation shows that even a relatively simplistic attack can have significant effects if it is executed at a sensitive time. The attackers in this case were able to deface Mizzima News because it was running a version of Joomla! that was known to be vulnerable. In effect, this was a preventable attack—a known vulnerability that was exploited by opportunistic attackers. However, the timing of the attack coincided with ongoing DDoS attacks, and the addition of a visible threat (defacement) compounded the effect on the political opposition and their supporters. The involvement of private individuals in cyber attacks during political events demonstrates the chaotic nature of cyberspace and shows that while it is possible that states may be instigating attacks, they cannot control outside participants from contributing to them, and such contributions can lead to unpredictable outcomes.[59]

Although we did not find evidence of state attribution in our investigation, it does not rule out the possibility that the SPDC is somehow involved in the recurring attacks against Burmese opposition groups. However, their involvement may be more subtle and indirect than speculations of elite military units leading cyber attacks on dissident Web sites convey. It is possible that the SPDC is engaged with individuals and groups in the Burmese hacker community and either subtly encourages them to participate in attacks against opposition groups or at least condones their actions. State-sanctioned patriotic hackers have been suspected in other cyber attacks originating from Russia, China, and Vietnam, but direct evidence is elusive.[60] The state may also be employing third-party actors to conduct cyber attacks through a crime-as-a-service model in which they hire criminal groups to perpetrate the attacks or rent necessary resources such as botnets from them.

The use of technical infrastructure related to criminal activities in seemingly politically motivated cyber attacks has been observed in high-profile cases such as attacks on Georgian government Web sites during the 2008 Russia-Georgia conflict.[61] This model of privateering is potentially attractive to nation-states because it permits them plausible deniability: actions take place in a criminal ecosystem that is removed from state entities and difficult—if not impossible—to trace back to them. Confirming these speculative scenarios in Burma is difficult, since much remains unknown about the attacks, the possible actors, and the motivations behind them. However, situating these events within the wider context of recent cyber attacks in other countries shows they are part of a troubling global trend that needs to be analyzed across both the technical and political complexities of cyberspace.[62]

Conclusion

Unlike Internet filtering at the ISP level that is limited to local control, cyber attacks conducted at strategically sensitive times have the ability to disrupt information flows to international audiences right when the content may have the most impact. States are obvious units of analysis when examining attribution and intent behind national filtering regimes. However, actors and their intentions are not as readily apparent in politically motivated cyber attacks. Despite the difficulties, due to the political nature of attacks against civil society organizations, many observers attribute these incidents to government and military entities. As a result, the attackers' capabilities are often overestimated, and their motivations are unknown. Although the issue of attribution is essential to analysis of such attacks, it remains the most difficult and ambiguous component of any investigation.

Our research illustrates the need to utilize a holistic approach that incorporates historical and political context into incident response and technical investigations, especially in cases where the attackers face little or no likelihood of being prosecuted. This analytical approach is especially applicable to civil society organizations that confront ongoing, politically motivated attacks originating from attackers who leverage geography, adversarial political relationships, and the lack of international cooperation to avoid prosecution. Careful technical analysis is required to properly assess the threat posed by attackers. However, if security incidents are treated as isolated cases focused solely on technical forensics, the bigger picture and broader implications of the attacks cannot be properly understood.

The struggle between information control and resistance in Burma takes place on a contested terrain that reveals unique characteristics of cyberspace that preclude simplistic explanations and frames. The opposition between state and citizen that is emphasized by images of military crackdowns on peaceful protesters can obfuscate the complexities of political power in cyberspace. The Burma case shows that even in a country with one of the world's most restrictive communications environments, an authoritarian state cannot maintain full control over the Internet without disconnecting from the global network all together. Conversely, the same dynamic properties of cyberspace that make it resistant to complete control are also what make vectors like denial of service attacks such effective and vexing threats against freedom of expression.

These attacks may be the product of users motivated by patriotism swarming in from the edges of the network to disrupt key information outlets, state-sanctioned military operations, or collusion between states and criminal groups operating in the shadows of the Internet. Any one or combination of these scenarios may be at work, making the study of these attacks all the more difficult.

Burma shows that Asian cyberspace cannot be simply classified as either a locus of control or resistance, but rather is better understood as the site of a constantly evolving and dynamic contest between a range of actors and agendas. Understanding how freedom of expression can be equally repressed and advocated in this environment requires studying it holistically and examining the subtle interrelations between the social, political, and technical facets of the network. Approaching the domain in this way presents significant practical and methodological difficulties for consortiums like the ONI, IWM, and the research and policy community at large, but confronting these challenges and peering into the subterranean depths of cyberspace are essential for revealing the contests being fought and the stakes involved in them.

Notes

1. Human Rights Watch, "Burma," 2009, http://www.hrw.org/en/world-report-2010/burma; Amnesty International, "Burma, Amnesty International Report 2009," http://report2009.amnesty .org/en/regions/asia-pacific/myanmar.

2. Larry Diamond, "Liberation Technology," *Journal of Democracy* 21, no. 3 (2010): 69–82.

3. Evgeny Morozov, *The Net Delusion: The Dark Side of Internet Freedom* (New York: PublicAffairs, 2011).

4. Mirdul Chowdhury, "The Role of the Internet in Burma's Saffron Revolution," Berkman Center for Internet and Society, September 28, 2008, http://cyber.law.harvard.edu/publications/2008/Role_of_the_Internet_in_Burmas_Saffron_Revolution; OpenNet Initiative, "Pulling the Plug: A Technical Review of the Internet Shutdown in Burma," October 15, 2007, http://opennet.net/research/bulletins/013.

5. The Democratic Voice of Burma Web site is http://www.dvb.no.

6. The Irrawaddy Web site is http://www.irrawaddy.org.

7. The Mizzima News Web site is http://www.mizzima.com.

8. A Web site defacement is an attack in which the visual content of a page is altered.

9. For a listing of reported attacks on Burmese opposition groups, see the DoS Watch project, http://www.doswatch.org/search/label/burma.

10. Committee to Protect Journalists, "Burma's Exile Media Hit by Cyber-attacks," September 27, 2010, http://cpj.org/2010/09/burmas-exile-media-hit-by-cyber-attacks.php.

11. The Information Warfare Monitor is a sister project to the OpenNet Initiative that studies the emergence of cyberspace as a strategic domain and analyzes politically motivated cyber attacks and espionage. See Information Warfare Monitor, http://www.infowar-monitor.net.

12. Freedom House, "Burma (Myanmar) Country Report 2010," http://www.freedomhouse.org/template.cfm?page=22&year=2010&country=7792.

13. Roy Greenslade, "How Burma Quashes Press Freedom," Guardian Greenslade Blog, September 26, 2007, http://www.guardian.co.uk/media/greenslade/2007/sep/26/howburmaquashespressfreedom.

14. Printers and Publishers Registration Act (1962), http://www.burmalibrary.org/docs6/Printers_and_Publishers_Registation_Act.pdf.

15. Article 32, Television and Video Law (The State Law and Order Restoration Council Law No. 8/96), July 26, 1996, http://www.blc-burma.org/html/Myanmar%20Law/lr_e_ml96_08.html.

16. Chowdhury, "The Role of the Internet in Burma's Saffron Revolution."

17. Ibid.

18. International Telecommunications Union (ITU), "Internet Indicators: Subscribers, Users and Broadband Subscribers," 2009 figures. http://www.itu.int/ITU-D/icteye/Reporting/ShowReportFrame.aspx?ReportName=/WTI/InformationTechnologyPublic&ReportFormat=HTML4.0&RP_intYear=2009&RP_intLanguageID=1&RP_bitLiveData=False.

19. See the Burma country profile in this volume; Reporters Without Borders, "Internet Enemies: Burma," 2010, http://www.rsf.org/en-ennemi26126-Burma.html.

20. Nart Villeneuve, "Fortinet for Who?" Nart Villeneuve: Malware Explorer, October 13, 2005, http://www.nartv.org/2005/10/13/fortinet-for-who/; United States Department of the Treasury, "Burma Sanctions," http://www.treasury.gov/resource-center/sanctions/Programs/pages/burma.aspx.

21. Reporters Without Borders, "Press Freedom Index 2010," 2010, http://en.rsf.org/press -freedom-index-2010,1034.html; Committee to Protect Journalists, "Ten Worst Countries to Be a Blogger," April 30, 2009, http://cpj.org/reports/2009/04/10-worst-countries-to-be-a-blogger.php.

22. Seth Mydans, "Steep Rise in Fuel Costs Prompts Rare Public Protest in Myanmar," *New York Times*, August 23, 2007, http://www.nytimes.com/2007/08/23/world/asia/23myanmar.html?_r=1&scp.

23. Ardeth Maung Thawnghmung and Maung Aung Myoe, "Myanmar in 2007," *Asian Survey* 48, no. 1 (2008): 13–19.

24. Ibid.

25. OpenNet Initiative, "Pulling the Plug."

26. OpenNet Initiative, "Nepal Country Profile," 2007, http://opennet.net/research/profiles/nepal.

27. James Cowie, "Egypt Leaves the Net," Renesys, January 27, 2011, http://www.renesys.com/blog/2011/01/egypt-leaves-the-internet.shtml.

28. Ronald Deibert and Rafal Rohozinski, "Good for Liberty, Bad for Security? Global Civil Society and the Securitization of the Internet," in *Access Denied: The Practice and Policy of Global Internet Filtering,* ed. Ronald Deibert, John Palfrey, Rafal Rohozinski, and Jonathan Zittrain (Cambridge, MA: MIT Press, 2008), 123–149.

29. Brian McCartan, "Myanmar on the Cyber-offensive," *Asia Times*, October 1, 2008, http://www.atimes.com/atimes/Southeast_Asia/JJ01Ae01.html.

30. Mizzima News also previously reported being the target of DDoS attacks on July 29, 2008. Saw Yan Nang, "The Irrawaddy Hopes to Defeat the Hackers Soon," The Irrawaddy, September 19, 2008, http://www.irrawaddy.org/article.php?art_id=14283; "Websites of Three Burmese News Agencies in Exile under Attack," Mizzima News, September 17, 2008, http://www.mizzima.com/news/regional/1052-websites-of-three-burmese-news-agencies-in-exile-under-attack.html; Connie Levett, "Burmese Dissident Websites Shut Down," The Age, September 20, 2008, http://www.theage.com.au/news/web/burmese-dissident-websites-shut-down/2008/09/19/1221935424916.html; and Kenneth Denby, "Dissident Websites Crippled by Burma on Anniversary of Revolt," *The Times*, September 22, 2008, http://technology.timesonline.co.uk/tol/news/tech_and_web/the_web/article4799375.ece.

31. "Burma's IT Generation Combats Regime Repression," The Irrawaddy, October 7, 2008, http://www.irrawaddy.org/print_article.php?art_id=14399; "Mizzima Websites Hacked," Mizzima News, October 1, 2008, http://www.mizzima.com/news/inside-burma/1092-mizzima-websites -hacked.html; McCartan, "Myanmar on the Cyber-offensive."

32. McCartan, "Myanmar on the Cyber-offensive."

33. "Mizzima Websites Hacked," Mizzima News; Saw Yan Naing, "Burmese Exile Media Web Site Again under Attack," The Irrawaddy, October 1, 2008, http://www.irrawaddy.org/article.php?art_id=14348.

34. "Mizzima Websites Hacked," Mizzima News.

35. "Hack Attempts Suspend Mizzima Websites," Mizzima News, October 10, 2008, http://mizzima-english.blogspot.com/2008/10/hack-attempts-suspend-mizzima-websites.html.

36. "Backdoor programs" refer to malicious software designed to provide attackers with unauthorized remote access to computer systems. For a detailed technical description of the c99shell backdoor program, see "Backdoor.PHP.C99Shell.w," Secure List, July 15, 2008, http://www.securelist.com/en/descriptions/old188613.

37. The user-agent header is sent by your browser to the Web server you are connecting to. The user-agent header commonly identifies the operating system and browser that you are using.

38. In fact, they appeared to be monitoring news of attacks on opposition Web sites, with one user posting this article into the IRC chat Myanmar ISP, "Military Government Paralyses Internet," October 9, 2008, http://www.myanmarisp.com/20080816/ICTN/ictnews0101/, authored by Reporters Without Borders, which details the ongoing attacks and suggests that the military and government were behind the attacks.

39. "Myanmar on the Cyber-offensive," BaganLand, http://baganland.blogspot.com/2008/09/myanmar-on-cyber-offensive.html.

40. Joomla! is an open-source content management system. See, Joomla! http://www.joomla.org/.

41. The following instructions demonstrate the simplicity of this browser exploit:

1. Go to URL target.com/index.php?option=com_user&view=reset&layout=confirm.
2. Write into field "token" char ' and click OK.
3. Write new password for admin.
4. Go to url: target.com/administrator/.
5. Login as admin with new password.

42. "Backdoor.PHP.C99Shell.w," Secure List, July 15, 2008, http://www.securelist.com/en/descriptions/old188613.

43. See Co.cc lookup, https://www.co.cc/whois/whois.php?domain=0verkill.

44. Moscow Aviation Institute, "Faculty of Applied Mathematics and Physics," http://www.mai.ru/english/fac_8/computer_eng.htm; Moscow Aviation Institute, "Informatics and Mathematics," http://www.mai.ru/english/fac_8/informatics_eng.htm.

45. U.S. Department of Treasury OFAC, "Nonproliferation: What You Need to Know about Treasury Sanctions," April 7, 2009, http://www.treas.gov/offices/enforcement/ofac/programs/wmd/wmd.pdf; Federation of American Scientists, "A Sourcebook on Allegations of Cooperation between Myanmar (Burma) and North Korea on Nuclear Projects," February 14, 2011, http://

www.fas.org/man/eprint/burma.pdf; Charles G. Billo and Welton Chang, "Cyber Warfare: An Analysis of the Means and Motivations of Selected Nation States," Institute for Security Technology Studies at Dartmouth College, December 2004, http://www.ists.dartmouth.edu/library/212 .pdf.

46. Htet Aung Kyaw, "Burma's Generals Are Afraid of Telephones and the Internet," *The Nation*, March 24, 2009, http://www.nationmultimedia.com/2009/03/24/opinion/opinion_30098633 .php.

47. Ibid.

48. See an archive of the oGc homepage at http://web.archive.org/web/20070227151313/http:// www.globalogc.org.

49. Myanmar Marine University, http://www.mot.gov.mm/mmu/organization.html.

50. Before initiating conversations with members of the IRC group, we identified ourselves as researchers at the University of Toronto and explained that we were analyzing attacks against Burmese independent media Web sites.

51. Paul Roberts, "Alleged Fluffi Bunni Leader Worked for Siemens," *Computer World*, May 8, 2003, http://www.computerworld.com/s/article/81043/Alleged_Fluffi_Bunni_leader_worked_for _Siemens; Lain Tomson, "Infosec Hit by Arrest and Virus Attack," April 30, 2003, V3.co.uk, http://www.v3.co.uk/vnunet/news/2122174/infosec-hit-arrest-virus-attack; Drew Cullen, "Fluffi Bunni Nabbed at Infosec," The Register, April 3, 2003, http://www.theregister.co.uk/2003/04/ 30/fluffi_bunni_nabbed_at_infosec/; Gillian Law and Paul Roberts, "U.K. Police Nab Fluffi Bunni Hacker," *Computer World*, April 30, 2003, http://www.computerworld.com/s/article/80811/U.K._ police_nab_Fluffi_Bunni_hacker?taxonomyId=017.

52. Myanmar IT Pros, October 23, 2008, http://www.myanmaritpro.com/forum/topics/1445004 :Topic:79509?commentId=1445004%3AComment%3A79990.

53. Myanmar IT Pros, September 9, 2009, http://www.myanmaritpro.com/forum/topics/1445004 :Topic:156949?commentId=1445004%3AComment%3A157606.

54. Myanmar IT Pros, August 10, 2009, http://www.myanmaritpro.com/forum/topics/1445004 :Topic:148136?commentId=1445004%3AComment%3A149799.

55. Arkar Moe, "Burmese IT Contest to Aid Junta?" The Irrawaddy, August 25, 2009, http://www .irrawaddy.org/article.php?art_id=16633.

56. Myanmar IT Pros, August 26, 2009, http://www.myanmaritpro.com/forum/topics/1445004 :Topic:152929?commentId=1445004%3AComment%3A153346.

57. Naval Post Graduate School, *Cyberterror Prospects and Implications*, October 1999, http://www .nps.edu/Academics/Centers/CTIW/files/Cyberterror%20Prospects%20and%20Implications .pdf.

58. Ronald Deibert, Rafal Rohozinski, and Masashi Crete-Nishihata, "Cyclones in Cyberspace: Information Shaping and Denial in the 2008 South Ossetia War," paper presented at 51st Annual

International Studies Association Convention, February 2010, New Orleans, LA; Jose Nazario, "Politically Motivated Denial of Service Attacks," in *The Virtual Battlefield: Perspectives on Cyber Warfare*, ed. Christian Czosseck and Kenneth Geers (Amsterdam: IOS Press, 2009), 163–181.

59. Deibert, Rohozinski, and Crete-Nishihata, "Cyclones in Cyberspace."

60. Ronald Deibert and Rafal Rohozinski, "Control and Subversion in Russian Cyberspace," in *Access Controlled: The Shaping of Power, Rights, and Rule in Cyberspace*, ed. Ronald Deibert, John Palfrey, Rafal Rohozinski, and Jonathan Zittrain (Cambridge, MA: MIT Press, 2010); Information Warfare Monitor, *Tracking GhostNet: Investigating a Cyber Espionage Network*, March 29, 2009, http://tracking-ghost.net; Information Warfare Monitor and Shadowserver Foundation, "Shadows in the Cloud: An Investigation into Cyber Espionage 2.0," April 6, 2010, http://shadows-in-the -cloud.net; Nart Villeneuve, "Vietnam and Aurora," Nart Villeneuve Malware Explorer, April 5, 2010, http://www.nartv.org/2010/04/05/vietnam-aurora.

61. Mike Johnson, "Georgian Websites under Attack—Don't Believe the Hype," Shadowserver Foundation, August 12, 2008, http://www.shadowserver.org/wiki/pmwiki.php/Calendar/20080812.

62. For further analysis of the global prevalence and effect of DDoS attacks against civil society groups, see Hal Roberts, Ethan Zuckerman, and John Palfrey, "Interconnected Contests: Distributed Denial of Service Attacks and Other Digital Control Measures in Asia," chapter 7 in this volume.

9   China and Global Internet Governance

A Tiger by the Tail

Milton L. Mueller

As of June 2010 the Chinese government claimed the country's number of "netizens," or Internet users, had increased to 430 million.[1] That very large number is only 32 percent of China's total population.[2] Already one of the biggest presences on the Internet, and with a long way to go yet, China and the Internet enjoy a complex and seemingly paradoxical relationship. Many Westerners have trouble making sense of the way China's socialist market economy (SME) combines heavy restrictions with vibrant growth, and globalized networking with an insistence on territorial sovereignty. Western observers have long abandoned the notion that the Internet was inherently uncontrollable and that its use would automatically overthrow dictatorships. They are now replacing that simplistic notion with an equally coarse inversion: the image of China as the constructor of an impregnable "Great Firewall," a place of omnipotent surveillance, a population susceptible to well-organized propaganda campaigns, and a source of pervasive and insidious cyber attacks and cyber espionage. It is a new Internet version of the Cold War.

The Internet in the People's Republic of China (PRC) strains and challenges the capacity of the Chinese Communist Party (CCP) to maintain control. And the fact that China needs to be linked to the external world, through the Internet as well as through trade, provides a double challenge. The international environment of Internet governance is freer, is private-sector based, and is more capitalistic than China's rulers would prefer. And, it is subject to U.S. hegemony. If one combines an analysis of the global politics of Internet governance with an understanding of the long-term status of China's reform process, one can understand better which factors facilitate and which place constraints on the party's ability to regulate the Internet. One can even, perhaps, understand how the further development of digital communications might contribute to a transformation of Chinese society.

This chapter outlines a general framework for understanding Internet politics and locating China within it. It then analyzes China's attempt to move against the grain of the current Internet governance regime, promoting sovereignty and intergovernmental institutions in opposition to the new, transnational, and private-sector-based

Internet governance institutions such as the Internet Corporation for Assigned Names and Numbers (ICANN) and the Regional Internet Registries (RIRs). The next section describes various interactions and spillover effects, both intended and unintended, between China's attempt to maintain its Great Firewall and the globalized operations that characterize the Internet, focusing in particular on the domain name system (DNS) and routing, and cyber espionage. A concluding section places these issues in a more general discussion of the tensions inherent in the Chinese "socialist market economy."

The Four Quadrants of Internet Politics and China's Place in Them

In another work I have described the politics of Internet governance using a space defined by two axes.[3] This conceptual scheme is predicated on recognizing that the Internet does indeed create a novel form of politics around communication and information policy. The novelty comes from the Internet's transnational scope, its massively increased scale of interaction, its distribution of control, its capacity to facilitate new forms of collective action, and the emergence of new, nonstate-based governance institutions native to the Internet.

The horizontal axis pertains to the status of the territorial nation-state in the governance of the Internet and communications technology generally. The vertical axis identifies the level of hierarchical control one is willing to countenance in the solution of Internet governance problems. Together, these axes form a four-quadrant space, which provides a useful schema for analyzing and classifying the various ideologies and policy systems related to the Internet.

In figure 9.1, the horizontal or nation-state axis locates one's view of the appropriate polity. Those on the right side of this axis prefer the traditional territorial nation-state as the institutional basis for governing the Internet. At the rightmost extreme stand those who would subordinate the Internet to national sovereignty completely—in effect, negating global networking altogether in favor of a bounded, analog telephone-network-like regime. At the left extreme, Internet governance decisions would be made by a globalized polity where national borders, national sovereignty, and national identity play almost no role.

The vertical or networking-hierarchy axis juxtaposes free association (at the top) with command and control (at the bottom). This reflects the degree to which one believes the problems associated with Internet governance should be solved using coercive and hierarchical mechanisms or left to the looser forms of association and disassociation among Internet users and suppliers. At the top of this axis, the shape of Internet governance would be defined by looser forms of *networked governance*; at the bottom, governance emerges from adherence to rules enforced by an authority. Of course, what makes Internet governance especially interesting is that there is no

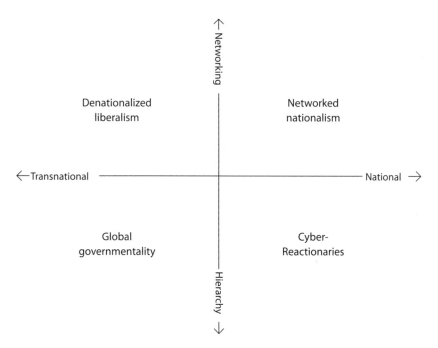

Figure 9.1
The quadrants of Internet politics.

universally recognized authority at the global level; therefore, advocates of hierarchy must also make choices regarding where they stand on the horizontal axis.

These two axes form a political space with four quadrants. In the lower-right quadrant, we have *cyber-conservatives* and outright *cyber-reactionaries*. In essence, these actors regret the rise of the Internet in most respects, and insofar as they tolerate its existence they strive to make it conform to the authority and parameters of the nation-state. Their intent is to realign control over the Internet's operational units and critical resources with the jurisdiction of the nation-state. Insofar as international policy is recognized as necessary, they believe that it should be handled by intergovernmental institutions and kept to the bare minimum required to protect or supplement domestic policy.

In the upper-right quadrant, which I call *networked nationalism*, the nation-state is still the dominant governance institution, but there is greater willingness to embrace the potential of networking and less of an attempt to impose territorial hierarchies on networked actors and network operations. National public policies and regulations are applied to actors within the territorial jurisdiction, but many loopholes and escape valves are left open because of transnational Internet access. States in this quadrant might cope with transnational problems through a mix of transgovernmental networks, delegation to private actors, or formal intergovernmental treaties, but international institutions remain rooted in states, and any organically evolved Internet institutions would have to be recognized by and subordinated to states. This quadrant is characterized by an acute tension between the boundaries of the national polity and the (transnational) boundaries of networked activity.

The lower-left quadrant encompasses those who advocate *global governmentality*—namely, hierarchical control of the Internet by means of new institutions that transcend the nation-state. These new institutions are most likely to be private-sector based and created to advance business interests, though they could also be multistakeholder and public-private partnerships and even democratic for some version of democracy not rooted in 20th-century nations.

The upper-left quadrant, which I call *denationalized liberalism*, also supports a transnational institutional framework but is less hierarchical in its approach to the need for order. This quadrant combines economic and social liberalism; its adherents recognize individual network participants, not states or corporations, as the fundamental source of legitimate Internet governance and propose to create new institutions around them. Its adherents valorize freedom and propose to rely primarily on peer-production processes, networked governance, and competitive markets to handle the issues of Internet governance. Hierarchical interventions would be limited to the minimum required to secure basic protections against theft, fraud, and coercion.

Within this political space, China (along with Burma, Russia, and other postcommunist nations such as Vietnam) is unambiguously cyber-nationalist. It strives mightily to reorder the Internet by filtering content and by licensing and regulating the providers of Internet services in order to make them conform to national policy. Its philosophy is clear from its own 2010 White Paper:

The Chinese government believes that the Internet is an important infrastructure facility for the nation. Within Chinese territory the Internet is under the jurisdiction of Chinese sovereignty. The Internet sovereignty of China should be respected and protected. Citizens of the People's Republic of China and foreign citizens, legal persons and other organizations within Chinese territory have the right and freedom to use the Internet; at the same time, they must obey the laws and regulations of China and conscientiously protect Internet security.[4]

Along with the emphasis on sovereignty, equally strong support for hierarchical control exists. Both the telecommunication infrastructure and the services that run on top of it are subject to strict licensing and entry restrictions, as well as outright censorship and repression:

No organization or individual may produce, duplicate, announce or disseminate information having the following contents: being against the cardinal principles set forth in the Constitution; endangering state security, divulging state secrets, subverting state power and jeopardizing national unification; damaging state honor and interests; instigating ethnic hatred or discrimination and jeopardizing ethnic unity; jeopardizing state religious policy, propagating heretical or superstitious ideas; spreading rumors, disrupting social order and stability; disseminating obscenity, pornography, gambling, violence, brutality and terror or abetting crime; humiliating or slandering others, trespassing on the lawful rights and interests of others; and other contents forbidden by laws and administrative regulations. These regulations are the legal basis for the protection of Internet information security within the territory of the People's Republic of China. All Chinese citizens, foreign citizens, legal persons and other organizations within the territory of China must obey these provisions.[5]

As a logical extension of its cyber-nationalism, China steadfastly supports a traditional, sovereignty-based communications governance regime in the international arena. It prefers an international regime organized around treaty-based intergovernmental organizations that rely on one-country, one-vote distributions of power. When China uses the word "democratic" in this context, it means one country, one vote. Its point of reference for "democracy" is not the rights and interests of the individual citizen, but is equality among sovereign states: "China believes that UN [United Nations] should be given full scope in international Internet administration and supports the establishment of an authoritative and just international Internet administration organization under the UN system through democratic procedures on a worldwide scale. All countries have equal rights in participating in the administration of the fundamental international resources of the Internet."[6]

Both the domestic and international aspects of China's approach to the Internet underscore the inevitability of its attempt to create a bordered Internet subject to national policy. The Great Firewall of China (GFW) is but one aspect of this; more important than the filtering of external information are the licensing requirements, extensive state ownership, and entry controls that can be imposed upon domestic Internet intermediaries and service providers, as well as the growing identification and surveillance of users and potential for severe, arbitrary punishment that can be imposed on them domestically. This leads to extensive self-regulation and self-censorship.

All these points refer to the Chinese Communist Party's theory of how things *should* be—their preferred state of affairs. That preferred reality, however, is undercut by the realities of the Internet. As Wang Chen, the State Council's chief information officer, put it, "the Internet is a global open-information system." In a speech before the Chinese parliament, he recognized the fact that

as long as our country's Internet is linked to the global Internet, there will be channels and means for all sorts of harmful foreign information to appear on our domestic Internet. As long as our Internet is open to the public, there will be channels and means for netizens to express all sorts of speech on the Internet. Judging from our country's social development, our country is currently in a period of social transformation, rapid development, and conspicuous contradictions. Unavoidably, actual contradictions and problems in our society are reported on the Internet. Judging from our country's Internet management practices, we are still in the process of exploration and improvement. Many weak links still exist in our work. These problems have weakened our ability to manage the Internet scientifically and effectively.[7]

In addition to those limitations on control, China is constrained by the need for economic development and productive exchanges with the rest of the world. Thus, in its experimentation with combinations of restriction and openness and its sensitivity to its economic interdependence with the developed world, China's approach to the Internet mirrors its strategic approach to openness to foreign investment and trade generally. With its aspiration to become a global leader in high technology, China simply cannot afford to turn its back on the Internet.

China's Predictable Clash with (and Adjustment to) the Current Internet Governance Regime

The current Internet governance regime clashes with China's preferences in two distinct ways. First, the legacy of denationalized liberalism associated with the Internet's early development still powerfully shapes the Internet's operations and the social, economic, and political norms associated with its use. Instead of traditional, intergovernmental institutions there are private-sector-based, transnational forms of governance and a widespread ethic of self-regulation and civil society support for Internet freedom. Second, the privileged role of the United States in the current Internet governance regime, especially its control over ICANN, rankles the Chinese. Although in many respects denationalized liberalism and U.S. preeminence are at odds with each other, it is not surprising that China sees them as related and mutually reinforcing. In China's state-centric view, Internet freedom and the U.S. doctrine of the "free flow of information" are merely tools that a hegemonic America uses to penetrate and subvert other states with its own worldviews and values. China's accusations that Hillary Clinton's "Internet freedom" initiatives are part of a calculated "information imperialism" flow logically from this perspective.[8] The Chinese view is given some credence, since U.S. "Internet freedom" initiatives are in fact rather selectively targeted at U.S. geopolitical rivals China and Iran, as opposed to other equally censorious countries that are allies of the United States.[9]

China and ICANN

To the Chinese state (in common with other cyber-nationalist and cyber-reactionary nation-states), ICANN is highly objectionable for two reasons: first, because of its status as a nonstate actor that supplants or competes with states in the exercise of policy-making and governance responsibilities; and second, because of its unilateral establishment by the United States and its contracts that make it beholden to the U.S. Department of Commerce. Initially, the Chinese also objected to ICANN because, as a private corporation free from intergovernmental diplomacy, the corporation allowed representatives of the government of Taiwan to participate openly and freely in ICANN activities and sit on its Governmental Advisory Commmittee (GAC). ICANN did not observe the protocols regarding the name affixed to Taiwan and used various other means of treating it as an independent state. Thus, after some early engagement with ICANN, China ceased sending representatives to its meetings in 2001.

During the World Summit on the Information Society (WSIS) from 2002 to 2005, China joined in the attack on ICANN. It made clear its support for a takeover of its functions by an intergovernmental institution such as the International Telecommunication Union (ITU). Adding to these tensions, members of the Chinese-language technical community (not all of whom lived in or were citizens of the PRC) were also frustrated with the slow development of new technical standards enabling the DNS to represent Chinese and other non-Roman scripts. Internationalized Domain Names (IDNs) represented not only a business and political opportunity for the Chinese, but a potential threat as well. U.S. companies such as VeriSign were licensing IDN technology and could use it to enter the Chinese market. The market for registration of Chinese-language domain names is potentially a very large one. If the Chinese government and its favored state enterprises were not in control of the standards for representing Chinese characters in the DNS and if they had no direct participation in the policy processes within ICANN for adding top-level domain names (TLDs) to the DNS root, this opportunity might be threatened.

During the ICANN-China freeze period, China mounted a challenge to ICANN that was less visible but far more radical and significant than the conference diplomacy of WSIS. It created what was, in effect, an alternate DNS root for Chinese-character domain names. China's national alternative to ICANN's global DNS root used the same technical approach pioneered by competing root operator New.Net to ensure that the new domains were globally compatible.[10] Chinese characters would appear as top-level domains inside China. If one of these Chinese-character domains was queried from outside China, the uniquely Chinese names would be rendered compatible with the global Internet by having the name servers add the globally recognized ICANN country code top-level domain, .cn, to the end of them. China created three new top-level domains in this fashion: Zhong guo, Gong si, and Wang luo. These additions were done some time in 2003 but were not widely publicized, and if inquiries were made, they were downplayed as "experimental" by the Chinese. In 2006, however, as ICANN began to develop new policies for the addition of top-level domains, the online version of *People's Daily* openly acknowledged the existence of these new domains and claimed that "[Chinese] Internet users don't have to surf the Web via the servers under the management of the Internet Corporation for Assigned Names and Numbers (ICANN) of the United States."[11]

Due to these preemptive moves, and because of China's realization after WSIS that ICANN was not going to go away, China and ICANN reached a mutual accommodation sometime in 2009. At the June 2009 ICANN meeting, the PRC officially returned to the GAC, sending a divisional director of the Ministry of Industry and Information Technology (MIIT) to represent it. ICANN also made concessions, agreeing to rename Taiwan as "Chinese Taipei" and (more substantively) to create a "fast track" for the recognition and creation of new "country code top level domains" (ccTLDs) in non-Roman scripts.[12] Unlike ICANN's new generic top-level domain program for ordinary businesses and organizations, these new "ccTLDs" did not have to wait two or three additional years while stringent policies and regulations governing their award and use were developed; nor did they have to pay six-figure application fees or recurring annual fees based on the number of registrations. Indeed, the whole concept of a "country code TLD" was based on an ISO standard assigning two-letter codes using the Roman alphabet to specific geographic territories. Since no such standard existed for the rest of the world's writing scripts, the characterization of these new top-level domains as "country codes" provided political cover for a land grab by national ccTLD monopolies. By giving countries such as China, Russia, and India a privileged and accelerated right to get new top-level domains representing their country names in native scripts, ICANN and the U.S. government were giving the world's states an economically valuable and politically powerful gift in order to keep them happy with the ICANN regime.

China and the Internet Governance Forum

When WSIS failed to bring about a major change in ICANN's status, China acceded to the creation of the Internet Governance Forum (IGF). The IGF is yet another new institution associated with the Internet that fails to conform to cyber-nationalist norms. Although nominally created under UN auspices, it is a multistakeholder environment that mixes governments, civil society, the Internet technical community, and business actors in nonbinding dialogue about Internet issues. All actors are afforded equal status. Within the IGF, China initially took a low profile. Its main accomplishment was to insist that the IGF directly grapple with the issue of U.S. unilateral control over critical Internet resources. On several occasions it has expressed sharp (and valid) criticism of efforts by the United States and its allies in the private sector to avoid confronting those issues in IGF meetings. At one point a frustrated China publicly expressed opposition to the renewal of the IGF after its initial five-year mandate expired because of its avoidance of the WSIS-related issues. That position was later moderated, and now seems to have been replaced with reliance on a longer-term war of attrition that attempts to make the IGF gradually become more intergovernmental and a standard part of the UN bureaucracy.

This war of attrition attained tangible success in late 2010. In the early days of the IGF, no one at the UN headquarters was paying much attention to the IGF or even to the Internet. This situation has changed. China has taken the lead in shaping the institutional environment for the IGF at the UN. Chinese diplomat Sha Zukang, who represented China during WSIS, became the United Nations' undersecretary-general for economic and social affairs on July 1, 2007. From that platform he has made a series of moves designed to bring the IGF more under the control of the UN system and make it more intergovernmental in character. China has the support of many Arab states and the BRICs in this regard. (Brazil, Russia, India, and China make up the BRICs.) While business interests and the United States thought they were minimizing damage by making the Committee on Science and Technology for Development (CSTD), a near-dormant entity within the UN Economic and Social Council (ECOSOC), responsible for WSIS follow-up, they were later outmaneuvered. The UN resolution renewing IGF was conditioned on a review and "improvement" process that made it more intergovernmental. In setting the parameters of the improvement process, Undersecretary Sha, with the support of other cyber-nationalist states, minimized the role of civil society and business. He also reinstituted the old way of excluding non-state actors from speaking during parts of the public consultations.

These moves actually do more to exclude the United Nations from the broader currents of Internet governance than to assert UN control over Internet governance. Without full and equal-status participation of Internet businesses and users, the United Nations is unlikely to have much influence and the IGF will not be much of a forum. But the changes bring a halt to the multistakeholder innovations and reforms that came from WSIS.

China and the Regional Internet Registries

The Regional Internet Registries (RIRs) manage and set policy for Internet Protocol (IP) address resources. Like ICANN, the RIRs are private, nonprofit corporations that have transnational governance responsibilities. Although they are not under the direct contractual authority of the U.S. Commerce Department, they do rely on ICANN for the initial allocations of large address blocks, which they subdelegate to Internet service providers (ISPs) and organizations in their regions. China has consistently attempted to make IP addresses conform to the governmental, sovereigntist model. Led by the Chinese director of the ITU's Telecommunication Standardization Bureau, Houlin Zhao, it has backed efforts by the ITU to compete with the RIRs.[13] It also supported a more recent attempt by the ITU to propose a parallel system of IPv6 address allocation based on country Internet registries.[14] Within its region, it has acquired addresses through its own National Internet Registry (NIR) rather than allowing ISPs and companies to go directly to the IP addressing authority for its region, the Asia Pacific Network Information Centre (APNIC). The cyber-nationalist pattern is consistent here, too.

International Incidents

The Chinese Communist Party has more direct authority over the domestic institutional environment than it does over the international regime. It has used this authority to create a comprehensive system of blocking/censorship, public-opinion management, and intermediary responsibility that has come to be known colloquially as the Great Firewall of China. Even so, its attempt to maintain and enforce cyber-nationalism is challenged domestically by four tendencies: the need for Internet operations to be globally coordinated and compatible; the ability of domestic actors to grasp the communicative opportunities of the Internet; the greater transparency fostered by Internet communications; and China's need to maintain trade relationships with the rest of the world.

The China country profile in this volume covers the domestic situation in more detail. This chapter focuses instead on the way China's attempt to maintain cyber-nationalism has interacted or conflicted with the globalized nature of Internet operations and governance. It describes the way the Chinese state's attempt to tamper with the domain name system to support censorship "spilled out" into the rest of the world. It looks next at a routing misconfiguration incident that created a minipanic in the United States. Then it shows how cyber espionage efforts traced to China are also shaping global attitudes toward Internet governance.

Exporting the Great Firewall?

DNS root servers tell Internet users where to find the information needed to connect to other domains. In March 2010, Internet users outside China found that their access to popular Web sites such as Facebook, YouTube, and Twitter was impaired. The problem, which was known to affect users in Chile and California, was eventually traced to their use of root servers located in China.[15]

The origins of this story go back to the early days of ICANN, when U.S. control of the DNS was becoming a global political issue. Root servers are the starting point for the hierarchical resolution process that makes domain names globally unique and matches IP addresses to domains. Because of the Internet's U.S. origins, all but three of the world's 13 root servers were located in the United States; a few were run by the U.S. military. Many national leaders (assuming they were aware of the problem) viewed this as an unacceptable kind of dependency on a foreign power. Although many of the people who were concerned about this had no idea what a DNS root server actually does, they were quite sure that they wanted one in their country. And there were, in fact, legitimate technical reasons supporting a greater geographical diversification of the root server infrastructure, such as greater resiliency in the face of outages and reduced latency in response times.

A zero-sum solution to this problem would have required taking root servers away from the United States and moving them to other countries. Aside from being a non-starter politically, given U.S. power and the lack of any institutionalized process for designating and removing root server operators, such a measure had the potential to create adjustment and compatibility issues. Therefore, leading DNS experts developed and implemented a technical modification that allowed existing root servers to multiply themselves with "instances" elsewhere in the world.[16] This was a positive-sum solution that used some aspects of the "anycast" service to make an authoritative name-server operator provide access to a single-named server in multiple locations.

China was one of the first countries to set up "mirrored" or "anycasted" root servers. There are now instances of three different root servers located in Beijing. And due to routing agreements among ISPs, it is possible that root-level domain name queries coming from sources outside China might make use of those root server instances in China.

What makes this interdependency interesting is that China relies heavily on domain name blocking to implement the GFW. As a result, its name servers will modify or tamper with responses to queries about where to find the blocked domains. If someone lives outside China and, because of network topography, happens to query a root name server hosted in China, that person's queries will pass through the Great Firewall, potentially subjecting the person to the same censorship imposed on Chinese citizens. Apparently, China's version of the "I" root was not visible to the rest of the world. In early March 2010, however, it seems to have become visible.[17] As a result, Chinese censorship "spilled out" and affected a number of users outside of China. Despite some countermeasures taken by the main root server operators, the problem happened again in June. Like the incident described in the next section, the Chinese impact on the rest of the world's Internet was almost certainly unintentional.

The BGP "Hijack"

U.S.–China Internet relations were inflamed again in November 2010, when the U.S.–China Economic and Security Review Commission (USCESRC) issued its report to Congress.[18] Discussing what was probably an unintentional routing-prefix configuration error that took place in April, the USCESRC stated that "a state-owned Chinese telecommunications firm 'hijacked' massive volumes of Internet traffic. For about 18 minutes on April 8, 2010, China Telecom advertised erroneous network traffic routes that instructed U.S. and other foreign Internet traffic to travel through Chinese servers."[19]

In technical jargon, this is a problem in the border gateway protocol (BGP) routing protocol, sometimes called "BGP hijacks" or more frequently known as "BGP leaks," in which an ISP announces a route it is not authorized to service and the route announcement is propagated to other ISPs and begins to affect routing patterns around the world. Inaccurate or unauthorized BGP route announcements happen frequently and are a well-known problem. While the USCESRC report did not explicitly assert that the prefix leak was intentional, the report framed the event as an "interception of Internet traffic" rather than as a routing configuration error. Those hostile overtones were picked up and amplified by the U.S. mass media, which publicized the idea that China had diverted "15 percent of the Internet" to its own country. The "15 percent of the Internet" claim confused Internet traffic volume with Internet route announcements—a completely false equation. Internet technical experts quickly weighed in to correct the understanding of the situation. According to Arbor Networks' Craig Labovitz, "This hijack had limited impact on the Internet routing infrastructure—most of the Internet ignored the hijack for various technical reasons."[20] Labovitz wrote that far from diverting "massive amounts of the Internet's traffic," there was "no statistically significant increase for either [of the two Chinese Internet service providers]. While we did observe modest changes in traffic volumes for carriers within China, the BGP hijack had limited impact on traffic volumes to or from the rest of the world."[21]

Both the incident and the reaction to it underscore the global interdependencies created by the Internet and the dangerous tendency for interstate rivalries to inflame mundane operational problems into military and political tensions. Correctly interpreted, the April 2010 Chinese routing hijack had little if anything to do with China and its geopolitical rivalry with the United States, but instead should be viewed as a spur for instituting more secure routing protocols on the Internet. Greater routing security is something that would benefit both China and the United States—and proper implementation of such a goal would require cooperation between the United States and China especially.

Cyber Espionage and the Blurring Line between State and Nonstate Actors

As China becomes a powerful state on the global scene it will—like other powerful states before it—engage in power and spying games with its rivals. Just as traditional, "meatspace" (i.e., physical) forms of spying and infiltration provide governments with ways to disrupt their enemies' plans or obtain valuable information, so does Internet-based espionage. Evidence in the West suggests that China has been especially active and effective at using cybercrime tactics to monitor and disrupt its enemies.

In early 2009 the Information Warfare Monitor (IWM) released one of the first unclassified reports detailing the activities of a cyber espionage effort.[22] The network, dubbed GhostNet, appeared to have been controlled from commercial Internet accounts located on the island of Hainan, China. A year later, another report from the IWM and the Shadowserver Foundation uncovered more extensive evidence of a China-based computer espionage network targeting India: its diplomatic missions, government departments, national security and defense groups, Indian academics, and journalists focused on China. The Office of the Tibetan Dalai Lama was also targeted.[23] Leaked State Department cables show that U.S. and German government agencies were becoming concerned about Chinese cyber espionage as early as 2006.[24]

The Google-China incident (covered in more detail in the China country profile in this volume) can be seen as a straightforward clash between China's domestic policy and Internet freedom in that it involved a transnational business founded on the free and indiscriminate dissemination of information demanded by users. It was that, but it was something more as well. Google's sudden questioning of its presence in China was triggered not by ongoing Chinese censorship but by a break-in to its corporate network that Google believed could be attributed to Chinese state-sponsored or state-directed actors. This break-in not only involved the theft of proprietary information but also seemed to target the e-mail accounts of human rights activists.

State Department cables released by Wikileaks provide support for the conclusion not only that China's government was involved in the break-ins, but also that China's government views the Internet in general and Google in particular as state-directed pieces that are being played in its geopolitical power competition with the United States:

A well-placed contact claims that the Chinese government coordinated the recent intrusions of Google systems. According to our contact, the closely held operations were directed at the Politburo Standing Committee level. . . . Chinese concerns over the recent Google threat to take down the company's Chinese-language search engine google.cn over censorship and hacking allegations were focused on the service's growing popularity among Chinese Internet users and a perception that the USG and Google were working in concert.[25]

Ties between China's leadership and Google rival Baidu are also asserted in the cables. The current dialogue over Chinese cyber espionage may be overlooking the extent to which China is subject to the same tactics from other countries, especially the United States. The State Department cables, for example, warn darkly of "potential linkages of China's top companies with the PRC [state]" and claim that such links "illustrate the government's use of its 'private sector' in support of information warfare objectives."[26] Coming from the United States, it sounds very much like the policeman at Rick's casino in the movie *Casablanca* proclaiming that he is "shocked, shocked to discover that gambling is going on here." The massive U.S. military-industrial complex and the deep, long-term ties between Internet technical experts, cyber security firms, and Defense Department and the Department of Homeland Security's research funding are almost exactly the same as those described in threatening terms in the State Department cables.

An inherent feature of the nation-state system of governance is that concepts of order and security apply first and foremost in the domestic sovereign's jurisdiction. Different, negotiable standards apply to outsiders. Because China believes that it is both necessary and justified to "manage" the information environment and control political activity, it makes sense that it would use cyber espionage to its fullest capacity to survey its international and domestic environment.

Ongoing Tensions between China's Sovereigntism and the Internet

To decode the paradox of the Chinese Internet we need to return to the dialogue within the international communist movement about the future of socialism. By the 1950s it was clear that true, thoroughgoing socialism—an economy devoid of private property, a price system, or markets—had failed economically and was simply unworkable. Leftist intellectuals contemplated two ways forward, one known as reform and the other as transformation. Reform did not mean, as many Westerners assume it does, a liberalization of economy and society that leads to convergence with the West. The communists referred to that path as *transformation*—the abandonment of communism and a move toward liberal democracy. A *reformed* communism would make socialism economically viable by permitting the existence of enough market forces and trade to deliver growth, while retaining the Leninist approach to centralized political control associated with classical communism. This is clearly the path that China has chosen. The whole point of China's reform process is to benefit from Western technology and from trade with the global market economy *without* converging into the West's liberal democratic governance model. Its opening and reform process was and is intended to deliver continued economic development without fundamental political change. Continued economic growth, they believe, makes political transformation unnecessary.

At least since the early 1990s, China's approach to information and communication technology has played a significant role in facilitating the achievement of these reform objectives. An early discourse among Chinese intellectuals about "informatization" set the stage for this. The CCP viewed information technology as the best way to scale up the control capabilities of the state to keep pace with its growth and greater wealth. In a typically pragmatic Chinese style, which has been described as "touching the stones to cross the river," the Chinese Communist Party has gone through repeated cycles of loosening control to foster development and growth, and then tightening restrictions to ensure that the party stays in control. The first step releases suppressed economic energy and generates growth; the second phase prunes the development so that it conforms to the parameters of the SME and does not threaten the stability and security of the political system.

An observation by the former Beijing bureau chief of the *Financial Times* dispels any notion that the economic development based on these reforms is inherently incompatible with party control:

If you benchmark the Chinese Communist Party against a definitional checklist authored by Robert Service, the veteran historian of the Soviet Union, the similarities are remarkable. As with communism in its heyday elsewhere, the party in China has eradicated or emasculated political rivals, eliminated the autonomy of the courts and media, restricted religion and civil society, denigrated rival versions of nationhood, centralized political power, established extensive networks of security police, and dispatched dissidents to labor camps. There is a good reason why the Chinese system is often described as "market-Leninism."[27]

Unfortunately, in the West there is a persistent refusal or inability to grasp and accept the meaning of the SME. Westerners, and especially American politicians and businesses, are constantly mistaking China's *reform* with *transformation*. As a result, they are repeatedly disappointed and angry with China's suppression of individual rights and its limited and fitful openings to foreign investment and free trade. United States policies that attempt to change China are usually based on the premise that the country's leaders are making false steps on the road to embracing liberal democratic norms and models. They are not. Zhao Ziyang and a few other Chinese leaders from the mid-1980s may have flirted with or embraced transformation, but the Tiananmen Square incident settled that issue decisively within China's party.[28] Since then, the CCP mainstream has reaffirmed the notion of the SME and has explicitly rejected convergence. One need not approve of this approach to accept its reality and form one's expectations based on it.

It would make sense, then, that the Chinese state's approach to information and communications technologies (ICTs) in general and the Internet in particular is neither to completely suppress it in order to preserve a brittle and unpopular regime, nor to provide the Internet-based economy and society free rein. It is a constant, iterative attempt to release productive forces and then corral them into supporting the continued control and dominance of the CCP. Rebecca MacKinnon has called this "networked authoritarianism,"[29] although I am not sure it is the best label. The term may attribute too much intentionality to China's approach. What is really going on is an improvised response to the contradictions of the socialist market economy. On one hand, the market economy part of the package thrives on open exchanges with foreigners and robust circulation of information, both of which deliver the economic development and growth needed for the CCP to maintain its legitimacy; the continued political grip of the CCP, on the other hand, requires limiting entry into the market for information services, constant monitoring and surveillance of communications, propaganda activities, repressive capabilities, and accurate targeting of political and social threats.

Note that the attempt to subject the Internet to hierarchical control relies in many respects on the unique capabilities of networked computers, whether it is the use of DNS blocking and deep packet inspection to filter Web and search-engine queries, the mobilization of armies of freelance propagandists to search for and intervene in public discourses critical of the government, the surreptitious use of cyber espionage, or the "identification and record-keeping" activities invoked by Wang Chen. In an information age, the label "networked authoritarianism" is practically redundant—if there is to be authoritarianism on this scale, how can it *not* be networked? Still, China's online economy and innovative capacity is certainly stunted by these self-limiting applications of ICTs. While China's huge domestic economy makes the growth of major Internet companies inevitable, it is hard to imagine major service innovations or globally competitive online service providers emerging from this environment.

The oscillation between progress and control appears regularly across a number of different economic sectors, including China's approach to telecommunications sector reform.[30] In sum, the experience of China and the Internet is the latest episode in the familiar tale of Chinese reform, which recalls the parable of the man who caught a tiger by the tail. As the tiger gallops and struggles along, the man finds it more and more demanding to maintain his grip. But if he lets go, the tiger will surely turn and destroy him. Unlike the man in the parable, the CCP is, to some extent, strengthened by the tiger's energy—but the tiger keeps getting bigger and bigger. How long this cycle can go on is difficult to know. For those who seek transformation of communist China the trick is to conceptualize how this self-reinforcing cycle works and how it might break down. One thing seems certain: for other governments, especially the United States, neither external intervention nor subversion directed from outside is likely to work. The CCP thrives on exploitation of nationalism and by positioning itself as the people's defender against the humiliations and dominations of foreigners. If anything can make the tiger and the man hanging onto its tail work together in harmony it would be that process.

Notes

1. China Network Information Center, "Internet Fundamental Data," June 30, 2010, http://www .cnnic.cn/en/index/0O/index.htm, accessed January 5, 2011.

2. Ibid.; U.S. CIA, *The World Factbook*, https://www.cia.gov/library/publications/the-world-factbook/ geos/ch.html.

3. Milton Mueller, *Networks and States: The Global Politics of Internet Governance* (Cambridge, MA: MIT Press, 2010).

4. Information Office of the State Council of the People's Republic of China, chapter 5, "The Internet in China," June 8, 2010, http://www.gov.cn/english/2010-06/08/content_1622956 .htm.

5. Ibid.

6. Information Office of the State Council of the People's Republic of China, chapter 6, "The Internet in China."

7. Wang Chen, "Development and Administration of Our Country's Internet," delivered on April 29, 2010, before the Standing Committee of the National People's Congress. Unofficial English translation is available at http://www.hrichina.org/public/contents/article?revision%5fid=175119 &item%5fid=175084.

8. Christopher Bodeen, "China Slams Clinton's Internet Speech: 'Information Imperialism,'" Associated Press, January 22, 2010, http://www.huffingtonpost.com/2010/01/22/china-slams -clintons-inte_n_432691.html.

9. Sami ben Gharbia, "The Internet Freedom Fallacy and the Arab Digital Activism," Samibengharbia.com, September 17, 2010, http://samibengharbia.com/2010/09/17/the-internet -freedom-fallacy-and-the-arab-digital-activism.

10. For a good discussion of this, see the comments appended to Rebecca MacKinnon, "China's New Domain Names: Lost in Translation," CircleID, February 28, 2006, http://www.circleid.com/ posts/chinas_new_domain_names_lost_in_translation/#1905. The blog itself understates the significance of the situation, but the comments on the post and the tests reported there clarify the situation.

11. "China Adds Top-Level Domain Names," *People's Daily* Online, February 28, 2006, http:// english.people.com.cn/200602/28/eng20060228_246712.html.

12. A country code is a top-level domain based on the ISO-3166 standard of two-letter codes, such as .cn for China, .fr for France, or .br for Brazil. They were created in the mid-1980s as alternatives to the so-called generic top-level domains (.com, .net, .org, .mil) at the insistence of some non-U.S. Internet developers. Not wanting to put himself in the position of deciding who or what qualified as a "country," Internet pioneer Jon Postel found an existing ISO standard, originally developed for postal uses, which assigned unique two-letter codes to each territory. Most of these territories correspond to nations, but many (e.g., .io for Indian Ocean) did not.

13. Houlin Zhao, "ITU and Internet Governance," input to the seventh meeting of the ITU Council Working Group on WSIS, December 12–14, 2004, Geneva, 30 November 2004. In this WSIS contribution Zhao wrote, "in addition to the current arrangements for allocation of IPv6 address by the RIRs, one could reserve a portion of the large IPv6 space for country-based assignments, that is, assign a block to a country at no cost, and let the country itself manage this kind of address in IPv6."

14. Sureswaran Ramadass, *A Study on the IPv6 Address Allocation and Distribution Methods* (Geneva: International Telecommunication Union, 2009).

15. Earl Zmijewski, "Accidentally Importing Censorship," Renesys Blog, March 30, 2010, http:// www.renesys.com/blog/2010/03/fouling-the-global-nest.shtml.

16. Tim Hardie, "Distributing Authoritative Name Servers via Shared Unicast Addresses," RFC 3258, April 2002.

17. Zmijewski, "Accidentally Importing Censorship."

18. U.S.–China Economic and Security Review Commission (USCESRC), *2010 Report to Congress of the U.S.–China Economic and Security Review Commission* at the 11th Congress, Second Session, November 2010.

19. U.S.–China Economic and Security Review Commission, Section 2, *2010 Report to Congress of the U.S.–China Economic and Security Review Commission*, November 2010, http://www.uscc.gov/ annual_report/2010/annual_report_full_10.pdf.

20. Craig Labovitz, "China Hijacks 15% of Internet Traffic?" Arbor Networks Security to the Core Blog, November 19, 2010, http://asert.arbornetworks.com/2010/11/china-hijacks-15-of-internet-traffic.

21. Craig Labovitz, "Additional Discussion of the April China BGP Hijack Incident," Arbor Networks Security to the Core Blog, November 22, 2010, http://asert.arbornetworks.com/2010/11/additional-discussion-of-the-april-china-bgp-hijack-incident.

22. Information Warfare Monitor, *Tracking Ghostnet: Investigating a Cyber-espionage Network*, March 29, 2009, http://www.tracking-ghost.net.

23. Information Warfare Monitor and the Shadowserver Foundation, *Shadows in the Cloud: Investigating Cyber Espionage 2.0*, April 6, 2010, http://shadows-in-the-cloud.net.

24. The German Federal Office for the Protection of the Constitution (BfV) delivered a briefing on its analysis of the cyber threat posed by the People's Republic of China (PRC), which appears to mirror conclusions drawn by the U.S. intelligence community. The BfV surmises that the intention of PRC actors is espionage, and the primary attack vector used in their malicious activity is socially engineered e-mail messages containing malware attachments and/or embedded links to hostile Web sites. From October 2006 to October 2007, 500 such e-mail operations were conducted against a wide range of German organizations, and the attacks appear to be increasing in scope and sophistication. See Wikileaks cable at "A Selection from the Cache of Diplomatic Dispatches," *New York Times*, November 28, 2010, http://www.nytimes.com/interactive/2010/11/28/world/20101128-cables-viewer.html#report/. Once on the site, click on "China" to get to the cable.

25. "US Embassy Cables: Google Hacking 'Directed by Chinese Politburo Itself,'" Latest China (The Guardian online China News), December 4, 2010, http://latestchina.com/article/?rid=24361.

26. "WikiLeaks Cables Reveal Fears over Chinese Cyber Warfare," Latest China (The Guardian online China News), December 4, 2010, http://latestchina.com/article/?rid=24367.

27. Richard McGregor, "Five Myths about the Chinese Communist Party—Market-Leninism Lives," *Foreign Policy* (online), January/February 2011, http://www.foreignpolicy.com/articles/2011/01/02/5_myths_about_the_chinese_communist_party.

28. Willy Wo-Lap Lam, *The Era of Zhao Ziyang: Power Struggle in China, 1986–88* (Hong Kong: A.B. Books and Stationery, 1989).

29. Rebecca MacKinnon, "China's Internet White Paper: Networked Authoritarianism in Action," RConversation Blog, June 15, 2010, http://rconversation.blogs.com/rconversation/2010/06/chinas-internet-white-paper-networked-authoritarianism.html.

30. Milton Mueller and Zixiang Tan, *China in the Information Age: Telecommunications and the Dilemmas of Reform* (Westport, CT: Praeger, 1996); and Irene S. Wu, *From Iron Fist to Invisible Hand: The Uneven Path of Telecommunications Reform in China* (Stanford, CA: Stanford University Press, 2009).

10 Corporate Accountability in Networked Asia

Rebecca MacKinnon

In 2010, Google's defiance of Chinese government censorship demands, followed by its decision to remove its Chinese search operations from mainland China, grabbed front-page headlines around the world. Human rights groups and socially responsible investors praised the global Internet giant for standing up to the Chinese government's censorship policies. China's sophisticated system of Internet censorship and control depends on the compliance of domestic and foreign corporate intermediaries, which are required by Chinese law to help authorities track user activity and to remove or prevent publication and transmission of politically sensitive content on or through their services.

Yet China is by no means the only Asian country where companies face government pressure to reveal user data or remove content in ways that violate internationally recognized human rights principles. Local and international human rights groups point to Vietnam, Burma, Thailand, and the Philippines as countries where "Chinese-style" Internet controls are increasingly deployed to silence or monitor dissent, often implemented by means of private-sector information and communication technologies (ICTs) service providers, carriers, and platforms.[1] Reporters Without Borders includes Thailand, Sri Lanka, Malaysia, Australia, and South Korea on its watch list of countries with surveillance trends heading in the wrong direction.[2]

Recent studies of global surveillance and censorship by the OpenNet Initiative (ONI) and others are showing that private-sector Internet and telecommunications companies play an increasingly important role in government efforts to control what citizens can or cannot do in cyberspace.[3] Even in Asia's most vibrant democracies such as South Korea and India, companies—domestic and foreign—face government demands for censorship and user-data handover in ways that violate Internet users' rights to free expression and privacy.

The idea that upholding free expression and privacy rights should be a component of "corporate social responsibility" (CSR)—alongside other corporate responsibilities including labor standards, environmental protection, and sustainability—is a new concept for nongovernmental organizations (NGOs), investors, companies, and governments in the industrialized West, let alone anywhere else.[4] In the first ONI volume, *Access Denied*, Jonathan Zittrain and John Palfrey called for an industry code of conduct.[5] In 2008 came the launch of the Global Network Initiative (GNI), a multi-stakeholder initiative through which companies not only make a commitment to core principles of free expression and privacy, but also agree to be evaluated independently on the extent to which they actually adhere to these principles.[6] In the second ONI volume, *Access Controlled*, Colin Maclay examined the challenges facing this newly formed organization, a core challenge being the recruitment of members.[7] As of this writing, only three companies, Google, Microsoft, and Yahoo!, have agreed to be held publicly accountable for the way in which they handle government demands for censorship and surveillance around the world. No other North American companies have made this public commitment, and no companies from any other continents or regions have yet been willing to make a similar public commitment to free expression and privacy as a core component of responsible business practice.

Yet other forms of CSR—including environmental, labor, and sustainability standards—are by no means foreign to Asian businesses, even in China.[8] Might public expectations for corporate accountability in the area of free speech and privacy also rise in Asia in the coming years—particularly if these expectations are fed by increased civil society activism, pushing for greater accountability and transparency by ICT companies around their interactions with governments? In this chapter I compare government censorship and surveillance demands faced by companies in authoritarian China alongside the challenges faced by companies in two neighboring democracies that also have robust ICT industries and markets: South Korea and India. I argue that efforts to hold companies other than Google, Yahoo!, and Microsoft accountable for free speech and privacy in authoritarian countries like China will face an uphill battle unless companies in Asia's democracies are pushed by domestic civil society actors to defend and protect user rights in a more robust manner than is currently the case.

China: "Networked Authoritarianism" and the Private Sector[9]

As ONI research over the past decade has shown, China has the world's most sophisticated system of Internet filtering, which blocks access to vast numbers of Web sites and online content hosted by companies and on computer servers located mainly outside China.[10] But filtering is only the top layer of the country's elaborate system of Internet censorship. For Web sites run by individuals or companies located inside China, the government has direct jurisdiction—and thus more powerful instruments of control. Why merely filter a Web page when you can get it removed from the Internet completely or prevent its publication or dissemination in the first place? Over the past decade as Internet penetration grew rapidly in China, government regulators have created strong negative incentives—including Web site registration requirements, the threat of jail sentences for individuals, and the cancellation of business licenses for companies—in order to keep certain kinds of content off the Internet.[11] Ronald Deibert and Rafal Rohozinski classify this approach to censorship as "second-generation Internet controls."[12] The Chinese government calls the system corporate "self-discipline," and hands out an annual award to companies that have done the best job of keeping their Web sites "harmonious" and free of sensitive content— ranging from the pornographic to the political.[13]

In Anglo-European legal parlance, the legal mechanism used to implement such a "self-discipline" system is a form of "intermediary liability."[14] It is the legal mechanism through which Google's Chinese search engine, Google.cn, was required to censor itself until Google redirected its simplified Chinese search engine offshore to Hong Kong.[15] All Internet companies operating within Chinese jurisdiction—domestic or foreign—are held liable for everything appearing on their search engines, blogging platforms, and social-networking services. They are also legally responsible for everything their users discuss or organize through chat clients and messaging services. In this way, much of the censorship and surveillance work is delegated and outsourced by the government to the private sector. If private companies fail to censor and monitor their users to the government's satisfaction, they will lose their business licenses and be forced to shut down.[16] All large Internet companies operating in China have entire departments of employees with hundreds of people whose sole job is to police users and censor content around the clock.[17]

Companies are also expected to play a role in the surveillance of Internet and mobile users. In a country like China where "crime" is defined broadly to include political dissent, companies with in-country operations and user data stored locally can easily find themselves complicit in the surveillance and jailing of political dissidents. The most notorious example of law enforcement compliance gone very wrong was when Yahoo!'s local Beijing staff gave to the Chinese police e-mail and user-account information of journalist Shi Tao, activist Wang Xiaoning, and at least two others engaged in political dissent.[18] There are other examples of how law enforcement compliance by foreign companies has compromised activists. In 2006, Skype partnered with a Chinese company to provide a localized version of its service, then found itself being used by Chinese authorities to track and log politically sensitive chat sessions by users inside China. This happened because Skype delegated law enforcement compliance to its local partner without sufficient attention to how the compliance was being carried out. The local partner, in turn, was merely following standard industry practice that is commonplace for domestic Chinese Internet companies.[19]

In this way, the private sector in China plays a key role in a political innovation that I call "networked authoritarianism."[20] Compared to classic 20th-century authoritarianism, this new form of Internet-age authoritarianism embraces the reality that even when extensive filtering regimes are put in place, people cannot be prevented from accessing and creating a broad range of Internet content and holding all kinds of conversations, including those related to politics and policy. Networked authoritarianism thus accepts and allows a lot more give and take between government and citizens than in a pre-Internet authoritarian state. The regime uses the Internet not only to extend its control but also to enhance its legitimacy. While one party remains in control, a wide range of conversations about the country's problems rage on Web sites and social-networking services. The government follows online chatter and sometimes people are able to use the Internet to call attention to social problems or injustices, and even manage to have an impact on government policies. As a result, the average person with Internet or mobile access has a much greater sense of freedom—and may even feel like he or she has the ability to speak and be heard—in ways that were not possible under classic authoritarianism. It also makes most people a lot less likely to join a movement calling for radical political change. Meanwhile, the government exercises targeted censorship focused on activities and conversations that pose the greatest threat to the regime's power, and also devotes considerable resources to proactively seeding and manipulating the nation's online discourse about domestic and international events.[21]

Thus, while over 500 million Chinese people are finding their lives greatly enhanced by the Internet, Communist Party control over the bureaucracy and courts has strengthened, and the regime's institutional commitments to protect the universal rights and freedoms of all its citizens have weakened.[22] According to a recent report by the Dui Hua Foundation, in 2008 arrests and indictments on charges of "endangering state security"—the most common charge used in cases of political, religious, or ethnic dissent—more than doubled for the second time in three years.[23] Meanwhile, the Chinese government has made clear in its 2010 Internet White Paper that the rapid nationwide expansion of Internet and mobile penetration is a strategic priority. The development of a vibrant indigenous Internet and telecommunications sector is critical for China's long-term global economic competitiveness.[24] At the same time, Chinese companies are fully expected to support and reinforce domestic political stability, and to ensure that ICTs will not be used in a manner that threatens Communist Party rule.[25]

The China case demonstrates how companies can be used as an opaque extension of state power, helping authoritarian regimes to control and manipulate citizens with a lighter hand than was possible in the pre-Internet age while still maintaining power and preventing viable opposition movements from emerging. But what about democracies? In democratic societies, can ICT companies be used as an opaque tool for incumbent leaders, ruling political parties, and other powerful groups to manipulate public discourse and marginalize critics? Trends in South Korea and India suggest that such a situation is possible and may already be happening to different degrees. To prevent creeping networked authoritarian tendencies in democratic societies, stronger strategic alliances between civil society and industry will be needed to push back against abuse of government power by means of digital networks and platforms.

South Korea: From Dictatorship to E-Democracy to "Free-Floating Control"[26]

After decades of dictatorship, South Korea underwent a successful transition to democracy in the 1990s. At the same time, thanks to a strong government emphasis on ICT investment over the past two decades, by 2009 more than 80 percent of South Koreans had become Internet users, with Internet access reaching more than 95 percent of households.[27] Upon his inauguration in 2003, late President Roh Moo-hyun was hailed in the international media as the world's first "Internet president" of the world's most advanced "Internet democracy."[28] His narrow election victory was widely credited to viral mobilization by his online supporters via citizen-media Web sites like OhmyNews.[29] Yet by 2009 domestic and international human rights groups were sounding the alarm about mounting and blatant violations of Korean citizens' right to free expression and privacy on the Internet.

In March 2010, Reporters Without Borders placed South Korea on its watch list, citing "a liberticidal legislative arsenal that is inducing netizens to practice self-censorship—all that in the name of the fight against dissemination of 'false information.'"[30] After visiting South Korea in May 2010 and meeting with local human rights organizations as well as government officials, the United Nations special rapporteur on freedom of expression, Frank La Rue, concluded, "I am concerned that in recent years, there has been a shrinking space for freedom of expression in the Republic of Korea." Online expression, he wrote in a press statement, was being squeezed by "arbitrary procedures for the deletion of information on the Internet" as a result of the broadening of regulatory requirements placed on Internet service providers (ISPs) and other content-hosting services.[31] He also cited South Korea's real-name identification requirement for Internet portals, which he concluded "has the potential to undermine individuals' right to express opinions, particularly criticisms of the Government, as well as the right to privacy."[32]

Laws requiring real-name registration tied to the National ID system for all users of Internet portals and services over a certain size, as well as other laws targeting "spread of rumors," defamation, and "campaigning" during an election period, were first enacted during the Roh administration.[33] The reasons for their enactment are familiar to many democratic societies in the Internet age: protecting innocent people against cyber harassment, cyber bullying, and cyber attack. By the middle of the first decade of the 21st century, cyber bullying had become a serious social problem in Korea: vicious cyber mobs had caused the suicide of several celebrities and turned ordinary citizens into national pariahs for being caught on cell-phone cameras engaging in offensive yet relatively common behavior.[34] South Korean government, industry, and society at large were by 2003 already beginning to feel the cost of sophisticated cyber attacks.[35] A 2006 poll revealed that 85 percent of South Korean high school students were under stress from cyber bullying.[36] Real-ID requirements on Internet platforms and enhanced surveillance capabilities were touted by policymakers as a solution to social problems and crimes that the Internet had enabled, amplified, and exacerbated.

However, South Korean human rights activists argue that since the current president, Lee Myung-bak, took office in 2008, government measures have had an increasingly adverse impact on free expression and privacy. The ruling party, they say, has used media and communications laws to maximize its own political advantage, resulting in a marked "chilling effect" on political speech.[37] Measures include deletion or "temporary blocking" of Internet postings that criticize the government and powerful individuals, and prosecutions of individuals for dissemination of information characterized as "false communication using electronic communication facilities for the purpose of derogating public interest."[38] Laws against dissemination of false information, combined with the real-name registration requirement for all Internet services with more than 100,000 visitors per day, have resulted in the identification and prosecution of a number of Internet users for speech that is supposed to be protected under international human rights norms. Examples include the arrest of a teenager who proposed a student strike on a popular forum, and the arrest of the influential economic commentator known as "Minerva" for posting articles critical of the government's currency policy.[39] The man who wrote pseudonymously as "Minerva," Park Dae-sung, was identified by government investigators because the Internet portal Daum was required by law to hand over records of the account holder's real identity and National ID number. He was eventually acquitted, but only after spending five months in jail. Human rights groups argued that his experience has had a chilling effect on other citizens who might otherwise be motivated to post critiques of government policies online.[40] In December 2010, South Korea's Constitutional Court ruled that the telecommunications law banning the spread of false information was unconstitutional, citing unclear definitions in the law of terms such as "false" and "public interest."[41] While this ruling was hailed by digital rights groups as a major victory, other laws, including the real-ID requirements, remain in force.

While the Internet initially had a politically disruptive and democratizing effect on South Korean politics, enabling a political insurgent to win election in 2002 by circumventing political narratives promoted by mainstream broadcast and print media, the Internet has been used by the current regime as part of its efforts to chill dissent and marginalize critics.[42] Scholar Kwang-Suk Lee describes this process as an evolution from a dictatorship reliant on centralized, hierarchical control to a democracy whose political establishment seeks, through laws passed by a democratically elected legislature, to develop a new "distributed and ubiquitous network model" of governance and manipulation of the public discourse, enabled by "positive technologies for free floating control" which "can hide under an ethical patina the real intention of control directed at establishing the new digital rule of cybersociety."[43]

In 2009, Google decided that it would not contribute to this trend. In April of that year the company announced that the local Korean section of its video-sharing service, YouTube, would disable users from uploading videos or posting comments because allowing them to do so without registering their real names and ID numbers was a violation of local law. The company cited a concern for South Korean Internet users' right to freedom of expression, stating on its official blog, "We believe that it is important for free expression that people have the right to remain anonymous, if they choose."[44]

Unnamed executives quoted in the press at the time indicated that South Korean companies resent being used as agents for the chilling of free expression in their country, but find themselves in a weaker position to resist given that their main customer base—and in many cases sole market—is domestic. In the wake of Google's announcement, The Hankyoreh news Web site quoted an unnamed executive at one of South Korea's major Internet portals who said, "When I saw Google's decision, I was jealous and at the same time deeply distressed. . . . South Korean businesses will have to endure criticism from users while following unwanted regulations."[45] The *Korea Times* quoted a similarly frustrated official from Daum, the country's second-largest Web portal: "The increasing government regulations can't help Korean Web portals if Internet users feel they're on a short leash. Korea is one of the few countries where local companies introduced enough quality services to stay ahead of global Internet giants in the market, but now it seems we may be losing some of our competitive edge."[46]

In China, where there is little hope of a fair hearing in the courts, no free media coverage, and no recourse to oppositional politics, executives can ill afford to stand up to the government. However, South Korean companies, operating in a democracy, are in a much stronger position to advocate on behalf of the rights of their users, challenge government orders in cases that are arguably unconstitutional or even illegal, and push for changes in law so that they will not be compelled to act as de facto opaque extensions of the ruling political power in a way that taints their own relationship with users and customers.

It appears that at least some attempts are being made in this direction. In April 2009, the *Korea Times* reported that K-Internet, an industry lobby of 150 Internet companies, protested against a controversial bill proposed in parliament by members of the ruling Grand National Party that would grant intelligence authorities greater powers to intercept user communications on mobile telephone networks and Internet services, requiring all ICT companies to maintain comprehensive logs of user and

customer communications. K-Internet argued that the bill "seems to be focused exces-
sively on improving the 'efficiency' of investigations and less on protecting communication freedoms and limiting threats to privacy, posing a serious threat to the
fundamental rights of citizens, limiting the business of communications operators and
needlessly increasing social costs." An "industry insider" was further quoted as saying,
"There is no fun in joking about Pakistan and China anymore, when our own government seems to have a similar approach to Internet users."[47] Korean ICT companies
clearly see a link between protecting users' and customers' rights and their long-term
brand reputation and commercial success. It is less clear whether civil liberties groups
and Korean businesses are seeking or finding ways to work together effectively, not
only to prevent further incursion but also to regain lost ground.

India: Systematizing Surveillance[48]

In contrast to South Korea's 82 percent Internet penetration as of 2009, India's Internet
penetration hovered around 5 percent. While small in percentage terms, that still
translates into nearly 60 million Internet users—larger than South Korea's roughly 40
million.[49] More broadly, India's telecommunications market is the fastest growing in
the world, with industry executives predicting that the number of Indian mobile
phone users could surpass one billion by 2015.[50] While India has a lively blogosphere
and large communities on Orkut, Facebook, and Twitter, Indian citizens also expect
their government to protect them from the spread of online crime, shield youth from
pornography in a country where traditional values remain important, and take measures to prevent ethnic and religious violence in a country with a highly complex and
volatile mix of religions and ethnicities. Internet and mobile technologies were used
to coordinate the 2008 Mumbai terrorist attacks.[51] Cyber attacks launched from China,
uncovered in 2009, exposed the need for improved cyber security.[52] Although these
are all serious concerns for any democracy in the Internet age, the Indian government's approach to addressing these problems has raised concerns from civil liberties
groups and industry.

The Information Technology Act of 2000 established the legal framework for filtering and regulating India's Internet, as well as the procedures by which ISPs and other
Internet content and service companies can be compelled to censor online material
or share information with government authorities.[53] Several incidents took place in
the early 21st century in which the government ordered ISPs to block specific blogs
and groups hosted on international services like Orkut, Yahoo Groups, and Blogger.
These filtering efforts proved counterproductive because ISPs lacked the technical
capacity to block individual subdomains, resulting in the blanket blocking of Blogger,
Yahoo Groups, and Orkut at different points in time. This in turn prompted widespread public outcry and ridicule in the Indian media and blogosphere. It also sparked

grassroots efforts to spread knowledge among Indian Internet users about circumvention technologies so that most people who really wanted to access the offending content could still manage to do so.[54]

By the end of the decade the Indian government had changed its strategy for dealing with problematic content posted on, or transmitted through, the services of Internet companies. Ham-fisted and overbroad ISP-level filtering gave way to direct demands to the companies themselves to hand over user data and delete content.[55] The Information Technology (Amendment) Act of 2008 facilitated this transition by empowering the state to direct any ICT service to block, intercept, monitor, or decrypt any information through any computer resource.[56] The act also requires companies to have a designated point of contact for content-blocking, removal, and data requests. Company officials who fail to comply with government requests can face fines and up to seven years in jail.[57] Analysts point out that the new act has made ISP-level filtering more difficult, while strengthening and systematizing surveillance processes.[58] While most critics acknowledge the legitimate role of law enforcement, they have called for more comprehensive rules and procedures to supervise the process by which government demands are made, in order to prevent privacy violations, foul play, and political abuse.[59]

It was against this backdrop in early August 2010 that the Indian government demanded that Research in Motion (RIM), maker of Blackberry smart phones, grant Indian security agencies access to all corporate e-mail and instant-messenger communications transmitted within or through Indian borders. Failure to comply by the end of the month would result in blockage of all encrypted Blackberry traffic on Indian networks.[60] Gaining access to Blackberry's consumer services sold locally over domestic mobile carriers was one thing, and RIM expressed willingness to help the Indian government in this regard.[61] However, given that even RIM itself cannot access user data on Blackberry Enterprise Services—it is transmitted in highly encrypted form and retained on the corporate customers' servers—full compliance with the government's order in its original form is difficult if not impossible.[62] The company reportedly offered Indian authorities manual access to its messenger service with a pledge of real-time automated access by early 2011 and gained a reprieve from punishment until that time.[63]

Indian authorities claim to have begun conversations with other global companies, including Google and Skype, neither of which would comment publicly because they say they had not yet received any formal government requests or orders. Meanwhile, by late 2010 concerns were mounting in the Indian business community about the economic implications of their government's threats.[64] "We need a more balanced approach for lawful interception," wrote S. Ramadorai, vice chairman of Tata Consultancy Services Limited. "Bans and calls for bans aren't a solution. They'll disconnect India from the rest of the world. We can't allow that to happen, because then terrorists will win without even firing a bullet."[65]

Google has demonstrated that while companies are not in a position to commit civil disobedience if they want to stay in a market, they may be able to contribute to greater accountability by releasing more information about the demands that government authorities are making and whether they have been complied with. In September 2010, Google released a transparency report showing that from January through June, the Indian government made 30 content-removal requests (totaling 125 items), 53.3 percent of which Google claims to have "fully or partially complied with." Fourteen hundred and thirty Indian government requests to Google for user data ranked India the third highest in the world (behind 2,435 by Brazil and 4,287 by the United States)—not counting China.[66] The number of requests made by the Indian government to other foreign or domestic operators is unknown.

The Google Transparency Report has brought up some interesting questions. What if other multinational companies operating in India, along with Indian companies, all released similar data? Would that provide concerned citizens with at least some of the ammunition they need to hold their government accountable and ensure that censorship and surveillance in a democracy are restricted to the absolute minimum needed to protect innocent citizens' lives when they are clearly endangered by specific online activities by specific individuals, and that these tactics are not being abused for broader political purposes? Should India's vibrant activist community mount a campaign demanding that all companies operating in India must release similar transparency reports? Might they even lobby for the passage of a law requiring it? Might that at least be a first step toward necessary accountability?

Indian digital rights activists worry that India's vibrant nongovernmental sector has failed to mobilize on issues of digital free expression and privacy. In 2003, Supreme Court advocate Pavan Duggal wrote, "There is a need to change people's mindset [where most] view IT in isolation to democracy."[67] The problem does not seem to have improved over the decade. In 2007 lawyer Raman Jit Singh Chima lamented an "apparent lack of interest amongst traditional Indian civil liberties organizations in anything to do with the Internet or digital civil liberties in general."[68] In a 2009 report summarizing the state of Internet rights in India, activists Gurumurthy Kasinathan and Parminder Jeet Singh concluded that "unfortunately, in India, while different groups engage with some of the issues . . . in a piecemeal manner, there is little recognition of how they connect and reinforce each other in the building of a new social paradigm—euphemistically called an *information society*—that may require a set of coordinated civil society responses."[69]

Even in China, business leaders have expressed concern in private and semipublic forums that excessive burdens imposed on companies by governments can adversely impact innovation, which ultimately hurts national competitiveness.[70] The nature of China's legal and political system, however, makes it nearly impossible for Chinese companies to challenge government demands in the courts, take the debate to the court of public opinion through the media, or make common cause with civil liberties activists. Their position is made even weaker, unfortunately, when neighboring democracies like India and South Korea—and many other democracies around the world—set legal, technical, and regulatory precedents for government-directed censorship and surveillance to be built within privately operated digital networks without sufficient public oversight, transparency, and accountability. Chinese media frequently cite South Korean examples in particular when arguing that China's Internet controls are in line with international practice.[71]

Corporate Social Responsibility

While it may be easier said than done, the idea of CSR—the notion that long-term corporate success requires the inclusion of environmental, sustainability, and human rights concerns in companies' core technologies, management, and business practices—is being embraced by publics around the world.[72] John Ruggie, special representative of the secretary-general of the United Nations on business and human rights, in examining how companies can and should be expected to contribute to human rights around the globe, concluded that while human rights are primarily the responsibility of the nation-state, companies must also respect, protect, and uphold internationally recognized human rights norms in the spheres of human life and activity over which their business exerts influence or on which it has an impact.[73] The problem is that most companies do not have systems or procedures in place to identify when they are doing harm, let alone processes to anticipate harm done by new business activities and technologies. The core work of genuine corporate social responsibility involves building such systems and mechanisms. Doing so generally requires working with outside stakeholders including environmental, labor, and human rights activists, socially responsible investors, industry groups, and governments.[74]

Concepts of CSR and "sustainable business" are taking root around Asia, albeit in different forms and guises in different Asian countries, given the region's tremendous variation in cultural, political, and economic contexts.[75] More Asian countries are shifting from a focus on labor-intensive manufacturing and export-oriented growth strategies. Governments around the region are placing growing emphasis on innovation in services, technology, and knowledge sectors as the key to economic growth and national competitiveness. The "knowledge-based corporation" is critical to South Korea's continued economic success and is considered by the Chinese and Indian governments to be an important driver of their nations' economic futures. Such companies have few tangible assets and rely heavily on intellectual property, innovative processes, and public reputation. Experts in business management point out that "reputational capital" is difficult to build and easy to lose, making it all the more important that such companies anticipate and seek to avoid problems that could damage their reputation and lead to loss of "legitimacy" with their target users and customers.[76]

In India, the idea that business has a duty to serve the greater social good has deep roots in Gandhi's "trusteeship" model.[77] The Tata Group, which owns a number of ICT-related businesses, proudly quotes its founder Jamshetji Nusserwanji Tata (1839–1904): "In a free enterprise, the community is not just another stakeholder in business, but is in fact the very purpose of its existence."[78] While Indian companies have traditionally equated "corporate social responsibility" with charitable donation, a growing number—pushed by a broad range of civil society groups from national and international NGOs to local grassroots movements—are recognizing the need to engage with a broad range of "stakeholders" affected by their business, including India's many vibrant NGOs and grassroots activist groups, representing the interests of affected communities and groups.[79] As Indian multinationals expand around the world and seek to sharpen their competitiveness, more of them are adopting international standards for corporate social responsibility in order to improve their reputational capital in foreign markets.[80]

In South Korea, research shows that consumers tend to reward companies with reputations for being "good" to their communities and to their workers, while being less inclined to base purchasing decisions on companies' environmental practices.[81] Yet the South Korean environmental movement, which blossomed after the political system democratized in the early 1990s, achieved substantial change through public campaigns, media tactics, and political strategy. Most importantly, over the course of two decades the South Korean environmental movement—with the support of a broader global movement—was successful in reframing national priorities and values away from an earlier "developmentalist" narrative, promoted by government and industry, that economic development should be achieved at all costs.[82] Over time, thanks to democratization and greater media freedoms, the public and policymakers alike came to embrace the notion that clean soil, air, and water and conservation of national resources were not only essential for people's health and well-being, but were ultimately necessary for the nation's continued economic success. This shift in values has been crucial to bringing about change in government policy and business practice.[83]

South Korean society—like all modern industrialized consumption-driven economies—struggles with the problem of how to truly walk the talk. But the critical first step was to reframe prevailing narratives of what national "success" should look like. Globally, the mounting public pressure on companies to act responsibly is due to a dramatic shift in public expectations. That, in turn, is thanks to civil society's success in reframing the public discourse. Again, implementation remains a constant struggle. But once the concept was firmly planted in the public consciousness, it took root and has continued to grow.

In China, corporate social responsibility has been driven primarily by government fiat, based on the urgent recognition that environmentally sustainable business practices are imperative for the nation's long-term competitiveness as well as its people's physical survival. In January 2008, China's State-Owned Assets Supervision and Administration Commission decreed that "Corporate Social Responsibility has become a key criterion worldwide when people assess the value of a company."[84] Chinese companies were ordered to adopt global best practices so that their value for investors would rise. The number of Chinese companies producing sustainability reports shot up—from a handful in 2006 to more than 600 by 2009. By 2010 more than 600 companies were also participating in the United Nations Global Compact.[85] An ICT company—China Mobile—became the first mainland Chinese company to meaningfully disclose its carbon dioxide emissions, and it was also the first to be listed on the Dow Jones Sustainability Index.[86] While it would be difficult to imagine China Mobile signing on to the Global Network Initiative principles of free expression and privacy in China's current political climate, it is significant that Chinese companies—and Chinese policymakers—now view adherence to global CSR standards and expectations as an important part of Chinese companies' investment value. Such changes point to some reason for hope in the event that free expression and privacy become a more mainstream and established component of CSR for corporations, socially responsible investors, and civil society groups in the world's industrialized democracies.

Conclusion

Asia's governments—like all governments around the world—are grappling with many difficult challenges that the Internet has created for law enforcement and national security. Meanwhile, not only do civil society groups face new issues in terms of learning and deploying all the latest digital technologies for advocacy and discourse, but activists also have to keep developing new strategies, new knowledge, and new capacities in the fight to preserve civil liberties in the digital realm.

There are many questions to which nobody yet has answers. How can free expression and privacy be integrated into public definitions and expectations of responsible business behavior? What will it take for a critical mass of ICT companies operating in Asia to become more assertive in defending users' rights to free expression and privacy? What will it take to compel more multinational companies beyond the three GNI members, Google, Yahoo!, and Microsoft, to stand up for their users' rights to free expression and privacy not only because it is the right thing to do but also because they understand that in the long run this is the most successful business strategy?

In *Big Business, Big Responsibilities: From Villains to Visionaries: How Companies Are Tackling the World's Greatest Challenges,* authors Andy Wales, Matthew Gorman, and

Dunstan Hope point out that the issues of free expression and privacy involve relationships between citizens, companies, governments, and laws that are different
from "traditional" CSR issues. In the case of environmental and labor practices, for
instance, citizens often work with governments to force companies to stop polluting
or improve treatment of workers, through the passage and enforcement of laws.
However when it comes to government-driven incursions on free expression and
privacy by means of censorship and surveillance, the problem lies with domestic
laws, regulations, or law enforcement practices that are not in line with international
human rights norms. Thus a "common cause" between citizens and companies is
necessary in order to achieve the desired goal of protecting citizens' rights from the
potential abuse of government power. "What we are witnessing," they observe, "is
an intriguing alliance between the user and the company in defense of human
rights."[87]

Environmental-protection and labor rights groups in countries such as South Korea
and India have historically had good reason to view corporations as adversaries whose
pursuit of profit has resulted in environmental degradation and human exploitation.
Democratically elected government is won over by civil society as an ally in imposing
standards and rules on the private sector. When it comes to Internet surveillance and
censorship, however, interests are aligned in a different way so that citizens need
corporate-owned digital intermediaries to help shield them from abuses of government power. Companies can do this by challenging—or at the very least publicly
exposing—government demands for censorship and surveillance, which, if not arguably unconstitutional or illegal according to domestic law, clearly infringe on rights
enshrined in the Universal Declaration of Human Rights and other international
covenants.

Finding common cause *with* the private sector *against* government abuse of citizen
rights does not come naturally to many civil society activists in Asia's democracies,
many of which have only recently emerged either from corporatist-authoritarian pasts
or from centralized systems of economic planning. As digital rights activists quoted
earlier in this chapter pointed out, joining forces with the business community is not
consistent with the anticapitalist culture of many Indian civil society groups. Similarly,
South Korean civil society groups came of age in a culture of often-violent labor protest
against corporate *chaebols* with close ties to the regime. Corporate managers have
equally large cultural and mental barriers preventing them from tapping the moral
force of civil society groups, who can potentially be powerful allies in helping companies stave off government interference of the sort that is likely to hamper their
ability to innovate and compete on a global scale.

Achieving common cause between civil society and business thus requires new
thinking, new attitudes, and new strategies on all sides. While these innovations will
not be accomplished easily, in countries where civil society and business succeed in

working together to promote transparent and accountable governance of digital networks, the result could be a win-win for citizens' rights *as well as* high-tech competitiveness. Multinational companies from India and South Korea might even gain a competitive and reputational edge with global customers by joining the Global Network Initiative—even ahead of many of their European and North American competitors.

Studies of CSR practices in Asia show that even in democracies, managers and investors prefer to avoid terms like "human rights" and "social justice," which tend to be culturally associated with Western-style moralism. Instead, proponents and practitioners of CSR in Asia tend to emphasize concepts like "sustainability," with a strong emphasis on why environmental and labor standards contribute positively to social stability as well as companies' long-term value.[88] Such arguments have proven economically compelling even to corporations and regulators in authoritarian regimes such as China. If civil society and businesses in Asia's democracies can successfully make the economic value case for upholding global standards for free expression and privacy in the governance of digital networks, and if ICT companies from those nations gain a competitive boost as a result, there may well be reason to be optimistic that something similar may even happen in China someday.

Notes

1. Ben Doherty, "Silence of the Dissenters: How South-east Asia Keeps Web Users in Line," *The Guardian,* October 21, 2010, http://www.guardian.co.uk/technology/2010/oct/21/internet-web -censorship-asia.

2. Reporters Without Borders, "Web 2.0 Versus Control 2.0," March 18, 2010, http://en.rsf.org/web -2-0-versus-control-2-0-18-03-2010,36697.

3. Ronald Deibert and Rafal Rohozinski, "Liberation vs. Control: The Future of Cyberspace," *Journal of Democracy* 21, no. 4 (October 2010): 43–57.

4. "New Responsibilities in the Networked Age," in Andy Wales, Matthew Gorman, and Dunstan Hope, *Big Business, Big Responsibilities: From Villains to Visionaries: How Companies Are Tackling the World's Greatest Challenges* (New York: Palgrave Macmillan, 2010), 87–102.

5. Jonathan Zittrain and John Palfrey, "Reluctant Gatekeepers: Corporate Ethics on a Filtered Internet," in *Access Denied: The Practice and Policy of Global Internet Filtering,* ed. Ronald J. Deibert, John Palfrey, Rafal Rohozinski, and Jonathan Zittrain (Cambridge, MA: MIT Press, 2008), 103–122.

6. Global Network Initiative, http://globalnetworkinitiative.org.

7. Colin M. Maclay, "Protecting Privacy and Expression Online," in *Access Controlled: The Shaping of Power, Rights, and Rules in Cyberspace,* ed. Ronald Deibert, John Palfrey, Rafal Rohozinski, and Jonathan Zittrain (Cambridge, MA: MIT Press, 2010), 87–108.

8. "The Government of Big Business," in Wales et al., *Big Business, Big Responsibilities*, 119–124.

9. This section borrows heavily from Rebecca MacKinnon, "Networked Authoritarianism in China and Beyond: Implications for Global Internet Freedom," a paper presented at Liberation Technology in Authoritarian Regimes Conference, sponsored by the Hoover Institution and the Center on Democracy, Development, and the Rule of Law (CDDRL), Stanford University, October 11–12, 2010, http://rconversation.blogs.com/MacKinnon_Libtech.pdf.

10. OpenNet Initiative, "China: Country Profile," in *Access Controlled*, 449–487.

11. Rebecca MacKinnon, "Flatter World and Thicker Walls? Blogs, Censorship and Civic Discourse in China," *Public Choice* 134, nos. 1–2 (January 2008): 31–46.

12. Ronald Deibert and Rafal Rohozinski, "Beyond Denial: Introducing the Next Generation of Internet Controls," in *Access Controlled*, 3–13.

13. Rebecca MacKinnon, "Are China's Demands for Internet 'Self Discipline' Spreading to the West?" McClatchy Newspapers syndicated service, January 18, 2010, http://www.mcclatchydc .com/2010/01/18/82469/commentary-are-chinas-demands.html.

14. Ethan Zuckerman, "Intermediary Censorship," in *Access Controlled*, 71–84.

15. Miguel Helft and David Barboza, "Google Shuts China Site in Dispute Over Censorship," *New York Times*, March 22, 2010, http://www.nytimes.com/2010/03/23/technology/23google.html? _r=1.

16. Rebecca MacKinnon, "China's Censorship 2.0: How Companies Censor Bloggers," *First Monday* (February 2006), http://firstmonday.org/htbin/cgiwrap/bin/ojs/index.php/fm/article/view/2378/ 2089.

17. Wen Yunchao, "The Art of Censorship," *Index on Censorship* 39, no. 1 (2010): 53–57.

18. For detailed analysis of the Yahoo! China case, see Rebecca MacKinnon, "Shi Tao, Yahoo!, and the Lessons for Corporate Social Responsibility," working paper presented December 2007 at the International Conference on Information Technology and Social Responsibility, Chinese University, Hong Kong, http://rconversation.blogs.com/YahooShiTaoLessons.pdf.

19. Nart Villeneuve, *Breaching Trust: An Analysis of Surveillance and Security Practices on China's TOM-Skype Platform*, Information Warfare Monitor and ONI Asia Joint Report (October 2008), http://www.nartv.org/mirror/breachingtrust.pdf.

20. MacKinnon, "Networked Authoritarianism in China and Beyond."

21. Kathrin Hille, "How China Polices the Internet," *Financial Times*, July 17, 2009, http://www .ft.com/cms/s/2/e716cfc6-71a1-11de-a821-00144feabdc0.html; David Bandurski, "China's Guerrilla War for the Web," *Far Eastern Economic Review*, July 2008, http://feer.wsj.com/essays/2008/ august/chinas-guerrilla-war-for-the-web.

22. Congressional-Executive Commission on China, *2009 Annual Report*, http://www.cecc.gov/ pages/annualRpt/annualRpt09/CECCannRpt2009.pdf.

23. "Chinese State Security Arrests, Indictments Doubled in 2008," *Dui Hua Human Rights Journal*, March 25, 2009, http://www.duihua.org/hrjournal/2009/03/chinese-state-security-arrests.html.

24. Information Office of the State Council of the People's Republic of China, *The Internet in China*, June 8, 2010, http://china.org.cn/government/whitepaper/node_7093508.htm.

25. David Talbot, "China: Our Internet Is Free Enough," *MIT Technology Review*, June 16, 2010, http://www.technologyreview.com/web/25592/page1/.

26. Please refer to the South Korea country profile in this volume for a comprehensive overview of South Korean laws and regulations aimed at controlling online speech.

27. International Telecommunication Union (ITU), "Internet Indicators: Subscribers, Users and Broadband Subscribers," 2009 figures, http://www.itu.int/ITU-D/icteye/Reporting/ShowReportFrame.aspx?ReportName=/WTI/InformationTechnologyPublic&ReportFormat=HTML4.0&RP_intYear=2009&RP_intLanguageID=1&RP_bitLiveData=False.

28. Jonathan Watts, "World's First Internet President Logs On," *The Guardian*, February 24, 2003, http://www.guardian.co.uk/technology/2003/feb/24/newmedia.koreanews.

29. Elizabeth Woyke, "OhmyNews Chooses Influence over Income," *Forbes*, April 3, 2009, http://www.forbes.com/2009/04/02/internet-media-video-technology-korea-09-media.html.

30. Reporters Without Borders, "Enemies of the Internet, Countries under Surveillance," March 12, 2010, http://en.rsf.org/IMG/pdf/Internet_enemies.pdf.

31. Frank La Rue, "Full Text of the Press Statement Delivered by the UN Special Rapporteur on the Promotion and Protection of the Right to Freedom of Opinion and Expression, Mr. Frank La Rue, after the Conclusion of His Visit to the Republic of Korea," May 17, 2010, http://www2.ohchr.org/english/issues/opinion/docs/ROK-Pressstatement17052010.pdf.

32. Ibid.

33. Eric Fish, "Is Internet Censorship Compatible with Democracy? Legal Restrictions of Online Speech in South Korea," *Asia-Pacific Journal on Human Rights and the Law* 10, no. 2 (2009): 43–96.

34. Jonathan Krim, "Subway Fracas Escalates into Test of the Internet's Power to Shame," *Washington Post*, July 7, 2005, http://www.washingtonpost.com/wp-dyn/content/article/2005/07/06/AR2005070601953.html.

35. "Korean Companies Still Open to Cyber Attacks," *Asia Times Online*, November 21, 2003, http://www.atimes.com/atimes/Korea/EK21Dg02.html.

36. "Cyber Bullying Campaign against Korean Singer Dies Down," Agence France-Presse, October 13, 2010, http://www.google.com/hostednews/afp/article/ALeqM5ig4StQI4mbvccWeFCGC5uuih UyAg?docId=CNG.9dd1a1176881e712993720a765eec626.1d1.

37. Joint Korean NGOs for the Official Visit of the Special Rapporteur to the Republic of Korea, *NGO Report on the Situation of Freedom of Opinion and Expression in the Republic of Korea since 2008*, April 2010, http://kctu.org/7978.

38. Byongil Oh, "Republic of Korea," *Global Information Society Watch 2009,* Association for Progressive Communications and Humanist Institute for Cooperation with Developing Countries, 150–152, www.apc.org/system/files/GISW2009Web_EN.pdf.

39. Ibid.

40. Matthias Schwartz, "The Troubles of Korea's Influential Economic Pundit," *Wired Magazine,* October 19, 2009, http://www.wired.com/magazine/2009/10/mf_minerva.

41. Song Jung-a, "S. Korean Court Rules on Internet Law," *Financial Times,* December 28, 2010, http://www.ft.com/cms/s/0/38b354a4-126d-11e0-b4c8-00144feabdc0.html.

42. Fish, "Is Internet Censorship Compatible with Democracy?"

43. Lee, Kwang-Suk, "Surveillant Institutional Eyes in Korea: From Discipline to a Digital Grid of Control," *The Information Society* 23, no. 2 (2007): 119–124.

44. Stephen Shankland, "YouTube Korea Squelches Uploads, Comments," *CNET,* April 13, 2009, http://news.cnet.com/8301-1023_3-10218419-93.html.

45. *The Hankyoreh,* "S. Korea May Clash with Google over Internet Regulation Differences," April 21, 2009, http://english.hani.co.kr/arti/english_edition/e_international/350252.html.

46. Kim Tong-hyung, "Google Avoids Regulations, Korean Portals Not So Lucky," *Korea Times,* April 27, 2009, http://www.koreatimes.co.kr/www/news/tech/tech_view.asp?newsIdx=43939 &categoryCode=129.

47. Kim Tong-hyung, "Is Korea Turning into an Internet Police State?" *Korea Times,* April 9, 2009, http://www.koreatimes.co.kr/www/news/tech/2010/05/133_42877.html.

48. Please refer to the India country profile in this volume for a comprehensive overview of Indian laws and regulations aimed at controlling online speech.

49. International Telecommunication Union (ITU), "Internet Indicators: Subscribers, Users and Broadband Subscribers."

50. "India to Have 'Billion Plus' Mobile Users by 2015: Executive," *Economic Times,* November 18, 2009, http://economictimes.indiatimes.com/News/Economy/Finance/India-to-have-billion -plus-mobile-users-by-2015-executive/articleshow/5242284.cms; Shilpa Kannan, "India's 3G Licence Bidders Bank on Big Change," BBC News, April 7, 2010, http://news.bbc.co.uk/2/hi /business/8607866.stm.

51. Noah Schachtman, "How Gadgets Helped Mumbai Attackers," *Wired Magazine,* December 1, 2008, http://www.wired.com/dangerroom/2008/12/the-gagdets-of/.

52. Mehul Srivastava and James Rupert, "China-Linked Hackers Attacked India, Researchers Say," *Bloomberg Business Week,* April 6, 2010, http://www.businessweek.com/news/2010-04-06/ researchers-find-china-linked-cyber-spy-ring-targeting-india.html; Information Warfare Monitor and the Shadowserver Foundation, *Shadows in the Cloud: An Investigation into Cyber Espionage 2.0,* April 6, 2010, http://www.shadows-in-the-cloud.net.

53. See the India country profile in this volume.

54. Nishant Shah, "Subject to Technology: Internet Pornography, Cyber-terrorism and the Indian State," *Inter-Asia Cultural Studies* 8, no. 3 (2007): 349–366.

55. Amol Sharma and Jessica Vascellaro, "Google and India Test the Limits of Liberty," *Wall Street Journal*, January 4, 2010, http://online.wsj.com/article/SB126239086161213013.html.

56. An annotated copy of the full text can be found at: http://cyberlaws.net/itamendments/IT%20ACT%20AMENDMENTS.PDF.

57. Sharma and Vascellaro, "Google and India Test the Limits."

58. "Govt Can't Ban Porn Websites for Obscenity," *Economic Times,* February 11, 2010, http://economictimes.indiatimes.com/infotech/internet/Govt-cant-ban-porn-websites-for-obscenity/articleshow/5558340.cms.

59. Sevanti Ninan, "In the Name of National Security," *The Hindu,* June 7, 2009, http://www.hindu.com/mag/2009/06/07/stories/2009060750090300.htm.

60. Vikas Bajaj, "India Warns It Will Block BlackBerry Traffic That It Can't Monitor," *New York Times,* August 12, 2010, http://www.nytimes.com/2010/08/13/technology/13rim.html.

61. Phred Dvorak, Amol Sharma, and Margaret Coker, "RIM Offered Security Fixes," *Wall Street Journal,* August 14, 2010, http://online.wsj.com/article/SB10001424052748703960004575427312899373090.html.

62. Andrew Vanacore, "BlackBerry CEO Suggests Route to Eavesdropping," *Associated Press*, September 27, 2010, http://www.msnbc.msn.com/id/39387290/ns/technology_and_science-security/.

63. "India Extends BlackBerry Access Deadline," Agence France-Presse, October 12, 2010, http://www.google.com/hostednews/afp/article/ALeqM5h9tMlmC3AyuCjurj2tA4rPZj0alg?docId=CNG.3af003c84a71aeca2db44ba857bb01cc.401.

64. Vikas Bajaj and Ian Austen, "India's Surveillance Plan Said to Deter Business," *New York Times*, September 27, 2010, http://www.nytimes.com/2010/09/28/business/global/28secure.html.

65. S. Ramadoral, "Don't Disconnect India," *Hindustan Times*, September 21, 2010, http://www.hindustantimes.com/News-Feed/columns/Don-t-disconnect-India/Article1-603075.aspx.

66. Google, "Google Transparency Report: Government Requests," http://www.google.com/transparencyreport/governmentrequests/.

67. Pavan Duggal, "Internet and Democracy in India: A Report," in *Rhetoric and Reality: The Internet Challenge for Democracy in Asia,* ed. Indrajit Banerjee (Singapore: Times Media Academic Publishing, 2003), 61–98.

68. Raman Jit Singh Chima, "The Regulation of the Internet with Relation to Speech and Expression by the Indian State," Social Science Research Network, April 25, 2008, http://papers.ssrn.com/sol3/papers.cfm?abstract_id=1237262.

69. Gurumurthy Kasinathan and Parminder Jeet Singh, "India," Global Information Society Watch 2009, Association for Progressive Communications and Humanist Institute for Cooperation with Developing Countries, 127–130, www.apc.org/system/files/GISW2009Web_EN.pdf.

70. "Edward Tian: Google Is China's Best Tool for Understanding the West," *China Digital Times,* April 15, 2010, http://chinadigitaltimes.net/2010/04/edward-tian-google-is-chinas-best-tool-for -understanding-the-west/.

71. See, for example, "China Not Alone in Internet Regulation," *China Daily,* December 3, 2009, http://www.chinadaily.com.cn/opinion/2009-12/03/content_9111690.htm.

72. Aron Cramer and Zachary Karabel, *Sustainable Excellence: The Future of Business in a Fast-Changing World* (New York: Rodale, 2010).

73. United Nations Human Rights Council, *Promotion and Protection of All Human Rights, Civil, Political, Economic, Social and Cultural Rights, Including the Right to Development—Protect, Respect and Remedy: A Framework for Business and Human Rights,* April 7, 2008, http://www.reports-and -materials.org/Ruggie-report-7-Apr-2008.pdf.

74. Ibid.

75. Aron Cramer and Jeremy Prepscius, "Corporate Social Responsibility in Asia," *Global Asia* 2, no. 3 (Winter 2007), http://globalasia.org/new/l.php?c=e113.

76. Marc Newsona and Craig Deegan, "Global Expectations and Their Association with Corporate Social Disclosure Practices in Australia, Singapore, and South Korea," *International Journal of Accounting* 37 (2002): 183–213.

77. Subratesh Ghosh, "Trusteeship in Industry: Gandhiji's Dream and Contemporary Reality," *Indian Journal of Industrial Relations* 25, no. 1 (July 1989): 35–44.

78. Tata company, "About" page, http://www.tata.com/aboutus/articles/inside.aspx?artid= 1U2QamAhqtA=.

79. Mahabir Narwal and Tejinder Sharma, "Perceptions of Corporate Social Responsibility in India: An Empirical Study," *Journal of Knowledge Globalization* 1, no. 1 (2008): 61–79.

80. Ibid.

81. Ki-Hoon Lee and Dongyoung Shin, "Consumers' Responses to CSR Activities: The Linkage between Increased Awareness and Purchase Intention," *Public Relations Review* 36, no. 2 (June 2010): 193–195.

82. Moon Chung-in and Lim Sung-hack, "Weaving through Paradoxes: Democratization, Globalization, and Environment Politics in South Korea," *East Asian Review* 15, no. 2 (Summer 2003): 43–70.

83. Ibid.

84. Cramer and Karabell, *Sustainable Excellence,* 82–83.

85. Ibid.

86. Wales et al., *Big Business, Big Responsibilities,* 119–124.

87. "New Responsibilities in the Networked Age," in Wales et al., *Big Business, Big Responsibilities.*

88. Cramer and Prepscius, "Corporate Social Responsibility in Asia"; Simon Powell and Jonathan Galligan, *Ethical Asia: Corporate Good Guys? It's All about Labour and Environment,* CLSA Asia-Pacific Markets, November 1, 2010, https://www.clsa.com/assets/files/reports/CLSA-Ethical-Asia.pdf.

Part II   Country Profiles and Regional Overview

Introduction to the Country Profiles

The country profiles that follow offer a synopsis of the findings and conclusions of OpenNet Initiative (ONI) research into the factors influencing specific countries' decisions to filter or abstain from filtering the Internet, as well as the impact, relevance, and efficacy of technical filtering in a broader context of Internet censorship.

These profiles cover a selection of countries in Asia where the ONI conducted technical testing and analysis from 2009 to 2010. Countries selected for in-depth analysis are those in which it is believed there is the most to learn about the extent and processes of Internet filtering.

The ONI employs a unique "fusion" methodology that combines fieldwork, technical research, and data mining, fusion, analysis, and visualization. Our aim is to uncover evidence of Internet content filtering in countries under investigation. The ONI's tests consist of running special software programs within countries under investigation that connect back to databases that contain lists of thousands of URLs, IPs, and keywords. The lists are broken down into two categories: Global lists include URLs, IPs, and keywords that are tested in every country and that help us make general comparisons of accessibility across countries. Global lists also provide a "snapshot" of accessibility to content typically blocked by filtering software programs, and they can help us understand whether particular software programs are being used in a specific context. Local lists are unique for each country and are usually made up of content in local languages. These are high-impact URLs, IPs, and keywords, meaning they have content that is likely to be targeted for filtering or that has been reported to have been so targeted.

Our aim is to run tests on each of the main Internet service providers (ISPs) in a country over an extended period of time—typically at least two weeks on at least two occasions. Our accessibility depends very much on our in-country testers, and for security and other reasons we are not always able to perform comprehensive tests, meaning in some cases we have only partial results on which to base inferences. Our specially designed software checks access both within the country and from one or more control locations simultaneously. Anomalies are analyzed, and determinations are made as to whether a site is accessible or not, and if the latter, how the inaccessibility occurs. In some instances, block pages—Web sites that explicitly confirm blocking—appear following requests for banned content. In other instances, connections are simply broken. In some cases, special filtering software is employed, while in others routers are manually configured to block.

Each country profile includes the summary results of the empirical testing for filtering. The technical filtering data alone, however, do not amount to a complete picture of Internet censorship and content regulation. A wide range of policies relating to media, speech, and expression also act to restrict expression on the Internet and formation of online communities. Legal and regulatory frameworks, including Internet law, the state of Internet access and infrastructure, the level of economic development, and the quality of governance institutions are central to determining which countries resort to filtering and how they choose to implement Internet content controls. A brief synopsis of each of these factors is included in each of the country summaries. Together, these sections are intended to offer a concise, accurate, and unbiased overview of Internet filtering and content regulation.

Each country is given a score on a five-point scale presented in the "Results at a Glance" table. The scores reflect the observed level of filtering in each of four themes:

1. *Political:* This category is focused primarily on Web sites that express views in opposition to those of the current government. Content more broadly related to human rights, freedom of expression, minority rights, and religious movements is also considered here.

2. *Social:* This group covers material related to sexuality, gambling, and illegal drugs and alcohol, as well as other topics that may be socially sensitive or perceived as offensive.

3. *Conflict and security:* Content related to armed conflicts, border disputes, separatist movements, and militant groups is included in this category.

4. *Internet tools:* Web sites that provide e-mail, Internet hosting, search, translation, Voice over Internet Protocol (VoIP) telephone service, and circumvention methods are grouped in this category.

The relative magnitude of filtering for each of the four themes is defined as follows:

1. *Pervasive filtering* is characterized by both its depth—a blocking regime that blocks a large portion of the targeted content in a given category—and its breadth—a blocking regime that includes filtering in several categories in a given theme.

2. *Substantial filtering* has either depth or breadth: either a number of categories are subject to a medium level of filtering, or a low level of filtering is carried out across many categories.

3. *Selective filtering* is narrowly targeted filtering that blocks a small number of specific sites across a few categories or filtering that targets a single category or issue.

4. *Suspected filtering* is indicated when connectivity abnormalities are present that suggest the presence of filtering, although diagnostic work was unable to confirm conclusively that inaccessibility of Web sites was the result of deliberate tampering.
5. *No evidence of filtering:* ONI testing did not uncover any evidence of Web sites being blocked.

The "Results at a Glance" table also includes a measure (low, medium, or high) of the observed transparency and consistency of blocking patterns. The transparency score given to each country is a qualitative measure based on the level at which the country openly engages in filtering. In cases where filtering takes place without open acknowledgment or where the practice of filtering is actively disguised to appear as network errors, the transparency score is low. In assigning the transparency score, we have also considered the presence of provisions to appeal or report instances of inappropriate blocking. Consistency measures the variation in filtering within a country across different ISPs—in some cases the availability of specific Web pages differs significantly depending on the ISP one uses to connect to the Internet.

An aggregate view of the level of development for each country is represented by the results of the first four indexes presented in the "Key Indicators" table: gross domestic product per capita, life expectancy, literacy rates, and the human development index.

The first three measures are drawn from the World Bank development indicators data set. The GDP measure, which captures the ability to purchase a standard basket of consumer goods, is expressed in constant 2005 international dollars. Life expectancy can be seen as a proxy for general health, and literacy an imperfect but reasonable indication of the quality of education. The human development index is constructed by the United Nations Development Program to reflect overall human well-being.

Governance is widely recognized to be a key determinant of economic success and human welfare. We therefore also include two measures of governance: rule of law and voice and accountability. These indexes are defined and compiled by researchers at the World Bank using an aggregation of the best available data. The authors of the indexes define them in the following way:

Rule of Law (RL) captures perceptions of the extent to which agents have confidence in and abide by the rules of society, in particular the quality of contract enforcement, property rights, the police, and the courts, as well as the likelihood of crime and violence.
Voice and Accountability (VA) captures perceptions of the extent to which a country's citizens are able to participate in selecting their government, as well as freedom of expression, freedom of association, and a free media.[1]

An aggregate view of the state of democracy is provided by the Economist Intelligence Unit's democracy index. This index is based on five categories: electoral process and pluralism, civil liberties, the functioning of government, political participation, and political culture. The 167 states included in this index are placed within one of four regime type categories: full democracies, flawed democracies, hybrid regimes, and authoritarian regimes.

We also include two measures of Internet accessibility provided by the International Telecommunication Union: the digital opportunity index (DOI) and Internet users as a percentage of the population. The DOI is based on 11 core information communications technology (ICT) indicators that are agreed upon by the International Telecommunication Union's Partnership on Measuring ICT for Development. These are grouped in three clusters by type: opportunity, infrastructure, and utilization. The DOI therefore captures the overall potential for and context of Internet availability rather than usage alone. The measure of Internet access, the Internet penetration rate, is simply the percentage of the population identified as active Internet users. Internet regulation and filtering practices are often dynamic processes, subject to frequent change, though we expect that the political climate and the aggregate view of the issues reflected in these summaries will change more slowly than the specific instances of filtering. As the context for content regulation and the practice of Internet filtering evolve, updates will be made to the country summaries, and new countries may be added. These updates will be available at http://www.opennet.net.

Note

1. Daniel Kaufmann, Aart Kraay, and Massimo Mastruzzi, "The Worldwide Governance Indicators: Methodology and Analytical Issues," World Bank Development Research Group Macroeconomics and Growth Team, September 2010. Available at http://papers.ssrn.com/sol3/papers.cfm?abstract_id=1682130.

Sources for Key Indicators

GDP per Capita, PPP (constant 2005 international dollars)

World Bank, "GDP per Capita, PPP (Constant 2005 International $)," 2009, drawn from *The World Bank Data: Indicators* database, http://data.worldbank.org/indicator/NY.GDP.PCAP.PP.KD.

Life Expectancy at Birth (years)

World Bank, "Life Expectancy at Birth, Total (Years)," 2008a, drawn from *The World Bank Data: Indicators* database, http://data.worldbank.org/indicator/SP.DYN.LE00.IN.

Literacy Rate

World Bank, "Literacy Rate, Adult Total (% of People Ages 15 and Above)," 2008b, drawn from *The World Bank Data: Indicators* database, http://data.worldbank.org/indicator/SE.ADT.LITR.ZS.

United Nations Development Program (UNDP), *Human Development Report 2009: Overcoming Barriers: Human Mobility and Development*, 2009, http://hdr.undp.org/en/media/HDR_2009_EN _Complete.pdf.

Human Development Index (ranking of 169)

United Nations Development Program (UNDP), *The Real Wealth of Nations: Pathways to Human Development*, 2010, http://hdr.undp.org/en/reports/global/hdr2010/.

Rule of Law (five-point scale)

World Bank, *Worldwide Governance Indicators 1996–2009,* 2009 (Washington, DC: World Bank), http://info.worldbank.org/governance/wgi/pdf/wgidataset.xls.

Voice and Accountability (five-point scale)

World Bank, *Worldwide Governance Indicators 1996–2009,* 2009 (Washington, DC: World Bank), http://info.worldbank.org/governance/wgi/pdf/wgidataset.xls.

Democracy Index (ranking of 167)

Economist Intelligence Unit, *Democracy Index 2010: Democracy in Retreat,* 2010, http://graphics .eiu.com/PDF/Democracy_Index_2010_web.pdf.

Digital Opportunity Index (ranking of 181)

International Telecommunication Union (ITU), *World Information Society 2007 Report: Beyond WSIS,* 2007, http://www.itu.int/osg/spu/publications/worldinformationsociety/2007/report.html.

Internet Penetration

International Telecommunication Union (ITU), "Internet Indicators: Subscribers, Users and Broadband Subscribers," 2009 figures, http://www.itu.int/ITU-D/icteye/Indicators/Indicators .aspx.

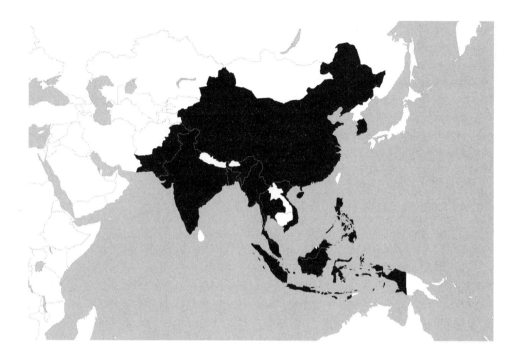

Asian cyberspace is the setting for a diverse range of information controls, contestations, and resistance. Governments across the region struggle to balance the rapid growth of information communication technologies (ICTs) with their concerns over social stability, national security, and cultural values. These tensions manifest themselves differently according to each state's context. The region is home to some of the least connected countries, such as Burma, and burgeoning ICT markets such as China and India. The spectrum of information controls across the region varies as well, with some of the world's strictest regimes of information control on one end and relatively unfettered communication environments on the other.

The continued growth of Internet connectivity in Asia, particularly in the mobile realm, has occurred alongside a growth in states' ability to monitor and control the flow of information. Countries such as Bangladesh, Indonesia, and Malaysia have seen dramatic increases in connectivity rates and mobile telephone ownership. However, as connectivity grows, so does the legal, regulatory, and technical capacity for states to monitor it. Both democratic and authoritarian states alike have expanded the scope of content that is considered illegal and have increased mechanisms to control it.

These have taken the form of centralized filtering mechanisms, increased power for regulators to monitor and censor content, and the prosecution of violators of content dissemination laws.

In 2009–2010, the OpenNet Initiative (ONI) conducted in-country testing of Internet filtering in Bangladesh, Burma, China, India, Indonesia, Malaysia, Pakistan, the Philippines, Singapore, South Korea, Thailand, and Vietnam. Testing results remain largely consistent with 2007–2008 findings and show that a spectrum of information filtering continues across Asian countries. Burma, China, and Vietnam maintain the most pervasive regimes of Internet filtering in the region, primarily targeting independent media and content related to politically sensitive issues, human rights, and political reform. On the other end of the spectrum, Singapore continues to symbolically block a limited number of pornography Web sites.

Filtering in South Korea and India focuses primarily on content related to national security and conflict issues—with South Korean Internet service providers (ISPs) extensively targeting online content related to North Korea and India targeting topics of Hindu extremism. Pakistan also focuses on blocking issues deemed sensitive to national security such as the Balochi conflict and independence movement, as well as religious content deemed blasphemous. Although previous ONI testing found no evidence of Internet filtering in Indonesia, recent testing revealed that ISPs are substantially filtering online pornography and selectively targeting political, blasphemous, and Internet-tool-related content. In Thailand filtering primarily concentrates on political content in reaction to sensitive events such as the 2009 political unrest that gripped the country. OpenNet Initiative testing found no evidence of Internet filtering in Bangladesh, Malaysia, or the Philippines.

Internet in Asia

Asia is home to one of the most connected countries in the world, and some of the least connected. In recent years, the region has seen tremendous growth, with several states identifying ICT growth as an integral part of their socioeconomic development. The mobile sector in particular has grown exponentially—an important development in countries with relatively underdeveloped fixed telecommunications infrastructure. In some countries, fixed infrastructure development has stagnated, eclipsed by the rapid rollout of mobile connectivity.

South Korea remains a world leader in Internet connectivity with one of the highest penetration rates and data transfer speeds in the world.[1] South Korea has penetration rates exceeding 81 percent[2] and an average broadband connection speed of 17 Mbps, the highest in the world and more than double the rate of second-ranked Hong Kong.[3] While not as high as South Korea, Malaysia also has a relatively substantial Internet penetration rate of 55.9 percent[4] and, like many in the region, a rapidly growing mobile sector. Malaysia's mobile penetration rate in 2009 was 106 percent, with 21 percent of subscribers using 3G technologies.[5] Vietnam has seen strong growth in both fixed and mobile connectivity, with broadband subscription rates growing at more than 40 percent annually[6] for the past two years and mobile penetration rates estimated to exceed 140 percent by the end of 2010.[7]

China remains one of the most significant examples of the growth of the Internet in Asia. Although its penetration rate is relatively modest at 28.9 percent, its total of almost 390 million Internet users in 2009 makes it the largest Internet population in the world.[8] Much like its neighbors in the region, China has experienced a dramatic growth in the mobile telephone sector. From having less than 100 million mobile phones in 2000, the country is estimated to approach one billion phones by the end of 2011.[9] The gap between urban and rural connectivity rates mirrors that of some of its neighbors. A 2008 initiative by the Ministry of Information and Industry sought to narrow this gap, extending broadband services to 92 percent of rural townships.[10] Despite improving the number of rural users to over 100 million by 2009, low incomes and lack of access make Internet connectivity still a luxury for many.[11]

In contrast, Burma remains one of the least connected countries on record, with government restrictions, slow connection speeds, and prohibitive costs contributing to a penetration rate of only 0.2 percent.[12] Fixed broadband subscriptions numbered roughly 15,000, representing a penetration rate of 0.03 percent.[13] In Bangladesh, similarly, the government has launched initiatives to expand the ICT sector as a means of driving socioeconomic development, but access remains relatively limited.[14] Penetration rates are below 0.4 percent of the population, and the fixed broadband subscription rate is 0.03 percent.[15] Despite this low level of fixed Internet access, the mobile market is growing rapidly, with a 37 percent penetration rate.[16]

Although India's penetration rate is low at just over 5 percent,[17] the country is experiencing a surge in mobile access. From roughly 10 million subscribers in 2002, the mobile market is expected to exceed 750 million by 2011.[18] Pakistan has seen a similar boom in its mobile and wireless market. While overall Internet penetration rate is only 11.3 percent,[19] mobile penetration exceeds 60 percent.[20] Pakistan was also home to the world's first countrywide deployment of the next-generation wireless technology, WiMAX.[21]

The case of Indonesia demonstrates the contribution that mobile technology can make in an environment with expensive and limited fixed connectivity. Given that the monthly cost for fixed broadband can be more than five times that of mobile access, subscription rates for fixed broadband are below 1 percent.[22] Growth of mobile subscriptions, however, was expected to exceed 20 percent in 2010, leading to more than three-quarters of the population having a mobile phone.[23] Thailand has similarly seen the number of mobile subscriptions more than double between 2004 and 2009.[24]

Legal and Regulatory Framework

The regulatory and legislative capacity of states to filter content and prosecute individuals for online content has steadily grown. Many states in the region have increased monitoring of content, expanded the range of content deemed unacceptable, and prosecuted more individuals for violating content rules. This trend has not been limited to authoritarian states in the region; democracies such as India and South Korea have also expanded their capacities to regulate content.

Efforts undertaken by Asian states to expand the legislative, regulatory, and technical capacities for Internet filtering include the creation of new groups tasked with monitoring content, new powers for existing groups to block content deemed illegal, and expansion of governments' capacity to control filtering mechanisms. In October 2009 the Indian Parliament passed an amendment to the Information Technology Act, expanding the powers of the central government to block Web sites considered a threat to national security or public order.[25] This amendment also expanded the mandate of the Indian Computer Emergency Response Team (CERT-IN) to coordinate all cyber security issues and to enhance cyber protection.[26] The Pakistan Telecommunication Authority has proposed that they be given access to a centralized filter to more effectively block Web sites containing offensive content rather than relying on orders to individual ISPs.[27] Similarly, the Indonesian Ministry of Communication and Information Technology began drafting a bill that includes plans for a monitoring team tasked with ordering ISPs to block content deemed illegal.[28] Thailand has seen already-existing legislation applied more frequently. Since the 2007 passage of the Computer-Related Offenses Act, the number of orders to shut down Web sites has steadily increased. While only two URLs were ordered blocked in the year the bill was passed, nearly 44,000 were ordered blocked in 2009.[29] In 2010 the Chinese government amended the 1988 State Secrets law to include all ICT companies operating in the country, requiring them to cooperate with the state in cases where state secrets are allegedly leaked online.[30] The regulations would require companies to block the distribution of such information and disclose records to state security organs.[31]

Many governments have expanded rules that prohibit content deemed libelous, hateful, blasphemous, or causing insult to religious or other social groups. This type of legislation was instituted in Bangladesh during the period of emergency rule and has remained in place since. The Emergency Power Rules established in 2007 forbid the use of the Internet to publish "provocative" material, primarily aimed at content critical of the ruling government or army.[32] However, since the end of emergency rule, the Information Communication and Technologies Act still prohibits content that is "false and vulgar" or that "may harm religious feelings," among other restrictions.[33] A bill drafted in late 2010 sought to extend punishment for crimes related to distribution of pornography online.[34] Indonesia has similar prohibitions against defamation in its Electronic Information and Transaction Law, which was unsuccessfully challenged in the Constitutional Court by a group of bloggers and media rights advocates.[35] Other sections of the same law prohibit dissemination of information intended to invoke hatred or hostility toward groups based on race, ethnicity, or religion, which caused the law to be invoked during the controversial "Everybody Draw Mohammed Day."[36] Controversy over the release of Indonesian celebrity sex videos led to a crackdown on pornographic Web sites and the government introducing the Trust Positive keyword-filtering system.[37] Pakistan has strict antiblasphemy laws, and the Supreme Court has ordered the Pakistan Telecommunication Authority to block access to Web sites with blasphemous content.[38]

This type of legislation is not unique to the authoritarian regimes of the region. South Korea's Telecommunications Business Act forbids communications that "harm the public peace and order or social morals and good customs."[39] Malaysia's Communications and Multimedia Act prohibits content deemed "indecent, obscene, false, menacing or offensive in character," with violators risking fines and jail time.[40] Filtering and takedown notices in Thailand also focus heavily on content deemed offensive, with the country's lèse-majesté laws targeting any negative remarks aimed at the monarchy. Combating this type of speech online has been deemed the top priority of Thailand's Ministry of Information and Technology.[41] More than three-quarters of the 75,000 orders blocking Web sites since the introduction of Thailand's Computer-Related Offenses Act in 2007 have been based on lèse-majesté laws.[42]

Alongside this increase in legislative and regulatory capacity has come the arrest of bloggers for content deemed politically sensitive, libelous, or against the public order. In Malaysia, numerous individuals have been charged for content posted online, including alleged insults to the monarchy[43] and the posting of a satirical article about the state power company.[44] In Bangladesh there have been several raids on television stations and newspapers critical of state officials, and journalists have been arrested for defaming the ruling government.[45]

Similarly, in South Korea individuals have been charged or investigated for posting online content identified as rumors, defamation, or misinformation. Online discussion following the sinking of a South Korean warship and the shelling of a South Korean island led to the arrest of several individuals charged with spreading "groundless rumors."[46] However, a December 2010 Constitutional Court ruling in the country may affect how such prosecutions are handled in the future. Following the acquittal of the blogger known as Minerva, the court ruled that the law under which bloggers had been prosecuted violated freedom of speech as guaranteed in the constitution.[47]

Numerous bloggers in China have also been imprisoned for posting content deemed controversial or politically sensitive. For example, a Twitter user was arrested for retweeting a sarcastic message about the recent naval conflict with Japan,[48] while an activist for families affected by the milk scandal was imprisoned for two and a half years.[49]

Internet Filtering

A spectrum of Internet filtering is found in Asia, ranging from some of the most pervasive censors of the Internet to relatively unfettered access. China and Burma rank
among the most severe censors anywhere in the world. In these states, content related
to opposition political movements, human rights, and pornography is widely blocked.
While the scope and breadth of this blocking may not be found throughout the region,
many other countries block similar content. For example, opposition political movements in Thailand and Vietnam are blocked, while Web sites deemed a threat to
national security in South Korea and India are targeted. For some states, social content
is the focus, with Indonesia and Pakistan concentrating their blocking on Web sites
deemed offensive to religious values. Bangladesh, Malaysia, and the Philippines do
not have systematic regimes of technical Internet filtering. However, Bangladesh in
two separate incidents in 2010 blocked YouTube for hosting politically sensitive
content[50] and Facebook for content deemed blasphemous.[51] In 2008, TMNet, a major
ISP in Malaysia, performed a DNS block on the controversial Web site Malaysia Today
following pressures from the government.[52]

There have been increasing challenges to the accessibility of online content from
a variety of sources. Google had a highly public conflict with the government of China
that culminated with the company refusing to continue censoring search results in
the country.[53] Research in Motion (RIM) pushed back against India's efforts to gain
access to the encrypted communications of BlackBerry users,[54] although it complied
with requests from the Indonesian government to block pornography on the devices.[55]

Popular sites such as Facebook, YouTube, Flickr, and Wikipedia have all experienced
some degree of control in South Korea, Pakistan, Bangladesh, and China. A December
2010 ruling by the Korean Communications Commission found that Facebook was in
violation of the country's laws protecting personal information.[56] Responding to an
online campaign to post drawings of the Prophet Mohammad in May 2010, the Pakistani government ordered ISPs to block access to Facebook for a month.[57] The campaign drew a similar response in Bangladesh, where the Telecommunications Regulatory
Commission temporarily blocked Facebook until the site removed the offending
images.[58] YouTube was targeted in Indonesia and Pakistan following the posting of a
controversial film by Dutch lawmaker Geert Wilders.[59] The Web site was also blocked
in Bangladesh "in the national interest" after video was posted of a contentious
meeting between the prime minister and army officers.[60]

The blocking of such sites can be selective. OpenNet Initiative testing shows that
South Korea has blocked the Twitter feed of the North Korean government, although
North Korea's YouTube and Facebook pages were still accessible. In China, ONI testing
in 2009 and 2010 found that the ISP CNLink had completely blocked Facebook and
Twitter. Filtering practices have also extended to the mobile realm, with several

countries challenging the accessibility of content on BlackBerry devices. Research in Motion agreed to implement a content-filtering system in Indonesia to ensure compliance with the country's antipornography laws.[61] Similarly, BlackBerry users in Pakistan reportedly found content inaccessible as the Pakistan Telecommunication Authority ordered blasphemous material blocked.[62]

The practice of "just-in-time" blocking has also been prevalent in the region. During anniversaries of highly sensitive events, such as the 60th anniversary of the founding of the People's Republic of China, the 50th anniversary of the Tibet Uprising, and the 20th anniversary of the Tiananmen Massacre, China has seen increases in the level of blocking.[63] Thailand also experienced an increase in blocking during the 2010 red shirt demonstrations. Following the introduction of a state of emergency in April 2010, the government introduced strict measures to control the media, including Internet content, particularly content related to opposition parties or sympathetic to protesters. OpenNet Initiative testing confirmed that Thai ISPs targeted a selection of the 36 Web sites ordered blocked by the government during this period.[64]

Filtering is often not applied consistently within countries. Different ISPs sometimes filter different content, or do not filter content at all times. For example, ONI testing in Thailand found that filtering between the two tested ISPs, TRUE and TOTNET, was inconsistent, with neither provider blocking all the sites on the government block list. Internet service providers tested in Indonesia showed a similar lack of uniformity, with blocked content differing across providers. While there were some variations in the number of sites filtered by ISPs in countries such as Pakistan and India, the content was similar in nature. Providers tested in Burma showed a distinct difference in the precision of their filtering—testing results showed that Myanmar Post and Telecommunication (MPT) blocked specific pages while Yatanarpon Teleport (or Myanmar Teleport, formerly known as Bagan Cybertech) often blocked entire domains. Filtering has also been intermittent in countries such as Pakistan, Bangladesh, and Thailand where censorship occurs in response to a crisis or controversy.

The degree of transparency about blocking that users experience also varies between countries. China's system of IP blocking combined with keyword filtering, which is unique in the world, can resemble network problems. When accessing a blocked site, users receive a network-timeout error page, leaving them uncertain about whether content is in fact blocked. Other countries, including South Korea and some Indonesian ISPs, explicitly inform users that the content they are trying to access is blocked by government order.

Surveillance

Internet service providers in Asia are increasingly required to monitor their users' access and retain information about their usage. This practice can be seen most prominently in Burma. Burmese Internet café owners are required to take screenshots of Web sites being visited.[65] Other countries, including China and Thailand, require Internet cafés to retain patron information and data usage records.

Surveillance has also extended into the mobile realm. The government of India confronted RIM over access to encrypted messages on BlackBerry devices, presenting the company with an ultimatum to grant access or face a ban on services.[66] Indonesia also expressed concern about its inability to monitor BlackBerry communications and requested that RIM set up local mirror servers to facilitate monitoring.

Some countries have expanded the requirements for Internet users to register with their real names before gaining access to services. In China, for example, users of some Web portals, Internet cafés, and mobile phones are required to present identification before gaining access.[67] Forum and chat-room users in South Korea have to register with their real names, a policy that led Google to disable features on the Korean-language version of YouTube to avoid the requirement.[68]

Cyber Attacks

Asian countries have also witnessed an increase in cyber attacks targeted at sensitive time periods, particularly during elections and anniversaries of key events. Burmese independent media Web sites regularly experience distributed denial of service (DDoS) attacks around anniversaries of political protests in the country such as the 2007 Saffron Revolution and the "8888" student uprising.[69] On October 25, 2010, two weeks before the first general elections in Burma since 1990, the primary ISP in the country, MPT, experienced large-scale DDoS attacks that significantly disrupted inbound and outbound traffic, rendering the Internet inaccessible.[70] The origin of and motivation behind the attacks remain unclear, but because of the timing there is speculation that they may be politically motivated. Controversial news site Malaysia Today reportedly faced a DDoS attack following published articles exposing government corruption.[71] In Vietnam, Web sites with content related to political reform hosted both within and outside of the country as well as dissidents in the country are frequently targets of DDoS attack.[72] For example, in April 2009, coinciding with the 24th anniversary of the fall of Saigon, the Web site of the Viet Tan, the Vietnam Reform Party, suffered a large-scale DDoS attack.[73]

Asian countries also continue to be primary sites for originating cyber attacks. In particular, a growing number of attacks have been attributed to sources originating from China, including targeted malware attacks on human rights groups[74] and media organizations,[75] and reports of attacks from numerous states such as Australia,[76] Japan,[77] Pakistan,[78] South Korea,[79] the United Kingdom,[80] and the United States.[81] Directly attributing any of these actions to the Chinese government is difficult, and the level of attacks sourced to the country should also be viewed within the context of China's growing Internet population, which is the biggest in the world.

Conclusion

While important variations exist across Asia, a trend of increasing controls in the context of growing connectivity is emerging in the region as a whole. This trend has not been limited to authoritarian countries. On the one hand, Burma, China, and Vietnam continue to expand and strengthen pervasive regimes of Internet controls, while on the other, South Korea imposes more restraints on the freedom of online speech than most other democracies, and Indonesia has begun to develop content controls for online pornographic material. This emerging trend reflects growing concerns over online content among governments in Asia as they struggle to balance the growth of information communication technologies with their interests of maintaining social stability and national security, as well as sustaining cultural values.

Both increasing connectivity and growing Internet controls have given rise to contestation over Asian cyberspace among different actors. Civil society actors, including netizens and activists, continue to use the Internet as a medium to broadcast their messages and to mobilize, organize, and resist state policies, while private actors struggle with obligations to governments in monitoring and filtering those very messages and forums of resistance. In India, such controls have tended to expand online civil society activism, while in Indonesia, a vibrant civil society including bloggers, media associations, women, and minority groups stands ready to challenge the imposition of regulations that could restrict online content freedoms.[82] In China, opposition from domestic and foreign PC makers as well as protests from angry netizens led the government to delay the "Green Dam" filtering program's installation in new computers.[83] At the same time, following a series of cyber attacks on its infrastructure and on e-mails of Chinese human rights activists, Google publicly challenged the country's filtering regime when it announced it would no longer comply with such regulations.[84]

Citizens also compete with one another over the shape of cyberspace. In Bangladesh, the promotion of an "Everyone Draw Mohammed Day" on Facebook gave rise to thousands of Bangladeshis protesting the social networking site and demanding an immediate ban, while other groups took to the streets after the country's telecommunication regulatory commission placed a temporary block on the Web site.[85] Other actors have sought to shape the Internet through cyber attacks that target opposition groups or forums for dissenting netizens. In Vietnam, cyber attacks on dissident groups and movements occur regularly, with the recent Vulcanbot and Vecebot botnets representing increasing sophistication of attacks.[86] There is some evidence that the perpetrators of the attacks are a pro–Vietnamese Communist Party hacking group concerned with reactionary online content.[87] In Burma, opposition media have seen a rise of cyber attacks on their Web sites, particularly on politically sensitive dates. Though some suspect such attacks to be state sanctioned, a lack of evidence makes state attribution difficult. Nonetheless, these attacks are consistent with the government's interest in strengthening Internet controls.

As states continue to promote information communication technologies and more citizens become connected to the Internet, netizens across the region may see a continuing rise of Internet controls. The contest over Asian cyberspace is expected to continue to intensify as actors with divergent interests compete with one another and vie for influence to shape the domain.

Notes

1. John D. Sutter, "Why Internet Connections Are Fastest in South Korea," CNN, March 31, 2010, http://articles.cnn.com/2010-03-31/tech/broadband.south.korea_1_broadband-plan-south-korea-broadband-internet?

2. International Telecommunication Union (ITU), "Internet Indicators: Subscribers, Users and Broadband Subscribers," 2009 figures, http://www.itu.int/ITU-D/icteye/Reporting/ShowReportFrame.aspx?ReportName=/WTI/InformationTechnologyPublic&ReportFormat=HTML4.0&RP_intYear=2009&RP_intLanguageID=1&RP_bitLiveData=False.

3. Darren Allan, "South Korea Tops Akamai Broadband Averages with 17 Mbps," Tech Watch, October 21, 2010, http://www.techwatch.co.uk/2010/10/21/south-korea-tops-akamai-broadband-averages-with-17mbps/.

4. ITU, "Internet Indicators: Subscribers, Users and Broadband Subscribers."

5. Note that mobile penetration rate is usually defined as the number of mobile subscriptions per person, so it can be higher than 100 percent. Paul Budde Communication Pty., Ltd., "Malaysia—Telecoms, Mobile and Broadband," May 2010, http://www.budde.com.au/Research/Malaysia-Telecoms-Mobile-and-Broadband.html.

6. Paul Budde Communication Pty., Ltd., "Vietnam—Telecoms, Mobile Broadband and Forecasts," June 2010, http://www.budde.com.au/Research/Vietnam-Telecoms-Mobile-Broadband-and-Forecasts.html.

7. Ibid.

8. ITU, "Internet Indicators: Subscribers, Users and Broadband Subscribers."

9. Ibid.

10. Ibid.

11. Ibid.

12. Ibid.

13. Ibid.

14. Ministry of Science and Information and Communication Technology, Government of the People's Republic of Bangladesh, "National Information and Communication Technology (ICT) Policy," October 2002, http://www.sdnbd.org/sdi/issues/IT-computer/itpolicy-bd-2002.htm.

15. ITU, "Internet Indicators: Subscribers, Users and Broadband Subscribers."

16. Paul Budde Communication Pty., Ltd., "Bangladesh—Telecoms, Mobile, Broadband and Forecasts," September 2010, http://www.budde.com.au/Research/Bangladesh-Telecoms-Mobile-Broadband-and-Forecasts.html.

17. ITU, "Internet Indicators: Subscribers, Users and Broadband Subscribers."

18. Paul Budde Communication Pty., Ltd., "India—Telecoms, Mobile, Broadband and Forecasts," July 2010, http://www.budde.com.au/Research/India-Telecoms-Mobile-Broadband-and-Forecasts.html.

19. ITU, "Internet Indicators: Subscribers, Users and Broadband Subscribers."

20. Paul Budde Communication Pty., Ltd., "PakistanTelecoms, Mobile Broadband and Forecasts," December 2010, http://www.budde.com.au/Research/Pakistan-Telecoms-Mobile-Broadband-and-Forecasts.html.

21. Wateen, "WiMAX," http://www.wateen.com/OurNetwork.aspx.

22. ITU, "Internet Indicators: Subscribers, Users and Broadband Subscribers."

23. Paul Budde Communication Pty., Ltd., "Indonesia—Telecoms, Mobile Broadband and Forecasts," March 2010, http://www.budde.com.au/Research/Indonesia-Telecoms-Mobile-Broadband-and-Forecasts.html.

24. ITU, "Mobile Cellular Subscriptions," http://www.itu.int/ITU-D/icteye/Reporting/ShowReportFrame.aspx?ReportName=/WTI/CellularSubscribersPublic&ReportFormat=HTML4.0&RP_intYear=2009&RP_intLanguageID=1&RP_bitLiveData=False.

25. "The Information Technology (Amendment) Act, 2008," February 5, 2009, http://www.mit.gov.in/sites/upload_files/dit/files/downloads/itact2000/it_amendment_act2008.pdf.

26. Vikas Asawat, "Information Technology (Amendment) Act, 2008: A New Vision through a New Change," March 2010, http://ssrn.com/abstract=1680152.

27. Aamir Attaa, "PTA to Devise Centralized Internet Censorship Practices," Pro Pakistani, June 23, 2010, http://propakistani.pk/2010/06/23/pta-to-devise-centralized-internet-censorship-practices/.

28. Ismira Lutfia, "Indonesia Web Monitoring Plan Panned," *Jakarta Globe*, February 16, 2010, http://www.thejakartaglobe.com/home/indonesia-web-monitoring-plan-panned/358890; Aubrey Belford, "Sex Tape Scandal Fixates Indonesia," *New York Times*, June 13, 2010, http://www.nytimes.com/2010/06/14/world/asia/14iht-sextape.html; and ICT Watch, "Indonesia Censorship," brief report presented at OpenNet Initiative Global Summit, Ottawa, Canada (June 2010), http://www.slideshare.net/donnybu/indonesian-internetcensorshipreport2010.

29. Siriphon Kusonsinwut, Sawatree Suksri, and Oraphin Yingyongpathana, "Situational Report on Control and Censorship of Online Media, through the Use of Laws and the Imposition of Thai State Policies," iLaw, http://ilaw.or.th/node/632.

30. Gillian Wong, "China Set to Tighten State-Secrets Law Forcing Internet Firms to Inform on Users," *Washington Post*, April 28, 2010, http://www.washingtonpost.com/wp-dyn/content/article/2010/04/27/AR2010042704503.html.

31. "Law of the People's Republic of China on Guarding State Secrets," adopted at the Third Meeting of the Standing Committee of the Seventh National People's Congress on September 5, 1988, and revised at the 14th Session of the Standing Committee of the 11th National People's Congress on April 29, 2010, http://www.npc.gov.cn/npc/xinwen/2010-04/29/content_1571588 .htm. Unofficial English translation is available at: http://www.hrichina.org/public/PDFs/PressReleases/20101001-StateSecretsLaw-EN.pdf.

32. Human Rights Watch, "World Report 2008—Bangladesh," January 31, 2008, http://www .unhcr.org/refworld/docid/47a87bf8c.html.

33. Tarek Mahmud, "Cyber Crime Detour: Facebook?" *Daily Star*, June 5, 2010, http://www .thedailystar.net/law/2010/06/01/life.htm.

34. "Draft Bill to Control Pornography to Be Placed at Next Cabinet Meeting for Approval," New Age, November 12, 2010, http://www.newagebd.com/2010/nov/12/nat.html; and Dhaka Mirror, "Law to Curb Cyber Crimes in Cards," October 13, 2010, http://www.dhakamirror .com/?p=18559.

35. Heru Andriyanto, "Teenager May Be Charged for Facebook Defamation," *Jakarta Globe*, July 9, 2009, http://www.thejakartaglobe.com/national/teenager-may-be-charged-for-facebook -defamation/317034.

36. Ardhi Surayadhi, "Pemerintah Akhirnya Keluarkan Perintah Blokir [Government Finally Removes the Command Block]" [Indonesian], DekiINET, http://us.detikinet.com/read/2010/05/20/135758/1360788/398/pemerintah-akhirnya-keluarkan-perintah-blokir.

37. Aubrey Belford, "Indonesia Finds Banning Pornography Is Difficult," *New York Times*, August 2, 2010, http://www.nytimes.com/2010/08/02/technology/02iht-indoporn02.html.

38. Alecks Pabico, "Blogspot Blanket Ban in Pakistan Appears to Be Lifted," Free Expression in Asian Cyberspace, May 4, 2006, http://freeexpressionasia.wordpress.com/2006/05/04/blogspot -blanket-ban-appears-to-be-lifted.

39. Telecommunications Business Act (wholly amended by presidential decree no. 13558 on August 10, 1991); and Decisions of the Korean Constitutional Court, Opinion14–1 KCCR 616, 99Hun-Ma480, June 27, 2002.

40. Malaysian Communications and Multimedia Act, 1998.

41. "Web Censoring Needs a Debate," *Bangkok Post*, January 6, 2009, http://www.bangkokpost .com/opinion/opinion/9202.

42. Kusonsinwut et al., "Situational Report on Control and Censorship of Online Media."

43. Charles Lourdes, "Six to Be Charged for Insulting Perak Sultan via Blogs, Postings (Update 2)," *The Star*, March 12, 2009, http://thestar.com.my/news/story.asp?sec=nation&file=/2009/3/12/nation/20090312194041.

44. Nurul Huda Jamaluddin, "Blogger 'Hassan Skodeng' to Face Charge Tomorrow," *Malay Mail*, September 1, 2010, http://www.mmail.com.my/content/48211-blogger-hassan-skodeng-face-charge -tomorrow.

45. International Freedom of Expression Exchange, "Hundreds of Police Shut Down Pro-opposition Newspaper," June 9, 2010, http://www.ifex.org/bangladesh/2010/06/09/opposition _hunt/.

46. Bae Ji-sook, "Prosecution Investigates Groundless Rumormongers," *Korea Times*, November 24, 2010, http://www.koreatimes.co.kr/www/news/nation/2010/11/117_76912.html.

47. Song Jung-a, "South Korean Court Rules on Internet Law," *Financial Times*, December 28, 2010, http://www.ft.com/cms/s/0/38b354a4-126d-11e0-b4c8-00144feabdc0.html.

48. Damian Grammaticas, "Chinese Woman Jailed over Twitter Post," BBC News, November 18, 2010, http://www.bbc.co.uk/news/world-asia-pacific-11784603.

49. Andrew Jacobs, "China Sentences Activist in Milk Scandal to Prison," *New York Times*, November 10, 2010, http://www.nytimes.com/2010/11/11/world/asia/11beijing.html.

50. "Bangladesh Imposes YouTube Block," BBC News, March 29, 2010, http://news.bbc.co.uk/2/ hi/7932659.stm.

51. "Bangladesh Blocks Facebook over Mohammed Cartoons," Agence France-Presse, May 29, 2010, http://www.google.com/hostednews/afp/article/ALeqM5ju8Kku2aAuieZmu1g3uUvBOFpHNA.

52. Nurbaiti Hamdan and Cheok Li Peng, "ISPs Ordered to Cut Access to *Malaysia Today* Website," August 28, 2008, *The Star*, http://thestar.com.my/news/story.asp?file=/2008/8/28/nation/ 22187596&sec=nation.

53. Andrew Jacobs and Miguel Helft, "Google, Citing Attack, Threatens to Exit China," *New York Times*, January 12, 2010, http://www.nytimes.com/2010/01/13/world/asia/13beijing.html?scp =3&sq=google%20china&st=cse.

54. "RIM Says No Access to Corporate Email in India," Reuters, January 27, 2011, http://in .reuters.com/article/2011/01/27/idINIndia-54445120110127.

55. "Blackberry Maker Says Will Filter Porn to Meet Indonesia Rules," Reuters, January 10, 2011, http://ca.reuters.com/article/businessNews/idCATRE7092DK20110110.

56. Martyn Williams, "Facebook in Breach of Korean Privacy Laws, Says Regulator," Computer World, December 8, 2010, http://www.computerworld.com/s/article/9200458/Facebook _in_breach_of_Korean_privacy_laws_says_regulator.

57. Waqar Gillani, "Pakistan: Court Blocks Facebook," *New York Times,* May 19, 2010, http:// www.nytimes.com/2010/05/20/world/asia/20briefs-Pakistan.html.

58. "Bangladesh Blocks Facebook over Mohammed Cartoons," Agence France-Presse, May 29, 2010, http://www.google.com/hostednews/afp/article/ALeqM5ju8Kku2aAuieZmu1g3uUvBOFpHNA.

59. "Indonesia Seeks to Block YouTube over Anti-Koran Film," Reuters, April 2, 2008, http:// uk.reuters.com/article/idUKJAK29880220080402; "Indonesia Blocks YouTube to Protest Islam

Film," CNN, April 8, 2008, http://www.cnn.com/2008/WORLD/asiapcf/04/08/indonesia.youtube/index.html.

60. "Bangladesh Imposes YouTube Block," BBC News, March 29, 2010, http://news.bbc.co.uk/2/hi/7932659.stm.

61. "Blackberry Maker Says Will Filter Porn to Meet Indonesia Rules," Reuters.

62. Muhammad Yasir, "BlackBerry Internet Services Yet to Be Restored," *Daily Times*, July 18, 2010, http://www.dailytimes.com.pk/default.asp?page=2010\07\18\story_18-7-2010_pg5_4.

63. Committee to Protect Journalists, "National Day Triggers Censorship, Cyber Attacks in China," September 22, 2009, http://cpj.org/2009/09/national-day-triggers-censorship-cyber-attacks-in.php; Tania Branigan, "China Blocks Twitter, Flickr and Hotmail Ahead of Tiananmen Anniversary," *The Guardian*, June 2, 2009, http://www.guardian.co.uk/technology/2009/jun/02/twitter-china; and "China Should Allow Access to Tibetan Areas," Foreign Correspondents' Club of China Statement, March 9, 2009, http://www.fccchina.org/2009/03/09/china-should-allow-access-to-tibetan-areas.

64. Anuchit Nyguen, "Thai Government Blocks Protest Web Site after Emergency Decree," *Bloomberg Business Week*, 7 April 2010, http://www.businessweek.com/news/2010-04-07/thai-government-blocks-protest-web-site-after-emergency-decree.html.

65. Kanbawza Win, "Fighting the Very Concept of Truth," *Asian Tribune*, October 1, 2010, http://www.asiantribune.com/news/2010/10/01/fighting-very-concept-truth.

66. Devidutta Tripathy and Krittivas Mukherjee, "RIM Gives India Access but Not to Secure E-mails," Reuters, January 13, 2011, http://www.reuters.com/article/2011/01/13/us-blackberry-india-idUSTRE70C1G920110113.

67. "Top 10: Please Show Your ID," *China Daily*, December 10, 2010, http://www2.chinadaily.com.cn/china/2010-12/10/content_11684998.htm.

68. Antone Gonsalves, "Google Scales Back YouTube Korea," *Information Week*, April 13, 2009, http://www.informationweek.com/news/internet/google/showArticle.jhtml?articleID=216500489.

69. See Nart Villeneuve and Masashi Crete-Nishihata, "Control and Resistance: Attacks on Burmese Opposition Media," chapter 8 in this volume.

70. Craig Labovitz, "Attack Severs Burma Internet," Arbor Networks, November 3, 2010, http://asert.arbornetworks.com/2010/11/attac-severs-myanmar-internet.

71. "M'sia Today Blocked 'To Stop Release of Documents,'" Malaysiakini, September 10, 2010, http://malaysiakini.com/news/142385.

72. Human Rights Watch, "Vietnam: Stop Cyber Attacks against Online Critics," May 26, 2010, http://www.hrw.org/en/news/2010/05/26/vietnam-stop-cyber-attacks-against-online-critics.

73. Viet Tan, "Denial of Service Cyber Attacks by the Vietnamese Government," April 27, 2010, http://www.viettan.org/spip.php?article9749.

74. Nart Villeneuve, "Human Rights and Malware Attacks," Nart Villeneuve: Malware Explorer, July 29, 2010, http://www.nartv.org/2010/07/29/human-rights-and-malware-attacks; Danny O'Brien, "That Nobel Invite? Mr. Malware Sent It," Committee to Protect Journalists, November 10, 2010, http://www.cpj.org/internet/2010/11/that-nobel-invite-mr-malware-sent-it.php.

75. "Warning on Fake Emails Targeting News Assistants," Foreign Correspondents' Club of China, September 21, 2009, http://www.fccchina.org/2009/09/21/warning-on-fake-emails-targeting-news -assistants; Nart Villeneuve and Greg Walton, "Targeted Malware Attack on Foreign Correspon- dents Based in China," Nart Villeneuve: Malware Explorer, September 29, 2009, http://www.nartv .org/2009/09/28/targeted-malware-attack-on-foreign-correspondent%E2%80%99s-based-in -china.

76. Brett Winterford, "Optus Customers Hit by China DDOS Attack," *SC Magazine*, April 15, 2010, http://www.securecomputing.net.au/News/172229,optus-customers-hit-by-china-ddos-attack .aspx; and Asher Moses, "Chinese Cyber Attackers Hit Optus," *Sydney Morning Herald*, April 15, 2010, http://www.smh.com.au/technology/security/chinese-cyber-attackers-hit-optus-20100415 -sgm8.html.

77. "Chinese Hackers Suspected of DDoS Attacks against Japan," The New New Internet, Sep- tember 27, 2010, http://www.thenewnewinternet.com/2010/09/27/chinese-hackers-suspected -of-ddos-attacks-against-japan; and "Japan Suspects Cyber Attacks Amid China Row: Media," Agence France-Press, September 17, 2010, http://www.google.com/hostednews/afp/article/ ALeqM5jrJX2uRX7gxO3zPa_dO-rE0FPbnA.

78. Rajeev Deshpande and Vishwa Mohan, "Pakistan, China Hackers Tried to Deface CWG Sites," *Times of India*, October 16, 2010, http://timesofindia.indiatimes.com/india/Pakistan-China -hackers-tried-to-deface-CWG-sites/articleshow/6755521.cms; and Indrani Bagchi, "China Mounts Cyber Attacks on Indian Sites," *Times of India*, May 5, 2008, http://timesofindia .indiatimes.com/India/China-mounts-cyber-attacks-on-Indian-sites/articleshow/3010288.cms.

79. "S. Korean Government Website Hit by Cyber Attacks," Agence France-Presse, June 9, 2010, http://www.google.com/hostednews/afp/article/ALeqM5j-cLHwEp033Jo3lRnOJSFM9L3z6Q.

80. David Hencke, "Whitehall Plans New Cyber Security Centre to Deter Foreign Hackers," *The Guardian*, June 14, 2009, http://www.guardian.co.uk/technology/2009/jun/14/government -security-cyber-crime-hacking.

81. Sam Diaz, "Law Firm That Sued Chinese Government Reports Cyber Attack," ZDNet, January 13, 2010, http://www.zdnet.com/blog/btl/law-firm-that-sued-chinese-government-reports-cyber -attack/29533; and Lolita Baldor, "Pentagon Takes Aim at China Cyber Threat," ABC News, August 19, 2010, http://abcnews.go.com/Politics/wireStory?id=11439149.

82. "Indonesia Passes Anti-porn Bill," BBC News, October 30, 2008, http://news.bbc.co.uk/2/ hi/7700150.stm; Peter Gelling, "Indonesia Passes Broad Anti-pornography Bill," *New York Times*, October 30, 2008, http://www.nytimes.com/2008/10/30/world/asia/30iht-indo.1.17378031.html; "Press Freedom Victim of Defamation Law's 'Inverted Logic,' Journalists Say," *Jakarta Globe*,

May 6, 2009, http://www.thejakartaglobe.com/justAdded/press-freedom-victim-of-defamation
-laws-inverted-logic-journalists-say-/275348.

83. Joe McDonald, "China Eases Internet Restrictions," Huffington Post, June 30, 2009, http://
www.huffingtonpost.com/2009/07/01/china-eases-internet-rest_n_223895.html.

84. "Google 'May Pull Out of China after Gmail Cyber Attack,'" BBC News, January 13, 2010,
http://news.bbc.co.uk/2/hi/8455712.stm.

85. "Facebook Blocked," *Daily Star*, May 30, 2010, http://www.thedailystar.net/newDesign/news
-details.php?nid=140613; and "Lift Ban on Facebook," *Daily Star*, May 31, 2010, http://www
.thedailystar.net/newDesign/news-details.php?nid=140815.

86. Viet Tan, "Denial of Service Cyber Attacks by the Vietnamese Government"; Neel Mehta,
"The Chilling Effects of Malware," Google Online Security Blog, March 30, 2010, http://
googleonlinesecurity.blogspot.com/2010/03/chilling-effects-of-malware.html; George Kurtz, "Vietnamese Speakers Targeted in Cyberattack," McAfee, March 30, 2010, http://siblog.mcafee.com/cto/
vietnamese-speakers-targeted-in-cyberattack; SecureWorks' Counter Threat Unit, "Vecebot Trojan
Analysis," SecureWorks, October 28, 2010, http://www.secureworks.com/research/threats/vecebot.

87. SecureWorks' Counter Threat Unit, "Vecebot Trojan Analysis"; Viet Tan, "Denial of Service
Cyber Attacks by the Vietnamese Government."

Bangladesh

Although Internet access in Bangladesh is not restricted by a national-level filtering regime, the state has twice intervened to block Web sites for hosting anti-Islamic content and content deemed subversive. Internet content is regulated by existing legal frameworks that restrict material deemed defamatory or offensive, as well as content that might challenge law and order.

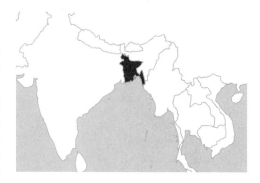

RESULTS AT A GLANCE

Filtering	No Evidence of Filtering	Suspected Filtering	Selective Filtering	Substantial Filtering	Pervasive Filtering
Political	•				
Social	•				
Conflict and security	•				
Internet tools	•				

OTHER FACTORS

	Low	Medium	High	Not Applicable
Transparency				•
Consistency				•

KEY INDICATORS	
GDP per capita, PPP (constant 2005 international dollars)	1,288
Life expectancy at birth, total (years)	66
Literacy rate, adult total (percent of people age 15+)	55.0
Human Development Index (out of 169)	129
Rule of Law (out of 5)	1.8
Voice and Accountability (out of 5)	2.1
Democracy Index (out of 167)	83 (Hybrid regime)
Digital Opportunity Index (out of 181)	134
Internet penetration rate (percentage of population)	0.4

Source by indicator: World Bank 2009, World Bank 2008a, World Bank 2008b, UNDP 2010, World Bank Worldwide Governance Indicators 2009, Economist Intelligence Unit 2010, ITU 2007, ITU 2009. See Introduction to the Country Profiles, pp. 222–223.

Background

The modern Bangladesh state (formerly East Pakistan) was created after the 1971 Bangladesh Liberation War when East Pakistan separated from West Pakistan. Following the independence movement, the new Bangladesh state was governed under military rule. In 1990 it reverted back to a democracy, but remained a volatile state.

In October 2006 a military-backed interim caretaker government was established in Bangladesh and remained in power until December 2008. On January 11, 2007, the military government declared a state of emergency and enacted the Special Powers Act, banning all political activism. Law-enforcement agencies, including the armed forces and the intelligence agencies, were given the right to preemptively detain anybody who they felt was going to violate the law. The political situation on the ground was tense, confrontational, and chaotic. Fundamental human rights were curtailed during the state of emergency, and at least 319 people died at the hands of legally constituted forces.[1]

The country returned to democratic rule after an alliance led by the Awami League gained a majority of seats in the December 29, 2008, national election. Since then the situation in Bangladesh has improved, although there was a brief return to instability in February 2009 when the Bangladesh Rifles (BDR), a paramilitary law-enforcement agency, staged a two-day mutiny over pay and work conditions and killed more than 70 people—primarily officers.[2] The BDR surrendered after Prime Minister Sheikh Hasina sent tanks to surround the force's headquarters in Dhaka.[3]

Today, Bangladesh is a secular democracy, with Islam as its largest religion. With two-thirds of its population working in the agricultural sector, the country is attempting to diversify its economy with industrial development as a priority. Although obstacles to growth exist (widespread poverty, corruption, etc.), Bangladesh's economy has been on an upward growth trajectory. In 2005, Goldman Sachs included Bangladesh in a list of promising destinations for investment—mentioning its high potential for future growth and for becoming one of the world's largest economies by 2025.[4]

Although concerns regarding Bangladesh's human rights situation have waned since the end of the state of emergency, harassment and intimidation continue. In 2010, a violent crackdown on labor activists, union leaders, and workers who were fighting for the right to organize unions and increase minimum wage became a cause for concern.[5] While Prime Minister Hasina has declared a commitment to human rights, including freedom of expression and access to information,[6] the government's commitment to this goal is unclear.

For the moment, the media and Internet appear to be free; however, government actions and existing legal frameworks suggest that opposition media are not always tolerated. In April 2010 the government shut down operations of Channel 1, the country's only privately owned pro-opposition television station, because of an illegal loan arrangement that the channel had made after it had defaulted on a loan.[7] Some believe that the government's decision to pull the plug on Channel 1 was politically motivated. In June 2010, 200 riot police raided the offices of *Amar Desh*, a critical and pro-opposition newspaper based in Dhaka. Police arrested Mahmudar Rahman, the editor of Amar Desh, who had written on extrajudicial killings in Bangladesh as well as corruption among state officials.[8] Rahman was charged and jailed under a number of counts, including sedition, and staff members were charged with a total of 20 counts of defamation for articles related to the ruling government.[9] The newspaper was canceled on the grounds that it was being published without an authorized publisher as per the 1973 Printing Presses and Publications Act. However, the Bangladeshi High Court removed the ban ten days later.

Internet in Bangladesh

The rapid growth of information and communication technologies (ICTs) in Bangladesh is providing new opportunities for the country's development. The government sees ICTs as enabling development and intends to use such technologies as a key driver of socioeconomic development.[10] This view is reflected in the government of Bangladesh's "Digital Bangladesh" plan to build a knowledge-based society and transform Bangladesh into a middle-income country by 2021.[11] It is also reflected in the National Information and Communication Technology Policy, which outlines issues of human resource development, development of ICT infrastructure, facilitation of research and development of ICTs, and development of ICT industries on a priority basis. The policy also highlights the importance of hardware industries, e-commerce, e-governance, and legal issues relating to ICTs, as well as the application of ICTs in areas such as health care, agriculture, social welfare, and transportation.[12] Ongoing initiatives are being taken to meet the goal of digitizing the country: special free Wi-Fi zones have been created for students at Shahjalal University and Dhaka University; textbooks have been published online; computer labs have been set up in 128 schools in 64 districts; and equal access has been ensured through the creation of community e-centers across the country.[13]

The number of Internet users in Bangladesh in 2009 was 617,300, representing a penetration rate of 0.38 percent. Fixed broadband subscriptions reached 50,000 users, representing a penetration rate of 0.03 percent.[14] Although 99 percent of homes lack a telephone line, the country's mobile market is undergoing rapid growth, and penetration is expected to continue to grow rapidly as a result of the large amount of private investment in the sector, lower handset and usage prices, and increasingly more affordable packages for low-income users.[15] As of June 2010, there were 60 million mobile subscribers in the country, representing a penetration rate of 37 percent.[16] In 2009, according to Bangladeshi Internet service providers (ISPs), there were around 4.5 million customers who used the Internet, with 90 percent of them connecting through mobile phone operators' wireless modems.[17]

Since the deregulation of very small aperture terminals (VSATs) by the government in February 2000, the number of ISPs has grown dramatically. As of November 2010, there were approximately 105 nationwide ISPs operating in Bangladesh.[18] In 2009 the market leaders for Internet service providers were Citycell and GrameenPhone.[19]

Mango and the Bangladesh Telecommunications Company Limited (BTCL) are the two international Internet gateway providers in the country. As of April 2008, all ISPs were required by regulation to route their international traffic to either provider, who would then send the traffic via the submarine cable or VSATs.[20]

In 2006, Bangladesh connected to the South East Asia–Middle East–Western Europe 4 (SEA-ME-WE 4) optical fiber submarine communications cable system—the primary Internet backbone between Southeast Asia, the Indian subcontinent, the Middle East, and Europe.[21] Since connecting to the SEA-ME-WE 4, the country has seen Internet bandwidth prices drop significantly. In 2008, the Bangladesh Telecommunication Regulatory Commission (BTRC)[22] slashed wholesale Internet bandwidth prices drastically, from BDT 80,000 (approximately USD 1,125) per Mbps to BDT 18,000 (approximately USD 250) per Mbps.[23] In 2009, after complaints that retail prices were still too high for slow, unreliable connections, the BTRC indicated that they were going to begin monitoring ISPs to ensure that retail prices reflected the reduced wholesale prices.[24] The Internet's speed in Bangladesh remains one of the slowest in the world. The average upload speed is 0.77 Mbps, and the average download speed is 0.87 Mbps.[25]

Although the government does not proactively filter Internet content, it has blocked Web sites on two occasions. On March 6, 2009, the government blocked access to YouTube for hosting a recording of a conversation between Prime Minister Hasina and Bangladeshi army officers in the aftermath of the BDR mutiny. In the conversation, army officials yelled angrily while the prime minister defended her decision to negotiate with the BDR during the course of the mutiny—a move that many believed gave border guards time to kill army officers and rape their wives.[26] Users reported that other file-hosting Web sites such as eSnips and Mediafire were also inaccessible. It was suspected that the Web sites were blocked by the firewalls at the international Internet gateway, since the sites were still available through proxy.[27] According to one senior government official, "The government can block any site that contains anti-state or subversive contents, which may cause unrest. We took the measure temporarily. It will be lifted soon."[28] The ban was lifted on March 12, 2009.

On May 29, 2010, the BTRC placed a temporary block on Facebook (which has close to one million Bangladeshi users)[29] because of content deemed offensive—in particular, caricatures of the Prophet Mohammed and Bangladeshi political leaders. On the day before the ban, thousands of Bangladeshis took to the streets of Dhaka to protest Facebook and the "Everyone Draw Mohammed Day" campaign being spread across the site. One of these protest organizers explained that "drawing caricatures of the Prophet Mohammed, peace be upon him, is an attack on Islam and is extremely humiliating for Islam."[30] That same day, three Islamic political parties demanded an immediate ban.[31] According to BTRC acting chairman Hasan Mahmud Delwar, the ban was imposed because the Web site "hurt the religious sentiments of the country's majority Muslim population."[32] The move to block the entire Web site as opposed to just the offending content was undertaken because the BTCL and Mango Telecom had not yet found a way to target the specific content.[33] An official explained that the ban would be lifted once a way to block offensive content was discovered. The decision to block the Web site angered many, including a group of Dhaka University students who subsequently took to the streets to protest.[34] On June 5, access was restored to Facebook after the company agreed to remove satirical cartoons of Mohammed and Bangladeshi politicians.[35]

Coincidently, the ban was imposed on the same day that the Rapid Action Battalion[36] arrested Mahbub Alam Rodin for posting satirical images of Bangladeshi politicians (including Prime Minister Hasina) on Facebook. Rodin was charged with "spreading malice and insulting the country's leaders."[37]

Legal and Regulatory Framework

The right to freedom of expression was severely curtailed during the state of emergency when the military-backed government imposed harsh restrictions on already-weakened media. Editors and journalists were told to exercise caution and were prohibited from publishing news critical of the government.[38] Under Section 5 of the Emergency Power Rules, citizens were prohibited from using the Internet and other print media to publish content deemed "provocative."[39] The government was given the power to censor "provocative" news content, seize publications, and confiscate media equipment.[40] The fear of detainment, harassment, and defamation charges under the Bangladesh Penal Code and Code of Criminal Procedure resulted in self-imposed censorship.[41]

Since the end of the state of emergency, the Bangladesh government has initiated some positive steps to reassert citizens' right to information and loosen the state's grip on media.[42] Examples of measures that facilitate access to information include the Right to Information Act, which enhances transparency and provides people with the right to access public information.[43] Nonetheless, Article 57 of the Information and Communication and Technologies Act still allows the state to regulate content, including Internet content. Under the act, offenders can face up to ten years imprisonment or a maximum fine of BDT 1 crore (approximately USD 140,500) for publishing content (including content in electronic form) that is "falsified or vulgar." This includes defamatory content, content that may harm law and order, and content that attacks religious beliefs.[44]

In general, there is a lack of a comprehensive cyber law in the country; however, it appears that authorities are working toward implementing one.[45] Cybercrime and online pornography have become an increasing concern for the Bangladesh state and the authorities who have been working on curbing such crimes. Authorities have voiced concerns about the need to acquire equipment to detect and identify people involved in cybercrime, the need to train law enforcement on how to curb cybercrimes and pornography, and the need to tighten regulation on Internet cafés. In 2010 a Pornography Control Bill was drafted and is currently pending cabinet approval. The draft bill proposes that offenders who commit cybercrime or a crime related to pornography could face five years imprisonment, a fine of BDT 50,000 (approximately USD 700), or both.[46]

Surveillance

In 2007, during the state of emergency, the Rapid Action Battalion conducted house-to-house searches in Dhaka, Chittagong, and Sylhet, and profiled more than 450,000 Internet subscribers to seek out Internet users with a fast connection.[47] ISPs reported that they had been instructed to provide a list of subscribers and details about them as well as the administrative passwords for all Internet gateway servers, and to assist in installing "traffic scanners" on gateway routers.[48] In another memo, ISPs were instructed to provide information about bandwidth lease and usage, details about clients, and copies of technical agreements with connectivity providers.[49] A BTRC official stated that the purpose of the crackdown was to track illegal Voice over Internet Protocol (VoIP) operators—however, he was unable to explain why house-to-house searches were being conducted.[50]

There have not been reports of surveillance since the end of the state of emergency. A notable exception is a 2009 Freedom House report that suggested that journalists' e-mails were being monitored and that some journalists had been required to submit their personal online passwords to intelligence officers during questioning.[51]

ONI Testing Results

In October 2009, testing was conducted on two Bangladeshi ISPs, BDCOM Online and GrameenPhone. BDCOM Online is a publicly owned company and provides Internet services to consumers and the majority of solutions for small- to large-scale ISPs in Bangladesh. GrameenPhone is a leading mobile operator and the largest ISP in Bangladesh with more than 23 million subscribers in urban and rural areas nationwide.[52] The tests revealed no evidence of filtering in any of the categories tested.

Conclusion

The Bangladeshi state sees ICTs as positive enablers of socioeconomic development and has been working toward digitizing the country. This effort has been reflected in state initiatives to strengthen equal access to ICTs across the country, including the installation of computer labs in schools and community e-centers, as well as developing Internet infrastructure for the country and making the Internet more affordable to citizens.

The current Bangladeshi government has reversed many of the rules that were in place during the state of emergency. The press has gained back much of the freedom it lost during that period. However, the government appears to maintain a distrust of opposition media, which is consistent with existing laws that regulate content, including Internet content. On two occasions, the state has blocked Web sites for "subversive" and anti-Islamic content. Nonetheless, ONI testing revealed no evidence of filtering on BDCOM Online and GrameenPhone, and there have been no reports of ongoing Web site filtering in Bangladesh.

Notes

1. "Next JS Must Review All Ordinances," *Daily Star*, December 13, 2008, http://www.thedailystar.net/story.php?nid=66906.

2. "Bangladesh Court Jails More Guards over Deadly Mutiny," BBC News, April 18, 2010, http://news.bbc.co.uk/2/hi/8628368.stm.

3. "Bangladesh Guard Mutiny Is Over," BBC News, February 26, 2009, http://news.bbc.co.uk/2/hi/7912392.stm.

4. Jim O'Neill, Roopa Purushothaman, Anna Stupnytska, and Dominic Wilson, *Global Economics Paper No. 134: How Solid Are the BRICs?* (New York: Goldman Sachs, 2005.)

5. Human Rights Watch, "Bangladesh: Stop Harassment and Intimidation of Apparel Worker Leaders," August 10, 2010, http://www.hrw.org/en/news/2010/08/10/bangladesh-stop-harassment-and-intimidation-apparel-worker-leaders; Shenal Shingavi, "Textile Strikes Rock Bangladesh," International Labor Rights Forum, August 24, 2010, http://www.laborrights.org/creating-a-sweatfree-world/sweatshops/news/12393; and "RMG Unrest Spreads in Ashulia, N'ganj," *Daily Star*, August 1, 2010, http://www.thedailystar.net/newDesign/news-details.php?nid=148902.

6. "PM Reiterates to Safeguard Human Rights," *Daily Star*, December 6, 2009, http://www.thedailystar.net/newDesign/latest_news.php?nid=20953.

7. "Bangladesh Shuts Down Opposition-Owned TV Channel," *Daily Times*, April 29, 2010, http://www.dailytimes.com.pk/default.asp?page=2010%5C04%5C29%5Cstory_29-4-2010_pg20_2.

8. International Freedom of Expression Exchange, "Hundreds of Police Shut Down Pro-opposition Newspaper," June 9, 2010, http://www.ifex.org/bangladesh/2010/06/09/opposition_hunt/.

9. Ibid.

10. Ministry of Science and Information and Communication Technology, Government of the People's Republic of Bangladesh, "National Information and Communication Technology (ICT) Policy," October 2002, http://www.sdnbd.org/sdi/issues/IT-computer/itpolicy-bd-2002.htm.

11. Bangladesh Board of Investment, Prime Minister's Office, "Digital Bangladesh," http://boi.gov.bd/about-bangladesh/government-and-policies/digital-bangladesh-overview.

12. Ministry of Science and Information and Communication Technology, "National Information and Communication Technology (ICT) Policy."

13. "What Need to Be Done for Digital Bangladesh," VOIP Bangladesh, February 18, 2010, http://voipbangladesh.com/bangladesh-internet/what-need-to-be-done-for-digital-bangladesh-287.html.

14. International Telecommunication Union (ITU), "Internet Indicators: Subscribers, Users and Broadband Subscribers," 2009 Figures, http://www.itu.int/ITU-D/icteye/Reporting/ShowReportFrame.aspx?ReportName=/WTI/InformationTechnologyPublic&ReportFormat=HTML4.0&RP_intYear=2009&RP_intLanguageID=1&RP_bitLiveData=False.

15. Paul Budde Communication Pty., Ltd., "2009 Bangladesh—Telecoms, Mobile, Broadband and Forecasts," September 2009, http://www.budde.com.au/Research/2009-Bangladesh-Telecoms-Mobile-Broadband-and-Forecasts.html.

16. Paul Budde Communication Pty., Ltd., "Bangladesh—Telecoms, Mobile, Broadband and Forecasts," September 2010, http://www.budde.com.au/Research/Bangladesh-Telecoms-Mobile-Broadband-and-Forecasts.html.

17. Ibid.

18. Bangladesh Telecommunication Regulatory Commission, "List of the ISP Licenses," http://www.btrc.gov.bd/licensing/operators/isp/nationwide_isp.pdf.

19. Md Hasan, "BTRC Moves to Discipline Internet," *Daily Star,* July 27, 2009, http://www.thedailystar.net/newDesign/news-details.php?nid=98772.

20. Rezwan, "Bangladesh: YouTube and File Sharing Sites Blocked," March 8, 2009, http://globalvoicesonline.org/2009/03/08/bangladesh-youtube-and-file-sharing-sites-blocked.

21. Ibid.

22. The Bangladesh Telecommunication Regulatory Commission is an independent commission responsible for regulating all issues related to telecommunications in Bangladesh.

23. "BTRC Cuts Bandwidth Charges," *Daily Star*, July 17, 2009, http://www.thedailystar.net/newDesign/news-details.php?nid=97233.

24. Ibid.

25. "World Speedtest.net Results," Speedtest.net, http://www.speedtest.net.

26. "Bangladesh Imposes YouTube Block," BBC News, March 29, 2010, http://news.bbc.co.uk/2/hi/7932659.stm.

27. "YouTube and Some File Sharing Sites Blocked in Bangladesh," E-Bangladesh, March 8, 2009, http://www.e-bangladesh.org/2009/03/08/youtube-and-some-file-sharing-sites-blocked-in-bangladesh.

28. "YouTube Blocked over Mutiny Tape," *Daily Star*, March 8, 2009, http://www.thedailystar.net/newDesign/latest_news.php?nid=15498.

29. Reporters Without Borders, "Access to Facebook Restored in Bangladesh," June 7, 2010, http://en.rsf.org/bangladesh-facebook-access-restored-in-31-05-2010,37627.html.

30. "Bangladesh Blocks Facebook over Mohammed Cartoons," Agence France-Presse, May 29, 2010, http://www.google.com/hostednews/afp/article/ALeqM5ju8Kku2aAuieZmu1g3uUvBOFpHNA.

31. "Facebook Blocked," *Daily Star*, May 30, 2010, http://www.thedailystar.net/newDesign/news-details.php?nid=140613.

32. Ibid.

33. Ibid.

34. "Lift Ban on Facebook," *Daily Star*, May 31, 2010, http://www.thedailystar.net/newDesign/news-details.php?nid=140815.

35. Reporters Without Borders, "Access to Facebook Restored in Bangladesh."

36. The Rapid Action Battalion is the anticrime and antiterrorism unit of Bangladesh Police.

37. "Bangladesh 'Blocks Facebook' over Political Cartoons," BBC News, May 30, 2010, http://www.bbc.co.uk/news/10192755.

38. Committee to Protect Journalists, "Attacks on the Press 2007: Bangladesh," February 5, 2008, http://www.cpj.org/2008/02/attacks-on-the-press-2007-bangladesh.php.

39. Human Rights Watch, *World Report 2008—Bangladesh*, January 31, 2008, http://www.unhcr.org/refworld/docid/47a87bf8c.html.

40. Committee to Protect Journalists, "Attacks on the Press 2007: Bangladesh."

41. Global Network for a Free Media, "The Media Environment in Bangladesh," http://www.freemedia.at/fileadmin/media/Documents/IPI_mission_reports/Bangladesh_Media_Environment_final.pdf.

42. Freedom House, *Freedom of the Press 2010—Bangladesh*, October 1, 2010, http://www.unhcr.org/refworld/docid/4ca5cc66a.html.

43. Shaheen Anam, "Freedom to Know," *Forum* 3, no. 6 (2009), http://www.thedailystar.net/forum/2009/june/freedom.htm.

44. "Cyber Crime Detour: Facebook?" *Daily Star*, June 5, 2010, http://www.thedailystar.net/law/2010/06/01/life.htm.

45. Zahurul Alam and Mohammed S. Chowdhury, "ICT-Driven Knowledge Economy in Bangladesh: Issues and Constraints," *Journal of Knowledge Management Practice* 10, no. 1 (2009).

46. "Law to Curb Cyber Crimes in Cards," *Dhaka Mirror*, October 13, 2010, http://www.dhakamirror.com/?p=18559.

47. "Crackdown on Internet Users in Bangladesh," E-Bangladesh, October 3, 2007, http://www.e-bangladesh.org/2007/10/03/crackdown-on-internet-users-in-bangladesh.

48. Ibid.

49. Ibid.

50. Ibid.

51. Freedom House, *Freedom of the Press 2010—Bangladesh*.

52. Grameenphone, "Grameenphone Crosses 23 Million Subscribers," December 29, 2009, http://www.grameenphone.com/index.php?id=523.

Burma

Burma's ruling military junta is attempting to expand Internet access in the country while maintaining a restrictive system of control. Although less than only 1 percent of the population has access to the Internet, the government maintains a tight grip over online content, and—as demonstrated by the shutdown of Internet access during the 2007 "Saffron Revolution"—is willing to take drastic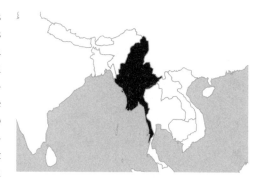
action to control the flow of information. Internet filtering in Burma is pervasive and extensively targets political and social content. Strict laws and regulations, along with surveillance, prohibit Internet users from freely accessing the Internet. Cyber attacks on the Web sites of opposition groups and media are frequent and typically occur on the anniversaries of significant political events, or during critical moments such as the 2010 election.

RESULTS AT A GLANCE

Filtering	No Evidence of Filtering	Suspected Filtering	Selective Filtering	Substantial Filtering	Pervasive Filtering
Political					•
Social				•	
Conflict and security				•	
Internet tools				•	

OTHER FACTORS

	Low	Medium	High	Not Applicable
Transparency		•		
Consistency		•		

KEY INDICATORS	
GDP per capita, PPP (constant 2005 international dollars)	854
Life expectancy at birth, total (years)	62
Literacy rate, adult total (percent of people age 15+)	91.9
Human Development Index (out of 169)	132
Rule of Law (out of 5)	1.0
Voice and Accountability (out of 5)	0.3
Democracy Index (out of 167)	163 (Authoritarian regime)
Digital Opportunity Index (out of 181)	179
Internet penetration rate (percentage of population)	0.2

Source by indicator: World Bank 2005, World Bank 2008a, World Bank 2008b, UNDP 2010, World Bank Worldwide Governance Indicators 2009, Economist Intelligence Unit 2010, ITU 2007, ITU 2009. See Introduction to the Country Profiles, pp. 222–223.

Background

The State Peace and Development Council (SPDC), the military government that rules the Union of Myanmar, maintains a tight stranglehold on the country's economic and political developments. The government polices Internet content through one of the most severe regimes of information control in the world. Despite barriers to access and very low connectivity, however, Internet users in Burma have managed to communicate valuable information to the outside world during explosive political events.

On August 19, 2007, precipitating what would become known as the Saffron Revolution, leaders of the 88 Generation student group organized a rally to protest a sudden sharp increase in fuel prices in Rangoon (Yangon).[1] Because the Burmese spend up to 70 percent of their monthly income on food alone,[2] the fuel-price hikes amid chronic inflation—which reached 30 percent in 2006 and 2007—were untenable.[3] Over the next month, leadership of the protests passed from former student leaders and a number of female activists to Buddhist monks, with participation swelling to an estimated crowd of 150,000 protesters on September 23.[4] Throughout the crisis, citizen journalists and bloggers continued to feed raw, graphic footage and eyewitness accounts to the outside world through the Internet. The violent crackdown that began on September 26 ultimately left up to 200 dead,[5] including a Japanese journalist whose death by gunshot was caught on video.[6] Burmese security forces raided monasteries, detaining and disrobing thousands of monks. Despite claims by official state media that only 91 people remained in detention as of December 2007, Human Rights Watch claimed the number to be in the hundreds.[7]

Between October and December 2008, around 300 individuals were sentenced to harsh prison terms for political crimes.[8] Most were tried by police prosecutors and convicted by judges operating from prison courts, including Insein prison—a prison run by the junta for the purpose of repressing political dissidents and notorious for its inhumane conditions.[9] In November, it was reported that 150 critics of the government had received imprisonment terms of two to 65 years.[10] According to the UN Special Rapporteur on the situation of human rights in Burma, 16 journalists and bloggers were in prison in March 2009.[11] As of 2010, there were an estimated 2,100 "prisoners of conscience" in Burma.[12]

A general election in Burma was held on November 7, 2010. It was the first election in Burma since 1990 when the National League for Democracy (NLD)—the major opposition party led by Aung San Suu Kyi—won a majority of 392 out of 492 seats. However, the State Law and Order Restoration (SPDC's predecessor) refused to hand over power to the NLD and imprisoned many of the NLD's members, including Suu Kyi.[13] The 2010 election was a part of the SPDC's plan to move the country from military to democratic rule under the "road map to democracy" plan. However, the general sentiment within the country was that the election would only consolidate military rule.[14]

In March 2010, the SPDC laid down ground rules for the election with controversial electoral laws and bylaws that undermined participation by opposition parties and prohibited those with criminal convictions from participating in the election.[15] These actions were understood by many as contrary to the democratic process because the move essentially prohibited the participation of many prodemocracy leaders who had been arrested in the aftermath of the 1990 election.

By October 2010, 40 political parties had been approved by the electoral commission to participate in the election, but observers predicted that the race would come down to three contenders: the National Democracy Force (established by former members of the NLD), the Union Solidarity and Development Party (USDP), and the National Unity Party (NUP). Both the USDP and the NUP had the full backing of the junta, with the USDP consisting of former military officers.[16] Due to draconian election laws and constraints imposed by the military's controversial constitution, as well as its size and budget, a USDP victory was expected. In the lead-up to the election, parties opposed to the junta complained about harassment, and Suu Kyi called for a boycott of the election. Foreign media and observers were barred from the country during the election.

On November 9, 2010, with 80 percent of all votes, the USDP was declared the winner of the general election.[17] The USDP claimed that 70 percent of eligible voters had participated in the election.[18] Although many opposition groups condemned the results by alleging massive fraud, the government of Burma declared the election to be a transition to democracy. Those who condemned the election pointed to illegitimate advance voting[19] and the fact that the Burmese constitution automatically reserves 25 percent of the seats in Parliament for military officials.[20]

Internet in Burma

A combination of government restrictions, slow connection speeds, and prohibitive costs has kept Internet access rates relatively low and stagnant in Burma. In 2009, there were an estimated 111,000 Internet users in Burma, representing a 0.2 percent penetration rate.[21] In the same year, there were 15,000 fixed broadband subscriptions, representing a 0.03 percent fixed broadband subscription penetration rate.[22]

Most users access the Internet in public access centers (PACs), which typically charge between USD 0.30 and 0.50 per hour.[23] Some PACs are owned by the Union Solidarity and Development Association (USDA), which operates Internet café services in their local township offices. Users and owners of PACs are subject to a number of state regulations.[24] Operators of PACs must record the names, identification numbers, and addresses of their customers. They are also required to take screenshots of a patron's computer every five minutes and maintain records of Internet usage to be sent to the Myanmar Information Communications Technology Development Corporation every two weeks. Internet café owners are required to arrange computer monitors in a way that makes them publically visible (that is, to restrict privacy) and to ensure that only state-run e-mail providers are used.[25] Access to political Web sites, as well as cybercrime (including acts against Burmese culture), are prohibited at Internet cafés.

Despite regular crackdowns, it is widely reported that most PAC owners ignore regulations and provide their customers with proxy servers, such as glite.sanyi.net, an alternative means of accessing blocked Web sites.[26] Informal bribe-paying arrangements between some PAC owners and government employees allows some PACs to operate illegally—which in turn allows owners to offer proxy tools and other services that are technically forbidden.[27]

Slow connection speeds and steep costs limit access significantly. In 2009, initial setup costs for broadband were approximately USD 200 for dial-up connection and USD 2,000 for ADSL.[28] The Internet connection speeds in homes, offices, and businesses were, respectively, 128 Kbps, 256 Kbps, and 512 Kbps.[29] Slow upload speeds are not only an indication of the lack of Internet capacity in Burma—they may also be of intentional design. For example, even after connectivity was resumed following the Internet shutdown during the Saffron Revolution, Internet speeds controlled with proxy-caching servers were slowed to 256 Kbps—a likely attempt by the government to prevent users from uploading videos and photos or sending large files and documents.[30] Although broadband subscribers can choose to pay according to access speeds, they also have to accept upload speeds that are half the download speeds in each subscription.[31] In Internet cafés, Internet speed tends to be slower because connection lines are shared by multiple computers.[32]

Slowdowns in Internet connection speeds are common in Burma. For example, a prolonged slowdown on the Burmese Internet service provider (ISP) Yatanarpon Teleport began on March 22, 2009, and continued until April 21.[33] Yatanarpon Teleport had announced that the submarine cable South East Asia–Middle East–Western Europe 3 (SEA-ME-WE 3) would be undergoing maintenance from March 21 to March 25, but both Yatanarpon Teleport and Ministry of Post and Telecommunications (MPT) shut down their service for several hours on the afternoon of March 22. For end users, the announced network maintenance resulted in frustration with delays (in addition to those caused by the use of circumvention tools) in accessing popular online services, while many Internet cafés were closed while waiting for the resumption of normal Internet access speeds. A similar slowdown occurred in February 2010.[34]

The Burmese government maintains a tight grip on the Internet, particularly during key moments, and continually strives to improve its means of controlling information. In April 2008, Mizzima News reported that the government had formulated a sector-based Internet shutdown strategy to deal with the constitutional referendum scheduled for May 10 so that as soon as information leaks began, Internet cafés and PACs would be cut off, followed by the commercial sector (and presumably the hospitality and tourism sector) if information continued to flow out.[35] Authorities planned both shutdowns of access and significant slowdowns in connection speeds,[36] a strategy that was made irrelevant in the wake of Cyclone Nargis.[37]

The Burmese government aggressively controls online content through filtering Web sites related to pornography, human rights, political reform, and politically sensitive topics. Web sites are filtered with technologies from U.S. companies Fortinet and Bluecoat,[38] despite an embargo that places limits on exports to Burma. Users often use proxy sites to access banned Web sites and free e-mail services and chat programs such as Gmail and Gtalk. However, proxy sites are also banned.

Despite the limitations imposed on society in Burma, the Internet has become an important tool for citizens to challenge the restrictions that are placed on them. For example, amid escalating tension and protests in September 2007, a small band of citizen bloggers and journalists fed graphic footage and eyewitness accounts to the outside world through the Internet.[39] Photographs and videos taken with cellular telephones and digital cameras were uploaded to the Internet, broadcast over television and radio, and spread across communities in Burma. Citizen journalists helped many generations of Burmese citizens link to each other through blogs and other forms of social media.[40] Although this effort was brought to a complete halt on September 29, 2007, when the SPDC completely shut down the country's Internet access for approximately two weeks, allowing only intermittent periods of connectivity,[41] the actions of "netizens" demonstrated that the tools of information technology can have a strong impact on the global coverage of events as they unfold. The subsequent Internet shutdown was the government's most direct and drastic option to cut off this bidirectional flow of information, to keep the picture of reality distorted for people both within the Burmese border and outside.

Although the Burmese ruling elite perceives the Internet as a source of instability and goes to great lengths to control access and content, they also see the Internet as an enabler of economic development. After signing the 2000 e-ASEAN Framework Agreement, Burma formed the e-National Task Force to support the development of information and communications technologies (ICTs).[42] Set to become Burma's largest IT development, Yatanarpon Cyber City in Pyin Oo Lwin is part of an ICT development master plan under the Initiative for ASEAN Integration.[43] The development of Yatanarpon Cyber City and the country's Internet infrastructure illustrates the regime's commitment to economic development in the realm of ICTs.

At the same time, some sources have charged Yatanarpon as being part of a plan to tighten control over the country's Internet and prevent users from gaining access to or distributing information critical of the regime.[44] In October 2010, Yatanarpon Teleport, the first Myanmar national Web portal, was launched in Yatanarpon. Its creation marked a major change in Burma's ICT development.

Prior to the launch of the national Web portal, the country's two ISPs were the state-owned MPT and the privately owned Yatanarpon Teleport (or Myanmar Teleport, formerly known as Bagan Cybertech), which was controlled by the Ministry of Communications, Posts, and Telegraphs. Internet requests would have to go through each of the ISPs, through the security gateway, and then through the military-controlled Hantharwaddy National Gateway before accessing the global Internet through the SEA-ME-WE 3 and China-Burma cross-border fiber-optic cables.[45] Under this system, all Internet requests were required to go through proxy servers located in Rangoon. Because military and government users shared ISPs with private users, Internet requests from military and government users also went through the Rangoon proxy servers, creating a bottleneck for government and military users.[46]

After the launch of Yatanarpon Teleport, the two main servers were no longer MPT and Yatanarpon, but MPT and a newly created Ministry of Defense ISP. Naypyitaw (a new ISP) and Yatanarpon Teleport are now under the Myanmar Post and Telecommunications ISP. Under this new ISP system, the Ministry of Defense ISP will serve only Ministry of Defense users, while the Naypyitaw ISP will serve other government ministries, and Yatanarpon will serve private civilian users. This new ISP system will minimize loading on the National Gateway as well as the main ISP, but Internet requests will have to pass through more ISPs servers—thus placing users under more screening and controls.[47]

As one report pointed out, segregating users into separate groups accessing the Internet through differentiated servers means that users will be subject to more screening and controls as the government will be given a better capacity to control traffic.[48] At a time of emergency, the government will only have to shut down the Yatanarpon ISP, as opposed to all ISPs, in order to block civilian users from the Internet. The Burma Media Association and Reporters Without Borders have expressed concern about the safety of users' login credentials because there are possibilities of sniffing (or "Man in the Middle")[49] attacks and DNS spoofing/poisoning.[50] These new developments demonstrate that the government intends to expand Burma's Internet access, while at the same time maintaining strict control over online activity.

Legal and Regulatory Frameworks

Despite the fact that the right to equal protection under the law, to freedom of expression and peaceful assembly, to education, and other fundamental rights are guaranteed in the Burmese constitution, the SPDC continues to violate these rights and freedoms.[51] Although the SPDC claims that 380 domestic laws are being reviewed for compliance with constitutional human rights provisions,[52] it continues to apply broad laws and regulations in order to punish citizens for any activity deemed detrimental to the national interest or the SPDC's grip on power.

All domestic radio and television stations, as well as daily newspapers, are state owned.[53] While more than 100 print publications are privately owned,[54] the Ministry of Information limits licensing to media outlets that agree only to print approved material and to submit to vigorous advance censorship by the Press Scrutiny and Registration Division.[55] For example, in the wake of Cyclone Nargis, media were prohibited from publishing stories that depicted devastation and human suffering.[56] Publishing license regulations issued by the Ministry of Information in 2005 are prodigious in scope, banning negative news and commentary about ASEAN, any "nonconstructive" criticism of government departments, coverage of national disasters and poverty that affect the public interest, and the citation of foreign news sources that are detrimental to the state.[57] In effect since 1962, the Printers and Publishers Registration Law applies to all "printed published matter" and requires the registration of all printing presses, printers, and publishers, as well as the submission of all books and newspapers as they are published.[58] Similar restrictions apply in the Video and Television Law, which stipulates three years of imprisonment in cases of "copying, distributing, hiring or exhibiting videotape" that has not received the prior approval of the Video Censor Board.[59]

Online access and content are stringently controlled through legal, regulatory, and economic constraints. As in other areas, state policies are difficult to access because they are rarely published or explained.

A terms-of-service rule for MPT users issued in 2000 provided a warning that online content would be subject to the same kind of strict filtering that the Press Scrutiny and Registration Division carries out. The terms state that users must obtain MPT's permission before creating Web pages, and users cannot post anything "detrimental" to the government or even simply related to politics.[60] Sharing registered Internet connections is punishable by revoked access and "legal action."[61] The MPT can also "amend and change regulations on the use of the Internet without prior notice."[62]

According to the 1996 Computer Science Development Law (CSDL), network-ready computers must be registered with the MPT. Failure to do so may result in fines and a prison sentence of seven to 15 years.[63] Under the 2004 Electronic Transactions Law, it is unlawful to use electronic transactions technology to receive or send information relating to state secrets or state security. It is also unlawful under Article 33 to use such technology to commit acts "detrimental to the security of the State or prevalence of law and order or community peace and tranquility or national solidarity or national economy or national culture."[64] Failure to abide by such laws can result in fines and a prison sentence of seven to 15 years.[65]

These laws have been invoked by the junta to prosecute Burmese activists and dissenters who use online tools to communicate or transmit information. In November 2008, closed courts, mostly operating out of Insein prison, applied the Electronic Transactions Law and the Television and Video Law to deliver sentences to 88 Generation activists, bloggers, and others.[66] That same month, Nay Phone Latt, a prominent Burmese blogger, was sentenced to more than 20 years of imprisonment by a special court in Insein prison: two years for defamation of the state under Article 505(b) of the Criminal Code and 18 years and six months for the violation of Article 32(b) of the Television and Video Law and Article 33(a) of the Electronics Transactions Law.[67] The Electronic Transactions Law also constituted part of the 59-year sentence handed to Maung Thura, comedian, film director, and blogger, who was convicted for circulating his footage of relief work after Cyclone Nargis on DVD and the Internet, as well for criticizing government aid efforts in interviews with overseas media.[68]

Surveillance

In Burma, the fear of surveillance is pervasive and embedded in daily life.[69] Offline, the state can effectively monitor its citizens through a dragnet that functions with the assistance of various civilian organizations it directly controls. These organizations include the USDA, which imposes mandatory membership on citizens in specific professions and is being cultivated as a "future military-controlled civilian government in Burma," with President Gen Than Shwe as its primary patron.[70] State and local Peace and Development Councils (PDCs) are also effective tools of social control. All households must provide their local ward PDCs with a list and photographs of all persons residing in the household and register any overnight guests before dark—a policy that is reinforced by regular midnight checks of homes.[71] Swan Arr Shin, another civilian organization, pays its members to conduct routine neighborhood surveillance and provide police assistance, delegating others to engage in violence against opposition figures for remuneration.[72] During the Saffron Revolution, intelligence officials videotaped and photographed protesters, and enlisted the help of PDCs, the USDA, and local law-enforcement authorities in identifying individuals for arrests in the ensuing crackdown.[73]

Because surveillance is more effective when there are fewer targets, a possible strategy of the Burmese regime may be to limit people's time online. During the October 2007 Internet shutdown, surveillance (or at least perceived surveillance) was attributed as a rationale for various government responses, including the government's policy of limiting Internet access to the curfew hours between 9:00 PM and 5:00 AM.[74] Not only would the late hours significantly reduce the number of users online (since most Burmese users do not have Internet at home), but it would also make the task of identifying targeted users easier for a government without much experience in tracking and investigating Internet usage.

While the government's aptitude at conducting online surveillance is not entirely clear, it appears to be pursuing a combination of methods to monitor the small proportion of its citizens that access the Internet. In addition to the constraints that Internet café owners are required to impose on their customers,[75] it has also been reported that most Internet cafés have installed local software to make each computer beep if it accesses a prodemocratic news media outlet outside the country. Owners must then intervene with the user or risk imprisonment.[76]

Government e-mail services—boosted by the blocking of many free Web-based e-mail services—are widely believed to be under surveillance, with delays of up to several days between the sending and receiving of e-mails, or with messages arriving without their original attachments.[77] Nay Phone Latt was allegedly convicted in part for storing a cartoon of General Than Shwe in his e-mail account.[78]

The military government's stringent filtering regime fosters fear and self-censorship. According to ONI sources, the banning of certain political blogs in mid-2007 sparked rumors that more would be banned if this trend continued, spurring many local bloggers to self-monitor their postings in the hope that their blogs would not be blacklisted.[79] Internet slowdowns fuel speculation of enhanced online monitoring, especially where users are required to click through pages equipped with network visibility applications (such as Bluecoat) that allow for monitoring of network activity and behavior intended to access the Internet.[80] Government workers are not exempt from surveillance—in 2010, two high-ranking government officials were sentenced to death for e-mailing documents abroad.[81]

Cyber Attacks

Beyond Internet filtering, there are also frequent cyber attacks on Web sites that host political content related to Burma, such as exiled independent Burmese media. These are typically distributed denial of service (DDoS) or defacement attacks, and appear to be politically motivated because the attacks are routinely launched on politically sensitive dates, such as the anniversary of the Saffron Revolution. It is widely believed that such attacks are state sanctioned; however, direct evidence of state attribution remains elusive. Nonetheless, attacks are consistent with the state's demonstrated interest in information control and censorship and are part of a pattern of ongoing attacks against opposition groups.[82]

On September 27, 2007, during the brutal crackdown on the Saffron Revolution, attackers infected The Irrawaddy's Web site with a Trojan virus, leaving the site inoperable.[83] Throughout 2008, persistent DDoS attacks on a number of Web sites belonging to overseas news organizations as well as community forums rendered these Web sites effectively inaccessible.[84] The September attacks coincided with the first anniversary of the Saffron Revolution. The DDoS attacks continued in 2009 and 2010.[85] Most notable were the attacks launched on the Web site of Mizzima News on the 21st anniversary of the 8888 Uprising (it was also reported that in the week leading up to the anniversary, the Internet speed in the country had been slowed down considerably);[86] and the DDoS attacks on Mizzima News, The Irrawaddy, and the Democratic Voice of Burma in September 2010. These attacks coincided with the anniversary of the Saffron Revolution.

The Irrawaddy reported that the attack on its Web site originated from a Chinese IP address and that the volume of the DDoS assault on its Web site was four Gbps— three Gbps larger than the 2008 assault.[87] The attack on Mizzima News was six Gbps and originated from China, Russia, the United States, and Turkey, while the attack on the Democratic Voice of Burma occurred at 120 Mbps and originated from Georgia, Israel, Kazakhstan, Russia, Ukraine, and Vietnam.[88]

On October 25, 2010, two weeks before the general election, MPT was subject to large-scale DDoS attacks.[89] By November 2, the sophisticated attacks had rendered Burma's Internet inaccessible.[90] The volume of the DDoS attack was ten to 15 Gbps, meaning that the attack transferred several hundred times more data than the 45 Mbps that the Internet in Burma can support.[91] This attack was significantly larger than the instances of DDoS attacks in Estonia in 2007 (814 Mbps) and against Georgian Web sites during the Russia-Georgia conflict of 2008.[92] In addition to the impact on individual Internet users, hospitals, hotels, media, and Internet cafés were also affected by the attacks.[93] However, unlike 2007, when it was obvious that the government had deliberately shut down the country's Internet access, government involvement in the case of the preelection DDoS attacks is unclear. International civil society groups accused the government of deliberately slowing down the Internet in the country in order to silence foreign media, which were prohibited from entering Burma.[94] However, domestic Burmese media did not attribute the slowdown to government action and, instead, reported the lower Internet speed as a result of attacks.[95]

ONI Testing Results

OpenNet Initiative testing was conducted on Yatanarpon Teleport and MPT at various periods in 2009 and 2010 and found evidence of extensive filtering. Findings revealed that the filtering practices of Yatanarpon Teleport and MPT remained largely consistent with previous ONI findings.

MPT focused on filtering political-reform Web sites, independent Burmese media, and human-rights content related to Burma. When users attempted to access these Web sites, they were redirected to a block page notifying them that "the URL you requested has been blocked." Users were not given the option of contacting a moderator to have the blocked Web site reevaluated. OpenNet Initiative testing found that MPT remains slightly more selective in its filtering practices than Yatanarpon Teleport, a finding that is consistent with previous results. Rather than blocking entire domains, MPT blocked specific pages of Web sites—for instance, blocking http://niknayman .blogspot.com, as opposed to http://blogspot.com.[96]

Yatanarpon Teleport continues to target the Web sites of independent Burmese media, content relating to political reform and human rights, free e-mail services, and circumvention tools. When users attempted to access these sites, they were redirected to a block page notifying them that "access has been denied . . . access to requested URL has been denied." At the bottom of the block page, users were given the option of contacting a moderator to have the blocked Web site reevaluated. In contrast to MPT, and consistent with previous ONI findings, Yatanarpon Teleport blocked entire domains. The result is that Web sites with content unrelated to Burma were often blocked.

Compared to MPT, Yatanarpon Teleport blocked significantly more Web sites in the "social" thematic category—ONI testing found that pornography and Web sites with content related to sex education and family planning were the two most filtered within the social thematic category. Yatanarpon Teleport filtered slightly more Web sites with political content than MPT, although both ISPs heavily filtered Web sites with political content, with the end result being approximately equivalent.

Consistent with previous ONI findings, Web sites with content related to human rights, women's rights, commentary and criticism, political transformation, political reform, free expression, media freedom, minority rights, and religious conversion continue to be a priority for blocking. Nongovernmental organizations with concerns about Burmese human-rights issues were blocked by Yatanarpon Teleport, including

Human Rights Watch, Amnesty International, and Burma Watch.[97] International news agencies were also filtered by Yatanarpon Teleport, including the Web sites of CNN, the *Times of India*, and the *Financial Times*. Both MPT and Yatanarpon Teleport also blocked regional news Web sites and forums, including Asian Tribune and Asia Observer, and independent Burmese media organizations, including The Irrawaddy, Mizzima News, and the Democratic Voice of Burma.

Yatanarpon Teleport continues to block a number of Internet tools such as multimedia-sharing Web sites (http://youtube.com, http://flickr.com, etc.) and social-media Web sites (http://twitter.com, http://mybloglog.com, etc.). Yatanarpon Teleport also heavily filters free Web-based e-mail services, anonymizers and circumvention tools (http://proxify.com, http://psiphon.civisec.org, http://tor.eff.org, etc.), and blogging services Web sites (http://blogger.com, http://livejournal.com, http://wordpress.com, etc.).

Conclusion

Despite the fact that less than 1 percent of Burma has access to the Internet, the Burmese military junta has targeted online independent media and dissent with the same commitment it has demonstrated to stifling traditional media and voices for reform. The government has demonstrated that it is willing to take extreme steps to maintain its control over the flow of information within and outside its borders, including shutting down Internet access entirely. Cyber attacks on opposition groups are frequent and occur at strategic moments. Although a lack of evidence makes state attribution difficult, these attacks remain consistent with the regime's interest in controlling information, as well as an overall pattern of ongoing attacks against opposition groups.

The Internet in Burma remains tightly controlled through state control of ISPs, state intervention through content filtering and various laws and regulations, and state-sanctioned surveillance. Despite the ability of a small group of Internet users to continue to disseminate information online, the pervasive climate of fear has compelled many to engage in self-censorship.

Notes

1. Seth Mydans, "Steep Rise in Fuel Costs Prompts Rare Public Protest in Myanmar," *New York Times*, August 22, 2007, http://www.nytimes.com/2007/08/23/world/asia/23myanmar.html?scp=1&sq=myanmar%20fuel%20price%20hike%20protest&st=cse.

2. "In Broken Economy, Burmese Improvise or Flee," *Washington Post*, August 16, 2008, http://www.washingtonpost.com/wp-dyn/content/article/2008/08/15/AR2008081503655.html.

3. Asian Development Bank, *Asian Development Outlook 2009: Myanmar,* http://www.adb.org/Documents/Books/ADO/2009/MYA.pdf.

4. Human Rights Watch, "Crackdown: Repression of the 2007 Popular Protests in Burma," December 8, 2007, http://www.hrw.org/sites/default/files/reports/burma1207web.pdf.

5. Justin McCurry, Alex Duval Smith, and Jonathan Watts, "How Junta Stemmed a Saffron Tide," *The Guardian,* September 30, 2007, http://www.guardian.co.uk/world/2007/sep/30/burma.justinmccurry.

6. David Batty, Ian MacKinnon, and Mark Tran, "Burma Video Shows Shooting of Japanese Journalist," *The Guardian,* September 28, 2007, http://www.guardian.co.uk/world/2007/sep/28/burma.marktran1.

7. Human Rights Watch, "Crackdown."

8. UN Human Rights Council, *Report of the Special Rapporteur on the Situation of Human Rights in Myanmar, Paulo Sérgio Pinheiro,* March 11, 2009, A/HRC/10/19, http://www.unhcr.org/refworld/docid/49d337b02.html.

9. Ibid.

10. Sharon Otterman, "Myanmar Gives Comedian 45-Year Sentence for Cyclone Comments," *New York Times,* November 21, 2008, http://www.nytimes.com/2008/11/22/world/asia/22myanmar.html?ref=world; *New York Times,* "Prison Terms for Activists in Myanmar," November 11, 2008, http://www.nytimes.com/2008/11/12/world/asia/12myanmar.html; and Saw Yan Naing, "Rangoon Trials Continue—At Least 19 Condemned Today," The Irrawaddy, November 13, 2008, http://irrawaddy.org/article.php?art_id=14628.

11. UN Economic and Social Council, *Situation of Human Rights in Myanmar: Report of the Special Rapporteur, Toma's Ojea Quintana,* A/HRC/10/19, March 11, 2009, http://www.reliefweb.int/rw/rwb.nsf/db900SID/SNAA-7Q97P5?OpenDocument.

12. United Nations General Assembly, *Situation of Human Rights in Burma,* September 15, 2010, A/65/368, http://www.securitycouncilreport.org/atf/cf/%7B65BFCF9B-6D27-4E9C-8CD3-CF6E4FF96FF9%7D/Myan%20A65%20368.pdf.

13. Suu Kyi was released on November 13, 2010, just days after the 2010 general election.

14. U Win Tin, "An 'Election' Burma's People Don't Need," *Washington Post,* September 9, 2009, http://www.washingtonpost.com/wp-dyn/content/article/2009/09/08/AR2009090802959.html; and "No Foreign Media or Observers for Burma Poll," BBC News, October 18, 2010, http://www.bbc.co.uk/news/world-asia-pacific-11563764.

15. Human Rights Watch, "Human Rights Watch Interactive Dialogue with the Special Rapporteur on the Situation of Human Rights in Burma," March 16, 2010, http://www.hrw.org/en/news/2010/03/16/human-rights-watch-interactive-dialogue-special-rapporteur-situation-human-rights-bu/.

16. Kyaw Thu, "Election to Be Three-Horse Race: NPA," *Myanmar Times*, August 16, 2010, http://www.mmtimes.com/2010/news/536/news009.html.

17. "Pro-military Party 'Wins' Burmese Election," BBC News, November 9, 2010, http://www.bbc.co.uk/news/world-asia-pacific-11715956.

18. Daniel Ten Kate and Supunnabul Suwannakij, "Burma's Junta Claims Election," The Age, November 10, 2010, http://www.theage.com.au/world/burmas-junta-claims-election-20101109-17m04.html.

19. Mong Palatino, "Myanmar Election: Junta-Backed Party Wins, Violence Erupts," Global Voices Online, November 9, 2010, http://globalvoicesonline.org/2010/11/09/myanmar-election-junta-backed-party-wins-violence-erupts/.

20. "Burma Refugees Flee to Thailand after Violent Clashes," *The Guardian*, November 9, 2010, http://www.guardian.co.uk/world/2010/nov/09/burma-refugees-flee-thailand-violence.

21. International Telecommunication Union (ITU), "Internet Indicators: Subscribers, Users and Broadband Subscribers," 2009 Figures, http://www.itu.int/ITU-D/icteye/Reporting/ShowReportFrame.aspx?ReportName=/WTI/InformationTechnologyPublic&ReportFormat=HTML4.0&RP_intYear=2009&RP_intLanguageID=1&RP_bitLiveData=False.

22. Ibid.

23. Soe Myint, "Bloggers in Burma Write at Great Risk," Committee to Protect Journalists, May 1, 2009, http://cpj.org/blog/2009/05/bloggers-in-burma-write-at-great-risk.php.

24. OpenNet Initiative Blog, "Burmese Regulations for Cybercafés Stringent as Expected," July 2, 2008, http://opennet.net/blog/2008/07/burmese-regulations-cybercafes-stringent-expected.

25. Ibid.

26. Daniel Pepper, "Aftermath of a Revolt: Myanmar's Lost Year," *New York Times*, October 4, 2008, http://www.nytimes.com/2008/10/05/weekinreview/05pepper.html?scp=2&sq=myanmar saffronrevolution&st=cse.

27. Ibid.

28. Digital Democracy, "Burma/Myanmar Report 2009," http://www.scribd.com/doc/41186709/Digital-Democracy-Burma-Myanmar-Report/; and "The Internet in Burma (1998–2009)," Mizzima News, December 24, 2009, http://www.mizzima.com/research/3202-the-internet-in-burma-1998-2009-.html.

29. "The Internet in Burma (1998–2009)."

30. OpenNet Initiative, "Pulling the Plug: A Technical Review of the Internet Shutdown in Burma," November 2007, http://opennet.net/research/bulletins/013.

31. OpenNet Initiative interview with PAC operator.

32. Reporters Without Borders, *2010 Annual Report—Burma*, http://en.rsf.org/internet-enemie-burma,36676.html.

33. OpenNet Initiative Blog, "Doubts Surface over Announced Internet Maintenance in Burma," March 24, 2009, http://opennet.net/blog/2009/03/doubts-surface-over-announced-internet-maintenance-burma; Lawi Weng, "Internet Slowdown to Continue at Least One More Day," The Irrawaddy, April 2, 2009, http://irrawaddy.org/article.php?art_id=15429.

34. Wai Moe and Min Lwin, "Burma's Internet Slows to a Stop," The Irrawaddy, February 2, 2010, http://www.irrawaddy.org/article.php?art_id=17725.

35. "Burma Authorities Planning Internet Cut-off," Mizzima News, April 28, 2008.

36. Ibid.

37. On May 2 and 3, 2008, Cyclone Nargis hit lower Burma and devastated Rangoon and much of the Irrawaddy Delta, with more than 138,000 dead or missing and millions in need of food, water, shelter, and medical care. See Seth Mydans, "Myanmar Rulers Still Impeding Access," *New York Times*, June 3, 2008, http://www.nytimes.com/2008/06/03/world/asia/03myanmar.html. After blocking aid for two critical weeks, the junta finally accepted relief efforts coordinated through the Tripartite Core Group. However, a year later, half a million people were still living in temporary shelters, more than 200,000 lacked local supplies of drinking water, and villagers were still coping with chronic food shortages and the slow resumption of farming and fishing. See Associated Press, "Villagers Still Struggle Year after Storm," The Irrawaddy, April 29, 2009, http://irrawaddy.org/article.php?art_id=15552.

38. Nart Villeneuve, "Fortinet for Who?" Nart Villeneuve: Internet Censorship Explorer, October 13, 2005, http://www.nartv.org/2005/10/13/fortinet-for-who/; OpenNet Initiative Blog, "Doubts Surface over Announced Internet Maintenance in Burma."

39. OpenNet Initiative, "Pulling the Plug."

40. Ibid.

41. Ibid.

42. The Association of Southeast Asian Nations e-ASEAN Initiative, "The Challenge of ICT Revolution," http://www.aseansec.org/7659.htm.

43. Min Lwin, "Junta Approves Investment in Cyber City," The Irrawaddy, July 29, 2008, http://www.irrawaddy.org/article.php?art_id=13614; and "Companies from 4 Countries to Invest in Myanmar Cyber City Project," Xinhua, September 12, 2007, http://news.xinhuanet.com/english/2007-09/12/content_6708999.htm.

44. Ibid.

45. Burma Media Association and Reporters Without Borders, *National Web Portal: Development or Repression?* November 2010, http://www.scribd.com/doc/41962598/National-Web-Portal-Development-or-Repression-Report.

46. Ibid.

47. Ibid.

48. Ibid.

49. For more on "Man in the Middle Attacks," see Burma Media Association and Reporters Without Borders, *National Web Portal*.

50. Ibid.

51. Constitution of the Republic of the Union of Myanmar (2008). Unofficial English translation is available at http://www.scribd.com/doc/7694880/Myanmar-Constitution-2008-English -version.

52. UN Economic and Social Council, *Report of the Special Rapporteur on the Situation of Human Rights in Myanmar, Tomás Ojea Quintana*, A/HRC/10/19, March 11, 2009, http://www2.ohchr.org/ english/bodies/hrcouncil/docs/10session/A.HRC.10.19.pdf.

53. Freedom House, *Burma (Myanmar) Country Report 2008*, http://www.freedomhouse.org/ template.cfm?page=22&year=2008&country=7363.

54. Roy Greenslade, "How Burma Quashes Press Freedom," Guardian Greenslade Blog, September 26, 2007, http://www.guardian.co.uk/media/greenslade/2007/sep/26/howburmaquashes pressfreedo.

55. Saw Yan Naing, "Suppressed," The Irrawaddy, 17(1): 2009, http://www.irrawaddy.org/article .php?art_id=15004.

56. "Burma: Crackdown on Opposition and Media," Article 19, May 22, 2008, http://www.unhcr .org/refworld/type,COUNTRYNEWS,ART19,MMR,483bcf452,0.html.

57. "More Publications Granted in Myanmar," People's Daily Online, June 6, 2006, http:// english.peopledaily.com.cn/200606/06/eng20060606_271309.html.

58. Printers and Publishers Registration Act (1962). Unofficial English translation is available at http://www.burmalibrary.org/docs6/Printers_and_Publishers_Registation_Act.pdf.

59. Television and Video Law (The State Law and Order Restoration Council Law No. 8/96), Article 32, July 26, 1996. Unofficial English translation is available at http://www.blc-burma.org/ html/Myanmar%20Law/lr_e_ml96_08.html.

60. "MPT Terms of Service," January 31, 2000, http://web.archive.org/web/20010220220441/ http://dfn.org/voices/burma/webregulations.htm.

61. Ibid.

62. Ibid.

63. Computer Science Development Law, Articles 27, 28, and 32, September 20, 1996. Unofficial English translation is available at http://www.blc-burma.org/HTML/Myanmar%20Law/lr_e _ml96_10.html.

64. Electronic Transactions Law (2004), Article 33. Unofficial English translation is available at http://www.burmalibrary.org/docs/Electronic-transactions.htm.

65. Ibid.

66. Jonathan Head, "Harsh Sentences for Burma Rebels," BBC News, November 11, 2008, http://news.bbc.co.uk/2/hi/asia-pacific/7721589.stm.

67. International Freedom of Expression Exchange, "Imprisoned Burmese Blogger Nay Phone Latt to Receive Top PEN Honor," April 14, 2010, http://www.ifex.org/awards/2010/04/14/award _to_imprisoned_blogger/; "Burma Blogger Jailed for 20 Years," BBC News, November 11, 2008, http://news.bbc.co.uk/2/hi/asia-pacific/7721271.stm. Other sources have reported that Nay Phone Latt was sentenced for offenses under the Computer Science Development Law. See Min Lwin, "Regime Tightens Reins on the Internet," The Irrawaddy, November 13, 2008, http://irrawaddy.org/article.php?art_id=14627.

68. International Freedom of Expression Exchange, "Comedian and Blogger 'Zarganar' Sentenced to 45 Years in Prison; Sports Journalist Zaw Thet Htwe Gets 15 Years," November 21, 2008, http://www.ifex.org/en/content/view/full/98774; Than Htike Oo, "Total Prison Term for Zarganar Climbs to 59 Years," Mizzima News, November 28, 2008, http://www.mizzima.com/news/inside -burma/1377-total-prison-term-for-zarganar-climbs-to-59-years-.html.

69. Tyler Chapman, "In Burma, Fear and Suspicion Prevail," Radio Free Asia, April 19, 2009, http://www.rfa.org/english/blog/burma_diary/rangoon-04172009150342.html.

70. Human Rights Watch, "Crackdown: Repression of the 2007 Popular Protests in Burma," December 8, 2007, http://www.hrw.org/sites/default/files/reports/burma1207web.pdf.

71. Ibid., 106.

72. Ibid.

73. Ibid.

74. OpenNet Initiative, "Pulling the Plug."

75. OpenNet Initiative Blog, "Burmese Regulations for Cybercafés Stringent as Expected."

76. Kanbawza Win, "Fighting the Very Concept of Truth," Asian Tribune, October 1, 2010, http://www.asiantribune.com/news/2010/10/01/fighting-very-concept-truth.

77. Ibid.; U.S. State Department Bureau of Democracy, Human Rights, and Labor, 2008 Country Reports on Human Rights Practices: Burma, February 25, 2009, http://www.state.gov/g/drl/rls/hrrpt/2008/eap/119035.htm.

78. Saw Yan Naing, "Young Burmese Blogger Sentenced to More Than 20 Years in Jail," The Irrawaddy, November 10, 2008, http://www.irrawaddy.org/article.php?art_id=14604.

79. OpenNet Initiative, "Pulling the Plug."

80. OpenNet Initiative Blog, "Doubts Surface over Announced Internet Maintenance in Burma."

81. Reporters Without Borders, 2010 Annual Report—Burma.

82. See Nart Villeneuve and Masashi Crete-Nishihata, "Control and Resistance: Attacks on Burmese Opposition Media," chapter 8 in this volume, on cyber attacks against independent

media Web sites in Burma; and Hal Roberts, Ethan Zuckerman, and John Palfrey, "Interconnected Contests: Distributed Denial of Service Attacks and Other Digital Control Measures in Asia," chapter 7 in this volume, on the global incidents of DDoS attacks against civil society organizations.

83. Brian McCartan, "Myanmar on the Cyber-offensive," *Asia Times*, October 1, 2008, http://www.atimes.com/atimes/Southeast_Asia/JJ01Ae01.html.

84. Attacks were launched against the Web sites of the Democratic Voice of Burma and Mizzima News in July; the community forums Mystery Zillion and Planet Myanmar in August; and the Web sites of The Irrawaddy, the Democratic Voice of Burma, and the New Era Journal in September. See Zarni, "Websites of Three Burmese News Agencies in Exile under Attack," Mizzima News, September 17, 2008, http://www.mizzima.com/news/regional/1052-websites-of-three-burmese-news-agencies-in-exile-under-attack.html.

85. In 2009 attacks were launched on the Web site of Ashin Mettacara (http://ashin-mettacara.com), a Burmese monk in exile, first on January 20 and 21 and again through DDoS attacks on March 11 and 15. These attacks occurred amid similar attacks on four other Web sites, including the People's Media Voice. See Muchacho Enfermo, "Burma: Sri Lanka–Based Myanmar Media Website Attacked Again," Ashin Mettacara, March 17, 2009, http://www.ashinmettacara.org/2009/01/burma-myanmar-sri-lanka-based-burmese.html. In 2010, the Web site of a Burmese army deserter (http://photayokeking.org)—set up in May 2008 to provide information about the Burmese military—was hit with DDoS attacks. As a result, the Web site was removed from the Los Angeles server that hosted it. See Alex Ellgee, "Another Opposition Website Shut Down by Hackers," The Irrawaddy, June 19, 2010, http://www.irrawaddy.org/article.php?art_id=18759&page=1.

86. "Fresh Attack on Mizzima Website," Mizzima, August 8, 2009, http://www.mizzima.com/news/inside-burma/2599-fresh-attack-on-mizzima-website.html.

87. "Irrawaddy: Cyber Attacks Seek to Suppress the Truth—Editorial," The Irrawaddy, September 30, 2009, http://www.irrawaddy.org/opinion_story.php?art_id=19593.

88. Ibid.; "Majority of Cyber Attacks Came from Chinese IP Addresses," The Irrawaddy, September 28, 2009, http://www.irrawaddy.org/article.php?art_id=19572.

89. "Burma Hit by Massive Net Attack Ahead of Election," BBC News, November 4, 2010, http://www.bbc.co.uk/news/technology-11693214.

90. Craig Labovitz, "Attack Severs Burma Internet," Arbor Networks, November 3, 2010, http://asert.arbornetworks.com/2010/11/attac-severs-myanmar-internet/.

91. Ibid.

92. Ibid.

93. "Burma Hit by Massive Net Attack Ahead of Election," BBC News.

94. "Myanmar Internet Link Continues to Meet with Interruption," Xinhua, November 3, 2010, http://news.xinhuanet.com/english2010/sci/2010-11/03/c_13589614.htm.

95. "Myanmar Junta Accused of Slowing Down Internet," *Globe and Mail,* November 1, 2010, http://www.theglobeandmail.com/news/technology/myanmar-junta-accused-of-slowing-down -internet/article1780445.

96. Data on global list URLs for MPT were not available at the time of this report. Although we were unable to determine whether global political pages were blocked by MPT, based on past ONI data and current field reports, it is highly likely that MPT filters international Web sites in manners consistent with previous testing results.

97. "Myanmar Junta Accused of Slowing Down Internet," *Globe and Mail.*

China

China maintains one of the most pervasive and sophisticated regimes of Internet filtering and information control in the world. The community of Chinese Internet users continues to grow, while the state simultaneously increases its capacity to restrict content that might threaten social stability or state control through tight regulations on domestic media, delegated liability for online content providers, just-in-time filtering, and "cleanup" campaigns.

RESULTS AT A GLANCE

Filtering	No Evidence of Filtering	Suspected Filtering	Selective Filtering	Substantial Filtering	Pervasive Filtering
Political					•
Social				•	
Conflict and security					•
Internet tools				•	

OTHER FACTORS

	Low	Medium	High	Not Applicable
Transparency	•			
Consistency			•	

KEY INDICATORS	
GDP per capita, PPP (constant 2005 international dollars)	6,200
Life expectancy at birth, total (years)	73
Literacy rate, adult total (percent of people age 15+)	93.7
Human Ddevelopment Index (out of 169)	89
Rule of Law (out of 5)	2.2
Voice and Accountability (out of 5)	0.8
Democracy Index (out of 167)	136 (Authoritarian regime)
Digital Opportunity Index (out of 181)	77
Internet penetration rate (percentage of population)	28.9

Source by indicator: World Bank 2009, World Bank 2008a, World Bank 2008b, UNDP 2010, World Bank Worldwide Governance Indicators 2009, Economist Intelligence Unit 2010, ITU 2007, ITU 2009. See Introduction to the Country Profiles, pp. 222–223.

Background

The People's Republic of China (PRC) is a one-party state ruled by the Chinese Communist Party (CCP). Since the opening of its economy under the leadership of Deng Xiaoping in the 1980s, the country has undergone drastic changes. These changes are especially apparent in the information communication technology (ICT) sector, which has become a subject of considerable significance within PRC policy and discourse.[1] With the total number of Chinese netizens surpassing 450 million at the end of 2010, the Internet has become increasingly embedded in Chinese society and progressively more central to the flow of information within and across Chinese borders.[2]

Although recent and current administrations have emphasized the importance of Internet development, Chinese policymakers are also wary of the potentially crippling effects that these changes could have on the CCP's ability to contain sensitive or threatening information.[3] As changing dynamics in China's relationship with the international community present new opportunities for increased dialogue, the CCP has focused significant energy on developing new ways of maintaining close regulation of the information accessed and disseminated within the PRC.

Since 2008, several milestones in China's development, domestic politics, and foreign relations have presented new challenges to the PRC government, and authorities have responded by launching rigorous campaigns to contain communications, monitor and control citizens' activities, and outweigh public criticism through proactive counterinformation campaigns.

On March 10, 2008, the anniversary of the 1959 Tibetan Uprising, protests erupted in the Tibetan capital of Lhasa, calling for improved human rights conditions, religious freedom, and, in some cases, political independence.[4] Shortly thereafter, with the international community's eyes on China during the lead-up to the Beijing Olympics, unprecedented protests broke out among Tibetan communities throughout China and around the world.[5] The Chinese government responded by initiating violent crackdowns in the Tibet Autonomous Region, clamping down on domestic and foreign media, and systematically blocking online content pertaining to the incident.[6]

As the Olympics drew nearer, China faced increasing international pressure to lessen censorship and honor its commitment to allow foreign media to report freely during the games. The official policy on foreign media restrictions during the Olympics, issued in 2006, considerably loosened control over foreign journalists, allowing them to travel and conduct interviews throughout China without registration or the official consent of local authorities.[7] However, while these new regulations represented an unprecedented level of freedom for foreign journalists working in China, the government continued to exercise strict control over domestic media, tightly limiting the availability of unbiased Chinese-language news.[8] Furthermore, though the PRC government had initially agreed to provide unfiltered Internet access to journalists during the Olympics, this promise was significantly compromised and redefined as pertaining only to "games-related" Web sites.[9] Numerous political and human-rights-focused Web sites remained blocked throughout the games. Following the Olympics, the new regulations on foreign media reporting in China remained temporarily in place. However, events of the coming year led to a series of tightened restrictions and intensified controls.

The year 2009 was a critical one in the trajectory of China's Internet restrictions and censorship. In April 2009 the State Council Information Office issued its first "National Human Rights Action Plan of China," which, in addition to numerous other commitments, promised that "the state will take effective measures to develop the press and publications industry and ensure that all channels are unblocked to guarantee citizens' right to be heard."[10] However, throughout the year China continued to tighten censorship and increase control over public media and discussion, showing little potential for progress toward this goal. In preparation for numerous important milestones, including the 60th anniversary of the PRC's founding, the 50th anniversary of the Tibetan Uprising and retreat of the Dalai Lama to India (and one year since the 2008 protests in Tibet organized on the same date), the 20th anniversary of the Tiananmen Massacre, and the tenth anniversary of the Falun Gong spiritual movement being outlawed, the ruling party began the year carefully poised to tighten restrictions surrounding these sensitive dates.[11]

In July 2009, violent clashes broke out in Urumqi, the capital of the western province of Xinjiang. The protests, which appeared to have started peacefully, began as a result of discontent among Uighur citizens following the murder of several Uighur workers in a Guangdong toy factory.[12] Though it is unclear what sparked the violence, conflict quickly erupted between Han and Uighur residents, leading to at least 197 deaths and more than 1,600 injuries.[13]

The Urumqi riots, China's most serious case of civil unrest in decades, led to severe and calculated clampdowns on local and national media and telecommunication networks. Unlike the case of the Tibetan protests of 2008, the Chinese government allowed—and even encouraged—foreign media coverage of the Xinjiang riots. However, journalists were confined to the city of Urumqi and permitted to cover violence instigated by Uighur citizens only. They were forbidden from reporting on the aftermath of the incidents, including the widespread and systematic interrogations and arrests of Uighurs, as well as the unexplained disappearance of dozens of detained suspects.[14] There were also cases of Chinese journalists being verbally and physically harassed while attempting to cover the news objectively.[15] Even more extreme, however, were the government's actions regarding Internet and telephone communications. The riots in Urumqi led immediately to drastic tightening of Internet censorship nationwide, including the blocking of Facebook, Twitter, and other social media sites, as well as a complete cutoff of all Internet and telephone access within the province of Xinjiang.[16]

Officials justified the Internet blocks as safety precautions, claiming, "We cut Internet connection in some areas of Urumqi in order to quench the riot quickly and prevent violence from spreading to other places."[17] They further asserted that the central government believed that World Uighur Congress Leader, Rebiya Kadeer, had "used the Internet and other means of communication to mastermind the riot," necessitating greater restrictions on the Internet to avoid further collaboration between separatist forces.[18] Although telephone communication and access to 31 state-sponsored Web sites were slowly restored, Xinjiang's Internet access remained effectively severed for ten months following the July 2009 riots.[19]

In January 2010, Google made a bold move by announcing it would no longer comply with the legal requirements of content filtering imposed on companies operating within the PRC.[20] Following a series of cyber attacks that targeted Google's infrastructure and the e-mail accounts of several Chinese human rights activists, Google publicly stated that it would seek to discuss the establishment of an unfiltered search engine in China, or else officially close down China-based Google.cn.[21] The attacks, which also hit a number of other Silicon Valley technology firms, led to responses from the central government that were largely dismissive of Google's accusations. Official reactions condemned the move as "financially driven," because of Google's inability to surpass Baidu.com as the number-one search engine in China.[22] Minister of the State Council Information Office Wang Chen defended China's censorship policies, maintaining that "properly guiding Internet opinion is a major measure for protecting Internet information security,"[23] and showed no signs that the government would be willing to negotiate with Google.

In March 2010, after a series of strained negotiations between Google and Chinese authorities, the company finally made good on its threat to stop filtering content, stating that it would redirect all traffic from Google.cn to its unfiltered Chinese-language site, Google.com.hk, based in Hong Kong. Later that month, there were numerous reports that the government had blocked both Google.cn and Google.com.hk, though blockings appeared to be somewhat sporadic.[24] In June 2010, Google's senior vice president, corporate development officer, and chief legal officer, David Drummond, said, "It's clear from conversations we have had with Chinese government officials that they find the redirect unacceptable."[25] To renew its ICP license and continue serving Chinese audiences (while still refusing to censor search results), Google altered its approach to include a link to the Hong Kong site on the Google.cn home page, rather than automatically redirecting users. Google's ICP license was successfully renewed on June 30.

The overall effect of Google's decision to take a public stance on Internet censorship and cease compliance with PRC censorship policies has been widely discussed among both the Chinese and international communities. Whether or not the company's actions serve to improve the overall online environment and Internet freedom for Chinese citizens is not entirely clear. However, Google's actions have directed widespread international attention to the censorship practices of the PRC government; heightened global awareness of issues surrounding targeted malware attacks, Internet controls, and human rights; and placed the actions of the Chinese authorities and their manipulation of cyberspace in the international spotlight.

Chinese leaders consider China to be one of the largest developing countries in the world—one that is following its own model of development, which suits its own national conditions and is shaped by its unique history, social system, and culture. Chinese leaders place great emphasis on equality and mutual respect for sovereignty in foreign relations and are particularly sensitive to criticisms of the Chinese state and its handling of its internal affairs.

In 2010, U.S. Secretary of State Hillary Clinton criticized the country for threatening the free flow of information. In her January speech on Internet freedom, Clinton remarked, "On their own, new technologies do not take sides in the struggle for freedom and progress, but the United States does. We stand for a single Internet where all of humanity has equal access to knowledge and ideas. And we recognize that the world's information infrastructure will become what we and others make of it."[26]

In response, an op-ed in the state-run *Global Times* accused the United States of using the notion of an unrestricted Internet as a disguised imposition of its values on other cultures—in other words, information imperialism. The op-ed argued that "countries disadvantaged by the unequal and undemocratic information flow have to protect their national interest, and take steps toward this. This is essential for their political stability as well as normal conduct of economic and social life. These facts about the difficulties of developing nations, though understood by politicians like Clinton, are not communicated to the people of Western countries. Instead, those politicians publicize and pursue their claims purely from a Western standpoint."[27] On the Chinese Foreign Ministry Web site, spokesperson Ma Zhaoxu officially stated, "We urge the US to respect facts and stop attacking China under the excuse of the so-called freedom of Internet."[28]

Internet in China

Like many of its neighbors in Asia, China has sought to balance the benefits that technological growth can bring to socioeconomic development with the potential risks to the government's control over media and information dissemination. Despite the rapid spread of Internet access throughout its vast population, China also has one of the largest and most sophisticated Internet filtering systems in the world.

Although access to the Internet in China is low relative to much of the world, it is growing rapidly and expanding into previously inaccessible regions. Despite a penetration rate of only 28.9 percent, the country's population means it has the most Internet users in the world.[29] The growth rate of China's user base has exceeded 20 percent for each year since 2006, reaching a peak of 53.3 percent in 2007.[30] Because the population has also grown since 2001, Internet users have increased more than tenfold—from 33 million to 388 million users by 2009.[31]

The majority of users access the Internet at home, although Internet cafés remain a means of access for an estimated one-third of users.[32] Broadband remains the most popular means of connectivity, with 103 million broadband users by 2009.[33]

Despite this large and growing population of users, Internet access is not evenly distributed. Most significant is the urban/rural divide, although this gap has closed in recent years as a result of initiatives to expand rural access.[34] As of January 2011, the China Internet Network Information Center reports that the number of urban Internet users was more than three times greater than the number of rural users.[35]

Other disparities in Internet access in China persist. The gender gap increased to more than 10 percent by 2010, with males making up 55.8 percent of users.[36] There is a significant age gap in access—almost 60 percent of users are under age 30, although the proportion of older users has increased.[37]

One area where China has seen tremendous growth and which offers the potential to alleviate the rural/urban imbalance is the mobile sector. Following the 2008 restructuring of China's telecom industry, the mobile services on offer expanded significantly. The number of mobile phones in use in China has multiplied almost tenfold in a decade, with an estimated one billion phones and a 73.5 percent penetration rate by

2010.[38] Mobile phones are a means of accessing the Internet for more than 300 million mobile users,[39] with over 10 percent of users accessing the Internet solely through their mobile phone.[40]

China's Internet users access a variety of resources online, including social networking, instant messaging, video sharing, and blogs. Search engines remain the primary use of the Internet, with 81.9 percent of users using these services.[41] Despite their dominance of the search-engine market throughout much of the world, Google is a distant second in China. China-based Baidu dominates the search-engine market with 75 percent market share compared to Google's 19 percent, particularly following Google's spat with CCP leadership over censorship and cyber attacks.[42] The use of instant messaging on mobile devices has grown, especially in regions with limited connectivity options.[43] Other services have also expanded. More than 3 million users use microblogging services,[44] and the country has the largest population of Voice over Internet Protocol (VoIP) users in the world.[45]

Access to the Internet in China is controlled by the Ministry of Industry and Information Technology (MIIT) and is provided by eight state-licensed Internet service providers (ISPs). The MIIT's mandate includes regulating telecommunications, Internet, and broadband as well as supervising IT development.[46] The telecommunications industry is dominated by a small group of state-owned companies. China Telecom Group is the largest telecommunications company in the country, controlling 70 percent of the local market.[47] China Telecom and the second-largest ISP, China Unicom, combined serve more than 20 percent of the world's total broadband users.[48] With six international backbone links, China's international bandwidth has grown consistently and now exceeds 1 million Mbps.[49]

A major restructuring of the telecom industry in China took place in 2008, with the six state-owned companies merged into three networks, greatly increasing the capacity of large firms to expand into wireless services.[50] By January 2009, the MIIT had issued 3G licenses to China Unicom and China Telecom using EVDO and WCDMA standards, as well as to China Mobile using the unproven TD-SCDMA standard unique to China.[51]

The expansion of Internet access has created a vibrant and dynamic online community throughout the country that has had a significant impact on public discourse, while also drawing the attention of government officials. Online discussion has frequently elevated local incidents to national prominence, with Web portals and forums dropping "information bombs" that have led to the tarnished reputations and dismissal of senior officials.[52] In an unpublished investigative report obtained by David Bandurski of the China Media Project, the vice president of People's Daily Online said that two-thirds of the few hundred secret internal reports that CCP top leaders give priority and action to are from the Internet Office of the State Council Information Office.[53]

The online community has broadened the capacity for collective action on a variety of fronts. Notable among these are so-called "human flesh search engines," which are massive online collective research projects. They have focused on conducting crowd-sourced investigations into a variety of incidents, from finding missing relatives to exposing corruption of government officials, although they have also strayed into questionable acts of vigilantism.[54] Discussion forums and blogs also offer new opportunities for organization and dissemination of information. Charter 08, a prodemocracy manifesto whose signatories included 2010 Nobel Peace Prize winner Liu Xiaobo, was circulated by e-mail and other means and had gathered 10,000 signatures by 2010.[55] However, these discussion forums are not the exclusive domain of those critical of government. The "Fifty Cent Party," named for the price individuals are rumored to be paid per post, is organized by the government to steer online discussion of sensitive topics.[56]

A variety of different Internet filtering mechanisms have been implemented. One such effort, the Green Dam Youth Escort project, was a far-reaching and ultimately unsuccessful attempt to implement filtering at the level of the user's computer. The project originally called for all new computers sold in China to come preinstalled with the Green Dam software to filter harmful online text and images to prevent them from being viewed by children.[57] However, ONI and Stop Badware researchers conducted an initial technical assessment of the software that found that Green Dam's filtering not only is ineffective at blocking pornographic content as a whole, but also includes unpredictable and disruptive blocking of political and religious content normally associated with the Great Firewall of China.[58] Following the findings, the MIIT delayed implementation and made installation of the software optional.[59] Despite the apparent failure of this initiative, a similar filtering package called Blue Dam was mandated for installation by all ISPs by September 2009.[60] This system included a graphic-filtering system, administration-management system, and Internet-behavior manager aimed at blocking content deemed inappropriate.[61]

Blog service providers also face requirements to ensure that there is no inappropriate content on their sites. These providers must install filters that prevent postings of thousands of keyword combinations, delete or conceal posts with sensitive comments, and cancel the accounts of bloggers deemed to have posted too many troublesome posts.[62] This discretion on the part of service providers has led to uneven patterns of filtering. A study of Chinese blog service providers demonstrated that there is substantial variation in censorship methods, the amount of content censored, and providers' transparency about deleting content.[63] Similar findings were reached in a Citizen Lab study of four popular search engines in China, which found significant variations in the level of transparency about filtering, actual content censored, and methods used, suggesting that there is no comprehensive system for determining censored content.[64]

China's dynamic system of Internet control is demonstrated by the rise of "just-in-time" filtering during key events. The 2009 violent protests between Uighur and Han residents of Urumqi saw Internet access in the Xinjiang autonomous region cut after videos and images of the protests spread online.[65] The 2010 awarding of the Nobel Peace Prize to activist Liu Xiaobo led to the blocking of sensitive keywords in search engines, blogging sites, and SMS text messages.[66] Notable anniversaries of sensitive events are a frequent target of filtering, including the 60th anniversary of the founding of the PRC,[67] the 20th anniversary of Tiananmen,[68] and the first anniversary of the 2008 Tibetan protests.[69] Such filtering has not been limited to domestic events—key Internet portals Sina.com and Netease.com blocked keyword searches of "Egypt" during that country's unrest in early 2011.[70]

The combination of rigorous technical filtering mechanisms and content providers' self-policing can often lead to self-censorship, with users unwilling to risk posting controversial content. Organizations like the China Internet Illegal Information Reporting Center (CIIRC), ostensibly a civil society organization, encourage the reporting of "illegal and harmful information" and send information about illegal content to the Ministry of Public Security.[71] As a result, commercial Web sites can elect to prevent the posting of controversial material rather than risk negative consequences later.[72] The pervasiveness of filtering at Internet cafés, a common method of access for many, means cafés are generally avoided for discussing sensitive topics online.[73] Further, many users have long assumed surveillance of communication tools like TOM-Skype,[74] thus discouraging their use.[75]

Legal and Regulatory Frameworks

The legal and regulatory frameworks that underpin China's Internet landscape are shaped by the PRC's desire to develop the Internet as a driver of the national economy while maintaining "state security and social harmony, state sovereignty and dignity, and the basic interests of the people."[76]

According to the June 2010 White Paper on Internet Policy, "The government has a basic policy regarding the Internet: active use, scientific development, law-based administration and ensured security. The Chinese government has from the outset abided by law-based administration of the Internet, and endeavored to create a healthy and harmonious Internet environment, and build an Internet that is more reliable, useful, and conducive to economic and social development."[77]

Regulations prohibit citizens from disseminating or accessing online content deemed subversive or harmful by the state. Laws and regulations that control online content distribute criminal and financial liability, licensing and registration requirements, and self-monitoring instructions to people at every stage of access—from the ISP to the Internet content provider to the end user.

Through Internet information service (IIS) providers and ISPs, the state regulates available online content and monitors Internet users. As laid out in Article 20 of the Measures for Managing Internet Information Services, IIS providers are directly responsible for content published on their services.[78] Specifically, IIS providers are prohibited from producing, reproducing, releasing, or disseminating information that falls under nine categories forbidden by the state, as laid out in Article 15 of the measures. Forbidden information ranges from content that undermines state security, social order, and national unity (such as information inciting ethnic hatred) to pornography. Internet information service providers who violate these measures or fail to monitor their Web sites and report violations can face fines, shutdown, criminal liability, and license revocation.[79] Commercial IIS providers must be licensed, while noncommercial IIS providers must report on their operations for official records. Electronic bulletin board services (including chat forums) are subject to similar regulations under the Rules on the Management of Internet Electronic Bulletin Services.[80]

Internet news information services have to abide by regulations laid out in the 2005 Provisions on the Administration of Internet News Information Services. The provision provides a complex regulatory scheme—only news originating from state-supervised news outlets can be posted online. Government-licensed and authorized news agencies are limited to covering specific subjects approved by the state, but they can at least conduct original reporting on "current events news information," defined as "reporting and commentary relating to politics, economics, military affairs, foreign affairs, and social and public affairs, as well as reporting and commentary relating to fast-breaking social events."[81] Web sites that are nongovernmental entities, or otherwise not licensed news agencies, are restricted from performing any journalistic function other than reprinting content from central news outlets or media under the direct control of provincial governments.[82]

Under Article 19 of this provision, there are 11 content categories that Internet news organizations are prohibited from posting or transmitting. These restrictions are similar to those regulating bulletin board services and IIS providers. Beyond formal controls such as policies, instructions, and defamation liability, the government also utilizes informal mechanisms to discipline media, ranging from editorial responsibility for content to economic incentives, intimidation, and other forms of pressure.[83]

The government has used this framework to bring social media in line with Internet content regulations. Under the January 1, 2008, "Provisions on the Management of Internet Audio and Video Programming Services,"[84] issued by the State Administration of Radio, Film, and Television (SARFT) and MIIT, Internet audiovisual program service providers that produce original content are required to obtain a broadcast production license and Internet news information services licenses regulated by the MIIT. Similarly, video service providers are also prohibited from allowing any individuals without a special license to upload content pertaining to "current events."[85] Audiovisual programs are further prevented from presenting content that pertains to all but one of the prohibitions listed under the 2005 provisions.[86] The Provision on Internet AV Programming Services was strengthened on March 30, 2009, with the addition of 21 additional types of content that Internet audiovisual service providers were required to edit or delete. These content categories range from sexually provocative or pornographic content; to content that promotes "a negative or decadent outlook, world view, or value system, or deliberate exaggeration of the ignorance and backwardness of ethic groups or social ills"; to content that calls "for religious extremism, provocation of conflict between religions, religious sects, or between believers and nonbelievers, hurting the feelings of the public," among others.[87] Within these updated rules, Internet AV program service providers are also mandated to "improve their program content administration systems by hiring well-qualified service personnel to review and filter content" so that content does not violate existing and new rules.[88]

With the explosion of an active blogosphere in China, the government implemented the Convention on Blog Service Discipline[89] in 2007, which was signed by blog service providers including the People's Daily Online, Sina, Sohu, Netease, Tencent, TOM, MSN China, and Qianlon.[90] According to the convention, blog service providers should "abide by state laws, regulations and policies, safeguard the legitimate blog users and the public interest." Blog providers must also have an end-user agreement with terms of service for the blogger to abstain from disseminating rumors or false information and to delete postings considered bad or illegal. The blog provider has to encourage real-name registration, supervise and manage content, and remove illegal content or cease blog services.[91]

Similarly, end users are also subject to content controls such as those as laid out in the rules of the National People's Congress (NPC) Standing Committee on Safeguarding Internet Security.[92] Violators of these rules can incur fines, content removal, and criminal liability. For example, on October 28, 2010, Twitter user Cheng Jianping was arrested for disturbing social order and sent to a labor camp for retweeting a sarcastic comment about the anti-Japanese protests in China, suggesting that the protesters attack the Japan pavilion at the Shanghai Expo.[93] In January 2011, blogger Lin Chenglong was arrested for spreading obscene material in his blog where he wrote about his experiences with prostitutes and posted obscene photos.[94] In 2010, Zhao Lianhai, an activist for families who suffered from the Chinese milk scandal and started the "Home for Kidney Stone Babies Web site" (http://jieshibaobao.com), had his Web site blocked and shut down. He was consequently charged with inciting social disorder and sentenced to two and a half years' imprisonment.[95] Seventy-seven netizens were reported imprisoned in 2009.[96]

In 2010, the Chinese government amended the 1988 Law on Guarding State Secrets (State Secrets Law) to require all ICT companies operating within the country to comply with measures to protect state secrets. "State secrets" are defined as matters of national security interests in the realm of political, economic, defense, and foreign affairs.[97] The revised law was passed in April, on the heels of the Google-China conflict, and took effect in October. Under Article 28 of the law, Internet and other public information network operators and service providers are required to cooperate with the state in investigating leaked secrets when the information involving the secret has been published on the Internet or other public information networks. In such cases, companies are required to cease transmission of the information immediately, and maintain and disclose records to public security organs, state security organs, or relevant departments that guard state secrets.[98] According to a Beijing-based lawyer, "Such regulation will leave users with no secrets at all, since the service providers have no means to resist the police."[99] In the past, the law has been invoked to target journalists, activists, and dissidents, like journalist Shi Tao, who sent an e-mail from his personal Yahoo! account to a prodemocracy group based in the United States, summarizing a government-issued directive on how to manage the 15th anniversary of the 1989 Tiananmen Square crackdown. He was subsequently arrested and imprisoned when Yahoo! disclosed his identity to authorities.[100]

Beyond legal restrictions to control Internet use, the state has also launched campaigns to clean up Internet use. These campaigns may be organized around a specific issue area (such as online gambling) during key politically sensitive events (such as the lead-up to the 17th Party Congress in 2007).[101] In 2010, Chinese authorities launched campaigns against online gambling and pornography and Web sites promoting or selling illegal drugs. In December 2009, authorities initiated an antipornography campaign that shut down more than 60,000 Web sites, deleted over 350 million pornographic and lewd online articles, pictures, and videos, and rounded up 4,965 suspects by the end of the year. Of these suspects, 1,332 were found criminally liable, and 58 were jailed for five or more years.[102] In the same year, the state launched a campaign against Web sites promoting or selling illegal drugs as a part of a nationwide effort to stamp out the production and distribution of counterfeit drugs or drugs that violated intellectual property rights.[103] As a result, 290 Web sites were shut down. Similarly, a February 2010 campaign against online gambling led to 3,430 suspects rounded up and 670 online gambling Web sites shut down.[104]

Surveillance

The PRC continues to refine Internet surveillance mechanisms to monitor users' activities. The Golden Shield project—a digital surveillance network with almost complete coverage across public security units nationwide—is the pillar of China's surveillance regime.[105] Its use of identification cards with scannable computer chips and photos further allows the state to effectively police citizens. Since 2006, local governments have been developing "Safe City" surveillance and communications networks that connect police stations through video surveillance, security cameras, and back-end data management facilities to specific locations including Internet cafés, financial centers, and entertainment areas. In recent years, the state has begun exploring real-name registration as a monitoring tool. Private companies, too, are often complicit in the state's surveillance regime.

Real-name registration (through ID cards) in Internet cafés illustrates how filtering and monitoring/surveillance are complementary processes that allow the state to manage the Internet. This is reflected in a recent speech, "Concerning the Development and Administration of Our Country's Internet," delivered to the Standing Committee of the National People's Congress on April 29, 2010.[106] The speaker claimed that in order to strengthen the basic management and security of the Internet, the state would have to implement the real-name system and improve the efficiency in handling harmful online information.[107]

In June 2010, the Chinese government released a white paper on Internet policy that insisted, "The Chinese government attaches great importance to protecting the safe flow of Internet information, actively guides people to manage Web sites in accordance with the law and use the Internet in a wholesome and correct way."[108] Following the release of the white paper, the government began to take active steps in strengthening security through the implementation of real-name registration across the country, including in Internet cafés.[109]

Because real-name registration removes the anonymity that allows citizens to make public comments without fear of state sanctions, it can lead to self-censorship among users.[110] Real-name registration policies also allow the state to track each user's Internet activities. In the summer of 2010, Internet users across cities in China were required to swipe their second-generation identity cards through an ID scanner in order to gain online access at Internet cafés.[111] In September 2010, real-name registration was expanded into the area of mobile phones so users are now required to show their identity card to purchase a SIM card.[112]

Prior to the white paper and the April 2010 speech, real-name registration had already been implemented on some Web sites. For instance, a few leading Web portals in China already require users to register their real names to post on message or bulletin boards. Sina requires users to register real names as well as identity cards in order to post comments on their site.[113] Since 2005, users of student-run university discussion forums have been required to register with their real identifying information before posting messages online.[114] In May 2010, the Chinese state was actively exploring ways to have all Internet users register their real names prior to posting on discussion forums or chat rooms.[115]

In December 2009, the China Internet Network Information Center (CNNIC), which operates under MIIT and is responsible for Internet affairs and China's domain name registry, announced that only businesses or organizations would be eligible for registering domain names ending in .cn.[116] The CNNIC stated that this control would eliminate abuse of .cn domain names by criminals. Because self-employed workers had been affected by the new rules, by February 2010 the CNNIC announced that they would allow individuals to register once again, but only if applicants registered for the domain with their government ID cards in person and attached a photograph to each application[117]—effectively ending anonymity in Web site registration. In opposition to the new reporting requirements, domain name registrar Go Daddy suspended registration for the .cn domain.[118]

Although there have been demonstrations against real-name registration on campus bulletin boards,[119] other efforts have embraced real-name registration on the grounds that it can empower citizens. A campaign launched by activist blogger Ai Aiwei on Twitter argued, "The fact that we try to cover our identity that we are so afraid of what we said has empowered the authoritarian state. We need to speak in public with transparency and demand the government to do the same. If we do not encourage such act and continue to live in fear, such fear would be exaggerated and we could not make any change."[120] In just a day, hundreds of Internet users had joined the campaign.[121]

Technically, Internet laws and regulations provide protection for individual privacy. However, state regulations require private actors to cooperate not only in monitoring and filtering online content but also in keeping records of personal user information and activities to be handed to authorities upon request.

Under the Measures for the Management of E-mail Services, e-mail service providers are required to keep personal information and e-mail addresses of users and can disclose such information with users' consent or when authorized for national security reasons or criminal investigations according to procedures stipulated by law.[122] Similarly, IIS providers, ISPs, and electronic bulletin board service providers are required to record users' information and activities. Internet service providers are obliged to record the addresses or domain names their users have accessed, while IISs are required to record the content of the information, the date such information was released, and the address or the domain name that hosted such information. Bulletin board service providers have to keep records of the contents, time of publication, and Web site names or addresses of the information published on their services, as well as user information.[123] All these services are required to store records for 60 days and provide records to authorities upon demand.[124]

Internet cafés, too, are heavily regulated and are required to install filtering software and record patron information and complete session logs for up to 60 days.[125] In August 2010, the Chinese government ordered that the installation of surveillance software in Internet cafés across Tibet be completed by the end of the month.[126]

Companies such as the China Mobile Communications Corporation (China's largest mobile phone company), Tencent, and Skype also monitor and store information about user activities. In a discussion on targeted advertising at the 2008 World Economy Forum, the CEO of China Mobile Communications Corporation, Wang

Jianzhou, announced that the company had access to the personal data of its users—including the user's exact whereabouts—which were given to the authorities on demand.[127] China's most popular instant messenger, QQ (owned by Tencent), was found to have installed a keyword-blocking program in their client software that monitored and recorded users' online communication. This information was given to authorities if required.[128]

In 2008, researcher Nart Villeneuve discovered that TOM-Skype, the Chinese-marketed version of Skype, had stored more than a million user records in seven types of log files stored on publicly accessible servers, including IP addresses, user names, and time-and-date stamps.[129] For call information logs dating from August 2007, the user name and phone number of the recipient were also logged, while content filter logs dating from August 2008 also contained full texts of chat messages (which themselves contained sensitive information such as e-mail addresses, passwords, and bank card numbers). With the information contained in the log files, it would be possible to conduct politically motivated surveillance by using simple social-networking tools to identify the relationships between users.[130]

Cyber Attacks

A growing number of countries, organizations, and companies have reported cyber attacks appearing to originate in China. These reports have ranged from instances of targeted malware attacks against human rights groups, distributed denial of service (DDoS) attacks against government Web sites, and high-profile attempts to compromise Google's e-mail system. While assessing attribution and motivation behind such attacks is perennially difficult, there is growing concern about the security risk posed by cyber attacks originating in China.

In January 2010, Google announced it would no longer censor search results on Google China (http://google.cn) following cyber attacks on its infrastructure.[131] Google claimed that the e-mail accounts of a number of human rights activists connected with China were compromised by the attack, which had also targeted dozens of other Silicon Valley firms.[132] Later reports suggested that the attackers had gained access to the password system controlling the access of millions of users of Google's services.[133] U.S. State Department cables leaked through Wikileaks implicated a senior member of China's government in this attack.[134] An MIIT spokesman denied the Chinese government's involvement, suggesting that in fact China was the world's primary victim of cyber attacks.[135] A compromise solution between Google and the government of China was eventually reached under which users in China were offered a link to Google's unfiltered Chinese-language search services based in Hong Kong.[136]

Google was not the only source to report attacks on human rights and civil society organizations working on issues related to China. Malicious e-mails purporting to

originate from the group Human Rights in China were sent to numerous other organizations that, if opened and executed, would install malware connected to a
command-and-control server located in China.[137] In a similar incident, staff at the
Committee to Protect Journalists received falsified e-mail invitations to the Nobel
Peace Prize awards ceremony of Chinese dissident Liu Xiabo containing malware
designed to contact servers in Bengbu, China.[138] These reports followed 2009's *Tracking
GhostNet* report by the Information Warfare Monitor, which identified an extensive
cyber espionage network that compromised thousands of computers, including some
at the private office of the Dalai Lama and several Tibetan nongovernmental organizations (NGOs), which contacted command-and-control servers located in China.[139]

Other organizations that do work in China have also reported malware infection.
Journalists and other staff of media organizations have been targeted with malware
attacks that made contact with servers in China. The Foreign Correspondents' Club
of China warned fellow journalists to be cautious following an e-mail-based malware
attack targeting media organizations.[140] Further investigation found a sophisticated
malware campaign that compromised users' computers and attempted to make contact
with servers at a university in Taiwan.[141] The increase in malware attacks targeting
foreign journalists occurred before the 60th anniversary of the founding of the People's
Republic of China, a sensitive political event that saw an increase in security
precautions.[142]

Cyber attacks attributed to sources in China have been identified by a variety of
different states. Reports from Australia,[143] Japan,[144] Pakistan,[145] South Korea,[146] the
United Kingdom,[147] and the United States[148] all point to the rise of cyber attacks originating from China. However, attribution of these incidents remains an ongoing challenge. While many of the targets of these attacks may reflect strategic interests for
China's government, the country also represents the largest single population of
Internet users and thus the greatest potential source of cyber-attack instigators.

ONI Testing Results

In 2010, the OpenNet Initiative conducted testing on a single Chinese ISP, CNLink
Networks. The testing results confirm that China maintains an advanced Internet
filtering system at the backbone level that is capable of blocking content through a
variety of methods, such as IP blocking, DNS tampering, and keyword filtering (TCP
resets).

Filtering in China is implemented at the backbone level through a method known
as keyword-based filtering, or TCP resets. This blocking method is unique to China and
works in part by inspecting the content of IP packets to determine if specific, sensitive
keywords are present. These keywords relate to historical events, banned groups, and
other topics considered sensitive or controversial by the Chinese government. A

keyword detected in either the header or the content of a message triggers the blocking mechanism and sends reset packets to both the source and destination IP addresses to disrupt and break the Internet user's connection.

The OpenNet Initiative found a lesser extent of Internet protocol (IP) blocking. Consistent with past ONI findings, transparency in Internet filtering remains low. There is no publicly available list of banned sites or mechanisms for users to petition to have a blocked site reviewed. When users attempt to access a blocked site, they receive a network timeout error page that does not indicate if or why the site has been blocked—it can appear to be the result of routine network errors.

Results indicate that the Chinese government continues to concentrate on blocking content that could potentially undermine the authority of the CCP as well as its control over social stability. It was found that CNLink Networks was extensively filtering Web sites critical of the ruling party. These sites include foreign and international media reporting on China in both foreign and local languages, such as Boxun (http://boxun.com), Ming Pao (http://www.mingpao.com), the Epoch Times (http://epochtimes.com), BBC Asia Pacific (http://news.bbc.co.uk/2/hi/asia-pacific), the Chinese-language BBC Zhongwen (http://news.bbc.co.uk/chinese/simp/hi/default.stm), Voice of America (http://voanews.com), and Radio Free Asia (both the English- and local-language versions of the site: http://rfa.org, http://rfa.org/mandarin, http://rfa.org/uyghur, and http://rfa.org/tibetan). Web sites belonging to human rights groups critical of the Chinese state are also extensively filtered, including those belonging to Human Rights in China (http://hrichina.org), Amnesty International (http://web.amnesty.org, http://amnesty.org.hk), Human Rights Watch (http://hrw.org, and http://www.hrw.org/chinese), and the China Labour Bulletin (http://clb.org.hk).

The filtering program of CNLink Networks also heavily emphasized Web sites focusing on politically sensitive issues related to China's national stability such as Uyghur, Tibetan, and Mongolian separatism and rights protection. Although these issues are all sensitive for the Chinese government, CNLink Networks filtered significantly more Web sites with content related to Tibet than the Uyghur minority or Mongolia. Among the Web sites blocked were http://savetibet.org, http://tibetanyouthcongress.org, http://friendsoftibet.org, http://www.uyghuramerican.org, and http://innermongolia.org. Falun Gong Web sites were also extensively filtered.

Web sites that challenge the reunification policy of the PRC—such as those calling for the formal independence of Taiwan—remain filtered, such as sites of the Taipei Economic and Cultural Office in New York (http://www.taipei.org), New Taiwan, Ilha Formosa, Taiwan Organization in the United States (http://taiwandc.org), and the main portal of the Taiwanese government (http://gov.tw). Web sites pertaining to politically sensitive events are also targeted, such as content related to Tiananmen Square (e.g., http://64memo.com, http://tiananmenvigil.org, and http://en.wikipedia.org/wiki/Tiananmen_Square_protests_of_1989).

While Web sites that challenge the political authority of the ruling party are the primary target of filtering on CNLink Networks, the ISP also blocks content that the government deems may harm the social fabric. Pornographic Web sites are heavily targeted, as well as online gambling (such as http://888casino.com and http://partypoker.com). This is consistent with the 2010 state crackdown on pornographic[149] and online gambling[150] content.

In contrast to previous ONI findings, testing results showed that China blocks access to major social media platforms such as Facebook, Twitter, and Blogspot. At the time of testing, other social media Web sites such as http://wordpress.com, http://wordpress.org, and http://flickr.com were accessible, though Wordpress blogs critical of the state or touching on political sensitive were blocked (such as http://chinaview .wordpress.com and http://seapa.wordpress.com). Web sites for circumvention tools were also found blocked, including http://gardennetworks.com, https://dongtaiwang .com, http://wujie.net, and http://peacefire.org.

Conclusion

Although the Chinese government views the Internet as a key engine of economic growth and an important platform for social and public services, it also sees the need to control the Internet to protect its domestic interests. With the largest number of Internet users in the world, the expanding scope of online content presents a major challenge for the Chinese government, which is intent on maintaining social order and stability in a context of rapid development and social transformation. Increasing contradictions arise out of these processes.[151] State authorities resist international criticism by pointing to China's developing country status and vulnerability to potential disorder.

The Chinese government maintains a strict and extensive approach to controlling the flow of information through a robust legal system that delegates filtering and monitoring responsibilities to domestic online service providers. Its content-control regulations impose self-censorship on users, which is reinforced by information campaigns and just-in-time filtering during sensitive moments. The mix of rapid development and a growing online population will remain persistent challenges to China's efforts at information control, and the state will continue to react with new measures for denying and shaping the flow of information in the country.

Notes

1. Will Foster, Milton Mueller, and Zixiang Tan, "China's New Internet Regulations: Two Steps Forward, One Step Back," *Communications of the ACM* 40, no. 12 (1997), http://portal.acm.org/citation.cfm?id=265565.

2. China Internet Network Information Center, *27th Statistical Survey Report on Internet Development in China* [in Chinese], January 19, 2011, http://research.cnnic.cn/html/1295338825d2556.html.

3. China Information Industry Trade Association—Information Security Subcommittee, *China Information Security Industry Development White Paper, 2005–2010* [in Chinese], http://www.itsec.gov.cn/sh/1341.htm.

4. Human Rights Watch, "China: Investigate Crackdown before Torch Relay's Passage through Tibet," March 24, 2008, http://www.hrw.org/en/news/2008/03/23/china-investigate-crackdown-torch-relay-s-passage-through-tibet.

5. Michael Bristow, "Tibet Anti-China Protests Spread," BBC News, March 17, 2008, http://news.bbc.co.uk/2/hi/asia-pacific/7300274.stm.

6. Human Rights Watch, "China: Investigate Crackdown before Torch Relay's Passage through Tibet."

7. Ministry of Foreign Affairs of the People's Republic of China, "Regulations on Reporting Activities by Foreign Journalists during the Beijing Olympic Games and the Preparatory Period," December 1, 2006, http://un.fmprc.gov.cn/eng/zxxx/t282169.htm.

8. OpenNet Initiative, "Country Profile: China," in *Access Controlled: The Shaping of Power, Rights, and Rule in Cyberspace*, ed. Ronald Deibert, John Palfrey, Rafal Rohozinski, and Jonathan Zittrain (Cambridge, MA: MIT Press, 2010), 449–487.

9. David Batty, "Media Face Web Censorship at Beijing Olympics," *The Guardian*, July 30, 2008, http://www.guardian.co.uk/world/2008/jul/30/china.olympicgames2008.

10. Information Office of the State Council of the People's Republic of China, *National Human Rights Action Plan of China (2009–2010)*, 2009, http://news.xinhuanet.com/english/2009-04/13/content_11177126.htm.

11. David Gelles, Joseph Menn, and Richard Waters, "Websites Blocked Ahead of Tiananmen Anniversary," *Financial Times*, June 3, 2009, http://www.ft.com/cms/s/0/e8b88790-4fc6-11de-a692-00144feabdc0.html#axzz1C9ZMGAcs; "There May Be Rising Mass Incidents in China in 2009 [in Chinese]," NF Daily, January 26, 2009, http://opinion.nfdaily.cn/content/2009-01/26/content_4867542.htm; Stan Schroeder, "China Blocks Twitter (and Almost Everything Else)," Mashable, June 2, 2009, http://mashable.com/2009/06/02/china-blocks-twitter-and-almost-everything-else.

12. Human Rights Watch, *We Are Afraid to Even Look for Them: Enforced Disappearances in the Wake of Xinjiang's Protests*, October 22, 2009, http://www.hrw.org/en/reports/2009/10/22/we-are-afraid-even-look-them.

13. Ibid.

14. Ibid.

15. UNESCO Bangkok, "China: Journalists Protest Savage Attacks on Colleagues," September 22, 2009, http://www.unescobkk.org/information/news-display/article/china-journalists-protest -savage-attacks-on-colleagues; Hong Kong Journalists Association, "Our Declaration for the Protest March on Liaison Office on 13 September, 2009," September 13, 2009, http://www.hkja .org.hk/site/portal/Site.aspx?id=A1-812&lang=en-US.

16. OpenNet Initiative Blog, "China Shuts Down Internet in Xinjiang Region after Riots," July 6, 2009, http://opennet.net/blog/2009/07/china-shuts-down-internet-xinjiang-region-after -riots.

17. Quoted in "Official: Internet Cut in Xinjiang to Prevent Riot from Spreading," Xinhua News Agency, July 7, 2009, http://news.xinhuanet.com/english/2009-07/07/content_11666802.htm.

18. Ibid.

19. "Accept the Delegation of Some Representatives of Xinjiang, the Media" [in Chinese], China News Service, March 7, 2010, http://www.chinanews.com/shipin/313/2010/0307/76.html.

20. "Google 'May Pull Out of China after Gmail Cyber Attack,'" BBC News, January 13, 2010, http://news.bbc.co.uk/2/hi/8455712.stm.

21. Ibid.

22. Chris Buckley and Lucy Hornby, "China Defends Censorship after Google Threat," Reuters, January 14, 2010, http://www.reuters.com/article/2010/01/14/us-china-usa-google -idUSTRE60C1TR20100114.

23. Ibid.

24. Kenneth Tan, "The Google.cn/Google.com.hk Lockdown Has Begun: ALL Search Queries Now End in a Connection Reset," Shanghaiist, March 30, 2010, http://shanghaiist.com/2010/03/30/ the_googlecn_googlecomhk_lockdown_h.php.

25. Google, "An Update on China," June 28, 2010, http://googleblog.blogspot.com/2010/06/ update-on-china.html.

26. Hillary Rodham Clinton, "Remarks on Internet Freedom," U.S. Department of State, January 21, 2010, http://www.state.gov/secretary/rm/2010/01/135519.htm.

27. "The Real Stake in 'Free Flow of Information,'" Global Times, January 22, 2010, http:// opinion.globaltimes.cn/editorial/2010-01/500324.html.

28. Ma Zhaoxu, "Foreign Ministry Spokesperson Ma Zhaoxu's Remarks on China-Related Speech by US Secretary of State on 'Internet Freedom,'" Ministry of Foreign Affairs of the People's Republic of China, January 22, 2010, http://www.fmprc.gov.cn/eng/xwfw/s2510/t653351.htm.

29. International Telecommunication Union (ITU), "Internet Indicators: Subscribers, Users and Broadband Subscribers," 2009 Figures, http://www.itu.int/ITU-D/icteye/Reporting/ ShowReportFrame.aspx?ReportName=/WTI/InformationTechnologyPublic&ReportFormat =HTML4.0&RP_intYear=2009&RP_intLanguageID=1&RP_bitLiveData=False.

30. Paul Budde Communication Pty., Ltd., "China—Key Statistics, Telecom Market, Regulatory Overview and Forecasts," July 7, 2010.

31. ITU, "Internet Indicators: Subscribers, Users and Broadband Subscribers"; China Internet Network Information Center, *27th Statistical Survey Report on Internet Development in China.*

32. China Internet Network Information Center, *27th Statistical Survey Report on Internet Development in China.*

33. ITU, "Internet Indicators: Subscribers, Users and Broadband Subscribers."

34. Paul Budde Communication Pty., Ltd., "China—Key Statistics, Telecom Market, Regulatory Overview and Forecasts."

35. Ibid.

36. China Internet Network Information Center, *27th Statistical Survey Report on Internet Development in China.*

37. Ibid.

38. Paul Budde Communication Pty., Ltd., "China—Key Statistics, Telecom Market, Regulatory Overview and Forecasts."

39. China Internet Network Information Center, *27th Statistical Survey Report on Internet Development in China.*

40. China Internet Network Information Center, *Statistical Report on Internet Development in China*, July 2010, http://www.cnnic.net.cn/uploadfiles/pdf/2010/8/24/93145.pdf.

41. China Internet Network Information Center, *27th Statistical Survey Report on Internet Development in China.*

42. "Search Engine Baidu Slams Google in China," AFP, January 20, 2011, http://www.nzherald.co.nz/technology/news/article.cfm?c_id=5&objectid=10700822.

43. China Internet Network Information Center, *27th Statistical Survey Report on Internet Development in China.*

44. Ibid.

45. Paul Budde Communication Pty., Ltd., "China—Key Statistics, Telecom Market, Regulatory Overview and Forecasts."

46. "Highlights of China's Institutional Restructuring Plan," *People's Daily*, March 16, 2008, http://english.peopledaily.com.cn/90001/90776/90785/6374104.html.

47. China Telecom USA, "Access China with CN2: The Internet for Business," http://www.chinatelecomusa.com/files/Chinausa_WP_FinalWeb.pdf.

48. Telegeography, "Broadband Provider Rankings: The Rise and Rise of China," July 28, 2010, http://www.telegeography.com/cu/article.php?article_id=33858.

49. China Internet Network Information Center, *27th Statistical Survey Report on Internet Development in China*.

50. Paul Budde Communication Pty., Ltd., "China—Key Statistics, Telecom Market, Regulatory Overview and Forecasts."

51. Sumner Lemon, "After Years of Delays, China Finally Issues 3G Licenses," *PC World*, January 7, 2009, http://www.pcworld.com/businesscenter/article/156612/after_years_of_delays_china _finally_issues_3g_licenses.html.

52. Alice Xin Liu, "Hu Yong Interview: The Digital Age, Orwell's 'Newspeak' and Chinese Media," Danwei, April 16, 2009, http://www.danwei.org/media/hu_yong_interview.php.

53. David Bandurski, "China's Guerrilla War for the Web," *Far Eastern Economic Review*, July 2008, http://testfeer.wsj-asia.com/essays/2008/august/chinas-guerrilla-war-for-the-web.

54. Ryan McLaughlin, "Human Flesh Search Engines—Crowd-Sourcing 'Justice,'" January 28, 2009, http://www.ryan-mclaughlin.com/blog/the-tech-dynasty/human-flesh-search-engines-crowd -sourcing-justice.

55. Vaclav Havel, Vaclav Maly, and Dana Nemcova, "A Nobel Prize for a Chinese Dissident," *New York Times*, September 20, 2010, http://www.nytimes.com/2010/09/21/opinion/21iht-edhavel .html?_r=2.

56. John Garnaut, "China's Plan to Use Internet for Propaganda," *The Age*, July 14, 2010, http:// www.theage.com.au/technology/technology-news/chinas-plan-to-use-internet-for-propaganda -20100713-109hc.html.

57. OpenNet Initiative, "China's Green Dam: The Implications of Government Control Encroaching on the Home PC," June 12, 2009, http://opennet.net/sites/opennet.net/files/GreenDam _bulletin.pdf.

58. Ibid.

59. Loretta Chao and Jason Dean, "Chinese Delay Plan for Censor Software," *Wall Street Journal*, July 1, 2009, http://online.wsj.com/article/SB124636491863372821.html.

60. Oiwan Lam, "China: Blue Dam Activated," Global Voices Advocacy, September 13, 2009, http://advocacy.globalvoicesonline.org/2009/09/13/china-blue-dam-activated.

61. Ibid.

62. Stephanie Wang and Robert Faris, "Welcome to the Machine," *Index on Censorship* 37, no. 2 (2008): 106–111.

63. Rebecca MacKinnon, "China's Censorship 2.0: How Companies Censor Bloggers," *First Monday* 14, no. 2 (2009), http://firstmonday.org/htbin/cgiwrap/bin/ojs/index.php/fm/article/ view/2378/2089.

64. Nart Villeneuve, "Search Monitor Project: Toward a Measure of Transparency," Citizen Lab Occasional Paper, June 2008, http://www.nartv.org/mirror/searchmonitor.pdf.

65. OpenNet Initiative Blog, "China Shuts Down Internet in Xinjian Region after Riots," July 6, 2009, http://opennet.net/blog/2009/07/china-shuts-down-internet-xinjiang-region-after -riots.

66. Steven Jiang, "China Blanks Nobel Peace Prize Searchers," CNN, "October 8, 2010, http:// edition.cnn.com/2010/WORLD/asiapcf/10/08/china.internet/?hpt=C1.

67. Committee to Protect Journalists, "National Day Triggers Censorship, Cyber Attacks in China," September 22, 2009, http://cpj.org/2009/09/national-day-triggers-censorship-cyber -attacks-in.php.

68. Tania Branigan, "China Blocks Twitter, Flickr and Hotmail Ahead of Tiananmen Anniversary," *The Guardian*, June 2, 2009, http://www.guardian.co.uk/technology/2009/jun/02/twitter -china.

69. Foreign Correspondents' Club of China, "China Should Allow Access to Tibetan Areas," March 9, 2009, http://www.fcchina.org/2009/03/09/china-should-allow-access-to-tibetan-areas.

70. Edward Wong and David Barboza, "Wary of Egypt Unrest, China Censors Web," *New York Times*, January 31, 2011, http://www.nytimes.com/2011/02/01/world/asia/01beijing.html.

71. China Internet Illegal Information Reporting Center, http://ciirc.china.cn.

72. Li Dan, "The Internet and Chinese Civil Society," *China Rights Forum,* no. 2 (2010): 96–104.

73. Rebecca MacKinnon, "China's Internet Censorship and Controls: The Context of Google's Approach in China," *China Rights Forum*, no. 2 (2010): 70–81.

74. Nart Villeneuve, *Breaching Trust: An Analysis of Surveillance and Security Practices on China's TOM-Skype Platform*, Information Warfare Monitor/ONI Asia, http://www.nartv.org/mirror/ breachingtrust.pdf.

75. MacKinnon, "China's Internet Censorship and Controls."

76. Information Office of the State Council of the People's Republic of China, *The Internet in China*, June 8, 2010, http://www.gov.cn/english/2010-06/08/content_1622956.htm

77. Ibid.

78. Measures for Managing Internet Information Services, Article 20 [in Chinese], issued by the State Council on September 25, 2000, effective October 1, 2000. Unofficial English translation is available at http://www.chinaculture.org/gb/en_aboutchina/2003-09/24/content_23369.htm.

79. Ibid.

80. Rules on the Management of Internet Electronic Bulletin Services [in Chinese], passed by the Fourth Ministry Affairs Meeting of the Ministry of Information Industry on October 8, 2000. Unofficial English translation is available at mesharpe.metapress.com/index/4T7361047374J2U0 .pdf.

81. Provisions on the Administration of News Information Services, Article 2 [in Chinese], issued by the Ministry of Information Industry and the State Council Information Office on September 25, 2005, http://www.isc.org.cn/20020417/ca315779.htm. Unofficial English translation is available at http://www.cecc.gov/pages/virtualAcad/index.phpd?showsingle=24396.

82. Provisions on the Administration of News Information Services, Article 11 [in Chinese], issued by the Ministry of Information Industry and the State Council Information Office on September 25, 2005, http://www.isc.org.cn/20020417/ca315779.htm. Unofficial English translation is available at http://www.cecc.gov/pages/virtualAcad/index.phpd?showsingle=24396.

83. Benjamin Liebman, "Watchdog or Demagogue? The Media in the Chinese Legal System," *Columbia Law Review,* January 2005: 41.

84. "Provisions on the Administration of News Information Services" [in Chinese], issued by the Ministry of Information Industry and the State Council Information Office on September 25, 2005, http://www.cecc.gov/pages/virtualAcad/index.php?showsingle-24396.

85. Ibid.

86. Ibid.

87. "Section 2, SARFT Notice for Strengthening the Administration of Internet Audio and Video Programming Content" [in Chinese] issued on March 30, 2009. Unofficial translation is available at http://www.sarft.gov.cn/articles/2009/03/30/20090330171107690049.html; "New Rules Imposed on Internet Video Content," Danwei, April 1, 2009, http://www.danwei.org/media_regulation/new_rules_imposed_on_internet.php.

88. "Section 3, SARFT Notice for Strengthening the Adminstration of Internet Audio and Video Programming Content."

89. Internet Society of China, "Internet Society of China Released 'Self-discipline Convention Blog Service' to Promote Orderly Development of Blog Service" [in Chinese], August 21, 2008, http://www.isc.org.cn/ShowArticle.php?id=7955.

90. Ibid.

91. Ibid.

92. For example, see "Rules of the NPC Standing Committee on Safeguarding Internet Security" [in Chinese], issued by the NPC Standing Committee on December 28, 2000. Unofficial English translation is available at http://www.guangshunda.com/en/Message.html.

93. Reporters Without Borders, "Woman Sentenced to a Year's Forced Labor over One Ironic Tweet," November 24, 2010, http://en.rsf.org/china-woman-sentenced-to-a-year-s-forced-24-11-2010,38886.html.

94. "Man Arrested for Obscene Blog," *China Times,* January 6, 2011, http://china.globaltimes.cn/society/2011-01/609726.html.

95. Bo Gu, "'I'm Innocent,' Roars Chinese Dad at Sentencing," NBC News, November 10, 2010, http://behindthewall.msnbc.msn.com/_nv/more/section/archive?date=2010/11.

96. Reporters Without Borders, "China," http://en.rsf.org/report-china,57.html.

97. Ibid.

98. "Law of the People's Republic of China on Guarding State Secrets," adopted at the Third Meeting of the Standing Committee of the Seventh National People's Congress on September 5, 1988, and revised at the 14th Session of the Standing Committee of the 11th National People's Congress on April 29, 2010, http://www.npc.gov.cn/npc/xinwen/2010-04/29/content_1571588 .htm. Unofficial English translation is available at http://www.hrichina.org/public/PDFs/ PressReleases/20101001-StateSecretsLaw-EN.pdf.

99. Quoted in Gillian Wong, "China Set to Tighten State Secrets Law Forcing Internet Firms to Inform on Users," *Washington Post*, April 28, 2010, http://www.washingtonpost.com/wp-dyn/ content/article/2010/04/27/AR2010042704503.html.

100. Human Rights in China, "HRIC Case Highlight: Shi Tao and Yahoo," http://www.hrichina .org/public/highlight; Human Rights in China, "Examples of Cases Involving Charges Related to State Secrets from 2007 to Present," July 24, 2009, http://hrichina.org/public/contents/ press?revision_id=170447&item_id=170446.

101. In the lead-up to the 17th party congress in 2007, an official announcement from the General Administration of Press and Publications indicated that it would clamp down on "illegal news coverage" and "false news" in order to create a healthy and harmonious environment for the congress. A crackdown on political news reporting, commentary, and Internet discussion followed. Media outlets were given instructions on what they could write about, while ISPs and individual Web sites disabled chat rooms and forums. See Peter Ford, "Why China Shut Down 18,401 Web Sites," *Christian Science Monitor*, September 25, 2007, http://www.csmonitor .com/2007/0925/p01s06-woap.html?page=1.

102. "China Shuts Over 60,000 Porn Websites This Year," Reuters, December 30, 2010, http:// www.reuters.com/article/2010/12/30/china-internet-idUSTOE6BT01T20101230.

103. "China Cracks Down on Illegal Online Drug Selling," *People's Daily,* November 25, 2010, http://english.people.com.cn/90001/90782/90872/7210365.html; "290 Websites Closed for Illicit Drug Promotion," *People's Daily*, November 17, 2010, http://english.peopledaily.com.cn/ 90001/90776/7202638.html.

104. "China Cracks Down on Online Gambling, Arrests 3,430," Xinhua News Agency, June 8, 2010, http://www.chinadaily.com.cn/bizchina/2010-06/08/content_9948601.htm.

105. "National Development and Reform Commission Issues National Approval for the 'Golden Shield' Construction Project at Management Conference" [in Chinese], Ministry of Public Security, November 17, 2006. For more discussion of the Golden Shield Project, see Greg Walton, "China's Golden Shield: Corporations and the Development of Surveillance Technology in the People's Republic of China, a Rights and Democracy Report," International Centre for Human Rights and Democratic Development, October 2001, http://www.dd-rd.ca/site/_PDF/publications/ globalization/CGS_ENG.PDF.

106. Wang Chen, "Development and Administration of Our Country's Internet," delivered on April 29, 2010, before the Standing Committee of the National People's Congress. Unofficial English translation is available at http://www.hrichina.org/public/contents/article?revision%5fid =175119&item%5fid=175084.

107. Ibid.

108. Information Office of the State Council of the People's Republic of China, *The Internet in China*.

109. "Top Ten: Please Show Your ID," *China Daily*, December 10, 2010, http://www2.chinadaily .com.cn/china/2010-12/10/content_11684998.htm.

110. Ibid.

111. Ibid.

112. "Real-name Registration Required for Mobile Users in China," Xinhua News Agency, September 1, 2010, http://news.xinhuanet.com/english2010/video/2010-09/01/c_13473049.htm.

113. See registration form at http://login.sina.com.cn/cgi/register/reg_sso_comment.php?entry =comment.

114. Philip P. Pan, "Chinese Crack Down on Student Web Sites," *Washington Post*, March 24, 2005, http://www.washingtonpost.com/wp-dyn/articles/A61334-2005Mar23.html.

115. Peter Foster, "China to Force Internet Users to Register Real Names," *The Telegraph*, May 5, 2010, http://www.telegraph.co.uk/news/worldnews/asia/china/7681709/China-to-force-internet -users-to-register-real-names.html.

116. China Internet Network Information Center, "The Notification about Further Enhancement of Auditing Domain Name Registration Information," December 14, 2009, http://www.cnnic.net .cn/html/Dir/2009/12/12/5750.htm.

117. MacKinnon, "China's Internet Censorship and Controls."

118. Chloe Albanesius, "Go Daddy Cuts Off Chinese Domain-Name Registration," *PC Magazine*, March 24, 2010, http://www.pcmag.com/article2/0,2817,2361779,00.asp.

119. Philip P. Pan, "Chinese Crack Down on Student Web Sites."

120. Oiwan Lam, "China: Radical Real Name Registration Campaign," *Global Voices*, June 15, 2010, http://advocacy.globalvoicesonline.org/2010/06/15/china-radical-real-name-registration -campaign.

121. Ibid.

122. Measures for the Management of E-mail Services, Article 3 [in Chinese], issued by the Ministry of Information Industry on November 7, 2005, effective March 30, 2006.

123. Rules on the Management of Internet Electronic Bulletin Services, Articles 14 and 15 [in Chinese], issued by the Ministry of Information Industry on October 7, 2000. Unofficial English translation is available at http://mesharpe.metapress.com/media/3g267jyuyj4urbm4ek0j/ contributions/4/t/7/3/4t7361047374j2u0_html/fulltext.html.

124. Measures for Managing Internet Information Services, Article 14 [in Chinese], issued by the State Council on September 25, 2000, effective October 1, 2000. Unofficial English translation is available at http://www.chinaculture.org/gb/en_aboutchina/2003-09/24/content_23369.htm.

125. Regulations on the Administration of Business Sites Providing Internet Services, Articles 19, 21, and 23 [in Chinese], issued by the State Council on September 29, 2002, effective November 15, 2002.

126. "China Tightens Internet Censorship in Tibet," *Tibetan Review,* August 5, 2010, http://www .tibetanreview.net/news.php?id=6834.

127. "China's Mobile Network: A Big Brother Surveillance Tool?" ABC News, January 28, 2008, http://www.abc.net.au/news/stories/2008/01/28/2147712.htm.

128. Matthew Robertson and Michelle Yu, "In Chinese Internet Rumble, User Rights Not the Focus," *The Epoch Times*, http://www.theepochtimes.com/n2/content/view/45580.

129. Villeneuve, *Breaching Trust.*

130. Ibid.

131. Google, "A New Approach to China," January 12, 2010, http://googleblog.blogspot.com/ 2010/01/new-approach-to-china.html.

132. Andrew Jacobs and Miguel Helft, "Google, Citing Attack, Threatens to Exit China," *New York Times*, January 12, 2010, http://www.nytimes.com/2010/01/13/world/asia/13beijing .html.

133. John Markoff, "Cyberattack on Google Said to Hit Password System," *New York Times*, April 19, 2010, http://www.nytimes.com/2010/04/20/technology/20google.html.

134. James Glanz and John Markoff, "Vast Hacking by a China Fearful of the Web," *New York Times*, December 4, 2010, http://www.nytimes.com/2010/12/05/world/asia/05wikileaks-china .html; Patrick Sawer, "Top Chinese Officials Ordered Attack on Google, Wikileaks Cables Claim," *The Telegraph*, December 4, 2010, http://www.telegraph.co.uk/news/worldnews/wikileaks/ 8181619/Top-Chinese-officials-ordered-attack-on-Google-Wikileaks-cables-claim.html.

135. Tania Branigan, "China Denies Involvement in Cyber Attacks on Google," *The Guardian*, January 25, 2010, http://www.guardian.co.uk/technology/2010/jan/25/china-denies-cyber-attacks -google.

136. Google, "An Update on China."

137. Nart Villeneuve, "Human Rights and Malware Attacks," Nart Villeneuve: Malware Explorer, July 29, 2010, http://www.nartv.org/2010/07/29/human-rights-and-malware-attacks.

138. Danny O'Brien, "That Nobel Invite? Mr. Malware Sent It," Committee to Protect Journalists, November 10, 2010, http://www.cpj.org/internet/2010/11/that-nobel-invite-mr-malware-sent-it .php.

139. "Tracking GhostNet: Investigating a Cyber Espionage Network," Information Warfare Monitor, March 29, 2009, http://www.tracking-ghost.net.

140. "Warning on Fake Emails Targeting News Assistants," Foreign Correspondents' Club of China, September 21, 2009, http://www.fccchina.org/2009/09/21/warning-on-fake-emails -targeting-news-assistants.

141. Nart Villeneuve and Greg Walton, "Targeted Malware Attack on Foreign Correspondents Based in China," Nart Villeneuve: Malware Explorer, September 29, 2009, http://www.nartv .org/2009/09/28/targeted-malware-attack-on-foreign-correspondent%E2%80%99s-based -in-china.

142. "National Day Triggers Censorship, Cyber Attacks in China," Committee to Protect Journalists, September 22, 2009, http://cpj.org/2009/09/national-day-triggers-censorship-cyber-attacks -in.php.

143. Brett Winterford, "Optus Customers Hit by China DDoS Attack," *SC Magazine*, April 15, 2010, http://www.securecomputing.net.au/News/172229,optus-customers-hit-by-china-ddos-attack .aspx; Asher Moses, "Chinese Cyber Attackers Hit Optus," *Sydney Morning Herald*, April 15, 2010, http://www.smh.com.au/technology/security/chinese-cyber-attackers-hit-optus-20100415-sgm8 .html.

144. "Chinese Hackers Suspected of DDoS Attacks Against Japan," The New New Internet, September 27, 2010, http://www.thenewnewinternet.com/2010/09/27/chinese-hackers-suspected -of-ddos-attacks-against-japan; "Japan Suspects Cyber Attacks Amid China Row: Media," Agence France-Press, September 17, 2010, http://www.google.com/hostednews/afp/article/ ALeqM5jrJX2uRX7gxO3zPa_dO-rE0FPbnA.

145. Rajeev Deshpande and Vishwa Mohan, "Pakistan, China Hackers Tried to Deface CWG Sites," *Times of India*, October 16, 2010, http://articles.timesofindia.indiatimes.com/2010-10-16/ india/28235934_1_cyber-security-hackers-official-agencies; Indrani Bagchi, "China Mounts Cyber Attacks on Indian Sites," *Times of India*, May 5, 2008, http://articles.timesofindia.indiatimes .com/2008-05-05/india/27760718_1_cyber-warfare-government-networks-china.

146. "S. Korean Government Website Hit by Cyber Attacks," Agence France-Presse, June 9, 2010, http://www.google.com/hostednews/afp/article/ALeqM5j-cLHwEp033Jo3lRnOJSFM9L3z6Q.

147. David Hencke, "Whitehall Plans New Cyber Security Centre to Deter Foreign Hackers," *The Guardian*, June 14, 2009, http://www.guardian.co.uk/technology/2009/jun/14/government -security-cyber-crime-hacking.

148. Sam Diaz, "Law Firm That Sued Chinese Government Reports Cyber Attack," ZDNet, January 13, 2010, http://www.zdnet.com/blog/btl/law-firm-that-sued-chinese-government-reports -cyber-attack/29533; Lolita Baldor, "Pentagon Takes Aim at China Cyber Threat," ABC News, August 19, 2010, http://abcnews.go.com/Politics/wireStory?id=11439149.

149. "China Cracks Down on Internet Pornography," *People's Daily,* December 30, 2010, http:// english.people.com.cn/90001/90776/90882/7246889.html.

150. "China Cracks Down on Online Gambling, Arrests 3,430," Xinhua.

151. See Wang Chen, "Development and Administration of Our Country's Internet."

India

A stable democracy with a strong tradition of press freedom, India nevertheless continues its regime of Internet filtering. However, India's selective censorship of blogs and other content, often under the guise of security, has also been met with significant opposition.

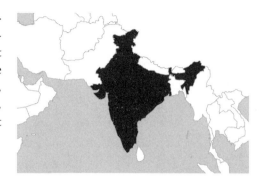

Filtering	No Evidence of Filtering	Suspected Filtering	Selective Filtering	Substantial Filtering	Pervasive Filtering
Political			•		
Social			•		
Conflict and security			•		
Internet tools			•		

	Low	Medium	High	Not Applicable
Transparency		•		
Consistency			•	

KEY INDICATORS	
GDP per capita, PPP (constant 2005 international dollars)	2,970
Life expectancy at birth, total (years)	64
Literacy rate, adult total (percent of people age 15+)	nd
Human Development Index (out of 169)	119
Rule of Law (out of 5)	2.5
Voice and Accountability (out of 5)	3.0
Democracy Index (out of 167)	40 (Flawed democracy)
Digital Opportunity Index (out of 181)	124
Internet penetration rate (percentage of population)	5.1

Source by indicator: World Bank 2009, World Bank 2008a, World Bank 2008b, UNDP 2010, World Bank Worldwide Governance Indicators 2009, Economist Intelligence Unit 2010, ITU 2007, ITU 2009. nd, no data. See Introduction to the Country Profiles, pp. 222–223.

Background

With a population of over one billion, India is the world's second most populous nation. The Indian government, a constitutional republic and representative democracy, generally respects the right to free speech and allows a wide array of political, social, and economic beliefs to be expressed. However, on targeted political and social conflicts, the government censors media and online discussion, particularly in areas of social unrest. In conflicts between castes and religious groups, and in the ongoing dispute with Pakistan over Kashmir, the state routinely censors material it believes could incite violence. Threats to journalists and bloggers come from political, religious, or ethnic nationalist groups. However, journalists are rarely detained as a means of censoring the press, and when they are held they are often quickly released.

Internet in India

Internet use in India reveals a great imbalance between urban and rural regions, although the gap has been diminishing during the past few years. Nearly 25 percent of India's population lives in cities (266 million), and 20 percent (52 million) of those are active Internet users (meaning they have used the Internet at least once in the past month).[1] By contrast, only 4.18 million among the rural population are active users; 54 percent of these rural users access the Internet through Internet cafés more than ten kilometers away from their villages. Seventy-eight percent of nonusers indicate that they are not aware of the Internet.[2] Language is another obstacle to using the Internet. Although there are 22 primary regional languages in India, most online content is in English, a language only 11 percent of the population speaks.[3] With approximately 61 million Internet users, India has an overall Internet penetration rate of 5.1 percent. However, its Internet subscription rate is low, at only 1.3 percent.[4]

Most Indians who access the Internet do so from Internet cafés. Home and work connections and school access points are less popular. Most Internet users in the country are male, middle-class, and young.[5] Almost half of the country's users are online at least four to six times per week.[6]

As of December 2009, approximately 370 Internet service providers (ISPs) were licensed to operate in the country.[7] According to an official Telecom Regulatory Authority of India report, Bharat Sanchar Nigam Limited (BSNL) and Mahanagar Telephone Nigam Limited (MTNL) were the market leaders, holding 57.84 percent and 13.81 percent of the market share respectively in June 2010.[8] In the mid-1980s, two state-owned corporations were formed to provide limited telecom services: Videsh Sanchar Nigam Limited (VSNL) for international long distance and Mahanagar Telephone Nigam Limited (MTNL) for Mumbai and Delhi. In 1995, VSNL became the first to provide Internet services to the country. In April 2002, the government authorized ISPs to offer Voice over Internet protocol (VoIP) services.[9]

In January 2007, the Department of Telecommunications (DOT) announced that it would install filtering mechanisms at India's international gateways. The head of the Internet Service Providers Association of India (ISPAI) said that these new "landing stations" would be able to block both specific Web sites at the subdomain level and unauthorized VoIP telephone systems.[10]

Legal and Regulatory Frameworks

India guarantees freedom of speech and expression in its constitution but reserves the authority to impose restrictions in the interests of national sovereignty, state security, foreign relations, public order, decency, and morality.[11] Each form of media—print, film, and television—is governed by its own regulatory apparatus. For example, print media are regulated by a board of press and government officials,[12] while films are regulated by a board appointed wholly by the government.[13] Private FM radio stations were legalized in 2000, but none of them are allowed to broadcast news or current affairs. The state continues to retain control over all AM radio stations.[14]

Until the late 1990s, the Indian government had control over all aspects of the telecommunications sector: policy, regulation, and operations.[15] The new Internet policy introduced in November 1998 allowed private companies to become ISPs and either lease transmission network capacity or build their own, thereby ending the monopoly over domestic long-distance networks of the Department of Telecoms.

However, most companies opted to use the lines already established by the government.[16]

In June 2000, the Indian Parliament created the Information Technology Act (IT Act) to provide a legal framework to regulate Internet use and commerce, including digital signatures, security, and hacking. The act criminalizes publication of obscene information electronically and grants police powers to search any premises without a warrant and arrest individuals in violation of the act.[17]

In December 2008, the Indian Parliament amended the IT Act; the amended act came into force on October 27, 2009.[18] The 2000 IT Act had criminalized the electroinc publication of obscene information, granting police powers to search premises without warrants and arrest individuals in violation of the act.[19] The 2008 amendment broadened content that could be blocked beyond online obscenity. The newly added Section 69A grants power to the central government, "in the interest of sovereignty and integrity of India, defense of India, security of the State, friendly relations with foreign states or public order," to issue directions to block public access to any information "generated, transmitted, received, stored or hosted in any computer resource."[20] Although Section 69A(2) requires procedures and safeguards to be prescribed when the government exercises this power,[21] these restrictions are unclear because they are not specified in the amendment. Critics claim that the amendment, which makes such sweeping changes in the existing regime, was passed "in an unprecedented hurry, without any discussion in both the houses of the Parliament."[22]

The Indian Computer Emergency Response Team (CERT-IN)[23] was set up by the Department of Information Technology under the amended IT Act to implement India's filtering regime.[24] In 2004, CERT-IN became operational to review complaints and act as the sole authority for issuing blocking instructions to the DOT.[25] Under the 2008 amendment of the IT Act, CERT-IN was assigned "the task of oversight of the Indian cyberspace for enhancing cyber protection, enabling security compliance and assurance in Government and critical sectors."[26] Only limited or specified individuals or institutions can make official complaints and recommendations for investigation to CERT-IN. These include high-ranking government officials, the police, government agencies, and "any others as may be specified by the Government."[27]

On July 13, 2006, CERT-IN ordered access to 17 Web sites blocked following the 2006 Mumbai train bombings, reportedly because the attackers were believed to have communicated by means of the blogosphere. The blocked Web sites included "American right-wing" sites (http://mypetjawa.mu.nu/, http://mackers-world.com/), Hindu extremist or "Hindutva" sites, and a defunct Web site supporting the formation of a "Dalit" homeland within India (http://www.dalitstan.org).[28]

In 2006, filtering requests also came from individuals protesting content they considered offensive or obscene. On October 10, 2006, media reported that the Bombay High

Court had directed the Maharashtra government to issue notice to Google for "alleged spread of hatred about India" on its social networking site Orkut, in response to a Public Interest Litigation (PIL) petition calling for the ban of Orkut for hosting a "We Hate India" community.[29] Similarly, in 2009, the Maharashtra government began examining legal options for censoring Google Earth, for fear that it could be used to facilitate terror attacks.[30] It was reported that the surviving gunman of the 2008 terror attacks in Mumbai claimed that Google satellite images had been used in planning the attacks.[31]

In November 2006, in response to protests over an "anti-Shivaji" community on Orkut, police banned Orkut, temporarily shut down Internet cafés where users were found using the site, and began an investigation under the IT Act and penal code provisions for obscene publications and religious insult offenses.[32] In December, a government official made a similar blocking request after a report that "obscene" material about "Hindu girls" was posted on Orkut.[33] In May 2007, although none of these efforts resulted in a comprehensive ban of Orkut, site officials reached an agreement with the Indian government to block "defamatory or inflammatory content" and to release the IP addresses of the offending parties to law enforcement.[34]

Many have argued that giving CERT-IN this power through executive order violates constitutional jurisprudence, holding that specific legislation must be passed before the government can encroach on individual rights. When CERT-IN has issued orders to block specific Web sites, no communication has been made to the public beforehand.[35] The blocking mechanism created under the IT Act provides for no review or appeal procedures, except in court, and is a permanent block.

Police commissioners, who can exercise the powers of executive magistrates in times of emergency, can also block Web sites containing material that constitutes a nuisance or threat to public safety under Section 155 of the Code of Criminal Procedure.[36] The first occurrence of such an action was in 2004, when Mumbai police blocked http://hinduunity.org on the grounds that it contained anti-Islamic material that could be inflammatory.[37] One of the nation's ISPs, Sify, refused to block the site on the basis that only CERT-IN had the authority to issue blocking orders.[38]

Filtering can also be mandated through licensing requirements. For example, ISPs seeking licenses to provide Internet services with the DOT "shall block Internet sites and/or individual subscribers, as identified and directed by the Telecom Authority from time to time" in the interests of "national security."[39] License agreements also require ISPs to prevent the transmission of obscene or otherwise "objectionable material."[40]

Surveillance

Section 69 of the IT Act empowers the central government to designate agencies and issue orders for interception, monitoring, and decryption in the interest of national security, public order, or preventing incitement of illegal acts. More specifically, Section 69B of the IT Act authorizes the central government to "monitor and collect traffic data or information through any computer resource for cyber security."[41] Within this authority, the law mandates that any intermediary or any person in charge of said computer resource called upon must "provide technical assistance and extend all facilities to such agency to enable online access," "intercept, monitor, or decrypt the information," and "provide information stored in computer resources."[42] Similar to Section 69A, the law requires that procedures and safeguards be applied when the government exercises such power, though the details of such procedures are not clear.

Concerned that terrorists may take advantage of the encryption in smart phones, the Indian government threatened to ban BlackBerry messaging and corporate e-mail services by August 31, 2010, unless Research in Motion (RIM) granted regulators access to encrypted user data. The deadline was first extended to October 2010, then to January 2011, for RIM and regulators to work on a feasible solution to address the national security concerns. As an interim solution, RIM agreed to host local servers and proposed a manual solution for messenger service.[43] In December 2010, India agreed to work with individual carriers to access data from BlackBerry devices, acknowledging RIM's assertion that they do not have access to individual users' encryption keys.[44]

According to Indian officials, the government also sent notices to Google and Skype, requiring them to set up local servers to allow full monitoring of encrypted e-mail and messenger communications.[45] It remains unclear how these service providers would comply with the direction.

ONI Testing Results

Results from OpenNet Initiative testing reveal that Indian ISPs selectively filter sites identified by government authorities. Over the course of 2009–2010, the ONI conducted testing on four major Indian ISPs: Bharti Airtel, Ltd.; Bharat Sanchar Nigam, Ltd. (BSNL); Tata Communications, Ltd.; and Mahanagar Telephone Nigam, Ltd. (MTNL). Testing done by the ONI found that BSNL blocked more Web sites than the other ISPs, which had only slight variations among them. Variations in blocking among ISPs suggest that CERT-IN and the DOT continue to rely on ISPs to implement filtering instructions.

When users attempt to access a blocked Web site on any of the four tested ISPs, they receive a "server not found" error page. This error page—also received in the instance of a genuine server error—gives users the impression that the Web sites are inaccessible as a result of routine network errors, rather than filtering.

OpenNet Initiative technical analysis revealed that these errors were the result of DNS tampering, a method of filtering that enables ISPs to target specific content. As a result, ISPs are able to block individual blogs (such as http://pajamaeditors.blogspot .com, http://commonfolkcommonsense.blogspot.com, and http://exposingtheleft

.blogspot.com) without blocking the host domain, http://blogspot.com, or any of the other blogs hosted on it.

While BSNL blocked more sites than the other ISPs, the ONI found that in general the level of filtering among ISPs was consistent with only slight variations. Further, the contents of filtered Web sites are similar across ISPs. For example, each ISP blocks a variety of extremist sites, such as Web sites of Hindu extremist groups (http://hinduunity.com and http://hinduunity.org) or Web sites with critical or extremist political (particularly "American right-wing") commentary (http://mypetjawa.mu.nu, http://mackers-world.com/). The OpenNet Initiative has found that these sites are consistently targeted for filtering by India. Web sites with information on human rights in India, Internet tools such as proxies, and content related to free expression are also targets of filtering. Data also showed that ISPs consistently filter pornography, but compared to other types of content, the number of blocked pornographic sites is small.

Technical analysis revealed evidence of collateral filtering on two ISPs: Bharti Airtel and MTNL. Collateral filtering is a result of IP-based blocking and refers to Web sites that are unintentionally filtered as a result of sharing the same IP address as a Web site that has been intentionally blocked. For example, 2006–2007 testing found that a site about American-Israeli rabbi Meir Kahane (http://kahane.org) was blocked because it shares the same IP address as the Hindu Unity Web site (http://hinduunity .com, http://hinduunity.org); 2009–2010 testing confirmed that the block was still in place. Similarly, during 2008–2009 testing a Web site for travel agents (http://www .positivespace.com) and a system administrator resource Web site (http://gwsystems .co.il) were found blocked as a result of sharing that same IP address with the Hindu Unity Web site.

Conclusion

Indian ISPs continue to selectively filter Web sites identified by authorities. However, government attempts at filtering have not been entirely effective because blocked content has quickly migrated to other Web sites and users have found ways to circumvent filtering. The government has also been criticized for a poor understanding of the technical feasibility of censorship and for haphazardly choosing which Web sites to block. There are still parts of the IT (Amendment) Act, including absolving intermediaries from being responsible for third-party-created content, that have not been tested since its enactment. This lack of action could signal stronger government monitoring in the future.

Notes

1. Internet and Mobile Association of India (IAMAI), "I-Cube 2009–2010: Internet in India," April 2010, http://www.iamai.in/Upload/Research/icube_new_curve_lowres_39.pdf.

2. IAMAI, "Internet for Rural India: 2009," August 2010, http://www.iamai.in/Upload/Research/Internet_for_Rural_India_44.pdf.

3. IAMAI, "I-Cube 2009–2010: Internet in India."

4. International Telecommunication Union (ITU), "Internet Indicators: Subscribers, Users and Broadband Subscribers," 2009 Figures, http://www.itu.int/ITU-D/icteye/Reporting/ShowReportFrame.aspx?ReportName=/WTI/InformationTechnologyPublic&ReportFormat=HTML4.0&RP_intYear=2009&RP_intLanguageID=1&RP_bitLiveData=False.

5. IAMAI, "I-Cube 2009–2010: Internet in India."

6. Ibid.

7. Department of Telecommunications, Ministry of Information and Technology India, "List of ISP Licensees as on 31.12.2009," December 31, 2009, http://www.dot.gov.in/isp/ISP_licences_31.12.09.doc.

8. Telecom Regulatory Authority of India, "Indian Telecom Services Performance Indicators April-June 2010," October 2010, http://www.trai.gov.in/WriteReadData/trai/upload/Reports/52/5octoberindicatorreporton13oct.pdf.

9. Rakesh Kumar Sharma and R. K. Yadav, "Reforms in Indian Telecom Sector," Indian MBA, http://www.indianmba.com/Faculty_Column/FC701/fc701.html.

10. Joji Thomas Philip and Moumita Bakshi Chatterjee, "Screening for Dangerous Blogs, Sites," India Times Infotech, December 5, 2006, http://www.digitalcommunities.com/articles/Security-and-Censorship-India-to-Clip.html.

11. Constitution Act of India (Ninety-Third Amendment), Article 19, http://lawmin.nic.in/coi.htm.

12. Indrajit Basu, "Security and Censorship: India to Clip the Wings of Internet," Digital Communities, January 26, 2007, http://www.digitalcommunities.com/articles/Security-and-Censorship-India-to-Clip.html.

13. Constitution Act of India (Ninety-Third Amendment), Article 19.

14. Press Council Act 1978, Articles 13–15, http://presscouncil.nic.in/act.htm.

15. Thankom G. Arun, "Regulation and Competition: Emerging Issues in an Indian Perspective," Centre on Regulation and Competition, October 2003, http://www.competition-regulation.org.uk/publications/working_papers/wp39.pdf.

16. Policy Guidelines for Setting up Community Radio Stations in India, Ministry of Information and Broadcasting, http://www.mib.nic.in/writereaddata/html_en_files/crs/CRBGUIDELINES041206.pdf; Subramanian Vincent, "Community Radio Gets Its Day," India Together, November 18, 2006, http://www.indiatogether.org/2006/nov/sbv-cradio.htm.

17. Information Technology (IT) Act 2000, Ministry of Information Technology, http://www.mit.gov.in/content/view-it-act-2000.

18. Enforcement of Information Technology (Amendment) Act 2008, Department of Information Technology, http://www.mit.gov.in/sites/upload_files/dit/files/downloads/itact2000/act301009.pdf.

19. IT Act, 2000, Article 67.

20. IT Act, 2008.

21. Ibid.

22. Comments by Pavan Duggal, President of Cyberlaws.net, http://www.cyberlaws.net/itamendments/index1.htm.

23. Indian Computer Emergency Response Team, http://www.cert-in.org.in.

24. Right to Information Act, 2005, Article 7(1), http://righttoinformation.gov.in/webactrti.htm.

25. Shivan Viv, "Internet Censorship in India: An RTI Application," National Highway, September 26, 2006, http://shivamvij.com/2006/09/26/internet-censorship-in-india-an-rti-application.

26. Vikas Asawat, "Information Technology (Amendment) Act, 2008: A New Vision through a New Change," March 17, 2010, http://ssrn.com/abstract=1680152.

27. Department of Telecommunications, Ministry of Communication and Information Technology, "Directions to Block Internet Websites," http://photos1.blogger.com/blogger/507/157/1600/Indian_censored_list.jpg.

28. Right to Information Act, 2005, Article 7(1).

29. Ibid., Article 8.

30. "Maharashtra Wants Google Earth Censored," *The Hindu*, March 10, 2009, http://www.hindu.com/holnus/004200903101511.htm.

31. "India's Own Version of Google Earth Causes Security Worries," *Economic Times*, March 11, 2009, http://economictimes.indiatimes.com/Infotech/Indias-own-version-of-Google-Earth-causes-security-worries-/articleshow/4250421.cms.

32. Viv, "Internet Censorship in India."

33. Department of Telecom, Ministry of Communication and Information Technology, "Directions to Block Internet Websites."

34. "Orkut's Tell-All Pact with Cops," *Economic Times*, May 1, 2007, http://articles.economictimes.indiatimes.com/2007-05-01/news/28459689_1_orkut-ip-addresses-mumbai-police.

35. John Ribeiro, "Orkut Comes under Fire in India," *InfoWorld*, October 12, 2006, http://www.infoworld.com/t/architecture/orkut-comes-under-fire-in-india-310.

36. Chinmayee Prasad, "Analysing Section 144, CrPC," National Law Institute University Bhopal, http://www.legalservicesindia.com/articles/crpc.htm.

37. Pratyush, "Orkut Blocked in Pune, PIL Filed against It for Running Anti Shivaji Community," India Daily, November 24, 2006, http://pratyush.instablogs.com/entry/orkut-blocked-in-pune -pil-filed-against-it-for-running-anti-shivaji-community/; "Orkut Forum on Shivaji Maharaj Blocked," Press Trust of India, November 18, 2006, http://www.expressindia.com/news/fullstory .php?newsid=77287.

38. Ministry of Communications and Information Technology, "Blocking of Website," September 22, 2003, http://pib.nic.in/archieve/lreleng/lyr2003/rsep2003/22092003/r2209200314.html.

39. Code of Criminal Procedure, 1973, Article 144, http://www.delhidistrictcourts.nic.in/CrPC .htm.

40. Priya Ganapati, "Mumbai Police Gag hinduunity.org," Rediff, May 27, 2004, http://ia.rediff .com/news/2004/may/26hindu.htm.

41. Information Technology (Amendment) Act 2008, http://www.mit.gov.in/sites/upload_files/ dit/files/downloads/itact2000/it_amendment_act2008.pdf.

42. Ibid.

43. Shauvik Ghosh, "Govt Gives RIM Time till Jan to Provide Data Access," October 12, 2010, Livemint, http://www.livemint.com/2010/10/11235823/Govt-gives-RIM-time-till-Jan-t.html.

44. Nancy Gohring, "RIM: India Agrees to Work with Enterprises for Data Access," PC World, December 3, 2010, http://www.pcworld.com/businesscenter/article/212462/rim_india_agrees _to_work_with_enterprises_for_data_access.html.

45. Devidutta Tripathy, "India to Decide on More Time to RIM for Data Access," Reuters, October 26, 2010, http://www.reuters.com/article/2010/10/26/india-rim-idUSSGE69P0IU20101026.

Indonesia

The Internet in Indonesia has been expanding rapidly. Although broadband subscriptions are relatively expensive, users have been accessing the Internet through mobile telephones and Internet cafés. As the Internet market continues to grow, the Indonesian government has become increasingly sensitive about pornographic and anti-Islamic online content. This concern has led to the

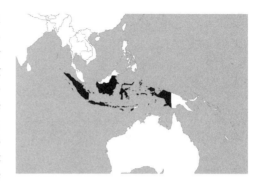

creation of a number of laws to regulate such content on the Internet and sparked discussions within the Ministry of Communication and Information Technology on how best to regulate content deemed "illegal" under the new laws. The circulation of two celebrity sex videos on the Internet sparked a government clampdown on pornographic Web content in the summer of 2010, despite opposition from the public.

RESULTS AT A GLANCE

Filtering	No Evidence of Filtering	Suspected Filtering	Selective Filtering	Substantial Filtering	Pervasive Filtering
Political			•		
Social				•	
Conflict and security	•				
Internet tools			•		

OTHER FACTORS

	Low	Medium	High	Not Applicable
Transparency			•	
Consistency	•			

KEY INDICATORS	
GDP per capita, PPP (constant 2005 international dollars)	3,813
Life expectancy at birth, total (years)	71
Literacy rate, adult total (percent of people age 15+)	92.0
Human Development Index (out of 169)	108
Rule of Law (out of 5)	1.9
Voice and Accountability (out of 5)	2.4
Democracy Index (out of 167)	60 (Flawed democracy)
Digital Opportunity Index (out of 181)	116
Internet penetration rate (percentage of population)	8.7

Source by indicator: World Bank 2009, World Bank 2008a, UNDP 2009, UNDP 2010, World Bank Worldwide Governance Indicators 2009, Economist Intelligence Unit 2010, ITU 2007, ITU 2009. See Introduction to the Country Profiles, pp. 222–223.

Background

The Asian Financial Crisis of 1997–1998 had a major effect on Indonesia's economy—the drying up of foreign direct investment, the collapse of the rupiah, mass unemployment, and rising inflation brought about major socioeconomic problems. Citizens demonstrated their discontent through major uprisings, which eventually led to the resignation of General Suharto in May 1998 and the end of three decades of United States–backed authoritarian rule.[1] Under Suharto, Indonesia was known as one of the "Asian Tigers" for its strong economic growth (with an annual average growth rate of 8 percent in the last decade of his regime).[2] However, government policies exacerbated socioeconomic cleavages and inequalities, and created tensions that were suppressed through repressive military measures.[3] The majority of people were excluded from political life in a climate in which social conflict, corruption, and repression of dissent were widespread. Some analysts suggest that although the financial crisis was the catalyst that triggered the breaking point of Suharto's rule, it was not the underlying cause.[4]

The end of the Suharto regime marked the beginning of rapid change and democratization in Indonesia. Although social unrest, separatist movements, corruption, terrorism, and political and economic instability hindered progress initially, conditions have since improved. The country experienced its first free parliamentary election in 1999 and its first directed presidential election in 2004.

One important outcome of democratization is the relative press freedom that Indonesian media and citizens enjoy today. However, although freedom of speech and of the press are protected by the constitution and Indonesia's press is considered among the freest in Southeast Asia,[5] full press freedom has been hindered by legal and regulatory restrictions (many of which have only recently been enacted).[6] Self-censorship is commonplace, and those who speak out risk violent attacks and intimidation.[7]

The country is secular with an ethnically and religiously diverse population. However, because of its predominantly Muslim population (as well as a conservative Muslim majority within government) the state is sensitive about indecency and blasphemy. The government has also expressed concern about media and Internet content that could spark social unrest. These concerns have had an adverse effect on full freedom of expression in the country.

Internet in Indonesia

As of August 2010, Indonesia had over 200 Internet service providers (ISPs).[8] The largest are Telkomsel and Indosat. Made up of roughly 17,000 islands, Indonesia does not have a centralized Web infrastructure and has several links to overseas networks.[9] Indonet receives its upstream bandwidth from San Francisco, London, and Hong Kong at a rate of 156 to 200 Mbps.[10] The country has two Internet exchange points (IXP), the Biznet Internet Exchange (BIX) and the Indonesia Internet Exchange (IIX). The IIX was the country's first IXP and is maintained by the Indonesian Internet Service Providers Association (APJII).

Internet usage in 2009 was reported to be 20 million with an 8.7 percent penetration rate.[11] Fixed broadband subscription rate was low, at 0.74 percent.[12] Many people access the Internet through mobile phones[13] or at privately owned Internet cafés (called warnets). Because broadband Internet is relatively expensive in Indonesia (USD 100 per month),[14] mobile plans and warnets are much more affordable alternatives. Indonesian mobile broadband plans are among the cheapest in the world (USD 17 per month).[15] As of September 2009, the mobile penetration rate of the country was 56.8 percent.[16] Warnets provide access to half of the country's Internet users, including those who are unable to afford individual access.[17] Warnets are obligated to record the identity cards of all visitors and to report the data to the Indonesia Security Incident Response team on Information Infrastructure.[18]

Facebook, Twitter, YouTube, and Wordpress are popular Web sites among Indonesian Internet users. As of April 2010, Indonesia had approximately 21 million Facebook users, making Indonesia the country with the third-largest number of Facebook users in the world.[19] As of the same month, Indonesia also had the largest number of Twitter users in Asia.[20] Blogging is another popular activity.

The state generally holds a positive attitude toward the Internet and views information and communication technologies (ICTs) as important tools for economic development. In 2001, the government announced its Five-Year Action Plan for the Development and Implementation of ICTs.[21] The plan addressed priorities for extending ICT benefits throughout Indonesia such as extending transparency and equal access to information, and facilitating Internet access to public services.[22] While the government supports the development of an Indonesian information society and greater Internet use for average citizens throughout the country,[23] it is very sensitive about pornographic and anti-Islamic content online and has censored such content on a number of occasions.

In April 2008, the Indonesian government ordered all ISPs to place a temporary ban on file-sharing video Web sites in order to prevent the dissemination of *Fitna*, an anti-Islamic film. The ban occurred amid the breakout of small-scale protests in Indonesia, including one outside of the Dutch embassy in Jakarta. The government cited fear of unrest within the nation as the reason for the ban.[24] This incident was the first time the country's ISPs had blocked access to a Web site, and many criticized the blocking technique that was deployed—ISPs blocked entire Web sites instead of the specific pages that contained the video.[25] This technique was utilized again in November 2009 when the government ordered ISPs to block a blog that contained an offensive cartoon of the Prophet Mohammed. One blogger complained that some ISPs simply blocked the entire Blogspot domain.[26]

The release of two homemade sex videos of three Indonesian celebrities in the summer of 2010 triggered a crackdown on pornographic Web content (the scandal was popularly known as "Peterporn" because singer Nazril Irham of the band Peter Pan was involved along with his high-profile girlfriends). As a part of this effort, the Ministry of Communications and Information Technology announced that Trust Positive—a government keyword filtering system that is already in place in many of the government's computer networks—would be adopted by ISPs.[27] Trust Positive, as well as a database of blacklisted and approved "whitelisted" Web sites, is available for download on the Ministry of Communications and Information Technology's Trust Positive Web site (http://trustpositif.depkominfo.go.id). According to the ministry, Trust Positive is not a gateway or a traffic relay for Indonesia Internet connection, and the ministry was not responsible for ISPs that use Trust Positive.[28] Trust Positive is made up of a database of top-level domains, URLs, and keywords that are placed in either a blacklist (negative and filtered content) or a white list (positive and trusted content).[29] The ministry encourages citizens to participate in developing the database by submitting URLs through e-mail or a complaint form.[30] The database can be found among three downloadable folders named "aplikasi" (application), "konfigurasi" (configuration), and "database." Within the "database" category there are three subfolders: "kaijian" (muslim/prayer), "pengaduan" (complaints), and "informasi" (information).[31] "Informasi" listed and contained information on approximately 43,000 blacklisted Web sites as of November 2010.

Internet filtering takes place through partnerships with the APJII and the Association of Indonesia's Internet Cafés (AWARI), to whom the Ministry of Communications and Information Technology drafts orders to apply censorship or filtering. There are currently three methods of Internet filtering: border gateway protocol,[32] DNS Nawala,[33] and Trust Positive.[34] In the first method, the administrator of the IIX places a URL onto an IIX system blacklist. The blacklist information is then distributed to all the ISPs connected to the IIX system, who then block the Web site. When end users try to connect to the blacklisted URL, they are denied access. In the second method, the administrator of the domain name server puts a URL onto a blacklist. Anyone (including warnets) may use DNS Nawala, a noncommercial domain name system–filtration program that was developed by Telkom in cooperation with AWARI, as a "self-censorship" mechanism. When users attempt to access a URL that has been filtered by DNS Nawala, the page is blocked.[35]

Legal and Regulatory Frameworks

The Indonesian government has drafted a number of laws to regulate content on the Internet. The first that laid out guidelines on prohibited online content was the 2008 Electronic Information and Transaction Law.[36] The law has been controversial, and many have expressed concern about the ways in which it limits freedom of expression. A major concern among bloggers and journalists is the prohibition of defamation— including online defamation—under Article 27(3) of the law, which allows police to detain any suspects and impose sentences of up to six years on offenders.[37] In December 2008, a group of Indonesian bloggers and media rights advocates (including the Legal Aid Center for the Press, the Independent Alliance of Journalists, and the Indonesian Legal Aid Foundation) requested a judicial review of the defamation article.[38] However, the Constitutional Court denied the request in 2009. A number of people have been charged under the law.[39]

Indonesia's Anti-Pornography Law[40] was passed in October 2008 despite wide opposition from various groups, including secular political parties, artists, women's groups, and non-Muslim minorities who saw the law as a threat to the country's cultural diversity and the rights of minority groups and women.[41] The bill defines pornography as "pictures, sketches, illustrations, photographs, writings, sound, sound image, moving animation, cartoons, conversations, gestures, or other forms of message through various forms of communication media and/or performances in public, which contain obscenity or sexual exploitation," and prohibits citizens from producing, making, reproducing, duplicating, distributing, broadcasting, importing, exporting, offering, trading in, leasing, and providing pornography.[42]

It also gives powers to government to prevent the creation, dissemination, and use of pornography. Under the law, any person found producing, creating, reproducing, copying, distributing, broadcasting, importing, or exporting pornography could face up to 12 years imprisonment or a fine of up to 6 billion rupiahs (approximately USD

663,495). Anyone downloading pornography faces up to four years imprisonment or a fine of up to 2 billion rupiah (approximately USD 221,165). In January 2011, Irham of the Peterporn affair was sentenced to three and a half years in jail for "giving an opportunity for others to spread, produce and prepare a pornographic video, despite denying that he had distributed the video tapes."[43] In 2009, women and minority-rights groups asked for a judicial review but their appeal was dismissed.

The Electronic Information and Transaction Law and the Anti-Pornography Law have both been invoked to block online content. Paragraph 2 of the Electronic Information and Transaction Law prohibits the dissemination of information that is intended to invoke hatred or hostility toward individuals or groups of people based on race, ethnicity, and religion. In 2010, the law was invoked when the Ministry of Communications and Information Technology ordered ISPs to block the "Everybody Draw Mohammed Day" Facebook group.[44] The antipornography law was used to justify the ministry's clampdown on pornographic Web sites during the Peterporn scandal.[45]

In February 2010, the Ministry of Communication and Information Technology announced a draft bill on regulating Internet content. Embedded within this was a plan to create a monitoring team that would have the power to order ISPs to block Web sites that contained content defined as illegal under the Electronic Information and Transaction Law and the antipornography law.[46] The idea was unpopular among the public because many saw the plan as a violation of existing media laws and as a threat to freedom of expression.[47] As a result of intense public scrutiny, the plan was put on hold. However, the online release of Peterporn in May 2010 breathed new life into the plan and was used as a justification for Internet content regulation.[48] On June 18, President Susilo Bambang Yudhoyono announced, "We have increasingly realized that our nation should not stay naked and be crushed by the information technology frenzy, because there will be many victims."[49] For the president, the scandal highlighted the need for further regulation of the Web.[50] On July 21, 2010, the Ministry of Communications and Information Technology ordered ISPs to block all pornographic Web sites before Ramadan and urged schools to install filters and warnets to use DNS Nawala to block access to pornographic content.[51] By late July, Trust Positive had been installed in all Internet-enabled computers that were supplied to villages under the government-sponsored Smart Village program.[52]

Amid the Peterporn scandal, the House of Representatives Commission ordered the ministry to resume work on the draft bill on regulating Internet content. As of June 2010, the ministry was in the process of revising the bill and was hoping to pass it by the end of the year.[53] The new draft revised the powers of the monitoring team so that they would respond to public complaints about content and would order ISPs to block such content only if the material could be deemed illegal under existing laws.[54]

Surveillance

Although the government of Indonesia has been actively attempting to regulate content online, there have not been many reported cases of surveillance on the Internet. Nonetheless, there have been instances of government-sanctioned raids and searches of warnets and schools. For instance, in February 2010, police raided warnets in Bandung in response to complaints from parents and teachers that children were missing school. Twenty-three warnets were raided, and 89 students were rounded up.[55] During the Peterporn scandal, police, with the help of teachers, searched mobile phones belonging to students and seized phones that contained the Peterporn videos. At the same time, the head of the Indonesian Education Ministry (Bandung Branch) ordered heads of schools to monitor students on mobile phones.[56]

It is too early to tell whether the government of Indonesia will move toward increased surveillance in order to tighten its grip over cyberspace. However, in the summer of 2010, an official from the Indonesian Telecommunications Regulatory Body expressed concern over the government's inability to monitor communications from BlackBerrys, since data were sent through Research in Motion's (RIM) servers and network operation centers (mostly located in Canada), as opposed to open networks.[57] An announcement followed from the Indonesian government that it was considering a ban on BlackBerry services as a means of pressuring RIM to establish a representative office in Indonesia, as well as a mirror server in the country.[58] In January 2011, RIM announced that it was committed to working with Indonesia's carriers to put in place a filtering solution to block pornographic sites—in effect, agreeing to comply with the country's antipornography law.[59]

ONI Testing Results

OpenNet Initiative testing was conducted on seven Indonesian ISPs—IndosatM2, Telkomsel, XL Axiata, Telkomnet, First Media, Biznet Networks, and Indonet—at various periods between 2009 and 2010. Evidence of filtering was found on Indosat, Telkomsel, and XL Axiata. Indosat and XL Axiata were found to be blocking significantly more Web sites than Telkomsel.

Technical analysis of the data from Indosat, Telkomsel, and XL Axiata indicates that Internet filtering is carried out through HTTP proxy blocking. This method of blocking uses a proxy to determine whether requests of Web sites should be permitted and modifies requests to blocked Web sites to resolve to a block page.

On Indosat, when attempts are made to access blocked Web sites, users are redirected to a block page informing them "Access Restricted by netSAFE." Similarly, attempts made by users to blocked Web sites on Telkomsel are redirected to a block page informing them that "access is denied due to security enforcement"—a reference to the Indonesian government's drive to restrict pornography during the month of Ramadan. On XL Axiata, users attempting to access blocked Web sites are simply redirected to a block page with an apology "Mohan Maaf" (translated as "I am sorry") with the URL of the requested Web site highlighted in red. Overall, testing revealed that Internet filtering in Indonesia is unsystematic and inconsistent, illustrated by the differences found in the level of filtering between ISPs.

Testing on IndosatM2[60] was performed by ONI between August 30 and November 30, 2010. Indosat was found to be primarily targeting Web sites with pornographic or adult content. However, it also directed filtering to content on free speech, including http://freespeech.org and http://freespeechcoalition.com—Web sites belonging to a U.S. online video network and free speech coalition group. Indosat also blocked a number of Internet tools, such as anonymizers and circumvention software Web sites (http://anonymizer.com, http://surfsecret.com, etc.), warez, search engines, hacking tools, peer-to-peer sites, and one free e-mail service (http://dcemail.com).

Testing on XL Axiata[61] was performed by ONI between August 30 and September 2, 2010. The contents of the blocked Web sites fell into three broad thematic categories: political, social, and Internet tools.

Similar to Indosat, XL Axiata focused its filtering on Web sites with content related to sex education, LBGT material, provocative attire, and pornography. Similar to Indosat, XL Axiata blocked content related to free speech, including http://freespeech.org and http://freespeechcoalition.com. Anonymizers and circumvention tools (http://anonymizer.com, http://surfsecret.com, and http://ultimate-anonymity.com) were also targeted by XL Axiata.

Testing on Telkomsel[62] was performed by ONI between August 30 and September 1, 2010. Only a limited number of Web sites were found to be blocked, all of which were related to pornography. This finding is in stark contrast to filtering performed by XL Axiata and Indosat—both of which heavily filtered pornographic Web sites.

OpenNet Initiative testing was conducted on Telkomnet, First Media, Biznet Networks, and Indonet before the release of "Peterporn" and the subsequent clampdown on pornographic Web content in the summer of 2010, a fact that may explain why no evidence of filtering was found on these ISPs. It is possible that filtering is now present on these ISPs that has not yet been confirmed by ONI tests. Testing was conducted by ONI on Telkomnet between October 12, 2009, and September 4, 2010; First Media between April 1 and November 30, 2010; Biznet Networks between April 1 and April 25, 2010; and Indonet between April 1 and April 25, 2010.

In November 2010, ONI retrieved the database of blacklisted and whitelisted Web sites, publicly available on the Ministry of Communications and Information Technology's Trust Positive Web site (http://trustpositif.depkominfo.go.id/files/downloads/). Of the listed URLs, ONI tested a sample of high-impact local Web sites on two ISPs: IndosatM2 and XL Axiata. The goal of this second round of testing was to determine whether content other than pornography was being filtered. High-impact local Web sites included sites that contained political or religious content, as well as social media sites (e.g., blogs and Facebook groups) and circumvention and anonymizer sites. Testing revealed that out of the URLs tested, IndosatM2 blocked a small number of blogs containing political criticism and commentary, religious conversion commentary, and religious criticism (e.g., http://indonbodoh.blogspot.com, http://beritamuslim.wordpress.com, and http://komiknabimuhammad.blogspot.com). It was found that XL Axiata was not blocking any of the tested URLs. While ONI testing determined that filtering was implemented by IndosatM2 and XL Axiata through HTTP proxy blocking, it was unable to ascertain whether the ISPs were using the Trust Positive filtering program.

Conclusion

Although the government of Indonesia holds a positive view about the Internet as a means for economic development, it has become increasingly concerned over the impact of access to information and has demonstrated an interest in increasing its control over offensive online content. The government regulates such content through legal and regulatory frameworks and through partnerships with ISPs and Internet cafés. During the "Peterporn" crisis in 2010, state officials expressed the need to protect the nation from offensive online content, and the government has since been developing and promoting mechanisms to ensure that Web content is adequately regulated. Although the government is tightening control over Web content, it is taking precautions to ensure that regulations abide by existing laws and that regulations are transparent. For example, databases of blacklisted Web sites are made available to the public. OpenNet Initiative testing found that ISP filtering heavily targets pornographic Web sites. However, filtering is unsystematic and inconsistent, as demonstrated by the differences in filtering among ISPs. It will be interesting to track how Internet filtering in Indonesia changes as the government develops more mechanisms to control Web content.

Notes

1. Bradley R. Simpson, *Economists with Guns: Authoritarian Development and U.S.-Indonesian Relations, 1960–1968* (Stanford, CA: Stanford University Press, 2008); "US Propped Up Suharto Despite Rights Abuses: Documents," Agence France-Presse, January 28, 2008, http://afp.google.com/article/ALeqM5gBus6P_G-L_m9i0uYBcRgEtt9Pvw.

2. Donald Greenlees, "Suharto's Legacy of Development and Corruption," *New York Times*, January 28, 2008, http://www.nytimes.com/2008/01/28/world/asia/28iht-suharto.1.9542684.html; Governance and Social Development Resource Center, *Helpdesk Research Report: Indonesian Finan-*

cial Crisis (1997–1998), March 30, 2009, http://www.docstoc.com/docs/44786587/Helpdesk
-Research-Report-Indonesian-Financial-Crisis-(1997-1998)-Date.

3. Michael Malley, "Class, Region, and Culture: The Sources of Social Conflict in Indonesia," in *Social Cohesion and Conflict Prevention in Asia: Managing Diversity through Development*, ed. Nat J. Colletta, Teck Ghee Lim, and Anita Kelles-Viitanen (Washington, D.C.: International Bank for Reconstruction, 2001), 349–381.

4. Governance and Social Development Resource Center, *Helpdesk Research Report*.

5. "Country Profile: Indonesia," BBC News, September 5, 2010, http://news.bbc.co.uk/2/hi/country_profiles/1260544.stm. For reports of violence and intimidation of the press, see "The Test of Indonesia's Press Freedom," Asia Sentinel, July 7, 2010, http://www.asiasentinel.com/index.php?option=com_content&task=view&id=2580&Itemid=189; James Balowski, "Indonesian Press, Freedom of Expression under Attack," Direct Action, August 2010, http://directaction.org.au/issue25/indonesian_press_freedom_of_expression_under_attack.

6. Human Rights Watch, *Turning Critics into Criminals*, May 3, 2010, http://www.hrw.org/en/reports/2010/05/04/turning-critics-criminals.

7. Freedom House, "Map of Press Freedom 2010: Indonesia," http://www.freedomhouse.org/template.cfm?page=363&year=2010&country=7841.

8. Reporters Without Borders, "Government Orders ISPs to Start Anti-porn Filtering," August 11, 2010, http://en.rsf.org/indonesia-government-orders-isps-to-start-11-08-2010,38118.html.

9. Aubrey Belford, "Indonesia Finds Banning Pornography Is Difficult," *New York Times*, August 1, 2010, http://www.nytimes.com/2010/08/02/technology/02iht-indoporn02.html?_r=2&src=busln.

10. Indonet, "Network," http://www.indo.net.id/network.php.

11. International Telecommunication Union (ITU), "Internet Indicators: Subscribers, Users and Broadband Subscribers," 2009 Figures, http://www.itu.int/ITU-D/icteye/Reporting/ShowReportFrame.aspx?ReportName=/WTI/InformationTechnologyPublic&ReportFormat=HTML4.0&RP_intYear=2009&RP_intLanguageID=1&RP_bitLiveData=False.

12. Ibid.

13. Yessar Rosendar, "Social Networks Lift Mobile Internet Use," *Jakarta Globe*, May 31, 2010, http://www.thejakartaglobe.com/business/social-networks-lift-mobile-internet-use/377990.

14. Thomas Crampton, "Indonesia: Where Blackberry Beats iPhone," Thomas Cramptom: Social Media in China and Across Asia, January 10, 2010, http://www.thomascrampton.com/indonesia/indonesia-iphone.

15. Ibid.

16. "Blackberry Beating iPhone in Indonesia by Mobile Ad Requests," InMobi, October 7, 2009, http://www.inmobi.com/press-releases/pressrelease/2009/10/07/blackberry-beating-iphone-in-indonesia-by-mobile-ad-requests.

17. Prodita Sabarinim, "The Changing Face of Internet Cafés," *Jakarta Post*, May 19, 2009, http://www.thejakartapost.com/news/2009/05/19/the-changing-face-internet-cafés.html.

18. *"Warung Internet Harus Mendata Identitas Pengunjungnya"* [All Internet Cafés Must Register Their Visitors' Identities], Tempo, August 30, 2006, http://www.tempointeraktif.com/hg/ekbis/2006/08/30/brk,20060830-82927,id.html.

19. Normitsu Onishi, "Debate on Internet's Limits Grows in Indonesia," *New York Times*, April 19, 2010, http://www.nytimes.com/2010/04/20/world/asia/20indonet.html.

20. Ibid.

21. Five-year Action Plan for the Development and Implementation of Information and Communication Technologies in Indonesia, Government of Indonesia's Action Plan to overcome the Digital Divide, Information and Communication Technologies in Indonesia under Presidential Instruction No. 6/2001, http://unpan1.un.org/intradoc/groups/public/documents/apcity/unpan002101.pdf.

22. Ibid.

23. International Telecommunication Union (ITU), "Indonesia Case Study," http://www.itu.int/ITU-D/ict/cs/indonesia/index.html.

24. "Indonesia Seeks to Block YouTube over Anti-Koran Film," Reuters, April 2, 2008, http://uk.reuters.com/article/2008/04/02/uk-dutch-islam-indonesia-idUKJAK29880220080402; "Indonesia Blocks YouTube to Protest Islam Film," CNN, April 8, 2008, http://www.cnn.com/2008/WORLD/asiapcf/04/08/indonesia.youtube/index.html.

25. "YouTube Accessible Again in Indonesia," Reporters Without Borders, April 14, 2008, http://en.rsf.org/indonesia-youtube-accessible-again-in-14-04-2008,26496.html.

26. Willy Sutrisno, "Indonesia Internet Censorship," Sutrisno.me, May 20, 2010, http://www.sutrisno.me/2010/05/indonesia-internet-censorship.html.

27. Belford, "Indonesia Finds Banning Pornography Is Difficult."

28. Ministry of Communications and Information Technology, "Trust Positive: About" [in Indonesian], http://www.trustpositif.depkominfo.go.id.

29. Ministry of Communications and Information Technology, "Trust Positive: Information Database" [in Indonesian], http://www.trustpositif.depkominfo.go.id.

30. Ministry of Communications and Information Technology, "Trust Positive: Search and Complaints" [in Indonesian], http://www.trustpositif.depkominfo.go.id.

31. Ministry of Communications and Information Technology, "Trust Positive: Directory" [in Indonesian], http://www.trustpositif.depkominfo.go.id/files/downloads.

32. ICT Watch, "Indonesia 'Internet Censorship,'" Brief Report Presented at OpenNet Initiative Global Summit, Ottawa, Canada (June 2010), http://www.slideshare.net/donnybu/indonesian-internetcensorshipreport2010.

33. Ibid.

34. For more information about Trust Positive, see Ministry of Communications and Information Technology, "Trust Positive: About" [in Indonesian], http://www.trustpositif.depkominfo.go.id/.

35. ICT Watch, "Indonesia 'Internet Censorship.'"

36. "Law of the Republic of Indonesia Number 11 Year 2008, About Information and Electronic Transactions" [in Indonesian], http://pih.depkominfo.go.id/default.aspx?page=detail _konten&jenis_konten=2&id_konten=2021.

37. Heru Andriyanto, "Teenager May Be Charged for Facebook Defamation," *Jakarta Globe*, July 9, 2009, http://www.thejakartaglobe.com/national/teenager-may-be-charged-for-facebook -defamation/317034.

38. "Press Freedom Victim of Defamation Law's 'Inverted Logic,' Journalists Say," *Jakarta Globe*, May 6, 2009, http://www.thejakartaglobe.com/justAdded/press-freedom-victim-of-defamation -laws-inverted-logic-journalists-say-/275348.

39. Freedom House, "Indonesian Sex Tape Scandal Reopens Debate on Free Speech," June 30, 2010, http://blog.freedomhouse.org/weblog/webtech.

40. "Law of the Republic of Indonesia Number 44 Year 2008 about Pornography" [in Indonesian], http://pih.depkominfo.go.id/userfiles/fkk/UU%2044%20Tahun%202008.pdf.

41. See "Indonesia Passes Anti-porn Bill," BBC News, October 30, 2008, http://news.bbc.co.uk/2/ hi/7700150.stm; Peter Gelling, "Indonesia Passes Broad Anti-pornography Bill," *New York Times*, October 30, 2008, http://www.nytimes.com/2008/10/30/world/asia/30iht-indo.1.17378031 .html; "Indonesia's New Anti-Porn Agenda," *Time*, http://www.time.com/time/world/ article/0,8599,1857090,00.html; and Olivia Rondonuwu, "Indonesia's Constitutional Court Defends Pornography Law," Reuters, March 25, 2010, http://www.reuters.com/article/ idUSTRE62O28R20100325.

42. "Law of the Republic of Indonesia Number 44 Year 2008 about Pornography."

43. "Indonesia Sex Tape Star Is Jailed," BBC News, January 31, 2011, http://www.bbc.co.uk/news/ world-asia-pacific-12321215.

44. Ardhi Surayadhi, "Government Finally Removes the Command Block" [in Indonesian], DetikINET, http://us.detikinet.com/read/2010/05/20/135758/1360788/398/pemerintah-akhirnya -keluarkan-perintah-blokir.

45. Balowski, "Indonesian Press, Freedom of Expression under Attack."

46. Ismira Lutfia, "Indonesia Web Monitoring Plan Panned," *Jakarta Globe*, February 16, 2010, http://www.thejakartaglobe.com/home/indonesia-web-monitoring-plan-panned/358890; Aubrey Belford, "Sex Tape Scandal Fixates Indonesia," *New York Times*, June 13, 2010, http://www .nytimes.com/2010/06/14/world/asia/14iht-sextape.html; ICT Watch, "Indonesia 'Indonesia Censorship.'" Presented at the OpenNet Initiative Global Summit, Ottawa, Canada (June 2010), http://www.slideshare.net/donnybu/indonesian-internetcensorshipreport2010.

47. Lutfia, "Indonesia Web Monitoring Plan Panned."

48. Belford, "Sex Tape Scandal Fixates Indonesia."

49. "Indonesia Must Resist Internet 'Frenzy': President," *Jakarta Globe*, June 18, 2010, http://www.thejakartaglobe.com/home/indonesia-must-resist-internet-frenzy-president/381267.

50. Ibid.

51. "Internet Cafes Given a Month to Block Porn Websites," *Jakarta Post*, August 2, 2010, http://www.thejakartapost.com/news/2010/08/02/internet-cafes-given-a-month-block-porn-websites.html-0.

52. Ismira Lutfia, "Indonesian Government Bid to Block Porn Sites Hits Technical, Political Snags," *Jakarta Globe*, July 29, 2010, http://www.thejakartaglobe.com/home/indonesian-government-bid-to-block-porn-sites-hits-technical-political-snags/388434.

53. Ibid.

54. Farouk Arnaz and Ismira Lutfia, "Two Held for Spreading Sex Video on Web," *Jakarta Globe*, June 18, 2010, http://www.thejakartaglobe.com/home/two-held-for-spreading-sex-video-on-web/381198.

55. "Indonesia Rounds Up Students in Cybercafés," *Taipei Times*, February 24, 2010, http://www.taipeitimes.com/News/lang/archives/2010/02/24/2003466435.

56. Muhammad Jusuf, "Police Raided Mobile Phone Students, Following the Widespread Circulation of Obscene Porn Videos in Public," All Voices, June 10, 2010, http://www.allvoices.com/contributed-news/6037182-police-raided-mobile-phone-students-following-the-widespread-circulation-of-obscene-porn-videos-in-public.

57. Dion Bisara and Bloomberg, "Indonesia Concern over BlackBerry Security," *Jakarta Globe*, August 4, 2010, http://www.thejakartaglobe.com/home/indonesian-concern-over-blackberry-security/389552.

58. Ibid.

59. "Blackberry Maker Says Will Filter Porn to Meet Indonesia Rules," Reuters, January 10, 2011, http://ca.reuters.com/article/businessNews/idCATRE7092DK20110110.

60. Indosat is a privately owned telecommunications company and is among the largest in the country. At the end of 2009, Indosat had 33.1 million subscribers. Of these, 660,000 were household subscribers, and 1,500 were corporate subscribers of Indosat's subsidiary ISPs, IndosatM2 and Lintasarta, respectively. See PT Indosat tbk., "Making Changes: 2009 Annual Report," http://www.indosat.com/template/media/editor/files/INDOSATAR09_English_Completed.pdf; IndosatM2, "IM2 Achieve Top Brand Award 2010: Award for the Fourth Time in a Row," February 2, 2010, http://www.indosatm2.com/index.php/corporate-information/corporate-news/id:124/im2-raih-top-brand-award-2010-penghargaan-untuk-keempat-kali-secara-berturut-turut; Lintasarta, "Lintasarta at a Glance," http://www.lintasarta.net/AboutLintasarta/LintasartaataGlance/tabid/61/language/en-US/Default.aspx.

61. XL Axiata is a privately owned telecommunications service operator in Indonesia that offers data communication, broadband Internet, mobile communication, and 3G services in Java, Bali, and Lombok, as well as main cities in and around Sumatra, Kalimantan, and Sulawesi. As a leading mobile service provider, XL Axiata has 31.4 million subscribers. See Axiata, "PT XL Axiata Tbk. (formerly known as PT Excelcomindo Pratama Tbk.)," http://www.axiata.com/operating -companies/indonesia.

62. Telkomsel is the largest telecommunication and network services provider in Indonesia. It is the only operator in Indonesia that covers the entire nation. Tekomsel is privately owned, and its parent company is PT Telekomunikasi Indonesia. At the end of 2009, Telkomsel had a customer base of 81.64 million. See PT Telekomunikasi Seluar, "2009 Annual Report," http://www .telkomsel.com/media/upload/pdf/AR2009.pdf.

Malaysia

The Malaysian government's 1998 pledge not to censor the Internet rings hollow a decade later. Since an unprecedented loss of voter confidence in the 2008 Malaysian general elections that was partly attributable to online dissent, the Malaysian government is now attuned to the political costs of a relatively uncensored Internet. It has since employed all means of control short of an outright technical filter of the Internet against cyber dissidents.

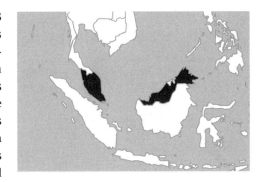

KEY INDICATORS	
GDP per capita, PPP (constant 2005 international dollars)	12,678
Life expectancy at birth, total (years)	74
Literacy rate, adult total (percent of people age 15+)	92.1
Human Development Index (out of 169)	57
Rule of Law (out of 5)	3.0
Voice and Accountability (out of 5)	2.0
Democracy Index (out of 167)	71 (Flawed democracy)
Digital Opportunity Index (out of 181)	57
Internet penetration rate (percentage of population)	55.9

Source by indicator: World Bank 2009, World Bank 2008a, World Bank 2008b, UNDP 2010, World Bank Worldwide Governance Indicators 2009, Economist Intelligence Unit 2010, ITU 2007, ITU 2009. See Introduction to the Country Profiles, pp. 222–223.

Background

In 1998, the Malaysian government pledged to refrain from censorship of the Internet as part of a financial calculation to attract foreign investment. This pledge was statutorily enshrined in Section 3(3) of the Communications and Multimedia Act of 1998 (CMA), which regulates telecommunications in Malaysia.[1] The pledge was repeated in a bill of guarantees attached to the main Malaysian IT development project aimed at reassuring foreign investors.[2] Thus the Internet initially offered a relatively unconstrained medium for opposition voices to flourish, allowing for the nascence of the active, vibrant, and mostly antigovernment Malaysian sociopolitical blogosphere.[3] This pledge of noncensorship of the Internet has been substantially eroded under the banner of preserving "racial harmony" in recent years, especially after a major political setback suffered by the ruling coalition in 2008.

Malaysia is an ethnically diverse country that has been governed by the same political coalition, Barisan Nasional (BN),[4] since independence from British colonial rule in 1957.[5] Malays make up 49.6 percent of the population, while 22.8 percent and 6.8 percent are Chinese and Indian, respectively.[6] The strength of the Malaysian government's appeal to "racial harmony" in justifying Internet regulation lies in the nation's historical experience with race relations. Race forms the "most prominent and pervasive line of cleavage in Malaysian politics, economics and society."[7] Racial tension, especially between the majority Malays and minority races over affirmative action, has been the source of the two most severe disruptions to social stability in Malaysia.[8]

The first incident in 1964 carved out Singapore as a separate state from the newly created Federation of Malaysia,[9] and the second, on May 13, 1969, led to at least 100 fatalities overnight.[10]

Given BN's uninterrupted rule since 1957, the litmus test of political strength in Malaysia's flawed constitutional democracy lies in a particular coalition's ability to maintain a two-thirds majority in the lower house of Parliament—the requisite majority for amending the Malaysian Federal Constitution.[11] Barisan Nasional has achieved this majority in almost every election since independence, in effect removing any real restriction on its legislative whims.[12] On the strength of this test, BN's political record is unblemished. It accounted for an unprecedented majority of 90.4 percent of all votes in the 2004 general elections.[13] In this context, BN's failure in the 2008 elections to secure the necessary number of seats in Parliament is unsurprisingly considered "a debacle."[14]

Running on a savvy online campaign, the opposition coalition, Pakatan Rakyat (PR),[15] became a meaningful political adversary to the incumbent BN for the first time in Malaysian history. In contrast to BN's three Web sites, PR was reported to have more than 7,500 Web sites and blogs, with little to no coverage in the mainstream media.[16] Underlying PR's heavy reliance on the Internet for campaigning in 2008 is Malaysia's long history of state censorship of the mainstream media.

Three main mechanisms of censorship and media control coexist and are wielded by the government in tandem. First, the Printing Presses and Publications Act of 1984 (PPPA) and CMA subject all offline media (i.e., newspapers, television, and radio stations) to licensing regimes granted at the unfettered and unreviewable discretion of various ministers.[17] Thus the mainstream media are forced to develop a norm of self-censorship to toe an opaque and undefined executive line. Also, the Malaysian government has not hesitated to employ coercive national security laws against critical publications and journalists.[18] Second, BN spearheaded a privatization campaign in 1998, enabling its component parties to acquire significant corporate stakes in the four main Malaysian daily newspapers. Third, the Malaysian government has taken the view that the role of the press is to act as agents and proponents, not critics, of national development.[19] Together, these factors restrict effective political campaigning against BN and create a deficit of objective, neutral reporting.

Internet in Malaysia

Since 1996, the Malaysian government has pursued an aggressive Internet implementation and development policy. The Multimedia Super Corridor (MSC) project was one of its most visible initiatives. The MSC is a strip of approximately 290 square miles of developed land meant to attract foreign IT research and development investors through tax breaks and infrastructural support—for example, connecting the area with high-speed fiber optic wires.[20] Affiliated projects include training an IT-literate Malaysian workforce through specialized school programs and providing consumers with financial incentives to purchase personal computers. As of 2009, Malaysia had more than 15 million Internet users, with a national penetration rate of 55.90 percent.[21] After Singapore and Brunei, Malaysia has the third-highest national penetration rate in Southeast Asia.[22]

Recently, the Malaysian government announced its aim to achieve household broadband penetration rates of 50 percent by the end of 2010 under its National Broadband Initiative program.[23] However, as of 2009, the fixed broadband penetration rate in Malaysia stood at a mere 6.08 percent, second in the region to Singapore's 23.7 percent.[24] In spite of the relatively slow uptake of broadband among Malaysians, the government has recently granted Worldwide Interoperability for Microwave Access (WiMAX) licenses to local network providers in a bid to improve overall connectivity to the Internet.[25]

The state maintains control over physical access to the Internet, requiring all Internet service providers (ISPs) to be licensed for operation. TMNet, a wholly owned subsidiary of a privatized branch of the state, dominates the ISP market with its 93 percent share.[26] By granting WiMAX licenses to four smaller, privately owned, and nonestablished ISP companies, the Malaysian government appeared to be reversing its trend of direct control over access to the Internet.[27] However, it would be premature to draw this conclusion. First, because WiMAX integrates telecommunication services onto a single platform with the result that a single state licensee provides fixed-line and mobile-phone coverage, television streaming, and broadband access, it is at least arguable that the need for direct state control through corporate stakeholding has been reduced. Second, YTL Communications, one of the four "independent" WiMAX licensees, is currently embroiled in controversy over an allegedly unfair governmental approval that enables it to operate in the "highly coveted 700MHz spectrum."[28]

Legal and Regulatory Framework

Although the Malaysian federal constitution guarantees the right to free speech, this freedom is immediately qualified.[29] Parliament is constitutionally permitted to restrict the right as it deems "necessary or expedient" for reasons of public order and national security.[30] As mentioned, this right is formally reinforced, where online content is concerned, in the 1998 pledge. However, the 2008 election results have provided an impetus for stricter scrutiny, which was made evident by the government's brief but thorough attempt in 2009 to implement a national-level filter on the Internet. The Malaysian government reportedly issued tenders to software companies for an Internet filter,[31] citing the need to "keep out pornographic materials and bloggers who inflame racial sentiments."[32] This blatant repudiation of its 1998 pledge drew many domestic and international objections, which led to the withdrawal of the proposal less than a week later.[33]

Currently, online news portals and bloggers are not governed by the existing registration and licensing regimes applicable to the mainstream media. However, because of the continuing growth and popularity of online media, the Malaysian government is planning to close this loophole. It announced plans in 2008 to register all "political bloggers."[34] This scheme has since been abandoned following vehement protests. However, on January 25, 2011, the Home Ministry revealed proposed amendments to the much-criticized Printing Presses and Publications Act that will bring online news Web sites within the act's licensing regime.[35] Malaysian civil society, bloggers, and journalists have resoundingly condemned the move.[36] The government's current position is unclear because statements from the Prime Minister's Department contradict the Home Ministry's claim of presenting these amendments to Parliament for its next sitting in March 2011.[37]

In addition, there has been a dramatic upsurge in the number of proceedings launched against individual bloggers and the popular, award-winning, independent online news portal Malaysiakini. The state has relied on three main methods in persecuting online dissidents.

First, it has exercised its draconian detention powers under numerous national security laws. Nathaniel Tan was the first Malaysian blogger to be detained on July 13, 2007, under the 1972 Official Secrets Act following corruption allegations against a deputy minister made in an anonymous comment left on his blog.[38] Subsequently, Raja Petra Kamarudin, who maintains the popular Malaysia Today blog, was detained in 2008 under the Internal Security Act (ISA) of 1960 for a controversial post alleging the Malaysian prime minister's complicity in the gruesome murder of a Mongolian model.[39] He has since fled the country after repeated threats of ISA incarceration and criminal prosecution for sedition.[40] Further, in December 2010 the government announced its intention to publish "cyber sedition guidelines" by January 2011. These guidelines are intended "to counter the rising trend in sedition and libel cases involving online media and social sites."[41] In response, free speech activists voiced concerns over the actual intention of these guidelines and their potential for increasing proceedings against cyber dissidents.[42]

Second, the state has launched defamation suits to silence and persecute online dissidents. A landmark defamation suit was initiated in early 2007 against two prominent bloggers, Jeff Ooi (now a member of Parliament) and Ahiruddin Attan, for allegedly libelous content concerning the *New Straits Times* newspaper on their blogs.[43] This is the first known defamation suit against bloggers and is broadly connected to the state because BN has substantial corporate control over *New Straits Times*.[44] Recently, another defamation suit has been initiated by the Malaysian Information Minister in his personal capacity against a political blogger who posted on rape allegations involving the Minister's former domestic help. [45]

The third method utilized by the state in persecuting bloggers involves the broad investigative and enforcement powers of the Malaysian Communications and Multimedia Commission (MCMC), the main regulatory authority of information technology and communications industries. [46] Under the CMA, there are two relevant offenses: Section 211 establishes a broad prohibition of online content that is "indecent, obscene, false, menacing, or offensive in character with intent to annoy, abuse, threaten or harass any person." [47] The other offense, under Section 233, relates to "improper use of network facilities," and criminalizes knowing use or permission for use of the Internet to communicate prohibited content as defined earlier in Section 211. [48] Contravention of either section may result in prosecution, and, if convicted, violators may be liable for a fine of up to MYR 50,000 (just over USD 16,000) and/or a maximum prison term of one year. [49]

The CMA grants MCMC power to conduct investigations, either upon receipt of complaints or on its own initiative, into potential commissions of both offenses, and it has wide discretion over the conduct of such investigations. [50] The number of MCMC investigations launched against online news portals and bloggers has increased more than tenfold from ten cases in 2005 to 133 in 2010. [51] Malaysiakini is a focal point of much of the MCMC's investigatory work, as one of its stories illustrated particularly well in September 2009. Malaysiakini reported on and posted videos of a controversial rally staged against proposed plans for constructing a Hindu temple in a mainly Malay-Muslim residential area. The videos featured protestors stomping on a severed cow head. [52] The incident has been considered offensive to racial and religious sensibilities, [53] in particular because of the sacred position reserved for cows in Hinduism, a belief held by many Malaysian Indians in lieu of the close identification of race and religion in Malaysia. [54] The organizers of this rally were subsequently charged under the Sedition Act for inciting racial hatred, [55] but ironically the MCMC saw fit to also initiate investigations and conduct "marathon" interview sessions lasting eight hours with Malaysiakini editors and staff on similar official grounds for publishing these videos. [56]

Recently, Malaysiakini again came under MCMC scrutiny for reporting on the 2010 annual general meeting of UMNO, the leading party in BN. [57] BN is not alone in its reliance on MCMC's wide powers in launching proceedings against its online critics. In September 2010, a PR-controlled state filed a complaint with MCMC against a blogger who claimed that funding for senior citizens' support programs had been improperly obtained from gambling sources, contrary to Islamic laws and beliefs. [58]

In response to increasing pressure to control online content, the MCMC has recently begun wielding its prosecutorial powers. [59] In March 2009, landmark court proceedings for "improper use of network facilities" were instigated by MCMC against bloggers who allegedly made disparaging comments about the involvement of a royal head of state in a tussle between BN and PR for control of a state government.[60] Two bloggers have since pled guilty. They had to pay fines of MYR 10,000 and MYR 8,000 (approximately USD 3,260 and USD 2,600), respectively. The other suits are still pending.[61] Similarly, in September 2010, Irwan Abdul Rahman, who started a satirical tongue-in-cheek blog mimicking The Onion News Network, was hauled up before the courts for the same offense after he posted a story highly critical of Tenaga Nasional Berhad, the country's main, state-owned energy provider.[62]

In the years since the 2008 elections, the incumbent BN has avoided repeating its 2008 mistake of ignoring the Internet and losing the digital race for votes.[63] Numerous by-elections since 2008 have seen BN effectively mobilizing online support, and its followers, dubbed "cybertroopers," have allegedly launched smear campaigns against Pakatan Rakyat candidates.[64] These are strongly reminiscent of government-sponsored information campaigns launched in other countries, such as Russia, China, and Iran.[65] On a constructive front, there are also signs of the Malaysian government using the Internet to engage with its electorate: thousands of citizens responded to the prime minister's invitation for suggestions on the proposed 2011 national budget on his blog.[66]

Surveillance

There is no express constitutional right to privacy in Malaysia, and the courts have declined to recognize it in common law.[67] Notwithstanding the absence of constitutional protection, the long-awaited Personal Data Protection Bill was passed in April 2010, prohibiting dissemination of personal information without consent in commercial transactions.[68] However, this act is severely limited because state action is expressly excluded from its scope.[69]

On the flipside, there are a wide range of legislative provisions empowering unsupervised and unreviewable governmental seizure and detention of information. The CMA criminalizes unlawful interception of communications but in the same breath requires ISPs to implement interception capabilities if required by a minister.[70] It also permits the MCMC to seize and retain, for as long as deemed necessary, any documents obtained pursuant to its investigations.[71] The Computer Crimes Act of 1997 and Anti-Corruption Act of the same year respectively permit a police inspector or the public prosecutor to dispense with judicial warrants in carrying out searches and seizures of electronic data for investigating cybercrimes or corruption where deemed reasonably necessary.[72] No subsequent judicial warrant is required under either act. In addition to these computer- and Internet-specific powers, the ISA is always available as a legal backstop, justifying searches, seizures, and detention in the name of national security.[73]

Evidence of ISP compliance with governmental interception requests stretches as far back as 1998, when the Malaysian government swiftly identified perpetrators behind an e-mail hoax with the cooperation of ISPs.[74] The government was spurred into action because the e-mail circulated a false but not implausible rumor that racial riots in neighboring Indonesia had spilled over to Malaysia, resulting in mass panic and binge buying of supplies in anticipation of a curfew.[75] More recently, a 2008 DNS block by the largest Malaysian ISP, TMNet, of the controversial Malaysia Today site demonstrates a degree of continued ISP compliance with governmental requests.[76] Subsequently, the site administrator, Raja Petra Kamarudin, has reported repeated distributed denial of service (DDoS) attacks between 2009 and 2010.[77] The most recent incident in September 2010 suggests pervasive (but unconfirmed) governmental monitoring—access to Malaysia Today was denied immediately after Raja Petra released documents illustrating rampant corruption within the federal government.[78] The rapid attack corroborates a 2010 announcement that the Malaysian government has created a specially designated cyber "task force" charged with monitoring the Internet for "blog postings deemed harmful to national unity."[79]

Although there are governmental plans to require ISPs to keep detailed records of their subscribers, as evidenced by a consultation paper and report issued by the MCMC, no rules appear to have been published to date.[80] In April 2011, the government announced the "1Malaysia" e-mail project, a "voluntary" service for all correspondence between the public and the state.[81] This project has been heavily criticized as expensive, superfluous, and a potential tool for state surveillance.[82] The public is well attuned to the government's heightened interest in the Internet, especially after the successful online coordination of five large rallies by means of blogs in 2007. This awareness of governmental monitoring is exemplified in precautions taken in 2010 by administrators of a Facebook protest page against governmental plans to build a MYR 5 billion (approximately USD 1.6 billion) 100-story tower in Malaysia. In organizing cake parties to mark the 263,000-member-strong page's one-month anniversary, they expressly advised against having banners, slogans, or leaders at each location to avoid arrest under the exceedingly broad Police Act.[83] These admonishments proved prescient, for university officials issued warnings to students who intended to host one such party, and security personnel dispersed another gathering.[84]

In general, Malaysians are accustomed to monitoring and surveillance by the government. Registration requirements are pervasive—each citizen is required by law to carry an identification card at all times,[85] and in 2006 registration was made compulsory for all prepaid mobile phone users under the CMA.[86] In 1998 the Malaysian government briefly toyed with requiring registration of all Internet café users but lifted this rule in 1999.[87] Today, the rule is arguably unnecessary because the combined effect of closed circuit television cameras installed after a spate of violent crimes[88] and the requirement of carrying one's identification card at all times renders it difficult to maintain anonymity in Malaysia without considerable effort.

ONI Testing Results

The OpenNet Initiative conducted testing over the course of September and October 2010 on two ISPs: TMNet, the main Malaysian ISP, and Macrolynx, a smaller specialist provider to Klang Valley, which has the highest density of Internet users and bloggers in Malaysia.[89] The tests revealed no evidence of filtering for any of the categories tested, which is unsurprising given the public climbdown of the Malaysian government from its 2009 filtering plans.

Conclusion

Malaysia has extended its practice of controlling all media of communication to the Internet. It joins a growing trend of state reliance on second- and third-generation control mechanisms through a complex combination of formal and informal methods, from applying existing laws to online content, to directly competing within cyber-informational space for voter attention. Significantly, the number of proceedings against individual bloggers has been increasing exponentially since the first cases in 2007 and is unlikely to abate. This trend is possibly the result of two factors. First, China has emerged as a model for controlling Internet content without sacrificing foreign investment interest. Second, the 2008 Malaysian elections unequivocally materialized BN's concerns over the destabilizing effect of cyber dissentients. Notably, the relatively tepid public response to 2010 official announcements of a governmental task force to scour the Internet may indicate a growing resignation to pervasive state monitoring and surveillance of the Internet in Malaysia.

Notes

1. Section 3(3), Malaysian Communications and Multimedia Act, 1998.

2. Point 7, Multimedia Super Corridor Bill of Guarantees, 1999.

3. This is self-defined by SoPoSentral, a directory of "sociopolitical" blogs in Malaysia, categorized as blogs on social, political, and financial issues pertaining to Malaysia.

4. Barisan Nasional translates to "National Front." BN is used here for readers who are accustomed to the regional abbreviation.

5. Malaysia has a federal government and 13 state governments. In this report, "Malaysian government" refers to the federal government unless indicated otherwise. Barisan Nasional is still in control of the federal government, though not of all 13 state governments.

6. Department of Statistics Malaysia, e-mail message to author on April 19, 2011 (based on 2010 census data).

7. Meredith L. Weiss, *Protest and Possibilities: Civil Society and Coalitions for Political Change in Malaysia* (Stanford, CA: Stanford University Press, 2006), 12.

8. Race-based affirmative action in favor of the majority Malays is constitutionally guaranteed in Malaysia and comes in the form of socioeconomic privileges. See Article 153, Malaysian Federal Constitution.

9. Richard Clutterbuck, *Conflict and Violence in Singapore and Malaysia, 1945–1983* (Singapore: Westview Press, 1985), 321.

10. The National Operations Council, *The May 13 Tragedy, A Report* (Kuala Lumpur, Malaysia: National Operations Council, 1969), 69.

11. See Article 159(3), Malaysian Federal Constitution.

12. Meredith L. Weiss, "Malaysia's 12th General Election: Causes and Consequences of the Opposition's Surge," *Asia Pacific Bulletin* 12 (2008): 1.

13. Abdul Rashid Moten and Tunku Mohar Mokhtar, "The 2004 General Elections in Malaysia," *Asian Survey* 46 (2004): 330.

14. Weiss, "Malaysia's 12th General Election," 1.

15. Translates from Malay as "people's pact" or "people's alliance." We use PR as an abbreviation to maintain regional consistency.

16. "How BN Lost the Media War," *New Straits Times*, April 2, 2008, http://findarticles.com/p/news-articles/new-straits-times/mi_8016/is_20080402/bn-lost-media-war/ai_n44396127/ (referring to a study conducted by Zentrum Future Studies Malaysia).

17. See Section 13(1), 13A, Malaysian Printing Presses and Publications Act.

18. *The Star* is the most widely read and circulated English national daily and was once a vocal critic of the Malaysian government. However, in 1987, *The Star* was one of the subjects of *Operasi Lalang* (i.e., "Operation Weeding Out"), an investigative campaign launched by the Malaysian government under its powers granted by the 1960 Internal Security Act. *The Star's* publication license was revoked briefly, but upon renewal of its license, *The Star* became far less politically attuned and has been criticized for being a pale version of its pre-1987 self. See Zaharom Nain and Wang Lay Kim, "Ownership, Control and the Malaysian Media," in *Who Owns the Media: Global Trends and Local Resistance*, ed. Pradip N. Thomas and Zaharom Nain (Penang, Malaysia: Zed Books, 2004), 249.

19. John Hilley, *Malaysia: Mahathirism, Hegemony and the New Opposition* (London: Zed Books, 2001), 123.

20. See MSC Malaysia National Rollout Phase 1, http://www.mscmalaysia.my/topic/12073058488660.

21. International Telecommunication Union (ITU), "Internet Indicators: Subscribers, Users and Broadband Subscribers," 2009 Figures, http://www.itu.int/ITU-D/icteye/Reporting/ShowReportFrame.aspx?ReportName=/WTI/InformationTechnologyPublic&ReportFormat=HTML4.0&RP_intYear=2009&RP_intLanguageID=1&RP_bitLiveData=False.

22. Ibid.

23. "Target: Broadband Penetration to Go Up to 50% by Next Year," Malaysiakini, November 10, 2009, http://malaysiakini.com/news/117064.

24. ITU, "Internet Indicators: Subscribers, Users and Broadband Subscribers."

25. "Government Believes Malaysia Will Become Major Hub for WiMAX Going Forward," Bernama, November 22, 2010, http://www.bernama.com/bernama/v5/newsbusiness.php?id=544499.

26. Telekom Malaysia is the "privatized branch of the state" referred to, the parent company of TMNet. The government maintains a 35.03 percent shareholding. See Telekom Malaysia, "TM—About TM—Background and Strength: Capital Structure," http://www.tm.com.my/ap/about/background/Pages/capital-structure.aspx; Telekom Malaysia, "TM—About TM—Background and Strength: Shareholding Structure," http://www.tm.com.my/ap/about/background/Pages/GroupCorporateStructure.aspx.

27. "Four Companies Successfully Obtain WiMAX Licences" [in Malay], Utusan Malaysia, March 16, 2007, http://www.skmm.gov.my/index.php?c=public&v=art_view&art_id=501.

28. "No Exclusive 700MHz Spectrum for YTL," Malaysiakini, November 30, 2010, http://malaysiakini.com/news/149640; Clara Chooi, "Rais Grilled in Parliament over YTL-700MH," *Malaysian Insider*, November 30, 2010, http://www.themalaysianinsider.com/malaysia/article/rais-grilled-in-parliament-over-ytl-700mhz-saga.

29. See Article 10(1)(a), Federal Constitution of Malaysia.

30. Ibid., Article 10(2)(a).

31. Yip Ai Tsin, "Rais Defends Internet Filter Plans," Malaysiakini, August 7, 2009, http://malaysiakini.com/news/110085.

32. "Gov't Mulls China-Style Net Censorship," Malaysiakini, August 6, 2009, http://www.malaysiakini.com/news/110048.

33. "No Plan to Filter Internet, Says Rais," Malaysiakini, August 12, 2009, http://www.malaysiakini.com/news/110397.

34. "Bloggers May Have to Reveal Identities," Malaysiakini, April 7, 2007, http://www.malaysiakini.com/news/65558.

35. "Online News Sites to Be Included under PPPA," Malaysiakini, January 25, 2011, http://www.malaysiakini.com/news/154483.

36. "Brickbats Hurled at Move to Control Online Media," Malaysiakini, January 26, 2011, http://www.malaysiakini.com/news/154520.

37. Aidila Razak, "No Change to Publishing Law in March: Liew," Malaysiakini, January 27, 2011, http://malaysiakini.com/news/154621.

38. "OSA Probe: Police Detains PKR Webmaster," Malaysiakini, July 13, 2007, http://www.malaysiakini.com/news/69917.

39. Andrew Ong, "Raja Petra Arrested under ISA," Malaysiakini, September 12, 2008, http://malaysiakini.com/news/89544.

40. See Malaysian Sedition Act, 1948.

41. Hazlan Zakaria, "Sedition Guidelines Will Now Apply to Online Media," Malaysiakini, January 24, 2011, http://www.malaysiakini.com/news/154301.

42. Chuah Siew Eng, "Proposed Cyber Sedition Law Is Undemocratic," Malaysiakini, December 3, 2010, http://www.malaysiakini.com/letters/149879.

43. Soon Li Tsin, "Bloggers Sued for Defamation," Malaysiakini, January 18, 2007, http://www.malaysiakini.com/news/62257.

44. Ming Kuok Lim, "Blogging and Democracy: Blogs in Malaysian Political Discourse" (PhD dissertation, Pennsylvania State University, 2009), 110–116, http://etda.libraries.psu.edu/theses/approved/WorldWideFiles/ETD-3818/LIM,_Doctoral_Dissertation_2009.pdf.

45. "PKR Activist Agrees Not to Blog Against Rais," Malaysiakini, March 21, 2011, http://www.malaysiakini.com/news/159200.

46. See Section 16, Malaysian Communications and Multimedia Commission Act, 1998.

47. Section 211(1), Malaysian Communications and Multimedia Act, 1998.

48. Ibid., Section 233.

49. Ibid., Sections 211(2) and 233(3).

50. Ibid., Sections 68, 69, and 70.

51. See MCMC List of Cases Investigated in 2005, 2010, http://www.skmm.gov.my/index.php?c=public&v=art_view&art_id=92.

52. Andrew Ong, "Temple Demo: Residents March with Cow's Head," Malaysiakini, August 28, 2009, http://malaysiakini.com/news/111628.

53. "PM Furious, Tells IGP to Act," Malaysiakini, August 28, 2009, http://malaysiakini.com/news/111669.

54. The Malaysian federal constitution itself identifies race with religion. See Article 160(1): "Malay" means a person who professes the religion of Islam. Additionally, many Hindus are Indians. See Saw Swee-Hock, The Population of Malaysia (Singapore: Institute of Southeast Asian Studies, 2007), 78–83. In Malaysia, 84.1 percent of Indians are Hindus, 100 percent of Malays are Muslims, and 76 percent of Chinese are Buddhists.

55. Kuek Ser Kuang Keng, "12 Charged over Cow-Head Protest," Malaysiakini, September 9, 2009, http://malaysiakini.com/news/112445.

56. "MCMC Quizzes Editor over Cow-Head Videos," Malaysiakini, September 5, 2009, http://malaysiakini.com/news/112204; "Cow-Head video: MCMC Comes A-calling Again," Malaysiakini, September 10, 2009, http://www.malaysiakini.com/news/112564.

57. "MCMC Targets Malaysiakini Again," Malaysiakini, October 22, 2010, http://malaysiakini.com/news/146121.

58. Susan Loone, "Penang Submits Complaint to MCMC against Blogger," Malaysiakini, September 21, 2010, http://www.malaysiakini.com/news/143210.

59. See Section 249, Malaysian Communications and Multimedia Act, 1998.

60. Charles Lourdes, "Six to Be Charged for Insulting Perak Sultan via Blogs, Postings (Update 2)," *The Star*, March 12, 2009, http://thestar.com.my/news/story.asp?sec=nation&file=/2009/3/12/nation/20090312194041; but see MCMC List of Prosecutions 2009, http://www.skmm.gov.my/index.php?c=public&v=art_view&art_id=92, which lists nine individuals.

61. MCMC List of Prosecutions 2009, http://www.skmm.gov.my/index.php?c=public&v=art_view&art_id=92.

62. Nurul Huda Jamaluddin, "Blogger 'Hassan Skodeng' to Face Charge Tomorrow," *Malay Mail*, September 1, 2010, http://www.mmail.com.my/content/48211-blogger-hassan-skodeng-face-charge-tomorrow.

63. "Alternative Media: BN vs. PR—Who's Winning?" *Malaysian Digest*, March 15, 2010, http://www.malaysiandigest.com/features/2541-alternative-media-bn-vs-pr-who-is-winning.html. (The report states that BN has more Twitter and Facebook fans overall: at 19,596 and 164,335 as opposed to PR's 17,176 and 109,472.)

64. For smear campaigns, see Hafiz Yatim, "Will the Mud Stick on Zaid?" Malaysiakini, April 20, 2010, http://malaysiakini.com/news/129741; Susan Loone, "Doctored Pic: Report Lodged against 'PAS Beruk,'" Malaysiakini, September 2, 2010, http://malaysiakini.com/news/141737. See also Malaysiakini, "Kit Siang: Why Are MCA Cybertroopers Attacking Me?" September 23, 2010, http://malaysiakini.com/news/143378.

65. Ronald J. Deibert and Rafal Rohozinski, "Control and Subversion in Russian Cyberspace," in *Access Controlled: The Shaping of Power, Rights, and Rule in Cyberspace,* ed. Ronald J. Deibert, John Palfrey, Rafal Rohozinksi, and Jonathan Zittrain (Cambridge, MA: MIT Press, 2010); David Bandurski, "China's Guerrilla War for the Web," *Far Eastern Economic Review* 171, no. 6 (July 2008), 41.

66. PM Invites Public to Share Ideas on Budget 2011," Malaysiakini, August 24, 2010, http://malaysiakini.com/news/140991; "Budget 2011: PM's Blog Flooded with Suggestions," Malaysiakini, September 24, 2010, http://malaysiakini.com/news/143527.

67. *Ultra Dimension v. Kook Wei Kuan* [2001] Malay. L. J. (Unreported) 751, at page 6. See also *Lew Cher Phow v. Pua Yong Yong* [2009] Malay. L. J. (Unreported) 1331.

68. "Parliament: Personal Data Protection Bill Passed," *The Star*, April 12, 2010, http://thestar .com.my/news/story.asp?file=/2010/4/5/nation/20100405210518&sec=nation. See also: Section 2, Personal Data Protection Bill, 2009. Note that the bill has not yet received royal assent.

69. See Section 3(1), Personal Data Protection Bill, 2009.

70. Section 234(1) and 265(1), Malaysian Communications Multimedia Act, 1998.

71. Ibid., Section 77(1).

72. See Section 10(2), Malaysian Computer Crimes Act, 1997; and Section 23(3), Anti-Corruption Act, 1997.

73. See Section 30(1), Malaysian Internal Security Act, 1960.

74. Thomas Fuller, "Press Curbed, Malaysians Go On-Line for News: Mahathir Caught in Web of Internet Awareness," *New York Times*, September 10, 1998, http://www.nytimes.com/1998/09/10/ news/10iht-malay.t_4.html?ref=thomasfuller.

75. Thomas Fuller, "Police Detain 2 over Spreading Internet Rumors: Virtual Riots in Malaysia," *New York Times*, August 12, 1998, http://www.nytimes.com/1998/08/12/news/12iht-malay.t_0 .html?ref=thomasfuller.

76. Nurbaiti Hamdan and Cheok Li Peng, "ISPs Ordered to Cut Access to *Malaysia Today* Website," August 28, 2008, *The Star*, http://thestar.com.my/news/story.asp?file=/2008/8/28/nation/ 22187596&sec=nation.

77. Raja Petra Kamarudin, "The Attacks on Malaysia Today," *Malaysia Today*, September 29, 2009, http://www.malaysia-today.net/archives/27311-the-attacks-on-malaysia-today-udpated -with-chinese-translation; Neville Spykerman, "Cyber Attack: Anwar's Blog Latest to Be Hit," *Malaysian Insider*, September 9, 2010, http://www.themalaysianinsider.com/malaysia/article/ fmt-malaysia-today-not-accessible-after-attacks.

78. "M'sia Today Blocked 'to Stop Release of Documents,'" Malaysiakini, September 10, 2010, http://malaysiakini.com/news/142385.

79. "Gov't to Monitor Internet for 'Harmful' Blogs," Malaysiakini, September 3, 2010, http:// malaysiakini.com/news/141893.

80. See MCMC Record Keeping Rules for the Communications and Multimedia Sector, Public Consultation Paper, August 2003; and MCMC Record Keeping Rules for the Communications and Multimedia Sector, A Report on the Public Consultation Paper, January 2004. See also Section 268, Malaysian Communications and Multimedia Act, 1998.

81. Hazlan Zakaria, "1Malaysia Email Not Entirely Free,'" Malaysiakini, April 21, 2011, http:// malaysiakini.com/news/162052.

82. "Better to Stick to Google, Yahoo or Hotmail," Malaysiakini, April 22, 2011, http:// malaysiakini.com/news/162146.

83. "Anti–100 Storey Tower Group Calls for 'Cake-Party,'" Malaysiakini, November 15, 2010, http://malaysiakini.com/news/148257. The Malaysian Police Act, 1976, sec. 27, requires gatherings of five or more persons to obtain police permits.

84. Aidila Razak, "When Eating Cake Is a 'Suspicious' Activity," Malaysiakini, November 16, 2010, http://www.malaysiakini.com/news/148415; Lee Long Hui and Lee Weng Keat, "Utar Warns Students over Anti-tower Cake Party," Malaysiakini, November 18, 2010, http://www.malaysiakini.com/news/148399.

85. See the national register established by Section 4(1), Malaysian National Registration Act, 1959. See also Regulation 3, Malaysian National Registration Regulations (Amendment 2001), requiring every person to register and obtain his/her identity card.

86. Postpaid mobile phone users would already have to register with mobile phone companies. Prepaid users were required to register under the Ministerial Direction on the Registration of Subscribers of Public Prepaid Cellular Services, Direction no. 1 of 2006, under CMA 1998.

87. "Cabinet: Cybercafes not Subjected to Restrictions," New Straits Times, March 18, 1999, 5.

88. Recently, the government has announced its intentions of installing more CCTV cameras to deter crime. See "CCTV Cameras to Be Fixed Nationwide to Fight Crime," Malaysiakini, December 22, 2010, http://malaysiakini.com/news/151486.

89. Jun E-Tan and Zawawi Ibrahim, Blogging and Democratization in Malaysia: A New Civil Society in the Making (Petaling Jaya, Malaysia: SIRD, 2008), 44.

Pakistan

In 2010, Pakistan made global head-lines for blocking Facebook and other Web sites in response to a contest pop-ularized on the social networking site to draw images of the Prophet Moham-mad. In general, Internet filtering in Pakistan remains both inconsistent and intermittent, with filtering pri-marily targeted at content deemed to be a threat to national security and at religious content considered blasphemous.

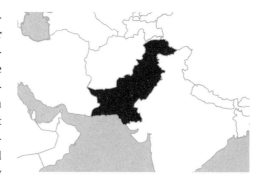

RESULTS AT A GLANCE

Filtering	No Evidence of Filtering	Suspected Filtering	Selective Filtering	Substantial Filtering	Pervasive Filtering
Political			•		
Social			•		
Conflict and security				•	
Internet tools			•		

OTHER FACTORS

	Low	Medium	High	Not Applicable
Transparency		•		
Consistency	•			

KEY INDICATORS	
GDP per capita, PPP (constant 2005 international dollars)	2,381
Life expectancy at birth, total (years)	67
Literacy rate, adult total (percent of people age 15+)	53.7
Human Development Index (of 169)	125
Rule of Law (of 5)	1.6
Voice and Accountability (of 5)	1.5
Democracy Index (of 167)	104 (Hybrid regime)
Digital Opportunity Index (of 181)	127
Internet penetration rate	11.3

Source by indicator: World Bank 2009, World Bank 2008a, World Bank 2008b, UNDP 2010, World Bank Worldwide Governance Indicators 2009, Economist Intelligence Unit 2010, ITU 2007, ITU 2009. See Introduction to the Country Profiles, pp. 222–223.

Background

Under General Pervez Musharraf's leadership (1999–2008), print and electronic media were often censored in cases where content was deemed to be antigovernment or anti-Islam. Government repression of media was particularly acute with regard to Baluchi and Sindhi political autonomy, as well as with content considered blasphemous or subversive.

In October 2007, Musharraf won an indirect, widely boycotted presidential election held while his two major political opponents were in exile.[1] Musharraf's eligibility to serve as president while still serving as army chief was challenged in court, to which Musharraf responded by suspending the constitution and placing the country under a state of emergency on November 3, 2007—shutting down all privately owned television and media outlets, arresting lawyers and judges, and jamming cell phone and Internet connections.[2] On August 18, 2008, Musharraf resigned from the presidency in order to avoid impeachment.[3] Elections were held on September 6, 2008, and Asif Ali Zardari, the husband of assassinated Pakistan People's Party (PPP) chair Benazir Bhutto, was elected Pakistan's new president.[4]

Pakistan is home to a vibrant civil society, including a large movement opposing and monitoring Internet and other censorship.[5] International human rights groups frequently report on persecution of journalists at the hands of Pakistani military and extremist groups. According to the Committee to Protect Journalists, at least five journalists and media workers were killed in 2009, and at least seven in 2010, representing an increase from previous years.[6]

Internet in Pakistan

Internet usage in 2009 was estimated to be at 20.4 million users, with an 11.3 percent penetration rate.[7] Since implementing a deregulation and market liberalization policy in 2003, Pakistan has seen considerable growth in its information and communication technology (ICT) sector. The aggressive pursuit of deregulation and market liberalization has been aimed at boosting Pakistan's economic modernization and creating an industry for software exports. Fierce competition and demand for service have seen Internet subscription charges drop. For example, DSL, which holds 64 percent of the market for Internet service, saw subscription charges drop from USD 55 to USD 15 per month by the end of 2008.[8] However, despite an increase in the implementation of fiber optic cables and wireless technologies, most of Pakistan relies on dial-up Internet connections.

There are approximately 130 Internet service providers (ISPs) in Pakistan. Some of the leading ISPs include Wateen, Paknet, Linkdotnet, Comsats, and Cybernet. In 2007, Wateen Telecom, a subsidiary of Warid Telecom, introduced Worldwide Interoperability for Microwave Access (WiMAX), a telecommunications technology that provides a third-generation (3G) wireless alternative to cable and DSL. Pakistan is the first country in the world to implement such technology, which is designed to provide high-performance, high-speed Internet access over a larger area than other wireless technologies that offer either greater coverage or greater bandwidth can provide.[9] Wateen was followed by Wi-Tribe, Mobilink Infinity, and Qubee in providing WiMAX to customers. Despite this state-of-the-art technology, WiMAX has about half as many subscribers as DSL, and about twice as much as EVDO. Internet subscriptions continue to remain low, with 3.7 million Internet subscriptions in 2009 at a 2 percent penetration rate.[10] Since 2006, DSL has remained the preferred form of broadband technology.

As of 2009, the largest Internet exchange point (IXP) in the country was the Pakistan Internet Exchange (PIE), a subsidiary of the Pakistan Telecommunication Company, Ltd. (PTCL), largely owned by the Pakistani government. It was created by the government in 2000 to provide a single core backbone for Pakistan by providing peering points for ISPs. The Pakistan Internet Exchange has three main nodes—in Karachi, Lahore, and Islamabad—as well as 42 smaller nodes, and it operates two submarine cables, the South East Asia–Middle East–Western Europe 3 (SEA-ME-WE 3) and the South East Asia–Middle East–Western Europe 4 (SEA-ME-WE 4).

The PTCL was the sole provider of bandwidth to the country until 2009, when an agreement between the Internet Service Providers Association of Pakistan and the

PTCL decided that ISPs would not be forced to buy bandwidth from the PTCL and were free to choose from third-party providers.[11] A second major company in Pakistan's Internet infrastructure is TransWorld, which owns and operates Pakistan's first and only privately owned submarine fiber optic cable system, the TW1, which has a capacity of 1.28 terabytes, more than is currently necessary for the nation.[12]

Internet filtering in Pakistan is regulated by the Pakistan Telecommunications Authority (PTA) and the Federal Investigation Agency (FIA) under the direction of the government, the Supreme Court of Pakistan, and the Ministry of Information Technology (MoIT).

On September 2, 2006, the MoIT announced the creation of the Inter-Ministerial Committee for the Evaluation of Web sites (IMCEW), responsible for monitoring and blocking Web sites containing blasphemous, pornographic, or antistate material.[13] The IMCEW is administered by the secretary of the MoIT and is composed of representatives from the MoIT, the PTA, the Ministry of the Interior, the cabinet, and other security agencies. Directives to block content are typically handed by the government or the Supreme Court through the IMCEW to the MoIT and PTA, who then pass the orders to individual ISPs. However, because there is no specific legal framework, directives can be given directly to the PTA and ISPs to block material without going through the IMCEW. The Deregulation Facilitation Unit is responsible for addressing the grievances that Internet users may have with this censorship body.[14]

Internet censorship in Pakistan has received worldwide attention because of the pervasive influence of religious groups. The government's often quick moves to filter certain material can be considered rash.

In 2006, the Supreme Court issued a directive that ordered the PTA to block access to 12 Web sites that included "blasphemous" cartoons depicting the Prophet Mohammad. Among this banned content was a Web site that was hosted on a Blogspot domain. Rather than blocking the offending Blogspot Web site, the PTA blocked access to the entire domain for approximately two months.[15] At the same time, the Supreme Court ordered police to register cases of publishing or posting of blasphemous images under article 295-C of the Pakistan Penal Code, under which blasphemy or defamation of the Prophet Mohammad is punishable by death.[16]

In 2008, the government issued an order to ISPs to block a URL and three IP addresses associated with a YouTube video clip of Geert Wilders, the Dutch lawmaker, considered "blasphemous" by the Pakistani government.[17] Because the PIE was unable to conduct a URL-specific block, it performed an IP-wide block, which had the unanticipated consequence of rendering the entire YouTube domain inaccessible to much of the world for approximately two hours.[18]

In May 2010, the PTA ordered ISPs to block Facebook, YouTube, and certain Flickr and Wikipedia pages when an Internet user created a Facebook page entitled "Post Drawings of the Prophet Mohammad Day."[19] The ban was ordered as a result of the

Islamic Lawyers Association's request for a court injunction to ban Facebook, while the other Web sites were later banned because of "objectionable material."[20] The blanket Facebook ban was lifted after the page in question was removed; however, the government stated that it would continue to block other Web sites that contained "blasphemous content."[21] In the following month, the government also ordered the PTA to monitor "offensive content" on Amazon, Bing, Google, Hotmail, MSN, Yahoo, and YouTube.[22]

Internet content that is critical of or draws negative attention toward the Pakistani government and armed forces is also a target of filtering. In 2009, President Zardari received widespread criticism after he passed a law prohibiting the spread of "ill motivated and concocted stories through emails and text messages against the civilian leadership" after a flood of jokes about his government were sent to the president's official e-mail.[23] In February 2010, YouTube was blocked by the PTA after videos of Zardari yelling at a public gathering were posted on the site.[24] In October 2010, the Pakistani army ordered videos of a Pakistani army officer beating a civilian in the Swat Valley to be removed from popular video-sharing Web sites.[25]

In addition to blasphemous material, Pakistan has blocked "antistate" content, Web sites promoting Baluchi and Sindhi human rights and political movements, and content regarding political autonomy and minorities. It has also blocked several Web sites regarding Pashtun secessionism.

Legal and Regulatory Frameworks

Former President Musharraf's crackdowns on the media included content prohibitions and enhanced government discretion toward licensing requirements in order to cultivate self-censorship. In 2002, Musharraf established the Pakistan Electronic Media Regulatory Authority (PEMRA) to facilitate and regulate private electronic media.[26] One of the PEMRA's first acts was to lay out the regulatory framework that ultimately served to support Musharraf's drive to control and restrict independent journalism.

In recent years, violence toward minorities, journalists, and bloggers has increased dramatically. In 2010, the Committee to Protect Journalists named Pakistan the deadliest country for journalists, with the deaths of six journalists and one media worker in the span of six months.[27] In 2009, seven journalists and one media worker were killed, and in 2008, six journalists were killed.[28]

Pakistan is considered to have some of the world's strictest laws regarding blasphemous material. In 1986 the penal code of 1860 was amended by the military regime of General Zia-ul-Haq. The amended laws prescribed life imprisonment or death for certain violations, and they have historically targeted Baluchi, Sindhi, Ahmadi, and Christian groups.[29] Minorities and those voicing divergent viewpoints continue to be targeted by extremist groups that use Pakistan's blasphemy laws to justify their brutal attacks. One of the most persecuted groups in Pakistan is the Ahmadiyya community. Ahmadis, who are declared non-Muslim by Pakistani law, suffer persecution and widespread censorship under Pakistan's blasphemy laws for their beliefs.[30] Most recently, on May 28, 2010, terrorists carried out two attacks on Ahmadi places of worship, killing more than 90 people.[31] In 2009 at least 50 members of the Ahmadiyya community were charged under the blasphemy law.[32] Since the amendment of the penal code, there have been approximately 700 blasphemy cases. In January 2011, Salman Taseer, the governor of Punjab province, was assassinated by one of his own guards, who condemned the politician's public opposition to the country's blasphemy laws.[33]

Actions taken by the government, especially in 2010, indicate a move toward a centralized monitoring and filtering system that is easy to manipulate through vague and easily amendable laws. The Prevention of Electronic Crimes Ordinance (PECO) came into effect on September 29, 2008.[34] The ordinance lays out offenses for electronic forgery, fraud, criminal data access, use of malicious code, cyber stalking, and cyber terrorism. It grants the government the ability to amend and add rules to the ordinance as it sees fit, as long as the changes are published in the government newspaper, the *Gazette of Pakistan*.[35]

In March 2010, the Pakistani government issued a directive allowing it to order the PTA, "in case of any national security situation, to order temporary or permanent termination of telecom services of any service provider, in any part or whole of Pakistan."[36] On June 3, 2010, the Lahore High Court ordered the PTA and the MoIT to devise methods to create a permanent system that would monitor and filter "blasphemous and objectionable content" on the Internet. By June 23, 2010, reports emerged that the PTA was in the process of developing regulations to define the filtering process, and that suggestions were made to create a centralized filter to block objectionable material.[37] These were immediately followed by orders from the Lahore High Court to the MoIC to ban 17 Web sites and to monitor Amazon, Bing, Google, Hotmail, MSN, Yahoo, and YouTube.[38] After the directive, evidence emerged that the PTCL was experimenting with transparent proxy servers in order to develop a more sophisticated censorship system. The evidence indicated that the PTCL was testing an advanced form of blocking known as CleanFeed, which would allow Pakistani authorities to block individual Web pages online as opposed to entire domains or Web sites.[39]

In November 2010, the Pakistani government released a draft policy that laid down the framework for a national plan to transform Pakistan's IT industry.[40] The draft policy uses vague language open to interpretation and misuse. It gives indirect control of the Country Code Top Level Domain for Pakistan, .pk, to the government. The draft policy also gives the government a free hand in enacting and amending legislation to support its goals, mentioning its ability to "take corrective actions as necessary."[41] According to the draft, free access to information and the sharing of divergent views and dialogue are promoted, except "in situations where the content poses a security risk or violated religious, social or cultural values," or disseminates blasphemous material, in which case the government has the ability to "take steps to block such traffic," and "necessary legislation would be enacted, as necessary, to support the aforementioned goals."[42] The final version of the policy was slated for release in December 2010; at the time of this writing it had not yet been released.

Surveillance

Internet surveillance in Pakistan is primarily conducted by the PIE under the auspices of the PTA. The PIE monitors all incoming and outgoing Internet traffic from Pakistan, as well as e-mail and keywords, and stores data for a specified amount of time.[43] Law enforcement agencies such as the FIA can be asked by the government to conduct surveillance and monitor content. Under PECO, ISPs are required to retain traffic data for a minimum of 90 days and may also be required to collect real-time data and record information while keeping their involvement with the government confidential.[44] The ordinance does not specify what kinds of actions constitute grounds for data collection and surveillance.

ONI Testing Results

OpenNet Initiative testing was conducted on two major ISPs: PTCL and CyberNet Internet Services. Consistent with 2007–2008 testing results, ONI testing found no uniform method of blocking between the two ISPs. Pakistan continues to filter content that is considered to threaten the country's internal security. This includes content relating to the Baluchi conflict and independence movement as well as religious content deemed blasphemous. Filtering in Pakistan is inconsistent between ISPs and is often intermittent.

Internet users on PTCL who attempt to access blocked content receive a block page informing them that the site in question is restricted, while CyberNet users attempting to access blocked content receive a network error page indicating that there are "no DNS records" for the site. This error page gives users the impression that the Web sites are inaccessible as a result of network errors or that they simply no longer exist. Technical analysis revealed that these errors were the result of a DNS look-up failure, which is consistent with 2007 and 2008 testing findings.

A form of collateral filtering, the blocking of additional content that is unintended and caused by imprecise filtering methods,[45] has long been a feature of Internet censorship in Pakistan. For example, in March 2007, in an attempt to comply with a Supreme Court order to filter blasphemous content "at all costs," the PTCL implemented a blanket IP address block at their Karachi PIE exchange that lasted for four days and affected the Akamai servers, leading to disruptions of Google, Yahoo, BBC, CNN, ESPN, and several other major Web sites.[46]

One of the most extreme examples of collateral filtering occurred in February 2008, when the Pakistani government attempted to block YouTube for hosting the Geert Wilders video clip.[47] The PTA issued an order to block access to a single video; in response, the PTCL redirected requests for YouTube videos to its own network. This rerouting was advertised to ISPs worldwide and was picked up by Hong Kong–based ISP PCCW, which then broadcast the redirect to other ISPs.[48] YouTube staffers worked with PCCW to restore access within two hours.[49] Access to YouTube in Pakistan was restored following YouTube's removal of the offending video.

The Web sites blocked by the two tested ISPs provide a representative snapshot of filtering practices in 2010, consisting mainly of Baluchi-related news, culture, and independence sites. Although ONI testing did not capture the intermittent blocks on Facebook and other sites in the wake of "Draw Mohammed Day," a related site, http://drawmohammed.com, was found blocked by CyberNet. Two other sites containing images of the Prophet were also found blocked by CyberNet: http://zombietime.com and http://prophet.rydasrecords.com. Among the handful of other sites blocked by CyberNet were http://themoviefitna.com (the Web site for Geert Wilders's anti-Islam film *Fitna*); http://michellemalkin.com (the site of right-wing American talk-show host Michelle Malkin); and http://www.faithfreedom.org (a site that calls itself a "grassroots movement of ex-Muslims"). PTCL was found to be blocking only three sites: http://hinduunity.com, http://hizb-ut-tahrir.org, and http://islamreview.com.

In 2008, the ONI observed that responsibility for implementing filtering in Pakistan had been shifted to the ISP level. Just as the ONI found a decrease in consistency between tests conducted in 2006–2007 and 2008, the most recent round of testing showed a further decrease in consistency between PTCL and CyberNet. Consistent with previous tests, 2010 ONI testing showed that the vast majority of Web sites with content related to independent media, social media, circumvention and anonymity tools, international human rights groups, Voice over Internet Protocol (VoIP) services, civil society groups, minority religions, Indian and Hindu human rights groups, Pakistani political parties, and sexual content (including pornography and LGBT content) were accessible across the ISPs tested.

Conclusion

Pakistanis currently have free access to a wide range of content, including most sexual, political, social, and religious sites on the Internet. Although the majority of filtering in Pakistan is intermittent—such as the occasional block on a major Web site like Blogspot or YouTube—the PTA continues to block sites containing content it considers to be blasphemous, anti-Islamic, or threatening to internal security. Online civil society activism that began in order to protect free expression in the country continues to expand as citizens utilize new media to disseminate information and organize.

Notes

1. Martina Smit, "Pervez Musharraf Wins Pakistan Election," *The Telegraph*, October 6, 2007, http://www.telegraph.co.uk/news/worldnews/1565320/Pervez-Musharraf-wins-Pakistan-election.html.

2. James Traub, "The Lawyers' Crusade," *New York Times Magazine*, June 1, 2008, http://www.nytimes.com/2008/06/01/magazine/01PAKISTAN-t.html.

3. Naween A. Mangi and Khalid Qayum, "Musharraf Quits as President to Avoid Impeachment," Bloomberg, August 18, 2008, http://www.bloomberg.com/apps/news?pid=newsarchive&sid=au6PGtmU44E0&refer=home.

4. "Timeline: Pakistan," BBC News, August 19, 2009, http://news.bbc.co.uk/2/hi/south_asia/country_profiles/1156716.stm.

5. For example, see Don't Block the Blog campaign, http://dbtb.org; Pakistan 451, http://pakistan451.wordpress.com; Bytesforall Pakistan ICT Policy Monitor Network, http://pakistanictpolicy.bytesforall.net.

6. Committee to Protect Journalists, "Journalists Killed in Pakistan since 1992," http://cpj.org/killed/asia/pakistan.

7. International Telecommunication Union (ITU), "Internet Indicators: Subscribers, Users and Broadband Subscribers," 2009 Figures, http://www.itu.int/ITU-D/icteye/Reporting/ShowReportFrame.aspx?ReportName=/WTI/InformationTechnologyPublic&ReportFormat=HTML4.0&RP_intYear=2009&RP_intLanguageID=1&RP_bitLiveData=False.

8. Pakistan Telecommunication Authority (PTA), "Value Added Services," August 23, 2009, http://www.pta.gov.pk/index.php?option=com_content&task=view&id=651&Itemid=604.

9. Mark Whitton, "What WiMAX Means for the Enterprise," TMCNet, April 2007, http://www.tmcnet.com/voip/0406/featurearticle-what-wimax-means-for-enterprise.htm.

10. ITU, "Internet Indicators."

11. Babar Bhatti, "End of PTCL Monopoly in Broadband," All Things Pakistan, May 23, 2009, http://pakistaniat.com/2009/05/23/broadband-pakistan/.

12. Transworld Associates, "TW1 Fiber Optic Cable Project," accessed November 29, 2010, http://www.tw1.com/index.php?action=text.

13. Don't Block the Blog, "Committee Formed to Block Websites," September 3, 2006, http://dbtb.org/2006/09/03/committee-formed-to-block-websites/.

14. Ministry of Information Technology, "De-regulation Policy for the Telecommunication Sector," July 2003, http://www.pta.gov.pk/media/telecom25092003.pdf.

15. Alecks Pabico, "Blogspot Blanket Ban in Pakistan Appears to Be Lifted," Free Expression in Asian Cyberspace, May 4, 2006, http://freeexpressionasia.wordpress.com/2006/05/04/blogspot -blanket-ban-appears-to-be-lifted.

16. Pakistan Penal Code, http://www.pakistani.org/pakistan/legislation/1860/actXLVof1860.html.

17. Stephen Graham, "Pakistan Lifts YouTube Ban," Huffington Post, February 26, 2008, http:// www.huffingtonpost.com/2008/02/26/pakistan-lifts-youtube-ba_n_88522.html.

18. Don't Block the Blog, "TWA Internet Backbone Blocks Only Blasphemous Video URL," February 24, 2008, http://dbtb.org/2008/02/24/twa-internet-backbone-blocks-only-blasphemous-video -url.

19. Waqar Gillani, "Pakistan: Court Blocks Facebook," *New York Times,* May 19, 2010, http:// www.nytimes.com/2010/05/20/world/asia/20briefs-Pakistan.html.

20. Zainab Jeewanjee, "Facebook Banned in Pakistan—May 2010," World Affairs Blog Network, May 20, 2010, http://pakistan.foreignpolicyblogs.com/2010/05/20/two-pakistans.

21. Declan Walsh, "Pakistan Lifts Facebook Ban but 'Blasphemous' Pages Stay Hidden," *The Guardian*, May 31, 2010, http://www.guardian.co.uk/world/2010/may/31/pakistan-lifts-facebook-ban.

22. Asif Shahzad, "Internet Censorship in Pakistan: Watching Google for Blasphemy," Associated Press, June 25, 2010, http://www.csmonitor.com/From-the-news-wires/2010/0625/Internet -censorship-in-Pakistan-Watching-Google-for-blasphemy.

23. Isambard Wilkinson, "Pakistan President Asif Zardari Bans Jokes Ridiculing Him," *The Telegraph,* July 21, 2009, http://www.telegraph.co.uk/news/worldnews/asia/pakistan/5878525/ Pakistan-president-Asif-Zardari-bans-jokes-ridiculing-him.html.

24. "Govt Blocks Site over Zardari 'Shut Up' Tape," *Times of India*, February 11, 2010, http://articles.timesofindia.indiatimes.com/2010-02-11/pakistan/28149197_1_president-asif -ali-zardari-youtube-blocks.

25. Jane Perlez, "Pakistani Army Chief Orders Video Inquiry," *New York Times*, October 7, 2010, http://www.nytimes.com/2010/10/08/world/asia/08islamabad.html.

26. PEMRA Pakistan, http://www.pemra.gov.pk/pemra.

27. Committee to Protect Journalists, "Thirty-two Journalists Killed in Pakistan Since 1992/ Motive Confirmed," http://cpj.org/killed/asia/pakistan.

28. Ibid.

29. "Blasphemy Laws in Pakistan," Rationalist International, May 20, 2010, http://www .rationalistinternational.net/Shaikh/blasphemy_laws_in_pakistan.htm.

30. Amjad Mahmood Khan, "Persecution of the Ahmadiyya Community in Pakistan: An Analysis under International Law and International Relations," *Harvard Human Rights Journal* 16 (2003), http://www.law.harvard.edu/students/orgs/hrj/iss16/khan.shtml.

31. "Attacks on Minorities in Pakistan: Growing Power of Fundamentalists in Punjab," South Asia Citizens Web, June 1, 2010, http://www.sacw.net/article1443.html.

32. Human Rights Watch, "Pakistan: Massacre of Minority Ahmadis," May 31, 2010, http://www .hrw.org/en/news/2010/05/31/pakistan-massacre-minority-ahmadis.

33. "Pakistani Governor Opposing Blasphemy Law Killed," CTV News, January 4, 2011, http:// www.ctv.ca/CTVNews/World/20110104/pakistan-assassination-110104.

34. Federal Investigation Agency, Government of Pakistan, "Prevention of Electronic Crimes Ordinance, 2007," http://www.fia.gov.pk/electronic_prevention_orde.pdf.

35. Ibid.

36. Aamir Attaa, "Government Regulates Jamming of Telecom Services Due to National Security," Pro Pakistani, February 12, 2010, http://propakistani.pk/2010/02/12/government-regulation -jamming-telecom-services-national-security.

37. Aamir Attaa, "PTA to Devise Centralized Internet Censorship Practices," Pro Pakistani, June 23, 2010, http://propakistani.pk/2010/06/23/pta-to-devise-centralized-internet-censorship -practices.

38. "Pakistan to Monitor Google and Yahoo for Blasphemy," BBC News, June 25, 2010, http:// www.bbc.co.uk/news/10418643.

39. Danny O'Brien, "In Pakistan, a Censor's Hand in Facebook, Twitter Woes?" Committee to Protect Journalists, June 21, 2010, http://cpj.org/internet/2010/06/facebook-twitter-woes-in -pakistan-may-offer-glimps.php.

40. Ministry of Information Technology, "National IT Policy (Revised 2010) Draft," November 2010, http://www.pcl.org.pk/policy/doc/Draft_National_IT_Policy_%282010%29.pdf.

41. Ibid.

42. Ibid.

43. Cecil J. Chen, "Bloggers Brace for Blackouts over CJ," *Daily Times*, March 17, 2007, www .dailytimes.com.pk/default.asp?page=2007\03\17\story_17-3-2007_pg12_9.

44. Prevention of Electronic Crimes Ordinance, 2009, http://www.na.gov.pk/ordinances/ ord2009/prevention_electronic_crime_ord2009_210809.pdf, accessed January 30, 2011.

45. Nart Villeneuve, "The Filtering Matrix: Integrated Mechanisms of Information Control and the Demarcation of Borders in Cyberspace," *First Monday* 11, no. 1 (2006), http://firstmonday .org/issues/issue11_1/villeneuve/index.html.

46. Adil Najam, "Google, Yahoo, BBC, CNN and Others Websites Blocked in Pakistan as PTCL Fumbles a Censorship Extravaganza," Pakistaniat, March 7, 2007, http://pakistaniat.com/ 2007/03/07/pakistan-blog-ban-block-ptcl-yahoo-google-cnn-websites-censorship-internet.

47. "Pakistan's Internet Has a Bad Weekend," OpenNet Initiative Blog, February 25, 2008, http://opennet.net/blog/2008/02/pakistan%E2%80%99s-internet-has-a-bad-weekend; Martin A. Brown, "Pakistan Hijacks YouTube," Renesys Blog, February 24, 2008, http://www.renesys.com/blog/2008/02/pakistan_hijacks_youtube_1.shtml.

48. Declan McCullagh, "How Pakistan Knocked YouTube Offline (and How to Make Sure It Never Happens Again)," CNet, February 25, 2008, http://news.cnet.com/8301-10784_3-9878655-7.html.

49. Brown, "Pakistan Hijacks YouTube."

South Korea

Despite the fact that South Korea has one of the most advanced information communication technology sectors in the world, online expression remains under the strict legal and technological control of the central government. The country is the global leader in Internet connectivity and speed, but its restrictions on what Internet users can access are substantial.

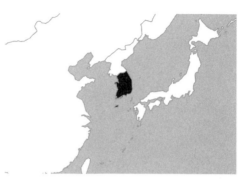

RESULTS AT A GLANCE

Filtering	No Evidence of Filtering	Suspected Filtering	Selective Filtering	Substantial Filtering	Pervasive Filtering
Political	•				
Social			•		
Conflict and security					•
Internet tools	•				

OTHER FACTORS

	Low	Medium	High	Not Applicable
Transparency			•	
Consistency			•	

KEY INDICATORS	
GDP per capita, PPP (constant 2005 international dollars)	25,493
Life expectancy at birth, total (years)	80
Literacy rate, adult total (percent of people age 15+)	99*
Human Development Index (out of 169)	12
Rule of Law (out of 5)	3.5
Voice and Accountability (out of 5)	3.2
Democracy Index (out of 167)	20 (Full democracy)
Digital Opportunity Index (out of 181)	1
Internet penetration rate (percentage of population)	81.5

*South Korea does not report literacy rate information. In previous years, the United Nations has assumed a literacy rate of 99 percent for the country. See United Nations Development Program, "Human Development Report 2009: Overcoming barriers: Human mobility and development," 2009, http://hdr.undp.org/en/media/HDR_2009_EN_Complete.pdf.

Source by indicator: World Bank 2009, World Bank 2008a, UNDP 2009, UNDP 2010, World Bank Worldwide Governance Indicators 2009, Economist Intelligence Unit 2010, ITU 2007, ITU 2009. See Introduction to the Country Profiles, pp. 222–223.

Background

The Republic of Korea (commonly referred to as South Korea) was established in 1948 and spent most of its first four decades under authoritarian rule. In response to massive protests in 1987, the government eventually enacted a democratic constitution that has endured to this day. South Korea has become one of the most vibrant democracies in the eastern hemisphere, and its human rights record has markedly improved since the 1990s. Today, South Korean citizens enjoy universal suffrage and broad constitutional freedoms, and they choose their leaders in free and fair multiparty elections.

The diplomatic policies of South Korea are heavily influenced by its relationship with the Democratic People's Republic of Korea (commonly referred to as North Korea). South Korea has been technically at war since the two sides fought to a stalemate in 1953. Since then the government has often been intolerant of dissident views, particularly from supporters of communism or of North Korea.[1] The National Security Law (NSL) is the epitome of the government's stance—thousands of South Koreans have been arrested under the anticommunist law since its enactment in 1948.[2] Although prosecutions under the NSL have significantly decreased since the late 20th century, there have been a few recent high-profile investigations using the law. At the start of the 21st century, South Korea attempted a new policy of engagement with

North Korea. Known as the Sunshine Policy, it was enacted by Kim Dae-jung, the 2000 Nobel Prize laureate who served as president from 1998 until 2003.[3] However, the frequent military provocations of North Korea continue to pose ongoing threats to security in South Korea. Today, freedom of expression online in South Korea, with its political and economic complexities, is confronting a new phase of controversy.

Internet in South Korea

South Korea is one of the most connected countries and most penetrated broadband markets in the world: by 2010, more than 81 percent of citizens had access to the Internet,[4] and more than 16 million people subscribed to broadband service.[5] Following heavy investment in broadband infrastructure after the Asian financial crisis in the late 1990s, South Korea now provides its citizens with a national network that carries data at average speeds of 17 Mbps, the highest in the world.[6] Its capital, Seoul, has been named "the bandwidth capital of the world," with its fast yet inexpensive broadband service.[7] Besides Seoul, major cities in South Korea also supply wireless broadband through Wibro and High-Speed Downlink Packet Access technologies. As a result of this broad coverage, over three-quarters of South Koreans use the Internet more than once per day.[8]

As of 2010, there were 126 Internet service providers (ISPs) in the country interconnected through five Internet exchange points (IXPs).[9] However, of these 126 ISPs, three (KT, formerly known as Korea Telecom, Hanaro Telecom, and Korea Thrunet) control almost 85 percent of the broadband market share.[10] KorNet—the largest broadband supplier—provides approximately half of the ADSL lines in the country, making it the largest ADSL supplier in the world.[11]

Legal and Regulatory Frameworks

Despite South Korea's political democracy and extensive Internet connectivity, freedom of online expression has fewer protections than other democracies have. Article 21 of the Korean constitution guarantees that "all citizens shall enjoy freedom of speech and the press," and prohibits censorship of speech and the press.[12] At the same time, Article 21 contains qualifications that "neither speech nor the press shall violate the honor or rights of other persons nor undermine public morals or social ethics."[13] Through Article 21, the constitution empowers the Korean government to regulate expression in news and broadcasting media.[14]

Laying the foundation for all digital and analog content regulation, Article 53(1) of the Telecommunications Business Act (1991) provides that "a person in use of telecommunications shall not make communications with contents that harm the public peace and order or social morals and good customs."[15] Harmful communications are to be determined by presidential decree,[16] and in the original formulation, harmful communications are referred to as content that aims at or abets a criminal act, aims at committing antistate activities, or impedes good customs and other aspects of social order.[17] Harmful communications can be further restricted by order of the Ministry of Information and Communication (MIC), which delegates this authority to the Information and Communication Ethics Committee (ICEC).[18] The ICEC was established under an amended Telecommunications Business Act (1995) to regulate the content of communications and inform state policy aimed at suppressing subversive communications and "promoting active and healthy information."[19]

In June 2002, the Supreme Court struck down the provisions of the Telecommunications Business Act defining "harmful" content and granted the government unlimited authority to regulate harmful Internet content.[20] The court held Article 53(1) to be insufficiently specific and clear, and Article 53(2) to violate the rule against blanket delegation.[21] In December 2002, the National Assembly amended Article 53 to prohibit content that is "illegal" rather than "harmful," while upholding the executive powers of the MIC and the delegated regulatory authority of the ICEC.[22] This provision was ultimately repealed with the 2007 amendment of the Act on Promotion of Information and Communications Network Utilization and Information Protection (Information Act),[23] although the definition referring to "illegal" material remains in place at least functionally.[24] Illegal information included in types of information to be reported continues to be defined as that which infringes on public interests and social order, specifically obscenity, defamation, violence or cruelty, and incitement to gambling.[25]

Specific laws to protect youth, national security, and other national priorities have informed the scope of content that is regulated by government-delegated bodies responsible for filtering. For example, the NSL[26] provides "up to seven years in prison for those who praise, encourage, disseminate or cooperate with antistate groups, members or those under their control."[27] Similarly, the directive to protect the country's youth from "harmful"[28] Internet content, broadly described as "immoral, violent, obscene, speculative and antisocial information,"[29] has been one of the central planks in South Korea's filtering policy. In accordance with the Juvenile Protection Act, ISPs are responsible for making inappropriate content inaccessible on their networks.[30] Web sites carrying adult content must warn visitors and require identification verification for access—measures meant to prevent minors under 19 from accessing pornographic material.[31]

In February 2008, the Korea Communications Commission (KCC) was created to consolidate the MIC and the Korean Broadcasting Commission (KBC). Under South Korea's current legal framework, regulation of Internet content is conducted primarily by two government agencies: the Korean Communications Standards Commission (KCSC; formerly KISCOM)[32] and the National Election Commission (NEC). The KCSC integrated the functions of the KBC and KISCOM[33] in February 2008.[34] Accordingly, the two KCSC subcommissions deal separately with broadcasting and telecommunications standards.[35]

At its inception, the ICEC was empowered to develop general principles or codes of telecommunications ethics, deliberate on and request the "correction" of information declared "harmful" by presidential decree, and operate centers reporting against unhealthy telecommunications activities.[36] The KCSC telecom subcommission continues to make determinations on "requests for correction" with respect to ISPs and Internet content providers (ICPs).[37] Thus the KCSC is empowered to make determinations on information "harmful" to youth under the Juvenile Protection Act,[38] as well as recommend action against Web sites containing "illegal" content, including pornography, information for cyber criminals, and gambling services, and Web sites that express support for communism or for the government of North Korea.[39] The scope of its authority extends to ordering the blocking or closure of Web sites, the deletion of offending messages, and/or the suspension of users identified as posting improper writing.[40] In addition to special advisory committees, the KCSC also mediates disputes over online defamation. The KCSC said it received 156,000 complaints in 2006 about Internet postings considered inaccurate, and 216,000 in 2007.[41]

With President Lee's full support, government ministries proposed a battery of legislation beginning in July 2008 that would create a framework for addressing defamation, "false rumors," and "malicious postings." In July 2008, the KCC introduced the Comprehensive Measures on Internet Information Protection, which instituted 50 changes to communications and Internet regulation.[42] In amendments to the Information Act, the South Korean government further expanded the already-significant regulatory authority of the KCC by adding to online providers' liability for their users' acts. The KCSC was authorized to force providers to delete content or suspend publishing for a minimum of 30 days upon receiving a complaint of "fraudulent" or "slanderous" postings, during which the commission would determine whether disputed articles should be removed permanently.[43] Internet portals that failed to block such postings would be subject to a fine of up to KRW 30 million (just over USD 26,500) or could be forced to shut down,[44] while portals or individuals involved in improperly manipulating Internet search results could be subject to imprisonment for up to one year and a fine of up to KRW 10 million (USD 8,800).[45] In cases of leaked personal information, the KCSC requires the portal to inform the victim of the privacy breach and report the matter to the KCC.

Following an approach taken toward other emergent forms of harmful or illegal content, ICPs have increasingly taken on responsibility for policing slanderous content. Although they were already legally compelled to set up constant in-house monitoring functions,[46] Korea's two largest Internet portals also implemented their own measures to curb postings considered to violate privacy. For example, Naver created a simplified process for users to quickly block "groundless rumors or postings," and Daum required users to click on a different box if they want to read other users' comments.[47]

In July 2008, Minister of Justice Kim Kyung-hwan introduced the crime of "cyber defamation," which punishes those who insult others through the Internet with up to two years imprisonment or a KRW 10 million (USD 8,800) fine.[48] Under this rubric, criminal law applies to defamation and threats, while penalties for cyber defamation and "cyber stalking" will be pursued under information and communication laws.[49] Public figures whose personal information is widely shared on the Internet are often the primary victims of online defamation, as in the cases of Tablo[50] and Choi Jin-sil.[51] Some have called for stronger defamation laws as a result of such incidents.[52]

Government prosecutors also pursued blogger Park Dae-sung on charges of "spreading false data in public with harmful intent" following his popular writings on economic matters during the 2008 economic crisis.[53] Using the pen name Minerva, Park had criticized government economic policy and gained notoriety for accurately predicting the fall of Lehman Brothers and the crash of the won.[54] Park was acquitted in 2009 and saw a subsequent appeal dropped following a December 2010 Constitutional Court ruling that struck down the law prohibiting the spread of "misleading information with the intention of damaging the public interest."[55] The court found that the definition of "public interest" was vague and that the law violated freedom of speech, although the government may still charge individuals with spreading misinformation under the NSL.[56]

On April 1, 2009, the National Assembly adopted a "three-strikes" approach to copyright infringement, particularly file sharing and downloading movie content.[57] In an amendment to Article 133 of the Copyright Law dealing with the "collection, abandonment, and deletion of illegal reproductions," the Minister of Culture, Sports, and Tourism would be authorized to shut down message boards that refuse to comply with more than three warnings to remove copyrighted content,[58] while users who upload such content may also have their accounts canceled.[59] These punitive measures could be taken regardless of whether a takedown request by a copyright holder has been issued.[60]

Social media sites whose "main purpose is to enable different people to interactively transmit works, etc. among themselves" are treated as "special types of online service providers" under Article 104 of the Copyright Law.[61] Under Article 104, providers are obliged to take "necessary measures" to intercept the illegal interactive transmission of copyrighted works upon the request of rights holders. Article 142(1) lays out fines to a maximum of KRW 30 million (USD 26,000) for these special providers who fail to take necessary measures, while other providers who "seriously damage" copyright enforcement as a result of their failure to take down reproductions or "interactive transmissions" are also subject to fines of up to KRW 10 million (USD 8,800).[62] Under the amended legislation, providers who have been fined under Article 142(1) twice and have failed to take necessary measures can be blocked upon the issuance of a third fine.[63]

South Korea's elections framework allows significant limits to be placed on political speech prior to and during elections in order to prevent corruption, promote equal opportunity, and minimize the "damages caused by distorted election news."[64] Elections are restricted by numerous detailed prohibitions on campaign-related activities that would be standard practice in many other democracies, including elected officials endorsing a candidate,[65] conducting public opinion polls within six days of an election,[66] setting limits on campaign locations, and posting campaign materials.

The election law also extends these restrictions to campaign activities conducted on information and communication networks. Article 93 of the Public Official Election Law makes it illegal for noncandidates to distribute information supporting, recommending, or opposing any political party or candidate.[67] Election commissions that discover such information posted online may demand that the Web site or hosting service delete, restrict, or suspend the relevant information.[68]

The NEC is responsible for controlling all aspects of Korean elections, from counting votes to monitoring the media and tracing campaign contributions.[69] The NEC has used its power to censor online media platforms to remove more than 100,000 election-related articles, comments, and blog entries from the Internet,[70] as well as more than 65,000 movies posted to video-sharing Web sites.[71] The NEC began censoring the Internet in the early 2000s, partly in reaction to the significant role the Internet played in the 2002 presidential election.[72] It currently has two divisions devoted to Internet regulation and censorship: the Internet Election News Deliberation Commission (IENDC),[73] which handles newspaper Web sites and other online media sources (or "Internet press"),[74] and the Cyber Censorship Team (CCT),[75] which monitors personal blogs, videos, message-board comments, and other Web sites.[76]

Violation of the law against advocating a candidate prior to the election period can be punished with a fine of up to KRW 4 million (USD 3,500) or two years in prison.[77] The line between campaigning and normal discussion is extremely vague, and the decision to censor is made at the discretion of the CCT's officers. This vagueness has had a chilling effect on online political discourse, especially on video-sharing sites, whose election-related content has been reduced to little more than videos produced by the campaigns themselves.[78] Between the 2002 and 2007 presidential elections, the total number of deletion requests for early campaigning skyrocketed, from 2,425 to 76,277.[79] Media have also reported that from June 2006 to May 2007, up to 19,000 online election-related messages were deleted, while the authors of 13 messages containing false rumors about candidates faced legal punishment.[80]

Several security incidents in late 2010 also led officials to crack down on the spread of misinformation online. In May 2010, a South Korean warship was sunk, an act widely labeled as North Korean provocation.[81] Despite an international investigation that found North Korea responsible, online discussion forums expressed doubt, suggesting the United States was to blame.[82] Government ministers responded by ordering a crackdown on the spread of "groundless rumors" online about the incident and charged an individual with libel for criticizing military action before the sinking.[83] In addition, Defense Ministry personnel brought prominent bloggers, Twitter users, and reporters to view the wreckage in an attempt to combat skepticism.[84] South Korean military leaders warned of the potential for cyber attacks from the North during the country's hosting of the G20 Summit in early November 2010.[85] A similar crackdown was launched following the November 2010 North Korean shelling of the South Korean island of Yeonpyeong, with the Supreme Prosecutors Office launching investigations into online rumors and arresting several individuals.[86] The National Police Agency's cybercrime team also expanded their crackdown on online posts sympathetic to North Korea, forcing Web site operators to delete 42,787 messages between January and June 2010.[87]

Surveillance

The South Korean constitution guarantees that the privacy of citizens (Article 17) and the privacy of their correspondence (Article 18) shall not be violated.[88] While most scholars believe that Article 17 forms the basis of a right to privacy,[89] the Supreme Court has also held that together with Article 10, guaranteeing human dignity and the right to pursue happiness, "these constitutional provisions not only guarantee the right to be let alone, which protects personal activity from invasion by others and public exposure, but also an active right to self-control over his or her personal information in a highly informatized modern society."[90]

Internet service providers are generally directed to gather the minimum amount of information necessary and are restricted from disclosing personal information beyond the scope of notification or collecting certain personal information, such as "political ideology, religion, and medical records," that would likely infringe upon the user's privacy without consent.[91] However, these protections do not apply where special provisions apply or other laws specify otherwise.

Real-name registration requirements have been a part of the South Korean Internet landscape since 2003, when the MIC sought the cooperation of four major Web portals (Yahoo Korea, Daum Communications, NHN, and NeoWiz) in developing real-name systems for their users.[92] While implicating deeper privacy concerns, the purported goal of real-name measures is to reduce abusive behavior on the Internet. A number of prominent cases (such as the suicides of a number of actresses) have made this a major issue for the Korean public.[93]

In 2004 election laws began requiring individuals who post comments on Web sites and message boards in support of, or in opposition to, a candidate to disclose their real names.[94] In 2005 the government implemented a rule that required e-mail or chat-service account holders to provide detailed information, including name, address, profession, and identification number.[95] This policy was tightened further by the MIC in July 2007 when users were required to register their real names and resident identification numbers with Web sites before posting comments or uploading video or audio clips on bulletin boards.[96] In December 2008, the KCC extended its reach to require all forum and chat room users to make verifiable real-name registrations.[97] Furthermore, an April 2009 amendment to the Information Act took effect, requiring Korea-domain Web sites with at least 100,000 visitors daily to confirm personal identities through real names and resident registration numbers.[98] Previously, real-name registration was required for news Web sites with more than 200,000 visitors a day or portals and user-generated content sites with over 300,000 daily visitors.[99] Rather than comply with the new registration system, Google disabled the features on the Korean-language YouTube site (http://kr.youtube.com) for uploading videos and comments.[100] The real-name registration provisions of the Public Official Elections Act were unsuccessfully challenged in July 2010 when the Constitutional Court found that the requirements did not violate principles against prior censorship and that they worked to prevent "social loss and side effects which arise out of the distortion of public opinion."[101]

In 2010, Facebook faced scrutiny from the KCC, which found that "Facebook violates the regulations on protection of privacy in information networks."[102] The KCC required Facebook to submit related documents and make improvements in line with the nation's Information and Communication Law—specifically Article 22 of the Act on Promotion of Information and Communication Network Utilization and Information Protection.[103] This article requires information and communication service providers to gain consent when gathering users' personal data.[104] Facebook indirectly responded by reciting the principle of its company that "the users have control of their personal information."[105]

Amendments to the 2007 Protection of Communications Secrets Act established extensive data retention requirements and expanded the government's surveillance capabilities.[106] These amendments require telecommunications companies and ISPs to retain access records and log files (including online transactions conducted; Web sites visited; time of access; and files downloaded, edited, read, and uploaded) for at least three months, along with date and time stamps, telephone numbers of callers and receivers, and GPS location information for 12 months.[107] The National Human Rights Commission of Korea (NHRCK) criticized these amendments, particularly the use of GPS information to locate users and the imposition of penalties for service providers who refuse to comply with requests for information despite existing provisions that allow gathering of evidence by search and seizure in ordinary investigations.[108]

In 2008, three years after a scandal over the illegal wiretapping of the cell phones of influential political figures forced them to destroy their equipment, the National

Intelligence Service asked for permission to resume the practice.[109] Messages sent by e-mail (after submission and receipt) are already considered by law enforcement authorities as "objects," subject to ordinary search and seizure requirements, rather than "means of communications" requiring wiretapping warrants and notification to parties within 30 days.[110]

ONI Testing Results

OpenNet Initiative testing conducted in 2010 found levels of filtering consistent with those of 2007–2008 testing: filtering in South Korea primarily targets social content and content related to conflict and security, particularly regarding North Korea.

In November 2010, ONI conducted testing on KT Corporation (formerly Korea Telecom), the biggest South Korean ISP. This testing found a select number of blocked Web sites, with the majority of blocked sites focused on issues related to North Korea. Additional blocking occurred with sites focused on dating, pornography, and gambling. These findings are closely consistent with the results of 2007–2008 ONI testing, with a marginal increase in the blocking of sites related to North Korea. New sites that were found to be blocked include North Korea's Twitter feed; however, a North Korea–focused YouTube channel and related Facebook pages were found to be accessible.

The method of blocking used by KT Corporation differed from past test results, although those results included the testing of additional ISPs not tested in this phase. While previous testing showed evidence of IP blocking and DNS tampering, the results of 2010 testing showed that filtering was carried out through HTTP Proxy blocking. Attempts to view these Web sites were redirected to a "block page" jointly hosted by Korea's National Police Agency and the KCSC.

In 2010, ONI testing found results consistent with those seen in 2007–2008, with evidence of filtering social content and content related to conflict and security. Although the overall rate of filtering is generally low, it is primarily targeted at content related to North Korea. In addition, the government's approach to regulating content is far more reliant on other measures, such as real-name registration, takedown orders, and laws prohibiting defamation and libel.

Conclusion

South Korea has one of the most advanced and connected Internet networks in the world. Its Internet speeds are the fastest, and its usage rates the highest. Nevertheless, South Korea's government imposes more constraints on the freedom of online speech than most other democratic countries. The wide range of information blocked, from elections-related discourse to discussion about North Korea, is subject to central filtering and censorship. South Korea may represent the future of the Internet: it represents a society that is both highly tech savvy and heavily monitored. As more technology is introduced and the hostile confrontation between North and South is prolonged, the paradoxical mix of an expanded base for online expression and the restriction of online voices will continue in South Korea.

Notes

1. "South Korea Country Profile," BBC News, November 23, 2010, http://news.bbc.co.uk/2/hi/asia-pacific/country_profiles/1123668.stm.

2. Reporters Without Borders, *Enemies of the Internet—Countries under Surveillance,* http://www.rsf.org/IMG/pdf/Internet_enemies.pdf.

3. "Kim Dae-Jung: Dedicated to Reconciliation," CNN, June 14, 2001, http://archives.cnn.com/2001/WORLD/asiapcf/east/06/12/bio.kim.daejung/.

4. International Telecommunication Union (ITU), "Internet Indicators: Subscribers, Users and Broadband Subscribers," 2009 Figures, http://www.itu.int/ITU-D/icteye/Reporting/ShowReportFrame.aspx?ReportName=/WTI/InformationTechnologyPublic&ReportFormat=HTML4.0&RP_intYear=2009&RP_intLanguageID=1&RP_bitLiveData=False.

5. Korea Internet and Security Agency, "2010 Survey on the Wireless Internet Usage Executive Summary," September 29, 2010, http://isis.kisa.or.kr/board/?pageId=060200&bbsId=3&itemId=788; Korea Internet and Security Agency, "Broadband Subscribers," http://isis.kisa.or.kr/eng/sub01/?pageId=010400.

6. Darren Allen, "South Korea Tops Akamai Broadband Averages with 17 Mbps," TechWatch, October 21, 2010, http://www.techwatch.co.uk/2010/10/21/south-korea-tops-akamai-broadband-averages-with-17mbps.

7. J.C. Hertz, "The Bandwidth Capital of the World," *Wired,* October 12, 2010, http://www.wired.com/wired/archive/10.08/korea.html.

8. National Internet Development Agency of Korea, "Survey on the Computer and Internet Usage," September 2008, http://isis.nida.or.kr.

9. National Internet Development Agency of Korea, "Korea Internet White Paper," 2010, http://isis.nida.or.kr/eng/ebook/ebook.html.

10. Paul Budde Communications Pty., Ltd., "South Korea Broadband Market—Overview and Statistics," July 24, 2010, http://www.budde.com.au/Research/South-Korea-Broadband-Market-Overview-Statistics-and-Forecasts.html.

11. Ibid.

12. Constitutional Court of Korea, Constitution of the Republic of Korea, Article 21, October 29, 1987, http://english.ccourt.go.kr/home/att_file/download/Constitution_of_the_Republic_of_Korea.pdf.

13. Ibid.

14. Ibid.

15. Telecommunications Business Act, wholly amended by presidential decree no. 13558 on August 10, 1991, Decisions of the Korean Constitutional Court, Opinion 14–1 KCCR 616, 99Hun-Ma480, June 27, 2002.

16. Ibid., Article 53(2).

17. Enforcement Decree of Telecommunications Business Act, Article 16, wholly amended by presidential decree no. 13558 on December 31, 1991, Decisions of the Korean Constitutional Court, Opinion 14–1 KCCR 616, 99Hun-Ma480, June 27, 2002, http://english.ccourt.go.kr/home/english/decisions/mgr_decision_view.jsp?seq=224&code=1&pg=1&sch_code=&sch_sel=sch_content&sch_txt=99Hun-Ma480&nScale=15.

18. Ibid.

19. Telecommunications Business Act, Law 4903, Article 53–2, January 5, 1995, http://www.itu.int/ITU-D/treg/Legislation/Korea/BusinessAct.htm.

20. "Decisions of the Korean Constitutional Court, Opinion 14–1 KCCR 616, 99Hun-Ma480," June 27, 2002, http://english.ccourt.go.kr/home/english/decisions/mgr_decision_view.jsp?seq=224&code=1&pg=1&sch_code=&sch_sel=sch_content&sch_txt=99Hun-Ma480&nScale=15.

21. Ibid.

22. Act on Promotion of Information and Communications Network Utilization and Information Protection, Law No. 8289, January 16, 2007, http://eng.kcc.go.kr/download.do?fileNm=TELECOMMUNICATIONS_BUSINESS_ACT.pdf; Privacy International and the GreenNet Educational Trust, "Silenced: An International Report on Censorship and Control of the Internet," September 2003, https://www.privacyinternational.org/survey/censorship/Silenced.pdf.

23. Ibid.

24. On its Web site, the Korea Communications Standards Commission defines illegal information as "all sorts of information against the positive law of the Republic of Korea, that is, information infringed upon the public interests and social orders." Korea Communications Standards Commission, "Subject of Report," http://www.singo.or.kr/eng/02_report/Subject_Report.php.

25. Ibid.

26. The NSL has been used to criminalize advocacy of communism and groups suspected of alignment with North Korea, although arrests under the NSL have become much less frequent in recent years. Nevertheless, the law continues to have a chilling effect on public discussion of North Korea and provides a justification for censorship of Web sites related to North Korea and communism. See Ser Myo-ja, "Security Law Marks 60 Years of Strife," *Korea JoongAng Daily*, September 1, 2008, http://joongangdaily.joins.com/article/view.asp?aid=2894346; Human Rights

Watch, "Retreat from Reform: Labor Rights and Freedom of Expression in South Korea," November 1, 1990, http://www.hrw.org/en/reports/1990/11/01/retreat-reform; Brad Adams, "South Korea Should Act Like It Knows," Human Rights Watch, April 13, 2006, http://www.hrw.org/en/news/2006/04/12/south-korea-should-act-it-knows; Brad Adams, "South Korea: Defend Human Rights," Human Rights Watch, January 15, 2008, http://www.hrw.org/en/news/2008/01/22/south-korea-defend-human-rights.

27. National Security Law, Article 7(1). Unofficial English translation is available at: http://www.hartford-hwp.com/archives/55a/205.html.

28. The standard of harm in the Enforcement Decree of the Juvenile Protection Act (JPA) was developed from "criteria for deliberation of media materials harmful to juveniles," which include provocative, obscene, antisocial, violent, or unethical materials that may harmfully affect youths' mental and physical health. See http://www.ccourt.go.kr/home/english/decisions/mgr_decision_view.jsp?seq=224&code=1.

29. Adams, "South Korea: Defend Human Rights."

30. Act on Promotion of Information and Communication Network Utilization and Information Protection (2001), Article 42.

31. Act on Promotion of Information and Communication Network Utilization and Information Protection (2001), Article 42; Korea Herald, "45 Websites Violate Youth Law," March 31, 2009.

32. Korea Communications Standards Commission (KCSC), http://www.singo.or.kr/eng/01_introduction/introduction.php.

33. KISCOM's mandate was originally established through the creation of the ICEC in 1995. See http://www.itu.int/ITU-D/treg/Legislation/Korea/BusinessAct.htm.

34. KCSC, "Chronology," http://www.icec.or.kr/eng/01_About/Chronology.php.

35. Telecommunications Business Act (1995), Law 4903, Article 53–2, January 5, 1995, http://www.itu.int/ITU-D/treg/Legislation/Korea/BusinessAct.htm.

36. Ibid.

37. For an explanation of the reporting process of suspected illegal content, see KCSC, "Report Process," http://www.singo.or.kr/eng/02_report/Process.php.

38. KCSC, "Committees," http://www.icec.or.kr/eng/02_Operation/Committees.php.

39. KCSC, "Subject of Report," http://www.singo.or.kr/eng/02_report/Subject_Report.php; Reporters Without Borders, South Korea—2004 Annual Report (2004), http://en.rsf.org/report-south-korea,59.html.

40. "Decisions of the Korean Constitutional Court, Opinion 14–1 KCCR 616, 99Hun-Ma480," June 27, 2002, http://english.ccourt.go.kr/home/english/decisions/mgr_decision_view.jsp?seq=224&code=1&pg=1&sch_code=&sch_sel=sch_content&sch_txt=99Hun-Ma480&nScale=15.

41. Kim Hyung-eun, "Do New Internet Regulations Curb Free Speech?" *Korea JoongAng Daily*, August 13, 2008, http://joongangdaily.joins.com/article/view.asp?aid=2893577.

42. Jung Ha-won, "Internet to Be Stripped of Anonymity," *Korea JoongAng Daily*, July 23, 2008, http://joongangdaily.joins.com/article/view.asp?aid=2892691.

43. Michael Fitzpatrick, "South Korea Wants to Gag the Noisy Internet Rabble," *Guardian*, October 8, 2008, http://www.guardian.co.uk/technology/2008/oct/09/news.internet; Kim Tong-hyung, "Cabinet Backs Crackdown on Cyber-bullying," *Korea Times*, July 22, 2008, http://www.koreatimes.co.kr/www/news/biz/2008/07/123_28003.html.

44. Park Sung-woo, "Court Says Web Portals Are Responsible for Comments," *Korea JoongAng Daily*, April 18, 2009, http://joongangdaily.joins.com/article/view.asp?aid=2903746.

45. Lee Sang-bok, "New Regulations Proposed for Internet Postings," *Korea JoongAng Daily*, August 21, 2008, http://joongangdaily.joins.com/article/view.asp?aid=2893939.

46. Kim Hyung-eun, "Do New Internet Regulations Curb Free Speech?"

47. Sung So-young, "Portals Beef Up Measures against Malicious Postings," *Korea JoongAng Daily*, October 23, 2008, http://joongangdaily.joins.com/article/view.asp?aid=2896433.

48. Ser Myo-ja, "GNP Files Bills to Alter the Nation's Media Landscape," *Korea JoongAng Daily*, December 4, 2008, http://joongangdaily.joins.com/article/view.asp?aid=2898166.

49. Lee Sang-eon and Chun In-sung, "Cyber Terror Sleuths Planning Internet Crackdown," *Korea JoongAng Daily*, October 6, 2008, http://joongangdaily.joins.com/article/view.asp?aid=2895724.

50. In 2010, Tablo, the leader of a Korean hip-hop band called Epik High, faced months-long doubt and accusation over the accuracy of his school records. An Internet group called "We Urge Tablo to Tell the Truth (Tajinyo)" raised suspicion in a television documentary produced to reveal the truth of Tablo's Stanford degree. Although his graduation from Stanford University was later verified, in August 2010 Tablo filed a libel suit against the bloggers, and a police investigation was opened. See Park Si-soo, "Tablo-Bashing Website Shut Down," *Korea Times*, October 22, 2010, http://www.koreatimes.co.kr/www/news/nation/2010/10/117_75055.html; *Korea Herald,* editorial, "Virus of Distrust," October 17, 2010, http://www.koreaherald.com/opinion/Detail.jsp?newsMLId=20101010000069; Park Si-soo, "Police Confirm Singer Tablo Graduated from Stanford," *Korea Times*, October 8, 2010, http://www.koreatimes.co.kr/www/news/nation/2010/10/117_74232.html; Kim Yoon-mi, "Tablo's Diploma Confirmed," October 8, 2010, http://www.koreaherald.com/entertainment/Detail.jsp?newsMLId=20101008000688.

51. In 2008, actress Choi Jin-sil committed suicide after suffering online harassment. See Choe Sang-hun, "Korean Star's Suicide Reignites Debate on Web Regulation," *New York Times*, October 12, 2008, http://www.nytimes.com/2008/10/13/technology/internet/13suicide.html.

52. "A Law for Choi Jin-sil," *Korea JoongAng Daily,* October 4, 2008, http://joongangdaily.joins.com/article/view.asp?aid=2895644.

53. Choe Sang-hun, "South Korea Frees Blogger Who Angered Government," *New York Times*, April 20, 2009, http://www.nytimes.com/2009/04/21/world/asia/21blogger.html; Oh Byung-sang, "After Minerva: Gaining Balance," *Korea JoongAng Daily*, April 24, 2009, http://joongangdaily.joins.com/article/view.asp?aid=2903946.

54. Ser Myo-ja, "Prognosticator 'Minerva' Is Acquitted by a Seoul Court," *Korea JoongAng Daily*, April 21, 2009, http://joongangdaily.joins.com/article/view.asp?aid=2903837.

55. Bae Ji-sook, "Prosecution Confirms 'Minerva' Innocent," *Korea Herald*, January 4, 2011, http://www.koreaherald.com/national/Detail.jsp?newsMLId=20110104000750.

56. Song Jung-a, "South Korean Court Rules on Internet Law," *Financial Times*, December 28, 2010, http://www.ft.com/cms/s/0/38b354a4-126d-11e0-b4c8-00144feabdc0.html.

57. "South Korea Passes Three-Strikes Internet Piracy Law," IP World, April 15, 2009, http://www.ipworld.com/ipwo/doc/view.htm?id=217097&searchCode=H. http://news.softpedia.com/news/File-Sharers-Cornered-Again-84010.shtml.

58. Proposed Amendment to Copyright Law of Korea, July 2008, Article 133–2(3). Unofficial English translation is available at http://ipleft.or.kr/bbs/view.php?board=ipleft_5&id=488&page=1&category1=3.

59. Ibid.

60. Nate Anderson, "South Korea Fits Itself for a '3 Strikes' Jackboot," Ars Technica, April 15, 2009, http://arstechnica.com/tech-policy/news/2009/04/korea-fits-itself-for-a-3-strikes-jackboot.ars.

61. Copyright Law of Korea, Article 104, http://eng.copyright.or.kr/law_01_01.html.

62. Ibid., Article 142(1).

63. Proposed Amendment to Copyright Law of Korea, Article 133–2(4)(1).

64. National Election Commission, "About IENDC," http://www.nec.go.kr/engvote/about/iendc.jsp.

65. Public Official Election Law, Act No. 8879, February 29, 2008, Article 86, http://www.nec.go.kr/english/NEC/Public_Official_Election.zip. Former President Roh Moo-hyun was charged by the NEC and impeached for violating this law. He was later reinstated as president. See "Obituary: Roh Moo-hyun," BBC News, May 23, 2009, http://news.bbc.co.uk/2/hi/asia-pacific/2535143.stm.

66. Public Official Election Law, Article 108.

67. Ibid., Article 93.

68. Ibid., Articles 82–84 (3–5).

69. ONI interview with an official from the IENDC.

70. National Election Commission, "The Overview of Cyber Crackdown Service Related to the 18th National Election."

71. Bruce Wallace, "Emotions Don't Reach S. Korea Voters," *Los Angeles Times*, December 15, 2007, http://articles.latimes.com/2007/dec/15/world/fg-korea15.

72. "The 2007 Korean Presidential Elections and Internet Censorship," Internet and Democracy Blog, January 16, 2008, http://blogs.law.harvard.edu/idblog/2008/01/16/the-2007-korean-presidential -elections-and-internet-censorship/.

73. The IENDC's mission is to ensure that newspaper Web sites, online news agencies, and other semiofficial online news sources are impartial in their campaign coverage and do not violate election laws. The IENDC has a great deal of discretion to decide what constitutes a violation of these rules and to censor the Internet press accordingly. Generally, it does so by contacting the relevant Internet press organizations and telling them to change their content or to issue a correction. See National Election Commission Web site, "About IENDC," http://www.nec.go.kr/ english/NEC/nec_IENDC01.html.

74. Public Official Election Law, Article 8–5(1). According to the NEC, IENDC bans the Internet media from doing the following: (1) Reporting on public opinion polls during the two- to three-week election period, or reporting on polls during any other period in a way the IENDC considers biased or inaccurate; (2) using headlines that "reduce, overstate or distort" election-related news; (3) reporting "distorted or false" news by "overstating, highlighting, cutting or hiding important facts that may have substantial impacts on the decisions of voters"; (4) falsely attributing any statements or other actions to candidates or political parties; (5) misinforming voters with reports on election results estimated without any reasonable basis; (6) failing to draw a sharp line between facts and opinions; (7) failing to equally represent different points of view when asking candidates or other people for their opinions; (8) modifying pictures or videos to create a negative portrayal of a candidate; (9) allowing opinion advertisements that support or oppose a particular party or candidate. See National Election Commission Web site, Internet Election News Deliberation Commission Regulation No. 1, Articles 1–18.

75. Since it started in 2002, the CCT polices blogs, personal Web sites, video postings, and message boards. Its three main tasks are to prevent damaging and untrue statements about candidates during an election, to maintain the prohibition against campaigning outside of election periods, and to ensure that all users make comments during an election with only their full, real names. All three tasks are usually executed by requesting that the Web site's hosting service delete or change offending content, potentially opening an investigation, and pressing charges if the hosting service refuses (ONI interview with an official from the Cyber Censorship Team). Monitoring is carried out by about 1,000 part-time workers who are hired nationwide 120 days before every election to run a search program to find and flag suspicious content (ONI interview with IENDC official).

76. ONI interview with an official from the Cyber Censorship Team.

77. Offending acts include posting long opinions of political parties on Web portals and Web sites, posting comments on online news articles, or any similar acts on personal Web sites or

blogs. However, the NEC has stated that "there is small chance that citizens will face legal charges for posting their opinion as they will be viewed flexibly in actual crackdowns." See Shin Hae-in, "Korea: Controversy Mounts over Ban on Internet Election," *Korea Herald*, June 25, 2007, http://www.asiamedia.ucla.edu/print.asp?parentid=72445.

78. Wallace, "Emotions Don't Reach S. Korea Voters."

79. Yoo Jae-il, Sohn Byung-kwon, et al., 'The 18 Political Scientists' Participatory Observation of the 18th Korean National Assembly Election in 2008," Purungil.

80. Shin Hae-in, "Korea: Controversy Mounts."

81. "Times Topics—he Cheonan (Ship)," *New York Times*, May 20, 2010, http://topics.nytimes.com/top/reference/timestopics/subjects/c/cheonan_ship/index.html.

82. Christian Oliver, "South Koreans Fear Unmasking of Online Critics," *Financial Times*, July 8, 2010, http://www.ft.com/cms/s/0/af902db6-8aac-11df-8e17-00144feab49a.html.

83. Bae Ji-sook, "Government Warns against 'Groundless Rumors,'" *Korea Times*, May 20, 2010, http://www.koreatimes.co.kr/www/news/nation/2010/05/117_66222.html.

84. Christian Oliver and Kang Buseong, "Seoul Turns to Twitter to Combat Skeptics," *Financial Times*, May 31, 2010.

85. Jung Sung-ki, "Military Leaders Warn of NK Cyber Attack," *Korea Times*, June 8, 2010, http://www.koreatimes.co.kr/www/news/nation/2010/06/113_67314.html.

86. Bae Ji-sook, "Prosecution Investigates Groundless Rumormongers," *Korea Times*, November 24, 2010, http://www.koreatimes.co.kr/www/news/nation/2010/11/117_76912.html.

87. Lee Tae-hoon, "Censorship on Pro-NK Websites Tight," *Korea Times*, September 9, 2010, http://www.koreatimes.co.kr/www/news/nation/2010/09/113_72788.html.

88. Constitution of the Republic of Korea, Articles 17–18, http://english.ccourt.go.kr/home/att_file/download/Constitution_of_the_Republic_of_Korea.pdf.

89. Soon Chul Huh, "Invasion of Privacy v. Commercial Speech: Regulation of Spam with a Comparative Constitutional Point of View," *Albany Law Review,* 2006, *70 Alb. L. Rev. 181.*

90. 96 Da 42789 (S. Korea 1998).

91. Act on Promotion of Information and Communications Network Utilization and Information Protection, Articles 22–24.

92. Winston Chai, "Real User IDs on Chat Groups: Korean Govt," ZDNet Asia, May 23, 2003, http://www.zdnetasia.com/real-user-ids-on-chat-groups-korean-govt-39133165.htm.

93. Choe Sang-Hun, "Web Rumors Tied to Korean Actress's Suicide," *New York Times*, October 2, 2008, http://www.nytimes.com/2008/10/03/world/asia/03actress.html.

94. Public Official Election Law, Article 82–6.

95. "Internet Real-Name System Boosts Cyber Security in S Korea," Xinhua, April 24, 2008, http://news.xinhuanet.com/english/2008-04/24/content_8039953.htm.

96. "Web Identification System Not Effective," *Korea Herald,* July 3, 2007.

97. Brian Lee, "What Happens When Intelligence Fails," *Korea JoongAng Daily,* September 28, 2008, http://joongangdaily.joins.com/article/view.asp?aid=2895216; Fitzpatrick, "South Korea Wants to Gag the Noisy Internet Rabble."

98. Antone Gonsalves, "Google Scales Back YouTube Korea," *Information Week*, April 13, 2009, http://www.informationweek.com/news/internet/google/showArticle.jhtml?articleID=216500489; Martyn Williams, "Google Disables Uploads, Comments on YouTube Korea," *PC World*, April 13, 2009, http://www.pcworld.com/article/162989/google_disables_uploads_comments_on_youtube_korea.html.

99. Kim Hyung-eun, "Do New Internet Regulations Curb Free Speech?" *Korea JoongAng Daily,* August 13, 2008, http://joongangdaily.joins.com/article/view.asp?aid=2893577.

100. Gonsalves, "Google Scales Back YouTube Korea."

101. Constitutional Court of Korea, "Real Name Verification of the Internet News Site Case," February 25, 2010, http://www.ccourt.go.kr/home/english/decisions/rcnt_decision_view.jsp?seq=513&pg=1&sch_sel=&sch_txt=&nScale=15&sch_code=9.

102. Martyn Williams, "Facebook in Breach of Korean Privacy Laws, Says Regulator," *Computer World*, December 8, 2010, http://www.computerworld.com/s/article/9200458/Facebook_in_breach_of_Korean_privacy_laws_says_regulator.

103. Act on Promotion of Information and Communications Network Utilization and Information Protection, Article 22, http://unpan1.un.org/intradoc/groups/public/documents/APCITY/UNPAN025694.pdf; Lee Min-hyung, "The KCC's Facebook Tackling," Digital Daily, December 14, 2010, http://www.ddaily.co.kr/news/news_view.php?uid=72089.

104. Ibid.

105. Jung Yuni, "Youtube, Facebook Sweating Hard Due to the Korean Market," ZD NET Korea, December 14, 2010, http://www.zdnet.co.kr/ArticleView.asp?artice_id=20101214153147.

106. "PHR2006—Republic of (South) Korea," Privacy International, December 18, 2007, https://www.privacyinternational.org/article/phr2006-republic-south-korea.

107. Asian Legal Resource Centre, "South Korea: Concerns about the Freedom of Expression and the Possible Resumption of Executions," June 4, 2009, http://www.alrc.net/doc/mainfile.php/alrc_st2009/562/http://www.humanrights.go.kr/english/activities/view_01.jsp?seqid=713&board_id=Press%20Releases.

108. National Human Rights Commission of Korea, "NHRCK Announces Opinion on Proposed Amendments to the Protection of Communications Secrets Act," January 30, 2008, http://www.humanrights.go.kr/english/download.jsp?board_id=Press%20Releases&filename=Communications%20Secrets%20Act.doc.

109. Brian Lee, "What Happens When Intelligence Fails," *Korea JoongAng Daily,* September 28, 2008, http://joongangdaily.joins.com/article/view.asp?aid=2895216; "S. Korean Spy Agency Admits Conducting Illegal Wiretapping," *People's Daily*, August 5, 2005, http://english.people .com.cn/200508/05/eng20050805_200519.html.

110. "Prosecutors Have Indiscriminate Access to Personal Email Communications," The Hankyoreh, April 24, 2009, http://english.hani.co.kr/arti/english_edition/e_national/351496.html.

Thailand

Amid political crisis, a deep social divide, and the uncertainty of royal succession, Thailand's Internet has become a contested terrain of various political views and movements. While the government has employed both legal and technological means to censor, filter, and control Internet content and communication, service providers and users resort to intermediary censorship and self-censorship, 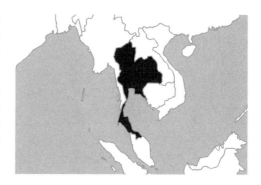 and dissidents resist the control, using evasion and circumvention tools and campaigning for freedom and transparency. Lèse-majesté, a deep-seated tradition in Thai society, has become a tool for clamping down on dissenting opinion and a basis for many online users to integrate state control into their own cyber behavior as they participate voluntarily in the surveillance and censorship of the Internet.

RESULTS AT A GLANCE

Filtering	No Evidence of Filtering	Suspected Filtering	Selective Filtering	Substantial Filtering	Pervasive Filtering
Political			•		
Social			•		
Conflict and security	•				
Internet tools			•		

OTHER FACTORS

	Low	Medium	High	Not Applicable
Transparency		•		
Consistency		•		

KEY INDICATORS	
GDP per capita, PPP (constant 2005 international dollars)	7,258
Life expectancy at birth, total (years)	63
Literacy rate, adult total (percent of people age 15+)	64.9
Human Development Index (out of 169)	92
Rule of Law (out of 5)	1.6
Voice and Accountability (out of 5)	1.5
Democracy Index (out of 167)	57 (Flawed democracy)
Digital Opportunity Index (out of 181)	151
Internet penetration rate (percentage of population)	25.8

Source by indicator: World Bank 2009, World Bank 2008a, World Bank 2008b, UNDP 2010, World Bank Worldwide Governance Indicators 2009, Economist Intelligence Unit 2010, ITU 2007, ITU 2009. See Introduction to the Country Profiles, pp. 222–223.

Background

Thai politics, long famous for coups and military dominance, shifted course in 2001 with the emergence of a single-party civilian government led by Prime Minister Thaksin Shinawatra and his Thai Rak Thai (TRT) Party. The TRT Party won landslide victories in two general elections in 2001 and 2005, becoming the second party in 73 years to form a single-party government. Thaksin, a former telecommunications tycoon who made his fortune from monopoly government concessions, was also the first prime minister to have completed a full four-year term in office. Despite his popularity, Thaksin is widely criticized for his authoritarian traits, outspokenness, and conflict of interest over his family business—Shin Corporation. A deal to sell a major stake in Shin Corporation to an investment firm owned by the Singaporean government mobilized a large number of the urban middle class to rally for Thaksin's resignation,[1] culminating in the formation of a royalist anti-Thaksin movement called the People's Alliance for Democracy (PAD), or the "yellow shirts." This public anger and protest was a prelude to the military coup that toppled Thaksin on September 19, 2006.[2]

Years of political turmoil followed the coup, and Thailand's political situation remains volatile. The rift between the United Front for Democracy against Dictatorship (UDD), or the "red shirts," which supports the ousted Thaksin, and the Yellow Shirts has deepened into a social divide. The opposing forces have become a reflection of the clash between an urban middle class on one side and the rural poor on the other.[3] Demands by the UDD for fresh elections resulted in a series of protests in Bangkok, with most of the protestors coming from outside the city. During April and May 2010, the demonstrations erupted into violence when military crackdowns were launched in order to disperse the antigovernment protestors.[4] Up to 90 people were killed and almost 2,000 were injured in the political mayhem that gripped the country between March 12 and May 19, 2010.[5] During the political unrest, the government issued a State of Emergency Decree on April 8, 2010, to block 36 Web sites that primarily had content sympathetic to the red shirts.[6] In addition to this state-sanctioned censorship, the Internet community in Thailand also appears to censor itself.

Internet in Thailand

The number of Internet users in Thailand has increased exponentially from 2.3 million in 2000 to 18.3 million in 2009,[7] resulting in an estimated penetration rate of 25.8 percent in 2009.[8] In 2010 international bandwidth for the entire country was 156,680 Mbps, while domestic bandwidth was 721,217 Mbps.[9] Nearly half of all Internet users are between 20 and 29 years old. Nearly half, 46.8 percent, of users access the Internet in educational institutions, 33.4 percent at home, and 29 percent at work.[10] Fifty-five percent of Internet users are concentrated in Bangkok and the greater Bangkok area.[11] Of these users, 43.5 percent access the Internet through broadband.[12]

According to the data from the National Electronics and Computer Technology Center (NECTEC), Thailand has six international Internet gateways (IIGs), which also serve as national Internet exchanges.[13] There are about 20 Internet service providers (ISPs) that are active and carrying Internet traffic. In 2010, TOTNET, TRUE, and 3BB dominated the market, holding market shares of 40.24 percent, 29.79 percent, and 25.60, respectively.[14] Half the operating ISPs are semiconcessionaires with 35 percent of their shares held by default by CAT Telecom,[15] a corporatized state enterprise and a long-standing international carrier monopoly.[16] The remaining ISPs are new operators that emerged as a result of the telecommunications reform following the establishment in 2004 of the National Telecommunications Commission (NTC), the country's first independent regulator of telecommunications. The commission has been issuing licenses for telecommunications services and Internet services since 2005. So far, a total of 130 licenses have been issued for telecommunications services, and 132 for Internet.[17] These figures reflect a two-tiered structure of Internet regulation. On one side, there are the prereform semiconcessionaires that are highly liable to CAT Telecom, which answers directly to the Ministry of Information and Communications Technology (MICT). On the other side, there are the postreform ISPs that operate under licenses issued from the NTC. This structure leads to somewhat of a double standard in Internet regulation and filtering.

The government has established the Government Information Network (GIN) to promote the level of information communication technology (ICT) employed in its agencies ranging from ministry level to department level. The main objective of this network is to create an e-government, which will pave the way for a government Internet gateway solely for state agencies.[18]

The top three most popular Web sites are sanook.com, kapook.com, and mthai.com, all of which are Web portals.[19] Thai users' primary purposes for accessing the Internet are to seek news and information (29.7 percent), to send e-mails (21.9 percent), and to engage in e-learning (8 percent).[20] The number of users accessing social networking Web sites has steadily increased. Within a span of nine months in 2010, the number of Facebook users in Thailand more than doubled from 2 million in January to more than 5 million in September.[21] The sharp increase in use and growth of awareness about Facebook can be attributed to the political crisis in March to May 2010. The extensive media censorship enforced under emergency decree triggered political discourse to move to the highly interactive and participatory platform. Given Facebook's recent announcement of 500 million active users worldwide,[22] this means that Thailand now accounts for more than 1 percent of the total active Facebook population worldwide.

Legal and Regulatory Frameworks

The MICT is responsible for ICT policy and oversight across the country. The second ICT master plan (2009–2013) aims to provide countrywide broadband, the so-called National Broadband Policy.[23] This is a part of the ICT Scheme 2020, which was drafted as a framework to develop the national ICT infrastructure. One of the main objectives of the master plan is to increase broadband Internet access to 80 percent of the population by 2015.[24]

The NTC is the country's telecommunications regulatory authority. Apart from its main responsibility in managing radio and telecommunication frequencies, the NTC also has the authority to grant licenses for Internet service, international Internet gateways, and Voice over Internet Protocol (VoIP) service.

An Internet filtering regime began in Thailand in 2002 with the establishment of a filtering unit within the MICT called the Cyber Inspector. The Cyber Inspector focused its filtering activity on issues such as pornography, negative comments about the monarchy, gambling, terrorism, and separatist movements.[25] However, its existence and role were widely questioned by the public because of a lack of legal grounds for filtering. The legalization of Internet filtering began in 2007 with the enactment of the controversial Computer Crime Act. This law was the first to be passed during the interim legislature appointed by the military junta. Apart from carrying broad-based provisions on content regulation, a tradition quite unusual for cybercrime law, this relatively new law also allows competent officials (who are appointed by the minister of ICT) to apply for court orders to seize computer equipment and to block

Web sites.[26] Furthermore, since 2008, an automatic URL filtering system has been installed at IIGs under CAT Telecom to filter objectionable materials, with lèse-majesté content being the prime target.[27]

Lèse-majesté, which refers to punishment for any negative public remarks about the monarchy, is strongly enforced in Thailand. The Thai criminal code specifies that whoever "defames, insults or threatens the King, Queen, the heir-apparent or the Regent" can be jailed for three to 15 years.[28] Although lèse-majesté was not included as a deterrent to Internet content in the law, it was incorporated under the broad provision of national security because the Thai nation-state is understood to rest on three pillars—the nation, the Buddhist religion, and the monarchy.[29] For this reason and because of the social divide between supporters of the monarchy and supporters of Thaksin Shinawatra, lèse-majesté has been increasingly invoked to censor Web sites. According to recent research, there was one court order to block two URLs in 2007, whereas in 2008 there were 13 court orders to block 2,071 URLs.[30] There were 64 orders in 2009 resulting in 28,705 Web sites ordered blocked. The number of Web sites ordered to be blocked rose to 43,908 in 2010.[31] Within three years after the enforcement of the Computer Crime Act, there have been 117 court orders to block access to 74,686 URLs.[32] Given the far-reaching power of this act, there is increasing evidence that this law is being employed as a political tool.[33]

A recent notable case of lèse-majesté being used to prosecute individuals for online actions is that of Chiranuch Premchaiporn, Web master of the popular online news portal Prachatai. Chiranuch was first charged in March 2009 under Section 15 of the Computer-Related Offenses act for intermediary liability or consent/negligence of operators for offenses to be committed. These charges were brought down because of alleged lèse-majesté comments posted on the Prachatai forum by users, which Chiranuch claims were removed immediately following the first notice from police. In September 2010, she was arrested and served new charges following reentry into Thailand after attending a Google-sponsored conference on Internet liberty. These further charges included lèse-majesté offenses for publishing an interview on Prachatai with a Thai man who was arrested and charged with lèse-majesté for refusing to stand during the royal anthem in a cinema.[34] A trial started in February 2011, with a verdict expected in April 2011. Chiranuch faces ten separate charges, each of which carries a maximum sentence of five years in jail. This case is a stark example of Thai legislation used to prosecute individuals for intermediary liability for lèse-majesté content and has raised concerns for freedom of expression in communities across the world.[35]

To bypass Internet censorship, many activists and dissidents use anonymizers and circumvention software.[36] With the recent enforcement of the State of Emergency Decree, online users and online service providers (OSPs) also self-censor or strictly monitor content to avoid prosecution under the Computer Crime Act. Public education and campaigns against the government's Internet control have also been carried out, mostly by the so-called Thai Netizen Network (TNN), a relatively new local nongovernmental organization (NGO) that advocates for Internet freedom. Increasingly, TNN has become allied with several international NGOs concerned with media freedom, including Freedom House and the Electronic Frontier Foundation.

Surveillance

Without an explicit privacy law in place, several data surveillance schemes have been administered since at least 1981 in Thailand without adequate legal safeguards, including the computerized and online civil registration system, a microchip national ID card system, a computerized criminal records database system, and surveillance cameras in public areas.[37] However, the public generally views these systems as part of the long-standing civil registration system and data infrastructure and not as surveillance schemes. For online surveillance, state-controlled IIGs and ISPs have been instructed to look into interactive communication in online forums hosted under their networks, focusing on lèse-majesté speech, and to give a 30-minute time frame for taking down such content. While the new surveillance scheme is not public knowledge, members of the public are unlikely to object to it, since filtering is rationalized on the grounds of lèse-majesté. More technologically savvy dissidents and civic workers have evaded the surveillance by relocating to host services overseas and by using circumvention software.

In a recent example of cybercrime law enforcement, local Internet advocates and media for the first time posited privacy rights as being undermined by law enforcers' zeal to track and crack down on sources of rumors surrounding the king's ailing condition.[38] This development followed the arrest of two suspects who posted the "problematic information (about the king)" in two popular online forums.[39] Prompted by this incident, the Department of Special Investigation (DSI) reportedly sought court orders to look into the e-mail communication of all the people who had posted on related topics on the two forums.[40]

Many Internet users also participate in online surveillance of lèse-majesté. For instance, a fan page called Social Sanction was developed for reporting lèse-majesté comments posted on Facebook.[41] A teenage girl was socially reprimanded after her damaging posts on the king were publicized on the Social Sanction page. Her admission to a prestigious university was denied on grounds of social misconduct, stemming from her "problematic" online speech.[42]

Although there is no comprehensive national law that addresses privacy in Thailand, there is a constitutional guarantee for the right to privacy in the section on protection of rights and liberties of citizens in the current constitution of 2007. Existing laws contain no direct stipulations about violation of "privacy" per se.[43] There is a section in the Freedom of Official Information Law (passed in 1997) that addresses protection of personal data kept in government files.[44]

A draft data protection law has been in existence since 1996 but has yet to materialize. In the latest development, in October 2009, the Cabinet agreed in principle to forward the draft law for Parliament reading.[45] The next step will be to appoint commissioners for the reading of the draft law. However, with other legislative priorities and inherent political instability, the draft law was sidestepped and has not yet made it to the legislative agenda.

Meanwhile, the new Cybercrime Law passed in 2007 has delegated full authority to state officials in surveillance, censorship, and control of Internet information and communication. For instance, Section 18 of this law authorized designated competent officials to do the following:

• Summon an alleged party to appear, report to, or send documents, information, or evidence.
• Request computer-based traffic information and other information that concerns Internet users from service providers and parties involved.
• Duplicate computer information and computer-based traffic information.
• Decrypt, censor, and access computer systems, computer information, computer-based traffic information, or equipment used to store computer information.
• Confiscate or "freeze" any computer system.[46]

The 2007 Computer Crime Act required all service providers—ISPs, OSPs, Web masters, Web moderators, and Internet cafés—to keep a log file of their users including IP addresses for 90 days.[47] This requirement necessitated setting up an identification and authentication clearance system for users as a condition for accessing the Internet—in other words, a surveillance system operated by service providers.

Findings from a series of focus groups on surveillance and privacy conducted in Bangkok found that there is a disparity with regard to public perception and knowledge of information privacy between different socioeconomic classes.[48] Those from the upper socioeconomic strata are generally more concerned with privacy rights and threats from personal data collection and use, and possess a greater understanding of information privacy, while those from a lower socioeconomic background tend to be less concerned with surveillance practices because they do not see privacy as being a part of their basic needs; rather, they are more concerned with making ends meet. The latter were also found to be less likely to challenge surveillance practices because they have less knowledge of surveillance technologies and a feeling of general powerlessness vis-à-vis the state.[49]

In recent years, new Internet applications such as social networking Web sites have emerged as popular communication tools among the younger generations in Thailand. Parallel to the emergence of such applications is the rise of new privacy challenges—for instance, the unintended consequences of posting sensitive personal information and confusion over privacy settings. While Thailand ranks in the top 20 fastest-growing user countries for Facebook, little awareness has been raised about the privacy implications of these popular applications.

There is a dearth of advocacy work in Thai civil society when it comes to privacy. Local NGOs working in the areas of information and communication are mainly focused on freedom of expression, freedom of information, consumer protection, intellectual property, and access rights. However, there is no identifiable civic entity whose main focus is privacy. The last time a privacy issue emerged at a public level, it was advocated by a consumer-protection NGO that viewed the mass texting of greeting messages from the then-incoming Prime Minister Abhisit Vejjajiva to all mobile phone users as a violation of privacy.[50]

ONI Testing Results

OpenNet Initiative conducted testing between April and May 2010 following Thailand's State of Emergency Decree invoked on April 8, 2010. Testing was conducted on two major Thai ISPs: TRUE and TOTNET. Results indicate that these ISPs primarily block content related to political opposition sites, pornography, gambling, and circumvention tools. A central focus of this blocking is on political content related to the red shirts and Thai-language content.

Testing by ONI on the 36 Web sites ordered blocked determined that neither TRUE nor TOTNET filtered the entirety of the Thai government's block list. TOTNET blocked only ten URLs from the list, and TOTNET filtered this same set and an additional 13 for a total of 23 URLs. The sites found blocked included pro–red shirt Web sites (http://thaipeoplevoice.org, http://sunshine.redthai.org, and http://xat.com/uddtoday) and news sites that provided updates on the unrest (http://prachatai.com and http://thaipeoplevoice.org). Pages on social media Web sites used by the red shirts to disseminate messages and organize demonstrations were also blocked on both ISPs, including the presence of the United Front for Democracy and Dictatorship on Twitter (http://twitter.com/uddtoday), Facebook (http://facebook.com/note.php?note_id=344691628328), and Ning (http://uddtoday.ning.com). Web sites belonging to the anticoup site (http://19sep.com) and the Patani United Liberation Organization (http://puloinfo.net) that were blocked in 2007 were found accessible in 2010 testing.

Technical analysis of the data from TRUE and TOTNET found that filtering was implemented similarly by both ISPs. Consistent with past ONI findings, when users on TRUE and TOTNET attempt to access blocked content they are redirected to an MICT block page. TRUE's block page notified users that the content was blocked by order of the emergency decree, whereas TOTNET's block page did not.

While both ISPs similarly implemented filtering, ONI found that filtering was inconsistent between them, and that the overall level of filtering on TOTNET was greater than that of TRUE in all categories where filtering was found. For instance, TOTNET blocked circumvention tools and anonymous proxy sites (e.g., http://proxify .com, http://anonymouse.com) and the online gambling Web site http://gamebookers .net, whereas TRUE did not. Testing results also show that the blocking of pornography remains inconsistent and observed a slight increase in the number of English-language pornography sites blocked. No Thai-related pornography sites were found blocked. The site http://sex.com was the only pornographic content from 2007 that continues to be blocked.

These overall results are consistent with findings from 2007 testing and show that filtering continues to be inconsistently practiced in Thailand and that government block lists are not uniformly implemented across ISPs.

Conclusion

As a result of highly volatile conditions and the politicization of online communication, Internet control in Thailand in the post-2006-coup period features a combination of approaches—technical, legal, and social. Conventional ISP-level filtering, based on state-mandated block lists, has been complemented by automatic URL filtering at the IIG level as well as filtering at other points in the network, particularly at the OSP level. Due to the enforcement of the new cybercrime law, which imposes severe intermediary liability, OSPs have emerged as important chokers for censorship, since they host social networking services, blogs, and online political forums—all of which constitute the much-needed public sphere in the climate of otherwise suppressed speech. Apart from filtering out problematic content and denying hosting space to politically risky content providers, OSPs also construct an identification clearance system to enable surveillance of users and potential rule breakers.

In addition to the new Cybercrime Law, which legalizes Internet blocking through court orders and helps enforce other filtering mechanisms, two other laws contribute directly to the new regime of Internet control: the State of Emergency Decree and lèse-majesté laws. While the former made censorship seem inevitable in the face of crisis, the latter, as an entrenched social norm, helped justify it. What is more alarming is how members of online communities engaged in cyber witch-hunting using lèse-majesté as a powerful rationale to publicly condemn and reprimand those who represent dissenting opinions.

Such controlling schemes have not only created a chilling effect in cyberspace as users and service providers resort to self-censorship and intermediary censorship, but have also given rise to struggles and resistance. More technologically capable dissidents have evaded the control using anonymizers and circumvention tools, while civic organizations advocating for online freedom of expression have introduced public education and regularly campaign against government Internet control, allied with international NGOs advocating on similar issues.

Notes

1. Shino Yuasa, "Anti-Thaksin Groups Launch Boycott over Temasek-Shin Corp Deal," Manager Online, March 9, 2006, http://manager.co.th/Home/ViewNews.aspx?NewsID=9490000033125.

2. Pasuk Phongpaichit and Chris Baker, "Thaksin's Populism," *Journal of Contemporary Asia* 38, no. 1 (2008): 62–83.

3. Economist Intelligence Unit Limited, *Country Report: Thailand*, Economist Intelligence Unit Limited, 2010.

4. "Army's Power at Peak since Crackdown," *Bangkok Post*, June 19, 2010, http://www .bangkokpost.com/news/local/39016/army-power-at-peak-since-crackdown.

5. Ibid.

6. Anuchit Nguyen, "Thai Government Blocks Protest Web Site after Emergency Decree," *Bloomberg Business Week*, April 7, 2010, http://www.businessweek.com/news/2010-04-07/thai -government-blocks-protest-web-site-after-emergency-decree.html.

7. National Electronics and Computer Technology Center, "Internet User in Thailand," November 15, 2010, http://internet.nectec.or.th/webstats/internetuser.iir?Sec=internetuser.

8. International Telecommunication Union (ITU), "Internet Indicators: Subscribers, Users and Broadband Subscribers," 2009 figures, http://www.itu.int/ITU-D/icteye/Reporting/ ShowReportFrame.aspx?ReportName=/WTI/InformationTechnologyPublic&ReportFormat =HTML4.0&RP_intYear=2009&RP_intLanguageID=1&RP_bitLiveData=False.

9. National Electronics and Computer Technology Center, "Thailand Internet Bandwidth," August 18, 2010, http://internet.nectec.or.th/webstats/bandwidth.iir?Sec=bandwidth.

10. Office of National Statistics, *ICT Household 2009*, Bangkok: Thana Press, 2010.

11. National Electronics and Computer Technology Center, *Internet Users Profile of Thailand 2552 (2009)*, http://pld.nectec.or.th/websrii/images/stories/documents/books/internetuser_2009.pdf.

12. Office of National Statistics, *ICT Household 2009*.

13. The six IIGs are CAT Telecom Plc, TOT Plc, TRUE Corporation, Thai Telephone and Telecommunications (TT&T), ADC, and CS Loxinfo. Of these six IIGs, CAT Telecom Plc and TOT Plc were former state enterprises and monopoly telecommunication companies, while TRUE and TT&T are long-time telecommunications concessionaires. Only ADC and CS Loxinfo are new market entrants after the telecommunications reform in 2005. For more discussion, see Thaweesak Koanantakool, "Important Internet Statistics of Thailand," August 24, 2007, Internet Information

Research Network Technology Lab, http://internet.nectec.or.th/document/pdf/20070824 _Important_Intenet_Statistics_of_Thailand.pdf.

14. National Telecommunication Commission of Thailand, *Telecommunication Market Report 2010*, Bangkok: NTC, 2010.

15. Pirongrong Ramasoota, "Internet and Democracy in Thailand," in *Rhetoric and Reality: The Internet Challenge for Democracy in Asia*, ed. Indrajit Banerjee (Singapore: Eastern Universities Press: 2003), 297.

16. Although CAT Telecom's shares are controlled by the Ministry of Finance, the entity is under the bureaucratic structure of the Ministry of Information and Communication Technology.

17. National Telecommunications Commission, Unpublished Data Submitted to the Commission in the reading of the Frequency Allocation Organization and Regulation of Broadcasting and Telecommunications draft law, 2010.

18. Ministry of Information, Communication and Technology, "Government Information Network: GIN," http://203.113.25.35/gin/rationale.htm.

19. Internet Innovation Research Center, "Web Rank by Country: Thailand," http://truehits.net/ index_ranking.php.

20. National Electronics and Computer Technology Center, *Internet Users Profile of Thailand 2552 (2009)*.

21. Jon Russell, "Analysis: Thailand Passes Five Million Facebook Users," Asian Correspondent, September 7, 2010, http://www.asiancorrespondent.com/39989/analysis-thailand-passes-5-million -facebook-users.

22. Figures obtained from Facebook press release available at http://www.facebook.com/press/ info.php?statistics, accessed February 7, 2011.

23. Ministry of Information, Communication, and Technology, "Broadband Policy," November 18, 2010, http://www.mict.go.th/article_attach/policy_Broadband.pdf.

24. Ibid.

25. See Pirongrong Ramasoota and Nithima Kananithinan, *Internet Content Regulation in Thailand*, 2003 Research report under the Media Reform Research Project. Supported by the Thailand Research Fund (TRF), http://www.tdri.or.th/reports/unpublished/media/number10.pdf.

26. Section 18, Thailand Computer-Related Offenses Act B.E. 2550, http://www.lib.su.ac.th/ ComputerLaw50.pdf.

27. The existence of this automatic URL filtering system is not common public knowledge. Its existence was discovered by OpenNet Asia research, which revealed that a group of computer science researchers from Kasetsart University in Bangkok were commissioned by CAT Telecom, a state enterprise that runs major IIGs, to design the filtering system. For further details see

Pirongrong Ramasoota, "Internet Politics in Thailand after the 2006 Coup: Regulation by Code and a Contested Ideological Terrain," chapter 5 in this volume.

28. Thai Criminal Code B.E. 2499 (1956), Article 112. Unofficial English translation is available at http://www.samuiforsale.com/Law-Texts/thailand-penal-code.html.

29. Somboon Suksamran, *Buddhism and Politics in Thailand*. Singapore: Institute of Southeast Asian Studies, 1982.

30. Siriphon Kusonsinwut, Sawatree Suksri, and Oraphin Yingyongpathana, "Situational Report on Control and Censorship of Online Media, through the Use of Laws and the Imposition of Thai State Policies," *iLaw*, http://ilaw.or.th/node/632.

31. Ibid.

32. Ibid.

33. Peter Leyland, "The Struggle for Freedom of Expression in Thailand: Media Moguls, the King, Citizen Politics and the Law," *Journal of Media Law* 2, no. 1 (2010): 115–137.

34. "Thailand: Moviegoer Faces Prison for Sitting during Anthem," *New York Times*, April 24, 2008, http://query.nytimes.com/gst/fullpage.html?res=9506E1DF1E31F937A15757C0A96E9C8B63&fta=y.

35. For further details on lèse-majesté in Thailand, see Pirongrong Ramasoota, "Internet Politics in Thailand after the 2006 Coup: Regulation by Code and a Contested Ideological Terrain," chapter 5 in this volume; see also Shawn W. Crispin, "Internet Freedom on Trial in Thailand," Committee to Protect Journalists, February 5, 2011, http://www.cpj.org/blog/2011/02/internet-freedom-on-trial-in-thailand.php; Simon Montlake, "Web Site Editor's Trail in Thailand a Test Case for Media Freedom," *Christian Science Monitor*, February 4, 2011, http://www.csmonitor.com/World/Asia-Pacific/2011/0204/Website-editor-s-trial-in-Thailand-a-test-case-for-media-freedom.

36. For instance, Freedom against Censorship Thailand (FACT), an NGO that advocates on freedom of expression online, has offered free downloads of circumvention software on their Web site. See http://facthai.wordpress.com/links/softwares/.

37. Pirongrong Ramasoota, "State Surveillance, Privacy and Social Control in Thailand (1358–1997)," 2000, PhD dissertation, Simon Fraser University, Canada.

38. "Data-Interception Technology Sparks Privacy vs Safety Arguments," *Bangkok Post*, January 21, 2010, http://www.bangkokpost.com/print/31829.

39. Richard Frost, "Thai Stocks, Baht Slump on King's Health Speculation," Bloomberg, http://www.bloomberg.com/apps/news?pid=newsarchive&sid=aWSLmdQccvyo.

40. In this incident, two stock brokers were arrested and charged with spreading online rumors on two online forums, http://prathathaiwebboard.co.th and http://sameskywebboard.co.th, about the king's deteriorating health. Their postings led to the panic selling in the local stock market in November 2009. The Computer Crime Act allows action against computer users spreading information deemed detrimental to national security or false information that could cause

panic among the public. See James Hookway, "Thai Police Arrest Two Accused of Violating Internet Laws," *Wall Street Journal*, November 3, 2009, http://online.wsj.com/article/SB125712550983721881.html.

41. Poowin Buyavejchewin, "Internet Politics: Internet as a Political Tour in Thailand," *Canadian Social Science* 6, no. 3 (2010); "Political Battles Go Online," *Bangkok Post,* January 8, 2010, http://m.bangkokpost.com/articledetail.php?channelID=1&articleID=188908.

42. "Political Battles Go Online," *Bangkok Post.*

43. Privacy abuses in Thailand have typically been framed in terms of trespass, defamation, or breach of trust or confidence. For analysis of privacy-related laws in Thailand, see Ramasoota, "State Surveillance, Privacy and Social Control in Thailand (1358–1997)."

44. Chapter 3: Personal Information, Official Information Act B.E. 2540, http://www.oic.go.th/content_eng/act.htm.

45. "Cabinet to Consider Data Protection Law" [in Thai], Chaopraya News, October 14, 2010, http://www.chaoprayanews.com/2010/10/14/.

46. Section 18, Thailand Computer-Related Offenses Act B.E. 2550, http://www.lib.su.ac.th/ComputerLaw50.pdf.

47. Section 26, Computer Crime Act B.E. 2550 (2007), issued June 10, 2007, effective July 18, 2007. Unofficial English translation is available at http://www.prachatai.com/english/node/117.

48. See Pirongrong Ramasoota Rananand, "Information Privacy in a Surveillance State: A Perspective from Thailand," in *Information Technology Ethics: Cultural Perspectives*, ed. Soraj Hongladarom and Charles Ess (Hershey, PA: Idea Group Reference, 2007).

49. Ibid.

50. Tulsathit Taptim, "Did Abhisit Text Himself into More Trouble?" *The Nation*, July 16, 2010, http://www.nationmultimedia.com/home/2010/07/16/politics/Did-Abhisit-text-himself-into-more-trouble-30133903.html.

Vietnam

The expansion of Internet use in the country has become a cause for concern for the government of Vietnam, which on one hand aspires to expand information and communication technologies for development purposes, and on the other, sees the Internet as a source of instability. The Vietnamese state has taken steps to control Internet use through legal and regulatory frameworks, and by  filtering content that it deems threatening to the regime, state unity, or national security. With the rise of social networking and blogging as tools to express dissent, the Internet has become a contested space in Vietnam: the government attempts to rival social networking sites such as Facebook through the development of a state-run social networking site on the one hand, while patriotic hackers launch cyber attacks on dissident Web sites on the other.

RESULTS AT A GLANCE

Filtering	No evidence of Filtering	Suspected Filtering	Selective Filtering	Substantial Filtering	Pervasive Filtering
Political					•
Social			•		
Conflict and security			•		
Internet tools				•	

OTHER FACTORS

	Low	Medium	High	Not Applicable
Transparency	•			
Consistency	•			

KEY INDICATORS	
GDP per capita, PPP (constant 2005 international dollars)	2,681
Life expectancy at birth, total (years)	74
Literacy rate, adult total (percent of people age 15+)	92.5
Human Development Index (out of 169)	113
Rule of Law (out of 5)	2.1
Voice and Accountability (out of 5)	1.0
Democracy Index (out of 167)	95 (Authoritarian regime)
Digital Opportunity Index (out of 181)	126
Internet penetration rate	26.6

Source by indicator: World Bank 2009, World Bank 2008a, World Bank 2008b, UNDP 2010, World Bank Worldwide Governance Indicators 2009, Economist Intelligence Unit 2010, ITU 2007, ITU 2009. See Introduction to the Country Profiles, pp. 222–223.

Background

Vietnam is a one-party state governed by the Communist Party of Vietnam. The party does not maintain a strict adherence to ideological orthodoxy.[1] Today, Vietnam is making a transition from a centrally planned economy to a market-oriented mixed economy. Since opening up its economy there has been an increased socioeconomic gap, which the government sees as a potential source of political instability.[2] The party maintains a tight grip on the Internet and information flows, and is sensitive to content that can cause social instability.

As a part of the country's development project, the government is promoting information and communication technologies (ICTs) and e-commerce. The government's commitment to ICTs can be seen in the country's Master Plan for ICT Development for 2005–2010, the creation of a National Steering Committee for ICT, and the creation of the Ministry of Information and Communication. However, the Communist Party of Vietnam sees the Internet as a threat to stability and actively seeks to monitor Internet content. After a period of relative openness and tolerance of independent voices and criticism in 2006 when liberal publications were established, the government clamped down on what it considers unlawful usage of the Internet. Because the ICT sector in Vietnam is changing constantly, it is difficult to describe the situation "on the ground" with complete accuracy.

Internet in Vietnam

Internet use in Vietnam is growing rapidly. In 2009, the country had an estimated 23,283,300 Internet users, with a penetration rate of 26.6 percent.[3] The country's broadband subscription rate is 3.6 percent.[4] Recently the home surpassed public access centers as the primary place that users access the Internet.[5] Prior to 2009, users primarily went to public access centers, such as Internet cafés or post offices. Access through mobile phones has also increased, reflecting competitive and attractive mobile phone packages.[6] A study conducted by Yahoo! and Kantar Media found that 71 percent of users in major cities such as Can Tho, Danang, Hanoi, and Ho Chi Min City accessed the Internet from their homes.[7] However, Internet cafés remain popular throughout the country, providing service to youth, online game players, and those who are unable to afford broadband access.

While any Vietnamese firm can operate as an Internet service provider (ISP), only companies that are state-owned can operate as Internet access service providers or Internet exchange providers. Formally, the Ministry of Posts and Telecommunications lists nine Internet access services providers, five Internet exchange providers, and 15 online service providers as licensed in Vietnam.[8] The state-owned ISP, the Vietnam Posts and Telecommunications (VNPT), dominates the broadband market. As of November 1, 2010, the VNPT held 74 percent of the market share, followed by Viettel with 11 percent, FPT Telecom with 10 percent, and SPT with 2 percent.[9]

State regulation determines how Internet connectivity in Vietnam is organized and managed, and facilitates Internet content filtering by limiting external access points that must be controlled.[10] Only Internet exchange points (IXPs) can connect to the international Internet, while online service providers (OSPs) and Internet content providers (ICPs) may connect to ISPs and IXPs.[11] At the edge of the network, Internet agents, such as Internet cafés, connect to their contracted ISPs.[12] Internet service providers may connect with each other and with IXPs, but private ISPs cannot connect with each other in peer arrangements.[13] Currently, IXPs can theoretically maintain independent connections to the international Internet, but it is not clear how many do so in practice. Internet connectivity in Vietnam is slow compared to other Asian countries—on average, broadband connection speed for downloading is 6.66 Mbps, and the speed for uploading is 3.77 Mbps.[14]

In Vietnam, Internet filtering happens at the domain name system (DNS) level, which means that instead of blocking a site, ISPs simply configure domain names to resolve to an invalid address or remove blocked Web sites from their DNS servers. It is widely known that blocking at the DNS level is subject to vulnerabilities, as this form of blocking can be easily circumvented by Internet users through the use of circumvention tools, proxy servers, and virtual private networks (VPNs) or simply by tampering with the DNS (for instance, changing a DNS provider to a publicly available one such as Google DNS).[15] There are many Vietnamese circumvention help sites whereby more advanced Internet users provide information on how to access blocked sites. One example is http://facebookviet.com, which provides instructions on how to access Facebook (which was blocked by ISPs after a government order in November 2009).[16] The countrywide block on the Web site was essentially irrelevant because it was so easily circumvented by users.[17] Filtering techniques are vulnerable because of their design, but the filtering regime is even further weakened by the fact that government orders to block Web sites are unevenly enforced by ISPs.[18]

Legal and Regulatory Frameworks

Vietnam's legal regulation of Internet access and content is multilayered and complex, and can occur at the level of National Assembly legislation, ministerial decisions, or through VNPT rules created for the management of the Internet infrastructure. Although Article 69 of the 1992 constitution of Vietnam states that "the citizen shall enjoy freedom of opinion and speech, freedom of the press, the right to be informed, and the right to assemble, form associations and hold demonstrations in accordance with the provisions of the law,"[19] state security laws and other regulations trump or eliminate these formal protections and guarantees. Freedom of expression and the right to assemble are constrained by the Criminal Code, which prohibits "abusing democratic freedoms to infringe upon the interests of the State" (Article 258), "conducting propaganda against the Socialist Republic" (Article 88), and "carrying out activities aimed at overthrowing the people's administration" (Article 79). These laws have been invoked to arrest people considered cyber dissidents such as prodemocracy bloggers.[20] Because of the harsh penalties for violation of such laws, self-censorship is commonplace in Vietnam.

Media in Vietnam are state owned and under tight control by the Vietnamese state. The 2006 Decree on Cultural and Information Activities subjects those who disseminate reactionary ideology, including revealing secrets (party, state, military, and economic), who deny revolutionary achievements, and who do not submit articles for review before publication to fines of up to 30 million dong (approximately USD 2,000).[21] These regulations appear to target journalists because criminal liability already exists for some of the proscribed activities, including the dissemination of state secrets. All information stored on, sent over, or retrieved from the Internet must comply with Vietnam's Press Law, Publication Law, and other laws, including state secrets and intellectual property protections.[22]

All domestic and foreign individuals and organizations involved in Internet activity in Vietnam are legally responsible for content created, disseminated, and stored. Just as ISPs and Internet cafés are required to install monitoring software and store information on users, users are also formally deputized to report content that opposes the state or threatens state security to the relevant authorities.[23] It is unlawful to host material that opposes the state; destabilizes Vietnam's security, economy, or social order; incites opposition to the state; discloses state secrets; infringes upon organizations' or individuals' rights; or interferes with the state's DNS servers.[24] Those who violate these Internet use rules are subject to a range of penalties. The National Assembly enacted the Law on Information Technology on June 22, 2006.[25]

On August 28, 2008, the state enacted Decree Number 97 on the Management, Supply, and Use of Internet Services and Electronic Information on the Internet,[26] which was strengthened in December by the Ministry of Information's Circular Number 7.[27] Under Article 6 of the decree, it is prohibited to use the Internet to oppose the government; to undermine the state and state unity, national security, public order, or social security; to incite violence or crime; or to damage the reputations of individuals and organizations.[28] Information about users violating Article 6 must be reported to the state.[29] To strengthen and clarify the contents in Decree 97, the Ministry of Information issued Circular Number 7 on December 18. Under Circular Number 7, blogs are restricted to only personal content, and providers of online social networking services (such as blogging platforms) are obligated to keep reports about users and provide such information to authorities every six months or upon request. Further reinforcing the law was the creation of the Administration Agency of Radio, Television, and Electronic Information under the Ministry of Information to monitor the Internet.

The initiatives of 2008 came on the heels of increased dissatisfaction among the population and growing instability in the country. In June 2008, inflation in Vietnam had reached 27 percent, and inflation for rice (a dietary staple) had reached 70 percent; within the first six months of 2008, 500 demonstrations had already taken place, despite restrictions on the right to strike.[30] In response to the growing instability, a crisis meeting of the party's Central Committee was called in July. The Vietnam Committee on Human Rights argues that it was within this context that the party started to intensify controls and repression.[31]

The state has become increasingly concerned about young people neglecting their studies for the Internet and, in particular, online gaming.[32] In 2006, Joint Document Number 60/2006, which regulates the production, supply, and use of online games in the country, was enacted.[33] In July 2010, after a public outcry over the negative effects of the Internet on youth—in particular, instances of youth engaging in murder and robbery for money to play online games—the Ministry of Information and Communication cracked down on online games by temporarily terminating their licensing and ordering ISPs to force shops that offered games to close by 11:00 PM.[34] In Hanoi, Internet retailers and businesses providing Internet service must be located at least 200 meters way from the entrance of any schools (up to high school) and can operate between 6:00 AM and 11:00 PM only.[35]

Surveillance

The Vietnamese government stringently monitors objectionable Internet activities. An Internet surveillance unit under the Ministry of Public Security is particularly interested in customers who access politically sensitive sites,[36] and firewalls have been deployed to block access to overseas Web sites that host sensitive content, such as international news and human rights Web sites.[37] In addition, under Decision Number 15 of 2010, domain servers in Hanoi are required to install a copy of the Internet Service Retailers Management Software, a government-controlled software developed by the National University of Hanoi.[38] Some believe that the software is for blocking as well as for surveillance.[39]

The growing popularity of social networking Web sites has prompted the Vietnamese government to develop its own, "Go.vn" (http://go.vn), in order to compete with other popular platforms. Go.vn is similar to Facebook, but it is government run, and users must register with official identification details, including government-issued identity numbers. Vietnamese officials have described Go.vn as being the country's biggest online investment so far, and it is expected that by 2015 Go.vn will boast more than 40 million registered users.[40] Some analysts believe that the site will strengthen the state's Web monitoring and surveillance capacities.

Cyber Attacks

Harassment, detainment, and imprisonment of bloggers as well as attacks on their Web sites and e-mails occur regularly in Vietnam.[41] *Viet Nam News*, a state-run newspaper, reported that more than 1,000 Web sites were attacked in 2009.[42] Although the newspaper attributed such attacks to a general lack of security protection for Vietnamese Web sites, many Web sites that have faced cyber attacks generally contain dissident content.[43] Web sites with content critical of the state (including blogs and discussion forums) that are hosted outside of Vietnam have had administrative passwords stolen or suffered dedicated denial of service (DDoS) attacks.[44] Viet Tan, the Vietnam Reform Party, often reports experiencing DDoS attacks. In April 2009, coinciding with the 24th anniversary of the Fall of Saigon, Viet Tan's Web site suffered a large-scale DDoS attack. Attackers compromised Web sites and installed a malicious program so that visitors executed the malicious script on their computers with instructions to attack the Viet Tan Web site. Viet Tan members have also reportedly received targeted malware attacks through e-mail.[45]

It is unclear who is behind the attacks and whether they are state sanctioned; however, cyber attacks have become instrumental to controlling online content and, as demonstrated recently by the Vulcanbot and the Vecebot botnets, have become increasingly sophisticated.

In December 2009 and October 2010, DDoS attacks were launched through a botnet on Web sites and blogs that expressed dissent. In the first instance, attackers compromised VPSKeys, a driver distributed by the Vietnamese Professional Society (VPS) to provide support to Vietnamese Windows users typing in Vietnamese, with a Trojan horse. The attackers then sent a fake e-mail from the VPS instructing users to download a VPSKeys software update that was, in fact, the compromised version. Once users installed the malicious software update, their computers would join the Vulcan botnet and be given instructions to perform DDoS attacks on dissident Web sites.[46] Vulcanbot's command-and-control servers were primarily located in Vietnam, and the botnet was thought to be part of a larger effort to attack the growing anti–bauxite-mining movement in Vietnam,[47] which had included the application of a firewall to three key Web sites (http://boxitvn.net, http://boxitvn.org, and http://boxitvn.info) the detaining of key organizers, and forged e-mails from organizers.[48] Tens of thousands of users were probably infected. According to a member of Google's security team, "These infected machines have been used both to spy on their owners as well as participate in distributed denial of service (DDoS) attacks against blogs containing messages of political dissent."[49]

In October 2010, SecureWorks discovered Trojan horse malware that was used to launch DDoS attacks against Vietnamese blogs and discussion forums that were critical of the government and the bauxite mining operations. The botnet's deployment coincided with "Vietnam Blogger Day," a coordinated online action to celebrate the release of Dieu Cay, a blogger and political prisoner. Dubbed Vecebot, the botnet infected between 10,000 and 20,000 host computers, most of them located in Vietnam.[50] SecureWorks has suggested that it is possible that the Vecebot attacks were a continuation of the Vulcanbot attacks. While many speculate that such attacks are state-sanctioned, there has been no solid evidence to connect such attacks to the Vietnamese government. There is, however, evidence that the perpetrators of the attacks may be a pro–Vietnamese Communist Party hacking group.[51] For SecureWorks, the Trojan is a new family of malware that appears to have political, as opposed to commercial, objectives.[52]

ONI Testing Results

In 2010, OpenNet Initiative testing was conducted on two major Vietnamese ISPs, FPT Telecom Corporation and Viettel Corporation. Founded in 1993 by Vietnam's Ministry of National Defense, Viettel is a military-owned Internet service provider that began offering Internet-access services to the public in 2002. As of November 2010, Viettel had captured 11 percent of the broadband market, making it the second largest ISP in the country after the Vietnam Posts and Telecommunications.[53] FPT Telecom is one of Vietnam's leading IT companies and telecom service providers. It is a joint-stock company that held 10 percent of the market share in November 2010, making it the third largest ISP in the country after Vietnam Posts and Telecommunications and Viettel.[54] Evidence of filtering was found on both ISPs, with Viettel blocking significantly more Web sites than FPT Telecom.

Testing on FPT Telecom was conducted by ONI in September 2010. The content of the blocked Web sites fell into four broad thematic categories: political, social, conflict and security, and Internet tools. Testing on Viettel was conducted by the ONI in October 2010. Like FPT Telecom, the content of Viettel's blocked Web sites fell into the same four broad thematic categories: political, social, conflict and security, and Internet tools.

When users attempt to access blocked Web sites on both ISPs, they encounter a standard network error page. Technical analysis of the data from each ISP revealed that these errors were the result of a form of DNS tampering, where the entries for blocked Web sites are removed from the ISPs' DNS servers.

The blocking pattern of the ISPs reflects the government's concerns about content that challenges its authority. Both ISPs filter Web sites with Vietnamese-language content that is critical of the Vietnamese Communist Party and that argues for political reform, such as http://x-cafevn.org and the Web site of the Viet Tan (http://viettan.org). Vietnamese-language Web sites operated outside of Vietnam are also a target of filtering. This includes Web sites that critique the party, such as the Web sites of the *Vietnam Daily News* based out of California (http://vietnamdaily.com) and the *Hướng Dương* based out of Australia (http://huongduong.com.au). Vietnamese-language news Web sites operating overseas that are not necessarily critical of the Vietnam state but contained news stories about Vietnam are also filtered by both ISPs, including Dân Việt (http://danviet.com.au), Vietmedia (http://vietmedia.net), and Việt Báo Online (http://vietbao.com). Two Web sites related to the Degar people in Vietnam—an ethnic minority with whom the state has had a history of conflict—are also blocked (http://montagnard-foundation.org and http://montagnards.org).

Web sites of international human rights groups were accessible with the exception of Human Rights Watch (http://hrw.org), which was found blocked on Viettel. FPT Telecom, which blocked Human Rights Watch in 2007–2008 testing, did not block the Web site in 2010 testing. English- or French-language Web sites with content on Vietnam were rarely blocked, with the exception of Radio Free Asia (http://rfa.org), which was blocked by both ISPs. Blocking of foreign media Web sites was infrequent and inconsistent. An exception is that both the English- and Vietnamese-language version of Voice of America were found blocked on Viettel and FPT.

OpenNet Initiative testing found inconsistencies in the level of filtering between the two ISPs. For instance, the Vietnamese-language news Web site of Vietnamese American Television (http://vietmaryland.com), which is critical of the Vietnamese government and based out of the United States, was found blocked on Viettel but not on FPT Telecom. The inconsistencies in the level of filtering between VNPT and FPT Telecom reflect previous findings from ONI testing in 2007–2008.

Both ISPs blocked significantly more political Web sites than social or conflict and security sites. FPT Telecom filtered only one Web site per category. The Web sites of the Vietnamese Youth Foundation (http://vnyouth.com) and the Federation of Associations of the Republic of Vietnam Navy and Merchant Marine (http://vietnamnavy.com) were found to be blocked on FPT Telecom. None of these Web sites were blocked in the 2007–2008 round of ONI testing. In the social category, Viettel blocked the Web site of the Vietnamese Youth Foundation (http://vnyouth.com) and Ngưới Việt, a local language news site (http://nguoi-viet.com). Viettel blocked two Web sites with content relating to the military and two Web sites with detailed content related to the Vietnamese navy and marines, http://vietnamnavy.com and http://tqlcvn.org. Neither ISP blocked pornographic content.

In the Internet tools category, both ISPs blocked Facebook (http://facebook.com). Both ISPs also targeted circumvention Web sites for filtering but differed in the specific sites they were blocking. For instance, Viettel filtered http://anonymizer.com, http://the-cloak.com, http://anonymouse.org/, https://megaproxy.com, http://proxyweb.net/, and http://inetprivacy.com, while FPT filtered only http://inetprivacy.com.

Conclusion

The government of Vietnam has committed to the advancement of ICTs as part of the country's development project. Internet penetration in Vietnam is expanding rapidly, with many citizens connecting to the Internet at home and through mobile phones. As the penetration rate continues to grow, the government is taking steps to ensure that the Internet is not being used in a way that can cause domestic instability. These controls are being accomplished through a robust legal and regulatory framework that lays down Internet use rules for private users and Internet services. The state further controls Internet use by monitoring users and filtering Web sites that contain questionable content.

Despite restrictions to free access, Vietnamese netizens continue to take advantage of the Internet as a space for expressing criticisms of the state. As a result, Vietnamese cyberspace has increasingly become a contested space among various actors, as illustrated by the cases of increasingly sophisticated cyber attacks launched against groups critical of the state.

Notes

1. U.S. Department of State, *Background Note: Vietnam*, November 30, 2010, http://www.state.gov/r/pa/ei/bgn/4130.htm.

2. "Vietnam Country Profile," BBC News, July 21, 2010, http://news.bbc.co.uk/2/hi/asia-pacific/country_profiles/1243338.stm.

3. International Telecommunication Union (ITU), "Internet Indicators: Subscribers, Users and Broadband Subscribers," 2009 Figures, http://www.itu.int/ITU-D/icteye/Reporting/ShowReportFrame.aspx?ReportName=/WTI/InformationTechnologyPublic&ReportFormat=HTML4.0&RP_intYear=2009&RP_intLanguageID=1&RP_bitLiveData=False.

4. Ibid.

5. Hien Nguyen, "Yahoo! Says Internet Access Trend in Vietnam to Change," *Saigon Times*, May 21, 2010, http://english.thesaigontimes.vn/Home/ict/internet/10410.

6. Tuyet An, "Greater Spending on the Internet," *Saigon Times*, June 30, 2010, http://english.thesaigontimes.vn/Home/ict/internet/11130.

7. Ibid.

8. Ministry of Information and Communications of the Socialist Republic of Vietnam, "Operators," http://english.mic.gov.vn/Statistics/staticstics_open/Trang/operators.aspx; Viet Nam Internet Center, "Diagram of the ISP Market" [in Vietnamese], http://www.thongkeinternet.vn/jsp/thuebao/chat_dt.jsp.

9. Viet Nam Internet Center, "Diagram of the ISP Market."

10. Decree No. 55/2001/ND-CP of the Government on the Management, Provision and Use of the Internet Services, Articles 27–38, http://www.business.gov.vn/assets/fbbc1d48c42d4f36a161a8a3d8749744.pdf.

11. Ibid., Article 27.

12. Ibid.

13. Ibid.

14. John E. Dunn, "Asian Cities Dominate Fast Broadband," *PC World*, October 24, 2010, http://www.pcworld.com/article/208550/asian_cities_dominate_fast_broadband.html; "World Speedtest.net Results," Speedtest.net, accessed December 21, 2010, http://www.speedtest.net.

15. Helen Clark, "Facebook in Vietnam: Why the Block Doesn't Work," Global Post, October 4, 2010, http://www.globalpost.com/dispatch/vietnam/100928/facebook-internet-china-press-freedom.

16. Reporters Without Borders, "Internet Enemies: Viet Nam," 2010, http://en.rsf.org/internet-enemie-viet-nam,36694.html.

17. Ibid.

18. Ibid.

19. 1992 Constitution of the Socialist Republic of Vietnam, Article 69, as amended December 25, 2001. Unofficial English translation is available at http://www.vietnamlaws.com/freelaws/Constitution92(aa01).pdf.

20. Reporters Without Borders, "Another Blogger Charged with 'Subversion' Faces Death Penalty," December 23, 2009, http://en.rsf.org/vietnam-another-blogger-charged-with-23-12-2009,35329; Amnesty International, "Closed: Truong Quoc Huy—Viet Nam," http://www.amnesty.org.uk/actions_details.asp?ActionID=362.

21. "Vietnam Readies Stricter Press Laws to Rein Back Aggressive Journalists," Southeast Asian Press Alliance (SEAPA), June 16, 2006, http://www.ifex.org/vietnam/2006/06/16/government _readies_stricter_press.

22. Decree No. 55/2001/ND-CP of the Government on the Management, Provision and Use of Internet Services, Article 6(1), issued August 23, 2001.

23. Decree No. 55/2001/ND-CP, Article 6(2); and Inter-Ministerial Joint Circular No. 02/2005/ TTLT-BCVT-VHTT-CA-KHDT of the Government on the Management, Provision and Use of Internet Services, http://english.mic.gov.vn/vbqppl/Lists/Vn%20bn%20QPPL/DispForm.aspx ?ID=6222.

24. Decision No. 27/2005/QD-BBCVT on Promulgating the Regulation on Management and the Use of Internet Resources, Article 2(2), http://english.mic.gov.vn/vbqppl/Lists/Vn%20bn%20 QPPL/DispForm.aspx?ID=6256.

25. "Vietnam Post and Telecommunication Sector Records Outstanding Achievements in 2006," Thai Press Reports, January 1, 2007.

26. Decree No. 97/2008/ND-CP on the Management, Supply, and Use of Internet Services and Electronic Information on the Internet, http://mic.gov.vn/vbqppl/Lists/Vn%20bn%20QPPL/ DispForm.aspx?ID=7012.

27. Circular No. 07 / 2008/TT-BTTTT on Guiding Some Contents on the Provision of Information on Personal Electronic Information in the Decree 97, http://mic.gov.vn/vbqppl/Lists/Vn%20 bn%20QPPL/DispForm.aspx?ID=7325.

28. Ann Binlot, "Vietnam Bloggers Face Government Crackdown," Time, December 30, 2008, http://www.time.com/time/world/article/0,8599,1869130,00.html.

29. Ibid.

30. For more on instability and dissatisfaction among workers, see "Hard Times Fall on a Once Investment-Rich Vietnam," Vancouver Sun, August 11, 2008, http://www.canada.com/story_print .html?id=a841b0da-a045-4a0a-80b6-19a58c36bbd1&sponsor=; "Political Stability vs. Democratic Freedom? Economic Crisis and Political Repression in Vietnam," in Hearing on Cambodia, Laos and Vietnam, Subcommission on Human Rights, European Parliament, August 25, 2008, Brussels, http://www.queme.net/eng/doc/2008-082513_Political_Stability_vs_Democratic_Freedom.pdf; "Vietnam: Year in Review 2008," Encyclopædia Britannica Online, 2010, http://www.britannica .com/EBchecked/topic/1493658/Vietnam-Year-In-Review-2008.

31. Vietnam Committee on Human Rights, "Political Stability vs Democratic Freedom?"

32. "In Pictures: Vietnam's Internet Addiction," BBC News, March 16, 2010, http://news.bbc .co.uk/2/hi/uk_news/8568855.stm.

33. Tran Ngoc Ca and Nguyen Thi Thu Huong, "Vietnam," in *Digital Review of Asia Pacific, 2009–2010*, ed. Shahid Akhtar and Patricia Arinto, http://www.idrc.ca/en/ev-141000-201-1-DO _TOPIC.html.

34. Associated Press, "Vietnam Restricts Online Games after Murder Cases," *Washington Times*, July 29, 2010, http://www.washingtontimes.com/news/2010/jul/29/vietnam-restricts-online-games -after-murder-cases.

35. Decision No. 15/2010/QD-UBND on Promulgating Stipulations on the Management, Provision, and Use of Internet Services at Retail Locations in Hanoi City. Unofficial English translation is available at http://www.viettan.org/spip.php?article9859.

36. "Vietnamese Security Ministry Establishes Special Unit to Tackle Internet Crime," BBC Monitoring International Reports, August 4, 2004.

37. Human Rights Watch, "Vietnam: Stop Cyber Attacks against Online Critics," May 26, 2010, http://www.hrw.org/en/news/2010/05/26/vietnam-stop-cyber-attacks-against-online-critics.

38. Robert McMillan, "Activists Worry about a New 'Green Dam' in Vietnam," *PC World*, June 4, 2010, http://www.pcworld.com/article/198064/activists_worry_about_a_new_green_dam_in _vietnam.html.

39. Ibid.

40. "In Vietnam, State 'Friends' You," *Wall Street Journal*, October 4, 2010, http://online.wsj.com/ article/SB10001424052748703305004575503561540612900.html#articleTabs%3Darticle.

41. For examples of arrests and detention of bloggers, as well as attacks against dissident blogs and Web sites in 2010, see Human Rights Watch, "Vietnam: Stop Cyber Attacks against Online Critics."

42. "Online Newspaper Hacking Case Sets Off Alarm Bells," *Việt Nam News,* November 24, 2010, http://vietnamnews.vnagency.com.vn/Social-Isssues/206033/Online-newspaper-hacking-case -sets-off-alarm-bells.html.

43. Viet Tan, "Denial of Service: Cyberattacks by the Vietnamese Government," April 27, 2010, http://www.viettan.org/spip.php?article9749.

44. For instance, boxitevn.info, blogosin.org, caotraonhanban.com, danchimviet.com, danluan. org, doi-thoai.com, dangvidan.org, dcctvn.net, hsiphu.com, minhbien.org, talawas.org, thongluan.org, viettan.org, ykien.net, vietbaosaigon.com, and xcafevn.org. See Human Rights Watch, "Vietnam: Stop Cyber Attacks against Online Critics."

45. Viet Tan, "Denial of Service."

46. Neel Mehta, "The Chilling Effects of Malware," Google Online Security Blog, March 30, 2010, http://googleonlinesecurity.blogspot.com/2010/03/chilling-effects-of-malware.html.

47. In 2009, mounting opposition to the mining of bauxite in the central highlands of Vietnam (by the government in partnership with the Chinese-run company Chalco) led to the creation

of Bauxite Vietnam, an opposition Web site hosted on a server in France. By December 2009, the site had attracted more than 20 million visitors. See "A Revolt of Sorts in Vietnam," Asia Times Online, November 2, 2010, http://www.atimes.com/atimes/Southeast_Asia/LK02Ae01 .html.

48. Viet Tan, "Denial of Service."

49. Mehta, "The Chilling Effects of Malware"; George Kurtz, "Vietnamese Speakers Targeted in Cyberattack," McAfee, March 30, 2010, http://siblog.mcafee.com/cto/vietnamese-speakers-targeted -in-cyberattack.

50. SecureWorks' Counter Threat Unit, "Vecebot Trojan Analysis," SecureWorks, October 28, 2010, http://www.secureworks.com/research/threats/vecebot/?threat=vecebot.

51. SecureWorks' Counter Threat Unit, "Vecebot Trojan Analysis"; Viet Tan, "Denial of Service."

52. SecureWorks' Counter Threat Unit, "Vecebot Trojan Analysis."

53. Ibid.

54. Viet Nam Internet Center, "Diagram of the ISP Market."

Glossary of Technical Terms

2G is the second generation of telecommunication technology for mobile networking.

3G is the third generation of telecommunication technology for mobile networking.

4G is the fourth generation of telecommunication technology for mobile networking.

403 (*403 Forbidden*) is the standard HTTP error code that occurs when a server will not allow a Web browser to access the file being requested.

404 (*404 Not Found*) is the standard HTTP error code that occurs when a server cannot find the file being requested.

ADSL (*asymmetric digital subscriber line*) is a technology that allows data to be sent over existing copper telephone lines.

Bandwidth is the amount of data that can flow in a given time.

Block page is the page delivered to the user when a request for a Web site is filtered, or blocked. Block pages take many forms and may be disguised as benign error pages or may bear the ISP's logo and further explanation of the block.

CCTV (*closed circuit television*) is the use of video cameras to transmit video from a specific place to a limited set of monitors. Signals for CCTV are not openly transmitted.

Circumvention refers to the general concept of using proxies and other tools to bypass Internet filtering.

DDoS attack (*distributed denial of service attack*) is an attempt to prevent users from accessing a specific computer resource, such as a Web site. DDoS attacks (sometimes called DoS, or denial of service, attacks) usually involve overwhelming the targeted computer with requests so that it is no longer able to communicate with its intended users.

Deep packet inspection is a form of computer network packet filtering that examines the data part (and possibly also the header) of a packet as it passes an inspection point, searching for protocol noncompliance, viruses, spam, intrusions, or predefined criteria to decide if the packet can pass or if it needs to be routed to a different destination, or for the purpose of collecting statistical information.

DNS (*domain name system*) is a hierarchical naming system for computers, services, or any resource participating in the Internet.

DNS tampering (*domain name system tampering*) is a method of blocking communication by preventing the conversion of domain names into IP addresses, effectively blocking access to the Web site.

Domain name is a label identifying a specific computer, service, or resource on the Internet.

DSL (*digital subscriber line*) is a family of technologies that provides digital data transmission over existing telephone wires.

EDGE (*Enhanced Data rates for GSM Evolution*), also known as EGPRS or Enhanced GPRS, is a GSM extension that improves data transmission rates by up to three times their original speed.

EVDO (*evolution-data optimized or evolution-data only*) is a telecommunications standard for the wireless transmission of data through radio.

GB (*gigabyte*) is a unit of digital information storage equal to 10^9 (1,000,000,000) bytes. However, this term is also often used to mean $1,024^3$ (1,073,741,824 bytes).

GPRS (*general packet radio service*) is service for mobile devices that divides data into packets for transmission purposes. It can be used with 2G and 3G wireless telephone technology operating on the GSM standard.

GPS (*Global Positioning System*) is a free global navigation satellite system that is used for both military and civilian purposes.

GSM (*Global System for Mobile Communications*) is a digital mobile phone standard used by as much as 80 percent of the global market. Its widespread use enables international roaming among different mobile phone operators.

HTTP (*Hypertext Transfer Protocol*) is a set of standards for exchanging text, images, sound, and video by means of the Internet.

HTTP proxy filtering blocks communication on the basis of the specific HTTP address or URL being requested.

ICP (*Internet Cache Protocol*) is a set of rules used to coordinate Web caches (places where duplications of online data are temporarily stored, enabling faster access and reducing bandwidth).

ICP (*Internet content provider*) is an online service provider that creates or provides informational, educational, or entertainment content.

ICT (*information and communication technology*) is an umbrella term that includes all technologies intended for the manipulation and communication of information.

IP address (*Internet Protocol address*) is a numerical identification assigned to devices participating in a computer network utilizing the Internet Protocol.

IRC (*Internet relay chat*) is a form of real-time Internet messaging.

ISP (*Internet service provider*) is a company that provides users with access to the Internet.

IT (*Information technology*) describes the use of computers, computer software, and other communications technologies to create and manage information.

IXP (*Internet exchange point*) is a shared facility that allows ISPs to exchange traffic with one another through free, mutual peering agreements.

KB (*kilobyte*) is a unit of digital information storage equal to either 1,000 bytes (10^3) or 1,024 bytes (2^{10}), depending on context.

Kbps (*kilobits per second*) is a measure of bandwidth on a data transmission medium.

LGBT is an acronym that refers to the lesbian, gay, bisexual, and transgender community. Sometime used to refer to anyone who is nonheterosexual.

MB (*megabyte*) is a unit of digital information storage equal to 10^6 (1,000,000) bytes.

Mbps (*megabits per second*) is a measure of bandwidth on a data transmission medium that is equal to 1,000,000 kilobits per second.

MP3 (*MPEG-1 Audio Layer 3*) is a digital audio encoding format that compresses audio data by a factor of 12 without losing noticeable sound quality.

P2P (*peer-to-peer*) is a computer network that uses diverse connectivity between participants in a network and the cumulative bandwidth of network participants rather than conventional centralized resources where a relatively low number of servers provide the core value to a service or application.

Portal If Web portal: is an online interface that allows Internet users to collect and view information (e-mail, weather, stock prices, etc.) from various sources in a visually unified way. If Intranet portal: is a single network-specific hub that provides unified access to information and applications, often for a private company or organization.

Proxy (also *Proxy server*) is a server that acts as a go-between for clients (such as Web browsers or other applications) and other servers. Proxy servers enable anonymous online activity and increase access speed through caching.

Reverse filtering (also called *geolocational filtering*) is a practice that occurs on the Web server hosting the content, as opposed to at a point along the way of the traffic flow, and is based on restricting requests based on geographical location of the originating Internet Protocol address. Copyright holders who want to restrict access to their content in certain markets often use reverse filtering. Examples include hulu.com, BBC.com, and other sites that syndicate commercial video and audio content that is subject to licensing.

SMS (*short message service*), also known as text message, is a communication service standardized in the GSM mobile communication system, allowing the exchange of short text messages between mobile devices.

Social networking sites are Web services that focus on communities of users with shared interests. Popular examples include Facebook, Twitter, MySpace, and Orkut.

TB   (*terabyte*) is a unit of digital information storage equal to 1 trillion (10^{12}) bytes, or 1,000 gigabytes.

TCP/IP   (*Transmission Control Protocol/Internet Protocol*) is the set of standards governing data transmission over the Internet.

TCP/IP content filtering   blocks communication on the basis of where packets of data are going to or coming from, and not on what they contain.

TCP/IP header filtering   blocks communication on the basis of the IP address and/or the port number (which gives clues as to the type of Web service being accessed) contained in the header of the data packet being sent.

Top-level domain   is the group of letters (usually two or three, but can include more) that follow the final dot in a domain name. Example: in opennet.net, the top-level domain is .net.

URL   (*Uniform Resource Locator*) is a string of characters that specify where a particular resource is located online and how to retrieve it. Also known as a Web address.

User ID   (*User Identification*) is a unique string of characters that identifies users of password-protected online services, such as e-mail or social networking sites.

VCD   (*Video Compact Disc*) is a digital compression standard that enables the storage of video on a compact disc.

VoIP   (*Voice over Internet Protocol*) is a technology that allows for voice communication over the Internet.

WAP   (*Wireless Application Protocol*) is a global standard for the transfer of information without using electrical conduits (wires). It allows for access to the Internet using mobile devices.

Warez   (derived from the plural of "ware," as in software) refers to copyrighted material that is distributed in violation of copyright law.

WiMAX   (*Worldwide Interoperability for Microwave Access*) is a wireless digital communications system that is meant to provide fixed and mobile Internet access for metropolitan area networks.

Index